Integrative Economic Ethics

Integrative Economic Ethics is a highly original work that progresses through a series of rational and philosophical arguments to address foundational issues concerning the relationship between ethics and the market economy. Rather than accepting market competition as a driver of ethical behaviour, the author shows that modern economies need to develop ethical principles that guide market competition, thus moving business ethics into the realms of political theory and civic rationality. Now in its fourth edition in the original German, this first English translation of Peter Ulrich's development of a new integrative approach to economic ethics will be of interest to all scholars and advanced students of business ethics, economics, and social and political philosophy.

PETER ULRICH is Full Professor of Economic and Business Ethics and Director of the Institute for Business Ethics at the University of St Gallen, Switzerland.

Integrative Economic Ethics

Foundations of a Civilized Market Economy

Peter Ulrich

CAMBRIDGE
UNIVERSITY PRESS

CAMBRIDGE UNIVERSITY PRESS
Cambridge, New York, Melbourne, Madrid, Cape Town, Singapore,
São Paulo, Delhi, Dubai, Tokyo, Mexico City

Cambridge University Press
The Edinburgh Building, Cambridge CB2 8RU, UK

Published in the United States of America by Cambridge University Press, New York

www.cambridge.org
Information on this title: www.cambridge.org/9780521172424

First published 2008
First paperback edition 2010

A catalogue record for this publication is available from the British Library

ISBN 978-0-521-87796-1 Hardback
ISBN 978-0-521-17242-4 Paperback

Contents

List of figures — *page* viii
Preface — ix
Translator's note — xii

Introduction: orientation in economic-ethical thinking — 1

Part I Fundamental concepts of modern ethics and the approach of integrative economic ethics — 11

1 The phenomenon of human morality: the normative logic of interpersonal relations — 13
1.1 The moral disposition as part of the conditio humana — 13
1.2 Morals and ethos as two sides of lived morality — 19
1.3 Modern ethics and the problem of relativism — 25
1.4 The humanistic core of the moral principle: the normative logic of interpersonal relations — 31
1.5 The developmental stages of moral consciousness — 37

2 The moral point of view: philosophical developmental lines of rational ethics — 43
2.1 The Golden Rule and the Judaeo-Christian commandment to love one's neighbour — 44
2.2 The standpoint of the impartial spectator (Adam Smith) — 48
2.3 The categorical imperative (Immanuel Kant) — 52
2.4 The rule-utilitarian generalization criterion — 57
2.5 Discourse ethics — 62

3 Morality and economic rationality: integrative economic ethics as the rational ethics of economic activity — 79
3.1 Economic ethics as applied ethics? — 80
3.2 Economic ethics as normative economics? — 89
3.3 The integrative approach: economic ethics as critical reflection on the foundations of economic reason — 100

Part II Reflections on the foundations of economic ethics I: a critique of economism 111

4 'Inherent necessity' of competition? A critique of economic determinism 115
4.1 The origins of modern market economy: the calvinistic ethos as a context of motivation 116
4.2 The systemic character of modern market economy: the 'free' market as a coercive context 120
4.3 The partiality of inherent necessity and the economic-ethical problem of reasonable expectation 131

5 'Morality' of the market? A critique of economic reductionism 147
5.1 Historical and doctrinal background I: the prestabilized harmony in the economic cosmos (classical period) 150
5.2 Historical and doctrinal background II: the utilitarian fiction of common good (early neoclassical period) 158
5.3 Methodological individualism and the normative logic of mutual advantage (pure economics) 166

Part III Reflections on the foundations of economic ethics II: rational economic activity and the lifeworld 185

6 The question of meaning: economic activity and the good life 189
6.1 The elementary sense of economic activity: securing the means of human subsistence 191
6.2 The advanced meaning of economic activity: furthering the abundance of human life 196
6.3 The discovery of personal meaning under conditions of competitive self-assertion 207

7 The question of legitimation: economic activity and the just social life 216
7.1 Fundamental moral rights as the ethical-political basis of legitimation 220
7.2 The well-ordered society and the conditions of legitimate inequality: on John Rawls's principles of justice 227
7.3 Economic citizenship rights as the basis of real freedom for all 240

Part IV A topology of economic ethics: the 'sites' of morality in economic life 269

8 Economic citizen's ethics 273
8.1 The basic problem of civic ethics: liberal society and republican virtue 276
8.2 Deliberative politics: the public sphere as the site of economic citizens' shared responsibility 288
8.3 Professional and private life as sites of economic citizens' self-commitment 303

9 Regulatory ethics 315
9.1 The basic problem of regulatory ethics: market logic and 'vital policy' 319
9.2 Deliberative order politics: the market framework as a site of morality – whose morality? 341
9.3 The global question: competition of national market frameworks or supranational sites of regulatory morality? 359

10 Corporate ethics 376
10.1 The basic problem of corporate ethics: 'profit principle' and legitimate business activity 379
10.2 Instrumentalist, charitable, corrective or integrative corporate ethics? 398
10.3 Deliberative corporate policy-making: the 'stakeholder dialogue' as a site of business morality 418
10.4 Elements of an integrative ethical programme for corporations 437

Bibliography 443
Index of subjects 471
Index of names 479

List of figures

Figure 0.1: Overview of the general systematics of integrative economic ethics *page* 6
Figure 1.1: The categories 'morals' and 'ethos' 25
Figure 1.2: Basic ethical concepts 31
Figure 1.3: Developmental stages of moral consciousness according to Lawrence Kohlberg 40
Figure 2.1: Developmental lines of the moral point of view 44
Figure 2.2: Basic types of rational action 68
Figure 3.1: The three-pole relationship of ethics, economics and comprehensive economic reason 80
Figure 3.2: The two-dimensional character of socio-economic rationality 107
Figure 3.3: Approaches to economic ethics 109
Figure 4.1: Lifeworld and economic system 129
Figure III.1: Two basic dimensions of economic activity in the service of life 186
Figure 7.1: Categories of human and civic rights 227
Figure 7.2: Four variants of the right to a basic income or to work 255
Figure IV.1: 'Sites' of the morality of economic activity 271
Figure 8.1: Ideal-typical basic models of civic virtue and civil society 279
Figure 9.1: The systematic dividing lines between paleo-, neo- and ordo-liberalism (ideal-typical conception) 323
Figure 10.1: Possible interpretations of entrepreneurial profit orientation 381
Figure 10.2: Corporate ethical approaches and their relationship to the profit principle 399
Figure 10.3: Internal two-stage conception of corporate ethics 411
Figure 10.4: Elements of an integrative ethics programme for corporations 442

Preface

At the beginning of the road leading to this book stood the creation of the first Chair of Economic and Business Ethics in the Economics or Business Faculty of a German-speaking university. This happened at the University of St Gallen in Switzerland in 1987. It was my privilege to take on this demanding task. My habilitation thesis *Transformation der ökonomischen Vernunft (Transformation of Economic Reason)* provided the foundation for the development of the St Gallen approach of *integrative economic ethics*, which differs fundamentally from existing international approaches. It is satisfied neither with the dominant concept of applied ethics in Anglo-Saxon countries, which employs ethics simply as a corrective *against* economic rationality, nor with 'moral economics' as a functionalist reduction of ethics *to* economics, such as is advocated by an influential school of economic thought in the German-speaking countries. The integrative approach endeavours rather to throw light upon the inherent normativity of economic rationality itself and to develop a comprehensive idea of ethically integrated economic rationality. The integrative approach also describes a third path beyond the usual alternatives in regard to the social framework in which a literally 'civilized' market economy must be embedded. Economic ethics is understood as what it implicitly or explicitly always inevitably is: a domain of political philosophy.

The book *Integrative Wirtschaftsethik* was published in the summer of 1997 after a developmental phase lasting ten years. In the intensive German-language debate on this young but highly topical discipline it met with a lively response. The integrative approach quickly established itself as one of the leading conceptions in its field. Interest in the book has also steadily grown outside the German-speaking world. That is why enquiries about an English edition have become more and more frequent. The reason, as far as I can see, is that no comparable overall conception exists to date in the Anglo-Saxon literature.

The English version presented here is based on the third revised German edition of 2001 but goes beyond this publication, as it includes improvements and topical new material planned for inclusion in a fourth

German edition (to be published in early 2008). Furthermore, the referenced literature has been comprehensively reworked for the English edition, in order to provide English sources wherever possible. This applies particularly to the original English sources and the standard English translations of works in other languages.

A project of this kind presupposes the commitment of an entire team over a longer period of time. Without the initiative of my research assistant Heiko Spitzeck, who stubbornly ignored my repeated hesitation and forged ahead, it would never have got off the ground. The next piece of good fortune was finding and winning James Fearns of the University of Konstanz as a professional translator for the project. As a native speaker of English who has lived for decades at Lake Constance doing interdisciplinary translation work in the humanities and social sciences, he was 'our man for the job'. His commitment to the difficult translation task was more than I could repay, in every sense of the word. He not only set about the search for suitable solutions to brain-teasing translation problems with great élan, but also used the resources of the University of Konstanz in order to identify a large part of the English translations and English originals of the literature quoted. His obliging nature and his calm and collected British manner made working with him a pleasure.

My research assistant Eric Patry also played an enormous part in the project. He took upon himself the complicated editorial process of preparing the text for publication and tirelessly supported me for months. That was great! Heiko Spitzeck, in the meantime in New York on a St Gallen scholarship, helped us further with the identification of English sources that could not be found in German or Swiss libraries. Likewise Florian Wettstein in Boston, MA, was always ready to provide assistance. Dorothea Baur, who is also a research assistant at our small Institute for Economic and Business Ethics in St Gallen, and Ulrich Thielemann, vice-president of the institute, were fully committed to critical reading of translated chapters as well as Eric. Finally, Eric, Dorothea and Ulrike Knobloch, lecturer at the institute, carefully worked out the indexes. I am deeply grateful for all of this support. And, of course, the support and almost never-ending patience of my wife Karin was just as indispensable.

That the outcome of this project can now be published by Cambridge University Press is in no small measure due to Paula Parish, Commissioning Editor of the publishing company. She promoted the evaluation process with so much goodwill. In this context I would also like to thank the three expert academic consultants for their favourable statements.

For readers who, like the above-mentioned consultants, are in a position to read both the English and the German versions of the text, it should be said that there are sometimes substantial differences between the texts, which are the result of changes in the content or of linguistic and stylistic modifications. They have either been formulated by me and checked by the translator or proposed by the translator in the interests of readability and authorized by me.

PETER ULRICH
St Gallen, Switzerland
June 2007

Translator's note

A number of concepts frequently used in the German literature on economic ethics have no direct equivalent in English or carry connotations and associations which may not be immediately evident to an English reader. The central term *Wirtschaftsethik* has been translated with 'economic ethics' when it is used in the sense of integrated ethics as advocated in this book. It has been translated with 'business ethics' where it specifically refers to one of the traditional approaches (business-oriented, instrumentalist, corrective, etc.) which the book challenges.

Wirtschaftsbürger has been translated as 'economic citizen' and *Wirtschaftsbürgerrechte* as 'economic citizenship rights', 'economic citizen's rights' or the 'civic rights of economic citizens'. These terms have in the meantime been well established in the English-language discussions on basic income and on multicultural economic communities. The terms *Wirtschaftsbürgerethik* and *Wirtschaftsbürgertugend* have no direct equivalents in English. The general, non-economic terms 'citizen virtue', 'citizen ethics' and 'citizen's ethics' are widely used in English, particularly in the context of the debate on republicanism. It has, therefore, been decided to coin the expressions 'economic citizen virtue' and 'economic citizen ('s) ethics' by extension.

The concepts of *Ordnungspolitik* and *Ordnungsethik* derive from the work of the ordoliberal school, particularly Walter Eucken and Franz Böhm, who insisted that the market economy is only a partial order which must be embedded in a higher overall order resting upon values beyond the economy. It is the function of the state to regulate the market (*Ordnungspolitik*) and to ensure that it operates in accordance with ethical standards which guarantee the human, social and ecological compatibility of economic activities (*Ordnungsethik*). *Ordnungsethik* is concerned with the normative questions of orientation and justification, *Ordnungspolitik* with the effective implementation of a corresponding overall conception of the market economy. *Ordnungsethik* has been translated as 'regulatory ethics' when it refers to the regulatory framework of the market established by the public authorities. In other contexts, such as corporate ethics, the term 'institutional ethics' is also used. Accordingly, *Ordnungspolitik* is generally translated as 'regulatory politics (or policy)' in the context of specific regulatory measures. In wider contexts 'institutional politics (or policy)' is also used. In complex adjectival constructions 'regulatory' is preferred ('regulatory political problems'). A further central idea of ordo-liberalism is Alexander Rüstow's concept of *Vitalpolitik*. Rüstow argues that the true purpose of the economy lies in the service of values beyond the economy, in the service of human dignity. *Vital* is whatever promotes the vita humana and a life which is worthy of a human being and hence *Vitalpolitik* takes into consideration 'all the factors on which the happiness, well-being and contentment of man truly depend' (Rüstow). It is translated here as 'vital policy', a term English readers have become familiar with as a result of its adoption (and modification) in the (translated) works of Michael Foucault. The adjectival form 'vital-political' has been hyphenated in order to distinguish it from the general English meaning (vital political issues etc.). A related concept also coined by Rüstow is the *Marktrand*. This term emphasizes that the market is only a means to an end, whereas the *Marktrand* designates those areas of human life which are an end in themselves and possess a human value of their own. They are 'a hundred times more important' (Rüstow) than the market itself, as they are decisive for the development of cultural and educational patterns and the moral and social guidelines of behaviour. *Marktrand* has been translated as 'the boundary of the market'.

The term *Ökonomismus* was probably first employed by Gerhard Weisser, for whom it meant the conviction that the postulates for the shaping of economic life can and must be drawn *from our economic thinking* alone. The advocates of *Ökonomismus* maintain the self-sufficiency and autonomy of economic rationality, which is forced upon us by the inherent logic of the market. They argue in a reductionist and deterministic fashion for a 'pure' and 'value-free' economics which has no place in its axiomatics for ethical categories. The term *Ökonomismus* is, therefore, negatively loaded. It has been translated directly as 'economism' with the corresponding derivative form 'economistic'.

Mention should also be made of the use of hyphenated adjectives (*ethisch-praktisch*, *politisch-ökonomisch*, etc.) which are at present much more widespread in German than in English literature. An English reader may perhaps find them stiff, but they have mostly been preserved and directly translated in the text (ethical-rational, etc.) as they serve a useful semantic purpose and can be found among academic writers (e.g. Lawrence Kohlberg) in the Anglo-Saxon world.

James Fearns

Introduction: orientation in economic-ethical thinking

> It has often been said that man must stand at the centre of the economy. This statement is certainly correct, but it is now necessary to make this general dictum more precise.[1]

Economic activity based on division of labour is a societal process designed to satisfy the human need to preserve and sustain the quality of life. It seems to lie in the nature of things that a rational social form of economic activity must be oriented towards *the service of life*[2] if it is to be meaningful. Consequently, in the words of Alfred Müller-Armack, man must indeed have a central place in the inherent logic of the economic system.

All well and good! In the practice and the theory of the modern market economy, however, we more and more frequently encounter what is called the inherent logic of the economy as a strangely anonymous and *coercive* logic. It occasionally contradicts our intuitions and governing ideas about the good life and just ways of living together in a well-ordered society of *free* and equal citizens. This logic condemns some people to unemployment and subjects others who are still on the labour market to increasingly hard pressure to perform at work. In this way it incessantly improves 'productivity' or what we regard as productivity, yet it still fails to provide everyone with what is minimally necessary for a life worthy of a human being at a national, let alone at a global, level. And it brings about a relentless economic growth, which creates high living and consuming standards for a part of the human race, but at an ecological expense which has long become a permanent problem. From the point of view of its conduciveness to a good life, the inherent logic of the 'modern' economy

[1] A. Müller-Armack, 'Die zweite Phase der sozialen Marktwirtschaft – Ihre Ergänzung durch das Leitbild einer neuen Gesellschaftspolitik' (1960), reprinted in *Genealogie der Sozialen Marktwirtschaft: Frühschriften und weiterführende Konzepte* (Berne *et al.*: Haupt, 1974), pp. 129–45, at p. 134.

[2] On this concept see n. 4 in the Introduction to Part III.

is evidently not the *whole* truth about economic reasonableness. What it lacks is the ethical dimension of rational (reasonable) economic action.

As a result, more and more people are beginning to doubt whether an economic rationalization process which is increasingly gaining a momentum of its own does actually operate in the service of life. The need for a fundamental reorientation in regard to economic progress and an ethically well-grounded containment of the market economy is growing. At the same time, however, the actual development is in the opposite direction, towards an increasingly radical independence of a 'free' market, which has meanwhile unleashed its forces worldwide. Questioning the acceptability of this development by no means implies a rejection of the market economy but only of its exaggeration towards a total market *society*. Not markets but citizens finally deserve to be free in modern society. The market economy must, therefore, be *civilized* in a literal sense.

This, in a few words, is the topical background to the growing recent calls for the new interdisciplinary field of *economic ethics*. Seen in this light, economic ethics is the focal point of an epochal challenge: How is economic rationality, as forced on us by the inherent logic of the market, to be firmly linked with ethical reason, by which we mean the normative logic of the reciprocal relationship between free human beings? This *civilizing* context of the market economy must be fundamentally clarified and redefined in the service of a future world fit to live in.

One might at first sight be surprised at the need for a new hybrid discipline called economic ethics. Are we not dealing here with one of the oldest questions of that venerable discipline which once arose, not by chance, out of moral philosophy and fittingly characterized itself until a hundred years ago as *political economy*? Well, in principle, yes. But this discipline has developed in the meantime into a 'pure' economics, which imagines it is 'value free' and no longer has a place in its axiomatics for ethical categories. Of course, the representatives of this discipline which has distanced itself so remarkably from all considerations of concrete service to life may well as citizens be just as concerned about the development of the real-world market economy as other thoughtful contemporaries; nevertheless, within the paradigms of their theoretical approach, they are scarcely able to comment reasonably on the increasingly evident divergence of the anonymous yet often strangely biased inherent logic of the market and the ethical logic of interpersonal relations. What is more, contemporary *mainstream economics* is, as we shall see, to a certain extent more a part of the problem than a sound basis for its solution. For it provides models only for the 'self-referential' functional logic of an idealized market system and consequently attempts to subsume the ethical problems of *social* economy purely and simply under economic *systems rationality*. Where human needs or social concerns cannot be adequately met in the abstract functional logic of the market economy system, or where they even contradict it in principle, 'pure' economics then argues often enough – and without reflecting on its own normative standpoint – *against* such demands for humanity and service to life in the economic practice of society.

The 'need for precision' which Alfred Müller-Armack referred to is consequently moving more and more into the centre of the socio-political discussion. There is much to be done in this respect in the field of traditional economic thinking. Above all, it is necessary to explore and clarify precisely the fundamental *difference* between the perspective of economic rationality, which has such powerful effects in the real world, and a perspective of ethical-practical reason which has still to be defined. It is evident that this requires an equally intensive examination of modern ethics and economics. Because of its (scientifically quite legitimate) paradigmatic restriction to the categories of economic rationality, pure economics lacks the indispensable philosophical ethical categories. Fortunately, contemporary philosophical ethics has made remarkable progress in terms of 'precision' in recent years and, as 'applied ethics', has begun to intervene more and more in the great practical and socio-political debates of our time. But, as will be shown, it is not enough simply to 'apply' ethics to the sphere of economic activity as the alternative to or corrective for economic rationality. Normativity always lies behind the economic logic of the market – consequently we have to lay it bare *within* economic thinking and to reflect upon it in the light of ethical reason. It is important to understand precisely the thought processes followed in accordance with the inherent logic of the market and to find the hiding places of its normative moments. This allows us to examine the practical (political) programme adopted in its name and to uncover its implicit circumvention of the ethical questions involved in economic action. This task, the critical reflection on the normative foundations of the inherent logic of the market, is the specific task of an economic ethics (worthy of the name), which is more than 'applied ethics' on the one hand and 'normative economics' on the other.

The approach described above characterizes the conception of *integrative economic ethics* presented in this book. This specific term is justified, even imposes itself upon us, because the approach proposed deviates substantially from the major positions represented in the international discourse on business and economic ethics. In accordance with the desire for a critical reflection on normative foundations mentioned above, the general methodical aim of this new conception of economic ethics can be defined as an ethically rational orientation in politico-economic thinking without abandoning reflection in the face of the implicit normativity of 'given' economic conditions. Since Kant's 'What is Orientation in Thinking?'[3] this means the methodically disciplined endeavour to achieve a justification of validity claims which is guided by reason and dispenses with all presuppositions. This, in turn, requires 'the ability to think for oneself and to make independent decisions'.[4] It is precisely this independence of moral judgement oriented on self-chosen principles which Kant describes as *autonomy* and defines as the constitutive capacity of a 'rational being'.[5] Whoever uses his tongue in this sense to speak rationally by 'speaking for himself because he has thought for himself and not merely repeated someone else'[6] is a 'mature' person. Only those who do not let others speak for them can be mature. Kant calls the reflective path to maturity and to autonomous orientation in thinking 'enlightenment' or 'man's emergence from his self-incurred immaturity'.[7] Autonomous, enlightened thinking and mature speaking are critical in the sense that they subject their own position, without reservation, to the requirement of justification by argument. In the possibility not simply to accept given conditions uncritically but to question them as to their ethical-rational justifiability, the most noble task of modern rational ethics is expressed: to assert the freedom of man to determine his own life.

Modern economic ethics cannot be satisfied with less than this fundamental self-requirement of modern ethics, particularly as critical reflection in the domain of economy must confront extremely influential ideologies and the viewpoints of powerful interest groups. To this extent a rational ethics of economic activity of the kind envisaged by integrative economic ethics is always at the same time an unconditional and comprehensive critique of ideology. Precisely because it refuses to draw back in the face of any supposed or actual inherent necessities, at least in its philosophical conceptions and intentions, it is the best antidote to

3 I. Kant, 'What is Orientation in Thinking?', in Kant, *Political Writings*, ed. H. Reiss, transl. H. B. Nisbet (Cambridge Edition of the Works of Immanuel Kant: Cambridge University Press, 1991), pp. 237–49. See also J. Mittelstrass, 'Was heisst: sich im Denken orientieren?', in O. Schwemmer (ed.), *Vernunft, Handlung und Erfahrung. Über die Grundlagen und Ziele der Wissenschaft* (Munich: Beck, 1981), pp. 117–32.

4 F. Oser/W. Althof, *Moralische Selbstbestimmung: Modelle der Entwicklung und Erziehung im Wertebereich*, 2nd edn (Stuttgart: Klett-Cotta, 1994), p. 51.

5 See I. Kant, 'Groundwork of the Metaphysics of Morals', in Kant, *Practical Philosophy*, transl. and ed. Mary J. Gregor (Cambridge Edition of the Works of Immanuel Kant: Cambridge University Press, 1996), pp. 37–108, at p. 99.

6 Th. Adorno, 'Kritik', in Adorno, *Kleine Schriften zur Gesellschaft* (Frankfurt: Suhrkamp, 1971), pp. 10–19, at p. 10.

7 I. Kant, 'An Answer to the Question: What Is Enlightenment?', in Kant, *Political Writings*, pp. 54–60, at p. 54.

ideologies of all kinds. Hence it aims to make a contribution to the development of mature and responsible economic citizens.

This obviously implies that integrative economic ethics does not intend to provide directly 'applicable' answers to specific questions of economic life or guidelines for politico-economic decisions. Its intention is rather to clarify the *form* of rational thinking about fundamental issues in economic ethics. The aim of providing a systematic elaboration and mediation of economic-ethical *orientation knowledge* sketched above is subsumed under four governing ideas, which are developed in the corresponding four parts of the book. Their characterization can, therefore, be linked to a brief survey of the structure of the book (Figure 0.1).

First, an attempt will be made to lay down a consistently pursued 'line of thought' founded on rational ethics. In comparison with other books on the subject, considerably more emphasis will be placed on a careful clarification of the moral point of view of rational economic ethics (Part I). A fundamental understanding of the moral point of view and a full awareness of the importance of methodically disciplined ethical reflection are indispensable preconditions for independent thinking on economic ethics. Two approaches are taken to the unfolding of this one perspective on ethics, for which a general validity is claimed, although it is of course open to criticism. First, the phenomenon of human morality, its constitutive significance for the nature of man and its universal basic structure are elucidated from the familiar perspective of real life experience (Chapter 1). Then the intellectual and philosophical developmental path of the moral point of view in the history of thought will be briefly traced from its first formulation to the most highly developed explication in discourse ethics (Chapter 2). At this point it will be possible to establish a sound basic conception for a rational ethics of economic action and to distinguish it from widespread but insufficient approaches in economic ethics, all of which abandon critical reflection at characteristic points (Chapter 3). The clarification of the resulting integrative approach to economic ethics will then lead us on to its three fundamental tasks, which provide the basis for the three subsequent parts of the book.

Second, in accordance with the proposed unconditional reflection on foundations, a critique of 'pure' economic reason (rationality) will be undertaken (Part II). It is necessary to discover why and how the inherent logic of the market supposedly succeeds, in its own eyes, in rejecting ethical claims in the sphere of economic action either as 'impossible' or even as 'unnecessary'; impossible because it seems as if we have no choice in view of market conditions, which are seen as coercive, and unnecessary because ethical questions about economic actions are apparently best 'looked after' within the categories of pure economic rationality. Behind

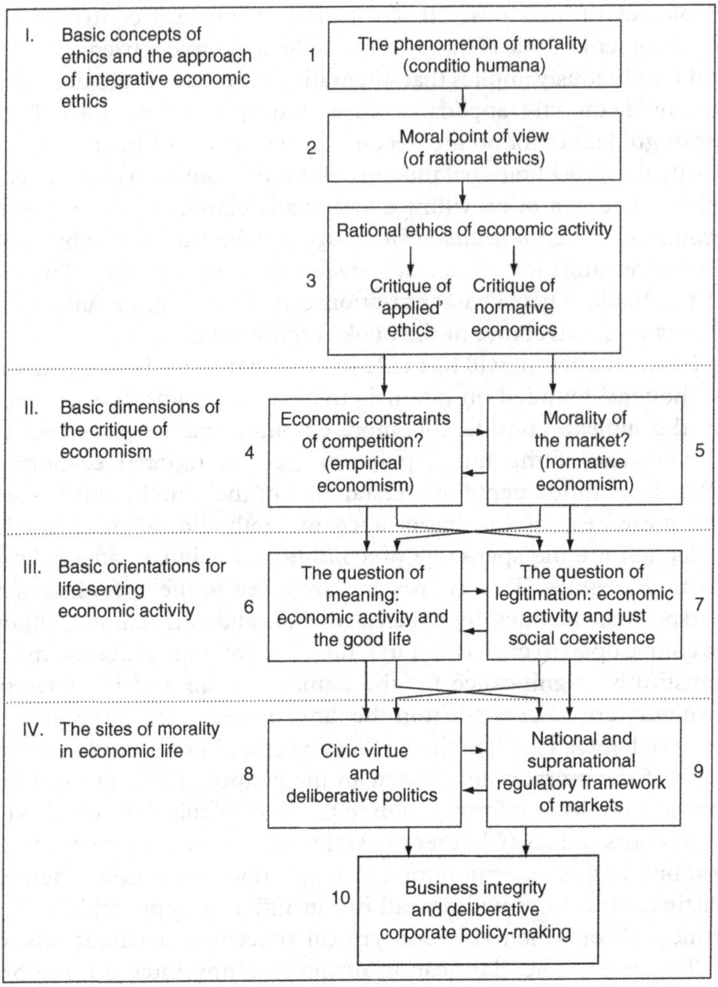

Figure 0.1. Overview of the general systematics of integrative economic ethics

this remarkable normative self-sufficiency of pure economics a tendency to economism shines through: the autonomy, absolutism and normative primacy of economic points of view. In this book the critique of *economism* is seen as an important task of reflection on the foundations of economic ethics, as economism is, as we shall see, the ultimate and perhaps most powerful major ideology of all time. Two fundamental manifestations of economism must be distinguished. The empirical variant, according to which ethics is more or less 'impossible' in economic affairs, thinks in terms of inherent necessity and the constraints of the circumstances (Chapter 4). The normative variant, according to which ethics is 'unnecessary', rests upon the conviction – whose many facets are historically well documented – that the market itself is the best guarantor for ethical correctness in business (Chapter 5). Both variants of economism will be subjected to a systematic examination in regard to their normative basis.

Once these economistic blind spots have been identified and overcome our vision is free for the treatment of the basic questions of practical reason in a 'civilized' economic life (Part III). The basic idea of the integrative approach in this regard aims to overcome the currently popular two-world conception of economic rationality and ethical reason in favour of an (integrative) idea of socio-economic rationality in which a rational-ethical point of view is already embedded. This guiding idea of rational economic action (already introduced in Chapter 3) at the same time defines the moral point of view of a rational ethics of economic activity. It serves as the starting point for the discussion of more concrete orientational viewpoints relevant to the two elementary ethical questions about an economy in the service of life: the question of the sense of economic activity in regard to the good life (Chapter 6) and the question of the legitimacy of the socio-economic conditions (relations) from the point of view of just forms of social life (Chapter 7). In both dimensions highly topical questions of a new orientation of economic and social policy for a future fit to live in are discussed. It is one of the distinctive marks of the integrative approach that it understands economic ethics in this sense as part of a political ethics which embeds a 'civilized' market economy in a well-ordered society of free citizens. In contrast, a great part of the international literature on business and economic ethics pays scant attention to the advanced – and exciting – political-philosophical discussion on foundational issues and even undercuts it systematically.[8]

Fourth, and finally, integrative economic ethics includes an ethical topology, i.e. a systematic treatment of the 'sites' of morality and socio-economic responsibility in the life of a modern society (Part IV). In accordance with the philosophical-ethical and political-philosophical horizon of reflection, it rests upon a deepened view of the relationship between individual and institutional ethics. In place of the customary (twofold) division of economic ethics into institutional ethics and corporate ethics, which by and large reflects only the familiar academic

[8] This critical assessment is shared from a philosophical standpoint by W. Kersting, 'Lexikalisch erfasst: Wirtschaftsethik und ethisches Wirtschaften', *Zeitschrift für Politik* 42 (1995), pp. 325–30, at p. 329.

distinction between political economy and business administration, it offers a differentiated conception of reciprocally related levels of responsibility. To this we add economic citizen's ethics as the third systematic 'site' of morality. This in itself combines individual-ethical elements with the politically and philosophically enlightened concept of a well-ordered society by taking up the indispensable idea of republican civic virtue. We propose consequently to characterize it as *republican liberalism*. With this concept certain reductionist elements of traditional political liberalism and, even more so, of economic neoliberalism are clarified and overcome. Moreover, a link is forged with the most progressive models of *deliberative politics*, which achieve a balance between the discourse-ethical ideal of free democratic politics and political realism (Chapter 8).

With the help of this fundamental critical orientation it is now possible to proceed to a precise, more sharply focused delimitation and critique of the most important regulatory political conceptions of the market economy (old or classical, ordo- and neoliberalism). This goes far beyond the customary systematics of the standard textbooks, whose approach to ethical and political questions seems vague and obsolete. It will be shown that none of the positions discussed does justice to the all-important primacy of the principle of service to life over the logic of the market. This is also true of the ordoliberal conception and the 'economic style' of the social market economy, in spite of their claims to the contrary. The dire consequences can be seen in the current symptoms of political disorientation in regard to the institutional framework of the market. In place of these approaches a formal concept of the normative tasks of a conception of order is presented, which is adequately specific from an ethical standpoint and is nonetheless open in regard to its actual fulfilment in the democratic process. As a particularly significant test of the various conceptions of political order, their treatment of the ethical and political challenge of globalization will be critically investigated (Chapter 9).

Corporate ethics will also be subjected to an unconditional fundamental reflection on its multi-layered inter-relations. First of all it will be shown – more consistently (and thoroughly) than in previously published accounts – why the so-called 'profit principle', which continues to run wild not only in the standard academic approach to business administration but also in corporate ethics, cannot be justified, even in the recent version of the shareholder value concept. In the light of their treatment of the profit principle, which is not a principle at all, four different basic conceptions of corporate ethics will be distinguished and discussed. We shall see that the integrative approach alone consistently avoids the economistic abandonment of reflection. Its central ideas of business integrity, republican sharing of responsibility for the institutional framework of market competition and deliberative corporate policy-making enable the clarification of the links to civic ethics as well as to institutional ethics, aiming at a deeper and more literal understanding of the nowadays widely used term 'corporate citizenship' (Chapter 10).

How far the proposed approach of an integrative economic ethics is sound enough to fulfil the task of bringing systematic order into an unbelievably complex topic is a question which is presented for discussion here. The book will achieve its goal if it helps us to find an orientation of economic-ethical thinking which is free of ideology and unconditionally guided by reason, as uncomfortable as this may be for certain brains of thought. A corresponding new veracity in dealing with the fundamental value questions of the economic 'creation of values' presupposes that the prevailing economistic circular thinking is seen through more and more and that the *whole* of economic reason is recognized as the decisive horizon for a civilized economy which has a life-serving future. This is an ideal which at the moment requires a great deal of autonomous self-reflection and occasionally the courage to contradict the *Zeitgeist*. But this fact need not speak against the practical orientational power of the perspectives outlined or against their closeness to life and their (critical) relationship to reality. Alois Riklin, who, as a former vice-chancellor of the University of St Gallen, played a decisive role in the creation of the first chair of economic and business ethics in a German-speaking country, put it in a nutshell: 'One is not realistic if one has no ideals.'[9]

[9] A. Riklin, *Verantwortung des Akademikers* (St Gallen: VGS, 1978), p. 201.

Part I

Fundamental concepts of modern ethics and the approach of integrative economic ethics

The difficulties involved in meeting the requirements for a rational foundation of a modern ethics are considerable. On the one hand, the traditional mere declarations of belief in moral concepts based on religious or dogmatic convictions can no longer fulfil the expectations of an 'ethics without metaphysics'[1] which can be justified by rational means alone. On the other hand, an ethical relativism is gaining ground – as a supposedly 'postmodern' reaction to the breakdown of traditional 'fixed values' and authoritative moral doctrines. This ethical relativism regards the rational foundation of moral obligations as impossible from the outset and virtually degrades moral issues to purely subjective questions of taste.

The main emphasis of the following introduction to a modern understanding of ethics is placed on the unfolding of a humanistic rational ethics that sees itself as a third way between dogmatism or fundamentalism on the one hand and relativism or scepticism on the other. As part of an enlightened 'cultivation of reason'[2] it pursues reflection on the *general* normative preconditions of the good life and just social relations of free and self-determined persons, which can be reasonably understood by all men of 'good will'.

We begin with the clarification of the *phenomenon of human morality* from the familiar perspective of those who have always participated in a moral community. The specifically modern idea of a rationally justifiable universal moral principle is already clearly present at this stage (Chapter 1). But it is only in what follows that we pursue the methodically demanding central ideas of an orientation in ethical thinking guided by reason in order to describe the most important developmental lines of the philosophical-ethical explication and justification of the rational moral

[1] See G. Patzig, *Ethik ohne Metaphysik*, 2nd edn (Göttingen: Vandenhoeck & Ruprecht, 1983).

[2] Kant, 'Metaphysics of Morals', p. 52.

point of view (Chapter 2). Finally, on this foundation, we tackle the task of clarifying how economic ethics can be conceived as rational ethics of economic activity and how the corresponding integrative ethics can be marked off from approaches which are insufficient from a rational ethical perspective (Chapter 3).

1 The phenomenon of human morality: the normative logic of interpersonal relations

Morality is a specifically human phenomenon about which everyone has intuitive preconceptions resulting from his own practical experience of life. Consequently, what is at issue in questions of morality and ethics can at first best be understood through its elementary significance for the personal and social life of man. We will begin with the determination of the moral disposition of man and its fundamental cultural-anthropological conditions (Section 1.1) and with the basic concepts of 'morality' and 'ethos' (Section 1.2). The basic concerns of modern philosophical ethics can then be elucidated from a cultural-historical perspective (Section 1.3). This is followed by an attempt to explicate the humanistic core of the universal moral principle, whose justification is the central issue of modern ethics (Section 1.4). From this vantage point it will then be possible to understand the developmental stages of moral consciousness, which every individual goes through in his progress towards becoming a (modern) person capable of moral judgement (Section 1.5).

1.1 The moral disposition as part of the conditio humana

Being human means freedom of choice.[1]

It is one of the fundamental 'conditions for the possibility of human existence'[2] and an indispensable aspect of the conditio humana that man – and that means in principle every single person – is a being whose behaviour, in contrast to that of other life forms, is not determined by the laws of nature. To a substantial degree it takes the form of deliberate *action*. The basis of man's ability to act is his freedom to develop a will of his own (freedom of the will) and *to take a stance*[3] on

[1] A. Portmann, *Um das Menschenbild* (Stuttgart: Reclam, 1964), p. 71.
[2] H. Plessner, 'Conditio Humana', in G. Mann/A. Heuss (eds.), *Propyläen Weltgeschichte*, 10 vols (Berlin/Frankfurt: Propyläen, 1964), vol. I, pp. 33–86, at p. 38.
[3] See A. Gehlen, *Man, his Nature and Place in the World* (New York: Columbia University Press, 1988; 1st edn German, Bonn, 1940), p. 3f.

the world, himself and the various possibilities for action (freedom of action). To take a stance means choosing an intellectual 'standpoint' from which we can judge our own actions and those of other persons. *Moral* judgements are involved when they refer to the constitutive 'conditions for the possibility of human existence' as such: that is to say to the inviolable freedom of all persons concerned.

Man is capable of taking a stance on himself and is, consequently, vitally dependent on the cultivation of his capacity for moral judgement and feeling as the basic precondition for his humanity. We characterize this fundamental state of man as his *moral disposition* or his general *morality*. This moral disposition is the basis for the irrefutable personal claim of man as a subject to regard himself in principle as free. We cannot dispute this personal claim without abandoning entirely the idea that man is in possession of free will and sound of mind, capable of taking stances and of accepting responsibility for his actions. In other words, we cannot deny the claim without denying ourselves. The ideas of morality and freedom are, therefore, inseparable:

> In the concept of morality freedom is seen as unconditional, as the unconditional claim to realize freedom for its own sake as the highest human good.[4]

As such an 'unconditional claim' the idea of morality is a concept of principle or reason.[5] We must assume and accept that every creature we recognize as human possesses the same disposition towards morality as ourselves and thus belongs to the specifically human community of beings who are in principle free and capable of self-determination. They are, consequently, also moral beings. For when we judge or address another person we always assume his autonomy and *soundness of mind*, i.e. his capacity for personal judgement of his own actions in the light of an idea of what is morally right.[6] At the same time, respect for the personal claim of another to see himself as a free subject is the basic moral condition of all legitimate claims we (in turn) can make on the actions of another person. From a moral point of view, interpersonal obligations can be founded only on the observation of the same inviolable freedom of all men in the sense of their right to pursue the 'possibility of human existence' to the full. This is in accordance with the autonomous *personal commitment* of every moral subject to the conditions of the general freedom of all men. Therefore, morality is the idea that renders personal freedom and interpersonal obligation compatible.

4 A. Pieper, *Einführung in die Ethik*, 2nd rev. edn (Tübingen: Francke, 1991), p. 44.
5 See ibid., p. 44.
6 For this reason people who are not sound of mind are regarded in the moral and legal sense (in legal procedures) as not responsible for their crimes.

In view of his unique 'world-openness'[7] man is existentially dependent on his capacity for morality. It is what permits him to take his life culturally 'into his own hands' in the first place and to lead it consciously, i.e. to orientate himself in his thinking and actions on self-determined ideas of the good life and a just and co-operative life with others. Man's openness to the world can be closed only normatively. Every supposedly objective 'ascertainment' of what man 'is' is inevitably already a part of his (inter-) subjective self-determination and thus the expression of a projection of what man *should* be or what he *wishes* to be for himself. Man 'is' what he makes or attempts to make of himself in the human community as a social, cultural and historical being.

From this principle of human autonomy it follows ultimately – at least within the framework of an 'ethics without metaphysics' (Patzig) – that we cannot find the *reasons* which lead us to regard certain moral validity claims as valid and obligatory in any instance outside ourselves. The sole instance is our moral disposition and hence our *willingness* to accept a moral self-commitment founded on the understanding of its human significance for ourselves and for others. We must already be in possession of this good will as such, before any justification of moral claims 'addresses' us. In this primacy of the moral 'will' over every justifiable normative 'ought' our autonomy and moral disposition are then expressed.[8]

However, this primacy must not be confused with a decisionist reduction of the moral 'ought' to an arbitrary individual 'will' in the sense of merely subjective preferences.[9] The indissoluble reflexive relationship between the (rationally) justified 'ought' and the moral 'will' must, rather, be taken into account. Good reasons (for what we should do) are nothing but ethically rational motives for what we wish to do as self-respecting persons of integrity.[10] What we should do for moral reasons is

[7] On this concept, which can be traced back to Max Scheler, see Gehlen, *Man*, p. 27; see also Plessner, 'Conditio Humana', p. 64 and A. Portmann, *Entlässt die Natur den Menschen?* (Munich: Piper, 1970), p. 205.

[8] See E. Tugendhat, *Vorlesungen über Ethik* (Frankfurt: Suhrkamp, 1993), p. 96f.

[9] It is not chance that such a non-cognitivist position, which ultimately reduces morality to subjective preferences (which are neither capable of nor require justification) and is thus equivalent to ethical relativism, can often be found among economists. A representative example is K. Homann, 'Konsensethik', in *Gabler Volkswirtschafts-Lexikon* (Wiesbaden: Gabler, 1996), pp. 614–17, who speaks of a non-cognitivist version of 'consensus ethics' in which the moral 'ought' is traced back to human 'will'. See also H. Kliemt, 'Individualism, Libertarianism and Non-Cognitivism', *Analyse & Kritik* 8 (1986), pp. 211–28.

[10] On this practical mediation of reasons and motives see E. Tugendhat, 'Gibt es eine moderne Moral?', *Zeitschrift für Philosophische Forschung* 50 (1996), pp. 323–38, at p. 331. As Tugendhat self-critically remarks, in his earlier writings he did not always maintain

in the final analysis, therefore, identical with what we can rationally want to do (autonomous duty ethics).[11]

But can we assume that people are usually morally 'responsive' and 'reasonable' when we know that they ultimately decide autonomously whether they wish to act morally? We can, of course, never know whether or how far people are willing in a certain situation to follow moral arguments, but we do at least know beyond doubt that all people are human beings like ourselves and, consequently, have morality, at least in principle, at their disposal. It is, therefore, quite legitimate to assume, in view of the need for self-respect and the membership of a social community held together by its sense of moral obligation, that every person of reasonably sound personality will in principle wish to lead his life in accordance with moral postulates, even though he does not succeed in doing so in every situation and at every moment of his life. We feel the identity-shaping need to belong to a community we regard as valuable and to see ourselves as respectable and decent people living in accordance with the community's moral standards. In this need we discover a fundamental, although possibly weak, motive for moral action, which normally makes it possible to make (reciprocal) moral 'claims' in our dealings with one another. But before we can be at all responsive to good reasons enabling us to see why we *should* act in a particular moral fashion, we must have an interest, already anchored in our personal identity, in understanding ourselves as members of a community and we must possess the *will* to act in accordance with its moral principles.

That good will is not merely an ivory-towered idealistic postulate but is deeply rooted in the conditio humana, is a fundamental fact of life founded on the social structure of all morality. From early childhood the world we live in, in which our moral sense develops, is replete with expectations and 'claims' of the important people in our lives not only in regard to our outward behaviour but also to our inner motives and value orientations. By internalizing these moral claims we develop our moral demands on ourselves (conscience); and by approving them and integrating them into our self-understanding we consolidate our – always vulnerable – feeling of self-esteem.

This, in turn, promotes the development of our moral expectations in regard to the attitudes and behaviour of others. We want to be treated

this identity of good reasons and ethically rational motives. This is the case, for example in Tugendhat, *Vorlesungen*, p. 29: 'That we wish to be a good member of society at all ... is ultimately an autonomous act on our part for which there can only be good motives but no good reasons.' To be correct this ought to read something like: '... for which the only good reasons are rational motives.'

11 On this point see the treatment of Kant in Section 2.3.

'decently' by them and recognized as full members of the social community we live in. There is in principle a (reciprocal) symmetry in these inter-personal expectations of the members of such a *moral community*, even if it is often overlaid by special role expectations which can indeed be asymmetrical (e.g. hierarchically organized). The phenomenon of morality finds its roots and, at the same time, its real-life practical meaning in this fundamental social structure of interpersonal claims and obligations:

> An attitude which is not integrated in the intersubjective structure of moral demands is not moral at all.[12]

This intersubjective basic structure of mutual moral expectations is so deeply anchored in the conditio humana that we can never completely 'opt out' of the moral community of our lifeworld, even if the selfish inclinations of our nature, to which we are also certainly subject, occasionally seduce us into behaving parasitically as moral *free riders*. We then profit from the moral consciousness and sense of obligation of other members of the moral community without ourselves behaving in a correspondingly social or cooperative way.[13] After all, we are neither angels nor devils, but human beings with all the consequent ambivalence and contradictions. (Devils know no ethics, angels have no need of it.) The fact that there is tension and often enough a discrepancy between our actions and our moral insights as to the way we ought to act does not make ethics – understood quite simply for the moment as the methodical search for a justified moral orientation – superfluous but, quite the contrary, really necessary in the practice of everyday life.

The anchoring of morality in the conditio humana rests on the interaction of two essential moments: (1) the affective moment of moral feelings and (2) the cognitive moment of the moral faculty of judgement and consciousness, which, as we shall see shortly, is fundamental to the first moment.

(1) The inescapability of our moral feelings

Morality is that particular dimension of human feeling in which men take an interest in the well-being of their fellow men and are 'affectively on the same wavelength'.[14] It is the soil in which both our respect for the personality of others and our own self-esteem grows or withers. The often very strong moral feelings we experience in early childhood are omnipresent throughout our lives; they are of paramount importance for our relations with others. Take, for example, the feelings of mutual

[12] Tugendhat, *Vorlesungen*, p. 64. [13] See ibid., p. 317f. [14] Ibid., p. 284.

respect or contempt, the approval or disapproval of the actions of others, shame over one's actions and indignation about the actions of others; hurt feelings or even humiliation of one's own self-esteem, resentment towards those responsible for injustice, lack of solidarity and disregard for interpersonal obligations and commitments; sympathy with others, feelings of guilt when we believe we have not fulfilled our duty towards others sufficiently or have acted wrongly when confronted with the needs or the vulnerability of another person.[15] Such omnipresent moral feelings remind us of the internalized expectations of the moral community of our lifeworld, whether it suits us or not at a certain moment. They themselves are always the expression of our moral capacity for judgement and thus presuppose its existence – and not vice versa.[16]

(2) The indisputability of our moral consciousness

That as human beings we are in principle capable of moral judgement is a fact we have already experienced well enough in our social life with others. As was mentioned briefly above, our moral capacity for judgement rests upon the culturally formed good will which has become part of our personal identity in the course of successful socialization, i.e. upon the will to belong to a moral community, to accept the corresponding moral obligations arising from interpersonal relations, and thus to be a good person in the sense of the prevailing morality of this community.[17] It may well be that our moral capacity for judgement is often clouded in specific situations or that our motivation to actually follow a moral insight in our actions is occasionally weak. But it is a well-known fact that precisely in such situations our moral consciousness tends to catch up with us, for instance, in the form of a 'bad conscience' (and is thus mediated by moral feelings!). Furthermore, a person who acts wrongly in terms of the moral conventions of his lifeworld and who is aware of his failings can know this and feel more or less shame for his actions only because he still belongs, as a result of the development of his personal and social identity, to the 'moral cosmos' of a certain social community.[18] We can possibly repress certain moral feelings for a time, but we cannot deny that we possess a consciousness of the possibility *in principle* to take a moral stance on our

[15] One of the most subtle descriptions to date of the social structure and the psychological variety of moral feelings stems from none other than Adam Smith, *The Theory of Moral Sentiments* (Glasgow Edition of the Works and Correspondence of Adam Smith, Oxford, 1976; 1st edn 1759). Smith's ethics will be specifically treated below in Section 2.2.

[16] See Tugendhat, *Vorlesungen*, p. 20f. For a similar point of view see J. Habermas, *The Inclusion of the Other* (Cambridge MA: MIT Press, 1998), p. 4f.

[17] See Tugendhat, *Vorlesungen*, p. 56ff. [18] See ibid., p. 61.

own actions or those of others, precisely because this moral consciousness is already present whenever we attempt to argue against its existence.[19]

A mental experiment can help us to demonstrate more clearly the practical indispensability of moral consciousness and sensitivity as a 'condition for the possibility of human existence' in everyday life. What would change in our relationship with ourselves and the world around us if the *categories* of moral judgement and feeling were alien to us? We could then perceive others only as objects of our natural drives, affects and needs and would no longer be capable of understanding and reflecting on ourselves and our actions in regard to their interpersonal significance. As a consequence, individuals could only behave towards each other in an instrumental way.[20] A literally inhuman 'social coldness' would prevail in which we would lose all respect for others as human subjects and our self-respect into the bargain. Our dealings with one another would then be merely 'animal' and devoid of every specifically 'human' quality. Of course, inhumanity in this sense occurs on a small and on a large scale again and again. But the existence of individuals with a lack of moral sense, with an underdeveloped or disturbed moral consciousness, serves only to prove that the moral disposition is not an instinct man possesses by nature but presupposes the unremitting cultivation of his *practical reason.* Whether valid moral norms 'exist' in the social world is, in the final analysis, a practical and not a theoretical problem. The justification of moral demands and norms has an 'irreducibly practical meaning',[21] which we can only clarify self-reflectively – and in no other way – as participants in a human community. In the words of Kant it is a matter of 'the practical use of reason with regard to freedom'.[22]

1.2 Morals and ethos as two sides of lived morality

Morality was made for man, not man for morality.[23]

We can now assume, then, that we possess in principle a more or less developed moral consciousness. But how do we know in specific situations what is morally right or wrong and consequently how we ought to act?

[19] This strictly reflexive transcendental-pragmatic line of justificatory argument, which was developed above all by Karl-Otto Apel, plays a fundamental role in discourse ethics. It will be treated in more detail in Section 2.5.

[20] See Tugendhat, *Vorlesungen*, p. 22. The instrumentalist view of interpersonal relations corresponds, as he has also noted (ibid., p. 62), to the economic contractual theory concept of the justification of society (contractualism). This will be dealt with later in Section 5.3.

[21] Tugendhat, 'Gibt es eine moderne Moral?', p. 331.

[22] Kant, 'Metaphysics of Morals', p. 108.

[23] W. Frankena, *Ethics* (Englewood Cliffs NJ: Prentice Hall, 1963), p. 37.

If our socio-cultural formation has proceeded in a reasonably 'healthy' way, we will have a more or less strongly developed 'inner voice' we usually characterize as our conscience, and which we follow or at least struggle with in situations of inner conflict. Which moral feelings and judgements determine our conscience in particular circumstances depends essentially on the socio-cultural context that has shaped our personality, especially during our childhood.[24] Thus, although all men possess the same disposition for morality, it expresses itself in a never-ending culturally and historically determined variety of actual moral conceptions.

When we turn our attention away from general human morality to a particular cultural and historical context in which our moral standards develop, we then speak of socially valid morals in the sense of a specific *moral tradition*. In accordance with the Latin root (*mos*, pl. *mores*: [good] morals, customs) this concept of morals characterizes the totality of the customary, currently effective moral concepts, judgements, principles and norms. They determine correct moral action in the practice of everyday life in a general manner binding on all members of a culture. In other words, these moral obligations regulate what 'one' can and cannot do and what one should not do. Moral judgements refer to the prevailing rules of a just, mutually supportive and considerate life together in a social community. Such socially valid rules of interpersonal relations take effect as *moral norms*. In contrast to legal norms, whose fulfilment can be enforced by law, the claim of moral laws to be binding depends, from the perspective of the participants in a social practice, on the acceptance of these norms by the great majority of a community or society: 'They are *valid* in as far as they are largely recognized within the motivational horizons of the individual conscience.'[25] As we shall see more precisely in the following section, this *social acceptance* must not be confused with the *rational validity (legitimacy)* of moral claims.

As long as our dealings with other people are restricted to those who essentially share our moral views because they have grown up in the same historical and cultural context and have been 'brought up' in the same or a similar fashion, we will normally understand each other's moral feelings and judgements perfectly well and have little reason to question the validity of our moral principles. But when people with very different moral conceptions encounter each other – and this will be more and more the normal case in an increasingly multicultural world – moral

[24] We will deal in more detail with the aspect of the formation of moral consciousness in the course of the development of the child to a 'mature' adult personality in Section 1.5.

[25] A. Anzenbacher, *Einführung in die Ethik* (Düsseldorf: Patmos, 1992), p. 110.

conflicts can easily arise as soon as the achievement of understanding on the principles of social coexistence or the correct way of living are at issue. Under these circumstances, whose moral concepts should be regarded as valid and who should be judged 'right' in the case of interpersonal conflict?

In the search for solutions to interpersonal conflicts we are always, in the final analysis, faced with the choice between the simple exercise of power and recourse to good reasons. In the first case the parties to the conflict do not see themselves as participants in a moral community or their conflict as a moral conflict between claims to validity which are capable of clarification. Instead the problem is reduced to the question of 'might is right' and leads to a ruthless (social Darwinist) state of war 'of every man against every man'.[26] Only when the parties to a conflict regard themselves in principle as members of the same moral universe of all human beings will they be in any way motivated to reach an agreement on a peaceful and just solution and so to abandon the power principle in favour of the moral principle in the solution of conflicts. In this second case the mere tolerance of the given power structure is replaced by the common will to find a (rational) justification for the moral rights of those concerned, in whose light we can answer for our actions to the others and to our own conscience.[27]

The essential subject matter of every robust moral conception is consequently the determination of interpersonal rights and duties in accordance with which the justification or *legitimacy* of conflicting personal claims can be tested. In principle, those actions can be regarded as legitimate (i.e. justified, well-grounded) which do not impinge on the moral rights of another person. If someone in a position of superior power is interested in the legitimacy of his actions, he will not enforce that power against weaker persons but will attempt to do justice to their moral rights out of a feeling of interpersonal commitment – and that means out of an awareness of the moral community he shares with people in need of protection. In a word, he autonomously subjects himself to the requirement of *solidarity* with those in need of protection.[28]

The consciousness with which a person is accustomed to justify his self-understanding, his conduct of life and his dealings with others depicts his

[26] This is the famous formulation of Thomas Hobbes (1651). See Thomas Hobbes, *Leviathan*, ed. Edwin Curley (Indianapolis: Hackett, 1994), p. 76.

[27] We take up the category of moral rights again in Section 1.4 (3). A further treatment of the concept of responsibility can be found in Sections 2.4 and 2.5 (3).

[28] See J. Habermas, *Inclusion of the Other*, p. 10: 'The 'solidarity' grounded in membership recalls the social bond that unites all persons: one person stands in for the other.'

ethos. Although this term contains a moral concept, it is employed nowadays as a specific category.[29] In the original concrete sense the Greek concept of ethos (with a short 'e') means 'habitat' (residence, domicile, abode), the most familiar place in our lives, the environment of our 'habits' and the mainstay of our inner stability. In this transferred sense it corresponds quite precisely with the Latin concept of *mores*. In a second transferred sense the concept of ethos (with a long 'e') also meant for the ancient Greeks 'virtues of character'.[30] In the contemporary usage ethos is normally used only in this second personal sense. It no longer characterizes a socially valid morality, but the subjective self-understanding and (character-shaping) convictions or the basic attitude of a person. Convictions which internalize morally good actions in a way that shapes personality are called virtues. Ethical *virtues* define a concept of 'moral competence';[31] they imply both a particular idea of a 'good person' (virtue ethics) and a corresponding projection of a good and successful life. This, in turn, largely determines what kinds of goods in the broadest sense of the concept are regarded as desirable (goods ethics, ethics of the good life).

The highest good can be defined formally as *happiness*, in whatever way we perceive it in accordance with our projection of the good life. Happiness is the sum total of what we desire for its own sake, as an ultimate goal, and not as the means to some even higher end.[32] Thus, when we sometimes feel 'perfectly happy' we would often like to perpetuate this state if we could. But human happiness is scarcely achievable as a permanent state; it can only be imagined as a meaningful journey, as an 'activity of the soul in accordance with virtue'.[33] What makes a good and happy life cannot be established in a generally valid way; it is a question of

[29] The conceptual distinction between the nouns 'morals' and 'ethos' is also maintained by some philosophers in the use of the adjectives 'moral' and 'ethical', in particular by J. Habermas, *Justification and Application: Remarks on Discourse Ethics* (Cambridge MA: MIT Press, 1993), p. 1ff. The latter conceptual practice is not followed here, as 'ethical' is at the same time the adjective corresponding to the concept of ethics and the maintenance of the distinction between the levels of a (conventional) ethos and the modern (supposedly post-conventional) ethics appears more important systematically than the distinction between morality and ethos. Consequently, in our usage, the adjective 'ethical' is strictly reserved for the scientific level of reflection on ethics. Accordingly, it makes little sense to say that an action or behaviour is 'unethical', as 'ethical' in our usage always refers only to the methodical level and *form* of justification and not to a particular *content* of morality or ethos.

[30] Aristotle, *Nichomachean Ethics* (Cambridge: Cambridge University Press, 2000), p. 23. Cf. the nuances in Piper, *Einführung*, p. 25f., Tugendhat, *Vorlesungen*, p. 34, and A. Rich, *Business and Economic Ethics: The Ethics of Economic Systems* (Leuven: Peeters, 2006), p. 11f.

[31] See Aristotle, *Nicomachean Ethics*, p. 26. [32] See ibid., p. 10f. [33] Ibid., p. 12.

the authenticity of the projected life plan of a person in the light of what he regards as desirable.[34]

One of the oldest and most difficult questions concerns the relationship between happiness and morality, the subjectively good life and the morally good (virtuous) life, self-fulfilment and consideration for others.[35] On the one hand it can hardly be denied that moral obligations sometimes stand in the way of the pursuit of our happiness, but on the other hand, personal happiness can scarcely be found outside the moral community shared with others. Consequently, the good life cannot simply be divorced from the idea of the morally good conduct of life. The achievement of a balance between the personal pursuit of happiness and moral consideration of the legitimate claims of others always takes place within our moral consciousness.[36] The ethos of a person who has achieved inner stability as a result of his social formation and life experience is characterized by such a (personally) beneficial balance he or she develops and maintains in his or her daily dealings with this tense relationship. The sustenance and perfection of this balance will then surely be regarded as an essential moment of personal happiness.

The indispensable substratum of a (personal) ethos lies in the normative obligations of a moral tradition which is internalized in the course of life and is assumed to be more or less self-evident. A particular ethos is thus a fact requiring cultural and historical interpretation in the same fashion as the moral tradition which forms its basis. The ethos of a person, a life community or a social group (e.g. a profession) is governed by a culture-specific idea of the good life. It includes all the normative fundamental convictions that determine self-understanding and personal role definition, provide inner meaning and motivation for actions in general or in a particular sphere of life (e.g. work ethic), and serve to justify those actions both individually and intersubjectively (legitimation). It can now be said that the ethos determines the demands that people or life communities make upon their all-embracing cultural identity, i.e. the subjective guidelines of authentic *will* and hence the core of what makes up the 'good will' of a person. The motivating force is, above all, the original (childhood) wish or social psychological need to draw our understanding of ourselves as good ('I'm ok') from our membership of the moral community we are born

[34] It is a well-known fact that the other side of the *conditio humana* usually catches up with us all too quickly, namely our existence as a (more or less civilized) being with needs, including among others the anthropological necessity for economic activity; consequently *economic ethics* makes up an essential part of the ethos of a life form, i.e. the basic attitude towards economic 'values' and the significance we attribute to them in regard to our good life.

[35] See M. Seel, *Versuch über die Form des Glücks* (Frankfurt: Suhrkamp, 1995), p. 13ff.

[36] See ibid., p. 43.

into.[37] We can develop and define our identity only in a meaningful community with others and so 'find ourselves' as independent and autonomous individuals.[38] In other words, the personal meaning of life cannot be discovered without a certain degree of community spirit. Consequently, a healthy ethos defines both our personal and our social identity:

- At the level of *personal identity* our unique, unmistakable and irreplaceable self, our autonomy (individualization), is formed. This permits the clarification of questions of the following kind: 'Who am I? How do I want to lead my life? What is the meaning of life for me?'
- At the level of *social identity* our social sense of belonging is stabilized in the form of membership of a moral community we consider 'valuable' and in which we recognize moral commitments as part of our identity (social integration). This permits the clarification of questions of the type: 'Whom do I feel at home with? Where can I find a meaningful place in the world? With whom do I share community spirit?'

Ideas of the good life, therefore, form the motivational background to moral action, but as a whole they neither need nor are accessible to a normative justification. In as far as they are available to us, they must be attractive enough to 'speak for themselves'.[39] The need for a rational foundation or justification of ideas of the good life shaped by ethos exists in a modern free society only if and as far as particular actions conflict with the claims of others or our own claims in regard to legitimacy and solidarity. In other words, justification is required only in regard to the question of whether a subjectively desired form of life includes 'socially acceptable' normative conditions for the involvement of others. No justification is required for the inner meaning (and content) of this form of life for the person who wishes to live that life. In a free society, intersubjectively valid norms of a just and solidary life in common determine the framework within which a pluralism in the forms of the good life chosen by individuals and groups is justified.[40] To this extent questions of morality enjoy primacy over questions of ethos. The aspects of ethos and morals thus prove to be interwoven. The former presents the motivational basis of a (more or less strong) will to behave in a moral fashion and the latter rationally justifies the normative obligations we should fulfil and marks the boundaries within

[37] See Tugendhat, *Vorlesungen*, p. 88ff.

[38] See K. Jaspers, *Einführung in die Philosophie*, 4th edn (Zurich: Artemis, 1963), p. 112; Engl. *Way to Wisdom: An Introduction to Philosophy* (New Haven: Yale University Press, 1951).

[39] F. Kambartel, 'Rekonstruktion und Rationalität. Zur normativen Grundlage einer Theorie der Wissenschaft', in Schwemmer (ed.), *Vernunft, Handlung und Erfahrung*, pp. 11–21, at p. 21.

[40] For a further consideration see Chapters 6 and 7.

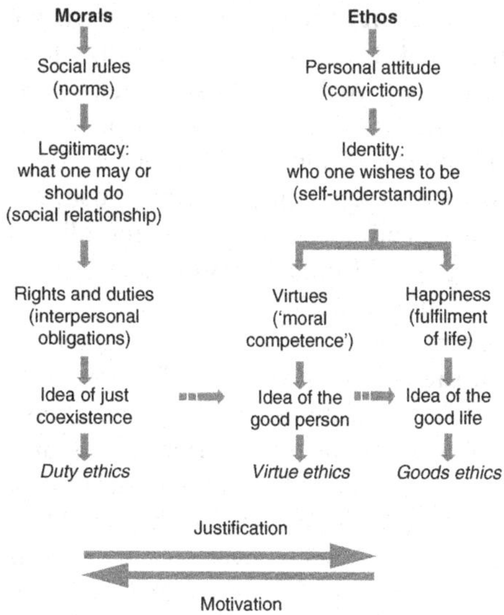

Figure 1.1. The categories 'morals' and 'ethos'

which we are free to pursue self-fulfilment in accordance with our personal ethos. Figure 1.1 schematically contrasts the two categories of morality and ethos developed here and illustrates the way they interlock.

1.3 Modern ethics and the problem of relativism

The rational foundation of moral principles and obligations is the central question of modern ethics. Ethics as a philosophical discipline can be distinguished from a particular ethos or the accepted morals of a social group by a qualified justification of moral claims. It does not refer to a different object of analysis but to a different level of reflection. Whereas ethos and morals denote traditional facts found in a variety of historical and cultural contexts, the purpose of ethics as a scientific, methodically disciplined form of reflection is a context-free critique and rational justification of moral ideas guided by reason:

> In accordance with a usage which is gradually becoming established we characterize 'morals' as the sum total of moral norms, value judgements and institutions, whereas we reserve the term 'ethics' ... for the philosophical examination of the problem field of morality.[41]

[41] Patzig, *Ethik ohne Metaphysik*, p. 4f.

In accordance with this delimitation of the concept, ethics is concerned with the reflective treatment of traditional (historically determined) forms of ethos as a whole.[42] As we have already seen, every ethos, particularly in the field of virtue (the idea of the good person), presupposes the existence of a moral conception. Consequently, the 'problem field of morality' (Patzig) does indeed occupy a central position in modern philosophical ethics; it deals with questions of the good life only in as far as they impinge upon the general formal conditions of an intersubjectively shared life form that requires rational justification.[43]

The demarcation of modern ethics from morals and ethos brings into the foreground an aspect of the historical process of rationalization and modernization, in which we, as ethically reflective beings, have always been involved.[44] The more traditional value orientations and norms dissolve as a result of the ongoing process of cultural, social and economic modernization (i.e. of rational questioning and reshaping of nearly all traditions), the more complex and confusing everyday life becomes. And the more frequently and diversely the different cultural traditions in the developing global society clash, the more indispensable ethics becomes as a contribution to the critical examination and advancement of moral traditions:

> Wherever traditional (worldly) wisdom and institutions have lost their self-evident validity, philosophical ethics, guided by the idea of a meaningful human life, attempts to arrive at generally valid statements about good and just actions in a methodical way, without final recourse to any religious or political authorities or to custom and tradition.[45]

Whereas in pre-modern societies moral teachings are founded on dogma, and the conventional, generally unquestioned, 'set values' anchored authoritatively in conscience are binding for all, in modern society all traditional validity claims, even the former certitudes of individual conscience, are in principle open to question and require a rational foundation.[46] This also applies to the residue of moral traditions which are not

[42] See above, note 29 in Section 1.2.

[43] For a remarkable attempt to establish a modern formal ethics of the good life see Seel, *Versuch über die Form des Glücks*.

[44] For a detailed treatment of the dimensions of the historical process of rationalization see P. Ulrich, *Transformation der ökonomischen Vernunft: Fortschrittsperspektiven der modernen Industriegesellschaft*, 3rd rev. edn (Berne *et al.*: Haupt, 1993; 1st edn 1986), p. 23ff.

[45] See the headword 'Ethik' in O. Höffe (ed.), *Lexikon der Ethik*, 4th edn (Munich: Beck, 1992), p. 61f.

[46] The fact that the individual conscience can be subjected to critical philosophical-ethical questioning by no means permits the conclusion that an argumentative or even a legal examination of conscience under unqualified pragmatic circumstances is reasonable.

yet 'questioned', at least not generally, since they will probably be perceived as behind the times by a growing part of the population unless they are critically integrated into the modern lifeworld. Otherwise they will then lose their normative force, and rightly so, in as far as their continued validity as points of orientation for moral action cannot be proved with good reasons at the level of objective ethical argumentation. This general orientation towards a rational grounding of moral obligations expresses no more and no less than the modern tendency towards rationalization of the entire practice of everyday life.

In a truly modern society, therefore, moral norms and standards worthy of recognition cannot exist without ethical-critical reflection. However, such critical reflection first of all creates an awareness of the *cultural relativity* of moral traditions and convictions of conscience: it all depends. With the first step in ethical-critical reflection it is already theoretically possible to imagine oneself as a 'native' of another cultural tradition, who, on occasion, might well judge moral questions differently. An ethics whose justificatory achievements fail to exceed the horizon of its own cultural tradition could do little to change that situation. Why should something be regarded as reasonable on its terms which in the eyes of the 'members' of different moral traditions is possibly only an expression of an historically evolved ethos they do not share, and which can, consequently, by no means be regarded as justified in a generally valid way outside the tradition it is embedded in?

From the standpoint of cultural history, the experience of the cultural relativity of moral traditions and the modern demand for a general rational foundation for the conduct of life has led to the collapse of nearly all traditional 'set values'. The epochal process of 'demystification of the world'[47] is only today being fully felt in many cultures throughout the world and even in the West it is by no means completed. But together with the accompanying abandonment of pre-modern ethical dogmatism

The subjection of the conscience to critical questioning applies without further qualification only to the level of a scientific argumentation without reference to real-life situations (i.e. is practically free of consequences and sanctions). At the legal level the extensive constitutional protection of individual freedom of conscience is to be preferred, as examinations of conscience before the courts (e.g. of the kind formerly practised in court cases against conscientious objectors with dubious results) have direct punitive consequences and hence cannot meet the requirements of a moral discourse which must take place without reference to specific practical actions. On this point see D. Böhler, 'Philosophischer Diskurs im Spannungsfeld von Theorie und Praxis', in K.-O. Apel/D. Böhler/K. Rebel (eds.), *Funkkolleg Praktische Philosophie/Ethik: Studientexte*, 3 vols. (Weinheim/Basle: Beltz, 1984), vol. II, pp. 313–55, at p. 344ff.

47 Cf. M. Weber, *From Max Weber: Essays in Sociology*, ed. H. H. Gerth and C. Wright Mills (London: Routledge, 1991; 1st edn 1948), p. 350, where the German 'Entzauberung' is unsatisfactorily translated as 'disenchantment'.

or anti-modern fundamentalism one of its primary effects has been to create an enormous loss of orientation or even of existential roots among modern men, as is most radically revealed in the philosophy of existentialism in the first half of the twentieth century. After the loss of the security provided by the tradition of divinely guaranteed, dogmatically fixed moral precepts and prohibitions, moral principles or obligations no longer seem to be justifiable at all, at least as long as the rational foundation of an ethics without metaphysics seems impossible. Nietzsche was the first to grasp clearly the sobering consequences of this disillusionment in regard to all moral dogmas:

> [It is] naïve [to behave] as if morals would survive the disappearance of the sanctioning God.[48]

Therefore, the perception of the cultural relativity of moral convictions leads almost inevitably to *ethical relativism* or *scepticism* and finally to *nihilism*. Whereas cultural relativism regards the actual differences in the various traditions of culture, ethos and morals as a given fact, it leaves the possibility of an ethical universalism open. Ethical (or normative) relativism, however, includes the conviction that omnicultural normative obligations (for example universal human rights) cannot be founded on reason. The ethical relativist draws the (mistaken) sceptical conclusion that it is in fact an ethical requirement of intercultural tolerance to desist from all kinds of morally motivated 'interference' in other cultural contexts (for example with protests against violations of human rights). But he inevitably ends up in a self-contradictory position, as he himself implicitly claims universal validity for the principle of tolerance he advocates. As he lacks a culturally invariant moral point of view from which he could criticize the prevailing moral traditions, it appears impossible for him to reach a decision on their validity or invalidity. Ultimately the subjective decision on a particular conviction is a matter of indifference to him – in contrast to the ethical dogmatists or fundamentalists.[49]

In spite of its self-understanding, ethical relativism has by no means stepped out of the long shadow of the old authoritative moral conception, as Nietzsche's dictum quoted above reveals. Ernst Tugendhat puts it in a nutshell:

[48] F. Nietzsche, *Werke*, vol. III, ed. K. Schlechta (Munich: Hanser, 1956), p. 484 (in the 'Nachlass'; own transl., not included in English editions).

[49] For a critique of ethical relativism see L. Kohlberg, *Essays on Moral Development, vol. I: The Philosophy of Moral Development* (San Francisco: Harper & Row, 1981), p. 105ff.; see also Oser/Althof, *Moralische Selbstbestimmung*, p. 124ff.

It appears just as naïve to believe that there is a book in heaven which contains all the answers to moral difficulties as to regard everything as arbitrary in the absence of such a book. Both viewpoints result from one and the same precondition, the orientation on an authoritarian morality.[50]

In the dilemma of choice between pre-modern dogmatism and ethical scepticism the *Zeitgeist* at the turn of the millennium is still shuttling back and forth between supposedly post-modern arbitrariness and the corresponding opportunism on the one hand, and all the newly burgeoning forms of fundamentalism on the other. These wish to compensate for the frightening loss of normative orientations and the exacting demands of modern life to find one's own orientations (in thought and action) by adopting a counter-enlightenment recourse to authoritative 'fixed values'.[51] As neither position can show how generally acceptable principles of a peaceful and dignified social coexistence between the supporters of different world views can be rationally founded, there is a danger that the 'irreconcilable conflict' between 'the various value spheres of the world' will break out, which Max Weber – himself an ethical sceptic and non-cognitivist[52] – saw looming on the horizon at the beginning of the twentieth century.[53] For where the terrain of ethical reflection guided by reason is abandoned and the readiness to search argumentatively for moral principles and rules of fair play between the different life projects and 'value spheres' is lacking, the way is opened to inhumanity and barbarity. This then leads to the discrimination of minorities and the systematic violation of human rights and ends in 'ethnic cleansing' or the holocaust. It is not by mere coincidence that the twentieth century experienced more of these horrors than the entire history of the human race before it, a fact largely explained by the intellectual situation of the epoch sketched above.

In this situation modern ethics acquires epochal significance as the founder of a universal orientation of human values. To this end it follows

[50] Tugendhat, *Vorlesungen*, p. 332.

[51] On the understanding of present-day fundamentalist currents as a reaction to the 'unreasonableness of thinking for oneself' in modern life see Th. Meyer, *Fundamentalismus – Aufstand gegen die Moderne* (Reinbek: Rowohlt, 1989).

[52] In the philosophical and epistemological debate ethical scepticism is often characterized as non-cognitivism. For a four-phase distinction in the levels of cognitivism and non-cognitivism from strong to weak see J. Habermas, *Inclusion of the Other*, p. 5ff. Weak non-cognitivism, which accepts rational motives in the sense of strategic rationality but not a rational moral point of view, has found widespread acceptance in positivistic and scientistic approaches, particularly in economic theory. This has, hitherto, made the relationship between economic theory and modern economic ethics difficult, as we shall see in Section 5.3.

[53] M. Weber, 'Science as a Vocation', in *From Max Weber*, pp. 129–56, at p. 147.

the only path still open: the 'third way' of practical reason, which steers us between the Scylla of counter-enlightenment fundamentalism and the Charybdis of scepticism and nihilism.[54] In harmony with the basic ideas of the enlightenment and of political-philosophical liberalism (in its unabbreviated form[55]), modern ethics searches for the multiplicity of legitimate value orientations in the unity of a 'culture of reason' (Kant). From the cultural-historical perspective (outlined above) the *search for the ethical in the rational* is in no way the expression of an ivory-towered academic rationalism remote from real life; on the contrary, it is the only practical chance for the pacification of a multicultural world which, in the absence of a minimal intercultural 'world ethos',[56] is at all times threatened by the violent clash of uncompromisingly propagated and fundamentalistically dogmatized moral systems, as experience shows.

The motivation to pursue a moral lifestyle can in the first place probably be built only on the foundations of a humanistic experience of ethos in one of the great world cultures and religions. However, if a circular reference back to a culturally biased ethos is to be avoided, an omnicultural, universally valid (minimal) ethics must necessarily presuppose the existence of a post-conventional moral point of view.[57] As it ought to be culturally invariant, such a general moral point of view cannot be founded on an instance outside the (self-) critical reason of man. For precisely this reason modern ethics is conceivable only 'within the limits of reason alone',[58] as *rational ethics.*[59] Without the assumption of a universal moral principle founded on rational ethics to which parties in dispute

[54] On this practical philosophical new beginning of ethics beyond dogmatism and nihilism see Ulrich, *Transformation*, p. 269ff.

[55] For a closer clarification of an unabbreviated understanding of political liberalism see Section 7.3.

[56] The concept of 'world ethos' or 'world ethic' coined by the ecumenical theologian Hans Küng accentuates a shared humanistic ethos which can be found already in the various moral conventions of the great world religions. See H. Küng, *Global Responsibility: In Search of a New World Ethic* (London: SCM/New York: Crossroad, 1991). For a further treatment, with impressive proofs for a growing awareness of the necessity for a global ethos, see his *A Global Ethic for Global Politics and Economics* (New York: Oxford University Press, 1998).

[57] On the distinction between conventional and post-conventional moral consciousness see Section 1.5.

[58] Following I. Kant, *Religion within the Limits of Reason Alone* (New York: Harper, 1960).

[59] The claims of a rational ethics can and should, in my opinion, be maintained – and here I am in obvious disagreement with Tugendhat, *Vorlesungen*, p. 70 – even when the primacy of the *will* to (practical) reason over every justifiable 'ought' is accepted. The concept of rational ethics need not be treated as equivalent to Kant's transcendental philosophical claim of an absolute justification of the categorical imperative, which Tugendhat (ibid., p. 88ff.) rightly rejects as a foundation for modern ethics. Although, as we shall see in Section 2.3, Kant does indeed explicate with the categorical imperative the moral principle of a *humanistic* rational ethics, his justificatory claim is still rooted in the

Morality =	Fundamental *disposition* of man in the sense of – his personal claim to moral self-determination (autonomy) – his moral sensitivity (vulnerability) and – his moral capacity for judgement (conscience) – independent of the plurality of the specific historical and cultural forms under which this basic human state has been cultivated → *conditio humana* = the 'nature' of man
Morals =	The *socially valid* moral rights, duties and behavioural norms – deriving from a culture-specific tradition, – which determine real-life practice – independently of whether the members of this tradition are aware of it or not → established *conventions* = lived morals
Ethos =	The subjective moral *consciousness* through which people – define their personal self-understanding and the conduct of their lives and – justify the moral principles on which their lives are based – independently of whether they have ethically good reasons or are the victims of ideological self-deception → personal *conviction* = self-conception in regard to identity and legitimacy
Ethics =	*Philosophical reflection* which (as modern rational ethics) attempts – to found a universally valid humanistic moral principle by means of practical reason – in the light of which the normative validity of moral claims can be critically considered as well as the further-reaching universal conditions and forms of the good life, just coexistence and responsible action – as independently as possible of moral traditions but in critical dialogue with them → universalistic and rational *moral point of view*

Figure 1.2. Basic ethical concepts

could appeal in order to clarify the justice of their claims rationally and impartially, it would be both impossible and superfluous to distinguish between ethos and ethics. This point will be further investigated in the following chapter.

Figure 1.2 briefly summarizes the basic ethical concepts elucidated to date.

1.4 The humanistic core of the moral principle: the normative logic of interpersonal relations

In what follows we speak of the 'moral principle' when we mean the fundamental universal idea of ethical practical reason itself, and we speak of the (rational) 'moral point of view'[60] when we refer to the

metaphysics of pure (divine) reason or 'a possible pure will' (in 'Metaphysics of Morals', p. 46) in which once again the primacy of an absolute moral law as an authoritative instance beyond (apriori) our moral autonomy is taken as given.

60 The concept of the moral point of view understood in a rational ethical sense stems from K. Baier, *Moral Point of View: Rational Basis of Ethics* (Ithaca/London: Cornell University Press, 1958).

philosophical-ethical forms of reflection on and justification of the moral principle. Although what is at issue is always the *one* moral principle, in the history of philosophy various attempts have been undertaken from different perspectives to define and justify the moral point of view. We will deal with the most important philosophical interpretations of the moral point of view in Chapter 2. For the moment we will attempt to come to grips directly with the humanistic core of the moral principle from the understanding of the phenomenon of the human moral disposition developed above and then (in Section 1.5) to show how the development of the personal moral consciousness, which runs an analogous course in all cultures even though the level achieved is (biographically) different for each individual, can be understood in terms of the moral principle.

Our task is to establish a rational foundation for an omnicultural post-conventional moral principle, whose universal validity can in principle be grasped in every culture that is accessible to reason, and hence cannot be disputed argumentatively. Logically, this requires the existence of a 'platform' which is independent of specific cultures. Such a rationally indisputable platform for modern ethics can be found at the culturally invariant level of the conditio humana in the fundamental intersubjective structure of all moral obligations. The rational moral point of view we are searching for can be explained reflexively by reference to the general *normative logic of interpersonal relations* we have always acceded to as moral beings.

In view of what has already been said above, we can immediately point to four closely interrelated, rationally indisputable, fundamental determinants of this universal logic of interpersonal obligations, or of the 'relation of rational beings to one another', as Kant[61] puts it, which are equally valid for all: (1) the equal vulnerability and need for protection of all men, (2) their equal ability to put themselves intellectually in the position of others, (3) the consequent reciprocity of legitimate moral claims, and finally, (4) the rational generalizability of moral reciprocity (principle of universalization).

(1) The vulnerability and need for protection of the human subject status

What is undoubtedly common to all men is their mental and physical vulnerability (fragility also in the psychological sense) and the corresponding claim to unconditional respect for and protection of the

[61] Kant, 'Metaphysics of Morals', p. 84.

'inviolability' of the identity, integrity and dignity of every individual. Our moral vulnerability reflects the profound human dependence on (self-) respect both for our unique individuality and our social membership of a community. The concept of *human dignity* characterizes the intact subject status of a person, which rests upon the regularly made experience that one's distinctive personality is not treated with disrespect or instrumentalized as the mere object of another's will.[62] Disregard of a person's dignity, i.e. of the preconditions for self-respect, comes down to humiliation. It is therefore essential for a decent society – long before it may become a just society – that its rules and institutions do not systematically humiliate anybody.[63] As inviolable subjects we merit both unconditional respect and protection of personality and, in equal measure, the solidarity of others (i.e. we are worthy of them), whenever we need them. In our childhood we have all made the inevitable, and in young years particularly painful, experience of the suffering involved when our subject status and dignity are violated by others, either through disrespect for our distinctive individuality or the denial of the solidarity needed from others. It is truly in accordance with our most elementary moral intuition, therefore, that careful and considerate handling of the extreme vulnerability of others is an essential aspect of 'human' coexistence.[64]

(2) *The capacity for imaginative role-taking*

All people are undoubtedly in a position to recognize another person as a person, to put themselves imaginatively in the position of another. As Adam Smith already realized, 'we can form no idea of the manner in which they are affected, but by conceiving what we ourselves should feel in the like situation'.[65] This human capacity for imaginative role-taking[66] is the cognitive root of our moral disposition. By putting ourselves

[62] Kant, 'Metaphysics of Morals', p. 84, already speaks in this sense of the 'idea of the *dignity* of a rational being who obeys no other law than that which he himself at the same time gives'.

[63] See A. Margalit, *The Decent Society* (Cambridge MA: Harvard University Press, 1996).

[64] See J. Habermas, 'Morality and Ethical Life: Does Hegel's Critique of Kant Apply to Discourse Ethics?', in Habermas, *Moral Consciousness and Communicative Action* (Cambridge: Polity, 1990), pp. 195–215, at p. 199; Habermas, *Justification and Application*, p. 109. Cf. also L. Wingert, *Gemeinsinn und Moral. Grundzüge einer intersubjektivistischen Moralkonzeption* (Frankfurt: Suhrkamp, 1993), pp. 15f., 166ff.

[65] Smith, *Moral Sentiments*, p. 9.

[66] This notion was introduced already in G. H. Mead, *Mind, Self and Society* (Chicago: University of Chicago Press, 1934), p. 254ff. See also J. Habermas, *Theory of Communicative Action*, 2 vols (Boston: Beacon Press, 1984), vol. II, p. 92ff.

imaginatively in the position of an alter ego it becomes possible for us both to show sympathy for his feelings and to achieve a critical self-reflection on our own actions by seeing 'with his eyes and from his station'.[67] This imaginative self-reflection from the standpoint of the other enables us to develop both our capacity for inter-personal relations and ties (social identity) and our 'self-image' and self-awareness (personal identity). For this reason our self-respect cannot be detached from the experience of being respected by others. This insight permits us to infer the deeper meaning of the concept of moral *integrity*: it can be literally understood as the intactness and wholeness of our moral self-relationship 'in view of' the reinforcing respect of those close to us. It allows us to look ourselves in the eye and to perceive ourselves as persons of integrity and hence as worthy of respect:

> The unconditional relations of mutual respect in which individuals confront one another as responsible acting persons are coeval with the phenomenon of self-respect, and thus with the consciousness of being worthy of the respect of others.[68]

(3) The interpersonal reciprocity of moral claims and rights

From the fact of intersubjective reversibility of perspectives we can also deduce the reciprocity of legitimate moral 'claims'. My moral claim to recognition and respect for my vulnerable subject status ('ego') stands symmetrically opposite to the same claim of the alter ego, as does my unconditional worthiness to be recognized as an 'inviolable' person. Consequently there is no 'private' or purely subjective morality; it is rather the case, as we have shown, that all moral claims, even our claims on ourselves have an intersubjective structure. Morality is 'irreducibly intersubjective'.[69]

The reciprocity of interpersonal expectations that corresponds to the intersubjective structure of all moral claims is expressed historically and culturally in a variety of forms as an *ethos of mutuality*.[70] As the renowned sociologist Alvin Gouldner has demonstrated empirically, the 'principle of

[67] Smith, *Moral Sentiments*, p. 110. [68] Habermas, *Justification and Application*, p. 46.
[69] Wingert, *Gemeinsinn und Moral*, p. 13.
[70] Reciprocity is fundamental not only to the symbolic ritual forms of interaction but also to language communication and the exchange of goods. The oldest symbolic ritual forms of interaction such as, for example, the reciprocal exchange of gifts arose in archaic society as mutual manifestations of a peaceful and friendly (not inimical) attitude in encounters between separate tribes or clans; they were not a form of economic exchange of goods but symbolized the *ethos* of reciprocity. See M. Mauss, *The Gift: Forms and Functions of Exchange in Archaic Societies*, transl. I. Cunnison (London: Cohen & West, 1966; French orig. 1924).

reciprocity' (a term probably first used by the ethnologist Malinowski in 1932) is in fact a universal element of all known cultures, also and not least when it is intended in the sense of the symmetry of reciprocal moral obligations.[71] Here we are interested only in the universal basic structure. Ego and alter ego cannot dispute each other's *moral right* (i.e. justified claim) to respect of the person without, as rational beings, at the same time revoking their own corresponding claim. The moral right of the one is the foundation for the *moral duty* of the other to observe this right and vice versa. It follows from this that they enjoy equal moral rights in regard to all the preconditions for the safeguarding of their human dignity and hence their personal identity and autonomy. To dispute this evident interpersonal symmetry of the moral rights and obligations existing between ego and alter ego would be tantamount to self-denial or pure cynicism.

(4) The rational generalizability of the moral principle of reciprocity

Every human being possesses a certain capacity for abstraction. This permits us to extend our insight into the reciprocal structure of interpersonal respect, which we have experienced in our dealings with the *concrete other*, intellectually to the *generalized other*.[72] The concretely experienced moral community of our lifeworld is generalized as the regulative idea[73] of the unlimited moral community of all men (human beings). The intellectual exchange of perspectives and roles with a particular communication and interaction partner leads to the regulative idea of *universal role reversibility*, which Lawrence Kohlberg, adapting George H. Mead, has characterized as *ideal role-taking*.[74] Consequently it is rationally compelling that every human being must be accorded a double status as an inviolable person: on the one hand 'without regard to the

[71] 'Contrary to some cultural relativists, it can be hypothesized that a norm of reciprocity is universal.' This norm is 'no less universal and important an element of culture than the incest taboo'. A.W. Gouldner, 'The Norm of Reciprocity: A Preliminary Statement', *American Sociological Review* 25 (1960), pp. 161–78, at p. 171.

[72] See Mead, *Mind, Self and Society*, p. 154ff. Mead's distinction between the concrete and the generalized other has recently been taken up again in the context of 'Gender Studies' and in a more specific sense by the philosopher S. Benhabib, *Situating the Self* (Cambridge: Polity, 1992), p. 148ff.

[73] Regulative ideas are orientational ideas which indicate the normative horizon for pragmatic steps in the right direction but can, however, never be fully realized under real circumstances on account of their ideal character.

[74] See Kohlberg, *Philosophy of Moral Development*, p. 199ff. He defines 'ideal role-taking' as the complete reversibility of perspectives. For the equivalent concept of the universal exchange of roles see Habermas, *Moral Consciousness and Communicative Action*, p. 65 and *Justification and Application*, p. 49f.

person'[75] (i.e. independently of gender, ethnic extraction, social origin or cultural background, religion, education, world view etc.[76]) in his *general equal status* as a human being, and, on the other hand, in his *concrete otherness* as a singular person, who may well always remain a stranger to us in every sense of the word.[77]

The *universalization principle* thus grows out of the principle of the moral reciprocity between concrete persons. Those moral claims or rights can be regarded as rationally justifiable which can be imaginatively generalized to encompass the unlimited moral community of all men and can so be accorded impartially to everyone to the same degree.[78] In other words, those claims enjoy general validity which every person who sees himself as a member of the universal moral community can assert against others in a rational way – and that now means precisely: when tested by the general principle of ideal role-taking or role reversal.[79]

The principle of generalized moral reciprocity (universalization principle) is the fundamental and universal *moral principle* we are looking for. We can, therefore, characterize it quite simply as the fundamental postulate of universal moral respect and reciprocity in dealing with interpersonal claims and rights.[80] It is the sole generally valid moral principle we

[75] Note that we use the expression 'without regard to the person' in a different sense than Max Weber. The point he wished to make was that persons are not valued for themselves but count only in regard to their function in the market or an organization; see M. Weber, *Economy and Society*, 2 vols (Berkeley: University of California Press, 1978), vol. I, pp. 600 and 636. See also Weber, *From Max Weber*, p. 334. Tugendhat, *Vorlesungen*, p. 83, speaks instead of 'any person at all' which however scarcely expresses equal respect for each individual in a better way.

[76] See Article Three of the German Basic Law (Constitution): 'No-one may be disadvantaged or favoured because of his sex, his parentage, his race, his language, his homeland and origin, his faith or his religious or political opinions.' Note that there is no limitation of this right to German citizens; the right applies universally to all people.

[77] For this 'moral universalism sensitive to difference' see Habermas, *Inclusion of the Other*, p. 40.

[78] This alone is the basis of the historically powerful idea of *universal human rights*. We will look at this in more detail in Section 7.1.

[79] If this general idea of the reversal of roles or perspectives is imagined as an inner mental experiment of an individual, it leads to Kant's categorical imperative (see Section 2.3); yet if the unlimited moral community is explicated as an ideal communicative community and the testing of the intersubjective reversibility of perspectives is correspondingly conceived of as the matter of an interpersonal argumentation, it leads to discourse ethics (see Section 2.5).

[80] Benhabib, *Situating the Self*, p. 29, speaks in a similar fashion of the moral principle as the 'principle of universal moral respect' and (without an entirely clear distinction between the two) of the 'principle of egalitarian reciprocity'; Tugendhat, *Vorlesungen*, p. 80, quite simply of the 'morality of universal respect'; and Habermas, *Inclusion of the Other*, p. 28 (and nearly identically p. 39), of the 'morality of equal respect and solidaristic responsibility for everyone'.

can define from the rational moral point of view.[81] By describing it as a rational moral point of view we claim that it is based neither on a subjective ethos nor on a culture-specific moral tradition to which there could be alternatives. Rather, it grows out of the normative logic of interpersonal or intersubjective relations. This normative logic is formal in the sense that it presumes the existence of no externally given material norm. In the universal reciprocal *form* or structure of the intersubjective relations in the moral community of all men of good will[82] the fundamental *norm* of a rational ethics free of metaphysics is itself reflexively revealed.[83]

In this approach, a formal and universalistic ethics does not search for its final justification by a process of deduction from something 'objective'[84] and absolutely valid outside ourselves. As we shall see in more detail in Chapter 2, it is founded solely on the process of strict reflection on the logically indisputable (although wilfully violable) moral implications of the 'mutual recognition of autonomous persons as beings of equal dignity'.[85] By explicating the fundamental implications of intersubjectivity rational ethics lays the foundation for rationally irrefutable normative obligations of a *humanistic minimal ethics* which is binding on all regardless of their cultural background. This is a possible starting point, 'within the limits of reason alone',[86] for a moral point of view that all people can recognize as valid and binding because it is rationally well founded.

1.5 The developmental stages of moral consciousness

The conception presented here of the moral principle as the quintessence of a universal normative logic of interpersonal relations is confirmed by the results of thirty years of research in moral psychology on the structure and development of moral consciousness, pioneered methodically by

81 On this idea, which was already developed by Kant, see Baier, *Moral Point of View*, p. 183ff.; see also Habermas, *Moral Consciousness*, p. 92f.

82 This can also be defined the other way round, as in Baier, *Moral Point of View*, p. 185: 'A person is of good will if he adopts the moral point of view as supreme.'

83 See Benhabib, *Situating the Self*, p. 38: 'In this sense universalizability is not only a *formal procedure* but involves the utopian projection of a way of life in which respect and reciprocity reign.'

84 Here we differ from Kant, who still understood the categorical imperative as an 'objective principle' and spoke of the 'moral law' as an 'objective practical law' which is 'indispensably necessary' ('Metaphysics of Morals', pp. 79, 78, 45). Hence Kant's transcendental philosophy contains a metaphysical remnant, namely the assumption of an absolute (i.e. divine?!) and pure practical reason which can be conceived of completely independently of the subjectivity of man. See the treatment of Kant in Section 2.3.

85 O. Höffe, 'Humanität', in Höffe (ed.), *Lexikon der Ethik*, 4th edn, p. 124.

86 Following Kant, *Religion within the Limits of Reason Alone*.

Jean Piaget[87] and developed and deepened, above all, by Lawrence Kohlberg.[88] Some special aspects of Kohlberg's much discussed theory are still the subject of dispute, but the core of his work – and this alone is relevant here – has withstood all criticisms and can be regarded from a conceptional and empirical standpoint as largely corroborated.[89]

As a moral psychologist Kohlberg provided empirical proof of the existence of a generally valid developmental sequence of various stages of moral consciousness. And as a moral philosopher he convincingly interpreted them in the light of a 'normative logic'[90] of morality. He describes the maturational process in the development of the cognitive structures and concepts used by individuals in order to judge moral issues, demonstrating that the sequence of the stages of development is the same for all individuals and all cultures. The central feature of this process of stage by stage extension of moral competence is, for Kohlberg, the cognitive ability of the individual to undertake an ideal (and hence also affective) reversal of roles: 'these stages represent successive modes of taking the role of others in social situations'.[91] This confirms the insight that all moral consciousness rests upon the perception of the intersubjective structure of moral claims and rights.

Each stage of moral consciousness is determined by a particular *formal* moral conception, a comprehensive thought pattern on which the formation of moral judgement is based; it involves a certain level of differentiation and organization in the perception of interpersonal relations and of the moral obligations relevant to them. It is possible to speak here of a universal developmental logic, in as far as (a) a distinct hierarchy of stages exists which every individual passes through in the same sequence, (b) no stage of this moral psychological development can be left out by any individual and (c) this concept of stages applies to the development of the moral consciousness of all people regardless of their culture and religion, precisely because it refers only to the formal structure of the

[87] See J. Piaget, *The Moral Judgement of the Child* (New York: Free Press, 1932). Piaget characterizes his comprehensive approach to research on the development of consciousness as genetic epistemology. See his *Genetic Epistemology* (New York: Columbia University Press, 1970).

[88] The most important writings can be found in Kohlberg, *Philosophy of Moral Development*. Of fundamental importance is the text 'From *Is* to *Ought*: How to Commit the Naturalistic Fallacy and Get Away with It in the Study of Moral Development', pp. 101–89.

[89] This is emphasized by the moral educationalist Fritz Oser, one of the most reputed Kohlberg experts in the German-speaking countries. See Oser/Althof, *Moralische Selbstbestimmung*, p. 142ff.

[90] Kohlberg, *Philosophy of Moral Development*, p. 133. [91] Ibid., p. 134.

formation of moral judgement, which has its roots in the general normative logic of interpersonal relations.[92]

The stage by stage unfolding of moral consciousness can be described more closely from three parallel, reciprocally interconnected points of view:

(1) as an extension of the *social perspective*: from an egocentric perception concentrated only on one's own needs and wishes (I) to the reciprocity of moral claims and rights in a moral community whose rights (interests, claims) are more and more comprehensively perceived (II) and finally to the perspective of the ideal moral point of view, which stands above every concrete social unit (III) – in brief, as a step for step *universalization* of the social perspective;
(2) as progress in *moral self-determination*: from blind obedience towards sanctioning authorities (I) to orientation on given social rules or laws (II) and finally to orientation on self-chosen moral principles (III) – in brief, as a step for step *autonomization* of the moral principle;
(3) as the development of *forms of justification* for one's own actions: from a hedonistic orientation on the self-referential consequences of an action (i.e. based on one's own feelings of pleasure and displeasure) (I) to the conformist orientation on socially valid conventions (i.e. justified by unquestioningly accepted norms) (II) and finally to a rational ethical orientation based on a post-conventional idea of interpersonal equal rights and justice (III) – in brief, as a step for step *ethical rationalization* of the justification of actions.

Kohlberg describes the three levels (I–III) of each developmental perspective as (I) pre-conventional, (II) conventional and (III) post-conventional levels of moral consciousness. Each level can be further subdivided into two stages (Figure 1.3). In what follows it will suffice to present a brief and graphic characterization of the individual stages.[93]

The *preconventional level* corresponds to the developmental level of a small child from about the age of four. In the *first stage* relationships with others are perceived primarily as power relationships without any clear understanding of moral claims. Actions are carried out from an egocentric

[92] See ibid., p. 130ff. An important objection to the claim to universality has been raised by feminist ethics. Kohlberg's definition of the moral stages is seen as orientating itself one-sidedly on the perspective of justice central to male moral consciousness (orientation on the generalized other), whereas the perspective of sympathy and care (orientation on the concrete other), which are more significant for the female moral consciousness, is neglected. The objection indicates the need to complement or to extend Kohlberg's conception, without, however, refuting it. Fundamental on this point is C. Gilligan, *In a Different Voice: Psychological Theory and Women's Development* (Cambridge MA: Harvard University Press, 1983). On the much discussed Kohlberg/Gilligan controversy see Benhabib, *Situating the Self*, p. 148ff.

[93] See Kohlberg, *Philosophy of Moral Development*, p. 147ff.

I	*Preconventional level* [level of the small child]		
	1st stage:	Heteronomous orientation on punishment and obedience (avoidance of pain)	
	2nd stage:	Instrumental orientation on mutual exchange of advantages (do ut des)	
II	*Conventional level* [level of the well socialized child]		
	3rd stage:	Interpersonal orientation on the moral expectations of others, particularly those in positions of authority ('good boy' or 'nice girl' orientation)	
	4th stage:	Social orientation on the maintenance of social order ('law and order')	
	Transitional stage [level of adolescence]		
	4 ½:	Purely subjective orientation: no longer socially orientated but still non-cognitive (ethical relativism and scepticism)	
III	*Postconventional level* [level of the mature adult]		
	5th stage:	Liberal orientation on the social contract between equal individuals (constitutionalism and contractualism)	
	6th stage:	Autonomous orientation on universal ethical principles (rational moral point of view)	

Figure 1.3. Developmental stages of moral consciousness according to Lawrence Kohlberg

perspective. Right is what superior authorities demand and what enables the child to avoid punishment (morality of obedience). In the *second stage* the child is for the first time capable of perceiving the reciprocity of legitimate interpersonal claims, but the perspective is still individualistic. Right is what serves to one's own advantage, but the other should also profit from the situation. Good is repaid with good, evil with evil ('tit for tat'). In the case of cooperative interaction this instrumental reciprocity takes the form of a mutually beneficial exchange of advantages, in the case of conflict it involves retaliation or revenge for the suffering inflicted, and in the neutral case it follows the motto 'live and let live' (mutual non-intervention).

The *conventional level* typically corresponds to the developmental level of a well socialized schoolchild from about the age of eight, who wishes to be a good person in accordance with the socially accepted standards. In the *third stage* the child knows and understands the moral expectations of those in positions of authority (parents, teachers etc.). It would like in principle to be a 'good boy' or a 'good girl' (Kohlberg), would like to live up to the expectations of the adults closely related to it and, when it fails to do so, it no longer experiences fear of punishment but feelings of guilt. In turn, however, it also claims the right to respect for its own moral expectations. Right is what corresponds to the accepted norms of good and bad behaviour in its own particular social community. In the *fourth stage* the social perspective of the concrete social community is extended to embrace the more abstract notion of society as a whole. What is right is now no longer defined by persons exercising direct authority but by impersonal socially accepted norms and rules and, in particular, the state laws. Good will no longer refers to the fulfilment of the expectations of other individuals, but primarily to the fulfilment of accepted or assigned duties (morality of duty) and the unquestioning observation of existing laws (legalism). The maintenance of the prevailing approved social order now achieves the status of a supreme norm. This completely uncritical, conformist orientation on the accepted rules ('law and order') is for a substantial part of humanity the highest stage of moral consciousness they achieve and it determines their lives as adults unless their moral development has been interrupted during adolescence.

The *post-conventional* level first describes the moral development of the 'mature and responsible' adult. The roles and norms learned in childhood lose their undisputed validity; they are questioned and considered justified only if there are supported by good reasons. This assumes the achievement of a moral point of view that stands above all traditional norms and permits a rational criticism of them. In the *fifth stage*, which approximately a quarter of all American citizens reach according to Kohlberg, the individual takes his orientation from the 'modern' idea of legitimization through contractual agreements between free and equal persons; hence the social order is also conceived of as a matter of a democratic social contract (constitutionalism). Legitimately concluded contracts must be observed (contractualism, i.e. contractual morality). Justifications may be based on notions of justice (observation of contractual rights) or of utility (for the benefit of all, or of the community). The ranking of these concepts (ideas, arguments) may be unclear and they may well stand alongside one another without any clear awareness of their categorial differences. Finally, in the *sixth stage*, this confusion is overcome. Now the idea of the equal dignity and equal basic rights of all people gains the upper hand over all notions of utility and it is consciously adopted as the universal principle of general and unconditional interpersonal respect. The individual now sees himself as an autonomous moral subject who judges in accordance with moral principles and tries to solve moral conflicts discursively and to reach agreement with others by presenting good and convincing arguments. This corresponds to the rational moral point of view – a stage which is reached by only a very small percentage of the population (less than 5% of the citizens of the USA according to Kohlberg's empirical research).[94]

[94] Ibid., p. 192.

In later publications Kohlberg modified this stage concept to include the *transitional stage 4½*, after reaching the conclusion that some of the individuals who pass beyond the conventional level during adolescence nonetheless fail to reach the level of post-conventional moral consciousness. Although they are capable of freeing themselves from the conformity of childhood and of questioning moral claims and normative standards, they still fail to find their way to an autonomous orientation on clearly recognized humanist principles. The personal loss of unquestioning childhood trust in given norms is objectified as a total collapse of all moral claims to validity. As an understanding of the intersubjective structure of interpersonal commitments is for the moment lacking or has not yet become an integrative element of personal self-understanding, the absolute necessity of general norms of interpersonal relations as a precondition for legitimate freedom and self-determination is not grasped. Choices in ethical questions are then supposedly subjective and arbitrary. Young people passing through the crisis of adolescence are typically at this instable ('shaky') transitional stage, until they finally, in favourable cases, take the step to a post-conventional orientation. This transitional stage corresponds to the *ethical relativism and scepticism* described in the previous section.

The ethical scepticism which so substantially shapes the *Zeitgeist* today indicates the existence of an epochal 'adolescent crisis of humanity'[95] during a period of cultural historical transition to the level of a generally accepted post-conventional ethics of autonomous and responsible persons – a process which must by no means be crowned with success. This perspective also permits us to understand the contemporary significance of the numerous calls for ethics and for a renaissance of practical-philosophical attempts to clarify and define a modern moral point of view.

[95] See K.-O. Apel, 'Zur geschichtlichen Entfaltung der ethischen Vernunft in der Philosophie (I)', in: Apel/Böhler/Rebel (eds.), *Funkkolleg*, vol. I, pp. 66–99, at pp. 84, 88. On the parallelism between the development of the individual consciousness (ontogenesis) and the cultural history of mankind (phylogenesis), which is already used systematically by Piaget, see Ulrich, *Transformation*, pp. 295f., 300ff.

2 The moral point of view: philosophical developmental lines of rational ethics

In the first chapter we adopted a phenomenological approach (i.e. from the meaning perspective of a participant in a familiar lifeworld practice) in order to work out the humanist core of the rational moral principle from the normative logic of interpersonal relations, independently, at this stage, of certain 'schools' of ethics. With this step alone, of course, we have not achieved a complete rational foundation of the moral principle. In the history of ethics the moral principle has also often been more intuitively grasped than rationally well-grounded; a number of developmental steps were necessary until, finally, in most recent times, modern philosophical ethics developed the categorial means for a convincing, strictly reflective explication of the moral point of view that can be regarded as a sufficient rational foundation.

In order to understand this reflective explication or justification of the moral point of view it is useful to trace briefly the most important intellectual and philosophical historical stages leading to it. It is basically possible to distinguish two elementary lines of development. Along the one line an increasing *differentiation between ethical and strategic reciprocity* takes place permitting a purification of rational ethics from aspects of interpersonal reciprocity that are external to morality. Along the other line there is a progressive *generalization of the reciprocity principle* from the concrete reciprocity of two opposites (alter and ego) to the abstract principle of universalization. Both lines of development are inextricably intertwined in the various interpretations of the moral point of view. For this reason we deal with them in chronological order. As pathmarks of the explication of the moral point of view we discuss in what follows the Golden Rule and the Judaeo-Christian commandment to love one's neighbour (Section 2.1), the impartial spectator according to Adam Smith (Section 2.2), Kant's categorical imperative (Section 2.3), the rule-utilitarian generalization criterion (Section 2.4) and, finally, discourse ethics (Section 2.5). As we shall see, the last mentioned approach is the first to succeed in finding a strictly reflective

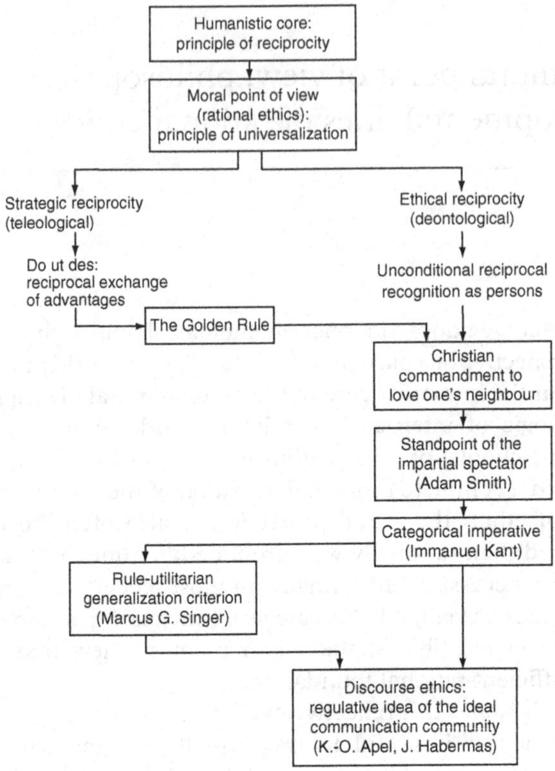

Figure 2.1. Developmental lines of the moral point of view

answer to the question of a fundamental moral-philosophical justification of rational ethics.

Figure 2.1 provides an overview. The horizontal dimension (from left to right) indicates the first, the vertical dimension the second line of development. Those concepts in the figure not yet been introduced will be dealt with later in the appropriate place.

2.1 The Golden Rule and the Judaeo-Christian commandment to love one's neighbour

Probably the oldest, most widely spread and to date most popular versionof the moral idea of reciprocity is the *Golden Rule*. It can be found in nearly identical form in virtually all high cultures: in old Hinduistic ethics, in Confucianism in China and Japan, in Greek antiquity, in Jewry, in the

Old and New Testaments of Christianity and in Islam.[1] In its positive form the Golden Rule runs:

Treat others as you would like to be treated.[2]

The negative version of the Golden Rule is more common:

Do nothing to others that you would not have them do to you.

In both the positive and the negative version of the Golden Rule the ideal reversal of roles and the ethos of reciprocity are expressed, but the justification of reciprocal interpersonal respect remains indeterminate. Particularly in the positive form it does not refer clearly to the moral principle (of unconditional mutual respect of all persons), but is guided, at least potentially, by arbitrary subjective expectations or even by egocentric strategic considerations[3] of personal advantage or utility. Certainly the standpoint of self-interest is not presented in the Golden Rule in its non-moral or pre-moral raw form of ruthless egoism indifferent to the personality of the other: it is rather morally disciplined, at least in part, by its integration in the social network that delimits the orientations of individual action. But the consideration of the other person does not (at least not evidently) follow independently of the cleverly calculated motive of obliging the other to treat oneself decently in return. One can speak here of a well-understood or enlightened self-interest:

The enlightened egoist ... knows that he cannot get the most out of life unless he pays attention to the needs of others on whose good will he depends.[4]

In as far as we are not dealing with the personal value of another but with the clever pursuit of one's own goals we can speak of a strategic orientation of action, as expressed in the popular motto 'honesty is the best policy'.[5] Or as the head of a company put it in a qualitative study of the business-ethical thought patterns of executives:

[1] The Golden Rule was formulated as early as the sixth century B.C., in its negative form, for example, by Confucius and even a little earlier, around 600 B.C., in Greek philosophy. On these and many other examples of its use see R. Wimmer, *Universalisierung in der Ethik* (Frankfurt: Suhrkamp, 1980), p. 254ff. and G. Enderle, 'Die Goldene Regel für Manager?', in Ch. Lattmann (ed.), *Ethik und Unternehmensführung* (Heidelberg: Physica, 1988), pp. 130–48.

[2] The following, more traditional form of the Golden Rule can be found in the New Testament: 'Therefore, all things whatsoever ye would that men should do unto you, do ye even so to them' (Matthew 7, 12; similarly Lucas 6, 31).

[3] On the strategic orientation of actions see Section 2.5.

[4] Baier, *Moral Point of View*, p. 188.

[5] See ibid., p. 188f. On this old maxim of the business ethos cf. Weber, *Economy and Society*, vol. I, p. 637; vol. II, p. 1206.

It is usually a question of giving up a short term advantage in favour of a long term advantage in the form of ethically correct behaviour which will pay off at some time in the future. Seen in this way the economy is right and the profit will be greater.[6]

Nonetheless the Golden Rule cannot simply be interpreted as the notion of a strict strategic reciprocity of interacting persons. It is adequate to speak of strategic reciprocity only when the motive of mutual 'consideration' is for both parties only the clever pursuit of personal interest under conditions of social interdependence in regard to the utility of an action, so that the consideration of the actor A for another person B assumes the *condition* that it pays off for A. The Golden Rule is different in as far as it requires the *unconditional* orientation on the mutual expectations of respect or non-harm, as the negative form, above all, demonstrates: A should not in principle expect B to put up with the side effects of selfish actions he himself in principle would not wish to suffer from – and vice versa.[7] The type of moral consciousness can readily be recognized here as it is characteristic of the conventional level of orientation on reciprocal expectations of good conduct in Kohlberg's stage conception (Stage Three).[8] The feeling of reciprocal moral commitment which is decisive for this stage and for the Golden Rule continues to be linked to the motive of fulfillment of one's own expectations. In the case of a sustained disappointment of this expectation a relapse to a pre-conventional 'an eye for an eye, a tooth for a tooth' attitude is conceivable, which repays good with good but also evil with evil (Stage Two).

It ought now to be clear, on the one hand, that the Golden Rule undoubtedly has a moral content (which marks it off from merely strategic reciprocity), but, on the other hand, that it is insufficient as the formulation of the post-conventional moral point of view. The systematic objection against the Golden Rule is that it is incapable of distinguishing

[6] On the form and distribution of this instrumental understanding of ethics (and on other thought patterns) see P. Ulrich/U. Thielemann, *Ethik und Erfolg: Unternehmensethische Denkmuster von Führungskräften – eine empirische Studie* (Berne *et al.*: Haupt, 1992), p. 46ff. For an overview in English see P. Ulrich /U. Thielemann, 'How Do Managers Think about Market Economies and Morality? Empirical Enquiries into Business-ethical Thinking Patterns', *Journal of Business Ethics* 12 (1993), pp. 879–98; reprinted in an abridged version in K. Gibson (ed.), *Business Ethics: People, Profit, and the Planet* (New York: McGraw-Hill, 2006), pp. 52–60.

[7] Hence the Golden Rule is a suitable basic norm demanding the internalization of external effects in one's own actions. On this point see Enderle, 'Goldene Regel', p. 139ff.

[8] See above, Section 1.5.

between strategic and ethical reciprocity – and hence between strategic and ethical rationality.[9]

That strategic and ethical reciprocity must be kept distinct follows logically from the fact that moral actions do not necessarily 'pay off'. Whenever the strategic and the ethical standpoint diverge and come into conflict, the question as to which standpoint is accorded priority is decisive: the strategic motive of the pursuit of personal advantage (utility) or the moral reasons requiring the recognition of the other as an autonomous person. It is possible to speak of ethical reciprocity (in accordance with the moral point of view) only when the mutual consideration is acknowledged for its own sake as being based on the unconditionally required – or to use Kant's formulation: the *categorical* – priority of the human dignity and autonomy of the other person over all egocentric calculations of personal utility. Practically, a principled moral position means quite simply that moral reasons are approved as enjoying priority per se over motives of personal interest. (In contrast the strict egoist has from the start no principles but only interests and aims he opportunistically pursues.[10]) This *primacy of ethics* (or more precisely: of the moral point of view) over all other possible points of view requires no further justification, as soon as it is admitted that the 'very raison d'être of a morality is to yield reasons which overrule the reasons of self interest'.[11]

In the Western tradition the next step from the Golden Rule to the principle of unconditional ethical reciprocity is probably first formulated in the *Judaeo-Christian commandment to love one's neighbour* (3rd book of Moses: Leviticus 19, 18):

Thou shalt love thy neighbour as thyself.

At first sight the commandment to love one's neighbour seems quite similar to the Golden Rule. In the second part of the commandment ('as thyself') one might assume the presence of the reciprocal motive of strategic cleverness. But the form is deceptive. Here it is not a question of making oneself 'loved' by showing love for a neighbour but of recognizing every human being, including ourselves, as being in principle worthy of love. In the required symmetry of love of one's neighbour and love of self the moral-psychological insight takes effect that our ability to respect

9 Probably the most thorough elucidation of the categorial differences between strategic and ethical rationality is to be found in K.-O. Apel, 'Lässt sich ethische Vernunft von strategischer Zweckrationalität unterscheiden?', in W. van Reijen/K.-O. Apel (eds.), *Rationales Handeln und Gesellschaftstheorie* (Bochum: Germinal, 1984), pp. 23–79. This categorial difference is important in economic ethics and we will return to it in Section 2.5.

10 See Baier, *Moral Point of View*, p. 190.

11 Ibid., p. 309.

others cannot be detached from our self-respect.[12] To adopt the moral point of view in the sense of the Judaeo-Christian commandment involves, on the one hand, the avoidance of pure egoism. But, on the other hand, it by no means involves the requirement to sacrifice oneself and to disregard one's own personality out of consideration for the needs of others.

It is interesting that in the Sermon on the Mount Jesus defended the unconditional ethical requirement of reciprocity in the commandment to love one's neighbour as oneself against any form of calculating strategic simplification, choosing the mentality of the publicans as an example. He also emphasized the universal validity of the commandment against attempts to restrict it to one's own community (Matthew 5, 43–46):

> Ye have heard that it hath been said, Thou shalt love thy neighbour, and hate thine enemy. But I say unto you, Love your enemies ... For if ye love them which love you, what reward have ye? Do not even the publicans the same? And if ye salute your brethren only, what do ye more than others? Do not even the publicans so?

This reveals, incidentally, that Judaeo-Christian ethics by no means contradicts the moral point of view in the sense of a modern rational ethics, but can, rather, be understood as one of its earliest 'prophetic' announcements. The commandment to love one's neighbour unconditionally is, however, justified metaphysically and religiously and hence does not provide a humanistic ethical, strictly reflective explication of the rational ethical moral point of view.

2.2 The standpoint of the impartial spectator (Adam Smith)

It was none other than the Scottish moral philosopher and founder of modern Political Economy, Adam Smith, who long before G. H. Mead first recognized the moral-psychological and philosophical significance of the ideally generalized reversal of roles and consequently, even earlier than Kant, the universalistic moral principle.[13] In his *Theory*

[12] See above Section 1.4.

[13] In contrast to the broad and sustained discussion on Smith in the Anglo-Saxon world, the debate on Smith's ethics in the German-speaking world has been restricted to a few authors, not least among them those writing on economic ethics. Among the established writers on the philosophical side, Tugendhat, *Vorlesungen*, p. 282ff., was one of the first to recognize and to deal productively with the outstanding *systematic* importance of Smith for the development of the modern moral point of view. For a more detailed treatment of what follows see P. Ulrich, 'Der kritische Adam Smith – im Spannungsfeld zwischen sittlichem Gefühl und ethischer Vernunft', in A. Meyer-Faje/P. Ulrich (eds.), *Der andere Adam Smith* (Berne *et al.*: Haupt, 1991), pp. 145–90. For an overview of the overall

of Moral Sentiments (1st edn 1759), a book which is not only too seldom read by economists and business administrators but is also regularly underestimated by contemporary philosophers of ethics, he depicts the universalistic moral point of view as the imaginary point of view of a *disinterested and impartial spectator*:

> We endeavour to examine our own conduct as we imagine any other fair and impartial spectator would examine it.[14]

The instance of morality to which Smith refers in his famous metaphor is clearly reason:

> It is *reason*, principle, conscience ... the great judge and arbiter of our conduct. (p. 137)

What matters in the moral justification of an action is the 'approbation of this *supposed* equitable judge' (p. 110; my italics), 'supposed' meaning here 'created in our imagination'). Moral feelings are the object of rational moral judgement, and the basis for our moral powers of judgement is, according to Smith, *sympathy* (p. 10ff.). By this he does not mean a specific actual feeling of affection but quite generally the formal capacity we nowadays prefer to call empathy (the general ability to share in another's emotions and feelings). Sympathy in that formal sense is the ability 'to change places in fancy' with another person (ideal role reversal!) and so 'to conceive or to be affected by what he feels' (p. 10).

The special strength of Smith's moral theory lies in the way he internally links ethical reason and moral sentiments in the concept of sympathy. Smith clearly recognized that moral sympathy for another person always presupposes a cognitive achievement:

> As we have no immediate experience of what other men feel, we can form no idea of the manner in which they are affected, but by conceiving what we ourselves should feel in the like situation. Though our brother is upon the rack, as long as we ourselves are at our ease, our senses will never inform us of what he suffers ... it is by the *imagination* only that we can form any conception of what are his sensations. Neither can that faculty help us to this any other way, than by *representing* to us what would be our own [sensations], if we were in his [our brother's] case. It is the *impressions* of our own senses only, not those of his, which our imaginations copy. By the imagination we place ourselves in his situation ... (p. 9; my italics)

ethical conception of Smith and the role of his economic thinking in it see also M. Patzen, 'Zur Diskussion des Adam-Smith-Problems – ein Überblick', in Meyer-Faje/Ulrich (eds.), *Der andere Adam Smith*, pp. 21–54.

14 Smith, *Moral Sentiments*, p. 110. The page numbers in brackets in the main text refer in what follows to this edition.

The sympathetic feelings constitute the sensitive experiential background; the evaluative reason (of the impartial spectator) offers the intelligible reflective horizon of suitable moral judgements and 'proper affections' (p. 16ff.). Sympathy, therefore, establishes both a rational and at the same time an affective reciprocity between interacting persons; Smith speaks of 'reflected passion' (p. 22), a phrase which again expresses the dominant role of reason as the instance of morality.[15] The formation of moral judgement occurs as follows:

> We either approve or disapprove of the conduct of another man according as we feel that, when we bring his case home to ourselves, we either can or cannot entirely sympathize with the sentiments and motives which directed it. And, in the same manner, we either approve or disapprove of our own conduct, according as we feel that, when we place ourselves in the situation of another man and view it, as it were, with his eyes and from his station, we either can or cannot entirely enter into and sympathize with the sentiments and motives which influenced it. (p. 109f.)

In the second sentence Smith makes it clear why the capacity for *critical self-reflection* on our own motives and actions arises from the 'sympathizing' reversal of roles with other persons, which empowers us in principle for moral self-commitment. In this passage Smith expressly states that in this way 'our first *moral criticisms* are exercised' (p. 112; my italics). He speaks in this context of the virtue of 'self-government' (p. 23) or 'self-command' (p. 237ff.). This in turn rests upon the 'social correspondence of moral feelings'.[16] On the one hand we develop a moral 'sense of duty' (p. 109ff.) towards other people, or a 'sense of demerit' (p. 74ff.) when we believe that we have violated or neglected our duties as they are defined as 'general rules' (p. 161ff.) in the moral community to which we belong (i.e. as social norms).[17] And, on the other hand, we develop a strong need to be *respected* by the members of this community as someone who 'deserves' to belong to it (p. 113). Because of the reciprocity of moral feelings this need for respect is indissolubly linked with our self-respect, i.e. our self-image as a person who is in principle good. For precisely this reason mere acceptance by the social environment, the 'opinion of all the real spectators' (p. 131), is generally insufficient. Our self-respect, guided

[15] On the interlocking of cognitive and affective reciprocity see also Section 1.1. With the abandonment of the one-sided empiricism of his predecessors in the important Scottish moral philosophy of the 18th century (notably Hutchison and Hume) Smith completes – twenty-five years before Kant – a Copernican turn to ethical criticism and cognitivism (rational ethics) without neglecting the role of moral feelings. On this point see Ulrich, 'Der kritische Adam Smith'.

[16] T. D. Campbell, *Adam Smith's Science of Morals* (London: Allan & Unwin, 1971), p. 94.

[17] See Smith, *Moral Sentiments*, pp. 109ff., 74ff., 161ff.

by our capacity for moral self-criticism, depends on the motives of our actions being found worthy of approval or praise by a morally competent, impartial, well-informed and just spectator:

> We are pleased not only with praise, but with having done what is praise-worthy. We are pleased to think that we have rendered ourselves the natural objects of approbation, though no approbation should ever actually be bestowed upon us ... (p. 115f.)

Smith thus distinguishes carefully between factual acceptance and normative recognition or 'praise-worthiness' (p. 114). By adopting the imagined point of view of the generalized ideal spectator we win that independence of the moral conventions of our social surroundings which Immanuel Kant only a few decades later would characterize as the moral autonomy of a person. What counts – one thinks one is hearing Kant's later words – is that every man should:

> ... act so as that the impartial spectator may enter into the principles of his conduct ... (p. 83).

For Smith, self-respect determined by the autonomous rational point of view (represented by the impartial spectator) is the indispensable critical antidote to our selfish tendency towards mere 'self-love' and 'selfish passions' (p. 40) to which the desire 'to be loved' from time to time corresponds:

> ... the natural misrepresentations of self-love [i.e. egocentrism P.U.] can be corrected only by the eye of this impartial spectator (p. 137).
>
> To disturb [another's] happiness merely because it stands in the way of our own ... is what no impartial spectator can go along with (p. 82).

In this way critical ethical reason is clearly able to reflect on and to control our egoistic interests, if only we are reasonable, i.e. if we possess the will to subject ourselves to the reasonable judgement of the impartial spectator. And for Smith that is ultimately the decisive point: Ethics is not a matter of our popularity in our own social reference groups but of our 'good will' in respecting 'the general rules of morality' and our corresponding 'universal benevolence':

> Our good will is circumscribed by no boundary, but may embrace the immensity of the universe (p. 235).

The second outstanding strength of Smith's conception of the moral point of view is, therefore, that he successfully develops the post-conventional moral principle of autonomous moral self-commitment without detaching the idea of personal autonomy in a moral-philosophical sense too much from its social context, as is later the case with Kant.

The systematic limitation of Smith's 'Theory of Moral Sentiments' as ethics is that it is primarily a descriptive theory in the sense of moral psychology. Although it observes and explains the structure of human morality in an extremely subtle way, it starts from a preconception rooted in natural law: the 'nature' of man as God's creature *is* unquestionably good and his moral consciousness is consequently right. As a result Smith does not even attempt to develop a normative foundation for the intellectual experiment of the impartial observer. Kant was the first to face explicitly the task of establishing a rational ethical foundation for the normative validity of the moral principle.

2.3 The categorical imperative (Immanuel Kant)

A few decades after Smith, Immanuel Kant further developed the metaphor of the impartial spectator – as the generalized other from whose imaginary standpoint we can recognize what is morally right – to the categorical imperative. How impressed Kant must have been by the formal, rational, and universal quality of Smith's moral theory is shown by his numerous, more or less literal, references to the great Scotsman.[18] It is striking how seamlessly the famous and still valid first sentence (after the preface) of his major ethical work, the *Groundwork of the Metaphysics of Morals* (1785), follows on the sentence of Smith just quoted above. It deals with a concept which was incidental for Smith but of central significance for Kant as the starting point of rational ethics, namely 'good will'.

> It is impossible to think of anything at all in the world, or indeed even beyond it, that could be considered good without limitation except a *good will.*[19]

In the same first paragraph Kant uses the concept of the impartial spectator. And in the following formulation from the 'Critique of Practical Reason' (1789) he undoubtedly takes up Smith's standpoint of the impartial spectator:

> What we are to call good must be an object of the faculty of desire in the judgement of every reasonable human being, and evil an object of aversion *in the eyes of everyone*; hence for this appraisal reason is needed.[20]

[18] For a detailed treatment of Kant's starting point from the perspective of the history of ideas and of the relationship between his moral philosophy and that of Smith see Ulrich, 'Der kritische Adam Smith', p. 153ff.

[19] Kant, 'Metaphysics of Morals', p. 49.

[20] I. Kant, 'Critique of Practical Reason', in Kant, *Practical Philosophy*, pp. 139–271, at p. 189 (my italics).

Whereas Smith still understood the conception of the generalized reversal of roles primarily as a criterion for the ethical examination of individual actions, Kant rendered the generalization principle more precise in the categorical imperative by requiring that it should be possible to raise the personal *maxims* of actions to the level of a generally valid rule or a general law:

So act that the maxim of your will could always hold at the same time as a principle in a giving of universal law.[21]

It is important here to interpret the concept of a maxim correctly. Kant means by it the subjective principles of action 'that contain a general determination of the will, having under it several practical rules'.[22] As opposed to the subordinate rules of action, which refer to concrete situational types, the maxims refer to subjective determinations of the will chosen by autonomous persons, who wish to adopt them consciously as guiding principles for their entire lives regardless of the changing concrete circumstances.[23] The reason for the universalistic validity claim of the basic formula of the categorical imperative quoted above lies entirely concealed in the humanistic ethical content of the maxims as self-determined moral principles (of the will). Because the maxims express a basic disposition which is independent of concrete circumstances, the generalization principle must, according to Kant, refer to the principles (of the will) as he understands them, and, consequently, only indirectly to actions or rules governing actions in specific situations. The necessary intellectual precondition is the freedom of the will (autonomy) of every person.[24]

If we now judge the maxims of an action morally, we do not assess its (context-dependent) external success, the achievements or competence of a person in certain roles (e.g. his profession), but the *entire person*, who is assumed to be reasonable and responsible for his actions in regard to the quality of his free will, which is the inner reason for the action:

[21] Kant, 'Practical Reason', p. 164. In the *Groundwork of the Metaphysics of Morals* the categorical imperative runs: 'Act only in accordance with that maxim of which you can at the same time will that it become a universal law.'

[22] Kant, 'Practical Reason', p. 153.

[23] On this point see O. Höffe, *Ethik und Politik: Grundmodelle und Probleme der praktischen Philosophie* (Frankfurt: Suhrkamp, 1979), p. 86ff.

[24] For Kant the human being is inherently free and 'can never think of the causality of his own will otherwise than under the idea of freedom' ('Metaphysics of Morals', p. 99). Only in as far as he belongs to the 'kingdom of freedom' (Kant also speaks of the 'kingdom of ends'), i.e. possesses freedom of will, is a human being different from the (other) animals, which belong entirely to the 'kingdom of nature', because their *behaviour* is entirely determined by instincts. Even though man also remains partially attached to the kingdom of nature (drives, affects), he alone can *act in accordance with reason*.

A good will . . . has its full worth in itself. Usefulness or fruitlessness can neither add anything to this worth nor take anything away from it.[25]

What we can 'will' as rational and autonomous persons is consequently synonymous with what we ought to do (universalistic maxim ethics as autonomous duty ethics). This is at the same time the standpoint of 'pure practical reason' (p. 47). With its means, 'carefully cleansed of everything empirical' (p. 45), Kant wishes to demonstrate the absolutely obligatory character of the categorical imperative as an 'objective' moral 'law' (p. 44, 55f.).[26] But Kant inevitably fails in this attempt at an ultimate justification, as he endeavours, in the metaphysical tradition, to sublate the practical conditions of *good will* into the pure logic of the normative ought. This leads to a heightening of the moral principle to a *must* which can be enforced by the supposed authority of absolute reason (whose reason?), as if practical reason could ultimately be guaranteed by an instance outside human freedom of will. Kant thus reinterprets the problem of motivation (of the will to reason!) as an 'absolute' problem of justification; ultimately he attempts to break down the indissoluble identity of the moral ought with the rational will. In order to arrive at a humanistic ethics free of metaphysics it is more fitting to start from the unavoidable primacy of the (rationally explicated) enlightened good will, as we have already seen above. Ethically rational motives for the will to act morally *are* sufficient reasons that we ought to act in a particular way.[27]

It is not, therefore, surprising that in the end Kant finds it necessary to concede that the irreducible conditions for the possibility of moral action, namely freedom of will (autonomy) and the idea of good will (morality), are an 'undeniable' 'fact of pure reason',[28] which can be discovered reflectively but is not capable of any further justification.[29] And indeed, if one abandons the metaphysical notion of the deduction of our moral

[25] Kant, 'Metaphysics of Morals', p. 50. The page numbers in brackets in the main text refer in what follows to this edition.

[26] Kant calls his approach to justification, which searches for the 'ground of obligation' of the moral principle prior to all empirical circumstances (which cannot justify an 'ought') in the ideal conditions for the possibility of the 'pure (good) will', *transcendental philosophy* (ibid., p. 46).

[27] See Section 1.1. [28] Kant, 'Practical Reason', pp. 164, 177.

[29] See Kant, 'Metaphysics of Morals', p. 101ff. On this 'extreme boundary of all practical philosophy' Kant frankly admits: 'It is impossible for us to explain how pure reason can be practical, and all the pains and labour of seeking an explanation of it are lost' (ibid., p. 107). Kant thus concedes that his transcendental philosophical attempt to establish an 'absolute' justification for the moral principle has basically failed, without, however, having clearly recognized that such a justification – but not a strictly reflective justification – is irrelevant because of the primacy of the will over the ought. But independently of this fact Kant succeeded, with the categorical imperative, in determining the rational ethical point of view correctly, as we can recognize from the normative logic of interpersonal relations.

'duty' from an absolute (divine?) reason, the question 'Why should I follow reason?' loses all meaning.[30] For we characterize as reasonable precisely the readiness implied in the 'Why' question to make our actions dependent on good reasons; 'to follow reason' is implicitly always exactly what we wish to do, if we are interested in justifying an action. And to ascertain this inner relationship strictly reflectively *is* the 'ultimate justification' Kant failed to find.[31]

Kant's remarkable 'fact of reason' ultimately expresses nothing other than the rationally irreducible conditio humana, the specifically human disposition for moral self-determination.[32] This shows that the formalistic rational ethics of Kant also has cultural-anthropological roots, although this is faded out in his transcendental philosophy.[33] In accordance with the practical sense of every image of man as a human self-projection, the conditio humana can, however, only be determined normatively, as we saw at the beginning. Accordingly, the 'fact' of human autonomy – or, as we could also say: the idea of the inalienable freedom of will of a person – has always been a moral idea; it is synonymous with 'the idea of the *dignity* of a rational being, who obeys no law other than that which he himself at the same time gives.'[34]

What is at issue in Kant's ethics is, therefore, nothing else than the 'relation of rational beings to one another',[35] namely 'the reciprocal recognition of human beings as beings of equal dignity'.[36] As the 'supreme principle of morality'[37] the categorical imperative is the imagined will of a transcendental subject, which is conceived as independent of all empirical and non-moral motives and consequently as good. It discerns the general moral duty (or 'moral law') in the universal reciprocal recognition of all human beings as persons with inviolable human dignity and the unconditional right to personal autonomy for its own sake. Thus, the true sense of the categorical imperative for the practice of everyday life lies in reminding us again and again of the unconditional and

[30] See Baier, *Moral Point of View*, p. 318.

[31] An undoubtedly more convincing treatment than Kant's of the so-called problem of ultimate justification in modern ethics in the context of discourse ethics can be found in the work of K.-O. Apel. See Section 2.5.

[32] Kant, 'Metaphysics of Morals', p. 87, formulates this as the membership of rational beings in the 'kingdom of ends' and not merely in the 'kingdom of nature'.

[33] On the 'anthropological basis', which Kant also inevitably makes use of, see O. Höffe, *Kategorische Rechtsprinzipien: Ein Kontrapunkt der Moderne* (Frankfurt: Suhrkamp, 1990), p. 127ff.

[34] Kant, 'Metaphysics of Morals', p. 84. On the concept of human dignity see Section 1.4.

[35] Ibid., p. 84. [36] O. Höffe, 'Humanität', p. 124.

[37] Kant, 'Metaphysics of Morals', p. 47.

universal primacy of the intrinsic value of a person – or his or her status as an end in itself – over all other aspects of social activity.

Only against this background it is possible to understand what the categorical imperative, defined in the above-mentioned formalistic basic formula as a universalizing principle related to maxims of action, has to do substantially with the moral point of view in the sense of the normative logic of inter-personal relations. Kant himself cannot clarify this relationship adequately with the help of the basic formula.[38] It is only in the second formula of the categorical imperative, the so-called formula of ends (which Kant expressly declares to be equivalent in meaning[39]), that the centrality of the universal intersubjective reciprocity of interpersonal respect and recognition is clearly expressed:

So act that you use humanity, whether in your own person or in the person of any other, always at the same time as an end, never merely as a means.[40]

What is meant by Kant's formulation 'always *at the same time* as an end, never *merely* as a means' is as follows: The categorical imperative does not forbid us entirely to include other people in our strategic calculations (as 'means' to our ends), otherwise every success-oriented rational action in the social world would be morally impermissible. But such action is always only legitimate (i.e. morally justified) under the precondition that the identity and dignity of the person as an inviolable subject with free will (as an 'end') is accorded priority unconditionally and at all times:

A human being, however, is not a thing and hence not something that can be used *merely* as a means.[41]

Interestingly enough, Kant elucidates the formula of ends with an (economic ethical) example from the labour market: 'Skill and diligence in work have a market price', for the (limited) use of human labour is legitimate; but the human being as a whole is 'raised above all price', as he may not be instrumentalized and 'has not merely a relative worth, that is, a price, but an inner worth, that is, dignity.'[42]

[38] The way in which Kant (ibid., p. 73ff.) attempts to elucidate the validity of the basic formula of the categorical imperative (general formulation of the moral law) with four standard examples by and large fails to take into account the social structure of morality and, consequently, the formal logic of interpersonal relations. As a result his examples have been almost unanimously dismissed as inadequate in the critical literature (and rightly so, in my opinion). However, this central reason for the weakness of Kant's attempted proofs has seldom been worked out sufficiently by the critics, as far as I can judge. See e.g. Wimmer, *Universalisierung in der Ethik*, p. 33ff., and Tugendhat, *Vorlesungen*, p. 149ff.

[39] Kant, 'Metaphysics of Morals', p. 85; see also Tugendhat, *Vorlesungen*, p. 148.

[40] Kant, 'Metaphysics of Morals', p. 80. [41] Ibid., p. 80. [42] Ibid., p. 84.

But how can we establish precisely whether the legitimacy conditions concerning the 'dignity' of a person are fulfilled in dealings with him or her and, consequently, whether these dealings are ethically acceptable? Kant's negatively formulated answer has seldom attracted attention: We must not 'make use of another human being' as a means to our ends, if he (as an autonomous subject) 'cannot possibly *agree to* my way of behaving toward him.'[43] Expressed positively: strategic (i.e. success-oriented) dealings with another person are legitimate only in as far as this person can agree to them out of her own free will.[44] Thus Kant basically took the first steps towards the regulative idea of legitimizing social action by searching for a rational consensus, which has been consistently pursued in recent times in discourse ethics (see Section 2.5).

2.4 The rule-utilitarian generalization criterion

In as far as ethics in the manner of Kant deals with the justification of an unconditional moral commitment it can be characterized as duty ethics or deontological ethics (Greek *déon*: duty, what is required); in as far as it is concerned with questions of the good life, it can be termed aspirational ethics or teleological ethics (Greek *télos*: aim, purpose).[45] But as we have already seen in Section 1.2, projections of the good life are always part of a more comprehensive ethos; they presume the existence of a moral conception, particularly in the dimension of virtue (idea of the good person). Approaches which attempt to establish the independence of the teleological aspect as a supposedly purely teleological ethics without a deontological basis – by judging the quality of an action or a rule of action solely from its consequences in regard to a non-moral criterion (such as happiness or the 'good life') – are based on a fundamental misunderstanding of the ethical (moral philosophical) perspective.[46] This is particularly true of utilitarian ethics as it has dominated ethical discourse in the Anglo-Saxon world until very recently. It sees the highest good and criterion in 'the

[43] Ibid., p. 80.

[44] What is meant by 'free will' here is the internal and external autonomy of a person who is willing to use his reason. In the same sense Tugendhat, *Vorlesungen*, p. 145f. More details on the relationship between orientation on success and orientation on reaching understanding are given in Section 2.5.

[45] The distinction between deontological and teleological ethics goes back to Frankena, *Ethics*.

[46] Instead of teleological ethics the term *consequentialist* ethics is also used. But then the reference to a supreme criterion of the good life is lost.

greatest happiness of the greatest number',[47] i.e. in the maximization of the 'common weal'. This vague *utilitarian principle* seems to present a kind of purely teleological generalization criterion, which apparently has no problems of justification in regard to duty ethics. And according to its advocates it offers an alternative to the (deontological) moral principle.

The endeavours to justify a teleological generalization principle derive from a well-known standard objection to the categorical imperative. According to this objection Kant's deontological ethics is a rigorous ethics of conviction. As it disregards all *consequences* of action,[48] it stands in the way of an *ethics of responsibility* on which concrete actions could be oriented.[49] A closer look reveals, however, that this objection misses the mark in several respects.

Firstly, the objection against an 'ethics of principled conviction' overlooks the fact that a deontological basis is indispensable for any kind of ethics of responsibility. The central idea of responsibility ethics, that the concrete consequences of actually available alternatives for action should be weighed up in a pragmatic way according to the situation, does not render deontologically justified maxims or principles superfluous. On the contrary, it presupposes their existence as normative criteria for the assessment of consequences. An 'ethics of responsibility without convictions' cannot be rationally conceived and is virtually meaningless. The justification of general criteria based on principles and the weighing up of what is situationally acceptable in terms of its consequences must be distinguished as two different levels of argumentation within a necessarily two-tiered conception of responsibility ethics.[50] For the judgement of the situational acceptability of an intention to act in the light of an ethical maxim,

[47] This is the famous utilitarian principle first formulated in 1776 by the founder of Utilitarianism, Jeremy Bentham, in his work *A Fragment on Government* (twelve years before the publication of Kant's Critique of Practical Reason). See J. Bentham, *A Commentary on the Commentaries and A Fragment on Government*, eds. J. H. Burns and H. L. A. Hart (London: Athlone Press, 1977), p. 393. A closer account of the utilitarian principle and its great significance in economic thinking follows in Section 5.2. On the deeper relationship between the teleological interpretation of the world and utilitarian ethics see Ulrich, *Transformation*, p. 180ff.

[48] G. Patzig, for example, accuses Kant of a 'sovereign disregard for all the consequences of duty-bound actions for the happiness of those concerned'. See G. Patzig, 'Ein Plädoyer für utilitaristische Grundsätze in der Ethik', *Neue Sammlung* 13 (1973), pp. 488–500, quoted from Höffe, *Ethik und Politik*, p. 85.

[49] The unfortunate juxtaposition of ethics of conviction and ethics of responsibility stems from M. Weber, 'Politics as a Vocation', in Weber, *From Max Weber*, pp. 77–128. Weber (p. 120) himself emphasizes, however: 'This is not to say that an ethic of ultimate ends [transl. note: this is a misleading translation of Weber's 'Gesinnungsethik', which means an ethics of principled convictions] is identical with irresponsibility, or that an ethic of responsibility is identical with unprincipled opportunism. Naturally nobody says that.'

[50] See Höffe, *Ethik und Politik*, p. 101.

considerations of the consequences which are as pragmatic and concrete as possible are certainly indispensable. They are indeed the actual *object* of moral judgement, but, without a circular argument, they cannot at the same time be the *criterion*. This must be justified independently of pragmatic questions, in the form of a general moral maxim and, ultimately, of the moral principle. It is precisely the purpose of generalizable maxims to guarantee in principle the indisposability and inviolability of human subjects as 'ends in themselves' (Kant). They serve as 'the decisive ... principle in accordance with which we respond to a given situation'[51] and by which the *legitimacy* of an action is to be judged, taking into account the concrete consequences to be expected for all concerned. In other words: If the concept is meant to be more than a rhetorical symptom of unprincipled opportunism, the ethics of responsibility can only be viewed as a deontologically well-founded ethics *oriented on principles*.

Secondly, according to Kant, precisely those maxims must be considered morally necessary which involve good will towards others and consequently promote their well-being or reduce their suffering out of a feeling of solidarity.[52] It is true that Kant's justification of the maxim of goodwill does not avail itself pragmatically of the empirically expected consequences of actions, but is derived solely from the inner structure of its rational generalizability for its own sake. Nonetheless, according to the maxim of goodwill, an action in a concrete situation, or even a rule for action in certain types of situation, requires as a matter of course the best possible and most responsible consideration of the expected consequences in regard to the promotion of the well-being of other persons.

Thirdly, the justification of the moral quality of an action cannot be based directly on its consequences, but only on the quality of the *principles* of our will on which it is founded, because the success and the side effects of our actions often depend on or are influenced by a complex multitude of forces that lie outside our control.[53] But we can only answer morally for those consequences which can be attributed normatively to our actions or failure to act (for example, failure to help someone in need).

To sum up: the sense of deontological ethics for the practice of everyday life lies and has always lain precisely in the clarification of generalizable principles according to which we wish to conduct our lives as responsible persons, and according to which we determine the ends of our actions and self-critically test their acceptability in concrete situations.

[51] Ibid., p. 92.

[52] Frankena, who is a clear advocate of the primacy of deontological ethics, regards the 'principle of benevolence' even as the moral 'prior principle' (*Ethics*, p. 37).

[53] See Höffe, *Ethik und Politik*, p. 89.

It must be admitted that Kant did not expressly bring up questions of the ethics of responsibility. (In this regard discourse ethics, which follows Kant's line on deontological ethics, has systematic advantages, as we shall see later.) Some moral philosophers, in particular Marcus G. Singer,[54] have therefore rejected Kant and disregarded the arguments presented above in a manner difficult to comprehend, proposing instead to make the direct consequences of regular actions in accordance with certain maxims the criterion of the universalization principle. The *consequentialist generalization principle* can be roughly expressed in the following (negative) basic form:

One should not carry out actions whose *general* implementation by any person has negative consequences.

Or in the following equally negative formulation of M. G. Singer:

The consequences of *everyone's* acting in a certain way must not be undesirable.[55]

Singer attempted to clarify the range and the conditions for the validity of this negative generalization criterion.[56] His proposal corresponds in principle to the rule-utilitarian form of the universalization principle, as formulated in the following popular test question:

What would happen if everyone acted in this way (in a certain situation)?

From a utilitarian point of view those rules should apply whose observation can be expected to lead to the greatest possible overall utility for the public good. In contrast to the older action utilitarianism, *rule utilitarianism* no longer applies this criterion to every single action but to rules of action for certain situational types. Although the rule itself is justified teleologically (i.e. in terms of its utility for public welfare, but without considering questions of justice), the duty to observe the rule (in every case!) is demanded deontologically.[57] From the point of view of rule

[54] M. G. Singer, *Generalization in Ethics* (London: Eyre and Spottiswoode, 1963).

[55] Ibid., p. 10 (my italics).

[56] On this point see also Wimmer, *Universalisierung*, p. 301ff.

[57] In the preface to the German translation of his *Generalization*, Singer rejects the interpretation of his approach as utilitarian as a 'misunderstanding': 'I am not a utilitarian.' This can be accepted in as far as it refers to a strict-action utilitarianism, because the conclusion from the undesirability of the overall consequences if *everyone* acted in a certain way to the norm that *no-one* should act in that way cannot in fact be justified with a consequentialist approach. From a utilitarian point of view it could at best be concluded that *not everybody* can act in this particular manner, as Singer emphasizes (German preface). But for precisely this reason Singer's position can be assigned to the rule-utilitarian school of thought, as it implies (as has been pointed out above) a specific deontological element according to which the rules must be observed by all independently of the circumstances of the individual case.

utilitarianism, rules which are not observed generally as a matter of principle serve no function and consequently lose their (narrow utilitarian) legitimation.[58]

As an illustration of the rule-utilitarian generalization criterion any case can be chosen involving the general observation of rules without an ethical value in themselves, such as traffic regulations. These are merely means for the achievement of higher traffic policy aims (for example, the minimization of the danger of accidents or negative social and ecological effects, optimal regulation of the flow of traffic, etc.). Nevertheless, the rule that a car driver must stop at red lights at a crossing in the middle of the night when the road is clear and the streets are empty remains in force, even though it no longer serves the ends mentioned above. The functional sense of the validity of such rules as a matter of principle is that the ends of 'the rules of a game' can only be achieved when the great majority of the 'players' actually follow them. Under this condition everyone can expect with a fair degree of confidence that the game will 'as a rule' take a 'regular' course. In order to guarantee the functioning of the rules their observation is ensured in principle, and pragmatic objections or exceptions in individual cases are generally excluded. *The rules of the game apply to everybody – or to nobody.*

The deontological moment, which is tacitly assumed in the rule-utilitarian generalization criterion, is the idea of equality of rights and of fair cooperation of all the participants in the collective maintenance of regular practice of the rules.[59] For this reason it is constitutive that the conditionally formulated test question (What would happen if ...) of rule utilitarianism is counterfactual; the obvious objection that usually *not everybody* would act in a particular way and that the consequences could be neglected if only *one individual* did act in that way is irrelevant.[60] What is important is rather the recognition in principle and by everybody of the basic norm that it is not legitimate for individuals to behave as free riders and to profit from the fact that the others do *not* behave in the same way. To this extent the

[58] The rule-utilitarian understanding of 'institutional ethics' in Karl Homann's work explains his firm conviction that 'the implementation of a norm leaves its mark on its validity'. See K. Homann/I. Pies, 'Wirtschaftsethik in der Moderne: Zur ökonomischen Theorie der Moral', *Ethik und Sozialwissenschaften* 5 (1994), pp. 3–12, at p. 5 and p. 11. Cf. Section 3.2 (2).

[59] Wimmer, *Universalisierung*, p. 318ff., accordingly proposes a reinterpretation of the rule-utilitarian generalization principle as a *fairness principle* which determines the normative conditions for the maintenance of a cooperative practice. The test question would then run something like: 'What gives you the right to refuse cooperation when you take advantage of results? Would not everyone of us have the same right, as we are all in the same situation as you?'

[60] See ibid., p. 300f.

rule-utilitarian generalization criterion involves a 'general practice of refraining'[61] from non-generalizable forms of action out of a sense of justice. It must, however, then be ensured that rules – before all considerations of collective functionality – actually do justice to all concerned.[62]

Furthermore, the rule-utilitarian generalization criterion also leaves open the question as to what is to be regarded as worth desiring or avoiding, i.e. the question of the ultimate criteria for the value or purpose of a generalizable action. In Chapter 5 we will examine in more detail the methodical paths taken by utilitarianism in the hope of avoiding the need to find a well-grounded answer to this question. At this point it is sufficient to realize that every truly well-grounded answer leads back ultimately to the (deontological) question of the general principles of morally good and proper action and hence to the idea of an impartial, rational, general will. Otherwise a naturalistic abandonment of reflection would occur involving a reduction of what is normatively right and 'ought' to be done to the actual 'will' of concrete persons (in the sense of arbitrary subjective preferences).

In summary it can be said that M. G. Singer – in contrast to the advocates of the widespread vulgar criticism of any kind of 'conviction ethics' – by no means succumbs to the mistaken idea that it is possible to formulate the moral principle in the form of a purely teleological or consequentialist generalization principle or to substitute the one for the other. The rule-utilitarian generalization principle also implicitly assumes the existence of the higher orientational horizon of a clarified moral principle. It may well serve its limited purpose in the determination of the functional rules of the game of social coexistence, without however being in a position to make statements of its own on their *ethical* quality. Taken by itself, the rule-utilitarian generalization criterion does not therefore present a properly understood form of the moral principle.

2.5 Discourse ethics

A properly understood version of the universalization principle and hence of the moral point of view, which is capable of integrating the teleological perspectives (generalizable consequences) into Kant's deontological justification (from the intrinsic moral value of a generalizable will), can be

[61] Ibid., p. 302. Note that under these purely negative criteria there is no place for solidarity or good will.

[62] This insight ultimately led John Rawls, originally an advocate of utilitarian ethics, to reject utilitarianism and to develop his theory of justice as fairness. On this critical turn in Rawls's approach see Section 5.3.

found within the framework of discourse ethics (or communicative ethics). This approach has been developed over the last three decades by Karl-Otto Apel[63] and Jürgen Habermas[64] in an interactive process which can scarcely be disentangled but nonetheless reveals differences in accentuation.

Let us begin with a simple question. Why has discourse, understood as that qualified form of speech serving the purpose of a rational understanding between the partners in a conversation, become the centrepiece of ethics? The experiential background (but not the direct basis for the justification) is once again provided by an anthropological constant: man is fundamentally a 'language animal'. Without linguistic concepts thinking and 'reasoning' (!) are impossible.[65] Even the most solitary thinking is an internalized discussion with oneself as the 'partner in conversation' in ideal role-taking.[66] Discourse is the process by which the intersubjective reversibility of perspectives in the community of subjects who are interested in the rational foundation of validity claims is *practically* tested by means of an exchange of arguments (good reasons) designed to achieve understanding. Reflection on the idealized structures of argumentative reciprocity suggests itself, therefore, as a means of uncovering the moral point of view.

The communicative ethos of reciprocity between interlocutors can probably even be seen in the history of man as the decisive root of the human moral disposition.[67] In the reciprocal relationship of persons who argue and reason with each other – and that means, quite literally, that they try to provide good reasons for or against validity claims – the principle of interpersonal reciprocity always takes the form of an 'immanent morality of

[63] See among other publications K.-O. Apel, *Towards a Transformation of Philosophy* (London: Routledge, 1980), especially the fundamental contribution 'The Apriori of the Communicative Community and the Foundations of Ethics', pp. 225–300. See also his *Diskurs und Verantwortung* (Frankfurt: Suhrkamp, 1988; no English translation available).

[64] See among other publications J. Habermas, 'Discourse Ethics: Notes on a Program of Philosophical Justification' in his *Moral Consciousness and Communicative Action*, pp. 43–115. See also his *Justification and Application*.

[65] As there can be no thinking without concepts, arguments which cannot be formulated are not arguments. This is the fundamental reason for the comprehensive change of paradigms in all epistemology and practical philosophy from the Cartesian subjectivist philosophy of consciousness to the intersubjectivist language philosophy Apel characterizes as a 'transformation of philosophy', to which he himself made essential contributions. See Apel, 'Der transzendentalhermeneutische Begriff der Sprache', in Apel, *Transformation der Philosophie*, vol. II (Frankfurt: Suhrkamp, 1976), pp. 330–57, at p. 354. This essay is not included in the English edition.

[66] On the regulative notion of ideal role-taking see Section 1.4.

[67] See J. Habermas, 'Konventionelle oder kommunikative Sittlichkeit?' in K.-O. Apel *et al.* (eds.), *Praktische Philosophie/Ethik I* (Frankfurt: Suhrkamp, 1980), p. 40; Habermas refers to Mead, *Mind, Self and Society*, pp. 160f., 234, 253ff., who emphasized the fundamental importance of communication for reciprocal role-taking.

speech.'[68] The indispensable 'normative condition for the possibility of argumentation'[69] and hence for reaching a mutual understanding is namely the reciprocal recognition of interlocutors as responsible (response-able!) persons who are willing and in principle able to speak rationally with one another. Anyone who begins to discuss seriously with other people (or even mentally with himself) always implicitly assumes the (passive) openness of the person spoken to for rational argument and his (active) ability to answer argumentatively. Otherwise his own attempts to argue would be meaningless and his language would be merely rhetorical or expressive. (One speaks rhetorically to a dog in order to influence it by the sound of the words, but one seldom argues with it. And one can speak expressively to the wall in order to give vent to feelings, but one seldom gets a rational answer, at best an echo.)

The starting point for discourse ethics is therefore the insight that *rational* communication inevitably presupposes the existence of a communicative *ethos*.[70] This opens up the possibility of explicating more precisely the idea of practical reason or ethical rationality, which remains rather indefinite in the Kantian tradition, as communicative rationality; and as such it has always to be understood as a communicative-ethical rationality. What Kant ultimately characterized as a mere (transcendental) 'fact of reason' now turns out to be a universally valid basic principle with the status of a rationally irreducible, indisputable normative condition for the possibility and validity of all argumentation: the principle of the reciprocal recognition of human beings as subjects between whom rational communication is fundamentally possible.[71]

But why can this typical precondition of all argumentation be regarded as a rationally irreducible[72] principle or normative a priori[73] of interpersonal understanding? To make this clear it is enough to reflect strictly on what we always presuppose normatively when we begin to argue. Apel characterizes this strict reflective justification as a transcendental-pragmatic 'final grounding'.[74] We cannot question the precondition of reciprocal recognition of partners to an argument as responsible subjects without ourselves assuming its existence in the act of (argumentative!) questioning. And we

[68] Habermas, 'Konventionelle oder kommunikative Sittlichkeit?', p. 42.
[69] Apel, *Diskurs und Verantwortung*, p. 101.
[70] For this reason Apel, *Transformation of Philosophy*, p. 259, speaks of the 'ethics of logic', which quite simply means the general primacy of practical reason over theoretical reason.
[71] Ibid., pp. 271, 274f., and Apel, *Diskurs und Verantwortung*, p. 115.
[72] See e.g. Apel, *Transformation of Philosophy*, p. 266. [73] Ibid., pp. 276, 280ff.
[74] Ibid., p. 262ff. See also Apel, 'Limits of Discourse Ethics? An Attempt at a Provisional Assessment', in Apel, *Selected Essays, vol. II: Ethics and the Theory of Rationality* (New Jersey: Humanities Press, 1996), pp. 192–219, at p. 195, where the term 'ultimate justification' is used instead of 'final grounding'.

thus become involved in a *pragmatic self-contradiction* between the content and the fact of our argumentation. But whatever cannot be meaningfully questioned represents a safe, rationally irreducible normative basis. In an attempt at *factual* argument in a real communicative situation we cannot avoid a (possibly) *counterfactual* 'anticipation' of an *ideal* language situation between responsible, rationally arguing persons.[75]

The crucial point is the following: the intellectually necessary assumption and regulative idea of the *ideal communicative community* is nothing other than the discourse-ethical interpretation of the moral point of view. It takes the place systematically of the transcendental rational subject in Kant, who tests the universalizability of his maxims of action (basic formula of the categorical imperative), or the impartial spectator in Smith, who judges the general approvability of reflected affects. The objects of the test of universalizability are now verbalized moral claims. The principle of universalization (the regulative idea of the universal reversal of roles in order to clarify legitimate claims) is operative in discourse ethics as the notion that in an assumedly unlimited argumentation community of all responsible persons of good will normative validity claims should be argumentatively justifiable to everyone and hence amenable to consensual agreement.[76]

It should, therefore, be clear that discourse ethics – in spite of a common misunderstanding to the contrary – cannot be understood concretistically as a particular (material) ethics with a special moral principle in the form of a 'consensus principle' (which is supposedly overestimated as a social principle of coordination). Discourse ethics is rather a particular form of *explication* of the general moral point of view in the shape of ideal discourse.[77] The particular categories in which discourse ethics

[75] See J. Habermas, 'Vorbereitende Bemerkungen zu einer Theorie der kommunikativen Kompetenz', in J. Habermas/N. Luhmann, *Theorie der Gesellschaft oder Sozialtechnologie – Was leistet die Systemforschung?* (Frankfurt: Luchterhand, 1971), pp. 101–41, at p. 122 (no English translation available).

[76] In discourse ethics, as always in ethics, it is a question only of *practical* claims (asserting a normative correctness), in contrast to theoretical claims to validity, which refer to the assertion of facts whose truth must be tested. Reflective language pragmatics can of course refer to the latter and be fruitfully applied epistemologically as *discourse theory of truth*. On this point see J. Habermas, 'A Reply', in A. Honneth and H. Joas (eds.), *Communicative Action: Essays on Jürgen Habermas', 'The Theory of Communicative Action'*, transl. J. Gaines and D. L. Jones (Oxford: Polity, 1991), pp. 214–64, at p. 232f.

[77] The concretistic misunderstanding of discourse ethics is revealed, for example, in the supposedly 'rigorous discourse ethical demands' that a 'coordination based predominantly on discourse' be postulated directly as a principle of social organization. It is understandable that a 'consensus ethics' misinterpreted in this way can then be met with the sceptical objection that it implies a 'nirvana approach' which operates with (over) powerful idealizations (like a kind of consensus ideology). But this misses the point of discourse ethics.

explicates the rational moral point of view are no longer – as was still the case with Kant – those of 'pure practical reason' but those of a (universally valid) *transcendental language pragmatics*.[78] It is correct to speak of pragmatics in as far as the approach – in contrast to Kant's transcendental philosophy – no longer assumes the existence of a metaphysical idea of absolute reason and of an 'objective' moral 'law'.[79] Instead, it reflects solely on the inevitable assumption of rationality in every real communicative situation and on the 'general structure of possible speech situations'.[80] The practical discourse must always be carried out in a practice that is hardly ever ideal. Discourse ethics systematically creates space, so to speak, for those concerned with moral questions and takes them seriously as subjects. In this way ethics finally leaves its pre-modern claim to authority as the 'guardian of morals' behind it without at the same time abandoning its regulative role as the 'guardian of rationality' in moral discourse, in which we as responsible citizens of a free society are always involved. What is more, it recognizes this specifically rational ethical role for the first time to the full extent.[81]

Besides, the lack of identity and the ineradicable tension between ideal and real communicative situations is not a special problem of discourse ethics, as all ethics is concerned with practical orientation in view of the lack of identity of 'is' and 'ought'.[82] It makes little sense, therefore, to object that discourse ethics is 'too idealistic'. As has been said, the practical significance of discourse ethics lies in the normative-critical orientational power of its procedural ideal of discursive clarification for

[78] See Apel, *Transformation of Philosophy*, p. 265. Occasionally he speaks more briefly of *transcendental pragmatics*. He thus follows the Kantian tradition of 'transcendental reflection' without preconditions and, as has been mentioned, raises the claim to a 'final grounding' of discourse ethics. Habermas, 'Vorbereitende Bemerkungen', p. 102, prefers the concept of universal pragmatics or formal pragmatics and rejects the qualification as a transcendental 'ultimate grounding'. See also J. Habermas, 'What is Universal Pragmatics?', in his *Communication and the Evolution of Society* (Oxford/Malden MA: Blackwell, 1991), pp. 1–68. See also Habermas, *Theory of Communicative Action*, vol. I, pp. 138, 328ff. and *Justification and Application*, p. 82.

[79] For a reservation about every *absolute* validity claim of any kind of moral 'ought' which is independent of the interpersonal structure of morality, as is typical of Kant's 'Metaphysics [!] of Morals', see Sections 1.1 and 2.3. A similar reservation probably lies behind Habermas's ('What is Universal Pragmatics?', p. 1f.) objection (in my opinion justified) to the overemphasis on the 'transcendental necessity' in Apel's claim of 'final grounding'. As far as I can see, however, Habermas has nowhere worked out the Kantian roots of the problem precisely, which explains the lack of clarity in his rather severe criticism of Apel, whom he accuses (in an exaggerated and in this form certainly not justified manner) of 'residual foundationalism' (Habermas, *Justification and Application*, p. 82).

[80] Habermas, 'Vorbereitende Bemerkungen', p. 102.

[81] On this point see Habermas, *Moral Consciousness and Communicative Action*, p. 1ff.

[82] On this double 'a priori of the communicative community' see Apel, *Transformation of Philosophy*, p. 280, and Ulrich, *Transformation*, p. 283ff.

real attempts to reach a mutual understanding in situations of conflicting validity claims, particularly for the peaceful and just solution of social conflicts. Specifically, at least four corresponding normative ideas can be reflectively grasped and practically enforced to good effect: (1) the necessary understanding-oriented attitude of those concerned; (2) their unreserved interest in legitimate action; (3) a differentiated concept of responsibility ethics; and last but not least (4) a political-ethical idea on the 'site' of morality in a modern society.

(1) Understanding-oriented attitude

The communicative ethos constitutive of all rational argumentation is first of all expressed in the readiness of all interlocutors (a) to make only those validity claims they truly regard as right, (b) to give reasons for them unreservedly, and (c) to be interested during the discourse only in arriving at a rational consensus by means of universalizable validity claims. The latter includes the readiness to be open for rational (counter) arguments of others and to accept no compulsion other than the 'typically uncompelled compulsion of the better argument'.[83] This elementarily determined understanding orientation quite simply expresses the Kantian precondition of 'good will' in a language pragmatic form. But this can now be more precisely understood as the basic disposition or attitude which reveals the normative basis of communicative rationality – or as *argumentational integrity*.[84]

This fundamental understanding orientation is categorically different from success orientation, which corresponds to the categories of technical rationality (instrumental and strategic rationality).[85] The three basic types of instrumental, strategic and communicative rationality of action provide together a complete systematics of the possible rational orientations of action, as the matrix in Figure 2.2 plausibly demonstrates.

Figure 2.2 illustrates first of all that the two action types of instrumental and strategic action share a purposive-rational orientation on given criteria of success (success orientation); they differ from one another only in

[83] Habermas, 'Vorbereitende Bemerkungen', p. 137.

[84] On the question of argumentational integrity see G. Blickle, *Kommunikationsethik im Management: Argumentationsintegrität als personal- und organisationspsychologisches Leitkonzept* (Stuttgart: Metzler-Poeschel, 1994), p. 10ff. This work is based on N. Groeben/M. Schreier/U. Christmann, *Argumentationsintegrität (I): Herleitung, Explikation und Binnenstrukturierung des Konstrukts*, Bericht N° 28 aus dem Sonderforschungsbereich 'Sprache und Situation' (Heidelberg/Mannheim: University of Heidelberg, 1990).

[85] See Habermas, *Theory of Communicative Action*, vol. I, p. 286; Habermas, 'Aspects of the Rationality of Action', in Th. F. Geraets (ed.), *Rationality Today* (Ottawa: Ottawa University Press, 1979), pp. 184–204, at p. 195ff.

Action situation \ Action orientation	*Oriented to success*	*Oriented to reaching understanding*
Non-social	Instrumental action	—
Social	Strategic action	Communicative action

Figure 2.2. Basic types of rational action[86]

regard to the preconditions of success-controlled action in specific situations. *Instrumental* rationality is technical rationality in a non-social action situation, in which the actor only deals with 'dead' objects he disposes of as means to his ends. In a social action situation, on the other hand, the actor is confronted by other, potentially 'self-willed' subjects, who, in contrast to mere objects, cannot be passively instrumentalized, as they may well pursue contrary aims and interests of their own. In the true sense of the word they remain 'unpredictable', so that the simple paradigm of success-controlled purposive action fails. A *strategic* uncertainty and interdependence is involved, as the success of the action of the actor does not depend on his manner of acting alone, but is influenced by that of his 'opponent'. Strategic action occurs, therefore, when, on the one hand, a person plans and attempts to achieve 'private' success, but, on the other hand, must take into account the socially interactive character of the determining circumstances (utility interdependence); consequently every actor is interested in influencing his opponent to his own ends.

The use of the expression 'opponent' in such situations involving success or utility interdependence indicates that we are in an area that is systematically treated in so-called game theory. One of the game-theoretical insights is that in certain situations it can be of advantage for all participants in the game to consider cooperation strategies instead of a policy of 'every man for himself'. This requires communication with the opponent and the achievement of agreement on the organization of mutual benefit. It must be noted, however, that as long as the strategic opponents unconditionally uphold their previous goals and only endeavour to maximize their own advantage they remain at the level of strategic bargaining aimed at reaching a 'balance of interests'[87] with the best possible results for themselves. In

[86] Source: Habermas, *Theory of Communicative Action*, vol. I, p. 285; Habermas, 'Aspects of the Rationality of Action', p. 195.

[87] On the discourse ethical criticism of this contractualist concept of the balance of interests see Section 5.3 (3).

other words, their attitudes are still strictly success and not understanding oriented.

The change from the strategic to the *communicative* type of rationality (and hence to a form of social coordination of actions which is in principle different) occurs only when the participants develop an understanding-oriented attitude. The other persons with whom a relationship of social interdependence exists will then no longer be regarded as mere objects of strategy, as opponents or fellow players who might interfere negatively or can perhaps be manipulated to contribute positively to the attempts to achieve personal success. They will be perceived instead as subjects with legitimate claims of their own. The moral interest in arriving at a consensus on conflicting validity claims by means of unconditional argumentation now acquires priority over the personal aims of the participants. The mutual desire of the players to influence each other for the achievement of individual goals is replaced by the wish to arrive at an ethically rational agreement[88] by means of argument. The decisive point – often misunderstood – is not closing down communicative processes by means of consent, but keeping them open for argumentative criticism. Discourse ethics does not describe a procedure for the achievement of consensus which guarantees (!) success but reflects on the normative conditions of the possibility of argumentative understanding processes.

(2) *Interest in legitimate action*

Contrary to a further standard misunderstanding, it must be pointed out that the shift from an attitude oriented strictly on success to an attitude oriented on reaching a mutual understanding by no means implies that the persons involved must completely abandon the pursuit of their personal aims and interests. The understanding-oriented coordination of actions does not exclude the circumstance that the participants may also be interested in their personal success. The understanding orientation acquires its practical significance precisely from the existence of plans of action presented by actors desirous of success.[89] In as far as the possible consequences of the realization of such plans affects others, they inevitably lead to problems of justification. For precisely this reason the *primary* 'interest' of the actors in a discursive clarification of the acceptability of their plans of action for all other participants is needed. A necessary rational ethical 'interest' is of course nothing other than a

[88] See J. Habermas, 'A Reply', pp. 240f., 249f.

[89] See Habermas, 'Aspects of the Rationality of Action', p. 196; similarly in *Theory of Communicative Action*, vol. I, pp. 100f., 285f.

moral self-commitment 'motivated' by reflective insight. In other words: the private pursuit of individual or special interests is subjected to the self-imposed normative condition of their legitimacy, i.e. their justification in regard to the preservation of the dignity and inviolable moral rights of all the persons involved.[90]

Thus, the conduct of moral persons is by no means characterized by categorical self-sacrifice or even self-disregard, but by the unconditional primacy of the moral interest in the legitimacy of actions over all private interests. Between the two equally problematic poles of inconsiderate self-interest (egoism) and heroic self-sacrifice (altruism) moral persons search for a third way of *legitimate self-assertion.* Then and only then will they renounce the pursuit of their further interests and goals when they recognize that these interests do not fulfil the conditions of legitimacy. But under the defined conditions of legitimacy the individual in a free and open society can pursue his personal interests in accordance with his own project of a good life. Accordingly the subjective preferences and interests of the participants in an action no longer constitute an unquestioned guideline for the achievement of a possible strategic 'balance of interests', but are regarded as claims whose acceptance as legitimate by the other participants must be tested. The object of the discursive test of legitimacy is to decide whether the responsibility can be accepted for the probable consequences of the realization of the claims in question with regard to all the persons potentially affected. The ethical criterion always is and remains, however, the deontological aspect of the moral rights of all concerned.

With the concept of an argumentatively and consensually legitimated pursuit of interests, discourse ethics achieves a development of the teleological-ethical perspective *within* a deontological ethics. As Habermas puts it, it has 'a built-in procedure that ensures awareness of consequences'.[91]

[90] We take up the question of concrete moral rights in Chapter 7.

[91] Habermas, *Moral Consciousness and Communicative Action*, p. 206. As Benhabib, *Situating the Self*, p. 35, has fittingly remarked, Habermas even tends to an all too consequentialist definition of the discourse ethical principle of universalization, in which the primacy of the deontological standpoint of the reciprocal recognition of persons in regard to their inviolable rights becomes blurred, as he defines the universalization principle directly in terms of the acceptability of consequences from the point of view of the private *interests* of all concerned: 'Thus every valid norm has to fulfil the following condition: (U) *All* affected can accept the consequences and the side effects its *general* observance can be anticipated to have for the satisfaction of *everyone's* interests (and these consequences are preferred to those of known alternative possibilities for regulation).' Habermas, *Moral Consciousness*, p. 65. This definition no longer needs to be understood in the sense of the deontological principle, but can be interpreted (although this is certainly contrary to the intention of Habermas) in a contract-theoretical way in the sense of *methodological individualism.* We will take a closer look at the fundamental differences between discourse ethics and economic contractual theory in Section 5.3.

What discourse ethics can provide is the clear integration of the two aspects in a lexical order. The understanding orientation enjoys normative primacy over the success orientation: legitimacy has priority over success.

(3) The three-stage concept of responsibility

As we have just made clear, a discursive test of the legitimacy of interests or claims on the basis of its 'built-in' consequentialist orientation (Habermas) aims precisely at securing the normative preconditions for responsible action. The reproach of (irresponsible?) 'conviction ethics' that is sometimes heard makes even less sense in regard to discourse ethics than to Kant. It is probably based on an inadequate concept of responsibility (without convictions?). As we have already seen above, responsibility ethics must always be understood as deontological ethics.[92]

With the regulative idea of the universal argumentative reciprocity between persons who recognize each other as responsible, discourse ethics literally explicates the normative (and linguistic!) core of responsible action as it is preserved in the concept of '*response*-ability': the idea that actors should answer unconditionally to those affected by their actions and take their legitimate claims into account. In this way it is first of all possible to achieve a discourse-ethical transformation of the often monologically narrow concept of responsibility (responsible decision-taking on behalf of those affected, i.e. paternalistic consideration of their interests) into a fundamentally *dialogical concept of responsibility* (decision-taking together with those affected, i.e. consensus-orientated communication on the legitimate claims of all concerned). In this sense a person acts responsibly, who faces up to the demands for justification or solidarity and to the criticism of all who are affected by his intended actions, in order to recognize their legitimate claims and to take them into account in his actions, instead of hiding behind the sweeping general justification of his 'responsibility to his own conscience'.

A specific problem of responsibility ethics in situations where reciprocity is lacking or incomplete remains to be dealt with.[93] There are situations in which reciprocal agreement between an actor and those affected by his actions cannot be easily achieved for a variety of reasons:

[92] See above Section 2.4.

[93] Hans Jonas also defines the concept of responsibility in terms of the 'non-reciprocal relationship'; see H. Jonas, *The Imperative of Responsibility: In Search of an Ethics for the Technological Age* (Chicago/London: University of Chicago Press, 1984), p. 94.

- because the *basic situation* does not permit the achievement of understanding (as in the case of the unborn, minors and others not responsible for their actions);
- because of *pragmatic difficulties* (e.g. the inability to determine or delimit the potentially affected, when the numbers are too large or there are spatial, temporal, technical or financial obstacles);
- or because the other actors lack the *personal motivation* to reach an understanding (strategic opponents!). In this case the bearer of responsibility cannot reckon lightly with the goodwill of other, possibly influential actors, if the practical consequences of the predictable disappointment of his naïve assumption could be highly problematic from an ethical point of view.

A further typical situation involving serious problems of responsibility is the dilemma of actors facing diverging and conflicting claims on their sense of responsibility. On the one hand there is usually a specific, organizationally defined *role responsibility* in the context of the accountable fulfillment of assigned executive duties, and, on the other, the ethically indivisible *civic responsibility*.[94] The dilemma consists in the contradiction between the fundamental 'legitimate interest in self-assertion'[95] and the possibly equally legitimate claims of those affected by organizational action. In such situations the bearer of a special role responsibility cannot and must not be expected simply to put aside his (or his organization's) interest in self-assertion.[96]

For these problematic situations Karl-Otto Apel proposes a 'supplementing principle'[97] of responsibility ethics as a so-called 'Part B' of discourse ethics. This requires actors to let their actions be guided by the *telos* (ethical goal) of the long-term 'approximative' realization of the normative conditions of discursive communication. This means that they must contribute to the realization of the 'historically contingent' preconditions of the ethical-political chances of reaching an understanding even when their actions are strategically oriented. The 'auxiliary principle' thus requires no more and no less than the 'moral strategy'[98] of accepting, within the given possibilities of the situation, a share of responsibility for the organization

[94] See the more detailed considerations on a modern civic ethics for economic agents, in particular on the idea of the institutional or organizational citizen, Section 8.3 (1).
[95] K.-O. Apel, 'Diskursethik vor der Problematik von Recht und Politik', in K.-O. Apel/M. Kettner (eds.), *Zur Anwendung der Diskursethik in Politik, Recht und Wissenschaft* (Frankfurt: Suhrkamp, 1992), pp. 29–61, at p. 35.
[96] Ibid., p. 35. [97] See Apel, 'Limits of Discourse Ethics?', pp. 208, 213.
[98] Ibid., p. 212.

of the social conditions of communication 'at all levels of human cooperation'.[99] According to Apel, what is at issue is the historical 'project of the discourse-ethical mobilization and organization of the collective shared responsibility of all for the consequences of our collective activities'.[100]

Although this project must be viewed very positively, it remains questionable whether it requires a special 'auxiliary principle' of responsibility ethics. According to our earlier considerations under (2) responsibility ethics is not to be understood as a complement to discourse ethics but as an orientation already implicit in practical discourse.[101] It is not only unclear what the 'auxiliary principle' achieves in terms of an additional normative orientation; it also creates normative problems itself in turn, which inevitably lead it back to the level of justificatory discourse. This becomes clear if one considers the 'mediation rule' which Apel proposes as a means of linking discourse ethics and responsibility ethics:

> as much prior concession as *possible* in the sense of reaching an understanding which is free of strategy; as many strategic reservations as *necessary* on the basis of a responsible calculation of risks.[102]

But what degree of understanding orientation is 'possible' in a concrete situation and at what point do reservations become 'necessary'? At precisely this point Apel makes a category mistake by reducing the *normative* problem (of the degree to which 'reservations' are legitimate in view of the conditions of strategic self-assertion of actors and the degree of communicative-ethical 'concessions' which can be *reasonably* expected) to an empirical problem of possibility. That we encounter resistance of all kinds in the real world, even and precisely in regard to our very best intentions, is normal. But as a rule only a tiny part of this resistance relates to natural law; it is predominantly determined by a historically established social practice. The desire to break or circumvent the resistance for strategic reasons means accepting it uncritically as a given inherent necessity instead of understanding it as an aspect of a normatively determined

[99] See Apel, 'Diskursethik vor der Problematik von Recht und Politik', p. 30. On the postulate of shared responsibility see Apel, *Diskurs und Verantwortung*, pp. 116, 271.

[100] Combined quotation from Apel, 'Diskursethik vor der Problematik von Recht und Politik', pp. 31 and 29.

[101] In a similar fashion Dieter Böhler raises the objection that responsibility ethics is 'less a complement ... as Apel misleadingly states, than a consequence' of discourse ethics. See D. Böhler, 'Diskursethik und Menschenwürdegrundsatz zwischen Idealisierung und Erfolgsverantwortung', in Apel/Kettner (eds.), *Zur Anwendung der Diskursethik in Politik, Recht und Wissenschaft*, pp. 201–31, at p. 204.

[102] Apel, 'Diskursethik vor der Problematik von Recht und Politik', p. 36. Similarly Apel, *Diskurs und Verantwortung*, p. 247ff.

practice which can in principle be changed and consequently putting its legitimacy up for discussion.[103]

In order to clarify the central ethical question of responsibility every person in a position of responsibility is thus 'forced' to participate, to the best of his ability, in a discourse with those affected by his actions, if only in his own mind. And such a mental attempt to reach an understanding with oneself is always 'possible'! There is no difference in principle between 'solitary' reflection with the intention of acting responsibly and the actual participation in a legitimation discourse – both require the basic communicative-ethical disposition of argumentative integrity and both must always take into account strategic aspects of the assessment and judgement of consequences in specific situations. Consequently there is no need for a special 'auxiliary principle' in order to formulate the following three-stage concept of a responsibility ethics transformed along the lines of discourse ethics:[104]

(a) When the preconditions for reciprocal understanding are fulfilled to a fair extent, a person acts responsibly who makes an effort to engage in a *real* legitimation discourse with those concerned.
(b) When the preconditions for reciprocal understanding cannot in principle be fulfilled, a person acts responsibly who, to the best of his ability, engages in a *proxy fictive* discourse with those concerned in 'solitary' reflection, in order to weigh their legitimate 'claims' against his own interests.
(c) When the preconditions for reciprocal understanding cannot be fulfilled at the moment for purely pragmatic reasons, a person acts responsibly who first of all acts as proxy and takes on the responsibility unilaterally in his mind, but at the same time orients his actions on the regulative idea of the long-term best possible realization of the unrestricted communicative conditions and accordingly accepts his *share of political responsibility*.[105]

At the third stage responsibility ethics points to the necessity of a political (institutional) ethics. It has to clarify the desirability of those institutional

[103] For this fundamental categorial distinction in economic ethics see U. Thielemann, 'Integrative Wirtschafts- und Unternehmensethik als Reflexion des spannungsreichen Verhältnisses von Einkommensstreben und Moral', *Berichte des Instituts für Wirtschaftsethik* N° 67 (St Gallen: Institute for Economic and Business Ethics, 1994). We will see this in more detail later in Sections 3.3 (1), 4.2 and 4.3, when dealing with the problem of inherent necessity.

[104] See Ulrich, *Transformation*, p. 321f.

[105] The postulate of political co-responsibility will be developed later in Sections 8.2, 8.3 and 10.2 (in the latter case as the political co-responsibility of the entrepreneur at the institutional level).

frameworks whose realization requires the acceptance of a share of responsibility.[106]

(4) *Public discourse as the 'site' of morality*

Practical processes of communication always take place within an institutional context. Although discursive processes are in the final analysis a question of the inner disposition of the participants, namely of their argumentative integrity, and not of external relationships of power, they usually depend upon 'a background of complementary institutions and normative contexts'.[107] Above all, the external (social) communicative conditions themselves require an adequate structural freedom from power and a normative openness, if the more or less counterfactual but unavoidable anticipation of an ideal speech situation (as we undertake it in every attempt to argue) should not remain unrealistic from the start and break down in the face of powerful resistance. It is, therefore, a matter of creating in each real communication community the best possible institutional conditions oriented on the regulative idea of the ideal communication community. Ideal discourse as such cannot be institutionalized. It must rather be understood as a mental (and in principle non-producible) 'meta-institution'[108] serving as a regulative idea for practical endeavours to shape the social conditions of communication in a manner that fosters argumentative solutions.[109]

[106] Against Apel's Part B of discourse ethics ('auxiliary principle') Habermas (*Justification and Application*, p. 85f.) points out that this goes beyond the scope of an action ethics and enters problem areas which require a much more comprehensive elucidation of constitutional and institutional principles. According to Habermas, Apel's teleological auxiliary principle has the 'undesirable consequence' that it attempts, within the framework of a moral theory, to address 'questions of political ethics "directly from above" through a super-principle, although these questions are not situated on the same level as the justification of the moral principle'. Habermas opposes this position in his major legal-philosophical study *Between Facts and Norms: Contributions to a Discourse Theory of Law and Democracy* (Cambridge MA: MIT Press, 1996).

[107] Habermas, *Justification and Application*, p. 33.

[108] See K.-O. Apel, 'Arnold Gehlens "Philosophie der Institutionen" und die Metainstitution der Sprache', in Apel, *Transformation der Philosophie*, vol. I (Frankfurt: Suhrkamp, 1976), pp. 197–221, at pp. 217, 221 (this essay is not included in the English edition).

[109] An objection must therefore be raised against Apel's standard formulation that it is a matter of 'realizing the ideal communication community in the real communication community'. (Apel, *Transformation of Philosophy*, p. 282). The wish to realize the regulative idea of the ideal communication community pragmatically is equivalent to a pragmatistic short-circuiting of the categorial difference and the necessary tension between the critical orientational idea and the 'implementable' practice and thus produces precisely that 'monstrous idealization' which Apel rather inappropriately ascribes to the institutional-ethical three-level heuristics of the present writer. On this point see n. 145 in Section 9.2.

A regulative idea of the *communicative rationalization of society* has thus been determined which presents nothing other than the political-ethical ideal horizon of a free democratic society of responsible citizens. At the same time, it overcomes the one-dimensional character of the usual technocratic perspectives of social rationalization.[110] Whereas technical rationalization always aims at extending the disposal and control over certain objects (and social technology correspondingly aims at the objectification and instrumental control of subjects!), communicative rationalization means the extension of the unconstrained communicative possibilities of responsible persons.

> Rationalization here means extirpating those relations of force that are inconspicuously set in the very structures of communication and that prevent conscious settlement of conflicts, and consensual regulation of conflicts, by means of intrapsychic as well as interpersonal communicative barriers.[111]

Discourse ethics thus points to the normative horizon for the *opening up*, in principle, of the social conditions for reaching understanding but not to their institutional *closure*. In other words, discourse ethics remains, even in the institutional-ethical context, a methodical form of reflection on the moral point of view – but it can never be an 'applicable' normative theory for the shaping of institutions.[112] As in the model of thought of discourse ethics the 'uncompelled compulsion of the better argument' (Habermas) alone should prevail, there is in principle no reason for excluding anybody at all from the discourse, who wishes to bring forward an argument, even if he is personally not directly affected by the consequences of the practical implementation of the disputed validity claims. In contrast, real institutions serve precisely the purpose of delimiting communication to a certain extent by determining rights of participation and procedural rules which narrow down the range of those entitled to take part in the argument and prestructure the argumentative process in order to arrive pragmatically at concrete results.

The legitimate regulation and partial closure of institutionalized communication is consequently always in itself a matter of practical political

[110] Habermas, *Theory of Communicative Action*, must be credited with moving beyond Max Weber's universal historical conception of modernization as technical rationalization and developing a systematic social-theoretical basic conception which is capable of integrating the perspectives of the communicative rationalization of the lifeworld and the functional (technical) rationalization of social subsystems.

[111] J. Habermas, 'Toward a Reconstruction of Historical Materialism', in his *Communication and the Evolution of Society*, p. 119f.

[112] In Section 3.1 we will return to this misunderstanding about the 'applicability' of discourse ethics, against which even its founders (especially Apel) are apparently not immune.

deliberation that has to be shaped in the light of the regulative idea of an ideal, power-free communication community. It is vital, therefore, to discern and to establish a level of 'open' social communication that takes normative priority over all other institutions as it alone guarantees the preconditions for the legitimate determination of partly closed social institutions. The regulative idea corresponding to this priority level is that of 'public discourse'[113] in the *unlimited public sphere involving all responsible (world-) citizens*. This embodies the final, intellectual instance ('meta-institution') or the ideal site of morality in a modern, open (world) society. There the ideal of 'the public use of man's reason'[114] already developed by Kant is more or less largely implemented in social practice as the unconstrained argumentation of a universal 'reasoning public'.

Seen in this light, 'publicity'[115] is itself not a delimitable part of a political system, but must be understood as the regulative 'bridging principle between politics and morality'.[116] All that can and must be regulated institutionally in regard to the specific meta-institution of the unlimited public sphere is the basic right of all persons to freedom of speech (i.e. to participation in the forum of public discourse) and the appropriate legal protection of this liberal basic right against the attempts of power and interest groups to exercise pressure, in as far as free speech is not circumscribed by even more fundamental rights to the protection of personality. What is at issue is the question of keeping public discourse open institutionally so that it can fulfil its indispensable critical function in an open society of subjecting all publicly relevant actions in principle to an equally public 'pressure of legitimation', i.e. to the 'uncompelled compulsion' to justify claims by argument. Alongside the executive, the legislative and the judicature, a watchful public sphere constitutes the necessary 'fourth power' in a free democratic society. Under its observation the practical *institutionalization of arrangements limiting communication* is legitimate, so that the circle of those entitled to participate in discourse is restricted to those who are affected in a certain way. The test criterion for an 'open society' (Karl Popper), however, is that even those

113 Habermas, *Justification and Application*, p. 203.

114 See I. Kant, 'What is Enlightenment?', p. 55. See also J. Rawls, 'The Idea of Public Reason' in his *Political Liberalism* (New York: Columbia University Press, 1993), pp. 212–54. For more on this point see Chapters 7 and 8.

115 See I. Kant, 'Toward perpetual peace', in Kant, *Practical Philosophy*, transl. and ed. M. J. Gregor (Cambridge: Cambridge Edition of the Works of Immanuel Kant, 1996), pp. 311–51, at p. 347ff.

116 J. Habermas, *The Structural Transformation of the Public Sphere*, transl. Th. Burger (Cambridge MA: MIT Press, 1989), p. 102. More details follow in Section 8.2.

limitations on communication which have already been publicly justified can be reversed politically, if contrary, better reasons are seen to be valid in public discourse.

In this way, in a first delimitation of the universe of discourse, it is possible to restrict the 'reasoning public' (Kant) to the citizens of a political unit (e.g. a national state). Although from a discourse ethical perspective this does not lead directly to a pragmatic concept, it does at least provide a regulative idea of ethically *rational politics*: the regulative idea of a political order as an unconstrained communication order of responsible citizens. This takes up the best intuitions and central ideas of modern political ethics as developed over the last 500 years in the ideals of political liberalism (emancipation from heteronomy through inviolable rights of personality and freedom) and democracy (general right of citizens to equal participation of all in deliberative political decision-making processes) and enables for the first time a justification of their specific communicative rationality. The unsurpassed free democratic central ideas have always aimed at equal rights for all citizens in regard to participation in *public communication* on the one hand and *private self-fulfilment* (the 'pursuit of happiness' according to the American constitution) on the other. Both of them are founded on a fundamental social consensus termed *constitution* in the basic order of democracy. The general priority of consensual legitimation over the private pursuit of success corresponds here to the institutional-ethical primacy of universal communication rights and opportunities of all responsible citizens over all further dispositional rights of individual actors.[117]

As an initial summary we can say that discourse ethics offers the most elaborate explication to date of the rational ethical point of view as the normative logic of interpersonal relations. It develops the explication consistently as the universal argumentative reciprocity between persons who recognize each other as responsible citizens. In comparison to earlier explications of the moral principle it acquires not only a superior reflective (universal pragmatic) justificatory force but also a wide-ranging critical-normative orientational force at the levels of personal responsibility ethics as well as institutional ethics in regard to the meta-institution of the unlimited public sphere as the ultimate site of morality in a free democratic society of responsible citizens.

[117] In Section 9.2 we will apply this institutional ethical principle to the institutional ethics of the market economy.

3 Morality and economic rationality: integrative economic ethics as the rational ethics of economic activity

In view of the understanding of ethics explicated above, modern economic ethics can be and has to be fundamentally developed as a rational ethics of economic activity. The basic systematic problem of modern economic ethics will be elaborated under this central idea and set off against two other approaches which have hitherto dominated the discussion.

At first sight it seems reasonable to conceive of economic ethics as 'applied' ethics for the areas of life and society in which the economy operates (Section 3.1). A closer look reveals, however, that such an understanding of economic ethics is inadequate. It is subject to the systematic misapprehension that 'the economic sphere' is an area still untouched by ethics into which morality must first be introduced and, what is more, as a complement or corrective which is external to the 'value free' inherent logic of the economy. This approach systematically ignores the fact that the inherent logic of the (market) economy, the extremely powerful economic rationality, itself implicitly or explicitly always claims a normative validity which inevitably comes into conflict with ethical rationality. Every conception of rationality has a normative significance, as it determines how people ought to act rationally. The position economic ethics as 'applied' ethics would like to fill is consequently already occupied; two competing normative logics are opposed to each other, whose relationship requires clarification.

The economic understanding of rationality is defined and cultivated paradigmatically in economic theory. The latter has always represented a normative theory of the 'correct' design of the economy. Such an ideal theory of rational economic activity corresponds precisely to its intellectual and historical origin in Political Economy (a thoroughly fitting name). This helps to understand a second approach to economic ethics which plays a prominent part in the discussions especially among German-speaking intellectuals: normative economics as an 'economic ethics' operating without ethical categories (Section 3.2). From the point of view of rational ethics, however, the resulting reduction of economic ethics to moral economics (in the sense of a 'pure' economic theory of morality) must be

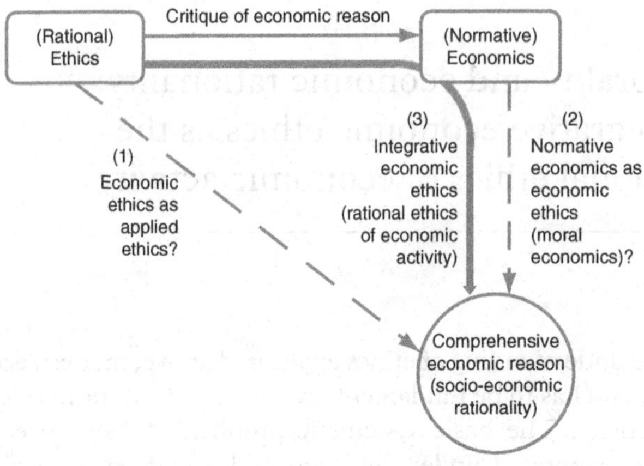

Figure 3.1. The three-pole relationship of ethics, economics and comprehensive economic reason

criticized as a normative exaggeration and exaltation of the 'economic principle'.

A rational ethics of economic activity can be satisfied neither with applied ethics nor with normative economics. Its core concern is an integrative approach which literally 'thinks together' the ethical rationality claim and the economic rationality claim instead of simply juxtaposing them symptomatically – as a theoretical duplication of the real starting position – or wishing to reduce the one claim to the other (Figure 3.1). Integrative economic ethics sees its fundamental task first of all in clarifying the categorial relationship between ethical and economic rationality and in solving the problem of their systematic mediation (Section 3.3). Along this path we will arrive at a comprehensive concept of economic reason – characterized henceforth as the regulative idea of socio-economic rationality – which already includes ethical rationality. At first only a general characterization of the integrative approach and of the basic systematic tasks of a rational ethics of economic activity will be undertaken. The detailed treatment of these tasks will be left to the later parts of the book.

3.1 Economic ethics as applied ethics?

In the modern world, new, complex and confusing problem areas have arisen that call for scientifically well-founded practical orientations and guidance. But most academic disciplines that once felt competent for this task have long retreated to 'value-free' theoretical conceptions, following a positivistic and scientistic[1] understanding and resulting in a merely (social-) technological relationship between theory and practice. Under these conditions of systematic helplessness in today's 'normal sciences', and in the face of the ethical-practical and socio-political challenges of the age, more and more hybrid forms of ethics are evolving, which see themselves as a kind of 'applied ethics' for specific areas. They endeavour to fill the gap left by the 'value-free' disciplines in regard to the ethical dimensions of practical problems (medical ethics, scientific ethics, technological ethics, ecological ethics, sport ethics, etc.). These 'area ethics' must therefore be primarily understood as practice-oriented compensatory phenomena.

This is also in principle the case with business and economic ethics. At first sight it seems to be a typical area of applied ethics comparable with the other forms of hybrid, specialized ethics. On the one hand, mainstream economics in its neoclassical form has long abandoned the classical tradition of political economy and, in accordance with its self-understanding as 'autonomous economics',[2] has emancipated itself totally from its mother discipline, practical philosophy.[3] On the other hand, every reasonably informed contemporary is aware of the epochal questions raised by the need for the reorientation of the economic style and order of industrial society towards the service of life. The established economic sciences obviously have little or nothing to offer of a sensible kind in this respect, as long as they restrict themselves to the cultivation of pure economic rationality (or what they regard as such). More and more people seem to be asking themselves fundamental questions in regard to the sense and legitimacy of the unbridled, increasingly self-referential global market dynamics in view of the incalculable side effects ('external effects') on the natural environment, the social lifeworld and our cultural inner world. The symptomatic 'call' for business ethics is not, therefore,

[1] Scientism involves the generalization of the natural science model of nomological theory (science in the narrow Anglo-Saxon sense of the word), which is interested in the formulation of generally valid, technologically implementable empirical laws to a single universal concept of science and its application to the humanities and social sciences. On the intellectual history and the epistemological background to the scientistic truncation of the practical dimension of 'modern' science see Ulrich, *Transformation*, pp. 145ff., 269ff.

[2] H. Albert, *Ökonomische Ideologie und politische Theorie*, 2nd edn (Göttingen: Otto Schwartz, 1972; 1st edn 1954), pp. 3 and 22. Albert coined or used the concept with critical intent. He spoke at the time explicitly of a 'supposedly autonomous economics' (p. 3).

[3] The main stages of this step-by-step emancipation of modern economics, which at certain points in its theoretical development is 'disturbed' by normative remnants or symptomatic aporias, is described in Ulrich, *Transformation*, p. 173ff. The most important aspects of the background to the rise, development and contemporary form of the paradigm of autonomous or pure economics are dealt with in Part II.

simply an intellectual fashion fallen from the heaven of an ivory-towered idealism, but is – analogous to the situation in other fields of area ethics – an expression of the increasing awareness and experience of very real ethical-practical problems. The trend towards specialized applied ethics does in fact largely determine the pre-understanding of Anglo-Saxon business ethics, but it is widespread in the discussion of the fundamental principles of economic ethics in German-speaking countries as well.[4] This might at first seem unproblematic, especially as the talk of 'applied ethics' is commonly found not only outside but also inside the discipline of philosophy, where the concept is usually understood in a very broad sense. Even the founders of discourse ethics now speak of 'the application of discourse ethics';[5] they believe that they have discerned a specific 'historically related problem of the application of discourse ethics'[6] and that they can or must distinguish between 'application discourses'[7] (in situational contexts) and 'justification discourses'. In this case it is necessary, as we shall shortly see, to defend discourse ethics against its founders. A closer look at the 'application models' of discourse ethics in fact reveals substantial problems both in general (1) and with specific reference to economic and business ethics (2).

(1) Application of discourse ethics?

No-one will doubt that the questions of ultimate foundation of the universal moral principle must be distinguished from context-specific concrete problems in regard to actions. But when, on this account, Habermas proposes a systematic distinction between 'justification' and 'application' discourse and regards 'different principles' as fundamentally necessary for the latter[8], a simple question suggests itself: What is at issue in an application discourse from a systematic point of view, if it is not, as

[4] The 'application model' of economic ethics was first classified as supposedly the only alternative to the 'economic foundational model' by the 'Economics and Ethics Committee' of the *Verein für Socialpolitik*; see K. Homann, H. Hesse *et al.*, 'Wirtschaftswissenschaft und Ethik', in H. Hesse (ed.), *Wirtschaftswissenschaft und Ethik* (Berlin: Duncker & Humblot, 1988), pp. 9–33. See also G. Enderle, 'Wirtschaftsethik als 'angewandte' Ethik', *Wirtschaft und Recht* 39 (1987), pp. 114–24; also his *Wirtschaftsethik im Werden: Ansätze und Problembereiche der Wirtschaftsethik* (Stuttgart: Akademie der Diözese Rottenburg-Stuttgart, 1988), p. 49ff. On 'corporate ethics as applied ethics' in Germany see, e.g., H. Steinmann/A. Löhr, *Grundlagen der Unternehmensethik*, 2nd rev. and exp. edn (Stuttgart: Schäffer-Poeschel, 1994), p. 94ff.

[5] See K.-O. Apel/M. Kettner (eds.), *Zur Anwendung der Diskursethik in Politik, Recht und Wissenschaft* (Frankfurt: Suhrkamp, 1992), Preface, p. 7.

[6] Particularly emphatically in the case of Apel, *Diskurs und Verantwortung*, p. 110ff.

[7] More in passing in the case of Habermas, *Justification and Application*, pp. 35ff., 120, 128f.

[8] See ibid., p. 128f.

in every moral discourse, argumentative communication on good reasons for alternative proposals for actions?

The situational problems concerned in the justification of legitimate forms of action might often be complex and not susceptible to satisfactory solutions in view of dilemmatic situations involving competing moral claims. But Habermas's (strikingly vague) thesis that 'application discourses require different data and principles from discourses of justification', namely an additional principle 'of appropriateness and the exhaustion of all relevant contextual features',[9] suggests that he has abandoned his own earlier insights. In *Moral Consciousness* he argued that testing the acceptability of the concrete situational consequences and with it the complete utilization of all information on the context of an intention to act is necessarily already 'built into' every legitimation or justification discourse.[10] Legitimation discourse is in this sense always application discourse – this differentiation makes no sense, at least when it is a matter of clarifying the rights (legitimacy) of conflicting claims of individuals.[11]

The doubts are not diminished by Habermas' elucidation of an additional 'principle of appropriateness', which he postulates for application discourses (application of what?):

> For within moral discourses, the principle of universalization necessitates the weighing of consequences and demands in general that all relevant features of the *given situation* be taken into account already in the justification of norms, but more especially in their application, as is explicitly required by the principle of

[9] See ibid., pp. 128–30. He refers to the work of his former student and colleague K. Günther, *Der Sinn für Angemessenheit: Anwendungsdiskurse in Moral und Recht* (Frankfurt: Suhrkamp, 1988).

[10] See Habermas, *Moral Consciousness and Communicative Action*, p. 206, and on this Section 2.5 (2).

[11] The separation of justification and application makes sense at best in regard to norms. 'No norm contains within itself the rules for its application. Yet moral justifications are pointless unless the decontextualization of the *general norms* used in justification is compensated for in the process of application' (Habermas, *Moral Consciousness*, p. 206, my italics). This may well be true, but the systematic error of Habermas and Günther seems to me to be that they regard the case of the justification of general norms and their application in concrete situations as paradigmatic for moral discourses per se, which is not appropriate for the treatment of the fundamental problem of the discursive clarification of the moral rights of persons and of the corresponding questions of legitimate action. What these *moral rights* are precisely and what they mean can always be clarified only in a concrete context. Only the general basic rights of all persons, i.e. the universal human and citizen's rights, can be decontextualized and hence normativized before every situative legitimation discourse (not: application discourse). But independently of the state of normativization every legitimation discourse must always elucidate all the moral rights of those concerned and can never restrict itself to the 'application' of norms of human rights which have already been declared binding.

appropriateness. And self-referential reflections on the reasonableness of moral demands already play a role within moral discourses.[12]

Here there is a danger of an abandonment of reflection in the face of empirically given circumstances, as Tugendhat has made clear:

> One can never question a moral judgement normatively by merely establishing its socio-economic conditions. A moral judgement can only be questioned normatively (and that means morally).[13]

Exactly! From a moral point of view actors are indeed required, precisely in adverse circumstances, to put up with personal disadvantages if the disadvantages are tolerable and disregard for the moral rights of the third party would be irresponsible. In order to clarify the degree to which an actor's renunciation of his own success in a given situation is 'appropriate'– and this can only mean justifiable – and to decide which consequences of one's pursuit of personal success those affected can be reasonably expected to accept, a justifying discourse on legitimacy and reasonableness is always and not merely 'occasionally indicated'.[14] All practical discourses on normative validity claims occur 'in given situations' and are justifying discourses in regard to the moral rights and norms which are valid in this situation.

In a different and even more problematic way than Habermas, Apel tends to favour a split between justifying discourse and 'the problem of application'. His frequent reference to the necessary 'realization of the application conditions of discourse ethics'[15] is disconcerting precisely from a discourse ethical point of view. The ideal discourse situation is neither realizable anywhere nor 'utopian'[16] for that reason; it is rather and remains a non-empirical (transcendental) regulative idea in the light of which we can indeed arrive at a normative-critical judgement of our communicative practice but which can never be empirically implemented. This, however, is exactly what Apel assumes when he optimistically speaks of 'the realization, *still pertinent*, of the conditions of application'.[17] One

[12] Habermas, *Justification and Application*, p. 86f. (my italics). What is vaguely translated by 'play a role' is in the German original 'sind gelegentlich am Platz', i.e. 'are occasionally indicated'. See below to this.

[13] Tugendhat, *Vorlesungen*, p. 16.

[14] The problem of reasonableness mentioned here is dealt with in Section 4.3. To the term 'occasionally' see n. 12 above.

[15] For example Apel, *Diskurs und Verantwortung*, p. 134.

[16] This is the obviously ambivalent position of Apel, ibid., p. 302.

[17] Apel, 'Limits of Discourse Ethics?', p. 207 (my italics). The translation 'still pertinent' is not quite adequate, as the original German expression 'noch ausstehend' means 'still to come' or '*not yet* fulfilled'. The more cautious formulation of an 'approximative' realization of ideals (which can never be fully realized) in the real communicative community, as is favoured, for example, by Böhler, 'Diskursethik und Menschenwürdegrundsatz',

cannot help thinking that Apel's notion of the 'application of discourse ethics' rests upon a latent concretistic (self-) misunderstanding. For him discourse ethics seems to provide a special 'basic norm for the ethics of consensus formation'[18] from which concrete obligations for a correct social practice can be directly (i.e. without discourse) gained through a situational application *after* its general philosophical justification. Instead, 'the basic norm' guiding actions in each particular situation has to be achieved *in the process* of lifeworld discourses. And these discursive processes need political institutions of democracy, of course. If, in contrast, one understands discourse ethics only as an excellent form of explication and justification of the moral point of view, as presented in Chapter 2, it cannot have a special basic norm at its disposal that brings up a 'problem of application'. After all, one cannot 'apply' the moral point of view as such; it is only a standpoint from which concrete moral judgements can be justified discursively.

The fact remains: in concrete situations rational ethics always deals only with the unconditional justification of situationally adequate guidelines for action from the moral point of view, but never with pragmatic problems of the application or even the 'implementation'[19] of guidelines for action justified beforehand. Consequently there can be neither situational 'application conditions' nor problems of responsibility that could be defined outside justification problems requiring a discursive solution.[20] Ethics provides critical-normative orientation knowledge and not 'implementable' dispositional knowledge[21] – it is not a social technique for a good cause.[22]

p. 205, still violates the regulative meaning of the *counterfactual* presuppositions from which we must inevitably start in argumentation. This is also pointed out by Habermas, *Facts and Norms*, p. 323.

18 Apel, *Diskurs und Verantwortung*, p. 101. Apel also speaks strikingly often elsewhere of 'basic norms' in regard to the conditions of possibility and validity of all argumentation, whose discovery is a strictly reflective process. See, for example, *Transformation of Philosophy*, p. 259. On the concretistic misinterpretation of discourse ethics see the treatment at the beginning of Section 2.5.

19 But this is the position of Apel, *Diskurs und Verantwortung*, p. 121.

20 Hence the formulation of a special 'Part B' (Apel) of discourse ethics reserved for responsibility ethics and applied in situations which lack the presuppositions for discourse is systematically impossible in the context of modern rational ethics. See Section 2.5 (3).

21 See J. Mittelstrass, *Wissenschaft als Lebensform* (Frankfurt: Suhrkamp, 1982), p. 19f.

22 This does not exclude the possibility that the argumentative process of developing ethical orientation knowledge can under certain circumstances require socio-technical support by means of a systematic procedural heuristics in the process of arriving at judgements in complex problem situations.

(2) *Economic ethics as applied ethics under market conditions?*

In the context of economic and business ethics the problem of 'applied ethics' presents itself, beyond what has been already said, in a specific form which distinguishes it fundamentally from other domains of ethics. In the case of the practical use of knowledge deriving from the natural sciences it may well lie 'in the nature of things' that a hybrid ethics has nothing to do with the inherent logic of the corresponding discipline, i.e. in regard to its fundamental thought patterns – and can simply be added as an external supplement. Ethics does then in fact serve the practical purpose of acting as a 'guardian of morals' by reflecting on the moral limits of the permissible application of the special knowledge concerned. The transfer of this 'complementarity system'[23] of a logic of science external to ethics, on the one hand, and an ethics 'alien to' the discipline in question on the other, leads us, however, in the case of economic ethics on the wrong track. The premise of a *two-world conception* of value-free economic theory and an economic ethics external to economics is fundamentally mistaken. The (mis-) understanding of economic ethics as 'applied' ethics rests upon the assumption that both the practical field of economy and the economic theory that provides its academic models are based on a value-free, or at least ethically neutral inherent logic untouched by normative claims.[24] From this perspective economic ethics is conceived of as a purely ethical corrective external to this inherent logic, which will put the economic necessities morally in their place without, however, questioning their normative premises.

In this manner Peter Koslowski sees 'ethics as corrective for economic failure' in regard to the market economy as a whole (market failure).[25] Similarly, and in spite of an essentially different philosophical and ethical basis, Horst Steinmann and his colleagues define corporate ethics as 'a situational corrective for the profit principle', whereby the latter is seen, in the tradition of a supposedly value-free business administration, as an

[23] For a critical viewpoint see K.-O. Apel, 'Die Konflikte unserer Zeit und das Erfordernis einer ethisch-politischen Grundorientierung', in K.-O. Apel *et al.* (eds.), *Reader zum Funkkolleg: Praktische Philosophie/Ethik*, vol. I (Frankfurt: Fischer, 1980), pp. 267–92, at p. 279f., and in *Diskurs und Verantwortung*, p. 26.

[24] Among others, Apel's former student and colleague, Dieter Böhler, misunderstands a discourse-ethical approach to economic ethics explicitly as a problem of the 'application' of discourse and responsibility ethics to a 'non-moral reality'. See D. Böhler, 'Über Diskursethik und (Markt-)Wirtschaftstheorie', in J. P. Brune/D. Böhler/W. Steden (eds.), *Moral und Sachzwang in der Marktwirtschaft* (Münster: LIT, 1995), pp. 125–43, at p. 129f.

[25] See P. Koslowski, *Principles of Ethical Economy* (Dordrecht/Boston/London: Kluwer, 2001), pp. 26ff.; also his 'Grundlinien der Wirtschaftsethik', *Zeitschrift für Wirtschafts- und Sozialwissenschaften* 109 (1989), pp. 345–83, at p. 353ff.

ethically neutral 'formal goal'.[26] The systematic role of a *corrective* economic and business ethics of this kind is always that of an 'antidote' against an excess of economic rationality. We are left with a compromise designed to restrict the domain of the inherent logic of the market economy (which itself is accepted without question) by means of a 'moral garden fence'.

There can, of course, be no objection as such to the postulate that the validity claims and the sphere of activity of the inherent logic of an unbridled economy should be set limits. It is in fact an indispensable initial impulse for the practical assertion of economic ethics in the real world. The systematic objection to (merely) corrective economic ethics is directed against the abandonment of reflection in the face of the given 'conditions of the market economy' and the economic understanding of rationality as such. Neither is subject to further questioning; both are simply presupposed in an unqualified manner. We speak of an abandonment of reflection here because we are dealing with historically determined and in principle alterable 'conditions' of a social practice. Their status quo is never ethically neutral but is always based on prior normative decisions, which as such must consequently be subjected to critical reflection. A renunciation of critical reflection amounts to a tacit affirmation of the status quo of the concretely given 'market economy conditions' and the societal interests which benefit from them.[27]

Let us take as a central example the common assertion that under the systematic conditions of the market economy the economic agents cannot help behaving strategically, i.e. by strictly pursuing their own success in a rational way, and that a 'realistic' economic ethics must take these 'conditions' into account. Apel also seems to adopt this position when he deals with the problem of the 'realization of the historico-social conditions for

[26] See H. Steinmann/B. Oppenrieder, 'Brauchen wir eine Unternehmensethik?', *Die Betriebswirtschaft* 45 (1985), pp. 170–83; H. Steinmann/A. Löhr, 'Unternehmensethik – eine "realistische Idee"', *Schmalenbachs Zeitschrift für betriebswirtschaftliche Forschung* 40 (1988), pp. 299–317; Steinmann/Löhr, 'Einleitung: Grundfragen und Problembestände einer Unternehmensethik', in H. Steinmann/A. Löhr (eds.), *Unternehmensethik*, 2nd rev. and exp. edn (Stuttgart: Schäffer-Poeschel, 1991), pp. 3–32. For an in-depth criticism of the 'profit principle' and corrective corporate ethics see Chapter 10.

[27] From the standpoint of discourse ethics M. Kettner warns against a 'false modesty' corresponding to the abandonment of reflection and the consequent 'secret alliance of practical [or rather 'applied', my suggestion] ethics with the maintenance of the social status quo'. See M. Kettner, 'Einleitung: Über einige Dilemmata angewandter Ethik', in: Apel/Kettner (eds.), *Zur Anwendung der Diskursethik*, pp. 9–28, at p. 21. With regard to the understanding of corporate ethics as applied ethics I have spoken of 'a false scientific programmatic modesty'; see P. Ulrich, 'Unternehmensethik – diesseits oder jenseits der betriebswirtschaftlichen Vernunft?', in Ch. Lattmann (ed.), *Ethik und Unternehmensführung* (Heidelberg: Physica, 1988), pp. 96–116, at p. 98.

the application of discourse ethics in a world primarily characterized by the strategic actions of systems of self-assertion'.[28] How one could even conceive such an approach remains a mystery. If it is *allowed* from the outset (normatively) that the subjects are foreordained to act in a primarily strategic rather than a communicative way, the best that can be 'realized' is a bargaining process, but certainly not a discourse. In the homo-oeconomicus-world according to Apel there cannot logically be any ethics to 'apply', as the normative decision has already been taken in advance. In contrast, wherever discourse ethics is to be applied in practice, the participants in a discourse must always be *expected*, in spite of contrary strategic interests, to encounter each other primarily with an understanding-oriented basic attitude, as this is the normative condition for the legitimation of the interests which they may justly pursue.[29] There remains at most the question how far they reasonably ought to be expected to put aside their own claims to self-assertion.

On closer examination, the merely corrective approach to economic ethics in general reveals a symptomatic inner contradiction due to the abandonment of reflection in the face of given economic 'conditions':

- On the one hand it is assumed that the 'market economy conditions' and the economic rationality immanent to them stand *outside the domain of ethical reflection* and must be conceived of as 'ethics free'[30] (two-world conception). It is thus assumed that there is a definable area of society in which the self-coordination of economic agents who behave in strict accordance with economic rationality functions in an ethically unproblematic manner, so that the regulation of their actions can be left to the free market: 'Under conditions of total competition ethics is superfluous.'[31]
- On the other hand *normative force* is at the same time implicitly attributed to the economic rationality principle (and the application conditions which go with it). It is assumed that market conditions are excellent wherever there is no evident failure of the market, i.e. wherever 'functioning' markets can be established. Behind this assumption the normative premise is concealed that the market principle as a principle of social coordination already has an ethical-normative content.

[28] Apel, *Diskurs und Verantwortung*, p. 134.
[29] On this premise, whose legitimacy has already been justified, see Section 2.5 (2).
[30] Koslowski, 'Grundlinien', p. 351.
[31] P. Koslowski, 'Über die Notwendigkeit von ethischen und zugleich ökonomischen Urteilen', *Orientierungen zur Wirtschafts- und Gesellschaftspolitik* 33 (1987), pp. 7–13, at p. 7. Koslowski comes to the conclusion that under ideal market conditions even the '*maximization* of profit' could be regarded as an 'ethically neutral motive' (my italics).

The proponents of corrective economic and business ethics fail to realize that regulatory decisions *for* ('functioning') market solutions require just as much ethical justification as decisions *against* market solutions. There is no good reason to restrict the application of the critical-normative reflection of economic ethics to situations 'outside the perfect market model'.[32] An economic ethics reduced by half in this way, which links the need for ethics to the condition of failure of the market, becomes entangled in a circular economistic argument[33] – for how is it possible to judge when the operation of the market is functioning well and when an 'economic failure' has occurred, without ethics and without reference to questions of value in real-life situations?[34]

It is evident, therefore, that on account of the abandonment of reflection in the face of the market principle the corrective approach – as the systematic consequence of 'applied' economic ethics – inevitably attributes to economic rationality and market economy conditions an unquestioned normative force and thus falls under suspicion of economism.[35] It also enlists the support, at least in part, of the second 'applied' conception of economic ethics, as normative economics, to which we now turn.

3.2 Economic ethics as normative economics?

Regardless of the interpretation of the concept we use, rationality is an orientational idea enabling sensible peoples to justify their preference for a particular action and to discover how they ought to act reasonably. The problem of rational economic activity – the economic rationality problem defined in unabbreviated form – always basically comprises an ethical and a technical dimension. On the one hand it is concerned with the determination of ethically rational (legitimate) purposes and principles of economic activity in view of possible alternative uses of limited resources; on the other hand it is about their technically rational (efficient) use as

[32] Ibid., p. 11. According to Koslowski under conditions of a perfectly functioning market 'ethics and ethical behaviour in the market are superfluous because the common good can be achieved without the tiresome approval of ethics'. But outside these 'ideal conditions' an 'ethics of economic activity' remains necessary (ibid.).

[33] On the concept of economism see the introductory remarks to Part II.

[34] The lack of a purely economic line of demarcation between an area of functioning market control which is to be kept free of ethics and an area of 'market failure' which requires ethical-political supervision is a central weakness of every theory of strictly (economic) liberal regulatory politics. This can easily lead to an obsessive ideological compulsion to raise 'conformity to the market' to the level of a categorical regulatory political principle, as we shall see in Chapter 9.

[35] The criticism of this variant of economism *concealed* behind the supposedly inescapable inherent logic of the 'market conditions' is the subject of the whole of Chapter 4.

means in regard to clarified purposes while observing the conditions of legitimacy. It is hence clear that political economy, as the classical tradition of economic thought appropriately called itself, was considered to be a part of moral philosophy from Aristotle to Adam Smith and the other fathers of modern economic theory.

From about 1870 on neoclassical 'pure economics'[36] no longer accepted this unified conception of (political) economy as moral philosophy, and instead eagerly strove for the establishment of a 'value-free' and objective science in emulation of the natural sciences. The consequence is the already mentioned two-world conception of pure economics on the one hand and an ethics which is external to the discipline on the other. This conception necessarily has an impact on the neoclassical understanding of economic rationality. There is no place in it for the ethical dimension. 'Pure' economic rationality is merely one half of economic reasonableness, namely its instrumental aspect equivalent to efficiency. This merely states *how* we should deal 'economically' with limited resources in view of a multiplicity of human needs which can be conceived of in principle as unlimited, namely by maximizing benefit (with a given quantity of resources) or minimizing costs (with a given quantity of goods to be produced). The concept of cost–benefit is formal and can be applied arbitrarily to any value orders. *To what end* and *for whom*, i.e. for which and whose 'preferences', the available resources should be efficiently employed in situations of interpersonal conflict is a question to which the concept of economic rationality understood in this way has nothing to say directly. It simply assumes that these decisions on values are given.

In the final analysis modern economic theory is no more and no less than the formal explication of this 'pure' economic rationality principle. What is astounding and in need of explanation is that modern economics has nevertheless maintained its traditional *explicative and normative double significance*[37] to the present day. On the one hand – as a science dealing with reality – it claims to *explain* empirical relationships, and, on the other hand – as an ideal theory of rational economic action – it claims to *justify* the normative orientation of actions. But the latter is logically

[36] The concept of 'pure economics' probably goes back to the French economist and founder of the Lausanne School of Economics (at Lake Geneva in Switzerland), Léon Walras, *Éléments d'économie politique pure, ou théorie de la richesse sociale* (1874), Engl. transl. *Elements of Pure Economics, or the theory of social wealth* (Cambridge MA: Harvard University Press, 1954). The term was also used by J. Schumpeter, *Das Wesen und der Hauptinhalt der theoretischen Nationalökonomie* (Leipzig: Duncker & Humblot, 1908), p. 23ff. The doctrinal history of the neoclassical turning point will be treated in more detail later in Section 5.2.

[37] See Albert, *Ökonomische Ideologie*, p. 14. See also Ulrich, *Transformation*, p. 197ff.

possible only in as far as normative remnants are hidden in an economics that is evidently not quite so 'pure' since the desired purification from all ethical aspects has *not* been completed. (And this is indeed the case, as we will show step by step.)

The approach to economic ethics as applied economics, most consistently represented by Karl Homann,[38] is also a part of this tradition. The resulting *moral economics* is explicitly characterized by Homann as an economic theory of morality.[39] In accordance with the normative-explicative double function of 'pure' economics, it can be interpreted in two directions that are not always clearly kept apart by the advocates of this approach: (1) as a functional explanation of 'moral' behaviour and (2) as 'pure' normative economics.[40]

(1) Explanation of 'moral behaviour' instead of economic ethics?

The explanatory intentions of an economic theory of morality are directed towards the functional analysis of 'morality'[41] from the cost–benefit perspective of rational economic agents. What is at issue is not the internal justification of morally motivated action, but the explanation, prediction and socio-technical utilization of its external effects. That the motives of moral action, like all motives, are also relevant for the *explanation* of empirically observable behaviour, is in itself trivial. The extent to which the explanatory motives possess moral quality can, however, never be recognized by means of such a moral-economic analysis. The attempt to 'explain' morality as such in a functionalist manner amounts to a category mistake, as moral action in the true sense can only be adequately *justified* from the moral point of view and can only be understood from this standpoint.

[38] From 1990–1999, Karl Homann held the earliest chair of business ethics in a German faculty of economics (University of Eichstätt-Ingolstadt).

[39] For a programmatic presentation of such an approach see Homann/Pies, 'Wirtschaftsethik in der Moderne'.

[40] In a single article Homann, for example, mentions the perspectives of 'explanation of moral behaviour', the 'usefulness of morality for society', the 'motivation of moral action' and 'moral justification founded on interest', without always clearly distinguishing between them. See K. Homann, 'Entstehung, Befolgung und Wandel moralischer Normen: Neuere Erklärungsansätze', in F. U. Pappi (ed.), *Wirtschaftsethik – Gesellschaftswissenschaftliche Perspektiven* (Kiel: Universität Kiel, 1989), pp. 47–64.

[41] Inverted commas are used here because the concept of morality cannot be separated from the good will of the person, as we have seen in Part I. The attempt to 'explain' morality itself by motives external to it fails to grasp the (rational) *foundation* of morality and amounts in the end to a category mistake, as will be shown in what follows.

However, the practical purpose of an economic analysis or 'explanation' of the 'function of morality in the modern economy'[42] obviously lies elsewhere. It is based on the morally sceptical working hypothesis that behind (supposedly) 'moral' motives ultimately the economic motives of the intelligent and sustained pursuit of vital interests are hidden, whether they be (a) the need for integration and cooperation in the social community internalized in the consciences of individuals during the process of socialization or even (b) consciously pursued purely egoistic interests.

(a) In the first case it is a question of analysing the objective functions of traditional moral conventions, which are at work behind the moral consciousness of the actors. Morality is here considered to be a culturally mediated functional mechanism, enabling us to cope with the task of controlling the socio-economic problems of society. According to this explanatory approach, which corresponds to the classical functionalist paradigm of cultural research, wherever morality in precisely this sense 'functions' it has achieved an intersubjectively binding character as conventional morality.[43] The 'requirement of a minimum morality in the economy'[44] should consequently be explained in a functional manner which can be linked up with the economic cost–benefit argument. Whereas moderate moral economists willingly concede the deontological intrinsic value of morality and emphasize that 'moral values ... cannot simply be merged without trace in economics',[45] the advocates of a stricter perspective of 'positive moral economics' occasionally equate the functional explanation of morality with economic ethics:

> Economic ethics ... turns on the question whether the internalization of certain norms by (the majority of) individuals is necessary for the survival of our political and/or economic system.[46]

[42] K. Homann, 'Wirtschaftsethik: Die Funktion der Moral in der modernen Wirtschaft', in J. Wieland (ed.), *Wirtschaftsethik und Theorie der Gesellschaft* (Frankfurt: Suhrkamp, 1993), pp. 52–3.

[43] On conventional moral consciousness see Section 1.5.

[44] J. Wieland, 'Die Ethik der Wirtschaft als Problem lokaler und konstitutioneller Gerechtigkeit', in his *Wirtschaftsethik und Theorie der Gesellschaft*, pp. 7–31, at p. 25. In the same sense G. Kirchgässner, 'Bemerkungen zur Minimalmoral', *Zeitschrift für Wirtschafts- und Sozialwissenschaften* 116 (1996), pp. 223–51.

[45] Wieland, 'Die Ethik der Wirtschaft', p. 17.

[46] G. Kirchgässner, *Homo oeconomicus: Das ökonomische Modell individuellen Verhaltens und seine Anwendung in den Wirtschafts- und Sozialwissenschaften* (Tübingen: Mohr Siebeck, 1991), p. 44.

This conceptual definition of economic ethics is at any rate explicitly proposed by G. Kirchgässner. His view constitutes the harshest variant of *functionalist* 'economic ethics' conceivable, as it declares the biologistic category of the survival of a politico-economic *system* to be the decisive normative-analytical point of view.[47]

(b) Kirchgässner's functionalist (mis-)understanding of economic ethics leads us to a second variant of explanatory moral economics. Here the explanatory endeavours are not directed towards the objective cultural function of morality, but to the possibility of a deliberate subjective use of morality for non-moral purposes.

> Moral behaviour itself becomes a strategy in the calculations of rational actors.[48]

Functionalist or instrumentalist business ethics might, for example, involve a certain 'moral' self-limitation which serves to strengthen the identification of employees with the aims of a firm and so improve their motivation, or to guarantee the acceptance of a potentially critical public sphere. In this way it works like a 'lubricating oil' and contributes to an increase in the economic rationality (efficiency) of business policy.[49] But the instrumentalization of the moral feelings of other persons by an actor whose intentions are not moral but strictly strategic amounts to a totally cynical treatment of other persons, as it only 'functions' as long as the instrumentalized persons do not see through the exploitation of their morality.[50]

[47] An 'economic ethics' of this kind could only have the practical function of ascertaining in a purely functional manner the 'right' norms that should be internalized by the 'majority of individuals' for the purpose of stabilizing the system. But such a 'value-free' (Kirchgässner, *Homo oeconomicus*, p. 3) research programme would do the groundwork for an elitist and heteronomous determination of moral norms and is from the start incompatible with the post-conventional understanding of morality as a solidary autonomous self-commitment which is appropriate for a modern free and democratic society. Such an elitist pre-understanding of morality as a heteronomous 'restriction' through which 'human behaviour' can be 'influenced' (p. 36) – by whom and to what end? – contrasts harshly with every properly understood liberal philosophy (see Section 7.2) and is certainly not intended by Kirchgässner. But instead of reflecting critically on the problem he flies in the face of the philosophical ethical facts and sweepingly discredits the 'emancipatory endeavours' of critical philosophy in the Kantian tradition of autonomous moral self-commitment, and specifically the work of the 'Frankfurt . . . , Erlangen, or Konstanz provenance', as 'elitist presumptuousness' (p. 42).

[48] Homann, 'Entstehung, Befolgung und Wandel', p. 50.

[49] The instrumentalist conception of corporate ethics is examined in more detail in Section 10.2 (1).

[50] The business administration strategies of 'symbolic' cultural management are based in part on precisely this cynical instrumental manipulation of the feelings of obligation of employees. See P. Ulrich, '"Symbolisches Management": Ethisch-kritische Anmerkungen zur gegenwärtigen Diskussion über Unternehmenskultur', in Ch. Lattmann (ed.), *Die Unternehmenskultur* (Heidelberg: Physica, 1990), pp. 277–302.

Morality thus turns out to be a 'cost reduction programme'[51] or as the moral economists put it in an almost formulaic manner: 'Ethics reduces transaction costs.'[52] What can be meant by ethics here is ultimately always only a *supposedly* or *apparently* moral activity. Truly moral motives are after all based on good reasons in the light of the moral rights of all those concerned and affected, as we have seen in Chapter 1. And such reasons cannot be derived from economic (benefit) motives and interests without making a category mistake, as ethical justification requires a basic disposition guided by understanding, whereas in the moral economic analysis the actors (as homines oeconomici) are assumed to be guided strictly by the desire for success. Rational action oriented towards success can perhaps be described from the point of view of an observer at best as *analogous* to moral behaviour. The explanation for such behaviour is then indeed that it 'pays off' economically for the actor, while in the case of immoral behaviour 'morality' obviously gives rise subjectively to more costs than benefits.

On the premise that people behave like homines oeconomici, which is ultimately only model-theoretical[53], a socio-technical 'application' of these interrelated moral-economic effects suggests itself. The authorities of political regulation could, for example, provide a *substitute* for the lack or weakness of moral intentions of persons by consciously creating, as far as possible, institutional restrictions with an analogous effect (economic incentives and disincentives) and thus strengthening the motives of personal interest. In this way the positive (functionally explanatory) moral economics leads to a normative institutional economics[54] for which the following 'programme for the shaping of society'[55] is characteristic:

> Shaping is achieved by changing the institutional arrangements, which lead to changes in costs, which in turn steer the actions of the actors in the desired direction by means of incentives.[56]

[51] Wieland, 'Die Ethik der Wirtschaft', p. 24. On the approach of an economic theory of 'moral goods' which analyses morality not only in terms of costs but also of benefits see J. Wieland, *Ökonomische Organisation, Allokation und Status* (Tübingen: Mohr Siebeck, 1996).

[52] In this sense K. Homann, 'Ethik und Ökonomik: Zur Theoriestrategie der Wirtschaftsethik', in Homann (ed.), *Wirtschaftsethische Perspektiven I* (Berlin: Duncker & Humblot, 1994), pp. 9–30, at p. 18. Similarly, although in the context of his (apart from that very different) approach of economic ethics as a corrective for market failure, Koslowski, 'Grundlinien der Wirtschaftsethik', p. 352: 'trust reduces transaction costs'; Homann, *Principles*, p. 26ff.

[53] More on this theoretical viewpoint in Section 4.2.

[54] See I. Pies, *Normative Institutionenökonomik: Zur Rationalisierung des politischen Liberalismus* (Tübingen: Mohr Siebeck, 1993).

[55] Homann, 'Wirtschaftsethik: Die Funktion der Moral', p. 43. [56] Ibid.

But what is the 'desired direction', who desires it and how ought it to be legitimized? On these decisive normative questions 'positive' moral economics has nothing of its own to say. Up to this point it is not concerned at all with economic ethics but with a social technique for the realization of 'good goals' that must be already justified from outside the moral and institutional economic approach – or so at least it seems. But the normative claim of 'normative economics' goes further, as we shall now see.

(2) Normative economics as economic ethics?

In as far as the moral-economic research programme explicitly describes itself as 'economic ethics', for example in the ideas of Karl Homann and his school, it lays claim to direct normative force by postulating the possibility of a total disburdenment of the individual from direct moral demands and their complete replacement by 'functional equivalents'[57] by means of the shaping of institutional incentives mentioned above. These are to be derived within the framework of 'normative institutional economics' entirely without ethical categories of norm justification. To this end Homann postulates:

> ... the development of morality from a general theory of rationality ..., which begins with 'weak' preconditions – interests instead of reason – and works with equally weak rationality requirements.[58]

Such a programme of 'moral justification founded on *interests*'[59] is equal to the reduction of morality to economic rationality, but this is impossible without making a category mistake. The systematic consequence is the claim to conduct 'economics as ethics with other means'.[60] On account of his homo oeconomicus premises, the moral economist, who is always also a methodical moral sceptic, even sees this in principle as the better ethics, precisely because it presents an 'ethics without morality'[61] and consequently requires the economic agents to accept no rationality claims other than the intelligent pursuit of their personal and private interests. An ethical-critical reflection on the legitimacy of existing interests does not take place.

[57] Ibid., p. 41.
[58] K. Homann, 'Philosophie und Ökonomik: Bemerkungen zur Interdisziplinarität', *Jahrbuch für neue politische Ökonomie*, vol. 7 (Tübingen: Mohr Siebeck, 1988), pp. 99–127, at p. 120.
[59] Homann, 'Entstehung, Befolgung und Wandel', p. 48.
[60] Homann, 'Ethik und Ökonomik', p. 13, and 'Wirtschaftsethik: Angewandte Ethik oder Ethik mit ökonomischer Methode', *Zeitschrift für Politik* 43 (1996), pp. 178–82, at p. 120.
[61] The concept is taken from A. Cortina, 'Ethik ohne Moral: Grenzen einer postkantischen Prinzipienethik?', in Apel/Kettner, *Zur Anwendung der Diskursethik*, pp. 278–95.

A corresponding 'economic ethics without morality' is, however, caught on the horns of a methodological dilemma. On the one hand it would like to operate completely without ethical-moral categories, but, on the other hand, without a deontological ethical minimum, it remains normatively as empty as the formal economic concepts of (subjectively indifferent) interests and preferences. But in this way the declared 'programme of moral *justification* founded on interests'[62] has in effect lost its object, as the individual preferences and interests in the economic paradigm are simply taken as given and in principle 'so accepted'[63] – there is nothing here which requires a justification or criticism with normative content or could be accessible to it (in purely economic categories). Consequently the moral economists as a rule hasten to declare the methodological decision in favour of an, in principle, uncritical attitude towards all individual preferences or claims to be ethically neutral, which is equivalent to a systematic exclusion of the question of ethical legitimacy. This enables them to rid themselves of a problem and to redefine the core ethical problem as quickly as possible as functionalistic:

> Economics is concerned with the common good, the solidarity of all people and the development of the individual freedom of all in community with others. There is no disagreement on the goal. But under the conditions of modern economy and society the *implementation* of this goal requires particular precautions ...[64]

Thus the question of the fundamental normative orientations of 'normative economics' is not adequately answered, but rather pushed aside as irrelevant – as if the brief additional reference to the key words 'common good', 'solidarity of all people' and 'individual freedom of all in the community' explained everything. Nowhere is the attempt undertaken to elaborate what these concepts mean in general and in regard to economic action in particular, to point out the explicitly justified deontological minimum on which their binding normative character is based or to indicate their systematic relationship to one another. And nevertheless the authors immediately continue in the second sentence quoted to speak

62 Homann, 'Entstehung, Befolgung und Wandel', p. 48, with changed emphasis (my emphasis).

63 Kirchgässner, *Homo oeconomicus*, p. 42.

64 K. Homann/F. Blome-Drees, *Wirtschafts- und Unternehmensethik* (Göttingen: Vandenhoeck & Ruprecht, 1992), p. 96. With remarkable inconsistency, they depart from their otherwise morally sceptical, non-cognitivistic position and supposedly even start 'in general from the fundamental principle of all morality, which can today be formulated as the solidarity of all people' (p. 15). The problem of ethical justification is dealt with even more rapidly and sweepingly in D. Aufderheide, *Unternehmer, Ethos und Ökonomik. Moral und unternehmerischer Gewinn aus der Sicht der Neuen Institutionenökonomik* (Berlin: Duncker & Humblot, 1995). In contrast to Homann, however, he concedes the existence of an ethical 'justification gap' (p. 201) in his 'moral-economic' approach (p. 200).

of only one (unequivocal?) 'goal' that apparently throws up only instrumental (socio-technical) questions of 'implementation'.

Such questions of institutional economics are of course perfectly legitimate. There would be no problem if Homann *et al.* restricted the issue and the claim of their approach explicitly to the clarification of functional rules for the implementation of an economic order whose normative validity was justified outside the scope of a purely economic approach. The approach could then orient itself directly on the rule-utilitarian generalization criterion and take as its starting point the requirement of the general enforceability of institutional incentive structures to ensure fair and equal treatment of all economic players in regard to regulatory criteria which have already been clarified and justified in rational ethical categories.[65] Of course, the moral-economic approach could then no longer describe itself as 'economic ethics' but would rather have to concede frankly that it presupposes an already existing justification of a robust and normatively substantial economic ethics.

But the moral economists are by no means willing to undertake such a methodical self-limitation of their approach. One must conclude that they wish the approach to be understood as an adequate and, from an economic-ethical point of view, sufficient justificational conception, in spite of its focus on the problem of implementation.[66] This might at first seem puzzling: what is there to be justified in an approach in which moral categories are literally alien? And what is the basis for the claim of functionalist economic ethics to develop normative orientational force? The solution to this puzzle can be found in the deep structures of the economic paradigm, which must be understood in terms of its doctrinal history. The whole of Chapter 5 will be devoted to fathoming these depths. For the moment it is sufficient to point out that the normative content lies concealed solely in the logic of the ideal market economy system and the corresponding economic rationality, as Karl Homann occasionally admits:

> Moral quality is attributed to the market and to competition for the sole reason that they are 'efficient'.[67]

We are dealing for the moment, therefore, with an as yet mysterious *internal morality of the market*. The obvious objection that the attempt

[65] On this point see Section 2.4.
[66] This is also assumed by W. Kersting, 'Moralphilosophie, angewandte Ethik und Ökonomismus. Bemerkungen zur wirtschaftsethischen Topologie', *Zeitschrift für Politik* 43 (1996), pp. 183–94, at p. 194.
[67] K. Homann, 'Wettbewerb und Moral', *Jahrbuch für christliche Sozialwissenschaften* 31 (1990), pp. 34–56, at p. 41.

to trace moral categories back totally to economic categories is a case of (mistaken) reductionism has at any rate always been expressly dismissed by Homann.[68] Later on he has at least conceded a *methodological economism* without, however, regarding it as normative economism.[69] But this methodological economism is a hypothetical construct serving purely analytical purposes and is therefore normatively non-binding. The retreat to it amounts to an admission (probably not intended) that functionalistic 'economic ethics' cannot justifiably claim normative validity. The claim is, nevertheless, implicitly assumed, as it is not possible solely on the basis of a methodological assumption to build up a 'normative economics' which can seriously claim to provide a 'moral justification founded on interest'.

This hidden normativity of methodological economism, which is not truly admitted but nevertheless assumed, and indeed the economic approach as such, will be examined in detail later. But first of all we will refer here to a second fundamental characteristic of 'normative economics' which is closely related to the reduction of the justificational problems of economic ethics to a problem of implementation in the context of institutional economics. It is Homann's repeatedly formulated basic 'determination of the tasks' of modern economic ethics and its characteristic emphasis on the (functional) conditions of the market economy:

> Business ethics (or corporate ethics) deals with the question of which moral norms and ideals can be effectively enforced (by the companies) *under the conditions of modern economy* and society.[70]

At first sight this circumscription of the basic problem of economic ethics could be classified under the approach to economic ethics as 'applied ethics' discussed in the previous section. But it must be noted here that for 'applied economics' the normative is always contained in the functional. Only those norms and ideals are accorded a normative claim to validity which 'can be enforced' economically. Consequently:

> Under the conditions of the modern age the implementation of a norm leaves its mark upon its validity.[71]

This thesis should not be understood empirically. What is meant by the 'conditions of modern economy and society' is not so much empirical

[68] See, for example, Homann, 'Ethik und Ökonomik', p. 19f., and Homann/Blome-Drees, *Wirtschafts- und Unternehmensethik*, p. 110.
[69] See Homann, 'Ethik mit ökonomischer Methode', p. 181. On the concept of economism see the introduction to Part II.
[70] Homann/Blome-Drees, *Wirtschafts- und Unternehmensethik*, p. 14 (my italics).
[71] Homann/Pies, 'Wirtschaftsethik in der Moderne', p. 5 (whole sentence in italics in the original).

resistance (practical constraints) as the normative 'conditions' of an *ideally functioning* society conceived of as being organized as a whole in accordance with the 'market principle'. But what is ideal about it is merely that it brings the given preferences of all individuals effectively into play. This is the sole and sufficient basis of the presupposed internal morality of the market.[72]

The systematic point of the conception of economic ethics as applied economics now becomes clear. Normative economics can see itself as ethics without morality in as far as it has always accepted pure economics as a normative ideal theory – based on the fundamental norm of a strict *normative individualism.* And this consists precisely in attributing the status of an ultimate normative binding character (not open to further critical questioning) to the factually given preferences of individuals. In the ideal model of society of 'economic ethics' as normative economics the solution of all problems of social coordination is left completely to the impersonal and in this sense entirely 'impartial' functioning of the normative logic of the market.[73] This logic functions 'impartially' by mediating harmoniously between the 'given' individual preferences without it being necessary to question critically any of the moral validity claims involved. Consequently, in the ideal market society, the *moral disposition* of persons is no longer necessary. It is sufficient for them to assert their *economic rationality* in the form of actions strictly oriented towards success and the maximization of personal benefit. The 'market principle' itself is the guarantee for ethically correct actions![74]

Instead of enquiring unconditionally into the *ethical conditions* under which the market economy system ought legitimately to function, the advocates of this position ultimately enquire only into the systemic *functional conditions* with the help of which all kinds of individual preferences can be asserted on the market, without restrictions and 'free of ethics'. From the standpoint of rational ethics the decisive abandonment of reflection occurs precisely here in the face of this basic norm of normative individualism. The approach thus indubitably fails to arrive at the moral point of view.

The integrative approach alone avoids the abandonment of reflection in the face of both the empirical 'conditions' of strategic self-assertion

[72] The proof of this thesis and of the following considerations is provided in Section 5.3.

[73] I adopt the formulation 'normative logic of the market' from U. Thielemann, *Das Prinzip Markt: Kritik der ökonomischen Tauschlogik* (Berne *et al.*: Haupt, 1996), p. 11ff.

[74] To this extent it appears perfectly consistent when Homann and his colleagues explicitly emphasize the advantages of 'economic imperialism'. See Homann, 'Wirtschaftsethik: Die Funktion der Moral', p. 42, and Homann/Blome-Drees, *Wirtschafts- und Unternehmensethik*, p. 110.

('applied ethics') and the ideal economic 'conditions' of normative individualism (normative economics) and opens up the entire range of basic questions of rational economic activity in a modern society unconditionally for critical reflection on their foundations.

3.3 The integrative approach: economic ethics as critical reflection on the foundations of economic reason

Virtually the whole of the international discussion among the experts on economic ethics takes place within the spectrum of the two approaches discussed above.[75] A third approach seems inconceivable both for 'pure' philosophers and for 'pure' economists. This is probably a symptom of the sustained influence of the two-world conception on both disciplines. Wolfgang Kersting, for example, follows up his critical comments on the approach of moral and institutional economics by doubting whether economic ethics as an independent research programme makes any sense at all:

> The present interest in economic ethics is at all events puzzling ... In order to grant economic ethics ethical independence [as an independent discipline] a normative field would have to be made recognizable which it could cultivate in its own right ...[76]

Kersting's ironical manner of speaking indicates his line of thought. He cannot make out a clearly delimited 'normative field' as the specific

[75] The report of Homann/Hesse *et al.*, 'Wirtschaftswissenschaft und Ethik', presented in 1988 in connection with the preparations for the establishment of the committee 'Wirtschaftswissenschaft und Ethik' in the *Verein für Socialpolitik* (see above n. 4 in Section 3.1), is typical of German-speaking countries. Following on from this came the first elaboration of the 'third way' of the fundamentally critical integrative approach in the inaugural lecture of the author. See P. Ulrich, 'Wirtschaftsethik als Wirtschaftswissenschaft: Standortbestimmungen im Verhältnis von Ethik und Ökonomie', *Berichte des Instituts für Wirtschaftsethik* N° 23 (St Gallen: Institute for Economic and Business Ethics, 1988). For further treatments see e.g. Ulrich, 'Wirtschaftsethik auf der Suche nach der verlorenen ökonomischen Vernunft', in Ulrich (ed.), *Auf der Suche nach einer modernen Wirtschaftsethik* (Berne *et al.*: Haupt, 1990), pp. 179–226; Ulrich, 'Integrative Wirtschafts- und Unternehmensethik – ein Rahmenkonzept', in Forum für Philosophie Bad Homburg/S. Blasche (eds.), *Markt und Moral* (Berne *et al.*: Haupt, 1994), pp. 75–107. In English, Ulrich, 'Towards an Ethically-Based Conception of Socio-Economic Rationality', *Praxiology: The International Annual of Practical Philosophy and Methodology, vol. 5: Human Action in Business*, ed. by W. Gasparski/L. V. Ryan (New Brunswick, N.J./London: Transaction, 1996), pp. 21–49; Ulrich, 'Integrative Economic Ethics – Towards a Conception of Socio-Economic Rationality', in P. Koslowski (ed.), *Contemporary Economic Ethics and Business Ethics* (Berlin/Heidelberg/New York: Springer, 2000), pp. 37–54; Ulrich, 'Ethics and Economics', in L. Zsolnai (ed.), *Ethics in the Economy: Handbook of Business Ethics* (Berne/Oxford: Peter Lang, 2002), pp. 9–37.

[76] Kersting, 'Moralphilosophie, angewandte Ethik und Ökonomismus', p. 191.

reflective content of economic ethics. But it exists nevertheless! Once it is fully realized that economic theory itself is essentially always an ideal and therefore normative theory of rational economic activity, the third – and ultimately the only thoroughgoing – systematic approach becomes evident. The crucial point is to overcome the abandonment of reflection in the two merely 'applied' approaches and to search for the normative first and foremost within economic thinking and action in order to make it accessible to ethical-critical reflection and argumentation. It is therefore the normative content of economic rationality itself which must be critically penetrated and elucidated. It should then be possible to integrate ethical rationality into a comprehensive regulative idea of rational economic activity. This is the only way to overcome the two-world conception of ethics and economics at its root and to grasp economic ethics as the rational ethics of economic activity – a task which however presupposes both a profound grasp of the economic approach and the history of economic thought just as a sound understanding of rational ethics and the moral point of view. The first requirement mentioned exceeds the competence of 'pure' philosophy, the second, that of 'pure' economics, which has battled for over a hundred years to emancipate itself from moral philosophy and, as a result, categorically resists philosophical-ethical reflection in its entire axiomatics.

Integrative economic ethics correspondingly takes as its starting point a critical reflection on the foundations of the normative 'conditions' of economic rationality. In accordance with the ambiguous concept of economic rationality it first of all faces two fundamental tasks. Its first basic object of reflection is the criticism of economic rationality or reason in the narrow sense of pure economics (1), its second is the clarification of a (discourse-) ethically grounded regulative idea of comprehensive economic reason or socio-economic rationality (2). A further task – which for the moment can only be defined in principle – is the determination of the major 'site' of morality to put the regulative idea of socio-economic rationality into practice (3).

(1) Critique of 'pure' economic reason

The first task of integrative economic ethics is, as has been said, to see through the alleged value-free condition or ethical neutrality of the market's inherent logic as it is understood in 'pure' economics by means of an ethical-critical elucidation of its normative basis. It will be necessary to show precisely the underhand means by which economics claims a normative force it nowhere justifies, in order then to present itself as the (better) 'economic ethics without morality'. The key word of this first task is: *critique of economism*. A start has already been made in the previous two sections if only in a programmatic manner until now.

As far as the basic *critical* orientation of economic ethics in general (in the philosophical sense) is concerned, we are dealing from a rational ethical point of view with something self-evident. It meets the approval of renowned representatives of American business ethics, as they are usually philosophers by training. Richard de George, for example, points critically to tendencies towards the instrumentalization (functionalization) of business ethics in no uncertain terms:

> Instruction in business ethics as an academic subject aims to produce critical ethical thinkers. But this is not what many who call for business ethics courses want.[77]

In the same sense Norman Bowie, a further leading American representative of his discipline, emphasizes that it is the aim of business and economic ethics:

> to produce a Kantian person – a rational, autonomous, moral agent who can take his or her place in a moral community.[78]

The Kantian way to a morally autonomous, mature and responsible person is clearly the way of critical rational ethics. Yet neither De George nor Bowie draws the systematic conclusion of a need for a rational ethics *of economic activity*. De George definitely questions 'the myth of amoral business',[79] but not the normative content of the logic of the market. In this regard almost the whole of Anglo-Saxon business ethics unquestionably remains entrapped in the approach to economic ethics as 'applied' ethics. Exceptions prove the rule. LaRue Tone Hosmer, a commuter between management theory and economic ethics, points to the 'moral content of microeconomic theory' and recognizes that what matters accordingly in economic ethics is to clarify theoretically the conflicting perspectives of ethics and economics instead of merely combining them in the applicational context.[80] Similarly R. Edward Freeman, who like Hosmer is active in the two 'worlds' of management theory and economic ethics, laid bare the customarily assumed 'separation thesis', which is

77 R. T. De George, 'Will Success Spoil Business Ethics?', in R. E. Freeman (ed.), *Business Ethics: The State of the Art* (New York/Oxford: Oxford University Press, 1991), pp. 42–56, at p. 49.

78 N. Bowie, 'Business Ethics as a Discipline: The Search for Legitimacy', in Freeman (ed.), *State of the Art*, pp. 17–41, at p. 31.

79 See R. T. De George, *Business Ethics*, 3rd edn (New York: Macmillan, 1990), p. 3ff.

80 See L. T. Hosmer, 'Managerial Ethics and Microeconomic Theory', *Journal of Business Ethics* 3 (1984), pp. 315–25, esp. 316f.

identical with the two-world-conception I criticized some years earlier. He correctly concludes:

> ... if the separation thesis cannot be maintained, the issue is what kind of moral content a theory has, not whether it has any moral content or not.[81]

Other investigations into the relationship between ethics and economics, particularly those by Amartya Sen or by Daniel M. Hausman and Michael S. McPherson, may go deeper into details, but the focus regularly remains on the mutual implications for the respective disciplines: functions of economic analysis for rational ethics and welfare economics on the one hand, and the role of morality as a *factor of influence* for positive economics on the other:

> Indeed, it would be rather absurd to devote much attention to the subject of ethics if it were really the case that ethical considerations would never affect people's actual behaviour.[82]
>
> Ethics has a role within positive economics because ethical commitments affect individual choices and hence economic outcomes, because economic institutions and policies affect ethical commitments, and because the terms in which economists conceptualize and explain individual choices have moral implications.[83]

Further conceptional steps in the direction of a fundamental critique of economic rationality itself, understood as the first systematic task of an economic ethics that does not fall short of its challenge, can be found in none of the authors mentioned.

But if integrative economic ethics now aims to overcome the two-world conception of ethics and pure economics with its long doctrinal and scientific history *from the bottom up* and to develop a comprehensive perspective on rational economic activity founded on ethics, it cannot simply place itself *alongside* pure economics in a complementary or corrective way. By proposing a foundational critique, economic ethics – and this is the most elementary significance of the 'integrative'

[81] R. E. Freeman, 'The Politics of Stakeholder Theory: Some Future Directions', *Business Ethics Quarterly* 4 (1994), pp. 401–21, at pp. 411f. and 413. Against this separation or the 'two-world conception' of 'pure' economic rationality and morality see Section 3.1 (2) and already Ulrich, *Transformation*, p. 343f. (1st edn 1986).

[82] A. Sen, *On Ethics and Economics* (Oxford/New York: Basil Blackwell, 1987), p. 52. Similarly p. 9: 'I would like to argue that economics, as it has emerged, can be made more productive by paying greater and more explicit attention to the ethical considerations that shape human behaviour and judgement.' More recently (and after the above book was written in 1997), Sen has balanced out that earlier bias with his much more normative *Development as Freedom* (Oxford: Oxford University Press, 1999).

[83] D. M. Hausman/M.S. McPherson, *Economic Analysis and Moral Philosophy* (Cambridge/New York: Cambridge University Press, 1996), p. 214f. The 'moral implications' mentioned by the authors relate only to the personal 'convictions of economic agents' (p. 219) but not the idea of economic rationality as such.

approach – inevitably becomes involved with the paradigmatic self-understanding of contemporary mainstream economics. 'Political' resistance from the established schools of thought must be reckoned with, particularly as the (not quite) 'autonomous economics' (H. Albert) has purposely cut itself off from philosophical-ethical moments of reflections as a result of its continual neoclassical 'purification'.[84] This presumably explains the strikingly defensive reaction of so many representatives of contemporary mainstream economics towards economic ethics. In as far as the latter cannot be absorbed as moral economics it is to a large degree excluded – as *the other of the inherent logic of the market*, situated on the opposite side of the established two-world conception instead of being recognized as its indubitable normative foundation.

If, however, one considers that pure economics itself is an ideal theory of rational action, it becomes clear that with modern (economic) ethics and modern economics *two competing normative logics* stand opposed to each other, both of which claim universal validity as the programme for the 'rationalization' of social practice: the normative logic of interpersonal relations on the one hand and the normative logic of the market on the other. Avowals of 'mutual recognition of the equal value and autonomy'[85] of the academic disciplines developing these two competing normative rationalization programmes may be pleasant enough at the personal level (between the representatives of the disciplines concerned), but they leave untouched the core problem of the clarification of the 'close' relationship between ethics and economics. Normativity is not the 'other side of the coin' of economic rationality, but its foundation.[86] Consequently the first systematic task of integrative economic ethics is to make this normative background accessible to argument from an ethical-critical perspective – namely as a *critique of pure economic reason* directed against economistic reductionism and circular argument, which are almost unavoidable as symptomatic consequences of the abandonment of reflection on the inner normativity of the 'pure' economic conception of rationality.

[84] I adopt this concept from H. G. Krüsselberg, 'Property-Rights-Theorie und Wohlfahrtsökonomik', in A. Schüller (ed.), *Property Rights und ökonomische Theorie* (Munich: Vahlen, 1983), pp. 45–77, at p. 58.

[85] Enderle, *Wirtschaftsethik im Werden*, p. 26, who at the same time (rightly) emphasizes that 'the relationship of ethics and economics cannot be understood as a non-relationship'. But if the mutual recognition of autonomy is interpreted as a principle of non-interference it leads to an 'indifference model' of the relationship between economics and economic ethics, which in the best possible case ends in non-committal reciprocal good will.

[86] See J. Mittelstrass, 'Wirtschaftsethik als wissenschaftliche Disziplin?', in G. Enderle (ed.), *Ethik und Wirtschaftswissenschaft* (Berlin: Duncker & Humblot, 1985), pp. 17–32, at p. 24.

The aim is to formulate a concept of properly understood economic rationality and this has to be seen as foundational work on the further development of economics in the direction of a 'declared departure from economism *within* economic theory along philosophical lines'.[87] Ultimately it is a question of the resumption of the unfinished methodological and foundational controversy over a modern paradigm of economics as a science, i.e. over the scope and method of economics.

(2) The idea of socio-economic rationality

The starting point for the integration of economic and ethical rationality is the clarification of the normative preconditions for rational economic activity, in a comprehensive sense of the concept, as legitimate *and* efficient action. It is a question of reconstructing the normative foundation of the economic understanding of rationality in terms of rational ethics. This means the establishment of a philosophically and ethically sound foundation of a different, expanded idea of economic rationality, so that it possesses ethical content already itself and can therefore serve as an *integrative* regulative idea of rational economic activity:

> The moral or ethical character is not added to the rational character of an action as something secondary, but is an integral part of that way of acting.[88]

Economic rationality in the 'given' form resulting from the historical development of its dogmas and theories ought therefore to be neither delimited externally nor merely applied, but transformed philosophically and ethically and thus brought to reason.[89] This is not intended disrespectfully in regard to the traditional economic conception of rationality, but simply expresses the indispensable primacy of ethics (as the normative logic of the *unconditional* reciprocal recognition of human beings) over economics (as the normative logic of the *conditional* cooperation of individuals acting in their own interests). The primacy of ethics is

[87] Ibid., p. 31 (my italics). See also J. Mittelstrass, 'Wirtschaftsethik oder der erklärte Abschied vom Ökonomismus auf philosophischen Wegen', in Ulrich (ed.), *Auf der Suche*, pp. 17–38.

[88] E. Herms, *Gesellschaft gestalten. Beiträge zur evangelischen Sozialethik* (Tübingen: Mohr Siebeck, 1991), p. 226. In a footnote on p. 226 Herms, a Protestant theologian, explicitly expresses his agreement with the programme of a 'transformation of economic reason' of the present author. (It is perhaps not pure chance that a Christian evangelical background is favourable for the idea of the ethical integration of economic rationality, as we shall see in Section 4.1.)

[89] This is the basic idea of a 'fundamental transformation of economic rationality' – or, more precisely, a transformation of the foundations of an economic conception of rationality from utilitarian to communicative ethics. Cf. Ulrich, *Transformation*, p. 13.

the central feature of a comprehensive perspective of rational economic activity and rational action per se.

How then can we precisely conceive the central idea of ethically rational economic activity, the regulative idea of socio-economic rationality, we are looking for? The unconditional basic moral requirement, which claims validity as the normative condition of all rational action, is legitimacy, as we have long known.[90] What is required, therefore, is an extension of the idea of economic rationality so that it already includes 'rational' legitimacy as a constitutive rational-ethical condition. This provides us with the fundamental orientational idea for the *ethical integration of economic rationality*.

The decisive point of integration can best be elucidated in terms of discourse ethics. The normative conditions for the possibility of rational economic activity in the sense of socio-economic rationality must be understood and reflectively grasped as the inescapable language-pragmatic preconditions for argumentative agreement on the legitimate claims of all participants in the process of the economic creation of values and of all others affected by it. This means quite simply that the question of an instrumentally rational treatment of the *scarcity* of resources and goods (efficiency) cannot be dissociated conceptually from the question of an ethically rational treatment of the social *conflicts* between those involved (legitimacy). The aspect of efficiency thematized in isolation in the neoclassical idea of pure economic rationality[91] is not therefore simply dropped, but – in Hegelian terms – 'sublated' in the more comprehensive socio-economic rationality. And this is unavoidable, as the rational solution of conflicting claims over the distribution of the (internal and external) costs and benefits of economic activity is a normative problem which cannot also be mastered within the categories of 'pure' economic rationality. Consequently, and in accordance with the primacy of ethics, in the conception of socio-economic rationality the ethical interest in a discursive clarification of the legitimacy conditions (i.e. the safeguard of the moral rights of all concerned) has priority over the private interests of economic agents in the employment of their resources in a way that is most efficient for them.

[90] See Section 2.5 (2).

[91] The neoclassical concept of economic rationality corresponds to the standard definition of pure economics in L. Robbins, *An Essay on the Nature and Significance of Economic Science*, 2nd edn (London: Macmillan, 1949), p. 16: 'Economics is the science which studies human behaviour as a relationship between ends and scarce means which have alternative uses.'

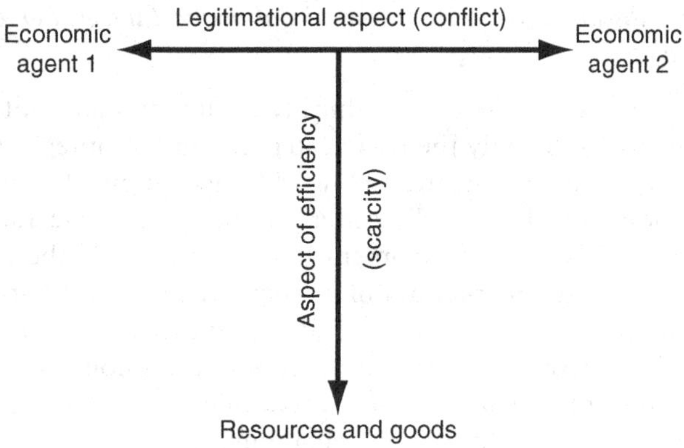

Figure 3.2. The two-dimensional character of socio-economic rationality

As Figure 3.2 illustrates, the idea of socio-economic rationality embeds the question of efficient economic activity in the question of the rational form of social relationships between all concerned. What is 'efficient' for the beneficiary of an economic action must by no means be so for those who do not share the benefits or are even affected by the social or ecological costs. The fallacy inherent to the neoclassical idea of economic rationality is the fictive notion of *general* efficiency for everybody which is supposedly definable in a social vacuum. This illusion must be abandoned, replaced by the practical everyday question 'efficient for whom in particular?', and answered from the standpoint of justice. Before this is done, there can be no question of economic reasonableness (socio-economic rationality) in the true sense of the word. Only those actions should therefore be regarded as (socio-)economically rational which are not only efficient for the actors themselves but also legitimately defensible with regard to all concerned. This leads us to the following *regulative idea of socio-economic rationality* founded on discourse ethics:

> Every action or institution can be regarded as socio-economically rational which free and responsible citizens (could) have – by deliberation among all concerned – consensually determined to be a legitimate way of creating value.

The addition 'could' is meant to show that the socio-economic conception of rationality has a completely different methodological status than the traditional neoclassical economic 'rational principle'. In contrast to the latter, it is not a decision criterion which can be applied purely analytically, but a fundamental regulative idea of economic-ethical discourse. The idea of socio-economic rationality formulates no more and no less than the moral point of view of a rational ethics of economic activity.

(3) *Public discourse as the site of the ethical-political integration of economics*

Of course, our work to date on an ethically meaningful concept of economic rationality fulfils only the basic categorial task of integrative economic ethics by overcoming the two-world conception of ethical and economic rationality. The guiding idea of socio-economic rationality developed here takes – for the moment only in principle – the (supposedly) 'pure' logic of the market out of its social vacuum and puts it back into the social context of ethically oriented deliberative processes between free citizens. The theoretically all-too-autonomous economic calculation is integrated conceptually into politico-economic communication on the normative conditions of a life-serving economy.

Here the practical significance of integrative economic ethics comes into view. The theoretical dissociation of autonomous economics from its ethical and political context, as it occurred in the neoclassical period from about 1870, mirrors in ideal-typical model form what actually happened in the real world, namely the dissociation of a largely autonomous economic system from the lifeworld. Since then the modern economic system has been essentially guided by its in-built, strangely anonymous 'inherent laws', which have developed a dynamics of their own and increasingly threaten to come into conflict with standpoints of practical reason in everyday life.[92] This growing tendency towards a *disintegration* of the economic system offered publicly under the euphemistic title of a 'free' market economy is definitely welcomed by interested circles, whereas it is encountered by an *integrative* economic ethics, claiming in principle to harness the dynamics of economic rationality in the service of life from an ethically justified point of view. The idea of socio-economic rationality can therefore also be understood as the (discourse-ethically explicated) governing idea of rational economic activity from the perspective of the lifeworld.

From this perspective economic ethics must undoubtedly be grasped as an aspect of *political ethics* with emancipatory intent, which first and foremost aims to secure or to recreate the preconditions for unconstrained political-economic deliberation between mature and responsible citizens. For as we have already seen, the unrestricted public sphere to which all responsible persons have access is the ultimate ideal 'site' of morality in modern society.[93] This is consequently also the ideal instance for shaping the political-economic system conditions in such a way that economic-ethical reflection, argumentation and action orientation can be

[92] This will be treated more closely in Chapter 4. [93] See Section 2.5 (4).

brought effectively into play at as many institutional 'sites' of morality as possible. It is the basic task of integrative economic ethics in the field of *institution ethics* to develop corresponding orientational ideas for the institutional inclusion (integration) of the system logics into the public reasoning of responsible citizens.

Let us pull the threads together: The approach of an integrative economic ethics aims, to put it briefly, at establishing an economic ethics without abandonment of reflection in the face of any kind of empirical or normative conditions of the market economy. It wishes to subject the entire normative substructure of the understanding of rational economic activity to an unconditional ethical reflection. In accordance with the

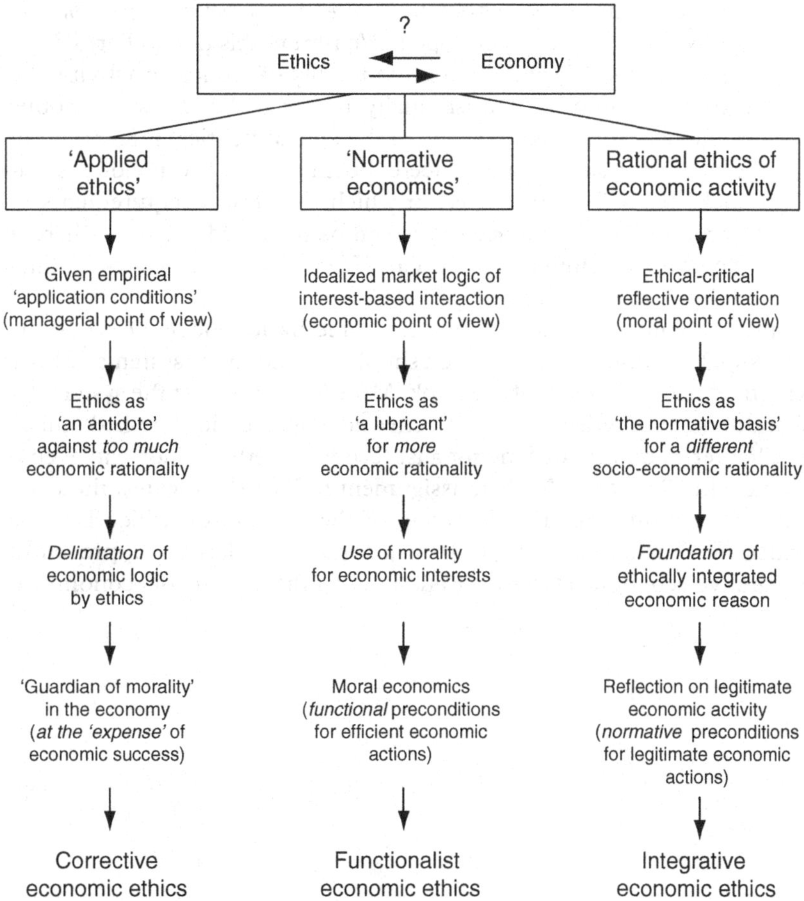

Figure 3.3. Approaches to economic ethics

three points sketched above, the orientational work to be done in economic ethics covers three general basic tasks, which also serve to define the topics reflected upon in the three following parts of the book:

(1) The critique of 'pure' economic reason: the normative background assumptions on which the claimed but not justified normative force of a supposedly value-free inherent logic of the market in the sense of mainstream economics is based will be unreservedly uncovered and subjected to critical argumentation. Part II of the book is devoted to the corresponding *critique of economism.*
(2) A true-to-life development of the idea of socio-economic rationality: the regulative idea is at first explicated abstractly as the moral point of view of a modern rational ethics of economic activity. In its light concrete guiding ideas about *rational economic activity from the life-world perspective* will be developed. We turn to this task in Part III.
(3) The discussion of possible sites of morality of economic activity: the institutional conditions must, finally, be clarified under which public discourse as the systematic site of the ethical-political integration of the economy can be guaranteed. Furthermore, the major institutional sites will be discussed in which the ethical requirements of an economy in the service of life can be mediated into the inherent logic of the economic system. Part IV deals with the corresponding *topology of economic ethics.*

Figure 3.3 sums up schematically the three basic models of economic ethics we have discussed. Attention should be paid to the systematic links with the further chapters of the book. More light is cast on the systematic abandonment of reflection of corrective economic ethics (applied ethics) in Chapter 4, on that of functionalist 'economic ethics' (normative economics) in Chapter 5. As their assignment to Part II indicates, these are only two variants, differing in reach, of the economism which is to be criticized. Finally, Chapters 6–10 will further develop the approach of integrative economic ethics over and beyond the critique of economism.

Part II

Reflections on the foundations of economic ethics I: a critique of economism

The first task of science is ... a critique of the popular metaphysics found in the common sense attitude.[1]

To put it briefly, *economism* is the belief of economic rationality in nothing but itself. Gerhard Weisser, who was probably the first to use the concept, has taken a critical look at the self-sufficient circularity of an economistic mode of thinking:

How do we arrive at postulates for economic policy? The opinion is still widespread today that the postulates for the shaping of economic life can and must be drawn *from our economic thinking*. (...) We call this *economism*.[2]

It is a phenomenon with a long dogmatic history rich in assumptions manifesting themselves in a variety of forms.[3] The three basic manifestations of economism are the development of a self-sufficient economic rationality, the representation of cost–benefit thinking as autonomous and absolute, and the elevation of the market logic to normative primacy, all of which lead to false totalities of a latently ideological kind.

- The *development of a self-sufficient economic rationality* in the absence of ethical considerations involves the isolation of a supposedly autonomous economic question from the question of rational action. As the object of knowledge of an *autonomous economics*, this is then analysed from a 'purely economic standpoint' as 'value-free' by excluding all

[1] G. Myrdal, *Das politische Element in der nationalökonomischen Doktrinbildung*, 2nd edn (Bonn-Bad Godesberg: Verlag Neue Gesellschaft, 1976), preface to the 1st German edn (Berlin 1932), not included in the English edn, p. XV.

[2] G. Weisser, 'Die Überwindung des Ökonomismus in der Wirtschaftswissenschaft', in Weisser, *Beiträge zur Gesellschaftspolitik* (Göttingen: Schwartz, 1978; 1st edn 1954), pp. 573–601, at p. 574. On the 'impossibility of economism' see also G. Weisser, *Wirtschaftspolitik als Wissenschaft: Erkenntniskritische Grundfragen der praktischen Nationalökonomie* (Stuttgart: Kohlhammer, 1934), p. 49ff. The concept of economism is also found early in W. Röpke, *Die Gesellschaftskrisis der Gegenwart* (Erlenbach-Zurich: Rentsch, 1942; 5th edn 1948), pp. 49 and 88.

[3] For a reasonably comprehensive treatment of the historical background to the dogmas of economism see Ulrich, *Tranformation*, p. 173ff.

'value-laden' socio-economic relationships. Consequently there is an abandonment of reflection on the normative preconditions of economic rationality, properly understood, and a 'non-relationship'[4] between autonomous economics and ethics is established (two-world conception). But the 'pure' economic idea of rationality always gives rise to a specific relationship between limited resources and the totality of all possible ends for their use.[5] The ethical neutralization involved in the purely economic approach is doomed to fail, as it presupposes, firstly, the unacceptable assumption that the means applied (natural resources, human labour, capital) possess no inherent value (restriction of the value aspect to the purposes of actions) and, secondly, the existence of an interest-neutral single criterion, assumed to be objectively defined, for the ends of economic activity (the fiction of the common good).[6]

- *The representation of cost–benefit thinking as autonomous and absolute* means the negation of the relational nature of the economic *aspect* of an action, and particularly of economic activity, in regard to orientations of meaning and purpose which are superordinate and external to pure economics. These are replaced by a tacit orientation on the normative idea of utility maximization under conditions of scarcity (idea of efficiency). Treating the aspect of efficiency as absolute and as an end in itself, however, turns it into an *economistic ideology*, which presents itself as 'pure' objective rationality. What is not objective and not rational about it is precisely the fact that it exaggeratedly elevates the economic 'rationality principle' to the principle of reason pure and simple. It thus represents the loss of methodological discipline in dealing with the validity conditions of rational economic argument ('economic rationalism'[7]).
- *The elevation of the market logic to normative primacy* as the determining principle for the social coordination of actions means the reduction of

4 Mittelstrass, *Abschied vom Ökonomismus*, p. 27. On this point see Section 3.1.

5 Cf. the neoclassical standard definition of pure economics in Robbins, *Essay*, p. 16: 'Economics is the science which studies human behaviour as a relationship between ends and scarce means which have alternative uses.'

6 The impossibility of an independent 'pure' economic approach and, consequently, of an 'economic standpoint' was thoroughly treated decades ago by established authors, in particular G. Myrdal, *The Political Element in the Development of Economic Theory* (London: Routledge & Kegan Paul, 1954); Albert, *Ökonomische Ideologie*, and G. Weisser, 'Wirtschaft', in W. Ziegenfuss (ed.), *Handbuch der Soziologie* (Stuttgart: Enke, 1956), pp. 970–1098, reprinted as a separate publication (Göttingen: Schwartz, 1989).

7 The concept of economic rationalism was already used by M. Weber, *The Protestant Ethic and the Spirit of Capitalism*, transl. T. Parsons (London: Unwin Hyman, 1930), pp. 26, 75; even more frequently in Weber, *Economy and Society*.

the normative logic of interpersonal relations (moral reciprocity) to the economic logic of mutual advantage. As the resulting conception of 'proper' regulatory politics reveals no awareness of the categorial limitations of its perspective on rationality or of the need for an ethical integration of the normative logic of the market, the latter is then elevated to the level of a 'principle' for a strictly economic ordering of the social world. Instead of the market being integrated into social relations in a proper fashion, there is a radical reversal of positions so that, in the end, the social relations are embedded in the market.[8] The disregard for the instrumental character of economic activity converts the economically active person into an 'economic person' (homo oeconomicus) and reduces his interpersonal relationships to relations of exchange. Thus, the idea of an efficient market economy is expanded conceptually into an ideology of a *total market society*.[9]

The various manifestations of economism can essentially be found in two typical, but clearly distinct lines of argument to which leading figures of the business world often have recourse when justifying unpopular measures: 'The market forces us to ...' *(inherent necessity thesis)* '... but it ultimately serves the well-being of all' *(common good thesis)*. These two fundamental economistic theses can be understood as symptomatic answers to the two basic questions of the *possibility* and the *necessity* of economic ethics under market economy conditions:

- The first basic question is concerned with the *problem of the 'room for manoeuvre'* for moral action in the market: Are ethical considerations and respects at all *possible* under the competitive conditions of the market economy? What is at issue here is the methodological status of the functional conditions of a modern economic system. The economistic answer to this question is that economic ethics is 'impossible' under the competitive conditions of the market economy because competition compels the strict observance of economic rationality (inherent necessity thesis). The basic theoretical assumption which must be critically examined is *economic determinism* (Chapter 4).
- The second basic question is concerned with the *problem of the 'morality of the market'*: Is the explicit consideration of ethical aspects in

[8] The most impressive treatment of this reversal of the relationship between economy and society stems from Karl Polanyi, if one leaves Marx out of account. See Polanyi, *The Great Transformation* (Boston: Beacon Press, 1957/2001; 1st edn 1944), p. 33ff. and especially p. 56f.

[9] On this dimension of the critique of economism see R. Blum, 'Die Zukunft des Homo oeconomicus', in B. Biervert/M. Held (eds.), *Das Menschenbild der ökonomischen Theorie* (Frankfurt/New York: Campus, 1991), pp. 111–31; along the same lines Rich, *Business and Economic Ethics*, p. 269ff., and even earlier Weisser, *Überwindung des Ökonomismus*.

economic actions at all *necessary* in the context of a modern economic system? Or does the 'invisible hand' of the 'free market' by itself lead to ethically good and fair results, as the advocates of economism hope? This question is about the normative content of the economic 'system rationality', namely whether the latter already possesses an adequate 'inner morality' or not. The economistic answer is positive: it states that a special economic ethics is 'unnecessary', as the market operates to the advantage of all participants (common good thesis), if only left alone to carry out its beneficial work. The basic theoretical assumption which must be subjected to an ideological critique here is *economic reductionism* (Chapter 5).

Neither of these two basic forms of economism have fallen like manna from (a theoretical) heaven. They are the result of complex historical developments in the real and the intellectual world. An understanding of them will consequently be facilitated by an historical approach which pays attention both to the actual historical background of far-reaching cultural and social changes as well as to the corresponding axiomatic and dogmatic developments in theoretical economic thinking. In view of the complexity and multilayered nature of the issue we must restrict the account to the main lines of development. Nonetheless, critical reflection on economism must necessarily be meticulous and thorough, if we are to sharpen our awareness of the basic economic-ethical problems. The decisive point is that the critique of economism, understood as critical reflection on the normative background convictions of what is claimed to be 'pure' economic rationality, is systematically the first fundamental task of integrative economics ethics. After all, it is the economistic intellectual blinkers which obstruct our view of the ethical challenges presented by the development of the market economy.

4 'Inherent necessity' of competition? A critique of economic determinism

Absolute inherent necessity – or more concisely in German: *Sachzwang* – exists only under the law of nature. This determines the objective relations between causes and effects. In the field of social practice, however, we are dealing with the inter-subjective relations between subjects who in principle possess a free will. Human subjects act deliberately, and this means that they pursue certain intentions when they have reasons for doing so. Reasons can never be compulsive, precisely because they are addressed to the reason of free and autonomous subjects. They only formulate why an action is meaningful or desirable for the person who intends to carry it out and thus justify the desired decision. We can always in principle contradict the justifications put forward or played through by us in an ideal reversal of roles; we do not have to 'follow' them on all accounts. The causes of an empirical situation can of course be part of a justification, but reasons as such never have the character of a determining cause.[1] Wherever this categorial difference is blurred and empirically given cause-effect relationships are presented directly as 'inherently necessary' reasons we are dealing with the abandonment of reflection in the face of tacitly assumed intentions which are not submitted to further examination. We are not then dealing with inherent objective necessities but with subjective mental constraints.

It is, however, possible that the intentional actions of one subject have direct or indirect objectively necessary effects on another, who then has difficulty in pursuing his intentions with an equally free degree of self-determination. This is particularly true of actions under market economy conditions, as will be shown later. Nevertheless, the *Sachzwänge* or objective necessities to which we are subjected as individuals under

[1] In this sense Kant distinguishes in a rather oddly formulated way between 'causality through freedom' (reasons) and 'causality in accordance with the laws of nature' (causes). See I. Kant, *Critique of Pure Reason*, ed. and transl. P. Guyer and A. W. Wood (Cambridge: Cambridge University Press, 1998), p. 484ff. [B 472].

such 'conditions' must be related to fundamental subjective intentions or mental constraints, which need to be scrutinized.

In what follows we will first trace the cultural and historical origins of the 'modern' economic notion of inherent necessity, as these reveal how the freedom of action in economic life can be regained at least conceptually (Section 4.1). Today, however, we encounter these motives of economic necessity not only in the realm of thought but also in the strangely anonymous and self-referential structures of the market economy as a 'system'. As a result the freedom of economic action can, at least in part, no longer be guaranteed directly and individually, but only indirectly through the political shaping of the systemic conditions (Section 4.2). Both for the ethical and political orientation of this formative political process and for the self-determination of the economic agents it is of decisive importance that the apparently empirical problem of *Sachzwang* is reconstructed as a normative problem of reasonable expectation, which is always the subject matter of an economic-ethical discourse (Section 4.3).

4.1 The origins of modern market economy: the calvinistic ethos as a context of motivation

In traditional pre-modern societies all economic activity was embedded in a well-established socio-cultural way of life in a twofold sense:

Firstly, economic *life* was totally permeated by the norms (i.e. the moral rules of behaviour) and customs which were valid for all other areas of life as well. Economic motives and interests were, so to speak, *normatively inhibited* and thoroughly subject to the guiding principles of the good life and just social co-existence in the lifeworld. An autonomous development of the motives of commercial acquisition independently of the shared meanings and value standards of the cultural context was literally unthinkable. Accordingly, the essence of all pre-modern economic doctrines – from Aristotle to the moral philosopher Adam Smith[2] – was economic ethics.

[2] Smith's work brings an epochal break with this tradition. In contrast to his *Theory of Moral Sentiments* (1759), *An Inquiry into the Nature and Causes of the Wealth of Nations* (1776) presents a world of thought which has achieved a partial autonomy in its conceptions. For this reason the moral philosopher Smith (who had a Calvinist upbringing!) became the founder of modern economics. A symptomatic consequence is the so-called *Adam-Smith-Problem*, i.e. the still unanswered question of the systematic relationship between his ethics and his political economy. Recent research has increasingly confirmed the insight that Smith's liberal political economy can ultimately be understood only against the background of his moral philosophy. On this point see the contributions in Meyer-Faje/Ulrich (eds.), *Der andere Adam Smith*, and, on the thesis presented here, especially the introduction of the editors, pp. 9–17.

Secondly, the *organization* of the economy also remained fully embedded in the traditional course of life and its institutions. Pre-modern society was a normatively closed society in which there were no separate spheres of everyday life with different rules. Accordingly, an economic sphere in which some kind of pure economic rationality applied was scarcely conceivable in this society and would literally not have made sense. In order to deprive ideas in this direction of a practical basis and to ensure total acceptance of the validity claims of the traditional or legally stipulated norms, the development of the structural autonomy of the economy and the expansion of economic activity were *institutionally shackled*. In the Late Middle Ages strict market regulations still provided for a spatial and temporal restriction of trade (guild system). Consequently the pre-modern local markets have little in common with the modern market economy, which cannot be traced back to them.[3] The traditional economy remains largely a subsistence economy, designed to satisfy the immediate needs of the local life community (family, clan and village). To produce and to work more than was necessary to this end would have seemed pointless to the people of that time. The local markets served only the subsidiary purpose of providing a place in which the scanty surplus of agrarian production and the specialized services or products of townsmen who were no longer agriculturally self-sufficient (tradesmen, merchants and sometimes professional people) could be put on offer.

The complex process of cultural and social modernization unfolded step by step in the West and led to what Karl Polanyi has termed 'the great transformation' which enabled the rise of the modern market economy. This again required fundamental and radical change both culturally and structurally (in the organization of society). From a cultural standpoint a profound religious and intellectual transformation, whose main lines were traced by Max Weber in his famous and to this day unsurpassed study 'The Protestant Ethic and the Spirit of Capitalism'[4] provided the context for an epochal revaluation of all values. The capitalist 'spirit' arises from 'the most spiritual forms of Christian piety' (p. 42) and these permeate all aspects of the conduct of life in radical

[3] As Polanyi, *Great Transformation*, p. 56ff., has shown, the immediate origins of the modern market economy are rather to be found in long-distance trade in which the merchant class was for the first time able to emancipate itself from the normative 'inhibitions' and institutional 'shackles' of the traditional economy. On this point cf. Ulrich, *Transformation*, p. 92ff.

[4] Weber, *Protestant Ethic*. The page numbers in brackets in the main text refer in what follows to Parsons' translation.

Protestantism.[5] Whereas Catholic medieval life was moulded by a characteristic this-worldly and other-worldly dichotomy together with the corresponding 'double morality' of secular and religious life, Protestantism, particularly in its Calvinist form, levelled out this dichotomy and subjected life in this world to the requirements of a 'worldly asceticism' (pp. 119f., 170f.). The 'other-worldly' asceticism of the Catholic tradition consisted of a retreat to the monastery; it was not a way of life open to everyman. Weber gets to the heart of the new situation with a quotation from the chronicler Sebastian Franck (1499–1542):

> You think you have escaped from the monastery; but everyone must now be a monk throughout his life.[6]

In Catholicism absolution through confession and indulgence served to ease the tension between religious duty and the sinfulness of humans in this world. 'Human' imperfection was permitted for Catholics, whereas the Calvinist was always in the service of God even in this world (pp. 117, 121).[7] The consequence is the duty to conduct a disciplined and purposeful life 'which served to increase the glory of God' (p. 114). It comprises, on the one hand, the higher value placed on tireless strenuous work as the main content of life and, on the other hand, moderation in the consumption of worldly goods and in the pleasures of life. Success in the world, and particularly in one's calling as a task set by God (p. 79), is then however interpreted as a 'sign of election' (p. 115). Although the believer cannot earn 'the election of grace' by his own efforts, the signs of success in his calling nonetheless mean 'that there are visible proofs that God

[5] As Weber (ibid., p. 36) shows, the Calvinist variant of Protestantism played a special part. Accordingly the map of early modern entrepreneurship largely corresponds with that of Calvinist (Pietist, Puritan, Zwinglian, etc., but not so much Lutheran) reformed areas in Switzerland (Calvin's town of Geneva and Zwingli's town of Zurich), Scotland, the Netherlands, and parts of Germany, and later New England (USA) and partly in England itself.

[6] Weber, M., 'The Evolution of the Capitalistic Spirit', in *General Economic History: Max Weber*, ed. I. J. Cohen, transl. F. H. Knight (New Brunswick/London: Transaction, 1981), pp. 352–69, at p. 366.

[7] The Protestant business ethicist Georg Wünsch advanced the following thesis as late as 1932: 'On the basis of the belief that God created the world and its order, the fact that man can only exist through economic activity (economy) must be recognized as a fact effected by God. The responsible affirmation of the *economic contingency* of human existence is grounded in the belief in creation. *Thus economic activity is service for the work of God.*' G. Wünsch, 'Wirtschaftsethik', in H. Gunkel, (ed.), *Religion in Geschichte und Gegenwart*, 2nd edn, vol. 6 (Tübingen: Mohr Siebeck, 1932), col. 1964–1971; reprinted in G. Brakelmann/T. Jähnichen (eds), *Die protestantischen Wurzel der sozialen Markwirtschaft: Ein Quellenband* (Gütersloh: Gütersloher Verlagshaus, 1994), pp. 275–83, at p. 275f. (my italics).

blessed his work'[8] and, in the favourable case, that he has achieved the desired 'certainty of salvation' (p. 115) for which the Calvinist strives along the lines of Calvin's doctrine of predestination:[9]

For if that God whose hand the Puritan sees in all the occurrences of life shows one of His elect a *chance of profit*, he must do it with a purpose. Hence the faithful Christian must follow the call by taking advantage of the opportunity. (p. 162; my italics)

What was formerly looked down upon, the 'uninhibited' pursuit of business interests and the resulting unconditional orientation towards private success, thus becomes the epitome of a virtuous and worthy way of life which is pleasing to God: that of the capitalist entrepreneur who can be identified by an investive attitude and a calculating rational conduct of life 'directed with foresight and caution towards the economic success' (p. 76). 'The important fact is always that a *calculation* of capital in terms of money is made' (p. 18). 'The practical result' of this 'release of acquisitive activity' is 'the accumulation of capital through ascetic compulsion to save' (p. 172). In as far as it is carried out legally, the entrepreneurial pursuit of profit is expressly included in activities designed to increase the glory and honour of God:

And since the success of work is the surest symptom that it pleases God, capitalist profit is one of the most important criteria for establishing that God's blessing rests on the enterprise. It is clear that this style of life is very closely related to the self-justification that is customary for bourgeois acquisition: profit and property appear not as ends in themselves but as indications of personal ability. Here has been attained the union of religious postulate and bourgeois style of life that promotes capitalism.[10]

In this business-oriented life project the resulting 'blessing of money' is a clear sign of God's blessing. As a paradoxical consequence not intended by Calvinism,[11] an ethically justified and far-reaching *moral disinhibition* or even an 'encouragement'[12] of actions free of direct ethical considerations

8 Weber, *Economy and Society*, vol. II, p. 1199.

9 The doctrine of predestination teaches the divine preordainment of the elect who will enter heaven ('election of grace') and of the condemned who are threatened with hell. On the doctrine of predestination and its practical significance see the succinct presentation in Weber, ibid., p. 1199f.

10 Ibid., p. 1200.

11 A distinction must be made between the actual historical development of Calvinism and the teachings of Calvin, who by no means spoke in favour of an uninhibited capitalism but rather emphasized the social obligations of the wealthy and encouraged official social measures of an almost modern kind in Geneva.

12 J. Meran, 'Ist es ökonomisch vernünftig, moralisch zu handeln?', in Ulrich (ed.), *Auf der Suche*, pp. 53–88, at p. 54ff., speaks in this sense of an 'encouragement model' of business ethics.

and guided 'purely' by principles of exchange value is achieved. This culminates ultimately in the justification of the so-called '*principle of economic acquisition*'[13] or the 'profit principle'. It elevates action focused strictly on the maximization of private advantage or profit to the epitome of economic rationality and even to the 'rational principle' pure and simple. In this way 'the providential interpretation of profit making justified the activities of the businessman.'[14] Thus 'private profitableness' (p. 162) wins a metaphysically elevated significance: the strict focussing of business activity 'on "impersonal" rational goals', imbued with the blessing of God, takes precedence over interpersonal orientations.[15] As a result the practical logic of the economy *(Sachlogik)* acquires a normative basis that both legitimates and motivates it. Weber thus uncovered the inner connection between 'the spirit of modern economic life' (p. 27), which first arose under Calvinist entrepreneurship and 'economic rationalism' (p. 75):

> It is not mere business astuteness ... it is an ethos (p. 51).
>
> In fact, the summum bonum of this ethic, the earning of more and more money with the strict avoidance of all spontaneous enjoyment of life ... is thought of so purely as an end in itself. (p. 53)

In this way the spiritual breeding ground for the autonomous development and the 'emancipation' of economic motives and interests from the control of the traditional lifeworld was cultivated. What was conceived of as the epitome of a self-disciplined way of life pleasing to God achieved autonomy in a way not really intended and became the driving force behind an increasingly self-referential dynamics of economic rationalization 'thought of purely as an end in itself'. The seeds are sown here for the cultivation of the notion of economic *Sachzwang* and its structural crystallization in an impersonally functioning economic system.

4.2 The systemic character of modern market economy: the 'free' market as a coercive context

Everybody does what is economically rational without orders or legal coercion [in the competitive system]; it does nobody any good to behave differently, and yet all *feel* they are free. Each individual is dependent on all the others, but this

[13] E. Gutenberg, *Grundlagen der Betriebswirtschaftslehre*, vol. I: *Die Produktion*, 22nd edn (Berlin/New York: Springer, 1976), p. 464ff.

[14] Weber, *Protestant Ethic*, p. 163. Parsons translates Weber's term 'verklärt' with 'justified', but it means a metaphysical idealization and in no way a rational justification. In the translation by P. Baehr and G. C. Wells (London: Penguin, 2002), 'verklärt' is translated with 'ethically transformed' (p. 110).

[15] Weber, *Economy and Society*, vol. II, p. 1200.

dependence is an objectified interdependence which impresses itself on the awareness of the individual in the form of prices, i.e. mathematical symbols, to which he can unhesitatingly raise his hat without feeling humiliated.[16]

The structural consequences of the radical cultural transformation sketched above were essentially effected in the political programme of *economic liberalism* that grew so strongly at the beginning of the 19th century.[17] The old market order based on the guild system was largely abolished, the markets opened ('free market') and the entire economy increasingly subjected to an 'unbridled' and far-reaching competition – a process that has not been concluded to this day. Its impact can be seen not only in the unending globalization of competition but also in the inclusion of more and more areas of the economy and everyday life in its sphere of influence.[18] At first only merchandising, trade and industrial production were affected, but subsequently increasingly abstract markets were created and established for factors of production which did not have the character of producible goods: the labour market, the market in land, property and housing, and the markets for capital, money and financial services.[19]

In each case the decisive structural change involves the transition from traditional norms and regulations to the principle of market coordination. Questions of meaning and value standards deriving from the lifeworld lose their direct relevance for the economic process. Whether they like it or not, economic agents now have to orientate themselves to the necessity of self-assertion in competition between suppliers of goods or factors of production (including their own labour) for buyers (i.e. in the case of the labour market: employers). The economic agents must rely on their self-assertion in competition at least in as far as they are existentially dependent on the continuing acquisition of income, either as employers who must achieve an adequate turnover in order to ensure the solvency and hence the profitability of their business, or as employees (i.e. employers of their own labour) who must 'earn' regular wages in order to cover their living expenses and those of their families. The practical use value of what individuals have to offer on the market does not count, at least not

[16] F. Böhm, 'Die Idee des Ordo im Denken Walter Euckens', *Ordo* 3 (1950), pp. XV–LXIX, reprinted in Böhm, *Freiheit und Ordnung in der Marktwirtschaft* (Baden-Baden: Nomos, 1980), p. 11f. (my italics).

[17] Together with the USA, Switzerland was the country in which liberalism achieved a political power unequalled in other countries, with its cultural starting point in the two radical Protestant cities of Zurich and Geneva. On the central role of Zurich in the European liberalism of the 19th century see G. A. Craig, *Triumph of Liberalism: Zurich in the Golden Age, 1830–1869* (London: Collier Macmillan, 1988).

[18] On globalization see the later treatment in Section 9.3.

[19] For details see Polanyi, *Great Transformation*, p. 68ff., and Ulrich, *Transformation*, p. 92ff.

directly; all that matters is the exchange value of their offer, i.e. the price they can get on the market. Their activities are no longer guided by subjective or inter-subjective considerations but by objective 'signals from the market'. What counts in the free market is what pays off.

As long as the economic agents wish to 'stay in the market' they are well advised not to allow personal motives and preferences to guide their actions but to decide 'objectively' on the basis of the impersonal data defined by the 'market forces' (for the employer, the relevant data are, for example, the number and the willingness to pay of potential buyers; market shares, price and cost structures of major competitors in comparison to his own business figures, etc.). This exclusion of 'market alien' considerations[20] is necessary for market agents in order to recognize and to maintain control over their strategic success factors and those of their competitors (benchmarking) at all times.

This is trivial, but it leads to a strange situation. Although every participant in the market is interested only in his private gain and his competitive position, he inevitably exerts a degree of *coercion* over his competitors, without any kind of personal interaction. This may be scarcely noticeable and merely marginal. Yet, as every participant in the market exerts this constraining pressure on every other and the process continues without limitation in the open markets, the reciprocal effects cumulate and ultimately acquire the character of an impersonal functional mechanism. No individual can be personally blamed for the constraints of competition; it is rather the ever-changing constellation of all the participants in the market, suppliers and buyers, which makes the behaviour we have sketched 'inevitable'. What economic liberalism has proclaimed as the 'free' market and has largely established in all modern societies – to differing degrees dependent on the cultural environment and the political relations of power – turns out to be an anonymous straitjacket for the economic agents under its sway. The system of the modern market economy is thus characterized by the compulsion to be competitive.

Competitiveness means the ability to outdo as many as possible of the competitors who offer goods, services or labour to potential buyers by achieving a comparative cost–benefit advantage (i.e. the same service for a lower price or additional benefits for the same price). Every supplier (or

20 Cf. Thielemann, 'A Brief Theory of the Market – Ethically Focused', *International Journal of Social Economics* 27/1 (2000), pp. 6–31, at p. 12ff., in accordance with Weber's concept of (market-) 'outside interests'. Weber, *Economy and Society*, vol. I, p. 139, regards as 'outside interests' all the motives 'which are not primarily oriented to the long-run profitability of the enterprise'.

every 'employee') who wishes 'to survive' in the market must at least outdo the least competitive rivals, who – on account of the limited purchasing power of potential customers and their accordingly restricted demand ('volume of the market') – fail to find a buyer and are consequently eliminated from the market. Employers must then declare their insolvency, whereas employees lose their jobs and their source of income. In other words, the market itself 'chooses' those economic agents who 'obey' it most insistently. Once again, it was Max Weber who was the first to recognize clearly this *selective function of the market*:

> Thus the capitalism of today, which has come to dominate economic life, educates and selects the economic subjects which it needs through a process of economic *survival of the fittest*.[21]

The market economy system rewards those who – 'on the basis of rigorous calculation'[22] – strictly strive to maximize their private success without consideration of the side-effects in the lifeworld, as they can then perhaps achieve the decisive comparative advantage in regard to services or costs and can so emerge as the winners in the tough competition with their rivals. Only those who survive this process of selection, which is strikingly reminiscent of the Calvinist concept of divine 'selection of grace', can remain free economic agents in the 'free' market. No-one can escape this self-contained inherent logic of the competitive system, unless he or she can dispose of independent sources of income (property, accumulated wealth). The literally forceful words of Weber are evidently as relevant today as they were in his own time:

> The capitalist economy of the present day is an immense cosmos into which the individual is born, and which presents itself to him, at least as an individual, as an unalterable order of things in which he must live. It *forces* the individual, *in so far* as he is involved in the system of market relationships, to conform to capitalistic rules of action. The manufacturer who in the long run acts counter to these norms will just as inevitably be eliminated from the economic scene as the worker who cannot or will not adapt himself to them will be thrown into the streets without a job.[23]

The motive of the pursuit of success in business, unleashed historically by Calvinism, has now hardened into an impersonal compulsion to succeed:

> Whoever does not adapt his manner of life to the conditions of capitalist success must go under or at least cannot rise.[24]

The logic of success in competition thus asserts itself in a coercive fashion. In this remarkable coercive context the personal freedom of the

[21] Weber, *Protestant Ethic*, p. 55. [22] Ibid., p. 76.
[23] Ibid., pp. 54–5 (my italics). [24] Ibid., p. 72.

economic agents, whether they are 'manufacturers' or merely employers of their own labour (and competitors on the labour market), is only the freedom to wish to be better – and that always means more successful in the market – than one's rivals and to understand this existential compulsion as something *one is permitted to follow*. Or in the striking words of the initiator of the neoliberal white paper 'Mut zum Aufbruch' ('Courage for a New Departure'):

The aim *must* be to *want* to be the best. (...) Not all can win, but all can try.[25]

Will and necessity are thus declared identical. The doctrine of the 'free' market economy seems here to breathe precisely the spirit of the 'insight into necessity' generally attributed by its followers solely to the Marxist ideology, which has long been 'punished' by history. But the ideologically forged identity of will and necessity in de Pury's ethos of the free entrepreneurial way of life falls apart again on sober consideration of the concealed structures of *Sachzwang*, as Max Weber realized more than a century ago:

The Puritan *wanted* to work in a calling [i.e. he felt 'called' to successful self-assertion in the market]; we are *forced* to do so.[26]

With those who do not 'want' to see the necessity or who fail in the hard competitive struggle in spite of giving their best – and many will 'naturally' fail – the market is 'merciless'. It soon shows them the 'red card'. In order to survive the process of selection the clever offerers continually strive to improve their competitive situation – and this is all that matters. Particularly when competition gets tougher the entrepreneurs are forced to improve their core competences[27], to develop new, if possible unrivalled products (product innovation), to improve the quality of their established products and to 'rationalize' their performance in order to save costs and to maintain their profit margin in spite of pressure on prices. Employees do the same, in principle, by incessantly improving their professional qualifications with the help of a good basic training, regular further training and a purposively planned 'curriculum vitae'.

25 D. de Pury, in 'David de Pury und wie er die Welt sieht' (Interview), *Tages-Anzeiger*, Zurich, 2 February 1996, p. 7 (my italics). We will return several times in Chapters 5, 6, and 9 to the white paper *Mut zum Aufbruch* (Zurich: Orell Füssli, 1995), which was published as 'a politico-economic agenda for Switzerland' by D. de Pury, H. Hauser and B. Schmid.

26 Weber, *Protestant Ethic*, p. 181.

27 See C. K. Prahalad/G. Hamel, 'The Core Competence of the Corporation', *Harvard Business Review* 68/3 (1990), pp. 79–91, at p. 91: 'Only if the company is conceived of as a hierarchy of core competencies, core products, and market-focused business units will it be fit to fight.'

They consequently choose their places of work primarily in accordance with their value as springboards for their future career.

The participant in the market who behaves in this achievement-oriented fashion and thus improves his competitive position of course also continually worsens the relative competitiveness of his rivals, which then prompts them to do the same to him as far as possible. This is the basis of the *efficiency function of the market* on which the much invoked economic 'superiority of the free market economy' over less 'liberal' economic systems or forms is in turn founded. As a result these too will in the long run all be eliminated in the international and intercultural 'competition of the institutional frameworks'. In accordance with the same principle of selection and increased efficiency in competition, the market forces assert themselves in more and more areas of life in society if they are not stopped by a stronger power. As the unintended consequence of intended actions (the striving for self-assertion) of the economic agents, the market thus develops its own self-referential and 'autonomous dynamics', and 'its participants do not look toward the persons of each other but only toward the commodity'.[28] The purely 'objective' quasi-natural 'laws of the market' confront the individuals who are 'subjected to'[29] competition in the form of an autonomous *functional logic* of the market which they are the less able to escape the more the market 'dominates' and the more intensive the competition is. What was in its cultural origins a religious or at least a religiously transfigured motive of free persons is converted into the coercive organizing principle of a market society. Weber has succinctly characterized this outcome as the 'masterless slavery'[30] of the market.

The Calvinist or Puritan could discover a higher meaning in this 'masterless' rule of the market. He was sure that behind the determining laws of the market the will of the creator reigned. The apparently autonomous market laws were ultimately an expression of divine law and the corresponding good order of the cosmos, including the 'economic order'.[31] For this reason 'the course of the world' is 'somehow *meaningful*, at least in so far as it touches upon the interests of men'.[32] But once the market has become sufficiently effective by exercising 'an inexorable power over the lives of men' it no longer needs religious motivation: the liberated forces of inherent necessity now dominate.[33]

[28] Weber, *Economy and Society*, vol. I, p. 636. [29] Ibid., vol. II, p. 1186
[30] Ibid. [31] Weber, *Protestant Ethic*, p. 160 [32] Weber, *From Max Weber*, p. 353.
[33] See Weber, *Protestant Ethic*, p. 181. In this sense he speaks here of the 'iron cage' of 'victorious capitalism'.

Weber's metaphor of 'masterless slavery' stands for the systemic character of market competition.[34] The systems-theoretical perspective of the market as developed by the classical political economists, and particularly Adam Smith, heralds the beginning of the intellectual detachment of the compelling inherent logic of market competition from religious and metaphysical justifications, as a moment of enlightened 'demystification of the world'.[35] The autonomous and anonymous dynamics of the market produces unintentional cumulative consequences (increased productivity, economic growth, improvement of living standards) which can be interpreted quite 'objectively' as a context of impersonal forces. It must be noted, however, that in the 'obvious and simple *system* of natural liberty',[36] as which Adam Smith characterized the coordinating mechanism of the market economy, a sign of the benevolent effects of the 'invisible hand' of God could be and was still seen. The early-modern liberal economic 'systems theory' is firmly based upon a *metaphysics of the system*.[37] Since this time it has been the intention of 'liberal' political economy to demonstrate theoretically that the determinism of the market, in which 'common people' usually see coercion, is ultimately to be understood as a guarantee for a free society and should consequently be made as effective as possible through 'deregulation'. Only then can it carry out its good work, which is not directly intended by the individual economic agents. The knowledge-constitutive interest guiding the 'liberal' theory of the market is always essentially to explain the unintentional functioning of the 'free' market as if it were meaningful and purposeful. The wonderful ability of the market for systemic self-control, supposedly explained in a purely theoretical fashion, in reality covers up and conceals the *natural teleology* of the well-ordered divine cosmos.[38]

[34] On the system character of the market see the detailed account in Thielemann, *Prinzip Markt*, pp. 27ff., 160ff., 288ff.; and his 'A Brief Theory'.

[35] Weber, *From Max Weber*, p. 350. There Weber's 'Entzauberung' is inadequately translated with 'disenchantment'. See also Weber, *Protestant Ethic*, p. 105, where 'Entzauberung' is translated by Parsons with 'the elimination of magic' (from the world).

[36] A. Smith, *An Enquiry into the Nature and Causes of the Wealth of Nations*, Glasgow Edition of the Works and Correspondence of Adam Smith, 2 vols. (Oxford: Oxford University Press, 1976), vol. II, p. 687 (my italics). Even earlier than Smith, Thomas Hobbes, *Leviathan*, p. 60f., interpreted the market economy as a system of barter agreements between individuals pursuing their own interests, without Smith's metaphysical implications.

[37] For systematic reasons this is first dealt with in more detail in Section 5.1.

[38] Naturalistic system theories always imply metaphysical-theological premises of a self-creating good order (self-organisation), which have been reinterpreted in a functional-rational manner. On this point see G. Keil, *Kritik des Naturalismus* (Berlin: de Gruyter, 1993), pp. 119ff, 145ff.

The normative content of such a naturalistic systems theory of the market lies hidden in the teleological fiction of a strangely impersonal *systems rationality*[39] which is completely detached from human reason and nevertheless seems to guide the market in a meaningful and purposive way. This capacity is attributed to the inherent logic of a self-regulating market. But whose reason and whose good purposes lie behind it all – if not those of a supra-human, divine reason and with it the wise preordainment built into the 'simple system of natural freedom' by the creator?

The naturalistic systems perspective of the 'free' market is, accordingly, the 'natural' perspective of those who wish to justify an economically determined market as normatively correct and meaningful, because they believe in the immanent meaningfulness and the evolutionary potential for progress of a well-ordered economic cosmos guided by an 'invisible hand'. The first advocates of this position were the Scottish enlightenment philosophers of the early modern period (David Hume, Adam Ferguson, Adam Smith, etc.) and even today there is still a rearguard defending the position among the paleo- and ultra-liberals. Among them we can name Friedrich A. von Hayek, who has dealt strikingly often with the unintended *good* effects of the self-interested actions of individuals under the conditions of the 'free' market. He has just as strikingly expressed a profound scepticism and even genuine resentment towards all claims to shape the social order in an ethically and politically rational fashion which differ from the supposedly 'natural' order.[40]

It goes without saying that the metaphysics of the market system, which has only been hinted at hitherto, is particularly attractive and convincing for those who themselves wish to lead a life aimed at business success on the market. The 'matter' looks very different from the perspective of those who do not really want this form of life but feel compelled to practise it in order to secure their subsistence. For them a 'free' market that is not integrated in an ethically justified principle of social order is an economic straitjacket which prevents them from realizing their life plans.[41]

39 Cf. the concept of system rationality as developed by Niklas Luhmann, *Zweckbegriff und Systemrationalität*, 2nd edn (Frankfurt: Suhrkamp, 1977; 1st edn 1968).

40 See, in particular, F. A. von Hayek, 'The Results of Human Action but not of Human Design', in von Hayek, *Studies in Philosophy, Politics, and Economics* (Chicago: University of Chicago Press, 1967), pp. 96–105. On various occasions Hayek refers to the famous passage in Adam Ferguson's *An Essay on the History of Civil Society* (Edinburgh: Edinburgh University Press, 1966; 1st edn 1767), p. 122, in which he writes: 'Nations stumble upon establishments, which are indeed the result of human action, but not the execution of any human design.' We examine the normative background to Hayek's position in more detail in Section 5.1.

41 We take up the problem of the asymmetric chances of alternative life plans in a market economy in Section 6.3.

From this perspective doubts about the anonymous 'systems rationality' of the market arise and make it conceivable that the inherent logic of the market need not necessarily represent the non plus ultra of a suprahuman rationality, but could quite simply be a euphemism for the literal irrationality of the uncontrolled systemic dynamics of the market forces. The decisive experience is that the overall results of the dynamics of competition are not good for everyone, but can be highly problematic for the unsuccessful. The practical consequence is the postulate that the repercussions of the market mechanism must be seen to require ethical-political regulation and that the market must be embedded in a truly meaningful social order.

Karl Marx, in his critique of the capitalist economy, was the first to work out this critical systemic perspective on the practical constraints of the market, affecting both 'capitalists' and workers alike, and to offer systematic proof of its unintended *negative* outcomes:

> Under free competition the immanent laws of capitalist production confront the individual capitalist as a coercive force external to him.[42]

He counterposes the belief in self-regulating systems rationality and the fundamental trust in a perfect natural teleology with a political programme designed to overcome the coercive relationships of a naturally and autonomously developing market society. It is not necessary to enter into the specific problematic aspects of Marx' critique of political economy here.[43] What is important in the present context is only the enlightened idea of calling, on principle, for the *primacy of politics over 'systems rationality'* and for a fundamental understanding of the economic system – rejecting market metaphysics – as a matter of socio-political formation. This, however, assumes in principle a perspective of social 'rationalization' which lies beyond systemic and functional rationality:

> It is not possible to question a system normatively simply by critically questioning the moral judgements which occur *within* this system in regard to their socio-economic *conditions*.[44]

What is needed instead is a dualistic theory of society which is capable of distinguishing between systems rationality and the ethical-practical reason regulating the lifeworld and of asserting the priority of the latter. A corresponding dualist conception of social rationalization has been

[42] K. Marx, *Capital*, transl. B. Fowkes, 3 vols (Harmondsworth: Penguin, 1976), vol. I, p. 381.

[43] For a brief criticism of Marx' paradigm of political economy see Ulrich, *Transformation*, pp. 351–3.

[44] Tugendhat, *Vorlesungen*, p. 16 (my italics). Cf. Section 3.1 (1).

	Lifeworld	*Economic (sub-) system*
Principle of coordination	Intentional: intersubjective coordination of subjective action orientations (relationship of meaning)	Functional: interlinking of objective consequences of action (relationship of effects)
Medium of coordination	Social validity claims (normative commitments)	Impersonal competitive constraints (market incentives)
Basis of social interaction	Shared convictions or communicatively achieved agreement	Mutual advantage without consent on norms (exchange contract)
Assumed action orientation of the participants	Communicative orientation (socially embedded orientation on meaning and ends)	Strict orientation on advantage (orientation on private success)
Participants' conception of rationality	Primarily communicative rationality (argumentative clarification of validity claims)	Primarily strategic rationality (self-assertion in competition)
Rationality perspective of an observer	–	Functional rationality of the system
Σ	Normative *social integration*	Functional *systems integration*

Figure 4.1. Lifeworld and economic system

developed by Jürgen Habermas following on Max Weber's theories of rationalization and modernization.[45] The basic distinction between system and lifeworld is presented in Figure 4.1 in a schematic form which assumes the integration of the economic system under the political. The former thus loses its 'compelling' self-referential character and becomes a *social subsystem* requiring rational organization. In other words, it is a 'functionally specified domain of action'[46] whose internal systemic coordination is only partial, as it is embedded in the social order.

The more or less extensive detachment of the economy from the norms and guiding principles of the lifeworld and its adjustment to the mechanisms of systemic integration has been called the 'uncoupling of system and lifeworld'[47] by Habermas. The accompanying development of a self-referential

[45] See Habermas, *Theory of Communicative Action*, especially vol. II, p. 113ff., and for a more nuanced treatment Habermas, 'A Reply', pp. 214–64; cf. Ulrich, *Transformation*, p. 68ff.

[46] Habermas, *Theory of Communicative Action*, vol. II, p. 115. As Habermas later pointed out more precisely in his 'Reply' (cf. the previous note), the conception of a politically constituted social subsystem permits an analytical system perspective but excludes an 'essentialist use' of the concept of a system in such a way, for example, that the market economy system could remain autonomous, exclusive and self-referential.

[47] See Habermas, *Theory of Communicative Action*, vol. II, p. 153ff.

subsystemic culture striving for functional rationality can be seen from this dualistic perspective as the central aspect of a *truncated* process of economic rationalization and modernization. Its problematic effect on the lifeworld is the permanent *intensification* of the 'competitive pressure' under which individuals find themselves in the market as well as an *extension* of the markets in a spatial (globalization) and in a quantitative sense (economic growth). As a result the corporations and entire national economies trying hard to hold their own in global competition are not only compelled to rationalize but also to grow.[48] The price paid for the one-dimensional 'systemic rationalization' is the resulting multidimensional intolerability of the economic development from a human, social and ecological point of view. The 'progress' of the market involves a progressive loss of meaning in the practice of everyday life. Claims to live a good life that cannot be translated into the categories of purchasing power and market demand merely disturb the autonomous economic process of rationalization.

The decisive question is whether the rampant growth of the structurally determined 'practical constraints' of competition can be subjected to limits set by the lifeworld. If our analysis of the *systemic causes* of the phenomenon of *Sachzwang* is correct, such a limitation is scarcely possible within the 'pure' logic of the system, as it is in the nature of the pressure to compete to grow unlimitedly. A change in the parameters of the system can at best influence the direction of the dynamic processes of rationalization and growth. The systematic 'site' for the limitation of competitive pressure is to be sought in *reasons rooted in the lifeworld* which lie behind and beyond the objectified forms of the 'established' social practice of the market economy. Whether the inherent necessities of the market economy system as a social order (market society) are dominant or whether, on the contrary, they are subject to a dominant and controlling social order (primacy of politics over the logic of the market) must be understood as a practical question of political will: an economic (systemic) determinism exists only in as far as it is socially and politically permitted. Absolute inherent necessities of the market which are literally free of all restrictions imposed by the lifeworld do not exist. It is rather the case that all the effective inherent necessities can ultimately be understood only as aspects of an economic and social order somebody has politically desired and put into practice. And this means that all 'inherent necessities', as far as they are not determined

[48] On the thesis of 'growth compulsion' see H. C. Binswanger, *Geld und Natur: Das wirtschaftliche Wachstum zwischen Ökonomie und Ökologie* (Stuttgart/Vienna: Weitbrecht, 1991), p. 83ff. For a systemic explanation of the compulsion to grow on which the above is based see Thielemann, *Prinzip Markt*, p. 312f.

by natural law, are an expression of institutionalized normative coercion which must be critically questioned. In as far as the market mechanism is institutionally 'liberated' it does indeed exercise compelling power over all who are existentially dependent upon it. For precisely this reason the institutional political decision as to where the market should rule and where not always requires justification and legitimation. And for the same reason, in a truly free society, the social intentions and ends pursued through the rule of the market (whose rule?) must always be open to criticism.

Taking the problem of *Sachzwang* seriously from an economic-ethical point of view means, under these circumstances, that we cannot be satisfied with an abandonment of reflection in the face of the empirically found conditions of self-assertion for the participants in competition but must persistently throw light upon the supposedly natural and self-referential dynamics of the economic system and its normative foundations – in order to make it accessible to ethical-critical argumentation.

4.3 The partiality of inherent necessity and the economic-ethical problem of reasonable expectation

My core experience was that that no human being can be voluntarily inhuman. This notion picked me up again and again when I had to do something that my nature actually shuddered at. (*The entrepreneur Wullnow in Peter Handke's play 'Die Unvernünftigen sterben aus' (1973)*)

The ultimate reason for the existence of the entire system dynamics of the market economy lies in the intentions motivating the actions of the human subjects 'who join in the game'. But whereas some of them want to act as 'entrepreneurs', others are forced to do so, as we have seen, because their existence depends on their self-assertion in the 'free' market. The voluntary upholders of the entire process of 'creative destruction'[49] inevitably force all the other persons 'entangled' in the market to submit to the mechanism of competition and to strive continually to maintain their competitiveness. When they do business all are forced, as 'rational' economic agents, to forget respect for each other, to assert themselves by behaving in a mutually unconcerned or indifferent way, to pursue their personal interests defined objectively by the market and to achieve the best possible advantage for themselves.

[49] See J. Schumpeter, *Capitalism, Socialism and Democracy* (London: Allen & Unwin, 1976), p. 81ff.

The general coercive context of the market economy thus seems to justify the tendency towards an unrestricted pursuit of personal advantage as objectively 'necessary' and to absolve the economic agents from the need to perceive moral demands arising from their actions. But the peculiar *partiality of the inherent necessities* (*Sachzwänge*) of the market is striking. Although they seemingly reflect the impartiality of the market's impersonal 'systems rationality', they nonetheless always justify forms of entrepreneurial life and action strictly serving the maximization of private success or profit and the interest in the best possible utilization of the capital of the investors that lie behind it. Their will to invest and to 'provide employment' then largely determines the chances of all economic agents 'without means of their own' to earn a living. But if the consideration of their needs does not pay off economically, they must then be excluded systematically from the market according to the (deterministically conceived) inherent logic of the system. If one follows the principles of systems rationality, the consideration of such 'outside interests' (Weber) would inevitably diminish the competitiveness of the entrepreneur who would then run the risk of being eliminated in the short or long term from the market. 'Outside interests', including morally justified claims, must consequently be interests alien to the system. On the other hand the interest in earning income and in utilizing the capital of those who have 'utilizable' capital in the widest sense (financial, material or human capital) at their disposal is in conformity with the system. What is ultimately concealed behind the coercive relations of the system is no more and no less than the subjectively intended 'necessity' to achieve profitability, as it is exerted today on the companies, in accordance with the shareholder-value doctrine, by the investors and administrators of the huge quantities of accumulated capital on the international financial markets.[50]

One of the few renowned economists to admit and reflect upon the structural asymmetry of interests in the (capitalist) market economy was Wilhelm Röpke, who, not by chance, was an important intellectual pioneer of ordoliberalism. He clearly recognized the asymmetry of the market:

> Yet the non-marketable value, while incomparably higher then the marketable one, is bound to lose unless we come to its assistance and put on its scale enough moral weight to make up for the deficiency of mercantile weight.[51]

[50] The shareholder-value concept is dealt with in Section 10.1 (4).

[51] W. Röpke, *A Humane Economy: The Social Framework of the Free Market*, transl. from the German *Jenseits von Angebot und Nachfrage* by E. Henderson (Chicago: Henry Regnery Co., 1960), p. 138. On the ordoliberal conception of the market economy see Section 9.1 (3).

The politico-economic analyses of the 'experts' on the economic system logic, who largely regard their evaluations as 'value free', nevertheless undoubtedly reflect the partiality of the inherent necessities of the market, as can be seen, for example, in the annual appraisal of the overall economic development by the German *Sachverständigenrat* (Board of [Economic] Experts). According to the assumed inherent logic of the market, the entrepreneurs who invest or disinvest, create or eliminate jobs, always behave rationally and 'efficiently', precisely because they rigorously pursue their interest in the 'long-run considerations of optimizing ... [the] profitability'[52] of the enterprise. In contrast to this all representatives of 'outside interests' or concerns automatically contradict the inherent logic of the market. That is why they are regularly confronted with 'objective' economic recommendations to moderate their claims or reproached for behaving in a mistaken and economically irrational way:

According to the neoclassical interpretative model the ascertainment of and accountability for abnormal behaviour is strikingly simple. Abnormal behaviour is only possible on the part of the trade unions (excessive wage demands) and the government (excessive taxation of profits) ... If the goals of stability are not reached it is consequently possible for the experts in economic policy, in an *apparently value free* political assessment, to confirm that the government and the trade unions *have violated the objective laws of the economy by their irresponsible behaviour in regard to the overall economic development.*[53]

The secret basic norm behind such 'value-free' representation of the interests of the one side and the attribution of (ir)responsibility and blame to the other is of course the notion that the inherent necessities of the market are as such good and right, and that the way they function is the way they ought to function. From this perspective the categorical business ethical postulate of Karl Homann makes sense:

The [economic] actors ought to behave in conformity with the system.[54]

In this principle of conformity to the system the supposedly 'value free' inherent logic of the market and the normative 'ought' are rendered identical. Concealed behind the general inherent constraints of the market on everybody lie the special normative 'constraints' (mental compulsions) of those who are interested in the 'long run profitability' (Weber) of their invested capital. The ideologically anonymized mental constraints

[52] Weber, *Economy and Society*, vol. I, p. 98.
[53] S. Katterle, *Alternativen zur neoliberalen Wende. Wirtschaftspolitik in der sozialstaatlichen Demokratie* (Bochum: SWI, 1989), p. 21ff. (my italics).
[54] Homann/Blome-Drees, *Wirtschafts- und Unternehmensethik*, p. 51; in the original the whole sentence is italicized for emphasis.

of the type 'We all have no choice ... competition forces us ...' result quite simply in a depoliticizing 'reinterpretation of the power structures of our social order, which are characterized by the domination of the interests of capital, as interest-neutral inherent necessities, to which all actors *reasonably* adapt'.[55] The one-dimensional argumentation within the logic of the system serves to conceal the normative decisions which underlie the system and to close it against requirements of ethical justification. The functional conditions of the existing economic system become the sole criterion of rationality and operate in the mental world of inherent necessity as a means of closing the door to economic-ethical discourse, which is then possible only in a truncated form as a discourse about inherent necessity 'under the conditions of the modern market economy'. The normatively fixed systemic conditions now themselves occupy the systematic place where ethical-critical reflection on other aspects of rational economic activity which are anchored in the lifeworld could begin. Under the 'dogmatism of the given'[56] it is not even necessary to come out into the open and admit that these other aspects are considered *undesirable*; it is sufficient to point out that under the given system conditions it is *impossible* to take them into account.

The position advocated by this theorem of the impossibility of economic ethics under systemic conditions can be characterized as *economic determinism*. As has been suggested, it is the version of economism which conceals its normative content behind notions of inherent necessity by abandoning reflection in the face of given empirical conditions and by implicitly ascribing normative character to those conditions as the sole criterion of 'rational' behaviour. We will take a closer look at the basic normative assumptions underlying the 'morality of the market' in Chapter 5. For the moment we will concentrate on the way in which this abandonment of reflection typically 'functions'. Two variants can be distinguished. In the first case the arguments against the possibility of moral action under the conditions of the system are strictly paradigmatic (1); in the second case a search for 'room for manoeuvre' is undertaken in a pragmatic manner (2).[57] Finally the systematic path which enables us to overcome both variants of the 'compulsory' abandonment of reflection will be illuminated: the interpretation of the problem of inherent necessity as a problem of reasonable expectation (3).

[55] Katterle, *Alternativen*, p. 22f. (my italics).
[56] Günther, *Sinn für Angemessenheit*, p. 71.
[57] Homann, 'Wettbewerb und Moral', p. 38, also distinguished between 'paradigmatic' and 'pragmatic' levels of argument.

(1) *The 'paradigmatic' art of dealing methodologically with inherent necessity*

The paradigmatic variant of the notion of inherent necessity cultivates economic determinism quite literally in its purest form. It is so pure that it has no interest whatsoever in concrete empirical circumstances. We are dealing, consequently, with a purely theoretical undertaking: that of *methodological economism.*[58] This theory does not formulate a (falsifiable) empirical hypothesis with reality explanatory intent, but rather a paradigmatic model assumption of an axiomatic ideal theory, that of 'pure' economics. It models the economic agent *as if*[59] he were a *homo oeconomicus*, who by definition knows no motives other than the motive of maximization of income or benefit, and it does so 'on analytic rather than empirical grounds':[60]

> In the research programme of economics ... the homo oeconomicus and his 'egoism' ... have the status of an assumption and not of a hypothesis. (...) The sentence 'Actors maximize their benefits under restrictions' is not an empirical assertion but the pre-empirical explanatory schema of economics.[61]

Understood in this way, the economic approach does not preoccupy itself with the empirical question whether human beings in fact behave in an economically rational way; instead it assumes axiomatically that their behaviour is in this sense *rationally determined* and focused on success. It is interested in how people *would possibly* act as strictly economic rational individuals. Pure economics explicates solely the idea of economic rationality – it unfolds the pure logic of rational action by strictly self-interested individuals. This 'as-if' assumption of rationality is defined as the pursuit of benefit maximization, so that rational behaviour can be unequivocally determined, assuming that in each situation requiring a decision the best alternative (i.e. maximizing benefits or minimizing costs) can be identified. The logical consequence is then:

[58] On this concept, which Homann expressly regards as valid for his 'paradigmatic' approach, see Section 3.2 (2).

[59] The model theoretical 'as if' construction was probably first developed by H. Vaihinger, *Die Philosophie des 'als ob'*, 8th edn (Leipzig: Meiner, 1922), engl. *The Philosophy of As If* (London: Routledge, 2000). It was taken over by E. Gutenberg, *Die Unternehmung als Gegenstand betriebswirtschaftlicher Theorie* (Berlin/Vienna: Gabler, 1929), p. 42. In general economics it was first propagated by M. Friedman, 'The Methodology of Positive Economics', in Friedman, *Essays in Positive Economics* (Chicago: University of Chicago Press, 1953), pp. 3–43. Recently the 'as-if' concept has increasingly come to be understood as the fundamental methodological characteristic of the *economic approach*; it has been elaborated particularly by G. Brennan/J. M. Buchanan, *The Reason of Rules: Constitutional Political Economy* (Cambridge: Cambridge University Press, 1985), p. 46ff. ('as if' p. 55).

[60] Brennan/Buchanan, *Reason of Rules*, p. 59.

[61] Homann, 'Philosophie und Ökonomik', p. 116, who adopts the methodological approach of Brennan/Buchanan completely.

Seen paradigmatically, the competitive process involves a quasi determined context from the initial endowment [of an economic agent] to the results on the market.[62]

This is correct – but only when 'seen' in this way! This strange rational 'determinism' is of course paradoxical, as it includes premises (that are by no means value-free) about the intentional, strictly rational and success-oriented actions of human subjects. At the same time, however, the 'quasi-determined context' is created with the help of the methodological assumption that these subjects have left their freedom of will in the dressing room before going on to the stage of the 'free' market as pure homines oeconomici, or rather as one-dimensional homunculi who are incapable of thinking and acting except in terms of acquisition and profit. The theoretical construct of economic determinism thus conceals the biased interests of those economic agents who wish to live as entrepreneurs behind an apparently impartial and value-free 'pure' economic rationality which is 'valid' for the paradigmatically modelled structure of inherent necessity in an ideal market. Methodological economism thus turns out, above all, to be a methodology involving the abandonment of reflection on the legitimation of the ends and interests guiding economic activity. In this way it simply raises the motive of personal benefit maximization to the level of a norm – which is nowhere justified – and declares it to be a 'compulsive' criterion for the actions of 'rational' subjects.

As long as it is an action of a human subject, even the strictest rational, success-oriented action is in reality always dependent on the subjective will to succeed and consequently on an in principle free choice of ends. For this reason it is also in principle accessible to argument. To this extent every determinist theory of human action goes wrong from the start – it is quite simply equivalent to a denial of the subject character of human beings. Economic determinism as an empirical hypothesis consequently makes no sense at all. The notion of inherent necessity can contribute nothing to the clarification of the question whether and how far it is right or wrong for the economic agents to ignore the moral claims of others on the market. Anyone who takes it as a basis for arguing against the possibility of moral action under market conditions is evidently confusing the purely model-theoretical character of economic determinism 'methodologically' with reality.

(2) The 'pragmatic' search for empirical room to manoeuvre

Those who wish to avoid the category mistake we have just pointed out are obviously obliged to abandon the theoretically modelled world of inherent necessity and to refer instead to pragmatic circumstances.

[62] Homann, 'Wettbewerb und Moral', p. 39.

Because economic determinism cannot exist in reality, the pragmatic approach takes as its starting point the idea that the market, 'realistically' considered, cannot function perfectly and is for this reason not absolutely deterministic in its effects. Accordingly, the objective 'inherent laws' of competition cannot have a full impact on individual economic calculations, either because 'gaps' in the rule of the market temporarily arise by chance[63] or because strategic uncertainties of a systematic and hence permanent kind exist, making it impossible for the economic agents to recognize the benefit-maximizing way of acting.[64] As a result, a spatially and temporally restricted *room for manoeuvre* exists in the market that economic agents who are aware of their responsibilities can and should use in order to take standpoints, and in particular ethical standpoints, into account which are not strictly rational in regard to private benefit. The decisive normative conclusion which is usually drawn from this perspective is that the economic agents bear ethical responsibility only within the empirical room for manoeuvre which exists for their actions:

Room for manoeuvre exists ... wherever the inherent necessities *do not completely determine* actions and *force* [the economic agent] to a mere reaction. (...) The greater ... the room for manoeuvre the greater the ethical responsibility of the actor is. (...) How great this room for manoeuvre is cannot be determined theoretically in advance, but must be decided empirically.[65]

[63] Most of the neoclassically influenced authors, including Homann/Blome-Drees, *Wirtschafts- und Unternehmensethik*, p. 53, tend to favour the thesis of a merely temporary, situative room for manoeuvre under competitive conditions. They explain occasional cases of room for manoeuvre for entrepreneurs solely in terms of 'gaps' in the overall regulatory framework of the market and regard them as the sole reason for the practical possibility of individual or corporate ethics.

[64] In decision theory every kind of uncertainty is characterized as 'strategic' which, in contrast to simple forms of uncertainty, cannot in principle be overcome by the acquisition of additional information, as it rests upon the *social interdependence* of the actions of 'rivals'; see Section 2.5 (1). But this precisely creates *systematic* room for manoeuvre, which is always present. Business managers, above all, argue for its existence, as it corresponds with the experience that even under hard competitive conditions alternative strategies for success always exist, which might possibly be differently evaluated from an ethical point of view. See, for example, A. Löhr, *Unternehmensethik und Betriebswirtschaftslehre: Untersuchungen zur theoretischen Stützung der Unternehmenspraxis* (Stuttgart: M & P Verlag für Wissenschaft und Forschung, 1991), p. 271ff.

[65] G. Enderle, *Handlungsorientierte Wirtschaftsethik* (Berne *et al.*: Haupt, 1993), p. 62 (my italics), who represents the 'pragmatic' form of economic determinism in an exemplary fashion. Similarly, Löhr, *Unternehmensethik und Betriebswirtschaftslehre*, p. 278, refers to the (supposedly) empirical character of the problem of room for manoeuvre, as do H. Steinmann/A. Zerfass, 'Privates Unternehmertum und öffentliches Interesse', in G.R. Wagner (ed.), *Betriebswirtschaftslehre und Umweltschutz* (Stuttgart: Schäffer-Poeschel, 1993), pp. 3–26, at p. 19. The authors mentioned dissociate themselves pragmatically to a certain extent from economic determinism, but they do not question its crypto-normative basis *as a matter of principle*. We deal with an inherently reductionist corporate ethics of this kind in Section 10.1 (3) and further in Section 10.2.

The answer to the question of the 'possibility' or 'impossibility' of morality in the market (and particularly of corporate ethics) then depends on *empirical* conditions and thus ultimately remains subject to the notion of inherent necessity.[66] The distinction between the conditions and the room for manoeuvre of economic activity, which at first sight seems self-evident and even trivial, implicitly contains the normative premise that the empirically given 'conditions of economic activity' as such determine the 'limits'[67] of what is morally possible. They should therefore be accepted and must only 'be perceived as realistically as possible'.[68] In this way whatever 'determines' actions *normatively* outside these supposed limits is a priori excluded as an object of ethical-critical reflection and potential change. Consequently, the uncomfortable but decisive ethical question whether the goals set or the given conditions for their realization are themselves legitimate or possibly demand moral protest can no longer be put. The pragmatic variant of the business-ethical (im-)possibility theorem thus also involves an abandonment of reflection in the face of the given conditions.

The pragmatic approach thus remains uncritical of given structures and, whether intentionally or not, proves to be structurally conservative. From this perspective what seems required ethically can all too quickly and sweepingly be judged to be 'unrealistic', 'utopian or 'heroic':

> If the conditions determining actions are played down ... a heroic ethics is then demanded according to which the actor could supposedly ignore all limits if he only wanted to.[69]

Such a sweeping justification of the inability to go against given conditions all too rapidly blurs over what is important for anyone who is seriously disposed to act morally. This involves subjecting one's personal pursuit of success to the ethical requirements of legitimation and responsibility and, after a conscientious and differentiated judgement of the concrete situation, deciding which 'limits' of the empirical conditions for success may be 'ignored' without intolerable consequences. It means, quite practically, making the supposed facticity of conditions determining one's own 'limited' room for manoeuvre the object of normative-critical reflection. The actor thus inevitably examines his own intentions and aims self-critically and can then reconsider whether it is really justifiable to carry out the action in question or whether he should

[66] As we have seen in Section 3.1, even Karl-Otto Apel makes this category mistake, which is characteristic of 'applied' (business) ethics in general.
[67] Enderle, *Handlungsorientierte Wirtschaftsethik*, p. 62.
[68] Ibid., p. 63. [69] Ibid., p. 63.

choose an alternative, more responsible action, which may perhaps be less beneficial for him personally but is nonetheless acceptable for all those affected, including himself, given the necessary good will! Every individual is in principle *capable* of rejecting inherent necessities. What is important is the question of the practical consequences he or she can be *reasonably expected* to accept. Why can it not be expected of an economic agent, or even be the enlightened intention of a subject who is also a moral person, that he or she should – at least to some extent and this side of heroism – abandon aims or strategies which turn out to be illegitimate or irresponsible in regard to all those involved? This has nothing to do with 'playing down' the empirical conditions for success, but is rather a matter of taking seriously or requiring the good will of the human subjects, which is constitutive of their basic moral disposition.

How far moral actions against one's own interests and the toleration of personal economic disadvantages can be regarded as reasonable within the system logic of the market is the truly 'compelling' ethical question. It cannot be answered merely by reference to empirical circumstances but only by means of a critical-normative, argumentative weighing up of all conflicting claims – including those concealed behind the system logic of the market – in conformity with the regulative idea of their universalizability.

(3) The reconstruction of the problem of inherent necessity as a problem of reasonable expectation

The principal argument against the theorem of the impossibility of moral action under market conditions insists upon the practical and socio-theoretical primacy of the perspective of action over the systems perspective.[70] After all, social systems always 'function' only as long as the personal bearers of functions 'play along'. And that depends in principle on what human subjects wish to achieve as participants in the market. Even the most radical representative of a systems theory of the market, Niklas Luhmann, does not dispute that the market economy is, in the final analysis, a system of social action whose function is fundamentally bound by the acquisitive intentions of the economic agents:

> Everybody calculates his relationship to another (in the market) *in accordance with his (private) relationship to money.*[71]

[70] J. Habermas, 'A Reply to my Critics', in J. P. Thompson/D. Held (eds.), *Habermas: Critical Debates* (Cambridge MA: MIT Press, 1982), pp. 219–83, at p. 268.

[71] N. Luhmann, *Die Wirtschaft der Gesellschaft* (Frankfurt: Suhrkamp, 1988), p. 241 (my italics).

Because of the impersonal mediation through 'money' the 'sociality of exchange is weakened'[72] but by no means abolished. The system itself only 'understands' – metaphorically speaking – the 'language' or the 'code' of monetary offers of payment, as this is its functional mechanism. But the persons acting in the market are thoroughly capable of understanding the reciprocal social effects in as far as they wish to attribute significance to them. For:

> Payments alone do not 'make' sense. Payments are rather bound by *reasons* for payments. In this way the necessary openness of the system for the (system) environment is established.[73]

It is not the market alone or the circumstances which force us to act in a particular way; it is rather our intentions and interests which encounter these circumstances and see in them an inherent necessity. And what is at issue in the market is, above all else, interest in profit and income. As Joseph Schumpeter accurately observed, 'firms and their managers' are just:

> ... *forced* ... *by their profit motive* to strain every nerve in order to maximize output and to minimize costs.[74]

Hence we are dealing less with a compulsion to maximize profits than with a reciprocal coercion of the economic agents as a result of their systemically linked orientation on income and profit. It is only the unquestioned acceptance of a presumed norm of income and profit maximization which 'forces' entrepreneurs of all kinds to consistently take advantage of the chances provided by the market. The apparent problem of the 'impossibility' of moral action under the practical constraints of competition thus turns out to be a thoroughly normative problem involving the conflict between various normative validity claims. A conceptual distinction should be made here between the normative claims in regard to (personal) *accountability* for the effects of actions on all concerned and the normative claims in regard to the *reasonableness* of moral demands on the economic actors requiring them to take the non-economic 'outside interests' into account.[75] The empirically misinterpreted 'problem of

[72] Luhmann, *Wirtschaft der Gesellschaft*, p. 241.

[73] J. Brewing, *Kritik der Unternehmensethik* (Berne *et al.*: Haupt, 1995), p. 44, following Luhmann, *Wirtschaft der Gesellschaft*, p. 59.

[74] Schumpeter, *Capitalism, Socialism and Democracy*, p. 78 (my italics).

[75] On this distinction see Th. Bausch, 'Wirtschaft und Ethik: Notizen zu einem dialogischen Brückenschlag', in Forum für Philosophie Bad Homburg (ed.), *Markt und Moral*, pp. 19–36, at p. 26. According to Bausch this conceptual distinction can be traced back to Dietrich Böhler.

(im)possibility' must therefore be reconstructed from the perspective of the actors as a problem of reasonable expectation.[76]

The fundamental ethical problem of legitimate action in the market can thus be generally understood as an entirely normative problem of potentially conflicting demands of accountability and of reasonable expectations between those involved in an economic action. There is clearly a symmetry between the two normative aspects of responsibility. The interest in self-assertion and success which the actor has must also be seriously considered as a 'candidate'[77] for possibly legitimate claims, i.e. for moral rights. As complex interdependencies can exist between the entrepreneurial willingness to invest and the fulfilment of the claims of affected persons, the interest of entrepreneurs and companies in economic self-assertion often has a very good chance of acceptance as a legitimate interest. The decisive point is, however, the obligation to justify such interests unconditionally, as they possibly conflict with other, equally legitimate claims. The proposed critical normative reconstruction of the problem of inherent necessity in the market economy is characterized by a balanced approach which neither favours a priori the rationality of entrepreneurial success in a biased fashion (as do economistic positions) nor denies (as moralistic positions sometimes do) the problem of the reasonableness of moral expectations on the entrepreneur. Instead, it understands the clarification and weighing up of all validity claims as the object of a discourse on responsibility and reasonableness based on the presentation of good reasons in each particular situation.

The decisive ethical criterion for the solution of problems of responsibility and reasonableness understood in this way can – as is always the case with normative problems – only be the argumentative universalizability of the validity claims in the sense of the intersubjective *reversibility of perspectives* between the actor and all those affected by his actions.[78] In discourse on reasonableness it is necessary in this way to

[76] See Thielemann, *Reflexion*, p. 9ff., and *Prinzip Markt*, pp. 261f., 288ff. Our conception of the problem of reasonable expectations must be distinguished from the position of Apel, who, as has been shown above (Section 3.1), remains within the limits of the approach of 'applied' discourse ethics. As a result Apel also misinterprets the problem of reasonable expectations as a problem of adverse empirical application conditions of (discourse or business) ethics; characteristically he speaks of the 'problem of the reasonableness of morality' as such, strangely translated as 'problem of the *exegebility of morality*' in Apel, 'Limits of Discourse Ethics?', p. 202. Habermas also speaks of the 'reasonableness of moral demands' as such and counterposes it to the 'given situation', *Justification and Application*, p. 87 (see the citation in note 12 of Section 3.1). He does, however, see in this a good reason for a normative solution, namely for 'the transition from morality to law', *Justification and Application*, p. 16.

[77] I take this formulation from Thielemann, *Prinzip Markt*, p. 130.

[78] Similarly Thielemann, *Prinzip Markt*, p. 262, from whom I take over the concept of reasonableness discourse.

clarify in each particular case the normative conditions under which the economic agents can be reasonably expected to turn down market opportunities, to refuse simply to 'function' as cogs in the wheel, and to take on the (co-)responsibility for the unintended systemic consequences of their actions.

With the help of normative orientational knowledge it is then possible to clarify, at least formally, the fundamental normative conditions for the reasonableness of moral demands on economic actors who are subject to the constraints of self-assertion in competitive situations. In order to overcome situational constraints of the market at the critical-normative level either a redefinition of our personal goals (preferences) or a political change in the basic external conditions of competition (restrictions) are, in principle, possible and necessary. The first starting point aims, at the individual level, at personal self-limitation (a); the second, at the institutional level, at political limitation of competition (b).

(a) Self-limitation It is precisely the normative function of the concept of purposes or *ends* to neutralize predecisions on the normative orientation of actions and to concentrate rational thinking on the means to the ends:

> The concept of ends characterizes those effects or the complex of effects which are meant to justify action and are thus always only a part of the overall complex of effects. Its 'theme' is not the realization of the specified effects but the relationship of their value to the values of side-effects (including the effects of other possibilities for action which must be abandoned when a particular commitment is chosen). The determination of ends implies that the value of the intended effects is sufficient to justify the action *regardless of the value or lack of value of the side-effects or the abandoned effects.*[79]

In other words, the setting of ends determines normatively 'a value relationship among the effects of action'[80] and we must justify this value relationship, on which we – as producers or consumers – base our economic activities, both to ourselves and to the other affected persons by giving good reasons for our decision. Should we reach the conclusion in an actual or imagined discourse with those affected that our choice of ends would 'force' us to do things we cannot approve of from a moral point of view either in regard to others or to our own principles of moral conduct, we must see it as our moral duty to give up the economic activity in question and to strive to find other forms of economic self-assertion.

[79] Luhmann, *Zweckbegriff und Systemrationalität*, p. 44 (italics in the original).
[80] Ibid., p. 44.

It can, in principle, be reasonably expected of us, firstly, that in such situations we change the concrete ends of our actions and the strategy by which we desire to achieve economic self-assertion. It is one of the standard insights of situational or contingency theoretical approaches to organization theory that the possibility exists, in principle, of making a strategic choice between constraints affecting the success of an organization or an economic agent. What this expresses is quite simply the logical primacy of our determination of ends over the practical constraints involved.

Secondly, it can, in principle, be reasonably expected that we renounce the claim to the strict maximization of personal benefits. Moreover, the strictly egoistic maximization of advantages or success is in principle not (even) a 'possibly' legitimate end, as it would be equivalent to a predetermined and fundamental disregard of all the value aspects opposed to it and hence of the primacy of legitimation over success.[81] In other words, it is possible and necessary to call for a *moral self-limitation* in the pursuit of personal success and benefit.[82] Self-assertion in competition by no means forces us to maximize uncompromisingly our private advantage in every situation. This is the decisive point at which motives in life other than the acquisitive intention are normatively 'admitted' to or excluded from the system.

Anyone who (like Handke's entrepreneur Wullnow in the quotation at the beginning of Section 4.3) goes against his better judgement in refusing to subject his pursuit of income to self-critical reflection and argumentation, thus abandoning reflection and repudiating the discourse on accountability and reasonable expectation, may in this way protect himself superficially from uncomfortable insights and moral claims on his actions. But when 'the earning of more and more money ... is thought of so purely as an end in itself'[83] and becomes an ingrained habit of thought and a normal attitude, the personality of an individual is in the long run almost inevitably deformed. The self-imposed 'notion of necessity', which serves the purpose of repressing identity threatening questions is then transformed into cynicism, into 'enlightened false consciousness', a

[81] For more detail on the significant consequences of this principle of reasonableness for corporate ethics see Chapter 10.

[82] On the scope of the (different) endeavours to justify self-limitation not for moral reasons but from motives of prudence see J. Elster, *Ulysses and the Sirens: Studies in Rationality and Irrationality* (Cambridge: Cambridge University Press, 1979), p. 36ff.; also C. Offe, 'Fessel und Bremse: moralische und institutionelle Aspekte 'intelligenter' Selbstbeschränkung' in A. Honneth *et al.* (eds.), *Zwischenbetrachtungen im Prozess der Aufklärung* (Frankfurt: Suhrkamp, 1989), pp. 739–74, at p. 784ff.

[83] Weber, *Protestant Ethic*, p. 53.

'self-cognizant accommodation which has sacrificed its better judgement to compulsions'[84]:

The compulsion to survive and desire to assert itself have demoralized enlightened consciousness. It is afflicted with the compulsion to put up with pre-established relations that it finds dubious, to accommodate itself to them, and finally even to carry out their business.[85]

Sloterdijk's concept of cynicism corresponds exactly to the attitude of strict maximization of success embodied with literary means in the figure of the entrepreneur Wullnow, who represses his moral feelings in favour of notions of inherent necessity and so reduces himself to a 'homunculus oeconomicus' whose actions are 'predetermined' and unfree. One could accordingly characterize methodological economism (Homann) as *methodological cynicism*, a point which is openly admitted, interestingly enough, by James M. Buchanan, probably the most consistent advocate of methodological economism (in the sense of the economic 'as if' approach).[86]

In contrast, in a rational discourse on the reasonableness of moral obligations, the precise purpose is to overcome the false alternatives of cynicism (which subordinates moral insights to the rationality of success) and moral heroism (which sacrifices self-assertion to moral conviction) and to clarify both the legitimate claims to self-assertion of the economic agents and the reasonableness of their self-limitation. But, as we have seen above, the effects of competition are in principle illimitable and are transmitted to innumerable economic agents. Consequently, in the question of the general conditions for the self-assertion of all agents, the 'site' of the economic-ethical discourse on the reasonableness of self-limitation can ultimately only be the public realm of all economic citizens.[87]

(b) The limitation of competition The more intensive competition is, the more it develops its inherently coercive character. In an imagined borderline case of total competition (i.e. totally without rules and limits), almost any consideration of 'outside interests' would be overdemanding for an entrepreneur. But when the economic disadvantages resulting

[84] P. Sloterdijk, *Critique of Cynical Reason* (London/New York: Verso, 1987), pp. 5 and 7.
[85] Sloterdijk, *Critique of Cynical Reason*, p. 6.
[86] See Brennan/Buchanan, *Reason of Rules*, pp. 47, 55 and 58. Methodological cynicism begins with the intellectual experiment as to whether an institutional arrangement would still function in the 'worst possible case', when all individuals behave as strictly self-interested homines oeconomici, and culminates in the normative conversion of this 'worst case' into the principle for the formation of a *good* society. On this 'homo oeconomicus' test of social institutions see Section 5.3 (1).
[87] The concept of economic citizenship will be developed in Section 7.3.

from the consideration of such interests are relatively slight for the individual actor, the abandonment of them can be reasonably expected. In such 'low-cost situations'[88] he may even be quite willing to give up the strict pursuit of his own interests. Consequently it is the ethical duty of institutional politics to set up legally binding 'rules of the game' and conditions limiting competition, which apply equally to all economic agents and thus generally exclude certain immoral options of strictly self-interested behaviour. In this way a normative framework can be established which determines and delimits the acceptability of the inherent necessities of competition between economic agents who attempt to assert themselves on the market by increasing their competitiveness. If legal norms clearly define what has absolute priority over the demands of competition, the economic players are then at least relieved, in extreme situations involving moral dilemmas, of the necessity to choose between personal and 'outside' interests and can be reasonably expected to follow the moral norms.[89] From this perspective institutional politics should be envisaged as *politics for the limitation of inherent necessities*. Only when the pressure of competition is restricted can individual self-limitation be reasonably expected.

We will deal in more detail in Chapter 9 with the manifold problems of institutional politics. For the moment a reference to the two (possible) approaches to the limitation of competition and its inherent necessities will suffice:

Firstly, institutional control over the *effective direction* of market competition is possible through the establishment of economic incentives and 'disincentives' which change the calculations of individual economic agents and consequently make the choice of alternative success strategies economically more interesting. The corresponding central idea of institutional ethics is to organize the price signals of the market in such a way that socially desired behaviour (e.g. environmental protection, energy saving measures, creation of employment) is 'rewarded' by the market or at least involves only slight cost disadvantages for individuals, whereas morally questionable behaviour is subject to sustained 'punishment', if not directly forbidden by law. The constraining effects of the market are then utilized as a controlling device in the service of superordinate ethical-political goals, which themselves of course require legitimation.

[88] On this point see H. Kliemt, 'The Veil of Insignificance', *European Journal of Political Economy* 2/3 (1986), pp. 333–44; G. Kirchgässner, 'Towards a Theory of Low-Cost Decisions', *European Journal of Political Economy* 8 (1992), pp. 305–20.

[89] See also M. Kettner, 'Wie ist eine diskursethische Begründung ökologischer Rechts- und Moralnormen möglich?', in J. Nida-Rümelin/D. v. d. Pfordten (eds.), *Ökologische Ethik und Rechtstheorie* (Baden-Baden: Nomos, 1995), pp. 301–23, at p. 302.

Secondly, where the problem is not so much the effective direction competitiveness takes as the coercive effect itself – perhaps because it is inevitably biased in favour of the 'entrepreneurial' life project and works against social forms of interaction and integration – competition as such must be restricted.[90] Because of the already mentioned self-dynamics of competition this is in principle possible only by means of *market restrictions*. It is after all not necessary that the principle of market co-ordination should dominate all spheres of life. An ethically oriented policy of market restriction can of course be perceived as a practical and rational postulate only as long as the market itself has not acquired an ideologically exaggerated normative status as the guarantor of a morally correct social order. This 'necessarily' leads us to the critique of the second, no less momentous manifestation of economism, namely the critique of the 'morality' of the market.

[90] On this thesis see Thielemann, *Prinzip Markt*, p. 339ff., and 'Brief Theory', p. 21ff.

5 'Morality' of the market? A critique of economic reductionism

> The cunning of the market leads to an overall economic benefit and thus to a good end which definitely stands up moral evaluation.[1]

Apart from economic determinism, according to which economic ethics seems systematically impossible (supposed *Sachzwänge*), there is a second, no less common objection that this endeavour is not only impossible but also systematically unnecessary and superfluous. Economic ethics is then passed off as being even damaging and dangerous, as it approaches in a moralizing fashion complex relationships which are best coordinated or should even be exclusively coordinated by the market itself. The anonymous functional logic of the competitive system is not then perceived as the problem but, on the contrary, as the solution of (almost) all ethical problems in society. The market itself is regarded as the best 'guarantor'[2] that everything is in the best of order from an ethical point of view. If only it is allowed to function, the market mechanism seems to be the great harmonizer, reconciling the conflicting interests of society of its own accord. Adam Smith was the first to put his finger on this function of competition as a (partial) substitute for normative social integration in a famous statement still enormously popular among 'liberal' economists and economic practitioners:

> It is not from the benevolence of the butcher, the brewer, or the baker that we expect our dinner, but from their regard to their own interest. We address ourselves, not to their humanity but to their self-love, and never talk to them of our own necessities, but of their advantages.[3]

[1] M. Gentz, 'Wirtschaftsethik in der Unternehmensführung', in J. Wieland (ed.), *Wirtschaftsethik und Theorie der Gesellschaft*, pp. 92–108, at p. 92f. (Dr Manfred Gentz has been a member of the board of directors of DaimlerChrysler and is now president of the Zurich Financial Services Group.)

[2] Ibid., p. 93. On the variants of this guarantor concept of the common good in the history of thought of political economy see Ulrich, 'Towards an Ethically-based Conception'.

[3] Smith, *Wealth of Nations*, p. 26f.

The exaggerated elevation of private interest to normative status as a principle serving the general good, which this central idea implies, need not apparently be regarded or justified as a normative postulate as long as it appears in the form of objective inherent necessity. If this were really the case, there would, on the one hand, be 'no place'[4] in the market for moral motives for their own sake; and, on the other hand, moral motives would be completely unnecessary, as the economic necessities themselves would ensure that everything turned out well for all participants in market activity. This potential for the harmonization of conflicting interests, the 'cunning of the market' (Gentz), consists in the supposed guarantee that when the economic agents eagerly pursue their private interests they will at the same time make the greatest possible contribution to the common good, as if everything were guided by an invisible hand (Adam Smith). The more efficiently the economy functions, the better it serves the common good (whatever that might be). The assumption that the pursuit of private interests automatically promotes the common good permits us to understand what is possibly the most radical, totally unrestricted normative transfiguration of competition, as it is propagated by Karl Homann:

> Competition is more solidary than sharing.[5]

If we assume that the 'common good' were an adequate criterion for the moral point of view (principle of universalization) and that it would best be served by the 'market principle', then liberal economics, by following this principle, would at the same time have the 'better ethics' – an 'ethics with other means'.[6] And this 'ethics with other means' would paradoxically achieve ethical-normative validity by strictly observing the functional conditions of the market system. The underlying assumption that moral questions can be totally and exhaustively transformed into economic questions[7] and can thus be reduced to economic categories must be characterized as *economic reductionism*. Economic reductionism can be recognized by its symptomatic and apparently 'logical' consequence that a 'remoralization'[8] of the economy is unnecessary and even ethically

[4] Homann, 'Philosophie und Ökonomik', p. 111.
[5] Homann/Blome-Drees, *Wirtschafts- und Unternehmensethik*, p. 111.
[6] Homann, 'Ethik und Ökonomik', p. 13.
[7] Homann (ibid., p. 16) is once again a good example: 'If economics is to be understood as ethics with other means, it must in principle be possible to reconstruct all economic analyses in terms of ethics. *The same applies the other way round.*' Or: 'Morality must be reformatted in the code of the economy, or translated into it', Homann, 'Wirtschaftsethik: Die Funktion der Moral', p. 47.
[8] See ibid., pp. 44, 33: 'A remoralization of the economy is out of the question' as 'every remoralization of action in differentiated sub-systems [of society] is not only disturbing; it even leads to an erosion of morality.'

questionable or 'socially damaging',[9] as economic-ethical problems are best solved by means of pure economism. This in turn would make an independent economic ethics which deviated from the logic and inherent morality of economism redundant; it would only 'disturb'[10] the beneficent operations of the invisible hand, the assumed inherent morality of the market.

The question that interests us here is: Why are so many economic practitioners and theorists so influenced by the 'neoliberal turn' that they are still willing, perhaps even more so than ever before, uncritically and docilely to accept the inherent necessities of the market as a guarantee for the ethical quality of economic activity? In what follows we will illuminate that the after-effects of the metaphysics of the market deeply rooted in the early 'modern economic ethos' (Weber) are of greater significance than we usually realize. Their systematic function is to free us from the obligation (treated in the last chapter) to unconditionally legitimize and take on full personal responsibility for our economic activities. They achieve this by creating the wonderful apparition of an impersonal and consequently impartial purposefulness of the market mechanism 'to the benefit of all'. This metaphysical *fiction of the common good* is still causing mischief in a variety of forms even today as far as it permits an economistic abandonment of reflection in the face of the ethical problems involved in justifying the ends and principles of economic activity – even after the untenability of economic determinism (the argument of inherent necessity) has been admitted.

It is consequently necessary to subject economic reductionism to an uncompromising ideological critique in the light of the central idea of integrative economic ethics, which is to integrate the ethical legitimating of the purposes of action under the concept of rational economic activity and to understand why the 'inherent logic' of the market as it is generally understood cannot of itself be a sufficient criterion of economic reason in an ethically adequate and meaningful sense. We will approach this task in three steps corresponding to the historical development of the theoretical concepts of economic reductionism: from the general normative convictions of the classical representatives of political economy (Section 5.1)

[9] D. Schneider, 'Unternehmensethik und Gewinnprinzip in der Betriebswirtschaftslehre', *Zeitschrift für betriebswirtschaftliche Forschung (ZfbF)* 42 (1990), pp. 869–91, at p. 883. See the rejoinder of P. Ulrich, 'Schwierigkeiten mit der unternehmensethischen Herausforderung', *Zeitschrift für betriebswirtschaftliche Forschung (ZfbF)* 43 (1991), pp. 529–36.

[10] This is also the position of E. Hoppmann, 'Moral und Marktsystem', *Ordo* 41 (1990), pp. 3–26; H. Giersch, 'Die Moral der offenen Märkte', *Frankfurter Allgemeine Zeitung*, No. 64, 16 March 1991, p. 13, quoted in Homann, 'Die Funktion der Moral', p. 32.

to the older neoclassical economics based on utilitarian principles (Section 5.2) and finally to the pure economics of the most recent versions of neoclassical theory, which are consistently built on an individualistic and contractarian (contract-ethical) foundation (Section. 5.3).

5.1 Historical and doctrinal background I: the prestabilized harmony in the economic cosmos (classical period)

The intellectual and spiritual roots of the metaphysics of the market are to be found in the 'spirit of capitalism' as unfolded by Max Weber.[11] The 'release of acquisitive activity'[12] and the corresponding trust in the 'invisible hand' of the market must be seen against the background of the theology of creation, according to which 'the world is a God-ordained, and hence somehow *meaningfully* and ethically oriented, cosmos.'[13] Behind the natural order of the cosmos the ordering hand of God can be assumed, who has purposefully arranged the course of nature in accordance with his plans. The interpretation of the entire cosmos as a great household (!) of God corresponds to this metaphysical-teleological aspect of the Christian world-view.[14] The cosmic *Oikos* is ruled by the planned purposes of the creator although these may at times remain unfathomable to our limited human understanding.

The resultant trust in a divinely *prestabilized harmony* (Leibniz) of the cosmic *Oikos*, as reflected in natural law, also determined the thinking of the classical advocates of liberal political economy. This is particularly true of the thinking of Adam Smith:

> In every part of the universe we observe means adjusted with the nicest artifice to the ends which they are intended to produce ...[15]

Particularly in the social world, however, this purposeful order is not always immediately evident. In his *Theory of Moral Sentiments*, for example, Smith observed something which at first appeared to him as an 'irregularity of sentiment',[16] namely the tendency of people to judge actions more in terms of their *success* than from the standpoint of the impartial spectator. But, of course, it was possible, within the framework

[11] See Section 4.1. [12] Weber, *Protestant Ethic*, p. 172.

[13] Weber, *From Max Weber*, p. 351. Probably the most comprehensive study of the theological background to liberal economics can still be found in A. Rüstow, *Das Versagen des Wirtschaftsliberalismus*, 3rd edn, ed. F. P. and M. Maier-Rigaud (Marburg: Metropolis, 2001; 1st edn 1945).

[14] See P. Koslowski, *Ethik des Kapitalismus*, 3rd edn (Tübingen: Mohr Siebeck, 1986), p. 31ff.

[15] Smith, *Moral Sentiments*, p. 87. [16] Ibid., pp. 93, 104ff.

of a teleological understanding of the world, to interpret this tendency, which seems at first sight so problematic for just social co-existence, as an expression of what 'is in reality the wisdom of God':[17]

Nature, however, when she implanted the seeds of this irregularity in the human breast, seems, as upon all other occasions, to have *intended* the happiness and perfection of the species.[18]

Accordingly the human pursuit of success must be a thoroughly 'salutary and useful irregularity'.[19] This conviction is the root of Smith's idea of placing the individual pursuit of economic success in the service of the good and just order. The next and final step is then to see free market economy as the 'natural economic order'[20] in order to be sure that the well-ordered ends of divine creation and the corresponding means to those ends will also have a beneficial effect in the 'economic cosmos' of the market.[21] With the application of this teleological world-view rooted in natural law and Christian belief (God as the great goal-setter) to the market economy the question of the ends of meaningful and just economic activity was also handed over to a higher instance. The impersonality and anonymity of the market mechanism now appeared as a sign that the great plans of the creator 'direct' the personal interest of his 'instruments' (Luther), i.e. human beings as economic agents, 'into the field of objective (impersonal) activity', as the higher ends of God 'could only be impersonal'.[22] The impersonal objectivity of the market signals can thus be interpreted as an expression of the supposed impartiality of the market.[23] Hence the anonymous coercive structure of the market itself guarantees that the human subjects do good because they are acting in

[17] Ibid., p. 87. On the deistic background to Smith see M. Büscher, 'Gott und Markt – religionsgeschichtliche Wurzeln Adam Smiths und die 'Invisible Hand' in der säkularisierten Industriegesellschaft', in Meyer-Faje/Ulrich (eds.), *Der andere Adam Smith*, pp. 123–44.

[18] Smith, *Moral Sentiments*, p. 105 (my italics). [19] Ibid., p. 105.

[20] The strikingly frequent use of the magic word 'natural' as the norm of what is right can be found in almost all of the economic theory of the classical and neoclassical periods and clearly indicates the natural law background to these convictions. On this point and the teleological world view it directly reflects see Ulrich, *Transformation*, p. 180ff.

[21] Weber, *Protestant Ethic*, p. 160, and *From Max Weber*, p. 355. The 'assumption of a correspondence between social and cosmic structure' is the root of all variants of 'social metaphysics'. It may be teleological or mechanistic, depending on the underlying cosmological conception. For this reason, as Koslowski (*Ethik des Kapitalismus*, pp. 29, 32) accurately points out, 'the type of economic theory a person advocates [is] always very closely linked to the standpoint he adopts in regard to the methodological or mechanistic conception of the cosmos'.

[22] Weber, *Protestant Ethic*, p. 108, n. 30.

[23] This reminds us of Smith's conception of the moral point of view as the ideal standpoint of an impartial spectator. On this see Section 2.2.

accordance with the unfathomable ends of God. Consequently they ought to let themselves be guided by these ends. In this way the *market* – and not the weak moral power of man – is interpreted as *the site of morality.*[24]

It is only against the background of this internal morality of the market guaranteed by a higher hand that Adam Smith's by no means unlimited trust in the 'simple system of natural liberty' can be understood.

All systems either of preference or restraint, therefore, being thus completely taken away, the obvious and simple system of natural liberty establishes itself of its own accord. Every man, as long as he does not violate the laws of justice, is left perfectly free to pursue his own interest in his own way, and to bring both his industry and capital into competition with those of any other man, or order of men ... According to the system of natural liberty, the sovereign has only three duties to attend to; three duties of great importance, indeed, but plain and intelligible to common understandings: first, the duty of protecting the society from the violence and invasion of other independent societies; secondly, *the duty of protecting, as far as possible, every member of the society from the injustice or oppression of every other member of it*, or the duty of establishing an exact administration of justice; and thirdly, the duty of erecting and maintaining certain publick works and certain publick institutions, which it can never be for the interest of any individual, or small number of individuals, to erect and maintain; because the profit could never repay the expense.[25]

Here Smith not only presupposes unequivocally the existence of a pre-stabilized harmony of the economic cosmos but also the exercise of justice under the rule of law. He elaborates its fundamental significance and its foundations in ethical virtue in an impressive passage of the *Theory of Moral Sentiments*:

Justice ... is the main pillar that upholds the whole edifice. If it is removed, the great, the immense fabric of human society ... must in moment crumble into atoms. In order to enforce the observation of justice, therefore, Nature has implanted in the human breast that consciousness of ill-desert, those terrors of merited punishment which attend upon its violation, as the great safeguards of the association of mankind, to protect the weak, to curb the violent, and to chastise the guilty.[26]

As a premise for the 'simple system of natural liberty' Smith, therefore, presupposes a truly complex image of man, namely as a citizen who is, on the one hand, a moral person with a very strong sense of justice and, on the other, a wealthy property owner who pursues his private economic 'interests', following as a matter of course the acquisitive principle ('to

24 For details on this 'cunning of the economic system' which is interpreted as meaningful in Smith's moral philosophy see Ulrich, 'Der kritische Adam Smith', p. 170ff.

25 Smith, *Wealth of Nations*, p. 687f. (my italics).

26 Ibid., p. 86.

bring both his industry and capital into competition'). These two thoroughly contrary aspects are imposingly synthesized in the Protestant economic ethos, which gains particular practical momentum in the form of the (early) modern *entrepreneurial ethos*. For when the creator 'shows one of His elect a chance of profit, he must do it with a purpose'.[27] As a result of this localization of the site of morality in the 'signs' the market gives the entrepreneur, and hence in his calculations of success, he can feel disburdened in principle of direct moral claims on his actions.

Consequently, liberal political economy could from the outset view the problem of legitimizing private entrepreneurial aims as solved in an impersonal fashion because it was subsumed under the inherent necessities of competition. For this reason Adam Smith could also rest assured that the businessman who:

> ... intends only his own gain ... is in this, as in many other cases, led by an *invisible hand* to promote an end which was no part of his intention.[28]

But what is this hidden purpose unintended by the economic agents yet guaranteed by a higher hand? It is, 'naturally', the common good. It was Smith who coined the metaphysical metaphor of the *invisible hand* for this notion of the impersonal (systemic!) integration of a society of free citizens through the unintended consequences of their actions in the pursuit of personal interest, yet he by no means discovered the idea it characterizes. He took it from Montesquieu, who had formulated it in the context of aspirations to political fame and had himself taken it from earlier philosophers.[29] Smith uses the famous metaphor of the invisible hand in his two major works *The Theory of Moral Sentiments* (1759) and *The Wealth of Nations* (1776) once in each and only in passing.[30] He is much more interested in the thoroughly modern issue of clarifying the way in which interlocking economic interests function systemically in the market as a *partial substitute* for the imperfect inter-subjective correspondence (reciprocity) of moral sentiments ('sympathy').[31] The

[27] Weber, *Protestant Ethic*, p. 162. [28] Smith, *Wealth of Nations*, p. 456 (my italics).

[29] Ch. de Montesquieu, *The Spirit of Laws*, ed. by D. W. Carrithers, based on Th. Naugent's translation (London: Nourse, 1750) of the first French ed. (Berkeley CA: University of California Press, 1977; orig. Geneva: Barillot, 1748), p. 122 [book III, chap. vii]: 'Each individual advances the public good, while he only thinks of promoting his own particular interest.' See also G. Streminger, *Der natürliche Lauf der Dinge: Essay zu Adam Smith und David Hume* (Marburg: Metropolis, 1995), p. 172f. On the politico-philosophical origins of the idea of the orientation on the common good incorporated in the pursuit of personal interest see A. O. Hirschman, *The Passions and the Interests: Political Arguments for Capitalism before its Triumph* (Princeton NJ: Princeton University Press, 1977).

[30] Smith, *Moral Sentiments*, p. 184; *Wealth of Nations*, p. 456.

[31] For details see Ulrich, 'Der kritische Adam Smith', p. 170ff.; on the correspondence of moral sentiments see Section 2.2.

integrative efficiency of the economic system in ethical matters can be only partial for Smith precisely because the invisible hand of God not only guides 'the simple system of natural liberty' in the market but also promotes the correspondence of moral sentiments with a view to achieving harmony between humans. Consequently Smith remains totally immune to all tendencies towards radicalism in the market or towards technocratic ideas of an autonomous 'free market' as the panacea for all the deficiencies of social organization, as they were later to become typical of the radical neo- and ultra-liberals of the 20th century.

Nonetheless, the metaphysics of the market seems to have substantially reduced the 'consciousness of ill-desert' in the 'breasts' (Adam Smith) of some contemporaries of bourgeois conviction in the very early stages of capitalist development, in spite of the all-too-evident social injustice of the time. The presupposition of justice, which was indispensable for Smith, was increasingly glossed over and the metaphysics of the market – sailing under the flag of an economistically truncated interpretation of Smith – acquired its historically decisive ideological function for economic liberalism and for its characteristic exaggeration of the normative status of the entrepreneurial pursuit of profit, as Max Weber has pointed out:

> With the consciousness of standing in the fullness of God's grace and being visibly blessed by Him (by the 'sign' of success), the bourgeois business man, as long as he remained within the bounds of formal correctness, was spotless and the use to which he put his wealth was not objectionable, could follow his pecuniary interests as he would and feel that he was fulfilling a duty in doing so.[32]

How little has changed in this regard for the representatives of classic and neoliberalism[33] can be documented by two typical quotations, one from an economic practitioner and the other from an economic theorist:

> There is no contradiction between what is required economically and what is morally right [for the entrepreneur in the market economy]; they coincide; it does not contradict morality, therefore, but is in fact *the moral duty of the entrepreneur* to do everything [sic!] which is in accordance with his company's rationale in order to keep the company 'fit'.[34]

[32] Weber, *Protestant Ethic*, p. 176–77. As late as 1932 the Protestant economic moral philosopher Georg Wünsch ('Wirtschaftsethik', p. 276) was convinced that 'economic activity serves the purposes of God' and tersely stated: 'The yardstick for the moral 'ought' is the autonomy of the economy.'

[33] On the dividing line between old and neoliberalism see Section 9.1.

[34] G. Habermann, 'Teilen oder produzieren? Bemerkungen zum Ethos des Unternehmers', *Neue Zürcher Zeitung*, N° 211, 11/12 September 1993, p. 31f. See the reply of P. Ulrich, 'Zwei Ebenen unternehmerischer Verantwortung', *Neue Zürcher Zeitung*, N° 232, 6 October 1993, p. 39.

Long-term profit maximization is ... not a privilege of the entrepreneurs for which they must continually apologize; it is rather their moral duty, because – presuming the existence of a suitable institutional framework – it is precisely this behaviour which best serves the interests of the consumers, the general public.[35]

This so-called principle of profit maximization has played such a basic ideological role in the past (and continues to do so today perhaps more than ever before) that justification or criticism of it is still of fundamental significance, particularly in regard to the question of the necessity or superfluity of economic ethics in present-day discussions.[36]

Liberal political economy has also failed to free itself of its paradigmatic predecision in favour of the 'market principle'. Since the days of Adam Smith it has repeatedly attempted to prove with new theoretical arguments that the 'natural' forces in the market cosmos are capable by themselves of harmonizing all social conflicts in regard to interests, values and norms, and of serving the general interest or public good, provided that man with his limited reason does not disturb this inherent harmony of the market system with interventionist measures. How deeply the *belief* in the free market is rooted in the religious cosmology was expressed above all by the classic French author Frédéric Bastiat (1801–1850) in his major work 'Harmonies économiques' (1849):

If the laws of providence are harmonious, they can be so only when they operate under conditions of *freedom*, for otherwise harmony is lacking. Therefore, when we perceive something inharmonious in the world, it cannot fail to correspond to some lack of freedom or justice.[37]

In the following credo Bastiat emphasizes that this is also particularly true of the social world:

I believe that He who designed the physical world has not seen fit to remain a stranger to the social world. I believe that His wisdom extends to human agents possessed of free will, that He has been able to bring them together and cause them to move in harmony, even as he has done with inert molecules. (...) I believe that the inevitable trend of society is toward a constantly rising physical, intellectual, and moral level shared by all mankind. I believe, if only man can win

[35] Homann/Blome/Drees, *Wirtschafts- und Unternehmensethik*, p. 38f. The role of the institutional framework of the market will be dealt with later, in Chapter 9.

[36] On the astounding persistence of belief in the *morality of the market* in the thinking of present-day economic practitioners see Ulrich/Thielemann, 'How Do Managers Think?'; for more details see Ulrich/Thielemann, *Ethik und Erfolg*, p. 34ff. For a critique of the 'profit principle' see Section 10.1.

[37] F. Bastiat, *Economic Harmonies*, transl. from the French by W. H. Boyers; ed. by G. B. de Huszar (Princeton NJ: Van Nostrand, 1964), p. xxxiv (my italics).

back his freedom of action and be allowed to follow his natural bent without interference, that his gradual, peaceful development is assured.[38]

In more recent years the twofold manifestation of the metaphysics of the market – complete trust in the internal morality of the market on the one hand, profound mistrust in the ethical-practical rationality of humans on the other – has been expressed with particular clarity by Friedrich A. von Hayek. He glorifies the 'spontaneous order of the market'[39] and its pre-eminent qualities as a knowledge creating 'discovery procedure'[40] in a kind of *revelation theory of the market*; at the same time he repeatedly warns against the dangers of 'constructivist' interventions in the 'natural' harmony of the market, emphasizing the inadequacy of human reason as a shaping force in economic life:

The interesting point about this [the order of the free market economy] is that men developed these rules without really understanding their functions.[41]

The ethical-political problem of embedding the market economy in a rational order is thus subliminally reduced to the naturalistic and evolutionistic postulate that the development of the system should be left to its own natural and fortuitous dynamics (postulate of *laissez-faire*):

The natural course of things cannot be entirely controlled by the impotent endeavours of man.[42]

We must mentally add: And that is the way it should be. The potentially heretical presumptuousness of man in believing that he can arrange the world better than God is the real 'basic error of constructivism', a conviction which explains the perceptibly moral emotional overtones of Hayek's writings on the topic.[43] For this kind of classic or paleoliberal natural law thinking any attempt to subject the natural evolution of the economic system to conscious rational shaping, for example with social or ecological intentions, will ultimately always be seen as a self-aggrandizement and elevation of man above the well-ordered divine creation, which he cannot 'really understand' (Hayek). What is more, social 'constructivism', whose worst form is seen in the ideas of socialism, is ultimately

[38] Ibid., p. xxxvi.
[39] See F.A. von Hayek, 'The Errors of Constructivism', in von Hayek, *New Studies in Philosophy, Politics, Economics and the History of Ideas* (Chicago: University of Chicago Press, 1978), pp. 3–22, at p. 15.
[40] Von Hayek, 'Competition as a Discovery Procedure', in Hayek, *New Studies*, pp. 179–90.
[41] Von Hayek, 'The Errors of Constructivism', p. 10.
[42] Smith, *Theory of Moral Sentiments*, p. 168.
[43] In this context one should also note the way Hayek speaks of the 'pretence of knowledge'. See Von Hayek, 'The Pretence of Knowledge', in his *New Studies*, pp. 23–34.

felt to be a form of blasphemy by all the metaphysicians of the market. The reverse of the almost unlimited (basic) trust of the classical liberal economists in the self-regulating power of the free market (*harmony economics*) is a deep-rooted, equally religious mistrust in the moral strength and practical reason of humans as immature 'children of God' (ethical scepticism), whose roots can again be found in Adam Smith:

> I have never known much good done by those who affected to trade for the public good.[44]

It is in any case not necessary to think of the common good in an economic and social cosmos guided by the invisible hand of God. It would not even meet with the approval of God, as 'God helps those who help themselves'.[45] This corresponds entirely to the Calvinist doctrine of predestination, according to which private success in life is a sign of election. As a result, it is not success in business which is morally suspect but the lack of success in business and social life: the 'punishment' of the market (including the labour market!) is the proof. Any pangs of conscience an entrepreneur who maximizes his success might have can be eased by the religiously guaranteed:

> comforting assurance that the unequal distribution of the goods of this world was a special dispensation of Divine Providence, which in these differences, as in particular grace, pursued secret ends unknown to men.[46]

Or to quote Smith once again:

> The administration of the great system of the universe, however, the care of the universal happiness of all rational and sensible beings, is the business of God and not of man.[47]

In the final analysis this explains not only the lack of moral inhibitions in the capitalist acquisitive spirit but also the striking social insensitivity towards the unsuccessful and those in need of help, which has always characterized economic liberalism. It probably also explains the crusading, dogmatic inflexibility with which the economic liberals of the 19th century defended their *laissez-faire* doctrine in spite of the ever-worsening social disharmony and conflict of the time. The result was the long-lasting repression of the social question and the consequent political radicalization at the beginning of the 20th century (fascism on the one hand, communism on the other) in industrial society and, furthermore, the aggravation of the international question of growing inequality and

[44] Smith, *Wealth of Nations*, p. 456. [45] Weber, *Protestant Ethic*, p. 115.
[46] Ibid., p. 177. [47] Smith, *Theory of Moral Sentiments*, p. 237.

instability in world trade due to the absolute and unconditional advocacy of the doctrine of free trade up to the outbreak of the First World War.

The highly questionable social and ethical aspects of the doctrine of laissez-faire and its catastrophic consequences for trade and politics world-wide – First World War, Black Friday, The Great Depression of the 1930s, the rise of fascism and communism as a reaction, and, finally, the Second World War and forty-five years of the Cold War and the Iron Curtain – profoundly impressed economic policy and economic theory after 1945. Practical consequences imbued with a clear will to shape and order the politico-economic sphere (Keynesianism, ordoliberalism and the Social Market Economy[48]) were drawn. But with the neoliberal turning point of the 1980s, which began with Reagonomics and Thatcherism and found expression in the debates of the 1990s on 'deregulation' and the 'unaffordability' of the welfare state, the old 'mystical readiness to accept the social consequences of economic improvement, whatever they might be'[49] made a comeback in radical neoliberal circles in the context of the growing toughness of global competition. This probably also provides a partial explanation for the hesitant attitude of economic-liberal circles towards the urgent need for an ecological reform of the market economy.

Those who have learnt the lessons of a reading of 20th century history will realize that, in view of the unsolved 'new' social questions of today (growing unemployment, the two-thirds society) and the (awesome) ecological and global problems we face, it is an urgent task of modern economic ethics and a truly liberal political economy to demystify the revival of market fundamentalism as the old worship of the market in a quite literal sense.

5.2 Historical and doctrinal background II: the utilitarian fiction of common good (early neoclassical period)

In the second half of the 19th century the anachronistic nature of the underlying assumptions of classical political economy deriving from metaphysics and natural law became increasingly conspicuous. Two aspects of the process of modernization played a significant role:

- *Economic modernization* during the 'great boom' effectuated by the unbridled dynamics of libertarian capitalism in an unprecedented quarter century of growth, which the renowned economic and social historian Eric Hobsbawm[50] dates from 1848–1875, brought with it the unpleasant side-effects of industrialization: the uprooting of the

[48] See Section 9.1. [49] Polanyi, *Great Transformation*, p. 33.
[50] E. J. Hobsbawm, *The Age of Capital, 1848–1875* (London: Encore, 1975).

agrarian population, the rise of an industrial labour force and the posing of the 'social question' mentioned above. In view of the growing awareness of the consequences of economic rationalization, the division of society into winners and losers, and the resulting ideological polarization between (economic) liberalism and the rising forces of socialism and Marxism, belief in the impartiality of the 'market principle' lost its innocence.

- *Cultural modernization*, which Weber impressively characterized as the 'demystification of the world',[51] and the tendency towards secularization it brought forth, has led since the beginning of the modern era to a progressive emancipation of science from the theological 'revelation church of knowledge'. In the last third of the 19th century this development had a profound impact on thinking in the humanities and social sciences. Political economy, which by and large continued to regard itself as value-oriented economic philosophy in the classical tradition until about 1870, no longer met the requirements of the new methodological ideal of a value-free nomological science taken over from the natural sciences (positivism and scientism).[52]

From about 1870 both elements played a part in the endeavours of the neoclassical thinkers to bring about a fundamental transformation of political economy into pure economics. The aim of establishing the

[51] Weber, *Protestant Ethic*, p. 105. Parsons translates Weber's 'Entzauberung' here with 'elimination of magic'.

[52] In the German-speaking countries the debate on the understanding of economics and the social sciences, well known as the 'value judgement dispute', was triggered off by Max Weber and was fought out in the *Verein für Sozialpolitik* in 1909. The 'Verein' originally stood for a *value-oriented*, socially and politically committed position, as its name recalls. Max Weber's call for a strict separation of (value free) science and normative postulates at first met with stiff resistance, but then gradually asserted itself, although by no means in the way Weber intended. In '"Objectivity" in Social Science and Social Policy', in *The Methodology of the Social Sciences: Max Weber*, transl. and ed. E. A. Shils and H. A. Finch (New York: Free Press, 1949), pp. 49–122, Weber presented a differentiated argument for an understanding of economics as a cultural science that was to be kept value-free internally but nevertheless clearly and indispensably value-based in its assumptions: 'There is no absolutely 'objective' scientific analysis of culture' (p. 72), for 'without the investigator's evaluative *ideas*, there would be no principle of selection of subject matter and no meaningful knowledge of the concrete reality ... Cultural science ... *involves* 'subjective' presuppositions ... to which we attach cultural *significance*' (p. 82). With great foresight Weber (p. 63ff.) argued against the 'one-sidedness of the economic approach' and its expansion to a 'general social science' (p. 67) and for a methodological approach to the knowledge-constitutive 'evaluative ideas'. At this early stage he already recognized the ideal-typical method *(as if)* as the adequate form of scientific understanding for the 'abstract economic theories' (p. 89ff.). But the neoclassical economism of the Anglo-Saxon type remained uninfluenced by Weber's conception, at first following instead the path via marginal utility theory and its hedonistic vulgar psychology to a shallow positivistic understanding of science, as we shall see in what follows.

reputation of economics as an impartial objective science befitting the times required, according to the new scientistic understanding of the discipline, the elimination of the socio-political problem of the distribution of wealth, as this could not be solved without value judgements. Consequently a process of mathematical formalization and progressive 'purification'[53] of economics from ideological premises was set in motion.

We cannot deal in detail with this development in the history of theory in its neoclassical phase here. It is sufficient to indicate the path taken in principle in the pursuit of a 'rationalization' of the normative foundations of the discipline. The neoclassics chose in fact to replace the old assumptions deriving from metaphysics and natural law with *utilitarian ethics*, which had become the dominant approach to a rational grounding of norms in the Anglo-Saxon world since the time of Jeremy Bentham.[54] Because of its fundamental affinity with economic thinking, namely its conception of calculatory rationality, it seemed ideally suited for 'application' in the sphere of economics. The new premises of neoclassical economics, which all derive from utilitarian ethics, can be classified under three elementary points: (1) ethical hedonism, (2) the utilitarian principle, and (3) the maximum theorem of the market economy.

(1) Ethical hedonism

It is assumed that the highest aim of the individual is the maximization of pleasure or utility.[55] Human needs are regarded as unlimited and the available goods are accordingly always scarce. We are dealing here in the first place with an assertion about the nature of man (psychological hedonism). But when the 'conclusion' is drawn that a greater degree of need satisfaction (by means of the available goods) is better than a lesser degree (ethical hedonism) a norm creeps in, namely the norm that the subjective satisfaction of needs *ought to be maximized.* This is by no means an ethically justified norm, but rather a naturalistic fallacy that shifts from (apparent) 'being' to an 'ought', as is illustrated by the famous opening sentences of Jeremy Bentham's utilitarian ethics:

[53] See Krüsselberg, 'Property-Rights-Theorie und Wohlfahrtsökonomik', p. 58.

[54] J. Bentham, *An Introduction to the Principles of Morals and Legislation*, ed. J. H. Burns and H. L. A. Hart (London: University of London, Athlone Press, 1970; 1st edn 1789).

[55] In the course of doctrinal history the hedonistic premises underlying utilitarian ethics and the subjectivistic equation of happiness, need satisfaction and utility of goods enter economics via the marginal utility theory (marginalistic revolution). On this point see B. Biervert/J. Wieland, 'Der ethische Gehalt ökonomischer Kategorien – Beispiel: Der Nutzen', in Biervert and Wieland (eds.), *Ökonomische Theorie und Ethik*, pp. 23–50.

> Nature has placed mankind under the governance of two sovereign masters, pain and pleasure. It is for them alone to point out what we ought to do as well as to determine what we shall do.[56]

The naturalistic fallacy lies in the equation of 'what we shall do' (empirical hypothesis) with 'what we ought to do' (normative requirement). This is not a case of unintentional faulty reasoning but of the old philosophical identification in natural law of 'what is natural' with 'what is ethically good'.

As we have seen above, the normative charge of the hedonistic premises is concealed as they are clothed in an axiomatic form. The maximization of utility is not directly demanded but is defined as 'rational' individual behaviour. But of course the characterization of a form of behaviour as rational itself has normative significance, as rationality is an orientational concept whose practical purpose is, in the final analysis, to tell us how we ought rationally to behave. How little the 'pure' economic concept of rationality has to do with reason in its full sense becomes clear, however, when one considers that according to the underlying ethical hedonism it is not the reason of human beings but their needs structure alone which is made the highest principle of right action, thereby reducing reason to a mere means to an end. The perspective of overcoming the scarcity of goods by means of a critical-rational cultivation of our needs, in other words by an approach to the art of the 'good life' that treats needs critically, lies outside the scope of economic rationality from the start; for homo oeconomicus the point of the good life is axiomatically pared down to the hedonistic goal of utility maximization. It is not the (economic-ethical) reflection on needs but alone the (technical) production of goods which appears 'necessary' and rational from an economic point of view.

(2) The utilitarian principle

We can speak of utilitarian *ethics* in as far as utilitarianism by no means advocates the egoistic principle of private maximization of utility. Its ethical criterion is rather the social maximization of utility for the well-being of all: 'the greatest happiness of the greatest number.'[57] This is the reason why the utilitarians saw themselves as social reformers and were characterized as Philosophical Radicals; they opposed metaphysical conceptions of harmony and laissez-faire postulates for the market and

[56] Bentham, *Principles*, p. 11. On the natural law background to utilitarian ethics see Ulrich, *Transformation*, p. 180ff.

[57] On utilitarian ethics see Section 2.4.

argued that the harmony of interests among men did not come about automatically but had to be created by means of a rational policy. And this rational policy was to take its bearings from the utilitarian principle.

The ethical-critical potential of the principle was still clearly expressed in the older welfare economics, particularly in the work of Pigou.[58] Following marginal utility theory, according to which the consumption of every additional unit of a good has a decreasing subjective utility for the recipient, Pigou could not escape the socially critical conclusion that an egalitarian social distribution of goods leads to the highest degree of overall utility for the economy. This theoretical finding, which is evidently not welcomed by some liberal economists, was probably an essential motive for the increasing exclusion of questions of distribution in more recent welfare theories and in economics in general.

This potentially egalitarian consequence of the utilitarian principle unfortunately lacks a sound ethical foundation. Hidden away in it there is a highly problematic normative assumption, the fiction of a definable 'general economic interest' or, more briefly, an *economic optimum*. The economy is implicitly conceived of as a collective subject which knows no interpersonal conflicts and should simply aim to maximize 'its' utility.

> The interest of the community then is, what? – the sum of the interests of the several members that compose it.[59]

The serious rational-ethical objection to this merely additive logic is that when the advantages (utility) for one person are balanced against the disadvantages ('external' costs) for another, the inviolable dignity and uninfringeable rights of individuals may possibly be disregarded and sacrificed to the 'general interests of society' or the *common good*. In other words: utilitarianism and, in its wake, neoclassical economics, at least in the older forms considered hitherto, are blind to the problem of justice. Again, this blind spot is not a product of chance, but an expression of the persisting influence of old natural law convictions on harmony, which proclaim that it is the duty of a higher instance than humankind to guarantee the existence of a just order in society.

In the vulgar economics[60] of practical economic policy the diffuse fiction of the common good is still sometimes up to mischief even

[58] A. C. Pigou, *The Economics of Welfare* (London: Macmillan, 1920; new edn 1960), p. 89ff.

[59] Bentham, *Principles*, p. 12.

[60] We can follow Myrdal and Albert in speaking of a vulgar version of the economistic fiction of a social utility maximum when – in contrast to the approach of pure economic theory – the (gross) national product is taken as the standard for utility maximization and hence for economic 'growth'.

today, particularly in the form of an all-embracing *growth ideology*. This postulates that economic growth is 'to the benefit of all' at least in the final analysis (which amounts to a long-term relativization of the fate of those who evidently lose out in the market economy). Prosperity through growth for all was the well-meant but essentially ideological slogan of the 1950s and 1960s, which even today still by and large constitutes de facto the highest aim of economic policy.[61] The utilitarian notion of the (growing) 'common good' instead of or even *as* justice and to this extent as an adequate legitimation of the market principle can still be found today among writers on business ethics who are otherwise critical of economism, for example Horst Steinmann and Albert Löhr. According to their surprisingly uncritical opinion:

> ... the legitimation of the market economy is based empirically (sic!) on its comparative advantage in terms of *efficiency*, which signifies a greater contribution to social peace. This is the core of the ethical legitimation of the market economy.[62]

Together with the criterion of 'social peace' the utilitarian fiction of the common good shows through here in a particularly unrealistic manner, as is demonstrated by current experience with growing social problems in most national economies which are evidently the consequence of the deregulation of the market and the intensification of competition. To praise the benefits (for all?) of an efficient market economy so sweepingly as a contribution to social peace is, under these circumstances, indicative of an ideological stance which ignores the issue of legitimation. Rather it was and probably still is the untiring rhetorical repetition of the utilitarian fiction of the common good itself which is meant to serve the maintenance of social peace. With its help it was in fact (and evidently still is) possible to exclude the value and interest related social problem of distribution substantially and 'sustainably' from economic theory and policy. The judgement of Tugendhat is, therefore, justified:

> Utilitarianism is the ideology of capitalism, for it (apparently) makes it possible to justify the growth of the economy morally without taking questions of distribution into account.[63]

[61] The position of Ludwig Erhard, the 'father' of the German 'Wirtschaftswunder' at that time, is, however, by no means one-sidedly oriented on growth. See his *Wohlstand für alle* (Düsseldorf: Econ, 1957) and below Section 9.1 (3).

[62] H. Steinmann/A. Löhr, 'Unternehmensethik als Ordnungselement in der Marktwirtschaft?', *Schmalenbachs Zeitschrift für betriebswirtschaftliche Forschung* 47 (1995), pp. 143–79, at p. 155 (my italics).

[63] Tugendhat, *Vorlesungen*, p. 327.

However, the economic growth of the 'mature' (national) economies now regularly falls behind the increase in productivity, tendencies towards a two-thirds society are becoming increasingly evident and the ecological limits of growth are looming on the horizon. Under these circumstances an ever-widening circle of concerned observers has become aware that what really matters ultimately is the question of justice, for example the just distribution of scarce opportunities for employment and of the available ecological resources under conditions of sustainable economic development.

The Nobel Prize winner Gunnar Myrdal was probably the first to recognize the ethical unacceptability of the idea of general utility maximization and the non-existence of a 'purely economic point of view' which would permit value-free decisions in political economy issues. He saw through utilitarianism as a 'new cloak for the teaching of natural law'[64] and criticized the economistic fiction of the common good of liberal economic theory thoroughly appropriately as a 'communistic fiction',[65] as 'the fiction of a purpose where there is only causal sequence'.[66] We can therefore follow Luhmann in stating baldly: 'The common good is not a conceivable end.'[67] The systematic consequences were first drawn decades later in more recent neoclassical economic theory as a response, above all, to external promptings from philosophical ethics, but even this response was only partial.[68]

(3) The market-economic maximum theorem

The utilitarian principle can be found in two forms in neoclassical economics. On the one hand, Bentham's idea of a utilitarian calculus was continued and took on actual theoretical shape in *welfare theory*. Its goal of achieving a value-free determination of a collective utility function (in older welfare economics) or of a collective order of preferences (in later welfare economics) has, however, been abandoned as impossible in principle – quite apart from the problems of pragmatic operationalization.[69] The attempt to split off the ethical problem of the political order entirely

[64] G. Myrdal, *The Political Element*, p. 27. Schumpeter similarly emphasizes as 'the essential point to grasp ... that utilitarianism was nothing but another natural law system'. J. Schumpeter, *History of Economic Analysis* (London: Allen & Unwin, 1954), p. 132.

[65] See Myrdal, *The Political Element*, pp. 54, 101, 115, 140ff.

[66] Ibid., p. 115. On the doctrinal history background to this fiction of a uniform economic agent in pre-classical (national) economic teaching and its utilitarian continuation in the older welfare theory see Ulrich, 'Towards an Ethically-based Conception'.

[67] Luhmann, *Zweckbegriff und Systemrationalität*, p. 180. [68] See Section 5.3.

[69] For an early thorough criticism see A. Bohnen, *Die utilitaristische Ethik als Grundlage der modernen Wohlfahrtsökonomik* (Göttingen: Schwartz, 1964).

from the question of the just shaping of social relationships and to reduce it to a problem of the maximization of social utility turned out to be a symptomatic 'professional error' of the neoclassical economists resulting from the overestimation of the significance of calculation:

It is so to speak a professional error of the economist that he pushes the problem of calculation into the centre of a debate which touches upon the foundations of the overall political order.[70]

The utilitarian fiction of an objective (national) economic optimum asserted itself in a much more central and influential if less obvious manner in the *general equilibrium theory*, the true paradigm of neo-classical economics.[71] The core statement of this ideal theory of the perfect market is that in a frictionless market (i.e. without transaction costs) with perfect competition a tendency towards a balance between supply and demand within and between all partial markets always exists and that the equilibrium price ('the natural price') is also the price which – independently of the distribution of purchasing power – brings about the economic optimum and hence the common good (maximum theorem).[72] With the equilibrium theory the 'belief in the optimality'[73] of an ideal market was dressed up in a highly formalized manner which created the impression of a 'social physics'[74] close in nature to the theoretical ideal of the natural sciences, but which in the final analysis served only as a cloak for a *mathematized metaphysics*.[75] In the standard normative application of the maximum theorem any consideration of welfare theory then remains superfluous. It is apparently enough to orient practical economic policy

[70] Albert, *Ökonomische Ideologie*, p. 111. Albert was one of the earliest and sharpest critics of the 'maximum theorem' in both equilibrium and welfare theory and of its vulgarization as an 'ideology of growth' (p. 1). In his later writings, however, he replaced this economistic error by a scientistic error of interpreting economics as an empirical-analytical social science, i.e. as a value-free theoretical and not practical social economy. On this see Ulrich, *Transformation*, pp. 234ff., 341ff.

[71] For a succinct presentation and critique of the model of a general equilibrium theory and its continuations see W. Holleis, *Das Ungleichgewicht der Gleichgewichtstheorie: Zur Diskussion um die neoklassische Wirtschaftstheorie* (Frankfurt/New York: Campus, 1985).

[72] Late versions of the utilitarian fiction of the common good based on equilibrium theory and the maximum theorem can be found in the economics of property rights, transaction cost economics and especially the Coase theorem, which even attempts to solve the problem of external effects from the standpoint of a 'purely' economic maximization of utility: R. Coase, 'The Problem of Social Cost', *The Journal of Law and Economics* 3 (1960), pp. 1–44. On this interpretation see Ulrich, *Transformation*, p. 250ff., and Thielemann, *Prinzip Markt*, p. 51ff.

[73] Albert, *Ökonomische Ideologie*, p. 68.

[74] Schumpeter, *History of Economic Analysis*, p. 827, saw in the general equilibrium theory of Léon Walras a work 'that will stand comparison with the achievements of theoretical physics'.

[75] On this point see Ulrich, *Transformation*, p. 202ff.

consistently on the 'market principle': from an economic point of view more market is always good!

The only problem is that 'Walras' wonderful ideal world'[76] is merely an axiomatically formulated ideal theory which – in view of the lack of justified normative premises – possesses neither normative force nor empirical substance. Rather, it serves as 'the core of economistic ideology' which, from an ethical point of view, culminates in a totally 'unjustified definition of an optimal state of the economy'.[77] Anyone who uses it as orientational knowledge to underlay his recommendations for the economic or political order is implicitly falling back on the old metaphysics of the market. This fact cannot be altered by the formal abstractness and precision of the theory. It would be more honest scientifically to abstain consistently from a normative application 'from a purely economic point of view' in as far as its methodical status is defined as that of an axiomatic 'as-if' theory. But if the claim to employ it as orientational knowledge is maintained, scientific correctness would then require its advocates to reflect critically and fundamentally on the unspoken value premises of the 'market principle' *within* (a once again political) economics.

5.3 Methodological individualism and the normative logic of mutual advantage (pure economics)

Both for an economic philosophy calling itself liberal and for the academic claim to be presenting a 'value-free' economic theory the insistent criticisms of a growing number of 'dissenting economists' on the margins of neoclassical mainstream economics gradually became painfully noticeable. The older neoclassical school had evidently not succeeded in 'purifying' its theory entirely of the remains of the metaphysical and natural law assumptions of the classical period.[78] A second stage of methodological rationalization was urgently needed for the discipline, based on a critical analysis of the utilitarian foundations of neoclassical theory. In spite of the already mentioned early criticisms (Myrdal, Weisser, Albert etc.), this happened on a wide front only in the 1970s. The decisive impulses came partly from the further development of welfare theory, partly from institutional and constitutional economics, but mainly from the philosophical-ethical discussions of the time.

76 W. Vogt, 'Zur Kritik der herrschenden Wirtschaftstheorie', in Vogt (ed.), *Seminar: Politische Ökonomie* (Frankfurt: Suhrkamp, 1973), pp. 108–205, at p. 188.
77 Albert, *Ökonomische Ideologie*, pp. 68 and 123.
78 See Krüsselberg, 'Property-Rights-Theorie und Wohlfahrtsökonomik', p. 58.

In the philosophical discussion on utilitarianism John Rawls,[79] who himself had been an advocate of utilitarian ethics, was the first to draw systematic consequences for social philosophy from the insight that the utilitarian calculus disregarded the fundamental liberal principle of the 'inviolability' (p. 3) of individual dignity and of the basic rights of every individual, because it allowed the disadvantages of some to be offset by the advantages of the many. With explicit reference to Kant (§ 40, p. 221ff.) he concluded that in a 'well-ordered' society of citizens (p. 4ff.) who are free and equal in regard to their rights and opportunities the primacy of justice – understood as equality of basic freedom, basic rights and life opportunities – over all calculations of (general) welfare is necessary in the interest of a free liberal quality of society. We will take a closer look at Rawls's conception of justice as fairness later.[80] What interests us here is in the first place only the systematic impulse he gave for the further development of neoclassical economics. And this rests less upon his intention of renewing the theory of justice than on his method. Rawls intention was, namely, to bring about a *contract theoretical turn* in social philosophy. Henceforth utilitarian ethics was to be abandoned, and the political philosophy of the social contract, which had been elucidated during the Enlightenment in various forms (Thomas Hobbes, John Locke, Jean-Jacques Rousseau, Immanuel Kant), was to be further developed as the normative basis of a liberal and democratic society.[81] Rawls thus triggered off a renaissance of political philosophy in the 1970s, which for methodological reasons also provided a basis for the further development of neoclassical economics and the renewal of the abandoned tradition of a liberal political economy of a neoliberal kind.

By means of certain methodological considerations, in particular a thought experiment (as if!) with a hypothetical 'original position', in which 'the veil of ignorance' deprives the members of society of a knowledge of their interests, Rawls replaces the morality of individuals, which is then no longer necessary, by an assumed impartial structural quality of the initial social situation. In this way Rawls deliberately reduces the problem of an ethical-rational solution of social conflict to the intelligent individual assurance of personal life opportunities in a situation of

[79] J. Rawls, *A Theory of Justice* (Cambridge, MA: Belknap Press of Harvard University Press, 1971; rev. edn 1999). Rawls's book is probably the most discussed work of the twentieth century on social philosophy worldwide and also among economists. The page numbers in brackets in the text refer to the 1999 edition.

[80] See below Section 7.2.

[81] For a comprehensive account of the theory of the social contract from Hobbes, Locke, Rousseau and Kant to Rawls and Buchanan see W. Kersting, *Die politische Philosophie des Gesellschaftsvertrags* (Darmstadt: Wissenschaftliche Buchgesellschaft, 1994).

strategic uncertainty about the future social position of individuals (p. 15f.). With the help of a methodological trick Rawls endeavours to trace the ethical reciprocity principle of unconditional mutual recognition among individuals back to the criterion of 'mutual benefit' and regards the result as synonymous with 'common benefit' (both p. 88), which permits individuals to pursue their personal advantage, i.e. to behave in an 'economically rational' manner.[82]

It is not surprising that Rawls's theory aroused lively interest among economic theorists, particular as a similarly radical reorientation occurred in welfare theory, parallel to but independently of the philosophical discussion on utilitarianism, as we shall see later (Paretian economics). It was, above all, James Buchanan who took up and radicalized Rawls's approach after having influenced him the other way round first.[83] Whereas in Rawls's conception the Kantian idea of the universal equal basic rights of all individuals still plays a part, Buchanan – who does not follow the tradition of Kant but that of Thomas Hobbes's variant of contract theory – does not impose any moral claims on the subjects, simply assuming that they will pursue their rational self-interest. As we shall see shortly, this premise, which Rawls also uses in his model of the original position, becomes axiomatic for a normative version of methodological individualism. Buchanan's major interest was to take it as a basis in order to finally achieve the foundation of a politico-economic 'liberalism without metaphysics'.[84]

The systematic result of the comprehensive transformation brought about by the contract theoretical turn has in the meantime become the paradigmatic basis for the thinking of the entire recent neoclassical school, which sees itself as the advocate of 'pure economics'. We are interested here only in its normative content, whose basis can be presented in summary by examining the new fundamental features which have replaced the three characteristic basic elements of the old utilitarian neoclassical thinking. The paradigmatic development leads:

[82] Rawls, *Theory of Justice* (rev. edn), p. 12, defines his 'concept of rationality ... as far as possible in the narrow sense, standard in economic theory, of taking the most effective means to given ends'. It must be noted, however, that Rawls clearly recognizes the moral dimension of individuals and assumes unconditional mutual recognition. In the context of the liberalism/communitarianism debate Rawls later undertook a substantial further development of his position, as we shall see in Section 7.2 and Chapter 8.

[83] J. M. Buchanan/G. Tullock, *The Calculus of Consent: Logical Foundations of Constitutional Democracy* (Ann Arbor: University of Michigan Press, 1962).

[84] Kersting, *Die politische Philosophie*, p. 330. The view advocated here by Kersting, that Buchanan 'succeeded', is not acceptable, as we shall see. At the end of his book Kersting comes to the same conclusion.

(1) in regard to the conception of the person from psychological hedonism to methodological and normative individualism;
(2) in regard to the conception of rationality from the utilitarian principle to the Pareto criterion;
(3) in regard to the conception of the market and society from the equilibrium theory to the (two-stage) contract theory.

In what follows we shall examine in relative detail the normative foundation of these three basic features, and particularly the last of them, as they contain the underlying economistic reductionist elements of contemporary economics, whose understanding is of decisive importance for an ideology-critical economic ethics.

(1) Methodological and normative individualism

Older neoclassical thinking was clearly based on a rather vulgar image of man still untouched by the more recent discussions in cultural anthropology: that of *psychological hedonism*. This was accompanied by an increasingly untenable scientific validity claim (as an economic behavioural hypothesis). As a result of Bentham's naturalistic fallacy cited above ('Nature has placed mankind') it also involved an uncritical normative turn towards *ethical hedonism* (as a maxim of good and proper action). Older neoclassical thinking was thus still bonded to the natural law tradition of the explicative and normative double function[85] of classical political economy. Its methodological status always remained strangely indefinite: how far the two implicit validity claims should also be made explicit had always been a source of dispute. But with the transition to methodological individualism both validity claims are radically dismissed and the discipline is restructured on a strictly axiomatic basis as an ideal typical 'as-if' model.[86] Accordingly, the new methodological credo is: 'Economics has no image of man.'[87] Reflective representatives of the economic approach avoid the potentially ideological circular argument involved in misunderstanding this credo as a fact and consider it cautiously as a mere approximation to the methodological ideal, as a regulative idea.[88]

[85] See Albert, *Ökonomische Ideologie*, p. 14. Cf. Section 3.2.
[86] This methodological conception has been dealt with above, in Section 4.3.
[87] For a critical review of the issues involved see M. Held, 'Die Ökonomik hat kein Menschenbild' – Institutionen, Normen, Menschenbild', in Biervert/Held (eds.), *Menschenbild*, pp. 10–41.
[88] The formulation of W. Kerber can, for example, be understood in this way: 'Homo oeconomicus: in the ideal case a concept without a fixed image of man.' W. Kerber, 'Homo oeconomicus: Zur Rechtfertigung eines umstrittenen Begriffs', in Biervert/Held (eds.), *Menschenbild*, pp. 56–75, at p. 59.

However, recent neoclassical thought goes far beyond the trivial assumption of methodological individualism that social phenomena can, in the final analysis, be understood only through the thinking and actions of the individuals involved.[89] It implies a central methodological as-if assumption, namely an assumption of rationality in the sense of the economic approach: 'I reckon, therefore I am' (to play on Descartes famous dictum) is the identity formula of the otherwise identityless 'homo oeconomicus'.[90] Its methodological aim is to introduce a (paradoxical) *rational determinism* which makes the actions and the behaviour of individuals calculable, 'as if' all individuals were homines oeconomici. Through this axiomatic model assumption pure economics eliminates from the start the ethical dimension of the problem of rational social practice and reduces it to the inter-personal coordination of private preference, following the utilitarian tradition of ignoring any kind of ethical-critical reflection and questioning. As a systematic consequence economics develops nothing other than a pure logic of the rational action of individuals who resolutely pursue the maximization of personal benefit – or, to put it differently, the logic of their individual self-assertion and conditional cooperation with one another (conditioned namely by the private benefit of each). Ultimately, individuals who strictly pursue their personal interests are inevitably 'mutually disinterested'.[91] They have no sense of moral community and consequently do not recognize any intersubjective obligations outside business relations. Hence they have no need of economic ethics.

As we have seen, such an axiomatic 'as-if' theory lacks both a well-grounded normative orientational force in regard to practical implementation and an empirical explanatory force (requiring falsifiability in the

[89] On the history of methodological individualism in economic theory see K. Arrow 'Methodological Individualism and Social Knowledge', *American Economic Review* 84 (1994), No. 2, pp. 1–9. He does not mention, however, Ludwig von Mises, *Human Action: A Treatise on Economics* (London: William Hodge, 1949), who was one of the first economists to base the discipline explicitly on methodological individualism. As we shall see, the concept has probably been most consistently developed by the Nobel Prize winner James Buchanan, particularly in *The Limits of Liberty: Between Anarchy and Leviathan* (Chicago/London: University of Chicago Press, 1975).

[90] In spite of all its methodological abstraction this assumption of rationality corresponds surprisingly precisely to the understanding of rationality and the accompanying naturalistic image of man in Thomas Hobbes, for whom 'reason ... is nothing but reckoning'. Hobbes, *Leviathan*, p. 22. On Hobbes's 'naturalistic conception of man' see the preface to the German edition (Frankfurt: Suhrkamp, 1984) by Iring Fetscher, p. XIXff.

[91] The definition of 'mutually disinterested rationality' as the basic characteristic of normative individualism stems from Rawls, *Theory of Justice* (rev. edn), pp. 11f., 125. In a similar, strictly individualistically based approach subjects are also defined as 'mutually unconcerned' in D. Gauthier, *Morals by Agreement* (Oxford: Clarendon, 1986), pp. 87ff., 326f.

real world).[92] But with the assumption of economic rationality how far are we then dealing with a 'useful fiction', as J.M. Buchanan, the most stringent advocate of methodological or rather normative individualism in economics, puts it? His answer is that the homo oeconomicus model is useful as a thought experiment designed to test proposed social rules or institutional orders in order to see whether they would still function in the 'worst case' when all those involved behaved like homines oeconomici.[93] This is the sole reason why such 'systematically cynical'[94] model assumptions are useful. Karl Homann has strikingly characterized this 'as-if' evaluation of institutional rules in regard to their resistance to strictly self-interested behaviour as the *homo-oeconomicus-test* (briefly: h.-o.-test).[95] In this respect the theoretical model is useful in politics, according to Buchanan.[96] The leap from the world of 'as-if' into normative practice thus seems to have succeeded.

What is decisive from a normative-ethical point of view is, however, the question of the socio-political ends of the social rules which are to be tested in regard to their capacity for 'h.-o.-resistance'. The crucial point is that according to the opinion of methodological individualists a statement of ethical-political ends – and hence also of economic ethics – is absolutely unnecessary. On the contrary, the h.-o.-test is precisely designed to discover an institutional arrangement (economic incentives and restrictions) under whose regime all individuals are allowed to behave in a strictly self-interested manner, as Brennan and Buchanan have made clear in a contribution with the illuminating title 'The Normative Purpose of Economic 'Science'':

[92] For the explanation of *actual* behaviour it is methodologically essential to reinterpret the 'as-if' model assumptions as real scientific behavioural hypotheses, which may be disproved by experience but inevitably lead back to a substantial image of man which is assumed to be 'realistic'. But then it seems plausible to base the explanatory efforts on a model of the actors which is closer to reality and unaffected by rational economic determinism. Those economists who follow Gary S. Becker, *The Economic Approach to Human Behavior* (Chicago: University of Chicago Press, 1976), and attempt to use modern economics directly as an empirical-analytical 'behavioural science' do then indeed usually plead for an enrichment of the 'homunculus oeconomicus' with empirical content, for example with psychological knowledge, in order to increase the real scientific explanatory and prognostic power of their models. See e.g. B. S. Frey, 'From Economic Imperialism to Social Science Inspiration', *Public Choice* 77 (1993), pp. 95–105.

[93] See Brennan/Buchanan, *Reason of Rules*, p. 51f.

[94] Ibid., pp. 55, 58. On this point see also Section 4.3 (3a) above.

[95] Homann/Blome-Drees, *Wirtschafts- und Unternehmensethik*, p. 95, and Homann/Pies, 'Wirtschaftsethik in der Moderne', p. 11.

[96] See Brennan/Buchanan, *Reason of Rules*, p. 50. The claim made here for political counselling guided by economic theory will be examined more specifically in Section 9.2 (2).

One calls for the homo oeconomicus assumption not because it is necessarily the most accurate model of human behaviour but because it is the appropriate model for testing whether institutions serve *to transform private interest into public.*[97]

Behind the methodological interest in the *worst case* a radical normative individualism in the form of a pre-scientific, knowledge-constitutive interest comes to light. Its practical goal is to relieve individuals as totally as possible of moral requirements, so that they can live out their assumed need for strict maximization of personal benefit (i.e. the old vulgar psychological hedonism!).[98] The internal 'worst case' of the model turns out to be intended as an external *best case*. The approach stands in the service of a social philosophy in which all that matters is the strictly individualistic foundation of social and political action. In the ideal case ethical-political legitimation claims are reduced totally to the private self-interested decisions of the individuals concerned. They cannot be expected to accept any ethos other than the egoism of bourgeois property owners! That a well-ordered society is nevertheless possible under these conditions is the basic economistic assumption of the entire approach.

The conscious or unconscious motivation behind the knowledge-constitutive interest of the methodological individualists stems ultimately from a quite specific, normatively determined conception of society, which must be understood in terms of its intellectual history, with a corresponding underlying image of man as its normative core, namely that of *possessive individualism.*[99] On taking a closer look, the supposedly open and 'rudimentary anthropology contained in the concept of the homo oeconomicus'[100] turns out to be by no means so value-neutral and non-normative as the frugal and formal axiomatics seems at first sight to suggest. By way of a preliminary conclusion we can say that the credo 'Economics has no image of man' must be replaced by the following more accurate and adequate statement: Pure economics is nothing but the explication of an image of man – Hobbes's 'reckoning' maximizer

97 G. Brennan/J. M. Buchanan, 'The Normative Purpose of Economic 'Science': Rediscovery of an Eighteenth Century Method', *International Journal of Law and Economics* 1 (1981), pp. 155–66, at p. 158; reprinted in Buchanan, *Economics Between Predictive Science and Moral Philosophy* (College Station: Texas University Press, 1987), pp. 51–65, at p. 59 (my italics); similarly Brennan/Buchanan, *Reason of Rules*, p. 53.

98 To call this 'private ethics' in contrast to 'social ethics' (Brennan/Buchanan, *Reason of Rules*, p. 47) not only borders in fact on cynicism but is also an expression of a lack of understanding of the social structure of all morality (cf. Section 1.1).

99 See C. B. Macpherson, *The Political Theory of Possessive Individualism* (Oxford: Clarendon, 1962). We will return to the characteristics corresponding to possessive individualism in the context of the question of the meaning of economic activity in Section 6.3. On the contrasting republican-ethical model of a free citizen see Section 8.1.

100 Kerber, 'Homo oeconomicus', p. 65.

of his personal benefit whose needs structure instrumentalizes his reason totally and allows it to shrink to a 'pure' economic rationality.

(2) The Pareto criterion

The Pareto criterion is named after the sociologist Vilfredo Pareto and can be traced back to his pioneering work at the end of the 19th century. It is the answer of recent welfare theory to the 'communistic fiction' of the utilitarian principle and the idea of an 'economic maximum' based upon it. According to the Pareto criterion only those social *changes* should be recognized as a collective (economic) welfare improvement through which the (subjectively evaluated) situation of at least one individual is improved without the situation of any other individual being worsened.[101] Thus every social (political) reform proposal is regarded as *Pareto efficient* which all those affected agree to solely because it is for them the most advantageous of the actually available alternatives and is to that extent 'to the advantage of all concerned'.[102] Vice versa, every proposal for a change of the social rules of the game is regarded as *Pareto inefficient* which provokes rejection (lack of 'acceptance') on the part of individual subjects because the change violates their vested rights as they see them.

Although the Paretian turn in welfare economics was set in motion independently of methodological individualism it runs completely parallel to it. It can be considered to be the elaborated formulation of normative individualism, which the methodological individualists also implicitly or explicitly claim for themselves with the practical interpretation of the h.-o.-test. As has been said, the principle message of individualism is, after all, that each individual should (be allowed to) maximize his personal benefit. Every possibility of questioning the 'given' preferences of individuals from an ethical-critical point of view is normatively excluded. No-one can be forced to act against his purely private interests and to renounce the maximization of his own advantages in favour of others. Consequently every affected person has a categorical and absolute *veto right*[103] in the defence of his interests or privileges. The Pareto criterion

101 In the utilitarian tradition of collective utility maximization a social state was originally defined as a so-called *Pareto optimum* in which the situation of no single individual could be improved further without worsening the situation of another individual. But the idea of maximization then loses its meaning, as there is any number of Pareto optima. For this reason nowadays the Pareto criterion is defined restrictedly only in terms of the Pareto efficiency of partial changes in social relationships.

102 Homann/Blome-Drees, *Wirtschafts- und Unternehmensethik*, p. 55.

103 This is expressly stated by the methodological individualists Homann and Blome-Drees, ibid., p. 56.

is, so to speak, an individualistically interpreted concept of the common good. According to this definition, what all concerned are interested in because it serves the private advantage of every single person embodies the general good. In other words: what is Pareto efficient is efficient for all. The idea of an anonymous, impartial economic rationality which is determinable independently of all questions of social distribution, that is to say the old economistic fiction of the common good, thus appears in a new form with an individualistic methodological basis. It is now clear why the methodological individualists are convinced they can claim to be serving the 'public interest' and hence the common good, as we have already seen under point (1) with the help of a quotation from Brennan and Buchanan.

The methodological individualists usually even characterize the Pareto criterion explicitly as an ethical principle. As Buchanan emphasizes:

> This Pareto rule is itself an ethical proposition.[104]

According to normative individualism whatever 'tends to emerge from the free choice of the individuals who are involved' is ethically good without the observation of any further conditions.[105] In the words of Karl Homann:

> Moral quality is accorded to the market and competition solely because they are 'efficient', i.e. because they alone are in a position to guarantee or even to improve the chances *of all individuals* to shape their lives according to their own ideas.[106]

'Pure' economics evidently believes it has found in the criterion of Pareto efficiency the magic formula which definitively permits the *reduction of legitimacy to efficiency*. The economistic trick used is straightforward: Pareto efficiency is simply defined as the approvability of a measure by all concerned out of rational self-interest (individual veto right!); consequently, in the opinion of the methodological-normative individualists, it meets the 'legitimation requirements of consensus'.[107]

What is wrong with the Paretian notion of the ethical dignity of the 'efficient' market? The problem and at the same time the root of economism lies in the contractualistic reduction of the concept of consensus and in the resulting relativity of the individual advantage contingent upon the initial position of the persons involved (*status-quo problem*). Legitimacy as a deontological-ethical concept implies that a social state or an action is worthy of recognition in the light of the moral rights of all those affected (which require clarification in each particular situation);

[104] Buchanan, *Economics Between*, p. 4. [105] Buchanan, *Limits of Liberty*, p. 6.
[106] Homann, 'Wettbewerb und Moral', p. 41 (my italics).
[107] Homann/Blome-Drees, *Wirtschafts- und Unternehmensethik*, p. 56.

the normative basis lies in the unconditional (categorical) reciprocal respect for all men as beings of equal worth with equal rights.[108] In contrast, the homines oeconomici who maximize their private benefit are mutually disinterested. They are interested only in achieving their personal benefit as smoothly and economically as possible. Their willingness to cooperate with others is therefore always conditioned by an egoistic cost–benefit calculation. As a result they do not arrive at a moral point of view, for which the primacy of good will is constitutive.[109] If Pareto efficiency is regarded as a sufficient legitimation criterion, ethical legitimacy (justifiability) is reduced to strategic acceptance (assertability). As this categorial difference cannot be perceived from the axiomatic basis of methodological and normative individualism, Paretian economics inevitably leads to a reduction of the regulative idea of ethical-rational consensus to strategic approval based on private advantage and hence to an economistic reduction of the ethical principle of universalization to a concept of *generalized mutual benefit*.

Whereas the ethical principle of universalization involves the unreserved recognition of the inviolable moral rights of every individual, measures oriented on the 'common good' in the sense of the Paretian 'advantage of all' are always subject to the reservation that the vested interests of all be maintained regardless of whether the *status quo* from which each individual starts out is just or not. The justice of the initial position remains unquestioned, as the Pareto criterion is only concerned with the relative advantageousness of *changes* in the situation. The Pareto criterion thus turns out to be status-quo conservative. The initial distribution of power, resources and purchasing power imposes its ethical legitimacy or illegitimacy indiscriminately on the terms of trade, the relationships of exchange. Those who have a lot to offer can demand a lot and those who have little must be satisfied with a correspondingly modest return. Thus Pareto efficiency as the criterion for the rational shaping of the social life of man implicitly replaces good reasons (moral principle) by factual power, by the right of the mightier to dictate the terms of trade to the weaker. The Pareto criterion is thus irrelevant when it comes to assessing the justice of a reform which is up for discussion or even of the 'given' determinants of a social situation.

The infiltration of power relationships into all market relationships is seen as an in principle inevitable result of what we might call *market internal effects*. This term can be applied as a conceptual parallel to the idea of the 'external effects' of market transactions on uninvolved third

108 On the concept of legitimacy see Section 2.5 (2). For more details see Chapter 7.
109 See Section 1.4.

parties, which are usually the only effects regarded as problematic from an economic-ethical point of view.[110] These 'market internal effects' are viewed as inherently logical and can at best be modified to some degree by a policy of (modest) compensation for the unequal starting positions of the participants in the market. The problems involved in this viewpoint were already touched upon at the beginning of the 20th century in debate in the *Verein für Socialpolitik* on the relationship of 'power and economic laws'.[111] But the debate failed by and large to go beyond the old natural law thinking and could consequently contribute little to the clarification of the issue. At all events, the market internal power relationships, which are so important from an economic-ethical point of view, are systematically blurred over in Paretian economics, and necessarily so, as they contradict the ethical dignity or at least neutrality (impartiality) claimed in the name of the Pareto criterion. In other words, this reductionist economistic approach gives rise to the impression that the market presents no internal ethical problems.[112]

Let us now turn to the third basic element of 'pure' economics, which builds upon the individualistic conception of the person (1) and the Paretian conception of rationality (2): the contractarian conception of society.

(3) Two-stage contract theory

The older neoclassical equilibrium theory had the formal character of an 'astronomy of the behavior of commodities',[113] which flows, anonymously and deterministically, without any social friction costs, as if in a 'social vacuum'.[114] In contrast, on the basis of methodological (and

[110] See Thielemann, *Prinzip Markt*, p. 273ff.

[111] See E. von Böhm-Bawerk, 'Macht oder ökonomisches Gesetz?', *Zeitschrift für Volkswirtschaft, Socialpolitik und Verwaltung* 23 (1914), pp. 205–71; reprinted as an independent publication Darmstadt 1975. In his approach Böhm-Bawerk maintains the naturalistic pseudo-contrast between 'natural pricing' (in the free market) and 'artificial interventions' and thus decides the answer in advance. On the naturalistic background to the blurring over of the market internal power factor see K. Rothschild, 'Macht: Die Lücke in der Preistheorie', in H. K. Schneider/Ch. Watrin (eds.), *Macht und ökonomisches Gesetz*, vol. II (Berlin: Duncker & Humblot, 1973), pp. 1097–111.

[112] This insight is significant from the point of view of institutional ethics and politics, as we shall see in Chapter 9.

[113] H. Albert, 'Die Problematik der ökonomischen Perspektive', *Zeitschrift für die gesamte Staatswissenschaft* 117 (1961), pp. 438–67, at p. 441. He follows K. E. Boulding, *The Skills of the Economist* (Cleveland: Howard Allen, 1958), p. 9: 'The economist sees the world not as men and things, but as commodities.'

[114] H. Albert, 'Politische Ökonomie und rationale Politik' (first publ. 1967), in Albert, *Aufklärung und Steuerung* (Hamburg: Hoffmann & Campe, 1976), pp. 91–122, at p. 120.

normative) individualism, an explication of the entire logic of the social interaction of individuals acting in a strictly self-interested way can be offered using the categories of Hobbesian contract theory. Rawls and Buchanan are the pioneers who bring about the corresponding comprehensive turn towards contract theory in the treatment of the problem of rational social cooperation and politics. We restrict our attention here to Buchanan's basic conception; we will take a closer look at Rawls's position in the next chapter.

First of all it is possible, on the basis of contract theory, to fetch the market process back ideally from the 'astronomy of the behaviour of commodities' (or rather the metaphysics) to the social world. As we know, in the market economy subjects conclude business deals, i.e. *exchange contracts*. When is such an exchange contract concluded? The contractualistic answer is quite simply: when both partners to the deal, the offerer and the demander of goods or services, reach an *agreement*, which is traditionally sealed by a handshake, or in modern terms, by a signature under a contract. But when do they reach an agreement? Only when the deal is advantageous for both parties, of course, or, to put it more precisely: when the most advantageous use of their scarce resources (the purchasing power of the buyer or the goods or services provided by the seller) is achieved. The conclusion of a deal is, therefore, quite simply the exchange of personal advantages between two mutually disinterested free economic agents who each endeavour to maximize their own benefit. The deal is then efficient for both parties precisely in the sense intended by the Pareto criterion. As all the exchange deals concluded in a 'free' market are formally voluntary and each individual hence acts to his own advantage, the market is by definition, and independently of the initial distribution of resources, efficient for all participants and consequently also Pareto efficient.

Thus the concept of Pareto efficiency can itself best be understood in terms of contract theory. From the point of view of methodological and normative individualism the actual conclusion of an exchange agreement is the only criterion there is for the efficiency of a market transaction.[115] What is more: 'efficient' then seems to be the equivalent of 'just'; in Buchanan's contractual theory both concepts are defined indiscriminately by the criterion of the voluntary agreement of all participants:

> We could easily say that the result or outcome is 'just' which reflects the voluntary agreement of participants.[116]

[115] See J. M. Buchanan, *Freedom in Constitutional Contract: Perspectives of a Political Economist* (College Station: Texas University Press, 1977), pp. 128f., 136f., 145f.

[116] Ibid., p. 129.

This thoroughly Hobbesian reductionist and individualistic 'contractual ethics' between homines oeconomici who strictly pursue their personal interests should not be confused with the rational ethical idea of a social contract in the sense of Kant, which is meant to justify the generalizable rights and duties of all members of society in a deontological sense. But it is precisely with the help of this category mistake that Hobbesian contractualistic economics deviously obtains its normative force. Otfried Höffe puts his finger on the categorial difference:

In Hobbes a contract is concluded because it is better for all concerned, in Kant, on the other hand, because it corresponds to practical reason, to the reciprocal recognition of individuals as persons and legal subjects.[117]

Although both conceptions contain the constitutive basic idea of a contract, namely the unanimous agreement between free individuals (veto right of every citizen), the critical-ethical aspect of the Kantian rational idea of the social contract is lacking in the individualistic Hobbesian conception which has provided the foundation for the Paretian concept of the common good ('benefit of all').

We need not dwell on the Hobbesian character of this contractual theory as long as it refers to the market with purely explanatory intent; it is adequate for its object or, we might say, it simply reflects the 'market principle' (without justifying it!). Business partners do not make presents to one another[118] – as soon as they do so instead of looking for their own advantage, they no longer encounter each other as businessmen but on the level of friendly interaction. They might quite conceivably be both friends and 'hard' business partners, for as homines oeconomici they see in the voluntary nature of business relationships a sufficient legitimation of their self-interested business behaviour, provided the conditions of business are reasonably fair. In the market a kind of 'exchange justice' seems to exist which corresponds to Hobbes' economistic reduction of the concept of justice:

The value of all things contracted for is measured by the appetite of the contractors; and therefore the just value is that which they be contented to give.[119]

With his equation of (economic) willingness to pay with (ethical) justice Hobbes was the first to make the decisive category mistake on which the entire Paretian 'ethics' of the market is based. The above mentioned *internal* ethical problems involved in exchange relationships between economic agents which can result from an unfair initial position (status-quo

[117] Höffe, *Ethik und Politik*, p. 211. For details on Kant see above Section 2.3.
[118] See Thielemann, *Prinzip Markt*, p. 43. [119] Hobbes, *Leviathan*, p. 94.

problem) are lost sight of in this Hobbesian world. From the economistic contractual point of view an ethical problem only arises as a result of the *external effects* of a transaction on third parties who do not participate in the deal and gain no advantage from it, but nevertheless involuntarily suffer disadvantages in the form of social or ecological costs.

The decisive point about Buchanan's contractarian approach is that he breaks through this traditional limitation of economic theory by introducing a two-stage conception of a social contract (at the primary constitutional level) and private exchange contracts (at the secondary post-constitutional level). The primacy of politics over the market is then guaranteed, at least superficially. As its name indicates, the *constitutional economics* founded by Buchanan attributes a constitutive role to the social contract (of the constitution) in relation to the market. In this social contract all citizens of a free democratic society should determine the rules (the basic framework) of the market by means of a unanimous agreement (veto right of each individual), under which private exchange contracts together with their external effects are to be regarded as legitimate. Negative external effects (social costs) of private transactions will only be tolerated by other citizens if they 'pay off' for them, either because they in turn profit from the contractual acceptance by others of the external effects of their own activities or because external effects which are regarded as intolerable are either compensated for legally or are completely excluded by the social contract. This Hobbesian social contract is, of course, quite simply the result of generalized mutual benefits among all citizens. If it materializes, such a contract is by definition and by the mere fact of its existence advantageous for all citizens, i.e. Pareto efficient. The remaining external effects which are possible accordingly seem to 'pay off' for all citizens and can therefore be regarded as legitimate.

At first sight we are in fact dealing here with a conception of the social constitution and legitimation of the market. This is no longer conceived of in evolutionist natural law terms (as in recent times in the work of Friedrich A. von Hayek) but in political and contractualistic terms. Buchanan's criticism of Hayek's late evolutionist form of the old liberal metaphysics of the market is correspondingly sharp and within its context thoroughly convincing.[120]

But Buchanan's purely Hobbesian conception of the social contract fails to solve the status-quo problem mentioned earlier, as the underlying

[120] See Buchanan, *Freedom in Constitutional Contract*, p. 30ff. A helpful comparative discussion of this point is given in V. Vanberg, *Liberaler Evolutionismus oder vertragstheoretischer Konstitutionalismus?* (Tübingen: Mohr Siebeck, 1981).

criterion of Pareto efficiency can refer meaningfully only to constitutional change; it assumes the legitimacy of the initial position. Accordingly Buchanan is caught up in a symptomatic dilemma which reflects the internal contradictions between the as-if approach of methodological individualism on the one hand and its normative turn in the form of the Pareto criterion on the other: the dilemma between (a) the criterion of factual agreement of individualism and (b) the fictional (as-if) constitutional consensus of methodological individualism.

(a) If Buchanan regards the *factual* acceptance or rejection as the criterion for the legitimation of the social contract as a whole, the given status quo of the distribution of social power and resources is then also to be seen as legitimate. Consequently, the lack of Pareto efficiency of contractual reforms on which no agreement is achieved is reinterpreted as agreement on the better merits of the status quo for all. Because of the veto rights of each individual the status quo cannot and may not be changed in the case of disagreement on reform.[121] Or to put it the other way round: Every reform is subject to the condition that it also 'pays off' for those who have been hitherto privileged. The conclusion is:

> Beyond agreement there is simply no place for the contractarian to go.[122]

Instead of constituting legitimate power and room for manoeuvre, the social contract has in reality precisely the opposite effect of making right dependent on the power of possibly unjustified vested interests. Here the image of man as the bourgeois property owner (possessive individualism) reappears. It has an impact on the understanding of society in such a way that the social relationship between individuals is one-sidedly seen as being of only secondary importance. Hobbes had already conceived of the relationship in this light. Socialization is only a means for the pursuit of personal advantage; it possesses no inter-subjective value of its own.[123] Homines oeconomici accept socialization only in as far as it is useful for them, which means that the normative primacy of individual self-assertion over any kind of social integration is taken as given. Buchanan's claim to have demonstrated the social *constitution* of individual freedom of exchange in the market thus proves invalid, as from this perspective society can be envisaged only as a *restriction*, as the external boundary of individual freedom. A natural and fortuitous arbitrary freedom thus

[121] On this point see also R. Kley, *Vertragstheorien der Gerechtigkeit: Eine philosophischen Kritik der Theorien von John Rawls, Robert Nozick und James Buchanan* (Berne *et al.*: Haupt, 1989), p. 144ff.

[122] Buchanan, *Freedom in Constitutional Contract*, p. 263.

[123] See Fetscher's preface to the German translation of Hobbes' *Leviathan* (1984), p. XX.

has the last word in the contractarian determination of the rules of social coexistence. These then do not unconditionally protect the equal rights of all citizens to freedom and the realization of their life opportunities against particularistic interests but serve instead the maintenance of the status quo: individual vested interests and the existing distribution of resources, power and property are protected against all kinds of claims for more justice. John Locke (1632–1702), the first radical liberal theoretician of the social contract, already argued along these lines:

> The great and chief end therefore, of Men's uniting into Commonwealths, and putting themselves under Government, is the *Preservation of their Property*.[124]

This economistically reduced conception of the free and democratic social contract expresses either the cynicism of the privileged (now of an ideological rather than a methodological kind)[125] or – and this is the only interpretation to make sense in the case of a serious theoretician like Buchanan – the continued influence of the old liberal, metaphysical, natural law notion of harmony according to which the 'natural' results of distribution in the course of history are guided by a higher hand and must consequently be justified. Hence it is not by chance that Buchanan defines the anarchic (pre-constitutional) initial situation in which the first social contract is established under model conditions as the result of a 'natural distribution' which represents the true balance of power of individual abilities and strengths and must consequently be accepted as a naturally just and unavoidable fact of life.[126] The true 'morality' of such a social Darwinist social philosophy is accurately characterized by Kley: 'Only those people deserve respect who know how to command respect.'[127] The influence of the Calvinist credo 'God helps those who help themselves'[128] is all too evident here.

(b) If, in view of the difficulties involved in normative individualism, Buchanan were to fall back on the 'as-if' methodology and the model of a *fictitious* social contract he would then have to go without the direct normative orientational force of the results. Instead he chooses a middle path which is designed to smuggle the intellectual experiment of the fictitious social contract into the factual social contract. On the one hand, as a consistent contractualist, he insists that only the factual

[124] J. Locke, *Two Treatises of Government* (Cambridge: Cambridge University Press, 1967), p. 368 (italics partly omitted).

[125] See point (1) of this section for Buchanan's conception of 'methodological cynicism'; on the concept of cynicism see the end of Section 4.3.

[126] See Buchanan, *Limits of Liberty*, pp. 8ff., 23ff. Cf. Kley, *Vertragstheorien*, p. 198ff., and Thielemann, *Prinzip Markt*, p. 227ff.

[127] Kley, *Vertragstheorien*, p. 199. [128] Weber, *Protestant Ethic*, p. 115.

approval of all concerned can legitimate real contracts. But, on the other hand, the intellectual experiment of the fictitious social contract can be used to enlighten the citizens as to their rational self interest when making actual choices, i.e. to help them become better homines oeconimici. The fictitious social contract then fulfils the practical role of a homo-oeconomicus-test (Homann) of all possible social contracts including those existing in reality. The pure economic rationality of the fictitious social contract thus functions as an instance serving the 'enlightenment' of real politics. But in this way the 'rational determinism' of the theoretical model becomes the criterion and the sufficient grounds for the justification of a just social contract; there is no systematic room in this conception for ethical-critical discussion leading to a justified factual approval or rejection by the citizens.[129]

Behind constitutional economics an economistic reduction of democratic politics to pure economic logic thus comes to light. Far from overcoming economic reductionism, it elevates itself to the ideology of a *market society* in which individuals encounter one another only as business partners.[130] In Hobbesian-Buchananian theory and 'ethics' of the social contract all the ethical-political categories that matter in the tradition of republicanism[131] (public spirit, priority of justice over private advantage, public use of practical reason) shrink to those of an economic theory of politics and democracy. Politics is merely the continuation of business with other means – no more, no less. In the end, constitutional economics simply turns out to be theoretical elaboration of a radical *political economism*.

Every conception of democratic politics can be defined as political economism which reduces the political ethics of a properly understood democracy to the economic logic of the market. This has long been precisely the case with the economic theory of politics and democracy which, thanks to Buchanan, has gained a prominent, indeed a constitutional place within economics. As early as 1940 Ludwig von Mises, the intellectual pioneer of political economism, argued that the market was the ideal model for democracy:

> It . . . has been said that the market is a democracy in which every penny is a ballot paper. The democratic electoral system could well be seen as an inadequate

[129] On 'rational determinism' cf. Section 4.3 (1).
[130] For a critical understanding of the concept of the market economy, which was probably first coined by Polanyi, *Great Transformation*, p. 71, see S. Katterle, 'Methodologischer Individualismus and Beyond', in Biervert/Held (eds.), *Menschenbild*, pp. 132–52, at p. 144.
[131] For more details see Chapter 8.

attempt to *copy* the constitution of the market in political life. In the market no votes are wasted.[132]

And Joseph Schumpeter, who is regarded as the true founder of the economic theory of democracy, comes up a little later with the short and simple assertion:

There exists no more democratic institution than a market.[133]

With this radical reversal of the priorities between the normative logic of inter-subjective relations, as we have defined rational ethics, and the crypto-normative (i.e. the concealed normative) logic of the market, economic reductionism has, in principle, reached its apogee. It will be the task of the following chapters to rethink this question of priorities from the bottom up and to discover an ethically and politically workable answer.

Let us draw a brief conclusion from the multi-faceted critique of economic reductionism presented above. The theoretical attempt to discover in the internal logic or 'morality' of the market an orientation towards the common good in an ethically meaningful sense has failed at all of the three developmental levels: (1) at the level of classical economics founded on metaphysics and natural law, (2) at the level of the older utilitarian, neoclassical economics, and (3) at the level of pure economics. It has failed in spite of its blossoming methodologically as radical individualism, becoming Pareto efficient and, in its contractual form, passing beyond the limits of the market into the sphere of politics. What is more, it has 'failed in an instructive manner', to use Kersting's expression.[134] The basic thesis of economic reductionism, that the explicit consideration of ethical points of view is 'not necessary' in the economy, has thus been disproved, even in its most elaborated form. The economic squaring of the ethical circle (of reflection) has failed.

The outcome of this critique of the economistic ideology is admittedly disagreeable for the 'pure' economists, as no-one, of course, would freely characterize himself or accept being unmasked as an economic

132 L. von Mises, *Nationalökonomie: Theorie des Handelns und Wirtschaftens* (Geneva: Union, 1940), p. 260 (my italics). As his *Human Action* (1949) is not a completely corresponding English edition, this formulation cannot be found there. Instead, a similar sentence exists in his book *Planned Chaos* (New York: Foundation for Economic Education, 1981), p. 30: 'The market is a democracy in which every penny gives a right to vote.'

133 Schumpeter, *Capitalism, Socialism and Democracy*, p. 184.

134 See Kersting, *Die politische Philosophie*, p. 348, and Thielemann, *Prinzip Markt*, p. 237, to whom I owe the reference to Kersting's accurate dictum.

reductionist.[135] But the outcome can hardly surprise anyone who is not led astray by the economistic category mistake. From a philosophical point of view ethical rationality (explicated as communicative rationality) and economic rationality (in the neoclassical sense of strategic success-oriented rationality) are from the start fundamentally different categories which cannot be reciprocally reduced to one another.[136] Wherever the reduction of freedom to barter, justice to Pareto efficiency, right to might, legitimacy to acceptance or morality to interest occurs we are ultimately dealing with economism pure and simple.

But if this is the case, we are faced, in the final analysis, with the choice between economistic reductionism and the inherent dualism of the conception of rationality of an unrestricted understanding of rational economic activity. As long as economic theory clings for paradigmatic reasons to its Hobbesian conception of 'pure' economic rationality it inevitably blurs over all the ethical aspects of an economic structure and order in the service of life; it fundamentally ignores the relevance of the lifeworld. It is thus forced to place the entire burden of social integration on the institutionalized interplay of mutually disinterested, merely self-interested homines oeconomici. It abandons the responsibility for all questions of reasonable economic activity in the lifeworld to the *purely systemic* networking of the activities of its restlessly active but literally unprincipled homunculi. We now take leave of this approach and its paradigmatic predecision in favour of the normative logic of the market, as anyone who takes seriously the claims of the lifeworld on rational economic activity which economism ignores needs ethics!

135 Homann, 'Ethik und Ökonomik', p. 348, for example, replies to the reproach of economic reductionism by explicitly stating that he has never 'taken up this position', although, according to all the criteria developed above, he is a model representative of it. As we have seen in Section 3.2, he in the meantime admits advocating 'methodical economism'; see Homann, 'Wirtschaftsethik', p. 181.

136 For a fundamental treatment of this point see Apel, 'Lässt sich ethische Vernunft', p. 31ff.

Part III

Reflections on the foundations of economic ethics II: rational economic activity and the lifeworld

There is an economy, because there are human persons.[1]

Economic activity means the creation of value. As is the case with all the technical terms of modern economics, the customary understanding of this widely used concept in business administration and (political) economics is now restricted to systemic functional relationships. Accordingly we are dealing with a purely quantitative factor, namely a monetarily evaluated net economic performance, i.e. value added, achieved in the market by means of work or service offered in return for payment, which effectively remains to a corporation, a branch or an entire national economy (in exchange with other national economies) after the deduction of costs which are also determined by the market. But the calculatory concept betrays its original ethical-qualitative meaning in the human life-context: the question of the value of economic activity in regard to the quality of life. In the final phase of the pre-modern (and that means here pre-systemic) cameralistic economy the relationship of economic activity to life values was still a matter of course. In 1835, for example, the 'Kameralistische Encyclopädie' offers the following definition:

> The contribution of goods to the achievement of the aims of man depends in fact on their suitability. The degree of suitability of a good for human ends is its value, which rises and falls in comparison with other goods and the importance of the end.[2]

For the cameralist economist Edward Baumstark the relationship between economic activity and the values of everyday life practice was so self-evident that in a note on the definition above he argued in an etymologically questionable but factually accurate fashion for the derivation of the

[1] Rich, *Economic and Business Ethics*, p. 271.

[2] E. Baumstark, *Kameralistische Encyclopädie* (Ruggell, Liechtenstein: Topos, 1975; first publ. 1835), p. 56, quoted from R. Rock/K. Rosenthal, *Marketing = Philosophie* (Frankfurt *et al.*: Peter Lang, 1986), p. 100. The use of the term 'cameralistics' or 'cameralist science' for the national economy derives from the equation of economics with the concepts of financial administration and (state) budgetary policy prevailing in the (financial) 'chambers' (camera) of the princes at the time.

The question of meaning	*The question of legitimation*
Which values should be created? → real-life practical and meaningful economic activity How do we *want* to live in the future? → cultural motives: attractive life form Is our economic activity *good for* ourselves? → the **good life** → Primacy of the lifeworld over the 'self-dynamics' of the economic system (direction of fulfilment)	*For whom* should values be created? → socially legitimate economic activity How *ought* we to live together? → social rules: well-ordered society Can we *account for* our economic activity to others? → **just social life** → Primacy of politics over the 'inherent necessities' of the market (normative preconditions)

Figure III.1. Two basic dimensions of economic activity in the service of life

German concept 'Wirtschaft' (economy) from 'Wertschaffen' (creation of value).[3] Be that as it may – the demand that economic activity should be reflected upon in terms of its quality as the 'creation of value for human ends' is nowadays by no means self-evident. Arthur Rich's straightforward characterization of the human existential grounds for economic activity quoted at the head of this chapter is a programmatic and for some provocative statement calling for resistance to the self-referential 'nature' of the 'modern' economic system and for critical advocacy of an ethical-rational orientation and justification of all economic activity. The decisive criterion of all economic activity should not be the creation of market value but – in spite of all the practical constraints involved – *the service of life*.[4]

This lifeworld perspective brings up two elementary questions (Figure III.1): which values should be created for whom? On the one hand it is necessary to ask about the beneficial effects of economic activity in regard to the good life (question of meaning), on the other hand about its acceptability (justifiability) for all concerned in regard to just social co-existence (question of legitimation). The question of meaning is of a teleological-ethical kind; it is concerned with the 'direction of human fulfilment'[5] and hence with the cultural motives of rational economic

[3] According to Rock/Rosenthal, *Marketing = Philosophie*, p. 101.

[4] Rich, *Economic and Business Ethics*, p. 277, following the equally important theologian and social moral philosopher Emil Brunner, *The Divine Imperative: A Study in Christian Ethics*, transl. O. Wyon (Philadelphia: Westminster Press, 1947); orig. *Das Gebot und die Ordnungen. Entwurf einer protestantisch-theologischen Ethik*, 4th edn (Zurich: Theologischer Verlag, 1978; 1st edn 1932), p. 402.

[5] Th. Rentsch, 'Wie ist eine menschliche Welt überhaupt möglich? Philosophische Anthropologie als Konstitutionsanalyse der humanen Welt', in Ch. Demmerling/G. Gabriel/Th. Rentsch (eds.), *Vernunft und Lebenspraxis, Philosophische Studien zu den Bedingungen einer rationalen Kultur* (Frankfurt: Suhrkamp, 1995), pp. 192–214, at p. 198.

activity in everyday life. The question of legitimation is of a deontological-ethical kind, concerned with the normative preconditions and the social rules of rational economic activity based upon them. There is no room for either of these points of view in a purely economic systemic rationality. The systemic logic of the market economy 'knows' neither meaning nor legitimation, but only functions. For precisely this reason the economic system needs 'instructions' pointing the way and providing legitimacy, as functionality is a relational matter: for what and for whom specifically is the 'value created by the system' efficient, beneficial or good?

As we have seen in Part II, it is the ideological function of economism to reduce the lifeworld categories to purely systemic categories, so that the functional rationality of the economic system seems already to be the whole of economic rationality and concepts such as 'utility maximization' and 'efficiency' can be reinterpreted as anonymous, self-sufficient criteria of economic rationality. In contrast, the two elementary questions posed above approach the issue of the practical 'grounds' for rational economic activity from a different perspective, namely that of *socio-economic rationality*.[6] They can consequently also be seen as the two key questions which challenge economism. The question of meaning focuses on the stated ends of economic activity, which economic determinism reduces to the maximization of profit or benefit in a closed system governed by inherent necessity. The question of legitimation focuses on the potential social conflict arising from competing claims of the economic agents and from the functional system constraints imposed upon them, which the economistic fiction of the common good ('to the advantage of all') blurs over.

The topical significance of this double perspective on economic activity in the service of life stems from the practical challenge to socio-economic rationality – a challenge largely created by the self-referential economic system dynamics itself. One could speak here of the dialectics of the economic rationalization process, which is in danger of 'progressively' losing its real-life practical meaning (orientation on 'human ends') and its fundamental social legitimation (through subjection to the democratic will of free and equal citizens). This manifests itself symptomatically in the contemporary dwindling of the formerly pronounced belief in progress in the 'advanced' market societies and in the growing awareness of an epochal crisis of meaning in these societies and even of the absurdity of the potentially uncontrollable dynamics of 'rationalization' in an unrestricted economic system. Under these circumstances, what matters

[6] For this notion see Section 3.3 (2).

nowadays is to re-establish a rational relationship between the standpoint of the (system-related) efficiency of economic activity and the standpoints of the real-life practical *meaning and justice* of the economic system.

In what follows we will deal first with the question of meaning (Chapter 6) and then with the question of legitimation (Chapter 7) in rational, life-serving economic activity for the fulfilment of human ends.

6 The question of meaning: economic activity and the good life

Ultimately, man should not ask what the meaning of his life is, but rather must recognize that it is *he* who is asked. In a word, each man is questioned by life; and he can only answer to life by *answering for* his own life; to life he can only respond by being responsible.[1]

Meaning must be understood as a fundamental category of human existence. Man is a being in search of meaning, and what is more, he possesses a 'will to meaning'[2] founded on his essential freedom of action and the consequent possibility and necessity of intentional (deliberate) self-determination. We can, therefore, speak of an 'apriori of meaning orientation on the basis of the teleological nature of man'[3] as a part of the universal conditio humana. Without a meaning context human life is impossible. Meaning fills human existence with significance by directing our existence towards what is essential in life, namely what we wish for in life as a whole. The truly strong motives which determine our strivings and aspirations in life are rooted in our teleological meaning structures. What we wish to make of our lives, what we expect from life, whether we are satisfied with what we achieve so that we 'feel good' about our lives or not depends on them.

Accordingly, when we talk about the meaning of an action we mean the ultimate or holistic purpose, which itself can no longer be interpreted functionally or instrumentally as a means to a further, higher end, i.e. the human intrinsic value of the *good life*. Questions of meaning always deal in essence with the fundamental intentions and highest value ideas which guide the human search for a fulfilled life for its own sake. If life in this sense succeeds and is 'good' we can speak of a fortunate or even blissful

[1] V. E. Frankl, *Man's Search of Meaning* (New York: Washington Square Press, 1963), p. 172.
[2] V. E. Frankl, *The Will to Meaning: Foundations and Applications of Logotherapy* (New York: Meridian, 1988).
[3] Rentsch, *Philosophische Anthropologie*, p. 199.

life – or simply of happiness. Aristotle defines happiness first of all quite formally as the ultimate goal or highest good of human endeavour, as we always strive for it 'for itself and never for the sake of anything else'.[4]

But what does happiness or the good life mean specifically? As we have seen in Chapter 1, the question refers to an *ethos* as the consciousness with which persons or groups customarily justify their cultural self-understanding and their conduct of life. Questions of meaning refer to value standards of a life form and these standards are specific to a culture or a personality. Within the limits of legitimacy, that is to say, of the observance of the moral rights of all others, they are neither capable of nor in need of generalization. Ultimately each and every human life is unique and irreplaceable. In the modern world, at least, every individual and every life community is free to and can indeed be expected to work out and pursue an (inter-) subjectively meaningful life plan of its own. We must not forget, however, that humans are fundamentally social beings. The discovery of meaning is a personal task related to the conduct of one's own life in the light of a carefully considered idea of the good life, but it also includes a conception of a just and solidary life together with others in a community which is invested with meaning.[5]

Within the legitimate framework of equal liberties and life opportunities for all the subjective search for and discovery of meaning and the corresponding conduct of life can and should be possible as a 'private affair' of the individual or the meaning community she or he feels attached to. Consequently modern economic ethics, as a universalistic rational ethics, cannot and will not claim the competence to make generally valid statements about the 'right' blueprint for life. But what can it then contribute to the meaning orientation of economic life?

The fundamental sense of the question about the meaning of economic life is that – even before the question of legitimation – it poses the first and basic ethical challenge to economism. It does so by opposing all the practical and theoretical tendencies towards an autonomous and autotelic, self-referential logic of the economy. Circular reasoning of this kind subsumes even the ends of economic activity under categories of 'pure' economics, such as 'utility maximization' or 'the achievement of competitive advantages'. The question of meaning breaks through this circularity of economistic argumentation with an instrumental view of the economy from the perspective of the lifeworld: the economy is always only a means in the service of higher and literally more *vital* ends.[6] And if

[4] Aristotle, *Nicomachean Ethics*, p. 11. [5] See Section 1.2.

[6] The ordoliberal theory, in particular, has emphasized this instrumental character of the market economy. This will be dealt with later, in Chapter 9.

they are to be meaningful, these can be determined only by the entirety of a subjectively right and well-cultivated lifeworld practice. Consequently, at a personal and societal as well as at a scientific level, economic life is ultimately to be reflected upon as a historically shaped cultural achievement that must be aligned with ever-changing horizons of meaning. As Max Weber emphasized long ago, 'meaningful' economy is, therefore, always social economy.[7]

The practice of an economic form *in the service of life* in the sense intended here will be possible only if certain structural preconditions can be implemented at the political level. Such an economy and the accompanying basic conditions can, furthermore, be established and prosper in a democratic society only if the majority of citizens really want it. They must have an enlightened and motivating idea as to how, if they had the choice, they would wish to act as reflective, purposeful economic agents in order to live a life acceptable to them without disregarding their responsibility towards others. Hence, cultural motives of the lifeworld must enjoy priority over questions of the organization of the economic system.

In view of this dependence of all economic activity on the context of a culturally desired life form, the elementary aspect of service to life contained in the quotation from Arthur Rich above reminds us that economic activity has in the first place a universal anthropologically constant reference to life. This permits a distinction between two elementary levels of meaningful economic activity in regard to the good life of individuals. It is a matter in the first place – at the level of an *economy of vital necessities* – of ensuring the bare means of universal human subsistence regardless of the cultural superstructure (Section 6.1). At an advanced stage the broadening of the abundance of human life (in whatever cultural or personal form) can come into the foreground as the goal of meaningful economic activity. Yet the transition to a corresponding *economy of abundance* (Section 6.2) does not happen automatically under the conditions of economic self-assertion in competition with others; it inevitably requires collective political decisions on changes in the socially desired life form (Section 6.3).

6.1 The elementary sense of economic activity: securing the means of human subsistence

The elementary meaning context of economic life is founded on the *conditio humana*, i.e. on the basic conditions of human existence in all

[7] And social economy in turn is for Weber always 'cultural science'. See Weber, '"Objectivity" in Social Science and Social Policy', p. 67.

the conceivable 'cultivated' forms. Man is subject to the absolute physical and psychological necessities of his nature as a creature of needs, whose satisfaction is indispensable for the maintenance of life at the most elementary level. Having enough to eat (food), being warm (clothing), enjoying good health (medical provision), having a 'home' to live in (housing) are undoubtedly basic needs of every human being; they are universal and indisputable, even though the possibilities and forms of their satisfaction are culture-specific, and consequently a long-standing subject of international endeavours to arrive at ethical-political, culture-independent norms.[8]

The fundamental significance of economic activity as 'service to life' consists, therefore, in the provision of all human beings with the necessary means of subsistence in the broadest sense of the word.[9] Humans differ from animals in this context in that they do not simply take the means of life directly from nature or live from hand to mouth, but must plan and develop to meet their needs and are consequently existentially dependent on the 'cultivation' of nature. From this perspective both cultural and economic life can equally be traced back to the origins of human society, a fact still expressed today in the term of culture (as agri-culture in its origin). Economic activity must itself be understood as a fundamental cultural achievement; it provides the framework within which the dignity of human existence[10] is not only 'technically' ensured but also culturally and normatively *defined*. Furthermore, not only how human needs are satisfied is culturally moulded and normatively determined, but also the definition of what basic human needs actually are, even though they are shared universally. There is no such thing as a 'pure' needy nature of humans; they are rather from the start the cultural subjects of their own 'nature'.[11] What is to be regarded as the human subsistence level is, consequently, not an objectively ascertainable, naturally given quantity but a constantly changing cultural norm and therefore in principle

[8] In addition to the basic needs mentioned above there are other needs which can be less clearly determined as they are more strongly influenced by specific cultural practices. They refer to the development of personality in accordance with human dignity and questions of social integration, whose socio-economic significance we will deal with in the context of human rights issues; see below Section 7.3 (1). They are regularly included in the international endeavours mentioned above, for example in the work of the International Labour Organization (ILO) in Geneva. See for instance Dh. Gai (ed.), *Decent Work: Objectives and Strategies* (Geneva: ILO, 2006).

[9] On the traditional orientation of economics on the necessities of life from Plato and Aristotle through the Christian Middle Ages to the Modern Period see U. Knobloch, *Theorie und Ethik des Konsums* (Berne *et al.*: Haupt, 1994), p. 43ff.

[10] On the concept of human dignity see Section 1.4.

[11] On the cultural nature of man and the historical relationships between culture and economy see the detailed treatment in Ulrich, *Transformation*, p. 31ff.

accessible to critical reflection and argumentation. And it is always indubitably a culturally determined social minimum.

The fact that what is existentially 'necessary' can be specified only in cultural terms in no way affects the applicability of these 'necessities' in principle to all mankind. Every individual enjoys a universal moral right to the provision of the necessities of life in accordance with the definition of the culturally determined social minimum of the society to which he or she belongs. This points to the relationship between the elementary meaning of economic activity, the safeguarding of the fundamentals of life for every person, and questions of basic rights and justice. We will return to this point later.[12]

What interests us at the moment is the meaning structure and the motives which lead to the recognition of, or the failure to recognize, the *social significance of economic activity*. This can plausibly be seen in the general prevention of existential neediness through the provision of sufficient 'means of life' for all the members of a society. And the 'progress' of an economy must accordingly be measured primarily by the degree to which it achieves this aim. The justification is easily found. As the production of the means of life in a social community or society involves the division of labour, that society must always 'necessarily' see itself as a *solidary community*, because the cooperation required by division of labour makes a purely individualistic calculation of economic performance impossible. Every product produced by division of labour is a 'social product'.[13] This gives rise to the problem of its just distribution. Those who do not participate directly in the production or supply of the means of life also 'earn' their share: the providers of other contributions to the community, the pensioners who have already fulfilled their obligations, the children who are preparing for a profession, the 'unemployed' who have been eliminated from working life through no fault of their own, the sick and the handicapped. Thus, in every community based on the division of labour, the distribution of goods is determined not only by the achievement principle but necessarily also by the principle of need. In a civilized society no-one will seriously dispute the obligation of the community to prevent death resulting from starvation or curable diseases, or suffering under inhuman conditions, with all the means at its disposal. The acceptance of such a state of affairs would be barbarous. But most societies are divided into two parts. Some of their members live below the culturally accepted social minimum, struggle against poverty and suffer from a degrading lack of the bare necessities of life, with 'too little to live

[12] See Chapter 7. [13] See Rich, *Business and Economic Ethics*, p. 410.

but too much to die', as the saying goes, whereas other, more fortunate individuals live in comfortable prosperity or even luxury. This must ultimately be evaluated as a symptom of politico-economic failure to carry out the elementary socio-economic task of efficiently providing all members of a society with the basic necessities of life. Solidarity is the touchstone by which the practical 'efficiency' of an economy of vital necessities must be measured.

Why are a considerable, and in most countries growing, number of the members of a society poor and what is the best starting point for the solution of the problem? Poverty is a complex phenomenon usually involving a wide variety of causes that cannot be explained and overcome in purely economic or individual terms but only by taking into account the overall life situation of those affected.[14] If one accepts the realistic assumption that very few people are voluntarily poor in the sense of suffering from a lack of basic necessities, then it is obvious that the decisive causes must be sought less in the unwillingness of individuals to achieve than in their social deprivation. This means that the opportunity to provide themselves with the necessities of life by their own efforts has, quite literally, been 'stolen' from them. The basic problem lies, therefore, in the 'helplessness' caused by their life conditions, in the lack of *real freedom*[15] (in spite of formal freedom) to help themselves. This applies equally to minority problems in 'highly developed' economies and to majority problems in underdeveloped or badly developed economies. The fact that in the 'advanced' and wealthy economies with an enormous productive potential there still exist entire population groups who live in more or less pronounced material need, and that the 'new poverty' has even increased statistically in recent years in the richest countries of the world, must be understood as the consequence of a growing structural incapacity for economic self-assertion, which is usually connected with the steadily growing existential dependence of most people on the market.

An economic policy – especially one designed to create jobs – which places its hopes in a forced increase of productivity and (quantitative) economic growth aggravates this basic problem rather than solving it. A merely *compensatory social policy* may assist the affected with transfer payments from the state and provide them with the purchasing power

[14] For an overview of the explanatory dimensions of poverty or prosperity see J. D. Sachs, *The End of Poverty: Economic Possibilities for Our Time* (London: Penguin, 2005).

[15] See Ph. Van Parijs, *Real Freedom for All: What (if anything) can justify capitalism?* (Oxford: Clarendon, 1995), p. 21ff. The conception of real freedom is taken up in Sections 7.2 and 7.3.

needed for survival; nevertheless it fails to fulfil the primary social task of an economy, as long as those concerned are not at the same time freed from their original 'structural passivity'.[16] Moreover, experience shows that the economic costs of a social policy that only tackles the symptoms increase overproportionally with economic progress (rationalization) and intensification of competition on the market. Ultimately such policies place too great a financial strain on economies engaged in global competition for attractive locations of investment and production. They make excessive demands on the willingness of the successful, financially better-off members of the community to show solidarity and to meet the social costs. Because of the one-dimensional economic progress ever broadening circles of the population are being reduced to a state of structural impotence ('the two-thirds society').

In contrast, an *emancipatory social policy* would primarily pursue the goal of enabling and empowering all who are capable of gainful employment to assert themselves economically – by guaranteeing the right to work and to acquire income and by providing general education and genuine offers of employment. This would make more sense from an ethical point of view as well as it would pave the way for a reduction of the social costs of compensatory payments.[17] The question usually occupying the foreground of the debate on the welfare state as to the level of provision that must be guaranteed to every citizen would then, in the long term, turn out to be secondary and financially less explosive. Discussion on the quantitative level of the social minimum to be guaranteed by the state is perfectly legitimate in view of the normative character of its definition. With regard to the question of economic acceptability it is, furthermore, quite conceivable that the provision of transfer payments by the welfare state should be linked to the assumption of suitable duties in order to help those concerned to overcome their structurally determined passivity and to ensure the reciprocity of citizens' rights and duties – as a giving and taking between the members of the community. The central idea should always be that the social significance of economic life consists in eliminating (at the roots, as far as possible) the existential need of all people, whereas the merely progressive 'modernization of poverty'[18] must be interpreted as an expression of continuing failure to achieve this goal.

[16] W. Hollstein, *Die Gegengesellschaft: Alternative Lebensformen*, 4th expanded edn (Bonn: Verlag Neue Gesellschaft, 1981), p. 154.

[17] On the central ideas of emancipatory social policy see for details Ulrich, *Transformation*, p. 467ff. The enabling and empowering approach to the struggle against poverty indicated above is dealt with more closely in Section 7.1.

[18] I. Illich, *The Right to Useful Employment and its Professional Enemies* (London: Boyars, 1978), p. 28ff.

6.2 The advanced meaning of economic activity: furthering the abundance of human life

The meaning of an economy in pursuit of the abundance of life (instead of goods only) will be examined in three stages. First of all we will develop the formal idea of meaningful economic life at this level, without regard to the real obstacles to its achievement. We will then contrast this idea with a symptomatic description of the 'normal' reality of the life form in 'advanced' industrial societies, illustrating the growing perversion of meaningfulness in the contemporary economy. Finally, in Section 6.3, we will attempt a systematic analysis of the basic problem and clarify the principal path towards a meaning orientation of economic activity in the lifeworld.

(1) The guiding idea of an economy of abundance

Once the satisfaction of the elementary and universal basic human needs has been ensured, the culture specific meaning context of particular historically determined economic forms and their contribution to the quality of life move into the foreground. It is not the never-ending increase in the quantity of available goods, but the emancipation of man from the need to concentrate all his energy on the provision of the bare necessities of life which makes cultural sense.[19] Beyond the elementary 'struggle for existence' and the satisfaction of fundamental existential needs the kingdom of scarcity comes to an end and the kingdom, not of overabundance but of the cultivation of 'higher' needs for the realization of personal life projects begins. Social variety and the abundance of opportunities for the free cultural development of the individual would then be the guiding idea which imparts meaning at an advanced and 'mature' economic level.[20] To take up the vision of the future presented by the brilliant economist John Maynard Keynes,[21] economic activity as a

[19] On the basic emancipatory meaning of the cultural-historical processes of rationalization and its various aspects (emancipation from the forces of nature, from social power and inner psychic compulsions) see Ulrich, *Transformation*, p. 55ff.

[20] The expression the 'abundance' of life seems to embody an age-old human dream. In antiquity Epicure points out 'that every being ... strives for an existential state which suits him best, by enjoying the greatest possible abundance of life'; Epikur, *Philosophie der Freude*, ed. J. Mewaldt (Stuttgart: Kröner, 1973), p. 24 (own translation from the editor's introduction). It occurs again later in the New Testament (John 10, 10), when Jesus says 'I am come that they might have life, and that they might have it more abundantly'. In Luther's translation of the Bible we find, instead of abundance, the equally fitting phrase 'volle Genüge' ('full sufficiency').

[21] J. M. Keynes, 'Economic Possibilities for Our Grandchildren', in Keynes, *Collected Writings, vol. IX, Essays in Persuasion* (London: Palgrave Macmillan, 1972; 1st edn 1930), pp. 321–32, at p. 325ff.

sign of progress would become more and more secondary, the problems of production and supply would in principle be solved, and human time and energy would be increasingly devoted to the more important matters of the good life: away from the troublesome need of having (enough) to the inner freedom and delights of cultivated being.[22]

The economy of abundance is based on the idea of making humans and not the market free – free for the essentials of a fulfilled life. It rests upon the holistic art of 'being satisfied with enough'. 'Enough' is not an economic but a cultural category, as it implies the insight:

> that no good would be served by having more, that more would not be better. 'Enough is as good as a feast', as the English say.[23]

The more we acquire material goods, the more important our ability to know what is enough for our lives becomes. Otherwise we will simply replace the old constraints of the economy of necessity with new self-created, ever-growing constraints resulting from the desire to have more and more. The subjectively felt scarcity of goods then becomes limitless and *avarice* threatens to dominate our lives. But:

> in greed humans lose their 'soul', their freedom, their composure, their inner peace, and thus that which makes them human.[24]

Being satisfied with 'enough' first frees us from the unauthentic 'imagined' goals of consumption and hence from the obsessive ideas which make us prisoners of the acquisitive compulsion to have (and to purchase) goods incessantly.[25] The potentially limitless need to satisfy the externally driven hunger for consumption steadily loses its coercive significance for the quality of life, however, the more truly liberating fulfilment in meaningful activity occupies the centre of our lives. But achieving *meaning through inner freedom* and autonomous self-determination requires – beyond provision for the existential basics – a well-developed ability to choose what is really good and beneficial for ourselves from the variety of options offered by the 'multi-option society'.[26] A selectively cultivated, moderate consumption along these lines can definitely contribute to the good life, but this does not depend directly on consumption as such:

> Consumption can bring lasting fulfilment. It consists in productive action (Fromm) which makes use of consumer goods to the extent that they enable or

[22] An allusion to E. Fromm, *To Have or To Be?* (New York *et al.*: Harper & Row, 1976).
[23] A. Gorz, *Critique of Economic Reason* (London and New York: Verso, 1989), p. 112.
[24] H. Küng, *A Global Ethic for Global Politics and Economics*, p. 234.
[25] On the dependence of the practical constraints to which we are subject on the goals we set and pursue see Section 4.3 (3).
[26] P. Gross, *Die Multioptionsgesellschaft* (Frankfurt: Suhrkamp, 1994).

facilitate intrinsically motivated personal activity, the unfolding of inner forces (. . .) The fulfilment produced in this way is immaterial. Although it is achieved with the help of material goods they are not its source. On the contrary, there are many good reasons for believing that the unfolding of inner forces requires only a minimum of goods; an excess of material stimulation leads to passivity, undermines the intrinsic motivation (Deci & Ryan) and weakens the lasting effects of fulfilment.[27]

The less we yield to the temptations of a merely quantitative increase in our consumption and the more we desire to cultivate, refine and qualitatively expand our range of experience, the more we need a clear and well-considered life project as an orientational horizon for the meaningful use of the economic means available to us. But this depends ultimately on our self-understanding, on our personal and social identity. If it is posed radically enough (i.e. down to the roots), the question of the kind of life we would like to lead cannot be separated from the question of the kind of person we wish to be:

When faced with crucial existential choices, someone who does not know what he wants to be will ultimately be led to pose the question, '*Who am I*, and who would I like to be?'[28]

Here we must recall our earlier treatment of the constitutive preconditions for the discovery of personal identity.[29] From early childhood the motives for the development of our self-understanding are shaped by our deep need to be recognized members of a moral community and to be seen by that community as worthy of recognition. The meaning of community with others is first necessary if we are to find ourselves as autonomous persons. No-one has better explained why this is so than Adam Smith with his interpretation of the 'social correspondence of moral sentiments'.[30] In order to achieve self-respect we must undertake the mental experiment of asking ourselves whether the motives for our actions would be worthy of respect from the standpoint of a morally competent impartial spectator. This criterion, worthiness of respect, precisely defines the wish to belong to a moral community of people we respect, as opposed to the merely instrumental interest in social acceptance as a means to the end of achieving our private superficial success as smoothly as possible.

[27] G. Scherhorn, 'Konsumverhalten', in G. Enderle *et al.* (eds.), *Lexikon der Wirtschaftsethik* (Freiburg i. Br.: Herder, 1993), col. 545–51, at p. 549, with reference to E. L. Deci/ M. R. Ryan, *Intrinsic Motivation and Self-determination in Human Behaviour* (New York: Plenum, 1985).

[28] Habermas, *Justification and Application*, p. 4. [29] See Section 1.2.

[30] Campbell, *Adam Smith's Science of Morals*, p. 94. See Section 2.2.

Ultimately we can arrive only at a good relationship to ourselves ('I'm okay') inside and not outside the reciprocity of interpersonal feelings and obligations. In other words, the need for individuation (personal identity through autonomy and self-realization) cannot be separated from the need for social integration (social identity through membership of an identifiable community). Without a 'social place in the world' a person cannot make his/her life 'habitable'[31] and fill it with meaning.

The more the concern for the satisfaction of the basic needs of life recedes into the background, the more the search for personal identity will be directed towards increasing the 'richness' and intensity of spiritual, intellectual and inter-personal experience. Neither want nor the desire for *objects* to satisfy our (real or imagined) needs will then dominate our 'interests' and guide our motivation, but the holistic development of our human *subject quality*, which can be found in the multiplicity of our singular human capabilities and potential for experience in the spheres of individuation *and* social commitment. The quality of our interpersonal relationships will increasingly become the decisive source of a meaningful life and the growth of personality – not only in our private long-term relationships but also in the context of self-discovery in a significant life-task or calling in accordance with our own inclinations and abilities. Full participation in the social process of work is then no longer merely a way of acquiring the means for survival (subsistence economy) or the necessary purchasing power for the market (market economy). Instead, work enables us to be useful members of the community, to 'cultivate' our abilities and personalities within it and to develop a healthy self-confidence.

For this reason the socially *productive* activity of man is, in principle, at least just as important as a meaning component of all cultures as the *consumerist* participation in the collective economic output, which (neoclassical) economic theory usually sees as the sole purpose. The intrinsic value of work is also important for working humans, in so far as it enables them to develop their ability to work autonomously.[32] All the important philosophers of the good life over the centuries agree that a happy fulfilled life does not simply fall into our laps with the acquisition of material goods or social success, but has rather to do with the inner meaningfulness and intrinsic human value of activities which are free, self-determined and essential for our self-understanding. More than 2000 years ago Aristotle

[31] We should recall here the original meaning of *ethos* as the place at the centre of our lives where we shape our *habits* and find our inner stability.

[32] On the significance of autonomous work for the good life see Seel, *Versuch über die Form des Glücks*, p. 142ff.

defined this state as 'activity of the soul in accordance with virtue'.[33] In the twentieth century Hannah Arendt approached the question from a particularly impressive cultural-historical perspective, demonstrating that the idea of the *vita activa*[34] is equivalent to liberation from the constraints of contemporary 'laborist' and consumerist life forms in which the 'value' of work lies only in its end product and hardly ever in its human significance for the worker himself. André Gorz's brilliant socio-economic analyses of the crisis of the 'work-based society' are also founded on the knowledge-guiding idea that the meaning of further economic rationalization must at long last be seen in 'making time available for these "higher activities" which are their own ends unto themselves, at one with the movement of life itself'.[35]

As the ancient Greeks clearly recognized, we can overcome our culturally reshaped 'neediness' along two fundamentally opposite paths to happiness: either along a materially productive path (which the work process itself possibly endows with meaning), by increasing the resources and goods which are useful for the satisfaction of our active and passive needs; or along a path which is *critical of needs*, by reflecting on our desires and reducing them to what is essential or even minimal for the meaning of our lives. An economy of abundance can be distinguished, in this regard, from an economy of merely material richness by the fact that it does not regard the satisfaction of needs through the uncritical accumulation of material goods as socio-economically rational; on the contrary, it approaches our needs in an intelligent self-critical fashion, sees through them and eliminates some of them as pseudo-needs. From this perspective the fundamental predecision of the traditional growth-oriented economy for the (bogus) productive fulfilment of 'given' needs appears as the expression of an economism which is blind to life.[36]

33 Aristotle, *Nicomachean Ethics*, p. 12.

34 H. Arendt, *The Human Condition* (Chicago: University of Chicago Press, 1958). Before Hannah Arendt, Karl Marx took up the Aristotelian ideal of autonomous activity (instead of heteronomously determined labour).

35 Gorz, *Critique of Economic Reason*, p. 94. Although he occupies a different political and ideological position, and his work is based on a less fundamental socio-economic analysis, Ralf Dahrendorf also develops a similar model of an 'activity society'. See R. Dahrendorf, *Die Chancen der Krise: Über die Zukunft des Liberalismus* (Stuttgart: DVA, 1983), p. 88.

36 This precisely is the basic idea of the philosophical approach to a rational critique of needs in F. Kambartel, 'Bemerkungen zum normativen Fundament der Ökonomie', in J. Mittelstrass (ed.), *Methodologische Probleme einer normativ-kritischen Gesellschaftstheorie* (Frankfurt: Suhrkamp, 1975), pp. 107–25; Mittelstrass 'Ist rationale Ökonomie als empirisch-quantitative Wissenschaft möglich?', in J. Mittelstrass (ed.), *Methodenprobleme der Wissenschaften vom gesellschaftlichen Handeln* (Frankfurt: Suhrkamp, 1979), pp. 299–319. Kambartel saw the rational critique of needs as a 'proto-economy', i.e. as

Cultural-historical movements have always swung back and forth between the two poles of life plans oriented on consumption and the pleasure principle (hedonism) and those oriented on contemplation and abstinence (asceticism), the tension between them often giving rise to mixed forms. The early modern Protestant ethic, for example, developed an extremely ascetic work ethos which, however, increasingly lost its original religious meaning (through the process of secularization) and became associated with a hedonistic pleasure-seeking culture. Without the latter the unbridled economic growth of industrial society would not have 'made sense'; but without the former the discipline needed for successful performance in the world of work would have been lacking.[37]

The spread of the consumerist-productivist conception of need satisfaction has not, however, rendered the alternative approach based on the critique of needs superfluous. On the contrary, the question of the degree of consumption and pleasure which is compatible with our vital need for personal individuation and social integration presents itself with growing urgency. Since antiquity moral philosophers have repeatedly attempted to explain a phenomenon that broad (but by no means all) strata of society have been able to experience in the industrial 'affluent society' of the last few decades: the *paradox of hedonism*.[38] It consists in the realization that the unrestrained pursuit of pleasure, the attempt to find happiness in the maximization of the satisfaction of material needs through the acquisition of consumer goods, quickly goes stale and fails to give life the desired 'meaning'. Consumerism, understood as a life form founded on boundless consumption, makes people passive and disappoints them, as it only pretends to give but in fact deprives the 'consumer' of significant meaningful experiences both in regard to the development of his own personality (personal identity) and to the experience of 'community spirit' through active participation in the social world (social identity).[39] Accordingly, consumption can contribute to a good and happy life only if it is enjoyed in moderation and alternates rhythmically with productive action (work). The less we are preoccupied with the satisfaction of basic existential needs and the more we can 'afford' the

the critical-normative foundation of a rational economy. On the characterization of the productive instead of the critical overcoming of pseudo-scarcity as economistic see especially his 'Bemerkungen', p. 117. The approach is, however, not sufficient as an economic ethical basis for rational economic activity. For a criticism see Ulrich, *Transformation*, p. 361ff.

37 As a supplement to Weber's *The Protestant Ethic*, see C. Campbell, *The Romantic Ethic and the Spirit of Modern Consumerism* (Oxford/Malden MA: Blackwell, 1987).

38 See Anzenbacher, *Einführung*, p. 158.

39 For a critique of consumerism and important literature on the topic see Ulrich, *Transformation*, p. 112ff.

numerous options for consumption available to us, the more important it evidently becomes to cultivate not only our forms of production but also those of consumption in view of a self-determined way to a fulfilled life.

Above all, the sense of fulfilment deriving from meaningful activity diminishes the relative significance of consumption for the 'satisfaction of our needs'. With the increasing satisfaction of our existential needs it ought to be easier for us – one might think – to develop a culture of self-critical reflection on our authentic needs and, without feeling that we have renounced something indispensable, to resist the calls of excessive hedonistic consumerism, which ignores the satisfaction of our genuine need for meaningful activity and tempts us instead to covet the luxuries which can be purchased on the market.[40] To put it in a nutshell: the phenomenon of the scarcity of the goods needed for survival might then be replaced by a sensitivity and feeling for the abundance of life: being instead of having.

(2) Symptoms of the consumerist reversal of meaningful life

The use of the irrealis above is justified, as the reality of the economically most advanced societies looks rather different today. They are by no means characterized by a general triumph over the lack of the necessities of life or the scarcity of essential goods, but – in analogy to the 'modernization of poverty' – by the persistent *modernization of scarcity*. The excessive production of goods which are inessential or completely superfluous is accompanied by a growing scarcity of resources and 'means of life' which are really essential for the quality of life. Wherever one looks, one can observe the remarkable fact that with the growth of the economy the feeling of scarcity increases rather than diminishes, even in regard to the essentials of life. Elementary goods such as living space, social security, adequate provision for old-age and medical treatment 'are eating up' an ever-growing share of available income and the real purchasing power of the lower and middle income groups is declining, making the fulfilment of the desires awakened by the growing range of consumer goods on the market more and more difficult to realize, while the national and local governments are suffering under a growing financial crisis.

On top of this, there is also a scarcity of employment, making life for the growing share of the population which has been eliminated against its will from the world of work as precarious as it was at a much lower level of economic development. Here we can observe world-wide one of the most striking symptoms of the paradoxical reversal of the meaning of economic

[40] For further consideration of this point see Section 8.3 (2).

progress. Now that the almost boundless productivity of the available means of production has, in principle, overcome the earlier scarcity of the means of subsistence for all mankind, the relationships of scarcity and the accompanying practical constraints are reversed. It is no longer the available goods, but paid *employment which is scarce*. It has long ceased to be the aim of economic policy to improve the overall quality of life by means of selective economic production; instead the sale of all kinds of goods and services must be increased, regardless of the need for them, so that increased production can then (supposedly) lead to the creation of workplaces of any kind whatever.[41] The first philosopher to fully recognize the absurdity of this development was probably Hannah Arendt, fifty years ago:

> The modern age has carried with it a theoretical glorification of labor and has resulted in a factual transformation of the whole of society into a laboring society. The fulfilment of the wish [liberation from labour through automation], therefore, like the fulfilment of wishes in fairy tales, comes at a moment when it can only be self-defeating. It is a society of laborers which is about to be liberated from the fetters of labor, and this society does no longer know of those other higher and more meaningful activities for the sake of which this freedom would deserve to be won. (. . .) What we are confronted with is the prospect of a society of laborers without labor, that is, without the only activity left to them. Surely, nothing could be worse.[42]

The policy of economic growth pursued as a (supposed) solution to the 'employment problem' has 'external effects' on the natural environment and the social lifeworld which bring about further, formerly unknown forms of scarcity, whose impact on daily life is increasingly drastic. *Ecological scarcity* affects almost all the natural resources (clean air, water, soil, forests, the genetic diversity of species, natural raw materials, and qualitatively unspoiled foodstuffs). *Social scarcity* in the form of socio-structural 'bottlenecks' in the supply of positional goods[43] that

41 We will come back to the 'problem of employment' in the context of justice in Section 7.3.

42 Arendt, *The Human Condition*, p. 4f. H. Arendt means by 'work' the industrial work based on extensive division of labour which is of little intrinsic value, heteronomous and possibly even 'slavish' (p. 81), in the sense of the Latin *labora*, incessantly repeated labours for the provision of the 'necessities of life', whereas by 'activity' or *vita activa* she means meaningful activity which usually 'goes on directly between men' (p. 7) or is a part of the *vita contemplativa*, the inner enrichment. According to Aristotle the precondition for both is 'freedom from the necessities of life and from compulsion by others' (p. 14).

43 On this point see F. Hirsch, *Social Limits to Growth* (London: Routledge & Kegan Paul, 1977). Positional goods are those which serve the satisfaction of higher needs, whose significance grows in the needs structure of the human subjects as the economy grows, for example the need for housing in 'high-class' residential areas, for travel, education and a career; the satisfaction of these needs quickly comes up against socio-structural, geographical or even ecological barriers. As a result, the cost of acquiring these positional

cannot be indefinitely increased (e.g. desirable educational qualifications and positions, good residential areas, living space and transportation) sours the supposed advantages of the 'affluent society'.[44] Furthermore, those who have work suffer under a new *scarcity of time*, which is rather remarkable in view of the continuous increase in productivity and the acceleration of economic processes (growing hustle and bustle in the working world in spite of or rather precisely because of 'faster' means of production, communication and transportation). All of this has led more and more people to dream of the 'new slowness'.[45]

In defence of the quality of their lives people are forced to make more and more advance investments of a material and immaterial kind in order to satisfy what are usually thoroughly elementary needs (e.g. in regard to the quality of foodstuffs, housing and work). Thus an objective need arises for the often cost-intensive *defensive consumption*[46] of formerly unnecessary goods (e.g. the purchase of mineral water instead of drinking tap water, the installation of technical security systems in view of growing public insecurity, the purchase of expensive housing in order to enjoy tranquillity, clean air and adequate living space, the investment of time and money in education and professional qualifications as a counter-strategy to the growing risk of unemployment, flight from the bustle of work and consumption to holidays which are urgently 'needed'). The result is an *objective* increase in the quantity of investments and goods which a person 'needs' for a tolerable life.

The same is true of the increase in *compensatory consumption*. This plays a particular role in connection with the lack of productive meaningfulness in places of work which have no intrinsic value but are entirely geared to the achievement of maximum output. Here the relationship of partial substitution between productive and consumptive satisfaction 'functions' in the opposite direction. People who are denied productive satisfaction at their place of work will usually attempt to compensate for the resulting inner emptiness all the more by purchasing consumer goods. This constellation is virtually the constitutive driving force behind the industrial way of life. On the one hand, at least in the case of less qualified places of work, monotonous, unchallenging, often 'mindless' work, which has been deprived of all appeal through rationalization and extreme division of labour, and whose sole value for the workers is seen

goods rises and they are increasingly reserved for the topmost layers of the hierarchy of social distribution. For the non-privileged the available quantity of more or less trivial goods increases, but the quality of life as a whole scarcely rises or even sinks.

44 See J. K. Galbraith, *The Affluent Society* (Boston: Houghton Mifflin, 1958).

45 See the novel by S. Nadolny, *The Discovery of Slowness* (New York: Penguin, 1987), to whom the concept is probably owed.

46 See F. Hirsch, *Social Limits to Growth*, p. 57ff.

in the acquisition of purchasing power for consumption (labourism). On the other hand, the concentration of the satisfaction of all the needs frustrated in the world of work on 'leisure time', where compensation for 'hard' work is sought in consumption (consumerism). But in comparison to the experiential quality of inherently meaningful activity, we find passive consumption in the long run to be shallow and trite rather than satisfying. As long as we fail to grasp the deeper causes of the *deceptive* 'experience of consumption', we will continue to be lead astray by advertising and the 'example' of others and to be *deceived* by the further temptations of compensatory consumption, without the increased consumption bringing any reduction of our desire. In this consumerist vicious circle the feeling of the scarcity of what we could acquire in relation to our needs tends to increase *subjectively* rather than to diminish.

Both objectively and subjectively, therefore, the dependence of people in the 'advanced' industrialist societies on scarce goods and advance investments of all kinds is increasing. The in principle conceivable *emancipation* from the 'necessities of life' and concentration on more important matters than economic activity, which Keynes saw as a prospect for his grandchildren, fails to take place or is reserved for a privileged minority. That is, in essence, the result of the failure to transform the old industrialist life into a cultivated life and economic style founded on the economy of abundance. And it has nowhere been more incisively expressed than in the work of Rudolf Bahro, formulated in a time which still showed sympathy for utopias:

> The *compensatory* interests, first of all, are the unavoidable reaction to the way that society restricts and stunts the growth, development, and confirmation of innumerable people at an early age. The corresponding needs are met with substitute satisfactions. People have to be indemnified, by possession and consumption of as many things and services as possible, with the greatest possible (exchange-) value, for the fact that they have an inadequate share in the proper human needs. The striving for power can also be classed with the compensatory interests, as a kind of higher derivative.
>
> The *emancipatory* interests, on the other hand, are oriented to the growth, differentiation and self-realization of the personality in all dimensions of human activity. (. . .) There are recognizable barriers from which men have always sought to emancipate themselves, in order to obtain access to something, and appropriate something, that is conceived time and again in the ideas of freedom, joy happiness, etc., which no cynical irony can expunge. The inexhaustible possibilities of human nature which themselves increase with cultural progress, are the innermost material of all utopias.[47]

[47] R. Bahro, *The Alternative in Eastern Europe* (London: NLB & Verso, 1978), p. 272f.

In this last word – utopia – Bahro also hits the nail on the head in regard to the feelings of most people about the situation today. It seems to be the case that, in spite of real economic progress in the highly developed national economies, society is failing more and more to acquire the cultural meaning corresponding to this level of development. We are confronted with a striking discrepancy: on the one hand there can in principle be scarcely any doubt that the enormous productivity of a modern market economy would permit the fulfilment of Keynes' vision of a society in which economic activity has become secondary and an economy of abundance can be realized; on the other hand, however, it is also indisputable that de facto most people all over the world are forced to continue living against their will in the 'conserved life form of an economy of poverty'[48] (although at different absolute levels). Their growing dissatisfaction with this situation is expressed in the symptoms of the much quoted 'crisis of meaning'. They fail to understand:

why despite the advanced stage of technological development the life of the individual is still determined by the dictates of professional careers, the ethics of status competition, and by the values of possessive individualism and available substitute gratifications: why the institutionalized struggle for existence, the discipline of alienated labor, and the eradication of sensuality and aesthetic gratification are perpetuated.[49]

The persistence of this state of affairs seems to make even less sense in view of the fact that the alternative project of a post-laborist (and post-consumerist) economic style permitting the realization of an active and full life must be regarded, in the words of Ralf Dahrendorf, as 'a liberal demand'.[50] Therefore, we must ask why, in regard to our cultural life projects, the majority of us remain imprisoned in a merely technologically modernizing form of the 'economy of poverty'. The clarification of the question leads us back to a fundamental structural problem which is connected with the coordinatory capacity of the market economy, i.e. with the basic mechanism of the economic system as such. It would 'make little sense' to ignore this context and unconcernedly recommend that people should give their lives a different direction from a cultural point of view in spite of it, as sometimes happens. Here too, integrative economic ethics must first critically expose the normative element concealed in the economic system itself by examining the systematic difficulties involved

48 J. Habermas, 'Technology and Science as "Ideology"', in his *Toward a Rational Society*, transl. J. Shapiro (Boston: Beacon Press, 1970), pp. 81–122, at p. 121.
49 Ibid., p. 121f.
50 Dahrendorf, *Chancen der Krise*, p. 96: 'The promotion of the activity society is a liberal demand.'

in bestowing a 'free' and personal meaning on life under the conditions of competitive self-assertion in the market economy.

6.3 The discovery of personal meaning under conditions of competitive self-assertion

As a thought experiment let us just imagine two different forms of life and mentality which are neither inimical to one another nor feel obliged to reciprocal solidarity but practise indifferent tolerance.[51] Let us further assume that the two styles of life are involved in a 'competition of cultures' in which the starting points are equal, so that both sides at first have the same resources and options at their disposal. These resources are modest and both sides depend upon meeting their existential needs by selling goods and services on the market.

The one group – we will call them the *self-limiters* – pursues an emancipatory life project in the sense of the economy of abundance sketched above. They attribute to economic activity merely an instrumental role in regard to the goal of the free development of their individual talents in the shape of self-determined, socially meaningful and responsible activities, and to the cultivation of interpersonal relationships and cultural forms of self-expression and experience. In material matters the life project of the self-limiters is by no means radically ascetic, but it is critical of needs. They certainly wish to work for a degree of prosperity, but reflect on its significance in terms of its serviceability for an existence guided by their overriding life project. For this reason their understanding of efficient economic activity is integrative in the sense that the benefit is not seen exclusively in the market value of the goods produced and the services offered. These are regarded instead as efficient only in as far as their 'vital' value (in the service of life) is found good according to the cultural standards of the group; in the same way the inherent value of work for working people is equally important. Nothing is produced simply because it can be sold and 'rationalization' exclusively with a view to minimizing costs plays no part in the considerations of the group. The aim is, instead, to optimize production under the holistic qualitative standpoint of service to life.

A considered self-limitation of the market orientation will play a particular part in the 'integrative' economic style of this group. After all, its aim is not the maximization of consumption but the provision of what is necessary and serviceable for their project of the good life and, over and

[51] We assume, therefore, completely in accordance with methodological and normative individualism, that the subjects are *mutually unconcerned*; see Section 5.3 (1).

beyond this, for a partial emancipation from competition. In their economic life they wish, therefore, to follow the slogan 'enough is enough'. For the self-limiters the true life-style consists in asserting themselves in economic competition to the extent that they are able to create the preconditions for the fulfilment of the good life by their own efforts, but they have no interest in making the production of 'the means of life' the main goal of life itself; on the contrary, their aim is to reduce their dependence on the market.[52] They seek a fine balance in order to arrive at a cultural 'society of liberated time'[53] built on the solid foundation of an economy of abundance. For them a 'wealth of time' is just as important as a moderate wealth of commodities.[54]

Let us now visit the second group in order to acquaint ourselves with a substantially different life project. We call them the *entrepreneurs* (who market their own personal resources and ability potential). Their socialization has taken a different course than that of the self-limiters. The idea of self-critical reflection on their needs and of 'opting out' partially from competition is completely alien to them. Early in life they have experienced great success in the struggle for self-assertion in all kinds of competition, which has made them 'hungry' for more success and has lastingly shaped their identity. Consequently they identify themselves to a great extent with the logic of covetousness, effort and market success – competition is fun! In the course of time the competitive stance becomes inextricably woven into their general life form and identity, an identity of flexible 'market orientation'[55] and possessive individualism ('I am what I have'[56]). In contrast to the self-limiters, whom they regard as 'softies' deficient in achievement orientation and toughness towards themselves, the 'entrepreneurs' hardly ever waste time thinking about a meaningful life form, as everything is already perfectly clear: a successful career in competition with people like themselves is the meaning of life for them. Accordingly, they consistently and continually invest in the improvement of their personal capacity for competition. They regard their personal biography as an entrepreneurial undertaking: always thinking in terms of the market, developing competitive advantages hard for others to imitate,

52 In this context Illich, *Right to Useful Employment*, p. 93, speaks of the ideal of 'modern subsistence'.
53 Following Gorz's project of a 'society of liberated time'. *Critique of Economic Reason*, p. 93.
54 J. P. Rinderspacher, 'Warum nicht auch mal sonntags arbeiten?', in K. W. Dahm *et al.* (eds.), *Sonntags nie? Die Zukunft des Wochenendes* (Frankfurt: Campus, 1989), pp. 13–42, at p. 34.
55 On the crystallization and the features of the 'marketing character' from a psychoanalytical point of view see Fromm, *To Have or To Be*, pp. 73, 147ff.; see also Tugendhat, *Vorlesungen*, p. 263ff.
56 Fromm, *To Have or To Be*, p. 77. On possessive individualism see Section 5.3 (1).

selling themselves as effectively as possible at all times and so increasing their success! To put it in the by no means fictional words a leading Swiss manager once chose to formulate the guiding principle of his life: 'The goal must be to want to be the best.'[57]

Accordingly, maximizing behaviour is the general principle: maximization of success, profit and benefits on the one hand, minimization of costs on the other. The motto runs: 'the more the better' – of everything! To pause at some stage, to lean back and to conclude that 'enough is enough' does not occur to them, as they have fully grasped the logic of competition and know that a comparative competitive advantage gained at an earlier stage can only be maintained with renewed efforts. In dynamic competition there are only 'winners' and 'losers' and movements up or down the ladder of success, but no chance of resting on one's laurels. On the contrary, the more the market dominates society, the more the principle of 'the winner takes it all' applies.[58] The market 'punishes' underachievers, and rightly so in view of its function as the guarantor of efficiency: 'Not everyone can win, but all can try.'[59]

But this authentic quotation on entrepreneurship fails to take the following into account: There are people who have no wish to participate unconditionally in the rat race for the maximization of success. The 'self-limiters', who consciously refrain from going beyond a certain degree of economic success because they would like to devote a substantial part of their time and energy to other ends outside competition, are then doomed from the start to be among the losers. There is no room for their life project alongside the uncontrollable expansion of the entrepreneurial pursuit of success, for, as has been said, 'the winner takes it all', or to repeat the formulation of Max Weber quoted earlier:

> Whoever does not adapt his life to the conditions of capitalist success must go under or at least cannot rise.[60]

The growing (negative) experience of the self-limiters will thus lead them either to voluntarily sacrifice their alternative life projects on the altar of the 'reality principle' and – against their original intentions, in flexible adaptation maybe until the 'corrosion' of their character[61] – to make the

[57] Pury, 'David de Pury', p. 7. At the time David de Pury was co-president of the Swedish-Swiss company Asea Brown Boveri (ABB) and the leading initiator of the sensational radical neoliberal White Book *Mut zum Aufbruch* (Courage for a New Departure), ed. Pury/Hauser/Schmid. See the comments made earlier in Section 4.2.

[58] See R. H. Frank/Ph. J. Cook, *The Winner-Take-All Society* (New York: Penguin, 1996).

[59] Pury, 'David de Pury', p. 7. [60] Weber, *The Protestant Ethic*, p. 72.

[61] See R. Sennett, *The Corrosion of Character: The Personal Consequences of Work in the New Capitalism* (New York: Norton, 1998); see also L. Boltanski/E. Chiapello, *The New Spirit of Capitalism*, transl. G. Elliott (London: Verso, 2005).

rat race of competitive self-assertion the main content of their lives or to accept their 'elimination' (Max Weber) in the long or short run from the market and their total exclusion from society. In this case they will then – together with other losers – quickly slide into a socially marginalized existence in which they are dependent on maintenance by public welfare and are unable to fulfil their life ideal of a voluntary self-limitation of needs based on a self-determined degree of self-assertion on the market. Instead of being able to practise an 'economy of abundance' the self-limiters are then faced with equally unsatisfactory alternatives, either – as 'opters-in' – to adapt their life form more or less unconditionally to that of the 'entrepreneurs', or – as total opters-out – to fall back into an 'economy of poverty'.

In view of this *structural asymmetry* of life chances it is not surprising that the tendency of the majority of people in the advanced industrial societies is to prefer the competitive life form, and this goes on parallel to the growing toughness of competition (particularly on the labour market) in a society in which the winner takes it all and the loser is left with virtually nothing. Under these conditions being able to 'opt in' and not to 'opt out' is the main concern and the primary goal of most young people nowadays, as those who fail to reach the first rung of the career ladder are faced with a highly unattractive future, living literally on the breadline.

All of this once again demonstrates that *competition is not a value-neutral instrument* for the efficient realization of all and any kinds of life scripts; on the contrary, it favours structurally a competitively and acquisitively oriented life form and as a result itself promotes the corresponding acquisitive mentality. Recently supporters of the 'entrepreneurial' attitude to life have even expressly demanded a furtherance of this process as a means to an end, for example in the preface to the neoliberal manifesto 'Mut zum Aufbruch' (Courage for a New Departure) mentioned above, which states that the White Book wishes:

> to contribute to a sharpening of the awareness of the necessity and urgency of this permanent *change in mentality* and to the realization of a change of course on a broad basis.[62]

In this way the supposedly value-neutral, merely efficient system of free competition acts like a fertilizer on its cultural humus soil, ensuring that only those plants flourish for which the competitively oriented fertilizer is good. As long as it remains unchecked, therefore, the free market is not merely an economic form but tends to become a comprehensive form of

[62] Pury/Hauser/Schmidt, *Mut zum Aufbruch*, p. 10; italics in the original.

society, a total market society with a clear tendency to subject all cultural life projects to its sway:[63]

Under the conditions of such a society individuals no longer strive for success on account of personal preferences or dispositions (perhaps because they are careerists or demons for work); instead, the overall state of society drives them in this direction. *Nobody* can live and survive here without striving for success. ... The pursuit of success in bourgeois society is not a habitus founded on personal predilections or inclinations but a form of behaviour required of *all* members of society by the system.[64]

Even such an important economist as Keynes was evidently unable to see through this social (positional) logic of competition sufficiently in order to recognize the naivety and illusory nature of his vision of a final solution of the economic problem within a hundred years 'for our grandchildren'. Instead he believed it would happen of its own accord that by the time of his grandchildren most people would only work a fifteen-hour week and would have time to cultivate 'the art of life'; only a minority who attach no value to such a life, namely the 'strenuous, purposeful money-makers' would then 'blindly pursue wealth'.[65]

The competitive asymmetry we have demonstrated between different life forms probably explains to a large degree the cultural-historical 'victory' of the bourgeois life form in the process of modernization, which first occurred in the 'West' and is being continually repeated not only in Western countries (in spite of occasional opposition of alternative movements[66]) but in more and more regions of the world. It is thus clear that the international variant of the economistic fiction of the common good, according to which 'free world trade is to the advantage of all countries', is

[63] See the considerations above, Section 4.3, on the partiality of inherent necessity. In misunderstanding itself as a 'value-free science', economics copies this partiality and usually rejects all reflection on its knowledge-constitutive interest. In its model the particular interests and perspectives of the entrepreneurial type are treated as axiomatic and generalized to represent the economic perspective pure and simple. Decades ago this was already recognized by the critical economist Werner Hofmann; see W. Hofmann, 'Zum Gesellschaftsbild der Nationalökonomie von heute', in his *Universität, Ideologie, Gesellschaft, Beiträge zur Wissenschaftssoziologie* (Frankfurt: Suhrkamp, 1969), pp. 92–116, at p. 101.

[64] Herms, *Gesellschaft gestalten*, p. 385; italics in the original.

[65] Keynes, 'Economic Possibilities for Our Grandchildren', p. 328ff.

[66] It is not chance that the colourful alternative scene of the economically less problematic 1970s has in the meantime been largely 'eliminated'. In a thoroughly favourable examination of the alternative scene Joseph Huber came quite early to the sobering conclusion: 'We [i.e. the alternative groups] are plugged in from top to bottom to the mega-machine [of the market society]; we should have no illusions about that.' J. Huber, *Wer soll das alles ändern? Die Alternativen der Alternativbewegung* (Berlin: Rotbuch, 1980), p. 45; for a sociological overview of the formerly many-facetted approaches of an alternative 'counter-society' see also Hollstein, *Gegengesellschaft.*

by no means accurate from a cultural point of view.[67] The competition of cultures has been decided in advance – step by step it will lead to the 'selection' of corresponding life forms world-wide, as far as its influence is not restricted by cultural-political measures. This is, furthermore, true quite generally for all competitive factors in the free global competition between economic locations. Consequently, wherever the free market is established, the impression will soon arise that throughout the world the people, or at least those who set the tone, will ardently desire a life form oriented on competition, achievement and acquisition of goods with all the trappings, even though it is much more hectic than their traditional culture. Cultures or individual groups of the 'native population' who are not willing or not able to pay the price for the more or less complete abandonment of their cultural traditions and fail to make themselves 'fit' for competition will be quickly classified as hopeless losers ('Africa, the lost continent').

The question of meaning, however, remains open, as a total 'market society' turns the means (production first of all of what is necessary for life and then of the preconditions for the abundance of life) into a literally meaningless or even nonsensical end in itself. Cut off from the entire meaning context of the lifeworld, the life form of an economy of poverty will be perpetuated. As only a few can 'win' and the majority must 'lose', this generalized social Darwinist life form becomes absurd: although it avails of a level of economic and technological productivity that could provide the basics of life for all mankind, it produces new poverty, in spite of the achievement orientation of most of those affected. The further symptoms of this reversal of meaning for the practice of everyday life become increasingly evident. How can we imagine a meaningful way out of this economistic vicious circle?

In principle, the answer is easy to find. If individuals, groups or even an entire culture cannot emancipate themselves from the competitive constraints on their preferred ways of life by own efforts without at the same time being entirely eliminated from the market, then it makes sense for all to work together so that each can enjoy a partial emancipation from the constraints of competition. To this end it is necessary to change the general conditions of life structurally in such a way that, on the one hand, all individuals, independently of their specific life projects, can work for and effectively secure the basic necessities of life within the market economy system, and, on the other hand, that they are left the free choice to live according to their authentic ideals of life beyond the necessary participation in social production (in the widest sense of the word). The

[67] See Section 5.2.

three fundamental, closely interconnected elements of such a structural reorganization of the conditions and chances of life in an advanced economy are

- a new, emancipatory *politics of time*:[68] partial liberation of life time through a general reduction of the length of working life for all might become attractive – with as much individual 'sovereignty'[69] as possible in regard to the distribution of the time worked over days, weeks, years and life phases. This would be equivalent to a more even distribution of the necessary and the available gainful employment;
- a new, emancipatory *politics of work*:[70] full employment in the traditional sense of a full-time job for everyone is no longer the (in the meantime unrealistic) goal, rather the continuous reduction of the generally possible and necessary work load in accordance with the progress of productivity will make sense. In contrast to the traditional, narrowly conceived 'employment policy' the politics of work must be understood as the comprehensive endeavour to create all the necessary basic conditions so that gainful employment can occupy a meaningful place in the lives of *all* individuals (acquisition of the necessary purchasing power, development of the personality and social integration);
- a new, emancipatory *social politics*:[71] it includes on the one hand basic economic security for all during life phases without gainful employment (childhood, education, illness, social service, involuntary unemployment, old age), and on the other hand a structural approach to social policy that does not merely react to symptoms by compensating for the consequences of the failure of individuals to assert themselves economically, but tackles the causes. This means preventing as far as possible a structural passivity of individuals and the resultant dependence on the support of the welfare services. The ethical basis for this policy is provided by the republican-liberal guiding idea of universalized economic citizenship rights to be established in the future.[72]

[68] See Gorz, *Critique of Economic Reason*, p. 190. Cf. the proposals of H. Ruh, 'Modelle einer neuen Zeiteinteilung für das Tätigsein der Menschen: Strategien zur Überwindung der Arbeitslosigkeit', in H. Würgler (ed.), *Arbeitszeit und Arbeitslosigkeit. Zur Diskussion der Beschäftigungspolitik in der Schweiz* (Zurich: Verlag der Fachvereine, 1994), pp. 135–52.

[69] See B. Teriet, 'Zeitsouveränität für eine flexible Lebensplanung', in J. Huber (ed.), *Anders arbeiten – anders wirtschaften* (Frankfurt: Fischer, 1979), pp. 150–7.

[70] See P. Ulrich, 'Arbeitspolitik jenseits des neoliberalen Ökonomismus – das Kernstück einer lebensdienlichen Sozialpolitik', *Jahrbuch für christliche Sozialwissenschaften* 38 (1997), pp. 136–52.

[71] For details see the chapter 'Begrenzung des sozialetatistischen Systems: emanzipatorische Sozialpolitik' (Restriction of the social state system: emancipatory social politics) in Ulrich, *Transformation*, p. 467ff.

[72] This guiding idea is dealt with in Section 7.3.

In the context of these and further structural reforms designed to bring about a cultural society of partially liberated time for all a new and sustainable variety of life forms could develop, since it would enable free citizens to choose more and more freely in the shaping of their lives. And forms of self-determined good life exist only in the plural.[73]

The necessary precondition is, however, that a collective political 'will to meaning' (Frankl) develops, both at a national and an international level, in order to pursue an emancipatory 'world domestic policy' of partial emancipation of all cultures from the self-referential competitive logic of globalized markets – on the basis of economic self-assertion in restricted competition with one another. The conclusion we must draw is, therefore, that a meaningful future for the market economy in the projected sense of an economy of abundance must ultimately be borne by a common cultural will to achieve or at least to concede life forms which are not primarily market-oriented.

One can, however, hardly escape the impression that as modern people we are not yet particularly well-equipped to cope with this cultural demand of the modern world; economic life is still characterized by an immature, so to speak 'adolescent',[74] treatment of the economic means at our disposal today. It is at all events surprising how many people continue to accept without question the functional self-dynamics of an economic system logic which is increasingly penetrating all areas of life, just as earlier generations uncritically accepted the given dogmatic claims to the meaning of tradition. One might almost think that Max Weber was right. He saw that 'victorious capitalism' was building the 'iron cage' of a new serfdom in which material goods would gain 'an increasing and finally an inexorable power over the lives of men as at no previous period in history'[75] until in the end 'the claims of the ethical postulate that the world is a somehow ethically *meaningfully* oriented cosmos'[76] would become redundant. But then the modern idea of freedom would also have become redundant and with it the task of practically determining the meaning of economic activity from a free standpoint. At last, from a

[73] See J. Habermas, *Theorie des kommunikativen Handelns*, vol. II (Frankfurt: Suhrkamp, 1981), p. 165 (the phrase 'exists only in the plural' is not found in the English translation. For the gap, see *Theory of Communicative Action*, vol. II, p. 108.

[74] The allusion here is to the metaphor of a 'crisis of adolescence' in the history of mankind before the transition to the post-conventional cultural level; see Section 1.5.

[75] Weber, *The Protestant Ethic*, p. 181f.

[76] M. Weber, 'Die Wirtschaft der Weltreligionen', in his *Gesammelte Aufsätze zur Religionssoziologie*, vol. I, 9th edn (Tübingen: Mohr Siebeck, 1988), p. 564; own translation from the German original.

lifeworld perspective, there is no meaningful alternative to meeting the epochal challenge of grasping economic activity in a manner befitting the times as a modern cultural form instead of simply accepting it as being driven by inescapable, inherently coercive, self-justifying system logic. It is, therefore, essential to foster awareness for the need to change course in a direction that culturally 'makes sense'.

7 The question of legitimation: economic activity and the just social life

From its beginnings economic activity has been a social event. The cooperative process of creating value based on division of labour and the interpersonal distribution of the goods produced has always been the focal point of social conflict. The same is true for the side-effects of the accompanying production of 'ungoods' or evils (such as, for example, environmental pollution). Decisions on conflicting claims can, in principle, be taken in two ways: either in accordance with the principle of power ('might is right') or in accordance with the moral principle. A third way, involving neither power nor morals, such as the advocates of economism believe they have found with the harmonistic fiction of a pure market solution, does not exist. As we have seen, the approach of the latter is only an ideologically disguised variant of the power principle, in which the status quo of vested rights is from the beginning 'methodologically' excluded from all critical questioning of the justice of claims.[1] In contrast, the moral principle subjects the regulation of conflicting claims and interests to the requirements of justice.

Regardless of the way it is defined in particular cases, the concept of justice takes up the issue of the quality of interpersonal or social relationships in the light of the *moral rights* of all persons – a category already introduced, which we will clarify more precisely in what follows.[2] A rather more specific meaning must be attributed to the concept of *legitimacy*. It establishes a connection between claims raised, the intended actions or the regulation of actions on the one hand and the moral rights of all concerned on the other. The question at issue is the moral justification of a claim, an action or a failure to act which have practical consequences in the lives of other persons. A way of acting can be characterized as legitimate if, after taking into account all the recognizable consequences, it observes the moral rights of those affected by the action (including the actor himself). If this is the case it can be said that the corresponding

[1] The allusion here is to methodological individualism; cf. Section 5.3.
[2] Cf. above Sections 1.2 and 1.4.

consequences of the action can be justified to all concerned as responsible and reasonable.[3]

Whereas the question of the meaning of economic activity deals with the direction of its fulfilment and its significance for the good life (choice of values to be created), the question of the legitimacy of economic activity is concerned with just social life (creation or destruction of value for whom?). Because economic action is by its very nature motivated by the desire for success, the normative condition of its legitimacy is a fundamental economic-ethical requirement; it is the basic ethical criterion for the 'social acceptability' of economic action. We can speak of the legitimate pursuit of success only if this is unconditionally subjected to the normative precondition that the moral rights of all concerned are protected. Legitimacy has primacy over success.[4] The legitimacy condition is constitutive precisely for the justification of the 'private economic' pursuit of success or profit, as whatever can be understood as a private matter in a society is always subject to public regulation and justification.

There are, consequently, two preconditions for the legitimacy of private forms of action and the justice of social relationships. Firstly, of course, they require the existence of *moral persons* who possess a 'sense of justice',[5] i.e. the ability to understand the justified claims of others and the good will to make justice the guideline for their own actions (justice as a personal virtue). People with a sense of justice also develop a moral interest in the legitimacy of their economic actions.

The sense of justice even of morally very sound persons can in the course of time be overtaxed and worn down if social life is not regulated by generally recognized principles of justice. Secondly, therefore, the practice of justice presumes the existence of what John Rawls calls a *well-ordered society*, a society 'in which institutions are just and this fact is publicly recognized'.[6] In a well-ordered society the norms of justice are valid for everyone and they are both morally and legally binding. The general moral obligation is the foundation for the binding legal character, and the latter supports the former. Legal norms justified in this way in turn require general implementation without respect of persons (political justice as an institutionalised basic structure of society). For this reason the fundamental moral rights of citizens in modern states are codified and protected by sanctions under national and to an increasing degree under

[3] See above, Section 4.3 (3). [4] See the earlier treatment in Section 2.5 (2).

[5] See Rawls, *Theory of Justice* (rev. edn), pp. 41, 274; Rawls, 'Kantian Constructivism in Moral Theory', *The Journal of Philosophy* 77/9 (1980), pp. 515–72, at pp. 521, 525.

[6] Rawls, *Theory of Justice* (rev. edn), p. 274. See also ibid., p. 397ff. and the more recent modifications in Rawls, 'Kantian Constructivism', pp. 521ff., 535ff. The concept of the well-ordered society is examined in more detail in Section 7.2.

international law. This is the only way to prevent or at least to contain discrimination (systematic unfair treatment to the disadvantage of particular groups), arbitrariness (misuse of power for personal advantage without concern for questions of justification) and free-riding (profiting in an unmoral, non-generalizable fashion from the moral behaviour of the majority). As a first approximation we can, therefore, characterize a well-ordered society as one in which no-one suffers from discrimination or the exercise of arbitrary power and free-riding is not normally possible.

The reciprocal interdependence of justice as a personal virtue (sense of justice) and as a basic institutional structure (well-ordered society) is rooted in the fact that the validity of legal rights and laws can ultimately be justified only by moral rights and that moral legitimacy (moral right) can accordingly never be subsumed under juridical legality (positive law). From a moral point of view positive law can be inadequate or even unjust. Consequently, the reference to laws which are 'in force' can never suffice as a justification of economic actions. Under the rule of law in a well-ordered society the moral *responsibility* of the economic agents remains fundamental; their actions must always be self-critically examined in regard to their legitimacy in the light of the moral rights of all concerned and their (argumentative) acceptability for others.

The real-life practical significance of questions of the legitimacy and justice of economic activity is revealed already in the attention frequently paid to them in public discussion, in both negative and positive cases. There was, for example, a world-wide positive response to the decision taken in 1993 by the jeans company Levi-Strauss to end the production of jeans in China on account of the continuing violations of human rights, even though it was cost-favourable and held out the promise of a huge market. The company followed its own ethical code, whose guiding principle must clearly be understood as a principle of legitimacy: 'We should not initiate or renew contractual relationships with countries in which fundamental human rights are violated.' In contrast, Shell, the company with the largest turnover in the world, had great difficulty in dealing with the question of legitimacy in 1995 when it announced its intention of sinking its obsolete oil platform Brent Spar in the North Sea and was then surprised by the international protests and boycotts initiated by Greenpeace.[7]

The (not so very) new social questions raised at the national and international level, in particular, bring up difficult problems of justice and legitimacy for the economic actors. Is it, for example, legitimate for

[7] For more details see Section 10.3 (1).

large, highly profitable companies to strive consistently for a further increase in profits by reducing staff, regardless of the consequences both for the dismissed employees and for the tax-payers who have to bear the social costs in view of the poor state of the labour market? Or, vice versa, would it not be legitimate to require companies which undertake mass dismissals to accept a share of the resulting social costs in accordance with the causer principle, in as far as these redundancies are not economically essential, and to reward companies which contribute to the avoidance or reduction of social costs through social innovation (e.g. working hours schemes) with tax benefits or lower social security contributions? And how far is it justifiable for a state which is endeavouring to increase its attractiveness as a location for new industry or to improve the international competitiveness of the national industry to accept as a consequence an increasingly unequal social distribution of income and wealth or even the marginalization of a growing part of the population who fail to meet the demands of competitiveness?

It is precisely in connection with problems of social distribution that the question of justice is often seen too narrowly, as the policies pursued are one-sidedly directed towards material compensation for the effects of unjust distribution, which only tackles the symptoms and leaves the causes untouched. There can be no doubt that such 'corrective justice'[8] is an indispensable component of any adequate conception of social justice. But it should always play only a subsidiary part; from a rational-ethical point of view priority must be given to the treatment of the causes, to the emancipation of people from social conditions and structures which create injustice.

The questions and aspects dealt with here should suffice to make it clear that issues of justice and legitimacy are extraordinarily complex. And in what follows there can be no question of offering patent remedies. It is necessary instead to reflect carefully on the normative foundations for judgements on the justice of actions or regulations which are rationally and ethically sound, in accordance with the guiding idea that what matters primarily is 'orientation in thinking' (Kant). We can take as our systematic starting point the insight we have already gained that the clarification of the preconditions for the legitimacy of the action of individual persons or companies is possible only in the context of a comprehensive conception of the well-ordered society. We will, therefore, proceed in three steps. First of all we will clarify more precisely what it means to have a moral right, consider which rights can be justifiably

[8] Tugendhat, *Vorlesungen*, p. 367.

regarded as general basic moral rights and examine their relationship to legal rights (Section 7.1). Then we will look at the conception of a well-ordered society and the normative conditions of legitimate inequality according to John Rawls (Section 7.2). This will lead us finally to the consideration of possible new basic rights of socio-economic citizenship (i.e. of the citizen with full civic rights and responsibilities in his/her economic life), which are more and more the focal point of present day socio-political discussions (Section 7.3).

7.1 Fundamental moral rights as the ethical-political basis of legitimation

In Chapter 1 we have already demonstrated that the moral point of view (as developed from the normative logic of interpersonal relations) rests upon the insight that all human beings have an equal and reciprocal moral right (i.e. justified claim) to respect of their personal dignity and to the recognition of their physical and psychological inviolability. It is on this insight that the idea of general human rights is based. But what it means precisely to possess a right in the context of a post-conventional 'morality of universal and equal respect'[9] is still an open question, as is the clarification of the specific contents to which the moral rights refer. The conceptual distinction between moral claims and rights expresses in the first place a difference in binding quality: 'claims' are claims to validity whose legitimacy must still be tested. The claims of a person A which are demonstrably justified and legitimate ought logically to be recognized and protected. They are thus the foundation for the moral obligation of all other ('natural' and legal or corporate) persons (N) to respect them. In the same sense it can also be said that any person N owes A respect for his legitimate claims and, vice versa, that A has the moral right to demand from everybody respect for a claim which is demonstrably legitimate.

The logical consequence is the idea constitutive of the concept of right that there must be an *instance* – beyond subjective discretion – which defines the moral rights of all individuals in an impartial manner, 'invests' persons with these rights and guarantees them as so-called 'positive' or legal rights, by ensuring their recognition with the threat of sanctions if they are not observed. The regulative idea is that this legal instance acts on the basis of general acceptance by all moral persons. Everyone can demand observation of his/her rights or, in the case of violation, take legal action before this instance. In a modern democratic state under the rule of

[9] Tugendhat, *Vorlesungen*, p. 336.

law a more or less elaborate system of judicial instances exists, so that questionable legal decisions can be referred to higher courts, re-examined and, if need be, revised.

The possibility of taking legal steps to protect rights is of particular importance in the case of basic human rights. Those elementary rights are characterized as *basic rights* which must first be fulfilled as essential preconditions for exercising or enjoying all further rights.[10] We are dealing in principle with all the inalienable conditions for safeguarding personal subject status and identity and hence the dignity of every human being. These basic rights must be understood as moral rights which can be justified as *universal human rights* before any positive (legal) rights come into play. Consequently their validity can never be questioned legally, although they require interpretation, confirmation and enforcement by constitutional and legal instances. The safeguarding of these general moral basic rights (which will be more closely defined later) is the minimal condition for every conception of justice and hence for every form of legitimate action. In order to protect them from violation, if need be even against despotic actions of the state, increasing efforts have been made in recent years to protect them under transnational and international law. This purpose is served, above all, by declarations on the binding nature of universal human rights and the creation of the corresponding instances of legal jurisdiction – a process which began in essence with the Bill of Rights of Virginia (1776) in the USA and the Déclaration des droits de l'homme et du citoyen (1789) in France and was consistently furthered after the Second World War in the various declarations of human rights (the Universal Declaration of Human Rights of the United Nations of 1948, the Convention for the Protection of Human Rights and Fundamental Freedoms of the European Council of 1954, the European Social Charter of 1961, etc.). The transnational organ with the most wide-ranging competence to take legal decisions to date is the European Court of Human Rights in Strasbourg. Furthermore, numerous larger and smaller idealistically oriented non-governmental organizations (NGOs) are committed to ensuring the observation of universal human rights throughout the world (e.g. Amnesty International).[11]

But does it make any sense, in view of these remarkable achievements and the general significance of law-giving and law-enforcing instances, to speak of *moral* rights in the contexts in which their establishment as legal

[10] See H. Shue, *Basic Rights: Subsistence, Affluence and U.S. Foreign Policy* (Princeton: Princeton University Press, 1980), p. 19f.

[11] For a survey of the conventions see I. Brownlie/G. S. Goodwin-Gill (eds.), *Basic Documents on Human Rights*, 5th edn (Oxford: Oxford University Press, 2006).

national and international rights has not yet succeeded? As long as they have not been given legal backing, the instance which safeguards these moral rights is at best an ideal instance without any powers of enforcement. And even if such an imagined instance can be defined, there is no way of making the claims asserted before it legally binding.[12]

Nonetheless the answer is absolutely clear: from an ethical point of view the idea of enforceable moral rights remains indispensable. Moral rights have the same systematic relationship to legal rights as post-conventional reflective judgements to constitutionally and politically established conventions. This depends to some extent on the principle of power and not on the moral principle alone. For precisely this reason moral rights necessarily provide the ultimate argumentative grounds and the fundamental normative criterion for all positive law and its future development. Even in states under the rule of law – quite apart from despotic regimes – it can still occasionally happen that in particular areas what is morally wrong can become a legal 'right'. This discrepancy and the possibility of error is the foundation for a moral right to *civil disobedience* to the law in cases of personal conflict of conscience, which cannot be legally abolished. In accepting this right every civilized constitutional state acknowledges its own moral fallibility and limits.[13] Moreover, the process of the development of 'positive' law usually limps behind the dynamics of social conditions which require legal regulation, thus creating legal gaps both at the national and the international level.

But what is the ideal instance for defining, granting and sanctioning moral rights? In the course of the history of ideas three possible answers have been given.[14] (a) Within the framework of a pre-modern traditional moral philosophy or, rather, moral theology the answer was easy. God alone as the creator could grant moral rights to his creatures. (b) As a result of the early modern tendency towards secularisation, and against the background of a deistic world-view, *natural law* gained ground as a second possibility. It regarded human beings as being equipped 'by nature' with certain inviolable human rights which neither needed to be granted nor could be denied by any instance of society.[15] The difficulty is that 'nature' speaks only through men, who must then interpret the normative will of nature themselves. What is apparently objectively read out of nature

[12] See Tugendhat, *Vorlesungen*, p. 348.

[13] See Rawls, *Theory of Justice* (rev. edn), p. 319ff.; R. Dworkin, *Taking Rights Seriously* (Cambridge MA: Harvard University Press, 1978), p. 206ff. J. Habermas, 'Civil Disobedience: Litmus Test for the Democratic Constitutional State', *Berkeley Journal of Sociology* 30 (1985), pp. 95–116.

[14] On what follows see Tugendhat, *Vorlesungen*, p. 344ff.

[15] On deistic and natural law thinking in the modern period see Section 5.1.

has inevitably been subjectively read or projected into it beforehand. Consequently, the problem of justification must then either be referred back to the moral theological representatives of God and their knowledge of revelation or (c) natural law must be grasped in a modern fashion as *rational law* requiring justification by rational ethical argument.

What is then the 'law-making' instance of modern rational ethics? We have already developed the answer in principle in Chapter 1. The instance or 'site' of morality in modern times is the universal moral community of all human subjects, the ideal meta-institution of the unlimited critical public discourse of all mature persons of good will.[16] Accordingly, it is the moral persons themselves who reciprocally grant and acknowledge the same rights as members of the moral community to one another, be it in the universal community of all humankind (human rights) or in a restricted community of members of an entity organized at a sub-state, state or supra-state level who mutually acknowledge that they have the same rights to participation in the res publica (citizens' rights).

The justification of concrete moral rights thus lies, beyond all political conventions on human rights and legally codified citizens' rights, in the domain of philosophical ethical justification, particularly in the form explicated by discourse ethics.[17] Both the determination of the contents and the overlaying juridical form of moral rights as positive (national or international) law must be seen as problems of ethical-political agreement. These problems should be dealt with under the horizon of the regulative idea of practical discourse, together with all the organizational and procedural questions which are a part of any kind of political ethics that human beings as mature and responsible subjects practice and observe.

From a discourse-ethical perspective it is clear that doubts about the universal validity of human rights usually result from narrow conventionalistic thinking, particularly when they are justified by reference to the 'Western' origin of the rights. It is indeed a fact that all the conventions on human rights have been more or less strongly influenced by certain occidental traditions as a result of their developmental history, but the (post-conventional) *idea* of universal human rights can by no means be questioned on this account. It is a matter of course that the interpretation and elaboration of the universally valid idea of human rights in terms of particular cultures, times and situations is a never-ending historical task

[16] See Section 2.5, particularly subsection (4).

[17] On this point see A. Cortina, 'Diskursethik und Menschenrechte', *Archiv für Rechts- und Sozialphilosophie* 76 (1990), pp. 37–49; in more detail J. Habermas, *Facts and Norms*.

which, again, can be fulfilled only in practical discourse in the *moral community* of all people of good will.

The normative core of the idea of universal human rights itself is derived directly from the elementary humanistic sense of the moral principle. The indubitable universality of the basic conditions of human existence (conditio humana) leads automatically to the normative idea of the equal inviolability of every human subject and the fundamentally equal value of all people, or, more briefly: the *moral equality* of all people; the legitimate claims of all individuals deserve the same consideration and are of equal value. In the moral 'right to equal concern and respect'[18] and the corresponding equal treatment we can recognize that 'most fundamental of rights'[19] which expresses nothing other than the one moral principle (universalization principle). All further specific human rights must be understood as an explication and interpretation of this one fundamental right.[20]

The moral idea of the equal treatment of all human beings *as* humans is therefore the constitutive, defining characteristic of universal human rights. The only necessary and sufficient grounds for the entitlement to claim universal human rights lies in membership of the human race, about which there can be no doubt (as there are no superhuman, half-human or subhuman human beings). The crucial point is that additional requirements for the recognition of the human rights of a particular person are not only unnecessary but impermissible. This moral prohibition of discrimination is so fundamental that it is expressly and comprehensively laid down in Article 2, paragraph 1 of the Universal Declaration of Human Rights:

18 Dworkin, *Taking Rights Seriously*, p. 180. 19 Ibid., p. xii.

20 In Rawls's original conception of a just society (*Theory of Justice*, rev. edn, p. 441ff.) moral equality, which he defines as 'equality as it applies to the respect which is owed to persons irrespective of their social position' (p. 447), is the expressly stated foundation. However, this rational ethical core (the Kantian side) of Rawls's theory of justice is in parts concealed rather than developed by his contract theoretical method (economic conception of rationality, Hobbesian conception of the social contract). As Dworkin (*Taking Rights Seriously*, p. 179ff.) has pointed out, the methodical construct of the *original position* and of the *veil of ignorance* prevailing in it fulfil precisely the function in Rawls' theory of reducing the moral right to equal treatment and the enjoyment of equal rights to a strategic calculation of benefits by the participants. And by this means economic contract theory *takes the place of* rational ethical justification. But this does not alter the fact that Rawls regards the right to equal treatment as the most fundamental of all rights as normatively given. For this reason – and in spite of the incompatibility of his methodical approach with the rational ethical perspective developed in this book – Rawls's principles of justice are thoroughly compatible with this perspective in regard to their normative content. It is, therefore, not necessary to enter more closely here into the conception of an original position in Rawls's methodical approach. On this point see Ulrich, *Transformation*, p. 256ff.

Everyone is entitled to all the rights and freedoms set forth in this Declaration, without distinction of any kind, such as race, colour, sex, language, religion, political or other opinion, national or social origin, property, birth or other status.

In the historical process of the crystallization and international codification of human rights a progressive differentiation and expansion of the areas of life which are expressly included is recognizable. It is, therefore, possible to speak of different 'generations' of codified basic rights.[21] In principle there are essentially three groups of basic human rights recognized and codified in the conventions on human rights of the 20th century:[22]

(a) the basic rights of inviolable personal freedom (of opinion, belief and action) and the corresponding equal protection of rights without respect of persons (negative rights of freedom and defence, rights of personality);
(b) basic rights of participation in the formation of the democratic political will (rights of political participation and citizenship);
(c) basic rights to a minimal degree of protection from existential need and social disadvantage, to conditions of life worthy of human beings and to adequate social welfare (rights to social protection and economic citizenship rights).

The three categories of basic rights can be distinguished in regard to the delimitation of the bearers of the rights. The rights of freedom and personality (a) apply unconditionally to all human beings; the rights of political participation (b) apply only to the citizens of a political community (res publica), who must also fulfil the corresponding civic duties: civil rights are 'rights *in rem publicam*',[23] limited to the country of origin but nonetheless universal rights of every person in that country. The delimitation of the bearers of rights of social participation (c) is more controversial. All persons are in principle to be entitled to these rights

[21] See J. Galtung, *Human Rights in Another Key* (Cambridge: Polity, 1994), p. 151ff. In accordance with the political groups which have each initiated a 'generation' of basic rights he distinguishes between 'blue' (liberal), 'red' (social), 'green' (ecological and life-world oriented) and 'coloured' (cultural and developmental) generations of rights.

[22] The following threefold division corresponds to the classical Anglo-Saxon distinction between civil, political and social rights according to Th. M. Marshall, 'Citizenship and Social Class', in Marshall (ed.), *Sociology at the Crossroads and Other Essays* (London: Heinemann, 1963), pp. 67–127, at p. 73ff. Without claiming historical precision Marshall assigns these three groups of basic rights to the 18th (bourgeois freedom rights), 19th (political citizens' rights) and 20th (social rights) centuries; the conception of 'generations' of rights can thus also be traced back to him.

[23] P. Koller, 'Menschen- und Bürgerrechte aus ethischer Perspektive', in B.S. Byrd/ J. Hruschka/J.C. Joerden (eds.), *Annual Review of Law and Ethics, vol. 3: Human Rights and the Rule of Law* (Berlin: Duncker & Humblot, 1995), pp. 49–68, at p. 60.

who have the right of residence in a community, actually live in it and are liable to taxation within it.[24] Here the circle of the bearers of moral rights is wider than that of citizens; it includes all the 'residents' in a well-ordered community and particularly the foreign workers with rights of residence.[25]

It is a characteristic feature of the legitimate fulfilment of moral basic rights in every modern society that in all three categories (a, b, c), regardless of the concrete realization within each circle of bearers, no form of inequality is permissible in principle, as this would amount to unjustifiable discrimination of individual members of a community in regard to the respect of their personality and private sphere (a), their status as citizens (b) or the elementary socio-economic conditions of life (c). Positively formulated, it is a matter of guaranteeing moral equality in the sense of private autonomy (a), political participation (b) and social equality of opportunity and security (c). Although the boundaries are fluid, we can speak in the case of the first category of rights (a) of general *personality rights* (rights of freedom and defence), in category (b) of *(political) citizenship rights* (rights of the political citizen) and in the category (c) of social and economic rights or, more precisely, of *(socio-) economic citizenship rights*. Furthermore, two contemporary developmental trends in category (a) deserve mention: on the one hand towards increased respect for personality rights in regard to self-determined cultural identity and identification in a pluralistic or multi-cultural society (cultural group rights)[26] and, on the other hand, towards ecological human rights of access to the natural resources necessary for life such as drinking water, unpolluted foods, clean air, protection from noise and

[24] The three delimitation criteria for rights of social participation must be regarded as complementary. A person with rights of citizenship and residence in a country who lives abroad will lay claim to his/her social rights of protection and participation (but not to his rights of citizenship) in the country in which he/she resides and pays taxes and not in the country of origin (residence principle). Refugees or asylum seekers with a recognized right of residence enjoy the right to the basic necessities of life but not necessarily the right to equality of opportunity in every respect (for example on the labour market) and to full participation in social prosperity as long as he does not share the citizens' duties of a tax-payer. As a guarantee of the right to the basic necessities of life, however, the recognition of the right of residence alone is sufficient. For a similar argumentation see G. Enderle, *Sicherung des Existenzminimums im nationalen und internationalen Kontext* (Berne *et al.*: Haupt, 1987), p. 214f.

[25] Michael Walzer goes beyond the customary practice and accords to foreign workers the right to the acquisition of citizenship in the country of residence and postulates the willingness of the native population to accept this as the legitimation condition for the employment of foreign workers. See M. Walzer, *Spheres of Justice: A Defense of Pluralism and Equality* (New York: Basic Books, 1983), p. 56ff.

[26] On this point see J. Donnelly, *Universal Human Rights in Theory and Practice* (Ithaca NY: Cornell University Press, 1989), p. 143ff.

Categories of human and civic rights	*Dimension of moral equality*	*Corresponding dimension of the well-ordered society*
Personality rights (of freedom, defence and affiliation)	Private autonomy and self-determined cultural communities	Individual liberty under the rule of law
Political citizenship rights (of political participation)	Political status and participation in the 'res publica'	Democracy
Economic citizenship rights (of existential security and shared prosperity)	Socio-economic living conditions and life chances	Social justice and welfare

Figure 7.1. Categories of human and civic rights

emissions which damage health, etc.[27] We will look in more detail at the proposed category of economic citizenship rights after the following clarification of the preconditions for a well-ordered society. Figure 7.1 summarizes the conception of the three categories of human and citizens' rights presented here, whereby the international dimension is left aside in each case.

7.2 The well-ordered society and the conditions of legitimate inequality: on John Rawls's principles of justice

The basic conception of human and citizens' rights sketched above, which largely follows the chronological 'generational history', has a disadvantage – a kind of congenital defect stemming from its historical development and leading again and again to misunderstandings, particularly in regard to the socio-economic rights. It neglects the essential reciprocal conditioning which occurs between the three categories of rights, as the social rights are seen merely additively as an appendix to the classical liberal rights of defence against the state and the democratic citizens' rights of participation in the political process.[28] This is, firstly, in accordance with the widespread notion that a contradiction exists between the postulates of individual freedom and social equality which

[27] In December 1994 the European Court of Human Rights for the first time affirmed the right to clean air, giving judgement in favour of a Spanish plaintiff who was inconvenienced by the strong smells from a nearby leather tannery. On the discussion at that time in regard to ecological human rights see M. Fitzmaurice, 'Environmental Protection and the International Court of Justice', in V. Lowe/M. Fitzmaurice (eds.), *Fifty Years of the International Court of Justice* (Cambridge: Cambridge University Press, 1996), pp. 293–315.

[28] See Shue, *Basic Rights*, p. 26, and the analogous critique of Habermas, *Facts and Norms*, p. 89.

can only be solved by compromise. This viewpoint is advocated in one-sided conceptions of economic liberalism ('more freedom – less state') but must be rejected as a fundamental misunderstanding, at least in one central point. The moral equality of all human beings implies in its essence their equal freedom and 'inviolability'. Properly understood, freedom can thus only be justified as *general freedom*, i.e. as the greatest possible equal freedom of all persons – anything else would be arbitrary freedom which would mean by 'freedom' merely the right of the stronger to an undisturbed and unlimited assertion of their own private interests without consideration of the equally legitimate claims to freedom of others.[29]

Secondly, the fact is blurred over that the idea of moral equality on which human rights are based applies indivisibly to all the conditions of autonomy, equal entitlement and equal treatment and not just to formal freedom and equality in a legal, constitutional sense. It also includes *real freedom*[30] in the sense of the socio-economic and socio-cultural preconditions for the realization of a personal life project within the framework of formal freedom and equality of opportunity. In contrast, radical libertarian conceptions[31] regard formal freedom and the protection of individuals from the attacks of others (negative freedom) as sufficient and reject the role of the public authorities as a guarantor of real freedom. But they are inevitably caught up in the contradiction that the real life possibilities of citizens to exercise their formal freedom and to pursue self-chosen ideals and purposes are in fact extremely different, depending on their social background and the economic means at their disposal. And this runs precisely counter to the universalistic claim of liberalism to ensure general freedom and a realizable equality of opportunity.[32] The real conditions and life chances or prospects[33] are of decisive importance for an

[29] For more details see Dworkin, *Taking Rights Seriously*, p. 266 ff.

[30] We will look more closely at Van Parijs's concept of real freedom, which we adopt here, in Section 7.3.

[31] In particular those of R. Nozick, *Anarchy, State and Utopia* (New York: Basic Books, 1974).

[32] See B. Manin, 'On Legitimacy and Political Deliberation', *Political Theory* 15 (1987), pp. 338–68, at p. 339.

[33] The conception of life chances and prospects hence plays an essential part in the thinking of truly liberal social philosophers such as Rawls, *Theory of Justice* (rev. edn), p. 6ff., and R. Dahrendorf, *Life Chances: Approaches to Social and Political Theory* (Chicago: Chicago University Press, 1979). Rawls in particular is less consistent in dealing with the existing differences in the conditions under which people live, as we shall see later.

unrestricted, consistent conception of *political liberalism*[34] – and it is the fundamental normative claim of a well-ordered society of free and equal citizens that these conditions are fair. The legitimacy conditions of 'economic freedom' in the true sense of the word must also be clarified within this horizon.

The heart of the well-ordered society as it is understood by political liberalism lies in the principles and rules of social coexistence among free and equal citizens in view of the 'fact of pluralism'[35] in conceptions of the good life. In this situation a basic social consensus on generally binding principles of equal coexistence is regarded as the necessary and at the same time sufficient legitimation condition for private life forms and actions. On the one hand – and in agreement with a properly understood concept of freedom – the claim to private autonomy is seen as being publicly constituted; it is both legitimated and limited by its need of social generalization. On the other hand, the ethical-political justification and consensus claims are at the same time limited by the basic consensus on this legitimate freedom to act in the private sphere. The justice and general validity of the political order is the foundation on which the private autonomy of the citizens in regard to their conception of the good is built. The *primacy of political justice* must, therefore, be regarded as a constitutive basic characteristic of all forms of political liberalism in the true sense of the word. This is indispensable for the successful interlocking of freedom and democracy, private autonomy and the political public sphere, 'reasonable disagreement'[36] (in regard to diverging but mutually respected conceptions of the good) and the limited claim to a consensus guided by reason (on the principles of just social coexistence). The political order of a society

[34] This is the declared self-characterization of the political-philosophical conception of Rawls in more recent years. See J. Rawls, 'The Idea of an Overlapping Consensus', *Oxford Journal of Legal Studies* 7 (1987), pp. 1–25, at p. 23ff. To prevent misunderstandings it must be said that the concept of political liberalism is of course used here as a philosophical concept. Actual parties which have the words 'liberal' or 'free' in their titles are not a priori assumed to hold particularly worthy normative positions. On the contrary they must be critically and unreservedly examined in order to discover whether they genuinely advocate liberal standpoints. It is an open secret that the results of such examinations would be rather disappointing, particularly where 'liberal' parties have more or less degenerated into representatives of particular interest groups in the economy, accordingly pursue a crude economic liberalism, and leave commitment to the original liberal goal of equality of opportunity and equal treatment of all citizens to other parties.

[35] Rawls, 'The Idea of an Overlapping Consensus', p. 1. See also W. Hinsch, 'Einleitung' to the German translation of Rawls, *Die Idee des politischen Liberalismus* (Frankfurt: Suhrkamp, 1992), pp. 9–44, at p. 22ff.

[36] See J. Rawls, 'The Domain of the Political and Overlapping Consensus', *New York University Law Review* 64 (1989), pp. 233–55, at p. 236; cf. Hinsch, 'Introduction', p. 25f.

which is well ordered in this sense has three closely related basic features:[37]

1. *Political basis consensus*:[38] the political order (more precisely defined as 'the basic structure of a modern constitutional democracy'[39]) regulating the just social life of free and equal citizens requires in principle the consensual legitimation *by* all citizens; a democratic constitution is thus a constitutive precondition of a liberal order (and to this extent cannot be simply understood as the external boundary of the freedom of the citizen).
2. *The political public sphere*: the political order (and with it the legitimation of all private and public forms of action) must be justifiable as impartial and just *before* all citizens; this necessarily implies an unrestricted opportunity for 'the public use of reason'[40] for the purpose of the critical and argumentative questioning and reform of all the political principles and rules of a well-ordered social coexistence.
3. *Neutrality in regard to conceptions of the good*: the political order should guarantee the same autonomy *for* all citizens in regard to their ideas on and actual forms of the good life, in as far as they respect the rules of just social coexistence and the equal right of all other conceptions of the good. It should not give preference to a particular life form but impartially guarantee this 'reasonable pluralism'[41] of freely chosen life plans and cultural identities in the sense of their having equal value and deserving equal treatment.[42] The indispensable basis consensus

[37] The following synthesis cannot be found directly in systematic form anywhere in Rawls's work, but would probably meet with his agreement. See the differing, partial characterizations of the well-ordered society in Rawls, *Theory of Justice* (rev.edn 1999), pp. 4ff., 397ff., Rawls, 'Kantian Constructivism', pp. 521ff., 535ff., Rawls, *Political Liberalism*, p. 35ff.

[38] Rawls, 'The Idea of an Overlapping Consensus', p. 1ff., and 'The Domain of the Political and Overlapping Consensus', pp. 233ff., does not speak of a basis consensus but of an overlapping consensus. But this term is unfortunate, as, in connection with Rawls's talk of the 'fact of pluralism', it suggests a conventionalistic misunderstanding in the sense of an exaggerated elevation of the actually existing partial agreement of all citizens on the conception of the good. Such a conventionalistic tendency is all too evident in Rawls's conception. See also A. Cortina, 'The General Public as the Locus of Ethics in Modern Society', in P. Ulrich/Ch. Sarasin (eds.), *Facing Public Interest: The Ethical Challenge to Business Policy and Corporate Communications* (Dordrecht/Boston/London: Kluwer, 1995), pp. 43–58, at p. 52f.

[39] J. Rawls, 'Justice as Fairness: Political not Metaphysical', *Philosophy and Public Affairs* 14 (1985), pp. 223–51, at p. 224.

[40] J. Rawls, 'The Basic Liberties and Their Priority', in S. M. McMurrin (ed.), *The Tanner Lectures on Human Values 1982* (Salt Lake City/Cambridge: University of Utah Press/ Cambridge University Press, 1983), pp. 3–87, at p. 10 (reprinted in *Political Liberalism*, p. 289ff., at p. 296); Rawls, 'The Idea of an Overlapping Consensus', p. 8; Rawls, 'Kantian Constructivism', p. 538ff., and, with more detail in Rawls, *Political Liberalism*, p. 212ff. With the postulate of the public use of reason Rawls draws explicitly on Kant, 'An Answer to the Question: What is Enlightenment?'.

[41] See Rawls, *Political Liberalism*, p. 24 (n. 27).

[42] See J. Rawls, 'The Priority of Right and Ideas of the Good', *Philosophy and Public Affairs* 17 (1988), pp. 251–76, at p. 260ff., reprinted in *Political Liberalism*, pp. 173–211, at p. 191ff.

(Point 1) and the public use of reason (Point 2) refer precisely to this 'neutral ground'[43] – and to it alone. For this reason Rawls' overlapping consensus must by no means remain utopian in real political life.[44]

As we have already seen above, a well-ordered society of this kind assumes the existence of citizens who have the quality of moral persons. Rawls, following the tradition of the two elementary dimensions of ethics, distinguishes between 'two moral powers', the 'capacity to act from a sense of justice' and the 'capacity to form and rationally to pursue a conception of the good'.[45] If we add the capacity to use public reason we arrive at the following: The citizens are free and equal citizens because they are in principle politically mature (i.e. capable of communicating rationally in a democratic political public sphere), have a sense of justice (i.e. are capable of understanding the primacy of justice over private autonomy) and are autonomous (i.e. capable of leading their lives in accordance with their conception of the good life). A well-ordered society in conformity with the principles of political liberalism, as developed by Rawls, cannot therefore be organized with strictly rational egoists (homines oeconomici) and thus stands in opposition to the axiomatics of economic theories of the social contract:[46]

> Political justifications are not addressed to *rational egoists*, who only take the claims of others into account in as far as they serve to their own advantage, but to rational *moral* persons who recognize one another as free and equal citizens and therefore acknowledge that political institutions must take the interests of all citizens equally into account.[47]

[43] Ibid., p. 262.

[44] See Rawls, 'The Idea of an Overlapping Consensus', p. 18ff. As we have seen in Section 6.3, however, the claim to impartiality or neutrality of the political order in regard to conceptions of the good life can by no means easily be made good in the context of a market economy (structural asymmetry of opportunities). Pursued to its logical conclusion Rawls's conception of the well-ordered society therefore has normative consequences, which have not as yet been drawn, or at least not unequivocally drawn, by Rawls himself. See Section 7.3.

[45] Rawls, 'Kantian Constructivism', p. 543. On the two corresponding basic dimensions of morality and ethos see Section 1.2.

[46] See Section 5.3 (3).

[47] Hinsch, 'Introduction', p. 17. When Rawls, *Theory of Justice* (rev. edn), p. 118ff., in his model of the original position, draws *the veil of ignorance* over the faces of individuals and hides their own interests from them, he does not do so because he assumes that they would look only for their own advantage but as a *methodical* construct ensuring impartiality. Impartial structural model conditions are designed to permit the analytical derivation of the principles of justice. (See above n. 20.) To this extent the model of the original position does not contradict Rawls' postulate that the citizens of a well-ordered society must be moral persons and it cannot therefore be used as an argument against this postulate.

Political liberalism thus assumes the primacy of citizens' rights and citizens' virtues (morality) over the logic of the market. We can even see the basic motive of Rawls's theory of justice in this claim. His starting point was, namely, the insight that utilitarian arguments about the public good, including the welfare theory criterion of Pareto efficiency, are not compatible with the categorical inviolability of the moral basic rights of all individuals.[48] For this reason Rawls regards the following two principles of justice, which form the core of his conception, as constitutive of every well-ordered society:[49]

First Principle
Each person is to have an equal right to the most extensive total system of equal basic liberties compatible with a similar system of liberty for all.
Second Principle
Social and economic inequalities are to be arranged so that they are both
(a) to the greatest benefit of the least advantaged, consistent with the just savings principle[50] and
(b) attached to offices and positions open to all under conditions of fair equality of opportunity.

The two *priority rules* defined by Rawls are just as important as these two principles of justice. The first principle, in particular, that of the greatest possible general liberty, has absolute priority over the second principle, that of difference. Inequalities in regard to basic liberties and rights are excluded in principle (first priority rule). Furthermore, in accordance with the inequality conditions (2b), 'fair opportunity' is lexically prior to all legitimate differences in individual life situations (second priority rule).[51] The difference principle can be interpreted as the principle which claims to define the legitimacy conditions of permissible social inequality and in this way aims to ensure the priority of social justice over Pareto efficiency. According to the difference principle all that matters is

[48] See ibid., p. 3ff.; on the Pareto criterion ibid., p. 58ff.; cf. the treatment in Section 5.3 (2).
[49] Ibid., p. 266. We keep to Rawls's earlier version of the two principles here, in spite of his later revision of the first principle (to 'Each person has the same indefeasible claim to a fully adequate scheme of equal basic liberties, which scheme is compatible with the same scheme of liberties for all') in *Justice as Fairness: A Restatement* (Cambridge MA/ London: Harvard University Press, 2001), § 13, p. 42ff. The newer version takes account of the fact that there is always a list of several basic liberties, whereas the original version suggests a *gradual* dimension of more or less freedom as such ('the most extensive ...'). This is exactly the point in regard to *real* freedom based on socio-economic conditions, but indeed not to *formal* liberties. See Section 7.3.
[50] The 'just savings principle' states that 'the long-term prospects of the least favored extending over future generations' must be considered. This means that each generation should 'put aside in each period of time a suitable amount of real capital accumulation' (Rawls, *Theory of Justice*, rev. edn, p. 252). The second principle of justice thus also requires that *intergenerational justice* may not be violated. We might say that economic prosperity must be ensured *in a sustainable fashion*.
[51] Ibid., pp. 214ff., 266ff.

the optimization of the *absolute* position of the worst-placed person. Social redistribution (from the privileged to the disadvantaged) is accordingly justified in as far as it permits an improvement in the situation of the least favoured; the status-quo conservative Pareto criterion would, of course, not allow this.[52] If, moreover, no state of social inequality can be determined which would, in absolute terms, be advantageous for the less fortunate in comparison to an egalitarian distribution of goods, then the egalitarian solution is to be preferred, as Rawls expressly states.[53] Vice versa, measures must also be regarded as legitimate which best improve the absolute position of the already advantaged and thus increase the relative inequality, as long as the absolute situation of the most disadvantaged can also be improved as a result.

Thus, the difference principle does not opt in a sweeping manner for or against a socio-political correction of existing social inequality, but, firstly, and categorically, subjects the legitimacy of social relationships to the condition of equal basic liberties for all and, secondly, makes inequality rigorously dependent on the condition that the best possible situation of the most disadvantaged can be achieved and sustained.[54] The normative burden of justification thus lies – in accordance with the principle of the moral equality of human beings – with those who wish to permit inequality. This leads Rawls to the following formulation:

> All social values – liberty and opportunity, income and wealth, and the social bases of self-respect – are to be distributed equally unless an unequal distribution of any, or all, of these values is to everyone's advantage.[55]

This last quotation points, however, to a lack of systematic conceptual clarity in two aspects of Rawls's theory of justice, which make it difficult to interpret their concrete significance for the practice of everyday life:

- Firstly, at level (2a) of the difference principle, justice is reduced to the *logic of advantage*. The criterion 'to everyone's advantage' cannot

[52] Ibid., p. 69f. [53] Ibid., p. 65f.

[54] As has been said, the principle of economic sustainability is contained in the 'principle of just saving' (Condition 2a). As Rawls himself makes clear (ibid., pp. 72, 132f.), the difference principle is an interpretation of the decision theoretical *maximin principle* in terms of justice theory. The methodical bridge is provided by the ideal original position with its veil of ignorance, which motivates all the participants to avoid risks and to accept the principle. There is, however, no rational ethical justification here for taking the principle as the decisive criterion for distribution, all the more so as the quality of life for individuals in many spheres does not depend unconditionally on the absolute resources available to them but on their relative position in the social hierarchy of distribution, as the positional economics of Fred Hirsch, *Social Limits to Growth*, has shown. For this criticism of the difference principle see also Ulrich, *Transformation*, p. 260ff.

[55] Rawls, *Theory of Justice* (rev. edn), p. 54.

simply be seen as equivalent to the 'final statement' quoted earlier, as it can be read in Pareto-economic terms.[56] In *A Theory of Justice* there are several examples of such lack of clarity or even confusions in the distinctions made between the principles of justice and the Pareto criterion.[57] This is evidently due to the 'disadvantageous' effects of the contractualistic approach in the original position, in which both the status quo problem and the categorial difference between justice and exchange of advantage are eliminated by definition.

– Secondly, and probably also as a negative consequence of the 'moral-free' original position, Rawls characterizes all the points named in the quotation – liberty, opportunity, income, wealth and even the preconditions for self-respect – without distinction as '*primary goods*'. He describes these goods vaguely as 'things which it is supposed a rational man wants whatever else he wants'.[58] However, in the economically oriented category of primary goods the difference between moral rights and goods is blurred over. Moral rights protect the basic preconditions for an unimpaired *subject status* (personality) of every individual and for the enjoyment of equal rights in social life; consequently they are capable of rational ethical generalization as human or citizens' rights, whereas goods are merely *objects* (or 'things') of subjective desire in the context of a certain conception of the good life (ethos).[59]

The concept of 'primary goods' thus undermines the essential categorial distinction between the constitutive *social conditions* of personal self-determination and the development and exercise of *individual preferences* on the basis of these guaranteed social conditions. The

[56] Rawls (ibid., p. 53) states that 'social and economic equalities are to be arranged so that they are both (a) reasonably expected to be *to everyone's advantage*, and (b) attached to positions and offices open to all' (my italics). Condition (a) is quite simply the Pareto-criterion, from which Rawls distances himself more precisely only later (ibid., p. 57ff.).

[57] Rawls (ibid., p. 65) asserts, for example, that 'the higher expectations of those better situated are just *if and only if* they work as part of a scheme which improves the expectations of the least advantaged members of society', without noticing that he has abandoned critical reflection at the point where the true problem of justice arises, namely at the starting place in society. A little later (ibid., p. 69f.) Rawls contradicts himself in writing: 'Justice is prior to efficiency and requires some changes that are not efficient in this sense. *Consistency obtains only in the sense that a perfectly just scheme is also efficient*' (my italics). On the categorial difference between Pareto efficiency and legitimacy see Section 5.3 (2).

[58] Ibid., p. 79; similarly p. 54. For a detailed list of primary goods see Rawls, *Political Liberalism*, p. 308f.

[59] On the philosophical distinction between moral rights and goods see Wingert, *Gemeinsinn und Moral*, p. 34f., 151f. For a critique of Rawls' disregard of this categorial difference see J. Habermas, 'Reconciliation through the Public Use of Reason: Remarks on John Rawls' Political Liberalism', *Journal of Philosophy* 92 (1995), pp. 109–31, at p. 114ff.

development of preferences for certain goods already assumes the freedom of choice of the person seeking to satisfy his needs within the framework of legitimate individual rights; vice versa, the possibility of exercising moral rights should never depend on the economic situation of an individual, as this would violate the basic right to moral equality. The 'intersubjective character of rights',[60] namely unconditional interpersonal respect and recognition, must ultimately prove its worth in the concrete situation. The guarantee of equal basic rights and opportunities thus is and remains a public matter with categorial priority in a well-ordered society and cannot be made dependent on the decisions of individuals following their personal preferences in economic situations in which resources may be severely limited. If this were the case, the poor and disadvantaged would in the end have to pay for the satisfaction of their basic material needs with a 'voluntary' sacrifice of their real liberties.

On closer examination it becomes apparent that the practical significance of Rawls's strange category of 'primary goods' lies precisely in the idea that under certain circumstances an improvement of the situation of the most disadvantaged could be achieved by their renunciation of certain rights and life prospects in return for more material goods. Rawls regards this as legitimate under two conditions. Firstly, those affected must be in a position to agree to the bargain, and, secondly, the 'basic liberties' must be excluded from such an exchange (first principle of justice). It is now clear why Rawls again and again postulates the optimization of the life prospects of all citizens on the one hand, but also assigns them to the sphere of the principle of difference on the other, and why, in all the final formulations of his first principle of justice, he speaks only of 'equal basic *liberties*'. Moreover, his 'list' of basic liberties contains only the elementary personality rights, political citizens' rights and 'the right to hold personal property' as the sole socio-economic basic right in his idea of a 'property-owning democracy'.[61] He also expressly declares that 'liberties not on the list ... are not basic' and cannot enjoy the priority and the protection of the first principle.[62]

Rawls has to assume, however, that the possibility of exercising the 'basic liberties' as he defines them is independent of the socio-economic situation of the individual; otherwise the category of basic liberties would no longer make sense.[63] He seems to be aware of the problem, as he deals

60 Habermas, *Facts and Norms*, p. 88. 61 See Rawls, *Restatement*, § 41, p. 135ff.

62 Cf. Rawls, *Theory of Justice* (rev. edn), p. 53. For a closer treatment of the priorities and an extension of the list of basic freedoms see Rawls, 'The Basic Liberties and their Priorities', p. 4ff.

63 For a criticism of this premise of Rawls from the point of view of a radical-liberal legal and social philosophy see I. Shapiro, *The Evolution of Rights in Liberal Theory* (Cambridge: Cambridge University Press, 1986), p. 218ff.

explicitly with the objection that in view of 'the social and economic inequalities likely to arise' in practice 'the basic liberties may prove to be merely formal, so to speak'.[64] But his very arguments illustrate the questionability of his premise that other liberties and life prospects beyond the elementary and the citizens' basic liberties relate to the subjective usefulness of liberty and are consequently a matter of individual maximization of advantages in accordance with the principle of Pareto efficiency:

> The basic liberties are a framework of legally protected paths and opportunities. Of course, ignorance and poverty, and the lack of material means generally, prevent people from exercising their rights and from taking advantage of these openings. But rather than counting these and similar obstacles as restricting a person's liberty, we count them as effecting the *worth of liberty*, that is the *usefulness to persons of their liberties*. (...) But the worth, or usefulness, of liberty is not the same for everyone.[65]

In other words, those whose urgent material needs are not satisfied will be happy, according to this dubious *economy of freedom*, to relinquish 'rights' which are not absolutely essential for life, as they have relatively less 'worth' in their eyes, and will choose instead to exchange them for the other primary goods they need. The orientation on the greatest possible advantage of the disadvantaged (in accordance with the principle of difference) accordingly suggests a market solution of the problem of the 'fair' distribution of goods – whereby the inalienable 'basic liberties' in Rawls's sense of course have to remain unaffected. This solution is then not only to the benefit of the most disadvantaged persons but also of their partners in the exchange. We can now understand why Rawls is convinced of the beneficial effects of the market, although this might at first sight seem surprising:

> A ... more significant advantage of a market system is that, given the requisite background institutions [of the well-ordered society], it is consistent with equal liberties and fair equality of opportunity.[66]

It is now definitively clear that Rawls's methodical reference to the assumption of economic rationality and contract theory, which we could at first consider as having no consequences in regard to the basic concept of the well-ordered society, in fact blurs over the categorial difference between justice and Pareto efficiency ('to the advantage of

64 Rawls, 'The Basic Liberties and their Priorities', p. 40; equally in *Political Liberalism*, p. 325.

65 Ibid., p. 40f., and again in *Political Liberalism*, p. 325f. (my italics). For a similar statement see Rawls, *Theory of Justice* (rev. edn), p. 179f.

66 Ibid., p. 240f.

all') at the decisive point, namely, where, for the sake of justice, it would have been necessary to uphold the primacy of the greatest possible *real* freedom of all and the 'fair equality of opportunity' over the exchange logic of the market. It is at least the case that the dividing line between the preconditions of justice, which must be *dictated* to the market, and the primary goods, whose allocation can in contrast be *left to* the market, becomes indistinct. Symptomatically, Rawls feels more and more compelled to state as a *premise* – called 'background justice'[67] – what was intended to be the *result* of his two principles of justice.[68]

It is not necessary here to look in detail at the difficult and shaky tightrope walk that Rawls undertakes when describing situations in which, in his opinion, an exchange of primary goods of very dissimilar quality (renunciation of rights in return for material goods) is legitimate. It is sufficient instead to realize why Rawls, as a philosopher of justice, does not devote more attention and care to the establishment and clarification of a less erratic and less reduced list of basic rights which are covered by his first principle of justice. The explanation is presumably that Rawls fails to maintain the fundamental categorial and normative difference between political liberalism as he understands it and economic (neo-) liberalism. This becomes clear wherever he deals with the role of markets and the 'competitive economy' in the context of the well-ordered society. His standpoint is surprisingly harmonistic and, as W. P. Mendonça has remarked,[69] sometimes even calls to mind Adam Smith's trust in the invisible hand. Rawls assumes, for example:

> that in a competitive economy (with or without private ownership) with an open class system excessive inequalities will not be the rule. Given the distribution of natural assets and the laws of motivation, great disparities will not long persist.[70]

He evidently understands a functioning market as a mechanism which favours the realization of the 'natural assets' of individuals. The reference to natural assets is significant as it reveals the presence of relicts of natural law thinking. Even though, as Rawls himself openly admits, the 'natural

[67] Rawls, *Political Liberalism*, p. 265ff.

[68] Rawls's arguments have not become clearer with his *Restatement* (p. 44): 'A free market system must be set within a framework of political and legal institutions that adjust the long run trend of economic forces so as to prevent excessive concentrations of property and wealth, especially those likely to lead to political domination.'

[69] See W. P. Mendonça, 'Zwischen Rechten und Gütern. Zur liberalistischen Verkürzung der praktischen Vernunft bei John Rawls', in Demmerling/Gabriel/Rentsch (eds.), *Vernunft und Lebenspraxis*, pp. 329–51, at p. 336.

[70] Rawls, *Theory of Justice* (rev. edn), p. 137.

assets' may well be very unevenly distributed, all that counts for him is that:

those who have the same level of talent and ability and the same willingness to use these gifts should have the same prospects of success *regardless of their social class of origin*, the class into which they are born and develop until the age of reason.[71]

Rawls obviously does not take the social constitution of personal abilities and of the willingness to make good use of them as his starting point, although he is fully aware of the problem:

... we cannot view the talents and abilities of individuals as fixed natural gifts. (...) Among the elements affecting the realization of natural capacities are social attitudes of encouragement and support and the institutions concerned with their training and use.[72]

Indeed! Nevertheless it seems to have no systematic consequences for Rawls (beyond the difference principle), as his argumentation is partly reminiscent of Buchanan and the libertarians who accept the 'natural distribution' of individual abilities as a given fact, even if it determines the real interpersonal and economic relationships.[73] Anyway, it is supposed to be *advantageous* for everybody in a societal cooperation according to the market logic of mutual benefit:

Such inequalities, we may assume, are inevitable, or else *necessary* or highly *advantageous* in maintaining effective social cooperation. Presumably there are various reasons for this, among which the need for *incentives* is but one.[74]

And therefore the whole problem with the basically unjust 'natural lottery'[75] as well as the social background of individuals finally seems to be more or less irrelevant in this Paretian world of mutual advantage:

While the distribution of wealth and income *need not be equal*, it must be *to everyone's advantage*.[76]

Even if we followed Rawls in accepting the inequalities in *personal* abilities as a given fact, his contractarian solution could still not be

[71] Rawls, *Restatement*, p. 44 (my italics). Nothing has changed here compared with an almost identical statement in *Theory of Justice* (rev. edn), p. 63.

[72] Rawls, 'The Basic Structure as a Subject', in A. I. Goldman/J. Kim (eds.), *Values and Morals* (Dordrecht: Reidel, 1978), pp. 47–71, § 5 at p. 55f.; reprinted in *Political Liberalism*, pp. 257–88, at pp. 269–70.

[73] See Buchanan, *The Limits of Liberty*, p. 8ff.; see also the treatment in Section 5.3 (3) above. The modern counterpoint to this understanding of liberalism, which is ultimately naturalistic and to this extent premodern, is provided by the conception of republican liberalism, which will be presented in Section 8.1.

[74] Rawls, 'The Basic Structure as a Subject', p. 56, repr. in *Political Liberalism*, p. 270 (my italics).

[75] Rawls, *Theory of Justice* (rev. edn), p. 64.

[76] Ibid., p. 53.

upheld normatively, as it overlooks the decisive *structural* disadvantages of the market system in regard to the 'fair equality of opportunity' for all conceptions of the good, namely the basic *asymmetry of opportunities* between the different life scripts under the competitive conditions of the market economy, as we have elaborated in Section 6.3.

This socio-economic objection is serious, as it disproves the assumption of Rawls, which is generally more characteristic of economic liberalism, that politics and economics can be kept completely apart – and also inevitably contradicts the thesis of the neutrality of political liberalism towards the different projects of the good life. Rawls's thesis of the neutrality of a political-liberal social order is thus met with an objection of a specifically economic-ethical kind which differs fundamentally from the well-known communitarian objection that every conception of justice is always dependent on a shared conception of the good. The economic-ethical counterpoint avoids the problematic consequence, involved in the communitarian approach, of doing without a post-conventional, universalistic idea of justice.[77] It is not the latter but the lack of a socio-economic substructure for the basic political-liberal conception of a well-ordered society which turns out to be the core problem.

If political liberalism takes its own claim to universal legitimacy and neutrality in regard to the 'fact of pluralism' of reasonable conceptions of the good seriously, it must also take the socio-economic conditions of real freedom and equality of opportunity which can be experienced in real life seriously – the two are inseparable. It is not enough to postulate the unconditional primacy of personality rights and political citizenship rights of individuals over the exchange of advantages in the market economy; their inalienable fundamental rights as economic citizens must also be established.

We may concede that Rawls occasionally makes demands in the direction of a conception of freedom for all which can be enjoyed in real life. He states, for example, that by 'fair (as opposed to formal) equality of opportunity' he also means 'equality of opportunity in economic activities', the 'free choice of occupation' and 'equal chances of education'.[78] Furthermore, he characterizes the 'wide dispersal of property' as 'a necessary condition ... if the fair value of equal liberties is to

[77] On communitarianism see Section 8.1.

[78] Rawls, *Theory of Justice* (rev. edn), p. 243. The following page numbers in brackets in the text refer to that book.

be maintained' (p. 245); the institutions which guarantee 'a fair equality of opportunity' are 'put in jeopardy when inequalities of wealth exceed a certain limit; and political liberty likewise tends to lose its value, and representative government to become such in appearance only' (p. 246).[79] In order to work against these processes political liberalism should support 'the taxation of inheritance and income at progressive rates' (p. 247) and the guarantee of a 'social minimum' for all citizens, for which Rawls proposes a 'negative income tax' (p. 243). In more recent contributions Rawls supports, in a general fashion and without clear reference to his theory, 'measures assuring to all citizens adequate all-purpose means to make effective use of their basic liberties and opportunities'.[80]

Thus Rawls at least confirms an extensive interpretation of a postulate he had already formulated towards the end of his major work in a surprisingly absolute fashion:

> In a well-ordered society then self-respect is secured by the public affirmation of the status of equal citizenship for all (p. 478).

Yet Rawls never developed a systematic conception of economic citizenship and the corresponding rights, so that the general postulates he indicates stand in an unqualified relationship to his theoretical conception: *the difference principle threatens to undermine the real substance of the freedom principle (the first principle of justice) to an uncontrollable degree.* In what follows we will, therefore, attempt – with Rawls but without his theoretical straitjacket – to study more closely the domain of those socio-economic citizenship rights which must be seen as the precondition for real freedom and consequently deserve to be included under the first principle of justice.

7.3 Economic citizenship rights as the basis of real freedom for all

The liberal dream of the 18th and early 19th centuries, a society of politically and economically free, responsible and equal citizens, has in the meantime largely faded in the face of the socio-economic realities

[79] This is the main reason why he argues for a 'property-owning democracy' and against 'welfare-state capitalism' in his *Restatement*, p. 139: 'One major difference is this: the background institutions of property-owning democracy work to disperse the ownership of wealth and capital, and thus to prevent a small part of society from controlling the economy, and indirectly, political life as well. By contrast, welfare-state capitalism permits a small class to have a near monopoly of the means of production.'

[80] Rawls, 'The Idea of an Overlapping Consensus', p. 18.

which the unconstrained market-based economization process has created and continues to produce. What was once conceived as a promise under the banner of the universalistic idea of the moral equality of all people has in fact been converted into an elitist programme of a privileged minority for the ideological purpose of defending its economic freedom of manoeuvre, vested interests and opportunities for acquisition and profit. The corresponding reduction of liberalism as it is actually practised to a more or less pure economic liberalism is accompanied by a relapse into a predominantly social-Darwinist concept of (arbitrary) freedom.

Against the background of an almost unbounded political economism the neoliberals put the case for a more or less total functionalization of the entire domain of politics for the economic ends of winning, sustaining or increasing competitive advantages in the regional, international and global competition over the location of industry. The less 'competitive' persons, in particular, suffer objectively and subjectively from a growing loss of security in regard to the economic basis of their existence (security of employment, maintenance of purchasing power and support from the welfare state). They also experience a growing structural dependence, which, in view of the all-powerful anonymous constraints of the system, prevents them from shaping their economic life autonomously and in accordance with self-defined existential needs. Rawls' political-liberal central idea of the 'rational autonomy'[81] of all citizens is faced in the liberalism of the real world with many people's 'economic unfreedom'[82] which often operates in very subtle ways. Its two basic manifestations are an underprivileged material existence (poverty) and the loss of the competence and power of individuals to help themselves (helplessness).[83]

The basic philosophical ideas of political liberalism, and specifically the fundamental conception of a well-ordered society, are, however, too important to allow us to submit resignedly to their erosion by a crude economic liberalism. Liberal thinkers with a clear understanding of the epochal social changes taking place today therefore look out for a third way between the two equally problematic extremes of an unbounded normative individualism[84] and a social *étatism* that limps behind in its attempts to deal with the symptomatic negative consequences of the

[81] Rawls, 'Kantian Constructivism', pp. 520, 527ff.

[82] Tugendhat, *Vorlesungen*, p. 360. 'Throughout the world a large part of humanity is economically unfree, i.e. they lack access to resources which would enable them either to survive at all or to lead lives "worthy of human beings". Many do not possess the positive freedom to do what is necessary in order to keep themselves and their children alive.'

[83] See Section 6.1. [84] On the concept of normative individualism see Section 5.3 (1).

economic processes. Beyond this old polarity, there is a perspective for a further development of the liberal project of society towards a *fully developed civil society*. Its elementary basic features can be summarized in the following three central ideas:

1. *Comprehensive citizenship*: citizens are neither merely political citizens (citoyen) nor merely property owners (bourgeois), but autonomous and at the same time socially integrated members of society. As the liberal idea of a self-determined conduct of life involving equal participation in the social process is decisive for citizenship status, it is a fundamental task of civil society to determine and guarantee this status independently of the socio-economic conditions of life. Ralf Dahrendorf has made the point: 'Citizenship is a non-economic concept. It defines people's standing independent of the relative value attached to their contribution to the economic process. The elements of citizenship are thus unconditional.'[85] Fully developed civic rights, pride in citizenship and, if need be, the readiness to stand up for one's beliefs, are all a part of this status.[86]
2. *Society as a network of egalitarian civil associations*: in civil society the citizens as social beings look after both their private and their communal affairs themselves. They do not primarily ask what others or the state can do for them but what they can do for the solution of public problems. The regulation of social life is left neither to the state nor to the market, but is primarily considered to be the task of communal or grass-roots democratic organizations.[87] Society functions as a complex and dynamic network of civil associations and forms of cooperation organized from the bottom to the top in accordance with the principle of subsidiarity. This offers the individuals a wide range of opportunities to participate and to integrate themselves, but always leaves them the freedom to choose when and where they wish to commit themselves and experience the feeling of belonging. At the same time this network also provides the fundamental 'civil' basis of political democracy.[88]

[85] R. Dahrendorf, 'The Changing Quality of Citizenship', in B. Van Steenbergen (ed.), *The Condition of Citizenship* (London: Sage, 1994), pp. 10–19, at p. 13.

[86] See R. Dahrendorf, *The Modern Social Conflict: An Essay on the Politics of Liberty* (New York/London: Weidenfeld & Nicolson, 1988), p. 29ff.

[87] This assumes the existence of a basic republican disposition. See Section 8.1.

[88] On this point see M. Walzer, 'The Civil Society Argument: A Path to Social Reconstruction', *Dissent* 38 (1991), pp. 293–304. Such forms of cooperation in civil society have acquired great significance, among other things, for the relatively gentle transition of countries like the Czech Republic and Hungary to democracy.

3. *Civilization of the market and of the state*: as citizenship status must be conceived of as involving comprehensive and real autonomy and shared responsibility, civil freedom can be reduced neither to economic nor to constitutional political (formal) freedom, but can be understood only as demanding real freedom and equality of opportunity. The independence of socio-economic conditions called for in point (1) assumes the 'sovereignty' of the citizen in regard to every form of power, including economic power (from property rights), and hence the precedence of the general (real) freedoms of the citizen over economic liberty. On this basis the primacy of politics over the economy and the harnessing of the market forces to the aims of society can also be realized: 'The rights of the citizen are those unconditional rights which go beyond the forces of the market and at the same time put them in their place.'[89] Or shorter: 'Citizenship cannot be marketed'[90] – the market economy has to be civilized.

It should be noted that the central idea of the civil society cannot be understood as a counter-model but as the logical further development of the political-liberal model of a well-ordered society, and, specifically, as a more comprehensive and consistent form of social liberalism. In accordance with point (3) we can readily define the ideal of a fully developed civil society by means of the guiding idea and criterion of a society in which all the members enjoy the greatest possible degree of freedom: *real freedom for all*.[91] Again it is Dahrendorf who puts his finger on the decisive challenge of liberalism understood in this way:

> However, basic human and civil rights have too little meaning for people who for reasons outside their control are unable to make use of them. They therefore lead to a series of *needs of empowerment which may also acquire the quality of rights.*
>
> What should or should not be included in these *enabling rights* is a legitimate subject of debate, and of political struggles. (...) As one pursues the argument one will soon enter T. H. Marshall's proper territory, that is, modern social policy and the entitlements which it conveys. (...) How much of people's *social status* should be removed from the vagaries of the market? Is there any plausible and practicable way of drawing the line between equality of opportunity and equality of results? Are there perhaps acceptable and unacceptable ways of delivering *social entitlements* of citizenship ...? (...) How and to what extent does the core of human and

89 R. Dahrendorf, 'Moralität, Institutionen und die Bürgergesellschaft', *Merkur* 7 (1992), pp. 557–68, at p. 567f.

90 R. Dahrendorf, 'Citizenship and Social Class', in M. Bulmer/A. M. Rees (eds.), *Citizenship Today: The Contemporary Relevance of T.H. Marshall* (London: Routledge, 1996), pp. 25–48, at p. 33.

91 See Van Parijs, *Real Freedom for All*, p. 23.

civil rights need to be backed up by a secondary set of lesser, but none the less, critical, entitlements?[92]

In regard to the full development of the civil society the socio-economic citizen's rights evidently present the core of the problem. The concept of the *economic citizen*, as it is used here, treats the citizen both as a moral person and as an economic agent who is interested in the legitimacy of his own business activities and those of other agents. His self-understanding consequently includes the corresponding virtue of the economic citizen.[93]

Economic citizens in this sense understand the unconditional exercise of the full citizenship status of all members of society, independently of their economic success or failure, as a legitimating condition just as fundamental for a liberal economic and social order as the equality of opportunity of all economic agents in competitive situations. Socio-economic civic rights are then quite simply the additional basic rights indicated by Dahrendorf which enable all citizens to maintain their unconditionally equal civic status even when they are unequally equipped to do so as economic agents. The decisive idea is that ensuring the socio-economic preconditions for a fully developed citizen status is not a question of caritas, of compensatory, charitable and paternal provision by the stronger or by the state for 'those genuinely in need', but must be understood as an *emancipatory* act designed to achieve real freedom as a general moral right of all economic citizens. The solidarity of the winners with the losers in competition must thus be seen as an integrative precondition and not as contrary to the liberal idea of order. The task of a truly liberal state under the rule of law is, accordingly, to achieve an economic order with full social commitment as the basis for a legal equality of all citizens which can be experienced in real life. Constitutional lawyers are usually fully aware of this indissoluble relationship:

> The social commitment [of the State] is not merely intended as noble provision for the poor, as a supplementary task which weakens or even falsifies the liberal substance: it rather involves the reciprocal relationship between economic freedom and legal freedom, between verbal and *real freedom*. (...) It contains the idea that the exercise of economic freedom requires an economic basis and a certain degree of stability and security, without which freedom remains empty declamation.[94]

[92] Dahrendorf, 'The Changing Quality of Citizenship', p. 13f. (my italics).
[93] We examine this ethical dimension of citizenship in Chapter 8.
[94] F. Gygi, 'Die schweizerische Wirtschaftsverfassung', *Zeitschrift für schweizerisches Recht*, N.F. 89 (1970), II, pp. 259–389, at p. 291 (my italics). NB that Gygi understands his account as an interpretation of the Swiss federal constitution.

Thus the freedom of the economic citizen not only includes negative freedom in the sense of the absence of external constraints, but also the positive freedom to perceive and take advantage of real options in the choice of economic actions. This always requires the possession of certain abilities and resources which facilitate self-determination.[95] Such an extended socio-economic concept of freedom characterizes precisely what Van Parijs means by real freedom.[96] The progressive sharpening of the asymmetry of opportunities among the different conceptions of the good life in the context of the rationalization process of the market economy and the need for growing self-assertion in competitive situations is forcing the as yet imperfect civil society of the present to decide, with epochal consequences for the future, either to bury the original liberal project of a society of free and equal citizens as a utopia which is 'incompatible with the market economy' or to develop civil rights further in the direction of modern economic citizenship rights.

In view of the paradigmatics of mainstream economics illustrated in Chapter 5, it is hardly surprising that the postulate of basic economic citizen rights seldom finds favour with the advocates of 'pure' economism.[97] What is more surprising or even alarming, however, is the fact that in more recent discussions on economic ethics, particularly in the German-speaking countries, there is little talk of socio-economic basic rights.[98] There is a lot to catch up on here, otherwise economic ethics could systematically undercut the basic conceptions of political ethics and fall behind in the debate on civil society instead of building on its results.

What then are the criteria we can apply to determine the basic rights of the economic citizen in specific situations? It must be recalled at the outset that from a rational ethical point of view there can be no question of developing a purely analytical systematics of these rights or of human rights in general which can be arrived at purely objectively – so to speak

[95] Cf. Tugendhat, *Vorlesungen*, p. 359.

[96] Van Parijs, *Real Freedom for All*, p. 22, defines the concept of real freedom as follows: 'I shall use the term *real freedom* to refer to a notion of freedom that incorporates all three components – security, self-ownership, and opportunity – in contrast to formal freedom, which only incorporates the first two.'

[97] See the examination in Section 9.3 (1) of the attitude of neoliberal economists towards the inclusion of 'social clauses' in the programme of the World Trade Organization, which ranges from scepticism to complete rejection.

[98] This is also pointed out by Enderle, *Handlungsorientierte Wirtschaftsethik*, p. 40, who is an early positive exception to the rule in the German-speaking countries. See particularly his work on the question of a right to a social minimum, *Sicherung des Existenzminimums*. From the perspective of philosophical ethics Tugendhat, *Vorlesungen*, p. 364ff., has recently called for comprehensive 'economic rights' as a consequence of a 'morality of equal respect' and as a conception of 'minimal justice'; at one point he also speaks of 'socio-economic rights' (p. 391).

outside the practical discourse of the moral community. In view of the complexity of economic and social-ethical interrelations we can at best come up with heuristic considerations as a preparation for discourse. Such considerations will more easily avoid the difficulties of a biased culture-specific context the more they can be systematized with the help of the elementary and universal socio-economic basic characteristics of the conditio humana. In the still relatively undeveloped discussions on this theme two corresponding approaches are recognizable: (1) the basic needs approach and (2) the basic capabilities approach.

(1) The basic needs approach

The concept of basic needs serves simply to characterize those needs which are in principle common to all people, independently of their culture specific formation, and whose satisfaction is consequently a precondition for a life worthy of a human being. As we have seen above, however, the needy nature of all people has always been culturally shaped.[99] It would therefore be a naturalistic misunderstanding if we were to conceive the determination of basic needs as a purely theoretical and not as an ethical and practical problem; what is called for is a heuristics of categories of needs which extends beyond specific cultures but which must nonetheless be interpreted in cultural terms. The International Labour Organization in Geneva, in particular, has worked along these lines, taking up the basic needs approach and applying it effectively to practical economic and social policies.[100]

The peace researcher Johan Galtung has proposed a comprehensive approach to the systematization of human rights which is oriented on basic needs.[101] He distinguishes between four fundamental classes of basic needs and the corresponding human rights: the needs of survival (avoidance of violence), of well-being (avoidance of misery), of identity (avoidance of alienation) and of freedom (avoidance of oppression). Galtung puts the bridging function of basic needs in regard to questions of human rights in a nutshell in the following words:

[99] See above Section 6.1.

[100] See ILO (ed.), *Employment, Growth and Basic Needs: A One-World Problem* (New York: Praeger, 1977). In the meantime, the ILO has gone further towards the paradigm of basic rights, especially with its programme on socio-economic security; see ILO (ed.), *Economic Security for a Better World* (Geneva: ILO, 2004). For the development of the basic needs approach and the path the discussion has taken see J. F. Weeks/E. W. Dore, 'Basic Needs: Journey of a Concept', in: M. E: Crahan (ed.), *Human Rights and Basic Needs in the Americas* (Washington D.C.: Georgetown University Press, 1982), pp. 13–149.

[101] See Galtung, *Human Rights*, pp. 57, 72.

> Where they are insulted human rights may have been violated or there may be a case for new human rights. (. . .) Basic human rights share with basic human needs a universal concern for everybody.[102]

Valuable though it is to test catalogues of human rights with the help of catalogues of basic needs, the approach is nonetheless insufficient as a justification of general rights, as Galtung himself realizes. Whereas the category of basic needs refer to something 'located inside individual human beings', as a part of their needy nature, the category of moral rights deals with the question of interpersonal obligations located *between* individuals.[103] There are, on the one hand, therefore, elementary human needs which do not have any direct relationship to interpersonal obligations and whose fulfilment can thus scarcely be guaranteed by human rights (e.g. the need for sleep or sexual satisfaction). On the other hand, there are essential, justifiable human rights which result purely from the normative logic of interpersonal relationships and can, consequently, be derived solely from the central ideas of just social coexistence without direct reference to the needy nature of human beings (e.g. the basic right to citizenship or free choice of occupation). Basic rights and basic needs are, therefore, fundamentally different categories and are not completely coextensive:

> The source of human rights is man's *moral* nature, which is only loosely linked to the 'human nature' defined by scientifically ascertainable means. Human rights are needed not for life but for a life of dignity . . . Violations of human rights deny one's *humanity*; they do not necessarily keep one from satisfying one's needs.[104]

For these reasons the basic needs approach will not be pursued any further here.

(2) The basic capabilities approach

We move closer to the interpersonal sphere and the socio-economic context with the idea that human rights should not be attached to specific individual basic needs but to the generally required personal basic abilities and the corresponding socio-structural preconditions for the capability of all human beings to take the responsibility themselves for the satisfaction of their needs in accordance with their life project. This approach corresponds well with the conception of real freedom explicated above and is also well-suited to integrate the conception of formal freedom. Formal entitlement and socio-cultural and socio-economic

[102] Ibid., pp. 55, 112. [103] Ibid., p. 56. [104] Donnelly, *Universal Human Rights*, p. 17.

capability are complementary. Only when they are taken together they bring about what can be characterized as the empowerment of the economic citizen to carry out self-determined actions.

This approach can be linked with ethical-critical intent to modern economic theory. The latter has long realized, on the basis of the economic theory of property rights, that the power of disposal over economic resources which an individual has to offer on the market is decisive for his ability to satisfy his needs.[105] On the market not only goods (objects) but also distinguishable rights of disposal over goods are exchanged, which is not always the same as the acquisition of (full) property rights in the sense of a complete set of dispositional rights. It is, for example, enough to rent a house in order to dispose of the usufructuary rights. Acquired rights of disposal give their owner powers to act and can serve either for immediate personal use in order to satisfy real life practical needs or for trading their entitlements as objects of exchange on the market. Property rights can, then, be regarded as (special, not necessarily generalizable) socio-economic 'rights of action'[106] and interaction. It is, therefore, clear that we must couple the empowerment of individuals to satisfy their (self-determined) needs with their entitlement to free disposition over a basic minimum of resources (ultimately purchasing power). We must see this as the central precondition which will enable them to lead a life worthy of a human being in accordance with their culturally determined needs, instead of trying to define specifically the needs which have to be fulfilled. It is only by making regular use of their empowerment to do things that people develop their personal capabilities.

The emancipatory approach which strives to enable and empower people to take their lives into their own hands first crystallized in the context of discussions on *development policy* as a critical alternative to economistic conceptions which sought ways of achieving economic growth and the integration of the underdeveloped and misdeveloped countries in the international market one-dimensionally and without any understanding of the socio-economic context.[107] It is not by chance

[105] It should be noted that within the economic paradigm the *right* of disposal is identical with the *power* of disposal, as an ethical-political legal concept is not conceivable in this context.

[106] H. Demsetz, 'The Exchange and Enforcement of Property Rights', *Journal of Law and Economics* 7 (1964), pp. 11–64. On the relevant literature and for a critical discussion of the economic theory of property rights see Ulrich, *Transformation*, p. 244ff.

[107] The context of underdevelopment serves to explain the heteronomous perspective of the empowerment approach; the assumed difference between the *instance* of empowerment

that the decisive contributions were made in the 1960s and 1970s by Latin American sociologists and theologians. Dependence theory[108] saw underdevelopment at first as a complex politico-economic phenomenon with three typical facets: (a) the external structural dependence of a country on the distribution of resources and the division of labour in the world economy, (b) the internal structural disintegration between the modern, market-oriented and the traditional subsistence economy sectors, and (c) the resulting structural power of a privileged minority over the oppressed majority of the population, who derive very little or no benefit from economic growth for the improvement of their life conditions. The theology of liberation has built on the dependence theory, but in place of its emphasis on exogenous and structural factors, however, it has underlined more strongly the endogenous socio-cultural factors involving lack of 'conscientization'.[109] It consequently promotes basic training and education of people aimed at creating an awareness of the transformability of conditions and self-reliance in their own capabilities and strengths. Although some of the radical ideas of liberation theology were and still are highly disputed, its understanding of development as a question of improving the capabilities of people and empowering them has in the meantime largely gained acceptance.

Among professional economists Amartya Sen was one of the first to understand poverty as the 'deprivation of basic capabilities' and to come to the logical conclusion that all persons must be accorded the basic right to the development of fundamental human capabilities and to the disposal over the resources which are indispensable for the conduct of a self-determined life.[110] The guarantee of this right, together with the promotion of the basic capabilities, is recognized as the best way of securing the livelihood and the human dignity of all people. Sen's approach has considerably influenced the UN Development Programme, which today simply

and those who are to be empowered or enabled reveals relicts of 'colonialistic' thinking even though the intention is emancipatory. The aim is precisely to overcome this heteronomy by means of genuine developmental *cooperation* between equal partners.

108 As the critical theses of the dependence theorists of the 1970s have been confirmed in essence by the manifest failure of the customary growth-oriented development aid policies, it will suffice here to refer to the still representative overview in the collection of essays in D. Senghaas (ed.), *Peripherer Kapitalismus: Analysen über Abhängigkeit und Unterentwicklung* (Frankfurt: Suhrkamp, 1974).

109 This is the keyword of liberation pedagogy (which is closely related to liberation theology) founded by the Brasilian educationist and social ethicist Paulo Freire, *Pedagogy of the Oppressed* (New York: Seabury, 1971). The socio-economic aspect of liberation theology is represented particularly by F. Hinkelammert, *The Ideological Weapons of Death: A Theological Critique of Capitalism* (Maryknoll NY: Orbis Books, 1986).

110 See Sen, *Development as Freedom*, p. 87ff.; path-breaking already his *Commodities and Capabilities* (Amsterdam: North-Holland Publishing, 1985).

defines development as 'a process of enhancing human capabilities – to expand choices and opportunities so that each person can lead a life of respect and value'.[111]

If we accept this viewpoint, it follows that the empowerment of people to develop and exercise general socio-economic basic capabilities provides the systematic criterion for the determination of economic citizenship rights. The basic capabilities approach is by no means relevant only to the developing countries but also to the 'advanced' industrial nations. Here too rapid economic structural change is increasingly creating new structural dependence, which makes the guarantee of socio-economic rights all the more urgent. As a result of market globalization and the limited ability of the welfare state to cope with the new developments practically all the countries in the world have been affected by the phenomenon of 'new poverty', social disintegration, marginalization and the structural powerlessness of those cut off from the means of gainful employment. The cause of this 'new' problem of poverty is to be seen less in the overtaxing of the welfare state than in the growing divide between structural dependence on the market for the provision of basic needs and the increased 'toughness' of the labour market as the place for acquiring the necessary purchasing power. However, even those strata of the population which are (still) among the beneficiaries of rationalization and globalization partly find themselves embroiled in new forms of structural dependence, as we have already seen above.[112]

In its closeness to the realities of socio-economic life and to the essence of human nature the entitlement and capability approach refers back to the considerations on an economy of abundance in the context of the question of the meaningfulness of economic activity (Chapter 6). It thus makes clear that we must approach the issue of socio-economic basic rights from two directions: on the one hand all people must be entitled to and be capable of *integrating* themselves into the processes of production and consumption in the market economy on the basis of equality of opportunity and, on the other hand, their entitlement and capability in regard to a (partial) *emancipation* from the functional constraints of the economic system must also be ensured. Neither the complete appropriation of people as functional elements of the economic systems logic nor total 'opting out' of the system will permit them to achieve a fully

[111] United Nations Development Programme (ed.), *Human Development Report* (New York/Oxford: Oxford University Press, 2000), p. 2.
[112] See Section 6.2 (3).

developed, both reasonably autonomous *and* socially integrated, 'rich' life in the fullest sense. Above all, it is necessary to find a more attractive and socially just alternative to the 'third-worldized' double economy of insiders within the economic system, who are well-paid but work hard, and outsiders, who have been 'released' from the systemic process of production and consumption, or, to put it more frankly, have been eliminated from the market and are dependent on social welfare and state support. The regulative idea of a dual life form for all citizens offers such an alternative. It combines the partial participation of all economic citizens in the economic process and partial emancipation from it in order to realize a new, generalizable, 'normal case' of socio-economic life in an advanced civil society.

If this model is accepted as meaningful, two general consequences follows for the form economic citizenship rights should take. They must (a) enable all citizens to acquire a comprehensive basic ability both to assert themselves within the economic system and to pursue autonomous self-realization in their lifeworld. However, (b) the rights to participate in the economic system and to share its 'fruits' must be conceived of as restricted participatory rights for the individual, so that they can be enjoyed as equal basic rights by all economic citizens.

Ad (a): the proposed orientation on comprehensive socio-economic basic capabilities makes the presentation of a systematic let alone a conclusive list difficult. One suitable heuristic perspective could be to follow the different biographical life phases and the areas of life essential for personal development and self-assertion in each phase (socialization, individualization and general education in childhood and youth; adult professional and family life and participation in public life; old age). Another conceivable order could be built upon the formal dimensions of capability to act. The following could then, for example, be distinguished as worthy of the status of socio-economically relevant[113] basic rights:

- the capability to understand one's own life context and to orient oneself in life (right to education);[114]

[113] Due to this restriction, the following list is less general than Martha Nussbaum's 'basic human functional capabilities'. See M. Nussbaum, 'Aristotelian Social Democracy', in R. B. Douglass / G. M. Mara / H. S. Richardson (eds.), *Liberalism and the Good* (New York *et al.*: Routledge, 1990), pp. 203–52, at p. 225.

[114] See Dahrendorf's justification, *Life Chances*, p. 174, of a 'civil right to education' which corresponds completely to Van Parijs's conception of *real freedom for all*: 'Equality of educational opportunity is a basic right of every citizen, as education is both a precondition and an aspect of full social and political participation.'

- the capability to develop one's own personality, self-awareness and self-respect and to make use of them effectively in the world of employment (right to inviolable identity and fitting participation in decision processes, specifically in economic life;[115])
- the capability to develop a sense of social belonging and to foster relationships with others as a respected person (right to social integration);
- the capability to exercise one's rights, particularly in the case of intolerable influence or interference of others (right to legal protection and fair trial);
- the capability to found and support a family (right to partnership, marriage, children and adequate social support for families);
- the capability to participate in social communication and democratic politics as a responsible citizen (right to participation in public communication);
- the capability to ensure one's own economic welfare by one's own efforts, whenever possible (right to professional training, right to work, fair working conditions and fair wages, but also the right to independent enterprise and private property, including access to appropriate investment credit;[116])
- the capability to lead a life worthy of a human being in accordance with one's self-respect even in situations of economic need (right to basic material security and social care).

What matters, ultimately, are all the capabilities and entitlements necessary in a justly ordered civil society for the pursuit of a coherent and successful life project, including suitable forms of economic existence and activity. The establishment of such fundamental points might even enable us to examine the actual state of the development of general conventions on human rights with a view to uncovering possible bias and discovering possible gaps. The basic capabilities approach can also help us to avoid the dangers of an unsystematic 'inflationary' expansion of the catalogues of human rights and to arrive at a limited number of truly fundamental basic rights which are worthy of being taken seriously.

Ad (b): if the various socio-economic basic rights are to have the character of real basic rights and are to be granted and guaranteed equally to all economic citizens, they must be conceived of as limited rights. The

[115] This leads, among other things, to the central idea of civil rights in organizations, i.e. the right to the protection of personality, to information and participation of dependent employees in organizations. See Section 10.3 (2).

[116] How useful a system of microcredits can be for overcoming poverty has been proven, for instance, by the Grameen Bank in Bangladesh and in many other countries. See the book of its founder and Nobel Peace Prize Laureate 2006 M. Yunus, *Banker to the Poor: Micro-Lending and the Battle against World Poverty* (New York: Public Affairs, 1999).

interdependence between universalizability and limitedness will be illustrated in what follows by the example of three central economic citizenship rights: firstly in regard to the right to property (b_1) and then in regard to two rights which must be considered together, as they are in part alternatives to one another: the right to a basic income and/or the right to employment (b_2).

(b_1) The *right to private property* is in principle fully justifiable as an economic citizenship right. But it is a striking fact that the first philosopher of political liberalism, John Locke (1632–1704), already emphasizes that this right is by no means unrestricted.[117] According to Locke every individual has an inalienable right to his own person. In accordance with the labourist legitimation of property he developed, every person has the right to the results of his labours (2nd Treatise, § 27). His philosophy of property thus implies a universalistic element: personal property should be accorded to every individual in relation to the work he invests. Consequently, legitimate private property is restricted to the amount which an individual is truly capable of amassing as a result of his own efforts (2nd Treatise, § 31) and which is 'necessary and useful to His being' (1st Treatise, § 86, p. 223):

> This measure did confine every Man's *Possession* to a very moderate Proportion, and such as he might appropriate to himself, without Injury to any Body in the first Ages of the World ... And the same measure may be allowed still, without prejudice to any Body, as full as the World seems.[118]

Locke saw very clearly that the introduction of money exploded the limitations set by natural law on the acquisition of property (2nd Treatise, § 37). But as he was unwilling to draw the obvious critical conclusions from his legitimation theory, he ultimately came closer to a justification of the unlimited accumulation of capital in private hands.[119] In regard to the justifiability of private property as an economic citizen's right, however, it is necessary to subject this position to a new ideological critique. The conception of the right to personal property as a *limited* socio-economic basic right implies the prevention of a concentration of property which would reduce the general right to property to a farce.

[117] See Locke, *Two Treatises of Government*, p. 303ff. The references in brackets in the text refer to Locke.

[118] Ibid., §36, pp. 310–11. Locke argues on the basis of the natural equality of all people in natural law, the Golden Rule and the Christian principle of neighbourly love.

[119] On this point see H. Holzhey, 'Locke's Begründung des Privateigentums in der Arbeit', in H. Holzhey/G. Kohler (eds.), *Eigentum und seine Gründe*, Studia philosophica, Supplementum 12 (Berne *et al.*: Haupt, 1983), pp. 19–34; A. Künzli, *Mein und Dein: Zur Ideengeschichte des Eigentumsfeindschaft* (Cologne: Bund-Verlag, 1986), p. 197ff. For a more comprehensive treatment see H. Medick, *Naturzustand und Naturgeschichte der bürgerlichen Gesellschaft* (Göttingen: Vandenhoeck & Ruprecht, 1973).

From a political-liberal point of view the limitation of the *right of inheritance* is even more clearly justifiable, as a lack of restrictions here has a serious adverse effect on the equality of opportunities at the outset and must therefore be regarded as a late feudal alien body in the liberal conception of society.[120]

In other words, the right to private property is a basic right only to a limited extent, namely in as far as it is restricted to a generalizable degree of private property.[121] If this condition is fulfilled, the ability of all citizens to acquire property should even be fostered.[122] In contrast, claims to property exceeding a generalizable degree can only be justified as special rights deriving from particular social performances or merit; in accordance with the categorical validity of all basic rights their legitimacy is bound by the reservation that they do not violate any general socio-economic citizenship rights of other persons.[123] The thesis of Tugendhat that 'the right to private property must be restricted to the extent that it violates other rights of the citizen'[124] can scarcely be refuted with good arguments, even though it sounds so provocative against the background of the traditional 'capitalist ethos' (Max Weber). An economic and business ethics that wants to get to the core of its subject matter will have to commit itself increasingly to an unreserved reflection on the complex fundamental questions of private property in a life-serving market economy.[125]

(b_2) We now turn our attention to the question of the justifiability of an economic citizenship *right to a basic income* and to the *right to employment*, as these two 'candidates' for the status of (alternative) basic rights have increasingly become the focus of the present-day debate on socio-political issues and on the institutional framework of the market. They must be considered each in its own right and also in regard to the relationship and the priorities which exist between them. The central significance and the liberal quality of these two proposals for the status of basic economic citizenship rights can be justified from the perspective of the capability

120 Rawls, *Theory of Justice* (rev. edn 1999), p. 245, also approves of progressive inheritance taxes. For this debate see also G. Erreygers/T. Vandevelde (eds.), *Is Inheritance Legitimate? Ethical and Economic Aspects of Wealth Transfers* (Berlin: Springer, 1997).

121 On the resulting necessary distinction between generalizable personal rights of property and functional rights of disposal over social productive capital see the systematic considerations in Ulrich, *Transformation*, p. 387ff.

122 Furthermore this is also demanded by Rawls, *Theory of Justice* (rev. edn), p. 244f.

123 On the distinction between general and special rights see Tugendhat, *Vorlesungen*, p. 338ff.

124 Ibid., p. 362.

125 Some additional remarks on property rights from the perspective of regulatory politics follow in Section 9.2 (3a).

	Unconditional right	*Conditional right*
1. Right to basic income	I. Unconditional basic income (Van Parijs)	II. Negative income tax (Friedman, Rawls and others)
2. Right to work	III. Defined working lifetime (Gorz)	IV. Subsidiary right to work on a second labour market

Figure 7.2. Four variants of the right to a basic income or to work

approach by their aim of enabling all citizens to participate in the social processes mediated by the market and/or of making them to some degree independent of the existential necessity of self-assertion on the (labour) market. Or in more drastic words: they help the citizens emancipate themselves from what can be called the 'tyranny'[126] of the labour market. The right to a basic income guarantees a minimum of purchasing power and thus the possibility of participating in social consumption on the market, whereas the right to (gainful) employment gives all citizens access to the labour market and thus not only recognizes their claim to acquire the basic material necessities of life by their own efforts (income-generating power), but also the immaterial claim to make a useful contribution to the social productive process and so to be recognized as full members of society.

If we distinguish, in regard to the two candidates for the status of basic rights, between the variants of unconditional and conditional right, i.e. a right which is directly tied to certain preconditions such as the fulfilment of certain services in return (civil duties), we arrive at the following fourfold table (Figure 7.2).

Variant I: Unconditional basic income

The central civic rights argument in favour of the unconditional guarantee of a basic income was already formulated by Thomas M. Marshall: 'a universal right to a real income which is not proportionate to the market value of the claimant' is part of full citizenship status.[127] The most consistent and thoroughly argued case to date for an unconditional basic income for all citizens has been presented by Philippe Van Parijs,

[126] Michael Walzer calls a principle of social distribution 'tyrannic' if it is not restricted to those spheres it is appropriate for but dominates other spheres, where it is not adequate, or even the whole life conditions of citizens; see Walzer, *Spheres of Justice*, p. 17ff.

[127] Marshall, 'Citizenship and Social Class', p. 100.

who defends it against almost all conceivable objections. His main argument is that only an unconditional basic income for all, which is independent of any service in return, of individual wealth or any other criteria, offers the opportunity for a free choice of a preferred life project.[128] No-one who takes the principle of the greatest possible real freedom for all citizens seriously can force a citizen to pursue a life form based on achievement and acquisition of income, but must accept the right of those citizens who so wish to lead a radically different life. From this point of view it is legitimate for individuals to be satisfied with the modest consumption their basic income (supplemented by their own labour) permits, so that they can win the freedom to devote their time to non-economic matters. In order to ensure that this does not remain a privilege of the wealthy but is open to as many citizens as possible, Van Parijs postulates, as a long-term view, the guarantee of the *greatest possible basic income* that is generalizable for all citizens.

The greatest possible basic income is defined by its *sustainability*, by the criterion that the incentives and efficiency needed to guarantee it must be permanently maintained (p. 38ff.).[129] Whether the greatest possible basic income is higher or lower than the income needed to guarantee a social minimum depends on the prevailing economic conditions. It should not, therefore, be confused with the conception of a social minimum guaranteed by the state, which rests upon the satisfaction of basic needs (p. 35). The focus is not primarily on social welfare but on economic citizenship as a basis for (or contribution to) real freedom for all. Consequently the right to an unconditional basic income – which is sometimes called 'citizen's dividend' or 'social dividend'[130] – by no means excludes its supplementation by public welfare assistance in the case of neediness. The higher this compensatory assistance is, however, the lower the economically 'sustainable' basic income becomes (p. 84). Conversely, the latter can be increased by the introduction of a general civic commitment to an obligatory, modestly remunerated community service in the social and health services, environmental protection, education or development aid programmes, etc. How this solidary civic obligation can and should be fulfilled in practice should, in turn, be regulated in accordance with

[128] See Van Parijs, *Real Freedom for All*, p. 32ff. Page numbers in brackets in the following text refer to that book.

[129] How high the 'greatest possible' general basic income can be is determined normatively in accordance with the principle of real freedom, namely by the social constellation of autonomously chosen life projects, whose realization is *willed* by the citizens. On the justification of this norm see below.

[130] This notion goes back to the first holder of the Chair of Political Economy at Oxford University, George D. H. Cole, in his *Principles of Economic Planning* (London: Macmillan, 1935).

the principle of real freedom of choice. All that matters is that one of the equally valuable forms of civic service should be carried out for the purpose of lowering the costs for the national budget and fostering public spirit and solidarity between the members of the civil society (p. 231).[131]

Both the precondition of economic sustainability and the prevention of the exploitation of the industrious by the lazy make it necessary, according to Van Parijs's further arguments, to find a market solution with corresponding wage incentives for the distribution of gainful employment. The higher the greatest possible basic income is, the lower the demand for gainful employment will be and the higher the wage incentives will have to be. In the ideal case of a balanced labour market the (monetary and other) incentives are such that nobody would have occasion to be envious of the advocates of a different life form, neither those with little or no employment in regard to those who prefer an acquisitive or 'entrepreneurial' life form,[132] nor vice versa, as the former would enjoy more freedom and leisure time. After all, each has the freedom to choose whether he prefers to take up the one or the other option or to seek a compromise between the two. Provided that the incentives and disincentives for income and taxation are properly regulated, an *undominated diversity* of lifestyle options can be created in a society which is largely free of compulsion and social envy (pp. 53f., 58ff., 77).

The unconditional basic income has a desired side-effect – it solves, in principle, the problem of unemployment, at least apart from situations of strong structural imbalance between demand and supply of labour. The demand for gainful employment would necessarily fall to a lesser or greater degree depending on the wage and tax incentives and disincentives. For precisely this reason voluntary unemployment then deserves exactly the same material 'compensation' as involuntary unemployment, as the renunciation of a place of work would contribute to the availability of employment for citizens who prefer a way of life involving work and a good income (p. 109ff.).[133] Van Parijs therefore gives the right to an unconditional basic income systematic priority over the *right to work*. He approves of the latter, but sees precisely in his conception of a general basic income the decisive socio-economic precondition for its realization (p. 125ff.).

[131] In Van Parijs's conception, however, the right to a general basic income is not made conditional on the fulfilment of a specific civic duty. These are two separate though complementary obligations, each unconditional in its own right.

[132] See above Section 6.3.

[133] The obvious objection that extensive voluntary unemployment would lead to a decline in the available national product would be invalid at least as long as a high level of *enforced* unemployment exists in an economy and the posts which have been voluntarily abandoned can be taken by others.

The model of Van Parijs, whose complex features cannot be developed fully here, may seem bold, but it is in principle only a consistent elaboration of Rawls's first principle of justice, which also postulates the greatest possible general freedom. And this is precisely the aim of Van Parijs, who extends the formal (civic) concept of freedom only to include the economic citizenship concept of real freedom (p. 25ff.).[134]

For the same reason some authors argue that, instead of an unconditional civic income, an unconditional *civic capital* endowment might be even more consistent and logical. The most prominent protagonists of such a one-time capital grant for every citizen (at birth or maturity) are Bruce Ackerman and Anne Alstott.[135] They see such 'stakeholding' as a universalized form of 'social inheritance', making inheritance a citizen's right in contrast to the traditional privilege of being born into a wealthy family. The latter corresponds much more to feudalism than to a modern society of free and equal citizens. The idea of an unconditional basic citizen's 'stake' in the societal capital stock inherited from the earlier generations perfectly suits the vision of a 'property-owning democracy' as distinguished from capitalism by Rawls[136] and proposed already by John Stuart Mill,[137] the leading political economist and liberal philosopher of the nineteenth century.

Obviously, 'basic income' and 'basic capital' are related conceptions, since income can be achieved from capital or vice versa be capitalized itself. Both variants imply some specific forms of paternalism (i.e. restrictions of possible use): on the one hand, a periodical but small basic income prevents the recipient from making 'entrepreneurial' or capital investments in an early stage of life; and on the other hand, with regard to basic capital, incapable as well as unlucky investors could easily and quickly lose their endowment and fall back into dependence on social security. It is not the place here to look at the ongoing debate in details.[138] But it might be plausible to combine the advantages of both approaches –

[134] See also his interpretation of Rawls's principle of difference, ibid., p. 94ff.

[135] B. Ackerman/A. Alstott, *The Stakeholder Society* (New Haven: Yale University Press, 1999).

[136] See above in Section 7.2.

[137] See J. St Mill, *Principles of Political Economy* (1848). Collected Works of John Stuart Mill, ed. J. M. Robson, vols. III–V (Toronto: University of Toronto Press, 1965ff.), Book II, Chap. 1–2, pp. 199–234. Cf. P. Ulrich, 'John Stuart Mills emanzipatorischer Liberalismus', in P. Ulrich/M. Assländer (eds.), *John Stuart Mill: Der vergessene politische Ökonom und Philosoph* (Berne *et al.*: Haupt, 2006), pp. 253–82.

[138] At present, the overall argumentation for an unconditional basic income is probably ahead. See C. Pateman, 'Democratizing Citizenship: Some advantages of a basic income', *Politics and Society* 32 (2004), pp. 89–106; J. Cunliffe & G. Erreygers, 'Basic Income? Basic Capital! Origins and Issues of a Debate', *Journal of Political Philosophy* 11 (2003), pp. 89–110.

freedom of choice between investment and consumption as offered by the basic capital together with the prudential continuity and security of a basic income – by means of a 'hybrid citizen's stake': why not, as a first step, combine a modest *time-limited* citizen's income (for one, two, three ... years of one's own choice in a life-time) with a citizen's *development* grant for qualified investment purposes (such as higher education, vocational training, or setting up a new business)?[139]

Variant II: Negative income tax

The idea of a negative income tax was probably first proposed by Milton Friedman[140] and has also met, for example with the approval of Rawls,[141] at least as a possible policy. Apart from technical and procedural differences, the only essential difference between this variant and the unconditional basic income is that its payment is bound by the *condition* that the income of those entitled to receive it falls below a determined level of taxable income. It does not therefore replace personally earned income, but it does nonetheless compensate for all forms of inadequate income regardless of the cause in each individual case. The scale of taxation then operates not only upwards for higher taxable income in the direction of growing 'positive' taxes, but also downwards in the 'negative' direction of a growing transfer of income to the less advantaged citizens. Together with the income acquired by employment this 'negative income tax' (NIT) should then guarantee the social minimum. The difference between the NIT and the traditional forms of public welfare (national assistance) is that a partial income acquired through employment increases overall income successively, so that both the incentive to work and the freedom to continue being employed are maintained as far as possible, in spite of dependence on public 'support'. As a result, the former rigorous separation between income acquired by personal effort and income from public assistance is replaced by a flowing transition in both directions.[142]

This conception is highly relevant today because it indicates a way of avoiding the choice between two consequences of the unbalanced labour market which are equally unacceptable from an economic-ethical

139 See S. White, 'The Citizen's Stake and Paternalism', *Politics and Society* 32 (2004), pp. 61–78.

140 M. Friedman, *Capitalism and Freedom* (Chicago/London: University of Chicago Press, 1962), pp. 190–5.

141 Rawls, *Theory of Justice* (rev. edn), p. 243.

142 See F.W. Scharpf, 'Für eine Subventionierung niedriger Erwerbseinkommen', *Wirtschaftsdienst* 74/3 (1994), pp. 111–18; Scharpf, 'Soziale Gerechtigkeit im globalen Kapitalismus', *Die neue Gesellschaft/Frankfurter Hefte* 40 (1993), pp. 544–7.

standpoint: the continental European 'real model' of chronic mass unemployment accompanied by relatively high wage levels and the Anglo-Saxon reality of a growing stratum of working poor, who find (casual) employment but cannot live a decent life on the income from it. With NIT the regulation of wage levels could be increasingly left to the market; the resulting additional low-paid jobs would reduce unemployment without those affected having to pay the price of an intolerably low income. If the condition of employment is abandoned and the conception expanded to include those who are unemployed and live entirely from (other) social transfers, this approach leads us to a conception which is even closer to that of the general basic income, namely the idea of a so-called *Bürgergeld* (civic income), which lumps more or less all social security benefits together in one universal transfer.[143] With the basic variant involving 'subsidization of low income' (Scharpf) and, even more so, with the extended variant guaranteeing a civic income it is possible at one sweep to replace numerous social security benefits which are tied to special criteria by a strikingly simple all-inclusive system, for which a single indicator already provided by the tax returns (available income) suffices. As it does away with complicated and degrading enquiries into the economic plight of citizens and with the unpleasant associations of humiliating dependence on charity, the concept corresponds to a real general economic citizenship right.

On taking a closer look, however, we can see that this conception gives rise not only to problems in regard to the justice of the tax system on which it is based but also to certain administrative difficulties, as the liability to tax or the entitlement to NIT can be established only a year after the need has arisen, so that some form of interim aid with a corresponding proof of need is necessary. Moreover, the comparison with the unconditional basic income (UBI) for all citizens is also not necessarily favourable for NIT in regard to the capacity of the national economy to finance it, as the UBI enables a correspondingly higher tax yield; in the case of equal net income the net burden for the state will in principle be the same.[144] From the standpoint of the greatest possible freedom for all the conception of the unconditional basic income is, therefore, all in all superior.

[143] The expression 'Bürgergeld' (civic income) was probably used for the first time by W. Engels/J. Mitschke/B. Starkoff, *Staatsbürgersteuer* (Wiesbaden: Karl Bräuer Institut, 1974). See also J. Mitschke, *Steuer- und Transferordnung aus einem Guss* (Baden-Baden: Nomos, 1985); Mitschke, 'Steuer- und Sozialpolitik für mehr reguläre Beschäftigung', *Wirtschaftsdienst* 75/2 (1995), pp. 75–84, especially p. 80ff.; W. Engels *et al.* (eds.), *Bürgersteuer – Entwurf einer Neuordnung von direkten Steuern und Sozialleistungen* (Bad Homburg: Schriftenreihe des Kronberger Kreises, 1986).

[144] See Van Parijs, *Real Freedom for All*, p. 57.

Variant III: Defined working lifetime

The two conceptions we have dealt with hitherto give priority to a right to a basic income and expect as a result indirect effects which can contribute to the solution of problems in the labour market. An argument against them which deserves careful consideration favours the primacy of the right to work. This argument, which was upheld among others by André Gorz for a long time,[145] approves the guarantee of a right to a basic income but rejects a dissociation from the right to work on account of the social character and human significance of participation in work in society. In the final analysis such a separation simply means that society withdraws from its moral obligation to provide every citizen who is willing to work with a place of work. The guarantee of a direct right to work alone exerts pressure on the instances of economic policy to *distribute justly* the scarce supply of reasonably meaningful and well-paid employment by means of a general reduction of working hours. In as far as this leads to the creation of new jobs, competition on the labour market will be lessened. But if there is no redistribution of gainful employment, the competition between the 'employees' in the struggle for good jobs will intensify in view of the continued improvement in levels of productivity; the growing army of losers who are unable to compete will then lead to a fundamental split in society between the employed and the (involuntarily) unemployed.

This process must be encountered, as it always has been in the past, by a partial conversion of the progress in productivity into a general reduction of working hours. It would be more desirable for all citizens to work less, rather than for a shrinking minority who possess competitive advantages on the labour market to work and earn unrestrictedly, while all the others, who are more or less excluded from attractive places of work, are given a basic income without working for it by way of 'compensation'. The consequence is the demand for an increasingly limited and hence generalizable number of normal working hours in return for improved productivity. For Gorz, at least according to his earlier position, this must involve both a right and an obligation to work. The fulfilment of the obligation to work a fixed number of hours brings with it a conditional right to income and thus ensures the coupling of the right to work with the right to a basic income. After all, it might be

[145] See Gorz, *Critique of Economic Reason*, p. 203ff. More recently, Gorz has changed his mind in as far as he sees the working life of more and more people as being precarious; see Gorz, *Reclaiming Work: Beyond the Wage-based Society* (Cambridge: Polity, 2000), p. 84ff., where he now argues for 'the *unconditional* right to a sufficient basic income' (p. 85; italics in the original).

simply a question of fair reciprocity and solidarity that all able and responsible citizens contribute to the social cooperation. Both a minimum workload and a guaranteed basic income are then constitutive for economic citizenship.[146]

Yet this line of argument does not take Van Parijs' highly developed conception of an unconditional basic income fully into account. A fair reciprocity between enjoying the economic benefits of social cooperation and making a productive contribution is certainly important, but only *against the background* (and not as a condition) of real freedom for all; otherwise the claim of fair reciprocity simply undermines the emancipatory sense of the unconditional basic income.[147] Moreover, Van Parijs's conception for its part includes the redistribution of gainful employment as one of its intended consequences.

Either way, in a working society much does indeed depend on gainful employment, which should be guaranteed to all for its own sake. Participation in work enables individuals to experience and respect themselves as useful members of society and also to 'earn' the respect and recognition of others in as far as they are engaged in a reasonably qualified and 'valuable' activity. A profession or occupation is also a significant source of learning and experience which permits us to develop and test our personal abilities, to improve self-confidence, to make social contacts and, in favourable cases, even to find the meaning of our lives, our 'calling'. Moreover, work also provides a desirable time structure for the lives of many people; the time spent at work creates the basis for the complementary enjoyment of 'leisure time'. Under all of these circumstances it is understandable that most people who have been culturally formed by industrial society for the moment still prefer, at least partially, to be in employment.

A basic right to work is particularly plausible when it is understood as a *right to participate* in the complex social cooperation based on division of labour and in the corresponding benefits.[148] It is then by no means merely a functional precondition for economic self-assertion, but rather an

[146] See S. White, 'Liberal Equality, Exploitation, and the Case for an Unconditional Basic Income', *Political Studies* (1997), pp. 312–26; White, *The Civic Minimum: On the Rights and Obligations of Economic Citizenship* (New York/Oxford: Oxford University Press, 2003), especially p. 202ff.

[147] See Ph. Van Parijs, 'Reciprocity and the Justification of an Unconditional Basic Income. Reply to Stuart White', *Political Studies* (1997), pp. 327–30; see also R. J. van der Veen, 'Real Freedom versus Reciprocity: Competing Views on the Justice of Unconditional Basic Income', *Political Studies* (1998), pp. 140–63.

[148] See F. Kambartel, 'Arbeit und Praxis. Zu den begrifflichen und methodischen Grundlagen einer aktuellen politischen Debatte', *Deutsche Zeitschrift für Philosophie* 41 (1993), pp. 239–49.

essential aspect of inter-personal relations and thus of mutual respect and recognition. As a moral right the claim to such active participation can hardly be rejected and it is not weakened by the standard objection that no party exists which can be sued for its enforcement. Even though there can be probably no legal guarantee of the observation of this basic right for individuals, it nonetheless obliges the instances responsible for economic policies to pursue a determined policy of just distribution of labour.

Under the conditions of a thoroughly rationalized economic system, however, it does not make much sense to seek the fulfilment of all expectations of self-realization and the good life in gainful employment; what matters most is rather a partial emancipation from the constraints of systemic labour.[149] The emancipatory goal today therefore requires both partial participation as a full member in the systemic process of production and also partial liberation from it, in order to achieve the dual life form for all postulated above. It also corresponds fully with the liberal criterion (the greatest possible freedom of individuals) to regulate the overall amount of time spent in gainful employment, to which the individual citizen is entitled or obliged (depending on the perspective). The distribution of working time over the week, the year, or even the entire working life need not be regulated then. More *time sovereignty*[150] is a part of personal autonomy. The central idea is therefore the conception of an overall general working lifetime, which can be continually reduced as productivity progresses. Every economic citizen could choose for himself how to distribute the amount of work on his 'work-time account'[151] over his lifetime. This would include the possibility of reaching an agreement with an employer to work in blocks of time, to do an agreed minimum of work by a certain age, or to choose, within a certain range, between a minimum and a maximum working lifetime. It would be important for individuals to be able to adapt the amount of work to be done to the phases of their lives (periods of education, further training, distribution of working time within the family, particularly during the upbringing of children).

149 See A. Gorz, *Farewell to the Working Class* (London: Pluto, 1982), p. 66ff.

150 See Teriet, 'Zeitsouveränität', and the postulation of a new 'time policy' in Section 6.3.

151 Gorz, *Critique of Economic Reason*, p. 148. A partly analogous system has proved its worth in the Swiss pension schemes for the retired and for surviving dependants (Alters- und Hinterlassenenversicherung = AHV). In a number of supplementary insurance schemes the individual citizen can hold an 'AHV-account'; if he becomes entitled to payment the amount is calculated on the basis of the years he has been in employment and the overall sum of his acquired income. In contrast to conventional pension schemes, the AHV is not based on income alone but also includes equivalent amounts for certain other costs of citizens, in particular for the years devoted to the upbringing of children.

Of course, this can be a real option only for those who have no private source of wealth if the income to which they have literally earned the right by the fulfilment of their social obligation to work is more or less evenly distributed over their lifetime, possibly in accordance with the personal preference of the recipient. Therefore a compensation system is necessary, in which work-time accounts are held on which individuals can draw at times when they are not gainfully employed, thus ensuring a steady supply of income at all times. In relation to the potential for real freedom which a corresponding labour policy would offer the administrative problems involved seem slight and perfectly soluble.

Variant IV: A second labour market

The idea of creating a second labour market has been widely discussed and practised in recent years in advanced industrial societies, for example in the German 'ABM' programme (Arbeitsbeschaffungsmassnahmen, i.e. public measures for the creation of employment). The concept involves the provision of offers of employment by the state or preferably the local community to people who, for whatever reason, are not capable of competing for jobs on the 'free' market. As far as possible the employment offered should not compete with the work available on the 'first labour market', but should supplement it by covering tasks which are socially meaningful though for financial reasons cannot be tackled by the private economic sector or by public institutions without the public employment measures. Typical examples of suitable activities are communal services in the area of infrastructure, social services or protection of the environment (or public-private partnerships in these areas). The jobs are not as well remunerated as those on the normal labour market, but the payment is high enough, on the one hand, to enable those employed to support themselves at least partially by their own efforts and low enough, on the other hand, to allow the public authorities to finance more employment opportunities than would be possible if it paid the wages offered on the market.

The conception of a second, supplementary labour market is based on three considerations.[152] Firstly, in spite of high levels of unemployment in all countries, there is a large unmet need for socially necessary and meaningful work which is not, however, 'interesting' from a commercial point of view. Secondly, it makes more sense economically to

[152] See A. Wagner/C. Weinkopf, 'Zweiter Arbeitsmarkt', *Die Neue Gesellschaft/Frankfurter Hefte* 41 (1994), pp. 606–11, at p. 607. For a detailed treatment see A. Wagner, 'Zweiter Arbeitsmarkt mit neuem Anspruch?', in H. Seifert (ed.), *Reform der Arbeitsmarktpolitik – Herausforderung für Politik und Wirtschaft* (Cologne: Bund-Verlag, 1995), pp. 206–40.

finance employment rather than unemployment when the provision of employment costs only slightly more than the 'compensation' for unemployment; the additional costs are counterbalanced by considerable additional benefits: the creation of value through the work performed, the maintenance and support of 'human capital' and the avoidance of poverty and social marginalization. Thirdly, the second labour market is a meaningful way of fighting the danger of a concentration of unemployment on certain (socially weak) groups and (structurally weak) regions and thus of counteracting definitive exclusion from the labour market through long-term unemployment. Local and national economic and social considerations are taken equally into account in the second labour market, although priority is clearly given to the aims of compensating for the numerous negative consequences of long-term unemployment and of improving the chances of the unemployed to be reintegrated into the first labour market.

From the point of view of our systematics we are dealing quite simply with a *conditional* right to work, which is linked, on the one hand, to the precondition of enduring personal lack of success on the normal labour market and, on the other hand, to the *obligation* to fulfil certain socially useful tasks, which are, however, both acceptable and beneficial to those affected. Furthermore, like other civic rights entitling individuals to receive compensatory welfare benefits, this conditional right to employment must be classified as a special social right for a clearly defined group of recipients, namely for those who are effectively excluded from the labour market, although they are in principle able to work, at least to a certain degree. Such social rights can be regarded as general civic rights only in the sense that everyone who suffers the corresponding fate has a legal claim to participate in the envisaged compensatory programme. From a moral point of view special social rights of this kind can be readily justified by the duty of the community to practise solidarity with those fellow citizens who, on account of handicaps, strokes of fate or sheer bad luck, are unable to take advantage of the emancipatory opportunities that general economic citizenship rights open up and consequently need social support, so that they can lead their lives under conditions fit for human beings. In comparison with general civic rights in the narrow sense, such 'targeted' social rights for the disadvantaged enjoy only subsidiary status but they are nonetheless indispensable in a civilized and solidary society.[153]

There is, however, a danger that under unfavourable general conditions a second labour market will become a second-*class* labour

[153] On this point and for a refutation of the usual objections to social rights see Tugendhat, *Vorlesungen*, pp. 361ff., 382ff.

market, which strengthens the stigmatization of those affected instead of eliminating it as desired. To prevent this happening it is necessary to offer the unemployed with corresponding qualifications reasonably well-qualified, socially recognized tasks which provide the opportunity for further qualification. It is also important that the wages paid enable those employed to lead a socially integrated life, as the second labour market would otherwise merely degenerate into a kind of 'administration of poverty'.[154] At all events this approach does not provide by itself an adequate conception in regard to the general economic citizen rights under consideration. It lacks the visionary orientational power for civil society of the other three approaches and can fulfil only a subsidiary supplementary function.

***

Which of the conceptions presented here or which combination of them should be preferred can remain an open question at this point. Ultimately a political decision will have to be taken which cannot be anticipated in all its aspects and with unequivocal reasons by economic ethics and political philosophy. From an ethical point of view the decisive test of basic economic citizen rights will always be the fulfilment of the three general criteria for basic rights: their universality, their priority over further rights and their mutual complementarity. This last criterion states that genuine basic rights cannot in principle conflict with one another, as they define categorical, indispensable possibility conditions for a life worthy of a human being. Accordingly, conflicts between socio-economic legal claims should be taken as an indication that we are dealing partly with non-universalizable claims which take second place to the more precisely delimitable universal and basic rights of economic citizens. The clarification of these general economic citizenship rights leads us to the normative core of every systematically justifiable, genuinely liberal economic and social order, in which a legitimate market economy must be embedded.

Let us try to take stock of the multifaceted questions of the justice and legitimacy of the market economy. There is much to be said in favour of seeing a socio-economically well-grounded continuation of the liberal conception of a well-ordered society of equally free citizens (Rawls, Dahrendorf) as a workable and path-breaking approach. The core of this approach is the emancipatory central idea of the greatest possible degree of real freedom and life opportunities for all (Van Parijs). The question of the lexical priority of this claim over the free market is of

[154] See Wagner/Weinkopf, 'Zweiter Arbeitsmarkt', p. 611.

fundamental significance. A decisive contribution in this direction can be made through the institutionalization of basic economic citizenship rights in one or the other form. A strong emancipatory conception of socio-economic rights takes as its starting point the criterion of the best possible empowerment (entitlement and capability) of the citizens (Sen) to realize their self-chosen life plans and thus at the same time to reduce fundamentally the need for redistributional welfare systems which compensate only after the fact for the symptoms of structural helplessness.

In view of the existing inequality of life conditions and life opportunities not only within society but also between the different parts of the world, the institutionalization of basic socio-economic citizenship rights in all countries of the world should represent a more sustainable and in the long term more permanent solution of global questions than the approaches of international compensatory redistribution of resources.[155] Under the conditions of global economic competition for the location of industry the realization of real freedom for all (Van Parijs) is in any case hardly limitable to the level of the single state. More than ever before it is Kant's vision of a cosmopolitan political constitution which stands at the end of the road.[156] It is, therefore, in accordance with the claim of genuine basic rights to universal application that in an age of global markets universal economic citizenship rights must also be understood ultimately as a constitutive element of a future civilized global economic order. Consequently, in the final analysis, we are called upon 'to realize that citizenship is either a universal project or a miserable cloak for privilege'.[157]

In conclusion, let us not forget that the concrete form of the basic rights of economic citizenship is and remains at all levels a never-ending matter of the public use of reason in the open communicative community of political, economic and global citizens who are ready to share the responsibility for the state of public order. Ethical-political questions of the legitimacy of social order and, in its frame, of economic activity must be answered in the form of democratic deliberation and decision-making

[155] For similar considerations oriented on basic rights see W. Kersting, 'Globale Rechtsordnung oder weltweite Verteilungsgerechtigkeit?', *Jahrbuch der deutschen Gesellschaft zur Erforschung des politischen Denkens* (Stuttgart: Metzler, 1996), pp. 197–246, especially p. 241ff. The global issue will be treated in more detail in Section 9.3.

[156] See I. Kant, 'Idea for a Universal History with a Cosmopolitan Purpose', in Kant, *Political Writings*, pp. 41–53.

[157] Dahrendorf, 'The Changing Quality of Citizenship', p. 16.

within the ideal horizon of the 'discourse model of legitimacy'.[158] How, in the light of this regulative idea, should rational political processes be conceived and which virtues of economic citizenship are preconditions for their realization? These are questions we will return to in the following chapter.

[158] Benhabib, *Situating the Self*, p. 82.

Part IV

A topology of economic ethics: the 'sites' of morality in economic life

In Chapter 3 we distinguished between three systematic tasks of integrative economic ethics: the critique of economism (a critique of 'pure' economic reason and its normative implications), the development of guiding ideas of rational economic activity from the lifeworld perspective (conception of socio-economic rationality) and, finally, the determination of the 'sites' of the systematic mediation between moral claims and the functional conditions of the economic system. Parts II and III of this book were devoted to the first two tasks; in this part we turn to the remaining issue of the 'sites' or the topology of economic ethics.[1]

On the whole, differences of opinion in economic ethics rest less upon different conceptions of morally correct action than on diverging ideas as to the correct 'site' of morality in or with reference to the market economy. Accordingly, the determination of the locations of morality is usually rooted in profound and comprehensive fundamental convictions deriving from economic and social philosophy involving both a clearly defined concept of man and a clearly defined idea of society. The fundamental topological question of economic ethics is ultimately concerned with the relationship between individual ethics and institutional ethics. The former deals with the responsibility for actions as far as it can be directly attributed or *ascribed* to the individual economic agents, the latter with the institutional points at which ethical 'landmarks' – legal norms and (dis-) incentives – can be *inscribed* into the economic and social order and thus indirectly mediated to the economic agents. It makes no sense in this context to set off individual ethics and regulatory ethics of a market economy against each other. The starting point must, rather, be a reciprocal relationship between the central conceptions concerning the moral demands that can fittingly be made on the actions of individuals (virtue or action ethics) and ideas on the correct design of the legal framework (regulatory ethics). On the one hand, economic agents who are subject to the existential requirements of self-assertion in a competitive

[1] The Greek concept *topos* means literally a 'place' or site. Topology is thus nothing other than the theory of the systematic ordering of *topoi* (plural form).

market economy can only be *reasonably expected* to accept the demands of virtue ethics within the framework of an institutional order that relieves them of the responsibility in difficult cases of moral dilemma which cannot be solved individually, as we have seen earlier.[2] And, on the other hand, in a modern democratic society of free and equal citizens, institutional arrangements can only be *justified* by the citizens themselves or at least to them.

If the basic assumptions in regard to the call for 'civic virtue' tend to be rather sceptical or pessimistic, the main burden for the mediation of morality and market logic will then fall on the economic and social order. But if scepticism is directed more towards the 'internal morality' inscribable in the institutions, a correspondingly higher demand for virtue must be made on the individual actors. In view of the problem of the inherent necessities of competition, however, economic ethics cannot be conceived purely as a matter of individual ethics. And, inversely, in view of the preconditions for the legitimacy of a free democratic society, it is no less possible to substitute institutional regulations entirely for the demand for individual ethical responsibility on the part of the economic agents.[3]

Between the dialectical poles of individual and regulatory ethics in economic action there is obviously no place for extreme positions in either direction. On the one hand requirements of personal virtue are indispensable in a free democratic society in as far as such a social order depends upon the cooperation of mature and responsible citizens. And, on the other hand, in a more or less pluralistic and anonymized advanced society in which individualistic attitudes to life are widespread, strong 'public spirit' and a pronounced willingness to practise solidarity of the kind traditionally found, and in part still found today, in *face to face* communities can hardly be expected.

It is then of decisive importance that the anonymous structural incentives of the economic and social order meet the limited willingness of the citizens to practise solidarity halfway by supporting them normatively and by making the personal consequences of solidarity tolerable. Without an ethically underpinned economic and social order in this sense the good will of responsible economic citizens would have 'no place' *(u-topia)* to act – but without such economic citizens both the shaping and the operation of all the institutional sites of morality for economic activities would have 'no subjects'.

[2] See Section 4.3 (3b).

[3] Precisely this indissoluble ethical relationship in regard to the question of legitimation is disregarded in the attempts of functionalistic 'economic ethics'. It tries to replace moral demands on individuals totally by control via incentives and restrictions. The resulting reduction of *regulatory ethics* to mere *institutional economics* is all the more problematic as the lack of ethical categories leads it to abandon the *justification* of the institutional regulations to the strategic clash of interests between actors from whom morality is not required (economic theory of democracy); see Sections 3.2 and 5.3 (3).

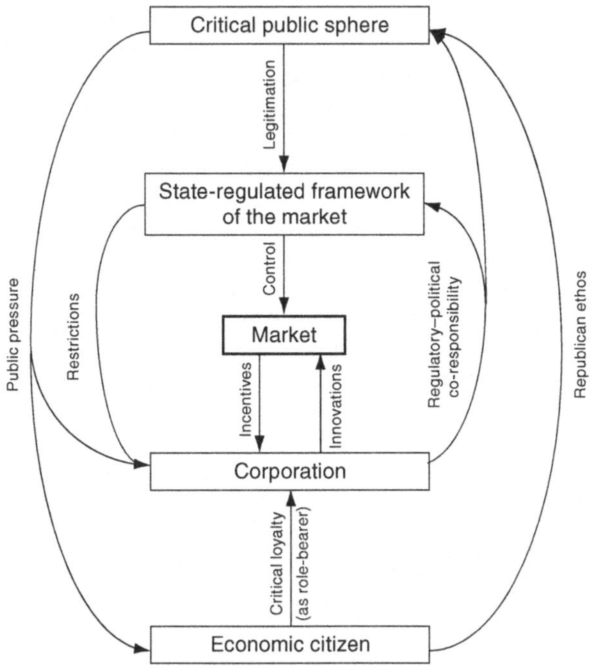

Figure IV.1. 'Sites' of the morality of economic activity

It is therefore necessary to clarify the indispensable virtue-ethical as well as the regulatory-ethical preconditions for responsible economic activities, paying attention to the way they dovetail. In principle five systematic 'sites' for the mediation of morality and market logic are conceivable (Figure IV.1): the individual economic citizen in his/her private and occupational activities (e.g. as an employee, consumer or investor) and in his/her public activities (as a citizen and participant in public discussion); the institutional framework of the market as determined by the state; the corporations which endeavour to operate successfully within this framework; and finally, the impersonal market mechanism itself to which an inherent morality is then attributed in the sense of a 'systems ethics'. We have already looked behind that presumed morality of the market in Chapter 5, with negative results. (Consequently this site is symbolically bracketed in Figure IV.1). We will therefore deal in what follows, in the context of an overall conception that takes into account the reciprocal relations, with the topoi of *economic citizen's ethics* including both the private and the public dimension (Chapter 8), *regulatory ethics* (Chapter 9) and *corporate ethics* (Chapter 10).

8 Economic citizen's ethics

The old Hobbesian dream of conceiving and founding a free society entirely on a 'system of ordered egoism',[1] without requiring any moral virtues of citizens, is still haunting us today in certain ideologies which call themselves liberal. As we have shown in Chapter 5, and particularly in Section 5.3, these ideologies amount to pure economic liberalism and political economism, as they understand politics merely as the continuation of business with other means. Behind this view lies a conception of citizens who are defined purely by their private legal claims and interests and are mutually indifferent to one another; they enter into social interaction only when it seems individually useful to them. John Rawls also believed at first that he could approve of this mutual indifference for the persons in his imaginary 'original position' behind the 'veil of ignorance' and that they need not be expected to follow any rationality other than pure economic rationality, i.e. the ability to pursue their own interests intelligently.[2]

As we have seen in Section 7.2, however, the later Rawls, in his revised perspective on political liberalism as a condition for a well-ordered society, expressly assumed the existence of moral persons who have a sense of justice and are capable of conducting their lives in accordance with a conception of the good. It is perfectly possible to interpret this 'surprising disappearance of economic rationality'[3] from Rawls's conception of a well-ordered society as an admission of the failure of all forms of political economism and as an expression of the insight that such a society cannot be created without *civic virtues*.[4] Rawls now makes political liberalism dependent upon an indispensable 'ideal of a good citizen of a democratic

1 Habermas, *Facts and Norms*, p. 90.

2 See Rawls, *Theory of Justice* (rev. edn), pp. 12ff, 123ff.

3 W. Kersting, 'Spannungsvolle Rationalitätsbegriffe in der politischen Philosophie von John Rawls', in K.-O. Apel/M. Kettner (eds.), *Die eine Vernunft und die vielen Rationalitäten* (Frankfurt: Suhrkamp, 1996), pp. 227–65, at p. 228.

4 Rawls at least saw the need to clarify the methodological function of the 'original position'. In *Political Liberalism*, p. 24f., he expressly emphasizes that the 'original position' in which the

state'.[5] The 'political virtues' he postulates, however, remain pale and vague. It is above all else remarkable that after three decades of work on a political philosophy starting from the premises of the homo oeconomicus (methodological individualism) Rawls, at the end of his journey, returns approvingly to a tradition of political philosophy and ethics which was originally completely alien to his approach, namely to 'classical republicanism'.[6] To put it in Kant's terms: Rawls's journey has led him from the economic-liberal concept of the citizen as the *bourgeois* who strictly pursues his own economic interests (possessive individualism in the abstract theoretical disguise of methodological individualism) to the republican-liberal concept of the citizen as the *citoyen*, who is characterized by his public spirit.[7]

From the perspective of the history of theory it is not the political-philosophical tradition of liberalism but of *republicanism* which has always debated the question at issue here: the question of the importance of civic virtues for the 'establishment of solidarity beyond particular interests',[8] i.e. for their integration into a well-ordered *res publica* which is seen as a public concern of free, equal and responsible citizens. In the last two hundred years, however, the republican intellectual tradition has been largely displaced by liberalism in all its nuances. Only recently has an unexpectedly broad-based 'rediscovery of the republican tradition' (Sewing) got under way. This development is not only an internal theoretical consequence of the ongoing debate on the (revised) Rawlsian conception but also, to a no lesser degree, a consequence of the growing practical experience of the most varied symptomatic problems resulting from the disappearance or lack of civic virtues in 'real existing' liberalism. Two recent lines of experience in particular have probably served to trigger this process.

- On the one hand, the problems which have arisen in connection with the transformation of the post-communist societies of Eastern Europe

fictitious social contract is presented cannot be understood as a form of justification but only as a hypothetical construct for analytical purposes, 'a device of representation'. He thus admits that the contract theoretical approach contributes nothing to a normative justification. This can result only from the reflective explication of the rational ethical content of the moral attitude of individuals and of the social structure which is represented by the 'original position'.

5 Rawls, 'The Priority of Right', p. 263; reprinted in *Political Liberalism*, p. 194f.

6 See Rawls, 'The Priority of Right', p. 272, reprinted in *Political Liberalism*, p. 205f. We will return to Rawls's qualification of his approval later.

7 The distinction between *bourgeois* and *citoyen* is found already in Kant. See 'On the Common Saying: That may be correct in theory but it is of no use in practice', in, *Practical Philosophy*, pp. 273–309, at p. 295.

8 W. Sewing, 'John G.A. Pocock und die Wiederentdeckung der republikanischen Tradition', preface in J. G. A. Pocock, *Die andere Bürgergesellschaft. Zur Dialektik von Tugend und Korruption* (Frankfurt/New York: Campus, 1993), pp. 7–32, at p. 8.

have revealed in time-lapse the fundamental significance and indispensability of a stable political culture and a *civil society* as preconditions for a sound socio-economic development. Their presence or absence explains to a large extent the widely varying degrees of success in the transformation of various countries. In Western societies as well the increasingly problematic consequences of an uncontrolled individualism, the corresponding diminution of the reservoirs of public spirit and the various manifestations of moral and social collapse are making themselves felt (corruption, new social issues, the rise of social Darwinist world views and political fundamentalism in all ideological directions which it was believed Western civilization had overcome).

- On the other hand, it is precisely the experience of these developments which, above all in the USA, has brought about or at least strengthened a countermovement against radical individualism: *communitarianism.*[9] The central idea shared by the different directions of the thoroughly heterogeneous communitarian movement is that the evolved social communities must regain their constitutive role both for the social and personal identity of individuals and for the organization of societal life. Communitarianism is, therefore, directed against the atomization of society (extreme individualism as falsely understood liberalism) and at the same time against tendencies of the state to take the responsibility of citizens for their own lives out of their hands. It stands outside the old systemic debate about 'more market versus more state' and refers back in essence to the third, occasionally forgotten, fundamental source of social integration: public spirit and solidarity. What is controversial, beyond the position of a radical economic liberalism (Hobbesianism), is less the fundamental need for these qualities than the complex question of an adequate relationship between the market, the state and the solidary communities of the lifeworld in modern society.

The political-philosophical debate between communitarianism and liberalism cannot be separated from the newly awakened interest in republicanism.[10] Some normative core ideas in the broad stream of

[9] The political movement is organized in *The Communitarian Network*, founded by Amitai Etzioni who has written the programmatic book *The Spirit of Community: Rights, Responsibilities and the Communitarian Agenda* (New York: Crown, 1993).

[10] Probably the most important original contributions to the academic debate on the relations between political liberalism, communitarianism and republicanism have been written by M. J. Sandel, *Liberalism and the Limits of Justice* (Cambridge/New York: Cambridge University Press, 1982); Sandel, 'The Procedural Republic and the Unencumbered Self', *Political Theory* 1 (1984), pp. 81–96; and Ch. Taylor, 'Cross-Purposes: The Liberal-Communitarian Debate', in N. L. Rosenblum (ed.), *Liberalism and the Moral Life* (Cambridge MA: Harvard University Press, 1989), pp. 159–82. In a

communitarian thought can be understood in part as a revitalization of old republican positions. At the same time, political liberalism is faced with the challenge of clarifying its own relationship to republicanism, which now suddenly appears in a more differentiated light. In this process significant republican traditions have been rediscovered *within* liberal thinking, particular in the domain of American constitutional history, which has for a long time been subjected to a one-sided liberal interpretation.

In what follows we will adopt both an historical and a systematic approach to the paradigmatic differences between republicanism and the rivalling political-philosophical thought patterns competing with it, as a background to a clear republican understanding of the indispensable civic virtues (Section 8.1). It will then be possible to explicate the unavoidable minimal demands on the virtue of the modern economic citizen at two 'sites' of morality on different levels: the level of the public use of reason in the context of a conception of political processes in a free democratic society which is republican in its orientation but pragmatically balanced (Section 8.2), and the level of the occupational and private life of the economic citizen (Section 8.3).

8.1 The basic problem of civic ethics: liberal society and republican virtue

A free and democratic society evidently cannot exist without 'civic sense' as a civilized sense of community. Civic ethos and a free democratic order (civic rights) are preconditions for one another. However, the corresponding civic virtues do not arise automatically in a free society, nor are they simply given by the nature of man – they must rather be recreated again and again in a process of continuous politico-cultural endeavour. The various forms of political and economic liberalism have, however, paid scant attention to this task as a result of their rootedness in the natural law tradition. It is not by chance that the model of thought of a – variously interpreted – hypothetical *natural state* ('original situation') has played such an outstanding part in political philosophy from Thomas Hobbes (1651) and John Locke (1690) to James Buchanan and John Rawls. The basic dividing line between the liberal and republican schools of thought can indeed be seen in the presence of a fundamental and

more recent work Sandel presents a detailed conception of 'republican citizenship'; see Sandel, *Democracy's Discontent: America in Search of a Political Philosophy* (Cambridge MA: Harvard University Press, 1996). For a review of the debate see the collection of contributions in S. Avineri/A. De-Shalit (eds.), *Communitarianism and Individualism* (Oxford/New York: Oxford University Press, 1992).

constant attachment to natural law thinking in the former and its total absence in the latter. It is characteristic of republican positions that their normative conceptions must always be understood as expressing an ideal *cultural state*, as ethical-practical postulates of a comprehensive *civic humanism*.

The term 'civic humanism' was first used by the historian Hans Baron[11] to characterize the political ideal of the Florentine republic in the fifteenth century, whose outstanding political philosopher was no less a figure than Niccolò Machiavelli (1469–1527). The Florentine renaissance itself looked back to the ancient Greek ideal of the *polis* as a community of free, equal, economically independent and politically active citizens, as depicted by Aristotle in his extolment of the democratic polis as the true site of moral and ethical development.[12] Aristotle sees man as a *zoon politicon*, as a political being with an innate disposition to pursue the *telos* of argumentative participation in the polis, for whom civic life is the highest good and, consequently, the embodiment of the good life.[13] From this perspective, therefore, the development of political civic virtues is virtually identical with the pursuit of a cultivated and fulfilled human life.[14]

Of course this teleological image of man is just as incompatible with modern philosophical anthropology as with the political-liberal principle of the neutrality of a just order towards the 'fact of pluralism' of legitimate life projects, particularly in the form advocated by Rawls.[15] Classical republicanism is also scarcely compatible with the reality of contemporary life, since people find only a limited part of their identity and life fulfilment in political and civic commitment, if they do not renounce it completely. In view of this fact, classical republicanism tends to make exaggerated

[11] See H. Baron, *The Crisis of the Early Italian Renaissance: Civic Humanism and Republican Liberty in an Age of Classicism and Tyranny* (Princeton: Princeton University Press, 1955). On this point and on the entire history of republicanism see the overview in Sewing, 'Pocock'.

[12] See Aristotle, *The Politics of Aristotle*, ed. by P. L. P. Simpson (Chapel Hill: University of North Carolina Press, 1997), Book III, p. 1275a-ff.

[13] For this reason republicans prefer federalist, grass-roots democratic political orders structured from the bottom to the top with as much autonomy as possible for the local community. In this regard the republican tradition has exercised its most sustained political influence on the USA, Switzerland and Holland, whereas in the larger European territorial states communal autonomy in particular has been sacrificed with the rise of centralized instances of national power.

[14] In the 20th century this Aristotelian tradition of the republican ethos has been brilliantly revived by Hannah Arendt, *The Human Condition*.

[15] This is the objection which Rawls, 'The Priority of Right', p. 272 (reprinted in *Political Liberalism*, p. 206), explicitly raised against classical civic humanism and the reason for his qualified approval of republicanism. It must indeed not be forgotten that in its early Aristotelian form the freedom of the few (male) propertied citizens involved the exclusion and oppression of women and slaves.

demands on the civic virtue of the citizen in a historically romanticising fashion. Together with the debate on the political system (market economy versus state-controlled economy) which has long dominated political discussion this may have been one of the major reasons for the waning of republican thought in the political philosophy of the 20th century.

Path-breaking pioneering work for the rediscovery of republicanism has been done by the historian John G. Pocock,[16] who has demonstrated the existence of an unbroken transatlantic tradition from Florentine republicanism via James Harrington,[17] the contemporary adversary of Thomas Hobbes in England, to an Anglo-Saxon republicanism of a liberal kind, whose influence on early American constitutional politics has long been underestimated. Following this line, American philosophers of law, above all Frank I. Michelman[18] and Cass R. Sunstein,[19] have presented illuminating studies in political and intellectual history which do away with the supposed fronts between liberalism and republicanism and reveal the modern synthesis of a liberal republicanism[20] in which enlightened (liberal!) philosophers such as Montesquieu (1689–1759), Rousseau (1712–1778) and Kant (1724–1804) are convincingly included.[21]

Against the background of the history of ideas touched upon here it is possible to develop the paradigm of a *republican liberalism* and to distinguish it systematically from economic liberalism (neoliberalism) as well as Rawlsian political liberalism on the one hand and communitarianism (which in its republican variant largely continues the tradition of classical civic humanism) on the other.[22] In the typology proposed here the term

16 J. G. A. Pocock, *The Machiavellian Moment: Florentine Political Thought and the Atlantic Republican Tradition* (Princeton NJ: Princeton University Press, 2003; 1st edn 1975); Pocock, 'Virtues, Rights and Manners. A Model for Historians of Political Thought', *Political Theory* 9 (1981), pp. 353–68.

17 Harrington's major work, the *Commonwealth of Oceana*, was first published in 1656.

18 See F. I. Michelman, 'The Supreme Court 1985 Term. Foreword: Traces of Self-Government', *Harvard Law Review* 100 (1986), pp. 4–77; Michelman, 'Law's Republic', *The Yale Law Journal* 97 (1988), pp. 1493–537.

19 See C. R. Sunstein, 'Beyond the Republican Revival', *The Yale Law Journal* 97 (1988), pp. 1539–90.

20 Sunstein, 'Republican Revival', p. 1541.

21 On the republican thinking of Montesquieu, Rousseau and Kant see the survey in H. Münkler, 'Politische Tugend. Bedarf die Demokratie einer sozio-moralischen Grundlegung?', in Münkler (ed.), *Die Chancen der Freiheit. Grundprobleme der Demokratie* (Munich/Zurich: Piper, 1992), pp. 25–46.

22 The term 'republican liberalism' was coined by the present author and Richard Dagger in 1997 independently and without knowledge of each other. See the first German edition of the present book (1997, p. 293ff.) and R. Dagger, *Civic Virtues: Rights, Citizenship, and Republican Liberalism* (New York/Oxford: Oxford University Press, 1997). Dagger goes deeply into the individual-ethical aspects of republican-liberal citizenship but does not consider the socio-economic side of the conception and the political consequences for a well-ordered society in a systematic way.

	Economic liberalism (neoliberalism)	*Republican liberalism (modern republicanism)*	*Communitarianism (classical 'civic humanism')*
Concept of the person	The unencumbered self (pre-social identity)	The autonomous self (self-committed identity)	The socially encumbered self (social identity)
Concept of freedom	Negative freedom (for the pursuit of private ends)	Negative and positive freedom (for participatory self-determination of legitimate ends)	Contextually determined positive freedom (in the context of communitarian ends)
Concept of the citizen	Property-owning citizen (bourgeois): 'I possess, therefore I am'	Political citizen (citoyen): 'I participate in the res publica, therefore I am'	Community citizen: 'I feel the spirit of the community, therefore I am'
Significance of civic virtue	None	Regulative	Constitutive
Dominant mode of socialization	Contractual benefit exchange (based on interests)	Civic rights and civic duties (based on justice)	Communitarian conception of the good (based on the community spirit)
Main political ordering principle	Pareto efficiency (balance of interests under status-quo conditions)	Justice (greatest possible equal freedom for all)	Value community (network of solidary communities)
Ideal of society	Total market society	Pluralistic civil society	Value-integrated civil society
Concept of the political process	Strategic competition between parties for power in the state (political market for votes)	Public use of reason by citizens enjoying equal rights (deliberative politics)	Federalist self-organization of the citizens from the bottom to the top (subsidiary politics)
Conception of ethics	Ethical scepticism (non-cognitivism)	Ethical universalism (cognitivism)	Conventionalism (cultural contextualism)

Figure 8.1. Ideal-typical basic models of civic virtue and civil society

'republican liberalism' is preferred to that of 'liberal republicanism' in order to indicate that this paradigm can be readily linked with the 'political liberalism' advocated by Rawls; the latter appears in the proposed framework as a paradigmatic mixed form primarily shaped by republican liberalism but blurring the lines of demarcation with economic liberalism at some points, as we have already seen in part and will now bring out more clearly.

The basic paradigmatic differences between the three politico-philosophical models counterposed schematically in Figure 8.1 relate to the general *concept of the person*. As Sandel first objected against (the early) Rawls, liberal positions are based upon the idea of an 'unencumbered self' whose personal identity is conceived, so to speak, as a pre-social identity which is independent of any social context.[23] If the autonomous individual is taken as 'given', liberalism is simply confused with individualism. It is noteworthy that none other than Frank H. Knight, the founder of the 'Chicago School of Economics', sharply highlighted what he called:

the most important single defect, amounting to a fallacy, in liberal individualism as a social philosophy. The most general and essential fact that makes such a position untenable as an exclusive principle of organization is that *liberalism takes the individual as given*, and views the social problem as one of right relations between given individuals. This is its fundamental error. (...) The individual cannot be a datum for the purposes of social policy, because he is largely formed in and by the social process, and the nature of the individual must be affected by any social action. Consequently, social policy must be judged by the kind of individuals that are produced by or under it, and not merely by the type of relations which subsist among individuals taken as they stand.[24]

This critique (by Knight as well as by Sandel) is concerned, above all, with the economic liberalism based on methodological individualism[25] and less with (the later) Rawls's political liberalism, which he revised not least because of Sandel's criticism. In this point Rawls's final approach can be included without hesitation under the republican position, regardless of his problematic methodical assumptions of rationality in regard to persons in the fictitious original position which we have commented on above.[26] Whereas in economic liberalism the needy nature of man instrumentalizes his reason and so reduces it to a rationality serving personal interests, political liberalism understands the person as both a self-interested and a moral being whose ethical reason reflects upon and controls personal interests. In accordance with the social structure of all morality, this assumes a constitutive role of the moral community for the self-understanding of the individual and thus a balance between personal and social identity.[27]

In this regard the decisive dividing line is not between republicanism and communitarianism on the one hand and liberalism on the other, but between economic and political liberalism. In economic liberalism the social context cannot be assigned a constitutive role in the formation of personal identity because it is conceived as subordinate to the unencumbered self and as a matter of purposive-rational choice. The

[23] See M. Sandel, *Liberalism and the Limits of Justice*, p. 54ff.; Sandel, 'The Procedural Republic and the Unencumbered Self'.

[24] F. H. Knight, *Freedom and Reform: Essays in Economics and Social Philosophy* (New York/London: Harper & Brothers, 1947), p. 69 (italics in the original).

[25] See Section 5.3. [26] See Section 7.2, especially n. 47.

[27] On this point see Sections 1.1 and 1.2.

unencumbered self enters into contractual social relations only when an exchange or social contract brings private advantage (instrumental understanding of society and politics). In the republican-liberal conception the situation is completely the reverse. Here the individual is conceived as a fundamentally social being, who is capable of (self-) critical reflection and hence of autonomous self-determination. The social context is accepted as antecedent to personal identity empirically, but not normatively; it has constitutive significance both for the development of personal identity (self-understanding) and for the ability to understand the social structure of moral obligations. The republican conception of the person and of the social context is also plausible in terms of moral psychology, in as far as the development of moral consciousness and the sense of personal identity passes through a childhood phase of identification with a moral community which is at first concrete and is subsequently conceived in an increasingly abstract fashion.[28]

Classical republicanism and civic humanism fail, however, to pass beyond a conventional moral consciousness (in Kohlberg's sense). They misunderstand personal identity as a self that is necessarily socially encumbered and thus overlook the possibility of a post-conventional moral consciousness and hence of an autonomous self in the Kantian sense of a morally self-committed identity (autonomous duty ethics).[29] The developmental psychological fact that personal identity is socially constituted must not be reinterpreted as the normative postulate of a primacy of the community over the person. This would deny the post-conventional possibility that an autonomous person can achieve a critical distance to the traditional values and norms of the community or society into which he/she has been socialized. Precisely this fundamental confusion between the constitutive significance of communities for the growth of personal identity and normative demands for conformity towards the traditional conceptions of what is good and morally right in a community regularly occurs in the thinking of value-conservative conventionalist communitarians, but not among modern republicans.[30]

[28] See the account of Kohlberg's developmental stages of moral consciousness in Section 1.5.

[29] On the conception of a socially encumbered self see Sandel, *Liberalism and the Limits of Justice*, p. 172.

[30] On this critique of communitarianism see also Benhabib, *Situating the Self*, p. 73f. Rainer Forst has proposed the term *substantialist communitarianism* for the philosophically anti-liberal and conventionalist tendencies, and the term *republican communitarianism* for the tendencies which are compatible with post-conventional and liberal claims. In the typology presented here the latter is described as modern republicanism and classified under republican liberalism (third column of Figure 8.1), whereas substantialist

The socio-philosophical consequences of the three different conceptions of the self are extraordinarily wide-reaching. First of all, as far as the *concept of freedom* is concerned, the economistic-liberal conception of the unencumbered self corresponds to the model of negative freedom. This sees freedom solely as the inviolability of naturally given private property rights and interests against intrusions by other natural and legal persons, particularly the state. It has consequently always regarded any form of ethical or social obligation and potentially even democracy itself as a restriction of freedom.[31] As a result, the citizen is simply defined as a property-owning citizen (bourgeois) whose private autonomy is legally protected. This self-understanding ('I possess therefore I am') leaves little room for a recognition of civic virtues beyond the capitalist ethos of a disciplined conduct of life (inner-worldly asceticism), of industrious capital accumulation and of contractual fidelity in business matters. In view of the assumed ideal of a total market society there is even no need for such recognition; the socially unencumbered homines oeconomici strictly pursue their own interests and remain mutually unconcerned.[32]

In contrast, republican liberalism is characterized by an understanding of freedom not only as negative (i.e. freedom from interference of others) but much more as positive freedom (i.e. to self-determination), or as a concept beyond this distinction.[33] Republican freedom is conceived as the politically constituted greatest possible equal freedom of all citizens. It includes, and is indeed a precondition for, their entitlement to active participation as citizens of the state *(citoyens)* in the democratic self-determination of a well-ordered life with others in a free society. Republican liberty consists in non-domination between the citizens

communitarianism is simply classified under communitarianism (right-hand column of Figure 8.1). See R. Forst, *Kontexte der Gerechtigkeit, Politische Philosophie jenseits von Liberalismus und Kommunitarismus* (Frankfurt: Suhrkamp, 1994), p. 161ff.

31 As Benjamin A. Barber, one of the leading American representatives of republicanism in democratic theory puts it, liberal democracy is thus a 'thin democracy' which always was and still is sceptical towards a broader and more committed republican participation in civic life. See B. Barber, *Strong Democracy: Participatory Politics for a New Age* (Berkeley: University of California Press, 1984), pp. 4, 29ff.

32 See the account in Section 4.1 (capitalist ethos) and Section 5.3 (possessive individualism and the ideal of the market society).

33 The distinction between negative and positive freedom, which goes back to I. Berlin, *Two Concepts of Liberty* (Oxford: Clarendon, 1958), reprinted in I. Berlin, *Liberty* (Oxford: Oxford University Press, 2002), pp. 166–217, is the starting point for the work of Charles Taylor, a further pioneer of the republican-communitarian critique of liberalism. See Taylor, 'What's Wrong with Negative Liberty?' in A. Ryan (ed.), *The Idea of Freedom: Essays in Honour of Isaiah Berlin* (Oxford: Oxford University Press, 1979), pp. 175–93. Reprinted in his *Philosophy and the Human Sciences* (Cambridge: Cambridge University Press, 1985), pp. 211–29; Taylor, 'Cross Purposes: The Liberal-Communitarian Debate', in N. L. Rosenblum (ed.), *Liberalism and the Moral Life* (Cambridge MA: Harvard University Press, 1989), pp. 159–82.

based on their shared emancipation from all kinds of arbitrary interference (by means of constitutionally and democratically controlled regulations) rather than total non-interference with others.[34]

The corresponding *self-understanding of the citizen* ('I participate in republican self-determination, therefore I am') includes the indispensable republican virtue of civic and political integrity. This means, quite literally, the voluntary renouncement, based on moral insight, of the separation of private action from the holistic self-understanding as a republican citizen. It also involves the readiness to shoulder a suitable share of the responsibility for the good and just order of the *res publica*, including the free development of the personality of the fellow citizens. The moral core of the *republican ethos* consists therefore – in precise contrast to the political economism of neoliberalism – in subordinating private interests on principle to the legitimacy condition of the res publica and submitting them to comment and criticism within the framework of the public use of reason by free citizens.[35]

This core postulate of modern republicanism certainly makes higher virtue-ethical demands on the citizen than economic liberalism, but these can be understood as the minimal individual-ethical demands without which a well-ordered society cannot be achieved. At all events republican-liberal ethics makes more modest demands on the virtue of the citizen than the substantialist forms of communitarianism and classical civic humanism in three respects:

- Firstly, republican-liberal ethics corresponds to a *formal* (rational) ethics that leaves the settlement of all material questions to the public use of reason (Kant, Rawls) by mature and responsible citizens of the res publica.[36] This stands in contrast to the communitarian claims on civic virtue, as far as they extend to a more or less uncritical subjection of the individual to the material conception of the good and to the spirit

[34] For the definition of republican liberty as non-domination see Ph. Pettit, *Republicanism: A Theory of Freedom and Government* (Oxford: Clarendon, 1997), p. 21ff. Also J. W. Maynor, *Republicanism in the Modern World* (Cambridge: Polity, 2003), p. 33ff.

[35] For concurring opinions on this core postulate of republicanism, which can be traced back to Montesquieu, see, among others, Pocock, 'Virtues, Rights and Manners', p. 358, Michelman, 'The Supreme Court', p. 18, Sunstein, 'Republican Revival', p. 1540, Münkler, 'Politische Tugend', p. 25. In the context of discourse on economic ethics the credit for first applying this postulate to republicanism, if only in a very brief form, is probably due to the Erlangen philosopher Paul Lorenzen. He defines republicans so to speak in terms of identity psychology as 'citizens for whom the justice of the state has become a part of their own lives'. See P. Lorenzen, 'Philosophische Fundierungsprobleme einer Wirtschafts- und Unternehmensethik', in Steinmann/Löhr (eds.), *Unternehmensethik*, pp. 35–67, especially p. 58ff. (quotation at p. 62).

[36] We will return to this point in Section 8.2.

of the community[37] and so largely disregard the modern citizen's legitimate claim to achieve a critical self-distance from the life community into which he/she is born.

- Secondly, the republican-liberal virtue claims are *restricted*, completely in Rawls' sense, to the call for political virtues. What matters primarily is to be a good citizen in the republican sense and this is not the same as the unrestricted moral demand to be a 'good person' in every respect and at all times.[38] In contrast to this clear limitation, communitarianism lacks a comparable criterion for the restriction of virtue claims, and consequently tends to make unlimited demands on the sense of community. In view of the structural problem of free riders, however, this leads to excessive demands on the citizens of modern society and to an underestimation of the regulatory-ethical challenges that have to be met politically.
- Thirdly, individual civic virtue has only a *regulative* (i.e. orientational) function for the creation of solidarity in society in the conception of republican-liberalism, whereas, in communitarianism, the 'we-feeling' and the public spirit of the citizens are required to play the constitutive (i.e. fundamental) role as the foundation of a functioning solidary community. In contrast, in the republican-liberal conception, this constitutive element is not based directly on civic virtue but on a republican constitution shaped in accordance with the principles of justice, a point already emphasized by Kant.[39] Republican virtue can now be quite simply defined as the citizens' willingness to subordinate their private interests under the republican constitution. This civic spirit is nevertheless an indispensable regulative factor, in whose light every citizen must self-critically examine his private and, especially, his civic actions.

As far as its demands on the virtue of the citizen are concerned, the republican-liberal way thus turns out to be a middle way: civic virtue neither bears the entire burden of solidarity in the community as in the communitarian project, nor is it rejected as entirely superfluous in favour of an (unrealizable) programme of social integration and 'legitimation' of politics based purely on self-interest as in the case of economic liberalism.

At this point we cannot avoid briefly taking a critical look at Kant's famous but problematic account of the relationship between the

[37] This is at the same time the already mentioned title of Etzioni's programmatic work of the communitarian movement.
[38] This republican distinction is already made by Aristotle, *Politics*, Book III, pp. 1276b–7b. On the concept of a 'good person' see the treatment in Section 1.2.
[39] See Kant, 'Toward Perpetual Peace', p. 322ff.

republican constitution and civic virtue. The constitution establishes and guarantees the inviolable civic rights and fair procedures in the development of informed political opinion, so that what matters in principle is, as Kant puts it, 'a good organization of a state (which is certainly within the capacity of human beings)'.[40] The critical regulative factor to which Kant must be referring with the 'capacity of human beings' can only be ethical-political reason, a point which should not be overlooked in the reading of his famous dictum:

> The problem of establishing a state, no matter how hard it may sound, is soluble even for a nation of devils (if only they have *understanding*) and goes like this: Given a multitude of *rational* beings all of whom need universal laws for their preservation but each of whom is inclined covertly to exempt himself from them, so to order this multitude and establish their constitution that, although in their private dispositions they strive against one another, these yet so check one another that in their public conduct the result is the same as if they had no such evil dispositions.[41]

Although it is obviously Kant's intention here to relieve the citizens of individual ethical demands on their virtue by means of 'legalized morality',[42] the indispensable republican ethical demand on the citizens is nonetheless present in the assumption that they must, *first of all*, be 'rational beings' with a moral sense for 'universal laws'. After all, they can only 'need' and 'establish' a constitutional state as moral beings. Only *afterwards*, when the republican constitution already exists, might it be sufficient for the citizens to possess mere understanding in the sense of strategic rationality (intelligent pursuit of their 'private dispositions' in which they 'strive against one another'). Kant's formulation can be read consistently only if it is interpreted to mean that he radically separates the ethical-rational justification from the legal implementation of the constitution. The *subject* who creates the constitution is conceived as an ethical-rational sovereign being clearly distinguished from the mass of normal citizens, who are merely the *objects* of the exercise of legal coercion and thus do not require any particular moral virtue.[43] Kant's transcendental idea of a republican constitutional state, whose coercive power is justly exercised but nonetheless

[40] Kant, 'Toward Perpetual Peace', p. 335. [41] Ibid. (my italics).

[42] W. Maihofer, 'Realität der Politik und Ethos der Republik', in Apel/Kettner (eds.), *Zur Anwendung der Diskursethik*, pp. 84–126, at p. 98.

[43] Kant, 'Toward Perpetual Peace', p. 324, does indeed understand republicanism as the principle of a rationally and ethically justifiable 'way a people is governed' independently of the question who actually possesses 'sovereign power'. Every ethical-rational sovereign is *capable* of ruling in the spirit of the republican idea of political justice; indeed, according to Kant, a non-democratic (autocratic or aristocratic) sovereign must first 'establish' the republic, which can then be governed in a democratic fashion. In contrast, Kant classifies a direct, revolutionary democracy established by force through the 'power of the people' as

lacks legitimation *by* all citizens (instead of merely *before* them), disregards the indissoluble inner relationship between the constitutional state and democracy. As Apel emphasizes, 'it must rather be possible to assume that the citizens of a constitutional state always have 'a sense of justice' (Rawls), for which, of course, additional motivation is necessary'.[44]

The republican-liberal point of view, to which we now return, differs from that of Kant in seeing the decisive motive for the indispensable political civic virtues as being rooted in a positive concept of freedom as civic freedom. This also involves the civic duty to participate actively in the public self-determination of the res publica, whose political institutions are perceived as a 'common bulwark of citizen dignity'.[45] Only if the citizens as the responsible 'sovereign' of a free-democratic constitution inscribe as much ethical content as possible into the rules of social co-existence to be implemented by the state can the political institutions of the republican constitution be assigned the role of providing the foundation for the good and just living together of all citizens. Here, once again, there is agreement with Kant. The persistent conceptional elucidation of this necessary, dialectical interaction between a minimal but indispensable civic virtue (individual ethics) on the one hand and a free and just constitution on the other (regulatory ethics) is the whole point of republican liberalism.

In regard to priorities in the *mode of socialization* republican liberalism clearly states, in accordance with the constitutive role of the constitution, the primacy of the justification and the general guarantee of the greatest possible set of equal civic rights for all. It also definitely foresees certain general civic duties.[46] Civic rights and duties have priority both over all private interests (whose legitimation is at issue here) and over communal conceptions of the good (whose peaceful and fair coexistence must be guaranteed in a pluralistic society). In contrast, the communitarian

'despotism', i.e. as 'the high-handed management of the state by laws the regent has himself given' (p. 324). Behind Kant's separation of a rational constitutional republic from a democratic rule achieved by force we can recognize Rousseau's problematic distinction between the *volonté générale* and the *volonté de tous*. On Rousseau's 'sin' against democratic theory and its discourse-ethical elucidation see Ulrich, *Transformation*, p. 308f.

44 Apel, 'Diskursethik vor der Problematik von Recht und Politik', p. 40.

45 Taylor, 'Cross Purposes: The Liberal-Communitarian Debate', pp. 159–82, at p. 165.

46 Republican civic duties cover the classical areas of military service in the defence of the republic (for men) and tax liability (for citizens with income and property) to finance public spending. Nowadays, in times of high tax burdens and state indebtedness, conceptions of obligatory general civic duties for restricted periods of time for both men and women are being discussed, often with a choice of the field of activity (community service in social, agrarian, ecological development or peace-promoting organizations etc. – or military service as a 'non-civil' civic duty). All of these can be readily assigned to the republican tradition. See also the considerations on civic duties in the context of the civil right to (gainful) employment or a basic income in Section 7.3.

precedence of a communal conception of the good (in the sense of concrete morals) over the principles of justice plays voluntarily or involuntarily into the hands of fundamentalist intolerance towards other life projects and concepts of value; and the economic-libertarian precedence of given private interests (balanced out by the exchange of advantages) over the principles of justice smoothes the way for the social Darwinist 'right of the stronger'.

In accordance with the republican-liberal view of the main *political ordering principle*, the equal basic freedoms of all citizens and the impartial rules of a just life together may never be subordinated to particular ideas of the good, be they cultural convictions arising from a 'communal spirit' or economic (utilitarian) considerations of the common good. A well-ordered modern society cannot and should not be held together either by the regulatory principle of a solidary and supportive community alone on the basis of a single shared conception of valid values and desirable goods (like a 'big family') or solely by the regulatory principle of Pareto efficiency, i.e. the 'market principle'.

Consequently the *ideal of society* in republican liberalism, that of a well-ordered pluralistic civil society, can be clearly distinguished both from the implicit ideal of economic liberalism, the total market society, and from the communitarian ideal of a civil society based on shared values. Moreover, from a philosophical-ethical point of view, the republican-liberal model alone can reach the post-conventional stage of the justification of norms in the sense of a rational-ethical universalism. Substantialist communitarianism, 'obsessed with cultural context', remains at the level of a conventional understanding of morality; and economic liberalism, 'forgetful of cultural context', does not pass beyond the morally sceptical or even the pre-conventional consciousness of the homo oeconomicus.[47]

Finally, particular importance must be attached to the only aspect of our topic presented in Figure 8.1 which we have not yet dealt with, and to which the entire following section will be devoted: the conception of the *political process*. For republican liberalism neither the economistic-liberal conception of the competition between political parties for power in the state as presented in the economic theory of democracy, nor the communitarian model of a grass-roots democratic, federalist self-organization of citizens are decisive determinants of the political process. What counts is rather the 'public use of reason' (Kant) within

[47] The characterization of substantialist communitarianism as 'obsessed with context' and of non-republican liberalism as 'forgetful of context' stems from Forst, *Kontexte der Gerechtigkeit*, p. 15.

the framework of a republican public sphere. Alongside the republican spirit (civic virtue) and the republican constitution this is the third fundamental and central idea of republicanism. The Kantian origin of the regulative idea of the public use of reason refers already to the profound underlying relationship between the political philosophy of republican liberalism and modern rational ethics. It is not, therefore, surprising that the republican conception of ethical-rational politics is being explicated and can be further developed most precisely today in the domain of discourse ethics: as a normatively and empirically meaningful conception of deliberative politics, as we shall see shortly. In the following section we shall attempt, on the basis of an ethically aware and at the same time pragmatic understanding of deliberative politics, to project a perspective of shared political responsibility for politically and economically committed citizens of republican conviction. They recognize the critical public sphere as the 'site' of morality – both as a site for testing the legitimation of their economic activities and, especially, as a site for the determination of the economic and socio-political conditions under which they can be reasonably expected to assert themselves in the market economy.

8.2 Deliberative politics: the public sphere as the site of economic citizens' shared responsibility

As a practice of civic self-legislation politics finds its paradigm not in the market but in dialogue.[48]

Kant was probably the first to grasp exactly the role of the critical public sphere as the systematic site of mediation between the moral principle (in the sense of rational ethics) and constitutional politics.[49] The critical public, understood as the ideal communicative community of free, equal and politically mature citizens, is at the same time the ideal site and highest instance of republican politics, in which those citizens who are politically active and take on their share of civic responsibility debate and regulate public affairs relating to their living together by way of argument. This informal 'reasoning public' is both (a) the site of morality in regard

[48] Habermas, *Facts and Norms*, p. 273.

[49] See the account at the end of Section 2.5 (4). It was Habermas, *Structural Transformation*, p. 102ff., who took up the central role of Kant's idea of the 'public use of reason' earlier than most contemporary ethical and political philosophers. On its significance for economic ethics see Ulrich/Thielemann, *Ethik und Erfolg*, p. 163ff.; Ulrich/Sarasin (eds.), *Facing Public Interest*; there especially Cortina, 'The General Public as the Locus of Ethics', and P. Ulrich, 'Business in the Nineties: Facing Public Interest', in Ulrich/Sarasin (eds.), *Facing Public Interest*, pp. 1–8.

to the justification of publicly relevant actions and also (b) the site of the (self-) enlightenment of free citizens.

Ad (a): *Justice*, as Kant emphasizes in his considerations on the relationship between morality and constitutional politics, can 'be thought only as publicly known'.[50] Every 'claim to a right' must have the 'capacity for publicity . . . since without it there would be no justice ... and so too no right, which is conferred only by justice.'[51] As the regulative idea or 'transcendental principle of publicity' he formulates:

> All actions relating to the rights of others are wrong if their maxim is incompatible with publicity.[52]

This principle, Kant continues, must be regarded as both ethical and juridical (constitutional):

> For a maxim that I cannot divulge without thereby defeating my own purpose, one that absolutely must be kept secret if it is to succeed and that I cannot publicly acknowledge without unavoidably arousing everyone's opposition to my project can derive this necessary and universal, hence a priori foreseeable, resistance of everyone to me only from the injustice with which it threatens everyone.[53]

Here Kant basically anticipates the later language pragmatic turn of discourse ethics. At that time, however, and in contrast to modern discourse ethics, Kant was not in a position to distinguish sharply between communication-oriented (ethical) and influence- or success-oriented (strategic) attitudes.[54] Let us put Kant's position on this point more precisely from a discourse ethical standpoint: 'maxims ... that I cannot divulge' are wrong not only on account of the actual 'resistance' they provoke in the public sphere (acceptance deficit) but also on account of their 'injustice', i.e. their lack of legitimacy in the sense of rational ethical justifiability for everybody. The mere factual existence of public opinion or even populist 'mob pressure' can by no means be regarded as a moral instance, as what matters is not simply empirical acceptance but the rationally justifiable legitimacy of a form of action in the sense of the moral principle. This does not exclude the possibility that good legitimatory reasons can develop a more or less powerful public argumentative force – that is their practical function. But in any case legitimacy can be clarified only with the help of an unconditional communication-oriented

[50] Kant, 'Toward Perpetual Peace', p. 347. [51] Ibid. [52] Ibid. [53] Ibid.

[54] See Section 2.5 (1). On the following critique of Kant's confusion of categories see also U. Thielemann, 'Die Differenz von Vertrags- und Diskursethik und die kategorialen Voraussetzungen ideologiekritischer Wirtschaftsethik', in J.-P. Harpes/W. Kuhlmann (eds.), *Zur Relevanz der Diskursethik: Anwendungsprobleme der Diskursethik in Wirtschaft und Politik* (Münster: Lit, 1997), pp. 271–312.

attitude, that is to say in a genuinely open process of argumentation. The critical public sphere is the site of morality only in as far as the legitimacy of all publicly relevant actions can be tested argumentatively by the 'arguing public', which is called upon 'to make public use of [its] reason in all matters'.[55] In other words: the 'public' can be the site of morality only when it is enlightened and guided by reason.

Ad (b): *Enlightenment* is nothing other than:

> man's emergence from his self-incurred immaturity. Immaturity is the inability to use one's own understanding without the guidance of another. This immaturity is self-incurred if its cause is not lack of understanding but lack of resolution and courage to use it without the guidance of another. The motto of enlightenment is therefore: Sapere aude! Have courage to use your own understanding![56]

However, as Kant soberly points out, the step to political maturity is 'difficult' for most people; 'it is so convenient to be immature'.[57] Only a minority of people are willing and able to free themselves by their own efforts from their political immaturity – what is needed is rather a public project for cultural and republican-political emancipation:

> Thus it is difficult for each separate individual to work his way out of the immaturity which has become almost second nature to him ... There is more chance of an entire public enlightening itself. This is indeed almost inevitable, if only the public concerned is left its freedom. For there will always be a few who think for themselves, even among those appointed as guardians of the common mass. Such guardians, once they have themselves thrown off the yoke of immaturity, will disseminate the spirit of rational respect for personal value and for the duty of all men to think for themselves.[58]

Kant conceives the emancipation of individuals towards political maturity and the social constitution of freedom in the republic – the freedom of politically responsible citizens to participate in public discourse – as necessarily interlocking:

> The public use of man's reason must always be free and it alone can bring about enlightenment among men.[59]

The public use of reason by free and responsible citizens alone can create the critical pressure of legitimation in the republic which will require the political instances to safeguard the public interest instead of merely

[55] Kant, 'What is Enlightenment?', p. 55. [56] Ibid., p. 54. [57] Ibid.

[58] Ibid., pp. 54–5. Here too the categorial difference between legitimation and the effects of the public sphere is still rather blurred. The ideal role of the 'public' as an instance of universalistic-ethical reason becomes clearer when Kant in the *Critique of Pure Reason*, p. 650, speaks of 'universal reason itself, in which everyone has a voice'.

[59] Kant, 'What is Enlightenment?', p. 55.

pursuing their own particular interests. The creation of the necessary pressure on the state to fulfil all its essential duties in regard to publicity, justification and accountability for all its decisions and actions is a fundamental task of a republican constitution. In this context the legal protection of the critical public sphere and the corresponding basic rights of freedom of opinion and freedom of the press, which must be restricted only for the protection of inviolable rights of personality, has a key role to play in states with a republican constitution. The public sphere, as the site of morality and enlightenment, must be free of domination and indivisible:

> The public sphere of civil society stood or fell with the principle of universal access. A public sphere from which specific groups would be eo ipso excluded was less than merely incomplete; it was not a public sphere at all.[60]

No matter how good the constitutional protection of an unrestricted critical public sphere is, it cannot of itself ensure that legitimation claims are observed in all publicly relevant processes and that the freedom guaranteed by the constitution is lived out politically in everyday life. This remains the indispensable role of the responsible citizens who follow their republican convictions and participate actively in the just regulation of public affairs. Here, once again, we have the dialectical reciprocity between a republican constitution and the indispensable republican civic virtues which we encountered in the previous section.

At this point we must note the systematic difference and the tense relationship between the reflective concept of the critical public sphere as the site of political morality on the one hand and the empirically observable conditions of 'real politics' on the other. In this context the *economic theory of democratic politics*, which was first developed by Joseph A. Schumpeter[61] and Anthony Downs,[62] wins suggestive power, particularly in the eyes of convinced moral sceptics. It accords closely with the concept of democracy as a strategic competition between parties for the vote of the citizens and hence for power in the state. Obviously, this perception is attributed to economic liberalism. The provocative basic premise of such 'another theory of democracy' (Schumpeter) is that in their political activities citizens do not in fact orient their behaviour on the desire for communication and mutual understanding but solely on the pursuit of their own interests. As a consequence, the commitment to politics would be purely instrumental, a kind of continuation of private business with public means. As far as this is the case, the economic theory

60 Habermas, *Structural Transformation*, p. 85.
61 Schumpeter, *Capitalism, Socialism and Democracy*, p. 269ff.
62 A. Downs, *An Economic Theory of Democracy* (New York: Harper, 1957).

of politics must be seen as realistic, and the (discourse) ethical idea of republican politics seems hopelessly utopian.[63]

A first reply to this position is that the supposed objection rests upon a methodological misunderstanding. As we have seen earlier pure economics and, consequently, a purely economic theory of democracy by no means have a direct empirical content; their homo oeconomicus premises have nothing to say about the citizen, how he 'really' is and how he acts politically, but have the status of axiomatic 'as-if' assumptions.[64] It can then also be shown that the economic theory of democracy, quite apart from its uselessness as a normative orientational model of rational politics, is hardly convincing as an explanatory approach both from a historical and a (contemporary) empirical and analytical point of view:

- In *historical* perspective the above-mentioned works of Pocock, Michelman, Sunstein and others impressively demonstrate how significant the republican tradition of civic virtue was in reality for the historical development of modern democratic constitutions and political cultures and how little of this historical development can be explained in the categories of individualist, property-owning liberalism.
- In an *empirical-analytical* perspective the economic theory of democracy on the axiomatic basis of methodological individualism inevitably comes up against the paradox of the rational voter.[65] What, namely, could be the rational motives of the homo oeconomicus who acts strictly in accordance with his personal interests for participating at all in democratic debates and voting? After all, the 'costs' in terms of the personal time and energy spent can scarcely be counterbalanced by the highly improbable 'benefits' deriving from contributing an opinion or voting, when his influence on the overall result remains absolutely marginal. It is perhaps conceivable that the failure to vote and general civic passivity might be explained in this way. But how do we explain the fact that a more or less greater number of citizens regularly exercise their right to participate in democratic processes whether it 'pays off' or not, thus revealing a republican disposition? The empirical evidence, therefore, refutes a purely economic theory of democracy, which has

[63] Schumpeter, *Capitalism, Socialism and Democracy*, p. 256, typically presented his descriptive 'evidence that accumulated against the hypothesis of rationality' (in the sense of ethical practical rationality) of the citizens in a section with the title 'Human *Nature* in Politics'.

[64] See Section 4.3. On the difficulties involved in reinterpreting the 'as-if' premises on the homo oeconomicus as empirical hypotheses see Section 5.3 (1) and in particular n. 92 of that section.

[65] Cf. A. Sen, 'Rational Fools', *Philosophy and Public Affairs* 6 (1977), pp. 317–44, at p. 328f.; on what follows see the illuminating review of the discussion in Habermas, *Facts and Norms*, p. 333ff.

'pushed the normative weight reduction too far'.[66] The empirical behaviour of active citizens can only be satisfactorily explained if other than purely self-interested motives, namely civic motives of ethical-political self-commitment, can be attributed to them.

Nor can this *deontological gap* in a purely economic perspective on civic behaviour be closed by the usual theoretical ad-hoc explanation of implausible attitudes in terms of 'meta-preferences'[67] (second-order preferences) or by the introduction of a category of 'expressive preferences'.[68] In both cases we are concerned by and large with a utilitarian reinterpretation, or rather misinterpretation, of the civic sense of duty and the rational-ethical ability of people to deal self-critically with the calculation of their personal interests in regard to their social generalizability. An adequate interpretation of this ability assumes the existence of a categorially completely different conception of an ethically competent person, who can be trusted to be capable of subordinating his spontaneous preferences to an autonomously chosen self-obligation and of *changing* them in processes of reflection and argumentation. Humans, as 'ethicising beings ... actively create and design conceptions of value and decide for or against them'.[69] In contradiction to the neoclassical-economic standard assumption, it is correct to say that human preferences are not simply 'given' but are constantly reworked and changed in an active critical examination of the vital questions of life, as C. C. von Weizsäcker pointed out earlier than most economists:

> An adult person may have sufficient insight to educate himself, to work on his own preferences.[70]

Jon Elster, above all others, has endeavoured to apply this human capacity for normative self-criticism and self-commitment fruitfully to the economic theory of democracy. Breaking with the purely economic paradigm in his approach, he assumes that normatively determined actions cannot be reduced to strategic actions in the pursuit of personal

[66] Habermas, *Facts and Norms*, p. 333.

[67] See Sen, 'Rational Fools'; J. C. Harsanyi, 'Morality and the Theory of Rational Behaviour', *Social Research* 44 (1977), pp. 626–56; T. C. Schelling, *Micromotives and Macrobehaviour* (New York: W. W. Norton, 1978).

[68] See G. Brennan/L. Lomasky, *Democracy and Decision: The Pure Theory of Electoral Preference* (Cambridge MA: Cambridge University Press, 1993), pp. 53, 81ff.

[69] On the emptiness of the idea of meta-preferences and the significance of moral restrictions see M. Tietzel, 'Moral und Wirtschaftstheorie', *Zeitschrift für Wirtschafts- und Sozialwissenschaften* 106 (1986), pp. 113–37, at p. 123.

[70] C. C. von Weizsäcker, 'Notes on Endogenous Change of Tastes', *Journal of Economic Theory* 3 (1971), pp. 345–72, at p. 371 (my italics). Weizsäcker drew the correct conclusion that, as a result, an 'endogenization' of the processes of preference formation is necessary in economics.

interest but represent an independent category of action based upon the priority of the intersubjective recognition of normative validity claims. At first Elster still adhered to a conventionalist understanding of morality which excluded the possibility of an ethical-rational, post-conventional justification and criticism of norms and operated merely with the concept of 'mixed motives'.[71] After revising his approach step by step Elster has arrived at a concept of ethical-rational self-commitment mediated by argument, which he has discovered, in a remarkable reconstruction of the events, to have been empirically effective in the constitutional assemblies of Philadelphia (1776) and Paris (1789–91).[72] More and more economists have in the meantime confirmed the empirical relevance of 'moral'[73] motives and argumentative processes in the explanation of the political behaviour of the citizen, for example Bruno S. Frey and Gebhard Kirchgässner in a study of a Swiss referendum (on a specific issue and not on the election of persons).[74] They assume that although the preferences of the citizens are 'given' at the post-constitutional level (of barter agreement), at the constitutional level (of voting on a partial constitutional reform) they cannot be assumed to have taken 'clearly fixed given preferences as their starting point'; only 'meta-preferences, i.e. those preferences which individuals have as to what their actual preferences *should* be', are 'given' in this case.[75] The authors come to the conclusion that an empirical connection in fact exists between the intensity of the (non-ideal) 'political discourse' *before* the voting on each particular issue and the readiness of the voters to choose 'altruistic' preferences which run counter to their private particular interests and to vote, for example, in favour of welfare policies from which they draw no personal benefit, but whose justice they recognize:

[71] See J. Elster, *The Cement of Society: A Study of Social Order* (New York: Cambridge University Press, 1989), particularly p. 97ff.; on 'mixed motives', ibid., p. 202ff.

[72] See J. Elster, 'The Possibility of Rational Politics', in D. Held (ed.), *Political Theory Today* (Oxford: Polity, 1991), pp. 115–42. In his concept of argumentative rationality Elster specifically follows Habermas. The analysis of the constitutional debates in Philadelphia and Paris referred to in the text can be found, according to Habermas, *Facts and Norms*, p. 338ff., in Elster's unpublished Storr Lectures, *Arguing and Bargaining in Two Constituent Assemblies*, Ms Yale Law School 1991. See also C. Offe/U. K. Preuss, 'Democratic Institutions and Moral Resources', in Held (ed.), *Political Theory Today*, pp. 143–71, especially p. 148ff.

[73] The inverted commas indicate that moral qualities as such elude all empirical-analytical explanations, let alone measurement, from the mere perspective of the observer. On this point see below Section 3.2 (1).

[74] See B. S. Frey/G. Kirchgässner, 'Diskursethik, Politische Ökonomie und Volksabstimmung', *Analyse und Kritik* 15, pp. 129–49.

[75] Ibid., p. 141 (my italics). On Buchanan's distinction between the constitutional and post-constitutional levels, to which the authors refer, see Section 5.3 (3).

It can be observed that in referenda (of this kind) the behaviour of the voters is more strongly altruistic than in other situations, for example those involving economic decisions. There is empirical evidence that citizens vote in favour of redistribution programmes although they themselves suffer a loss of income as a result. In such referenda they thus act 'more morally' than would be expected if they took into account the preferences which otherwise guide their daily lives.[76]

To put it briefly: it is empirically evident that at least a limited claim on the civic virtue of the citizens can be regarded as thoroughly realistic. In particular, it is clear that the formal 'reasonable demand' on the citizens that they should be *open for preference-changing public reasoning* can in fact be met in real political life.[77] Therefore, in recent years a conception of the political process under the heading 'deliberative politics' has moved into the foreground of scientific and philosophical discussions on politics; it tries to find a balance between the all too sceptical homo oeconomicus premises on the one hand and the all too idealizing expectations of virtue in classical republicanism on the other.[78] The practical goal of a conception of the formation of the public will based on rational deliberation is to uphold the regulative idea of a 'reasoning public' as explicated in Kant and in discourse ethics but to expect the citizen to pay the price of political morality 'only in small coins'.[79]

The conception of deliberative democracy follows seamlessly on from the above mentioned historical and empirical outcomes, although the founders of the approach at first developed their ideas in the context of

[76] Frey/Kirchgässner, 'Diskursethik', p. 141. The authors' understanding of discourse ethics is, incidentally, full of category mistakes, as they imagine its perspective to be 'the implementation (sic) of 'true' generalizable interests (sic!)' and tend to reduce the practical significance of 'discourse' to its *influence* on the subsequent behaviour of citizens when taking decisions, which alone can be empirically measured. But this does not affect the validity of their study in the point at issue here and it need not concern us any further.

[77] On the 'significance which normative elements have as part of social reality' (p. 71) and on the empirical evidentness of the argumentative public sphere (equality, openness, discursivity) see B. Peters, 'Der Sinn von Öffentlichkeit', in F. Neidhardt (ed.), *Öffentlichkeit, öffentliche Meinung, soziale Bewegung*, Special Issue of *Kölner Zeitschrift für Soziologie und Sozialpsychologie* (Opladen: Westdeutscher Verlag, 1994), pp. 42–76.

[78] See the influential works of B. Manin, 'On Legitimacy and Political Deliberation', *Political Theory* 15 (1987), pp. 338–68; Sunstein, 'Republican Revival', p. 1548ff.; J. Cohen, 'Deliberation and Democratic Legitimacy', in A. Hamlin/Ph. Pettit (eds.), *The Good Polity: Normative Analysis of the State* (Oxford: Basil Blackwell, 1989), pp. 17–34; J. Habermas, 'Three Normative Models of Democracy', in S. Benhabib (ed.), *Democracy and Difference: Contesting the Boundaries of the Political* (Princeton: Princeton University Press, 1996), pp. 21–30; S. Benhabib, *Facts and Norms*, p. 272ff.; S. Benhabib, 'Toward a Deliberative Model of Democratic Legitimacy', in Benhabib (ed.), *Democracy and Difference*, pp. 67–94; Forst, *Kontexte der Gerechtigkeit*, p. 191ff.

[79] J. Habermas, 'Popular Sovereignty as Procedure', in Habermas, *Facts and Norms*, pp. 463–90, at p. 487 (Rehg translates 'in kleiner Münze' not quite adequately with 'in small increments').

a critical examination of Rousseau's *volonté de tous.*[80] Rousseau also followed the tradition of atomistic (possessive) individualism in assuming that the citizens have an already fixed, pre-socially determined individual will when they engage in political interaction, which can accordingly no longer be conceived as a process of the formation of will but only as a procedure of voting on the 'given' preferences. Between the empirically resulting, aggregate overall or majority will *(volonté de tous)* and the rational idea of a general will *(volonté générale)* a mediatory element is lacking. Precisely this lack of mediation is the source both of Rousseau's rationalistic sin of dissociating the intended *rational legitimation* completely from the empirical preferences of the citizens on the one hand and of Hobbes empirical error in separating the contractualistic *procedural legitimation* totally from any kind of ethical-political rational idea on the other. Against this background the mediatory deliberative conception of the democratic process can be characterized by four central ideas.

(1) Argumentative clarification of preferences

The political attitudes and opinions of the citizens should not be exogenously given outside the democratic process, but endogenously presented within it for discussion and clarification in regard to their public acceptability.[81] The well-considered political 'preferences' of the citizens are the result of a deliberative process in the political public sphere and not previously determined choices. Thus, the democratic process does not serve, at least not primarily, the strategic implementation of predetermined private preferences or a balance of interests based on power structures. It serves instead the discursive formation of the public will both in regard to claims or needs worthy of social recognition and their importance for the common good and in regard to a just social order.[82] The gentle 'coercion' to present good reasons publicly in this process in itself promotes the ability of the citizens to reflect on their own preferences and standpoints.[83] It can be assumed that at the beginning of a public debate the citizens do not usually have a completely clear subjective order of preferences and are consequently ready to *change their original preferences* on the basis of new information, evaluations and arguments, in as far as the original preferences are

[80] Particularly Manin, 'On Legitimacy', p. 341ff.
[81] See Manin, 'On Legitimacy', p. 344f.; Sunstein, 'Republican Revival', p. 1548f.
[82] See N. Fraser, 'Struggles over Needs', in his *Unruly Practices: Power, Discourse and Gender in Contemporary Social Theory* (Minnesota: Minnesota University Press, 1989), pp. 161–87.
[83] See Benhabib, 'Toward a Deliberative Model', p. 71f.

self-contradictory – and accordingly ill-considered – or even publicly unacceptable – and thus illegitimate – on account of intolerable consequences for other citizens.[84]

(2) Deliberative procedural legitimation

The source of the legitimacy of democratic decisions is not the mere representation of all predetermined opinions in a 'speechless' procedure for the determination of majorities but rather the deliberative quality of the process leading to the formation of the public will.[85] Deliberative processes in which as many citizens as possible participate under fair communicative conditions[86] justify the assumption that 'some *degree* of practical rationality'[87] can be achieved, which provides a sufficient basis for the political legitimacy of the results. This assumption of legitimacy is weaker than the ideal claim of a universal ethical-rational ability to reach consensus (the regulative idea of discourse ethics) but still stronger than anything purely socio-technical (voting) procedures can bring forth. The structures and procedures of deliberative politics – in particular measures guaranteeing the power-free expression of public opinion, equal access to information, fair opportunities of presenting arguments for all concerned, uniform requirements in regard to the justificatory quality of validity claims, clearly defined modalities for decision-taking and the revisability of earlier decisions[88] – cannot be directly regarded as sufficient sources of legitimation in themselves. The deliberative procedures do not provide a guarantee but rather a 'crutch' for public reason. They only offer the opportunity (which the citizens must grasp) for a reasonably rational political debate. And they keep the legitimation process open: *contestability is more important than (temporary) consent.*[89] The more varied

[84] Manin, 'On Legitimacy', p. 349f. [85] Ibid., p. 351f.

[86] Not the least of which include equal political *rights* of communication and participation for all citizens.

[87] Benhabib, 'Toward a Deliberative Model', p. 71 (my italics). The 'degree' of the ethical rational content remains, however, undetermined as it cannot be assumed that the participants constantly strive to reach agreement. It is rather the case that 'mixed motives' are involved and a limited willingness to submit personal interests self-critically to discussion.

[88] For details see Habermas, *Facts and Norms*, p. 305ff. It must be noted that such procedures (a) are of a pragmatic kind, but (b) should permit the achievement of a consensus in the light of the regulative idea of ideal discourse. Yet the *ideal* discourse procedure as such is not open to further analysis and cannot therefore be directly operationalized with procedural techniques. On this point see Ulrich, *Transformation*, p. 293.

[89] See Pettit, *Republicanism*, pp. ix, 183ff.

and lively the social network of formal institutions and of 'arenas'[90] spontaneously created by politically committed citizens in the constitutionally protected open space of the public sphere, the better the development of ethical-political deliberation and 'public' reason.

(3) *Consensus-based regulation of dissent*

In a complexly organized, culturally pluralistic society a multiplicity of sources or occasions will give rise to almost unbridgeable ideological and political disagreements. It can scarcely be expected that these can be overcome by means of a comprehensive agreement achieved by argument. Under these circumstances it is important, above all, to reach an agreement on fair and binding rules for dealing with political dissent and to maintain a 'civilized culture' of debate. To this end it is enough to arrive at a basic political consensus on the formal principles and procedures for regulating conflict; beyond this, deliberative democracy does not assume the need for agreement on concrete value orientations in regard to the good life. Nor do material conflicts of interest necessarily require a consensual solution involving shared convictions; it is sufficient if they are resolved by *compromise.* In contrast to a merely strategic compromise (as the result of bargaining under given relationships of power), a compromise achieved by deliberation rests upon a basic consensus on fair conditions. It should take into account the moral rights and concrete problems of self-assertion of all concerned and, by making equal demands on all, it should be reasonable and, for this reason, acceptable to all parties.[91]

(4) *The public constitution of the private sphere*

A free society should guarantee its citizens the greatest possible degree of private free space. What is regarded as private, however, must be the same for all concerned and is, consequently, a necessary part of a basic political consensus in a well-ordered society. The delimitation of the private from the public in the sense of the definition and legal guarantee of legitimate free space for the pursuit of private interests must be regarded – analogous to the regulation of the areas of permissible dissent – as an indispensable

[90] Habermas, *Facts and Norms*, p. 299.

[91] According to Habermas, *Facts and Norms*, p. 283, such compromises serve to 'take into consideration strategically asserted particular interests in a manner compatible with the common good'.

object of deliberative politics.[92] Those activities are truly private whose social and ecological acceptability is guaranteed; this implies, however, regular control and a sufficient degree of public transparency in the affairs the citizens regard as private. All claims based on a pre-political definition of what is private or attempts to deny the need for accountability and control through public deliberation are forms of arbitrary privatism. A priori restrictions of the domain of public debate are not possible according to the conception of deliberative democracy, as the whole point of the exercise is to discover legitimate reasons for the privatization (i.e. depoliticization and legal transfer to the field of private law) of certain areas of action.[93]

The 'public use of reason'[94] takes effect in this deliberative conception in as far as the formal *minimum claims on republican civic virtue* implicit in the four central ideas treated above are met, namely:

- firstly, a fundamental willingness of the citizens *to reflect* on their preferences and attitudes involving a certain degree of self-critical open-mindedness which will enable them, if need be, to change their position;
- secondly, a fundamental willingness *to reach an agreement* on impartial, fair principles and procedural rules regulating the deliberative process. A particular degree of good will is required for the clarification of this basic consensus, as the participants must be prepared to renounce the use of their power potential in the pursuit of their own interests;
- thirdly, a willingness *to compromise* in areas of dissent which, beside the good will to arrive at a basic consensus on fair rules for finding compromises, also requires a permanent mutual acceptance of limited areas of disagreement;
- fourthly, a willingness *to accept the need for legitimation*, i.e. the willingness to submit 'private' actions unconditionally to the test of public legitimation. This includes the renunciation of an a priori privatism,

[92] See Habermas, *Facts and Norms*, p. 28.

[93] See Habermas, *Facts and Norms*, p. 312ff., and also Benhabib, *Situating the Self*, p. 95ff.

[94] It should now be clear that the deliberative model of politics involves a substantially wider understanding of the 'public use of reason' than that advocated by John Rawls, *Political Liberalism*, p. 212ff. Rawls remains by and large within the framework of the economic-liberal premises of pre-politically determined political preferences; furthermore, he postulates a strict restriction of the topics of public discourse to fundamental questions of the organization (constitution) of the well-ordered society and thus advocates the idea that the public and the private spheres can be separated a priori. Deliberative aspects of an active 'strong democracy' (Barber) can scarcely be found in Rawls's conception. See Manin, 'On Legitimacy', p. 347f., and Benhabib, 'Toward a Deliberative Model', p. 74ff.

adequate forms of 'publicity' and accountability for publicly relevant activities.

As is particularly clear from the last point, these deliberative civic virtues must also be seen to a high degree as formal minimum requirements of economic citizen virtue. Civic virtues are economic citizen virtues in as far as business activities have a de facto (and not merely de jure) public relevance. In contrast, the idea of a neat and tidy separation between the political citizen (as homo politicus) and the economic citizen (as homo oeconomicus) turns out to be the symptomatic expression of a privatistically reduced self-understanding of the bourgeois who has lost his awareness of the priority and indivisibility of his status as a citoyen. The core of a republican economic ethics consists precisely in reflecting on the indispensable republican civic ethos *in* the self-understanding of the economic agents and putting it into practice. From this point of view, all economic agents essentially share a responsibility that cannot be delegated. Their shared responsibility refers to the quality of societal processes of deliberation, particularly in regard to debates concerned with the general economic, social and political conditions for the legitimate pursuit of private economic interests.

As these civic *minima moralia* are of a formal (procedural) kind, and thus only determine the basic disposition required for the practical clarification of specific obligations in the public process of deliberation, they are largely open in regard to the concrete value orientations of responsible economic citizens participating in the deliberative process. The fact that economic and social reforms achieved by deliberation can, to 'some degree' (Benhabib), be assumed to be an expression of public reason and hence to be legitimated by their *impartiality* does not necessarily mean – even when the assumption is correct – that all economic agents are affected by them to an equal degree. It is rather the point of reforms of the general social conditions for private economic activity that they change the relative competitive position of those who produce or consume differently on the market, and that they are *not*, therefore, *competitively neutral* in relation to the status quo.[95]

By way of illustration we can take the introduction of taxes and levies on energy designed to steer its use in an ecologically meaningful direction. Such measures obviously have a greater financial impact on

[95] Homann/Blome-Drees, *Wirtschafts- und Unternehmensethik*, p. 114, mistakenly assume the competitive neutrality of rules regulating market competition which have a moral content. For a criticism see also M. Kettner, 'Rentabilität und Moralität. Offene Probleme in Karl Homann's Wirtschafts- und Unternehmensethik', in Forum für Philosophie Bad Homburg (ed.), *Markt und Moral*, pp. 241–67, at p. 250ff. We will return to the consequences for the institutional framework in Section 9.2 (2).

energy-intensive branches of the economy and also on citizens with a high consumption of the sources of energy in their private lives. And this is quite deliberate, as precisely these groups should be provided with a particularly strong regulatory incentive to change a behaviour which is evidently not 'economical' in every sense of the word. Particularly strong demands are, therefore, made on the economic citizen virtue of those who are affected most, should they agree to the corresponding reforms. Are these demands reasonable?

The answer is: basically, yes! Opposition to changed *general* conditions for the legitimate pursuit of private interests in defence of an existing but privileging (i.e. not universalizable) 'customary right', by referring to the *specific* impact in case of its loss, cannot, in principle, be regarded as an acceptable form of civic resistance to publicly meaningful and reasonable institutional reform. Otherwise arbitrariness in the defence of unfair competitive advantages by claiming them to be one's 'vested rights' or simply 'inherently necessary' would prevail. This in turn would make the implementation of general rules valid for all participants in market competition completely impossible. What is justifiable in regard to the demands which can be reasonably made on the specially affected competitors is at best the arrangement of short-term transitional modifications in their favour or permanent institutional measures designed to reduce competition generally.[96] The legitimacy of the institutional framework must ultimately rest upon the elimination of all those undeserved competitive advantages of market players derived from unjustified privileges or moral free riding, so that success in competition is decided by market performance under equal competitive conditions, even though they make different 'demands' on the economic agents.

If we view the situation realistically, however, we cannot ignore the fact that powerful lobbies often fight with all the means at their disposal against legitimate and impartial institutional reforms in order to maintain unfair competitive advantages (based on non-universalizable free-rider strategies). They sometimes also misuse their economic power in everyday political life in order to assert their particularistic interests. Often enough their self-interested strategies are ultimately successful and regulatory reforms are defeated, although in terms of the 'public use of reason' they ought to be viewed quite clearly as legitimate and sensible. The fatal consequence is the discouragement of the willingness to accept civic commitments in economic affairs, even among the undetermined but certainly substantial number of citizens in countries with a reasonably sound republican and democratic

[96] See Section 4.3 (3b) and the further development of this point in Section 9.2 (3c).

tradition whose readiness to share responsibility for the res publica is beyond doubt.[97] If their republican civic virtues are not occasionally encouraged and reinforced, they will be undermined by a sense of impotent idealism and disillusionment in the face of the reality of political life or pushed aside by the everyday concerns arising from the hard struggle for economic self-assertion. It need not surprise us, then, if the majority of people sooner or later give up the fight for the realization of civic virtue in political and economic life.

For this reason we must here call to mind once again the point of republicanism developed earlier, namely the necessary dialectical interaction between republican conviction (the virtue-ethical aspect) and the republican constitution (the regulatory ethical aspect). Beside general restrictions on competition, the exercise of economic citizen virtues in everyday business life requires *institutional 'backing'*. The following points should be considered:

- the greatest possible constitutional neutralization of economic power in the process of public deliberation, so that the personal civic involvement of economic citizens is not cancelled out by the open or concealed threat of sanctions on the part of those in positions of economic power, who disapprove of the actions of citizens which run counter to their interests, and on whom the citizens are existentially dependent (e.g. as employees or tenants);[98]
- general education in civics at all school levels and the creation of suitable local and regional arenas or forums for civic debate on the important economic and social issues of daily life, together with direct democratic initiative and referendum rights;[99]
- constitutional provision for economic citizenship rights, in particular information, communication and complaint rights, which – as structural components of their empowerment – enable them to participate as truly equal and informed citizens in public debates and to defend their legitimate claims;[100]

[97] According to a qualitative empirical study of 60 top managers in Switzerland, a segment of the population particularly subject to role strain in economic matters, about 10% of those questioned nonetheless revealed a pattern of economic-ethical thought which was strongly influenced by republican thinking. See Ulrich/Thielemann, *Ethik und Erfolg*, English short-version in their 'How Do Managers Think?'.

[98] On the application of this postulate in regard to property rights see Section 7.3 (2b) and Section 9.2 (3a).

[99] As an example the highly developed use of direct democratic processes in the Swiss referendum system is worth mentioning. See also the pragmatic proposals for the institutionalization of 'public talk', which in part make use of the new information technology, in Barber, *Strong Democracy*, p. 261ff. and Barber, 'An American Civic Forum: Civil Society between Market Individuals and the Political Community', *Social Philosophy and Policy* 13 (1996), pp. 269–83.

[100] See above Section 7.3.

– conversely, the clear constitutional accountability of those who take publicly relevant decisions in both the private and public sphere, their responsibility to bear the burden of proof for the compatibility of their actions with the public interest, to fulfil their legal obligation to provide meaningful information and to account for their actions.[101]

Even if such institutional backing for the practice of economic citizen virtue is to some extent forthcoming, it will not on its own suffice to counterbalance the lack of competitive neutrality of politico-economic measures. Institutional measures will never dispense with the need for all responsible economic citizens to be active in the public sphere and to strengthen meaningful institutional reforms by providing good reasons for their legitimation as well as their implementation. Understood in this way, the public use of reason by economic citizens of republican conviction can contribute substantially to the political realization of justified reforms, even against the united opposition of those who have no interest in the legitimacy of their particularistic interests. It can supply sustainable and scarcely refutable arguments which put pressure on the instances of economic and political power to legitimate their actions.

8.3 Professional and private life as sites of economic citizens' self-commitment

The economic citizen is not only a 'private citizen' but he has of course a right to a private life away from the spotlights of the critical public sphere, in as far as it is in accordance with the general legitimacy conditions. It is essential from a republican-liberal point of view, however, that the economic citizens should autonomously and responsibly live up to the principles of the public use of reason as thoroughly as possible to their 'private' economic life as well. In regard to this *demand for integrity* and thus for an undivided life-form of the economic citizen the question also arises as to how the corresponding expectations of civic virtue can be kept within modest limits, so that the citizen need only pay the price 'in small coins' (Habermas).

Before we take a closer look at this ethical 'coinage' in exemplary areas of private economic life, it is necessary to acquire a more precise picture of the general premises legitimating economic action. What does this mean in concrete terms?

[101] On this point see also U. Beck, *Politik in der Risikogesellschaft* (Frankfurt: Suhrkamp, 1991), p. 15: 'It will be necessary to *establish the attribution of responsibility* at all levels and with all means.' See the proposals made there.

The core of these legitimating premises is the unconditional readiness of economic citizens of republican conviction to accept the fundamental primacy of the principles and rules of just co-existence in society, as determined by the public use of reason (i.e. by the processes of deliberative democracy), over (particular) personal interests which cannot be generally justified. The direct practical consequence of this readiness is the moral duty *to renounce the maximization of strictly private benefits* in personal actions.[102]

The consequence is logically inevitable: the strict maximization of personal benefit cannot be a legitimate orientation for action, as it means quite precisely that all competing value standpoints, including the moral rights of others, must be subordinated without examination to personal benefit, which is accorded absolute priority as the criterion for action. In contrast, the minimal ethics of the economic citizen at the private level involves the recognition of the categorical primacy of the moral rights of all those affected by his actions and the observation of their legitimate claims (in relation to his own legitimate claims), since his activities are only private in a formal and legal sense. This implies that a responsible economic citizen will examine each of his intentions to act at the start, in order to discover whether the practical consequences are acceptable to those affected and can be advocated with good reasons, regardless of whether the claims of the others are 'announced' or not. For even in the cases where there are no objections or manifest opposition the responsible economic citizen will not disregard the legitimate claims of others; he would think it unfair to gain an economic advantage in this way.

Those who reflect on and accept the republican principle of legitimate economic action will recognize the moral duty of every economic citizen to practice the autonomous *self-limitation* of his endeavours to achieve private advantage, benefit or success and to see this not as a restriction but as the fundamental ethical basis (legitimacy condition) of his private freedom of action in economic matters. What is more, in situations, for example in professional life, in which the temptation to take unfair advantage of others spontaneously is predictable, he will, if he is serious about his responsibilities, take steps beforehand to commit himself to well-considered and firm principles – following the famous example of Ulysses. He knew he could not trust his own moral strength in the face of approaching temptations and ordered his crew to tie him to the mast before sailing past the enticing sirens.

The pioneers of republicanism have always revealed a total awareness of these dangers in their understanding of *corruption* as the opposite of

[102] On this point see Section 4.3 (3a).

republican self-limitation and as the symptomatic manifestation of its absence. Frank Michelman follows John G. A. Pocock in defining corruption clearly and concisely as 'the subversion, within the political motivation of any participant, of the general good by particular interest',[103] i.e. quite simply as the reverse of the republican order of priorities:

> Depending on the actions of the citizens, the *res publica*, the polity, is threatened, apart from the menace of external enemies, above all by the danger of corruption, the decline of *virtù* among those citizens who place their passions and their interest before the common good.[104]

Corruption is manifested wherever the 'private' civic virtue of an agent is weak, so that he succumbs to the temptation to take advantage of others who are dependent on his decisions with the intention of enriching himself unfairly. The danger is typically present in the case of office-holders[105] in high professional positions, who (as the passively corrupted) accept the confidential payment of bribe money or substantial 'presents' in non-monetary form from market competitors (as the active corruptors) 'in return for' a 'favourable' decision.

In the light of the republican principle what is reprehensible about such passive corruptibility and the active misuse of it is self-evident. The ethical problems involved go far beyond the fact that corruption is, first of all, a serious abuse of office on the part of the corrupted office-holder. If corruption becomes a widespread, almost 'normal' aspect of business behaviour, it has disastrous, almost uncontrollable effects on the entire economic life of a country. It destroys the fairness of competition in the market economy, undermines the normative validity of the generally binding impartial rules of a well-ordered society as a whole and seriously impairs the confidence of honest citizens in the justice of the political order. In view of these unacceptable consequences, the state, the industrial associations and every single organisation based on division of labour are called upon to root out, as far as possible, the potential structural sources of corruption, such as false incentives (i.e. tax deductions for bribes) or lack of transparency (inadequate regulations on publicity and control). They must also endeavour to strengthen the civic virtue of endangered office-holders by institutional means, for example:

- enforcement by the state of tax and penal regulations with the threat of high legal penalties in order to inhibit corruption;

[103] Michelman, 'The Supreme Court', p. 40. [104] Sewing, 'Pocock', p. 17.

[105] The normal case is a state official who must, for example, give permission for certain activities in the private sector of the economy; but analogous situations can occur with the holders of positions in large companies, where there is a lack of transparency.

- general agreements on the collective self-commitment of entire branches of the economy to corruption-free procedures for the submission of tenders and the award of contracts, which are consistently implemented by suitable industrial organs (at the national and, as far as possible, the international level) in order to guarantee fair competition for contracts;
- an ethics codex with clear compliance regulations and corresponding control mechanisms at the level of each company, particularly the large international companies, and at the level of the professional associations of particularly endangered professions.[106]

In the absence of sound and sufficiently broad-based republican civic virtues, however, even the most energetic institutional measures at all levels, assuming they could be realized at all, would scarcely be able to eradicate the evils of corruption. The degree of corruption is, therefore, possibly the best single indicator for the state of health of the economic civic virtues in the res publica of a society.[107]

Let us now leave this murky counterpoint to the republican civic virtues and sketch briefly some further perspectives of civic self-limitation in economic affairs in three areas of private economic life that are more or less important for most people: (1) in their professional lives as 'institutional citizens', (2) in their behaviour as consumers, and (3) in their behaviour as 'private' investors of capital.

(1) The economic citizen as an institution citizen

The concept of the 'institution citizen'[108] or 'organizational citizen' transfers the republican conception of a state or economic citizen to the situation of an employee in a hierarchically structured, complex organization based on the division of labour. The great majority of the working population today works in such an organization on the basis of an employment contract which regulates their responsibility for a more or less narrowly defined function or partial task depending on their qualifications and position in the hierarchy of the company. In accordance with the organizational principle of the necessarily equal scope of task, competence and responsibility, a partial task corresponds to an

[106] On this point see also Section 10.3 (3).

[107] Cf. Th. Maak/P. Ulrich, 'Korruption – die Unterwanderung des Gemeinwohls durch Partikularinteressen: Eine republikanisch-ethische Perspektive', in M. Pieth/P. Eigen (eds.), *Korruption im internationalen Geschäftsverkehr: Bestandsaufnahme, Bekämpfung, Prävention* (Neuwied: Luchterhand, 1999), pp. 103–19.

[108] P. R. Nielsen, 'Arendt's Action Philosophy and the Manager as Eichmann, Richard III, Faust or Institution Citizen', *California Management Review* 26 (1984), pp. 191–201.

organizationally restricted partial responsibility. Such an organizational partial or (functional) *role responsibility* can under certain circumstances conflict with the (ethical) *civic responsibility* of the role-bearer for all of the consequences (and not merely the functional results) of his actions.

Civic responsibility is indivisible. Economic citizens with republican convictions should certainly be loyal to their employers in the fulfilment of the tasks agreed on in their contracts. But where there is a danger that the 'blind' fulfilment of internal company duties can lead to the violation of the moral rights of others or the shared republican responsibility for the public good, the more broadly defined civic responsibility must, according to the republican principle, enjoy priority over the limited role responsibility. After all, the employee has not sold himself 'lock, stock and barrel' to his employer, but has only placed his labour at the disposal of the employer for restricted tasks which are legally defined in a proper employment contract; the resulting authority of the employer to issue directives is equally restricted. It is perfectly legitimate to object to business activities, internal company procedures and regulations or the directives of superiors which the employee regards as morally unacceptable. An organizational citizen may even feel called upon to raise a word of protest, although this, of course, requires *civic courage*. The economic citizen of republican conviction also preserves his fundamental moral autonomy as an institutional citizen and observes a *critical loyalty* towards the organization which employs him.

Because of the hierarchical dependence in which every employee finds himself, however, this principled republican attitude can possibly result in a demand for an almost heroic display of virtue if the employee faces a personal dilemma by having to choose between his responsibility as a citizen and as a member of an organisation. The situation is particularly serious for the employee if:

- his superiors issue directives whose implementation involves actions or omissions which are morally wrong (e.g. when employees are required to participate in illegal or unfair business activities);
- if a superior forbids him to pass on information to higher instances about irresponsible occurrences in the organization which have come to his knowledge (e.g. cases of bribery in the purchase or sale of goods or unfair treatment of other employees);
- if the employee has acquired knowledge of reprehensible or at least morally questionable occurrences in the organization of which his superior is unaware and considers whether he should keep his knowledge secret or follow his personal moral convictions and take the initiative in order to bring the occurrences to light and ensure that they are stopped.

In such situations the employee concerned must choose between the voice of his conscience and the role expectations of the organization. He is faced with this tricky problem resulting from his dependent position within the hierarchy, which may tempt him to behave opportunistically. Insensitive loyalty and the 'blind' fulfilment of duty[109] without consideration of the moral aspects are usually rewarded in accordance with the internal company criteria requiring success, whereas the ethically aware employee who follows his conscience must reckon with negative sanctions on the part of his superiors. These can range from financial disadvantages resulting from refusal of promotion to downright dismissal.

In this situation institutional citizens need *institutional backing* which guarantees that they are not required to demonstrate a heroic denial of their own existential interests. They should suffer no personal disadvantages for their ethically motivated commitment or at least should pay for their civic courage only 'in small coins' (Habermas). In principle, suitable support for establishing such 'low-cost situations'[110] can be offered from three sides: (a) from their colleagues at their place of work or in their professional association, (b) from the company itself, or (c) from the critical public sphere in as far as it has the institutions of the state on its side.

Ad (a): the support of other members of the company or professional colleagues can foster the courage of the critically loyal institutional citizen and decisively strengthen his argumentative position. Solidarity is a source of strength! If the organization has a works committee, it can support the colleague who is in a moral dilemma by making his problem a general concern of the entire workforce as represented in the committee or even of an employees' organization which extends beyond the company (trade union). The representatives of qualified professional groups are seldom organized to the same degree; but they may possibly be members of a professional association which, in a favourable case, has laid down a binding *professional code of ethics*. Doctors, engineers, lawyers and trustees typically have this institutionalized form of self-regulation in their professions. If a member of a profession who is caught

109 The 'blind fulfilment of duty', in which the employee adheres strictly to his organizational function, corresponds to the unconditional 'blind obedience' which is required only in strictly authoritarian (e.g. military) or totalitarian (e.g. fascist) institutions and is unworthy of a society of free citizens. Hannah Arendt has examined this phenomenon in the exemplary case of the interaction between Eichmann's idea of the unconditional fulfilment of duties and the 'structurally evil' totalitarian structures of National Socialism. See H. Arendt, *Eichmann in Jerusalem: A Report on the Banality of Evil* (New York: Penguin, 1994; 1st edn 1963).

110 See the treatment in Section 4.3 (3b).

on the horns of a moral dilemma can convince his superior or the management of the company that he would clearly violate a professional code which is binding for him if he carried out the problematic directive, this should normally make a lasting impression on his employer. If this appeal does not lead to a solution within the company the employee can call upon his professional association to intervene directly with the management.

It would be a particularly welcome development if, as a consequence and expression of the growing professionalization of management, the top managers in the business world founded more and more professional organizations with a professional ethos, a corresponding binding code of behaviour, and courts of arbitration to ensure its implementation within the profession. As every truly professional ethics involves the self-commitment of the professional group to the service of the public good (instead of serving only particularist interests), the top managers who followed the guidelines of their professional body would then establish the republican principle of critical loyalty as the autonomous basis for their management activities in a particularly effective manner.

Ad (b): a management which itself adopts a republican-ethical stance will see the removal or even the prevention of false incentives for 'organized internal irresponsibility'[111] which encourage opportunism as an important task and will implement a well-considered overall conception of 'organized responsibility'[112] based on management and leadership ethics. Such a conception will include, on the one hand, a clearly defined and guaranteed *institutional civic right to express critical opinions*. On the other hand, suitable sanction-free channels of communication will give the employee, as a responsible institutional citizen, a fair chance of standing by his own ethical judgement in spite of his dependent position in the company hierarchy. If necessary it must be possible for him to object to morally intolerable or questionable occurrences[113] at an early defined 'normative faultline that appears with (the) ability to say no'.[114]

Ad (c): only after the means of support sketched in (a) and (b) have been exhausted and the top management of the organization continues to deny or disregard a substantial moral problem will the institutional citizen feel justified and possibly morally obliged to take the last course open to him and make the problem known publicly in those special cases where

[111] Following the subtitle of U. Beck, *Gegengifte: Die organisierte Unverantwortlichkeit* (Frankfurt: Suhrkamp, 1988).

[112] T. Tuleja, *Beyond the Bottom Line* (New York: Facts on File, 1985), p. 177.

[113] Institutional citizen's rights will be treated in detail in Section 10.3 (3). Here we are interested in the problem only from the standpoint of civic ethics.

[114] Habermas, *Facts and Norms*, p. 324.

the protection of the higher interests of the res publica is at stake. Then he will raise the alarm by *whistle-blowing*, so that ultimately public pressure is exerted on the organization to legitimate its actions.[115]

(2) The economic citizen as a critical consumer

Those who have become accustomed, as economic citizens of republican conviction, to subject their own preferences and opinions to critical questioning and to weigh up their decisions carefully will also reflect critically on their preferences as 'private' consumers. They will do so in two regards: firstly, as regards the point of their preferences in terms of the good life (authenticity of needs) and secondly, as regards the legitimacy of their preferences from a social and ecological standpoint (generalizability of behaviour). The two aspects, the ability to accept responsibility for oneself (autonomy) and towards others (empathy), are ultimately indivisible.[116] In both dimensions the central issue is the competence for critical self-reflection and the will to commit oneself rationally to forms and degrees of consumption which do justice both to authentic personal needs and to the standpoints of a generalizable life style. The central feature is the integration of personal consumer needs and preferences in the self-concept of an autonomous and socially embedded personality.[117] For this reason consumers with a sense of responsibility will not only reflect on their personal behaviour as consumers but, as they are aware of the effectiveness of making common cause, will go further and 'signalize' their position to the market, the political world and possibly also to their fellow citizens.

The capacity for self-critical reflection on and self-determination of personal preferences was discussed many years ago by the philosopher Harry Frankfurt.[118] He coined the term 'second-order preferences' long before economists took it up as 'meta-preferences', thus reducing it to a category of methodological individualism that has in the meantime been gradually broadened again.[119] As we have seen earlier, the decisive point lies in a holistic approach to life which goes beyond merely economic

[115] See for instance De George, *Business Ethics*, Chapter 10, p. 200ff. One of the most informative books on the subject has been written (in German) by K. M. Leisinger, *Whistleblowing and Corporate Reputation Management* (Munich-Mering: Hampp, 2003).

[116] See G. Scherhorn, 'Autonomie and Empathie. Die Bedeutung der Freiheit für das verantwortliche Handeln: Zur Entwicklung eines neuen Menschenbildes', in Biervert/Held (eds.), *Menschenbild*, pp. 153–72; see also Scherhorn, 'Konsumverhalten'.

[117] See Scherhorn, 'Autonomie und Empathie', p. 166.

[118] H. Frankfurt, 'Freedom of the Will and the Concept of a Person', *Journal of Philosophy* 68 (1971), pp. 5–20.

[119] See above Section 8.2.

categories, accepts a limited but adequate satisfaction of material needs and finds fulfilment in meaningful activity.[120]

The more active a person is in this sense, the more inner energy he will find for reflection on his preferences as a consumer and for his republican commitment to public affairs and the common good. On the other hand there is a kind of competitive relationship between the concentration on private consumption and commitment to public affairs. Of course not only consumption but also political commitment can sometimes be a rather disappointing experience. Consequently, in both individual biography and cultural history, phases of privatistic consumer orientation are often followed by phases of public commitment in a cycle of disappointed expectations, as Albert O. Hirschman[121] has shown in an original study. He too emphasizes the fundamental significance of a person's critical judgement of his own experiences and decisions in regard to the formation of new and different preferences in such processes.[122]

An everyday life that is totally permeated by advertisers' promises of happiness through consumption, requires of course enormous inner strength, both to resist the temptations of the omnipresent display of goods and to reflect autonomously on the right choice among them. Here again the thoughtful consumer needs institutional backing! A basic requirement is the protection of the consumer provided by the legal framework, in particular the duty of producers to declare the contents of their products fully,[123] the limitation of advertising directed at children who are not yet capable of adopting a critical stance towards advertising methods and the total prohibition of advertising for products which are damaging to the health of consumers. An important role in the protection of the consumer will also be played by consumer organizations and even by the initiatives of individual 'consumer advocates'.[124] The protective measures will include information for consumers (improvement of market transparency according to systematic criteria[125] and

[120] See Section 6.2 (1).

[121] See A. O. Hirschman, *Shifting Involvements: Private Interest and Public Action* (Princeton NJ: Princeton University Press, 1982).

[122] See ibid., p. 6.

[123] The duty to declare the contents of goods is particularly important in regard to foodstuffs and the methods of their production (conventional or biological and dynamic cultivation, genetically engineered changes, etc.) and has already become legally binding in some countries (e.g. in the Swiss Foodstuff Regulations of 1995).

[124] The most famous example is the American consumers' advocate Ralph Nader, who initiated the campaign 'Unsafe at Any Speed' against the VW Beetle in the 1960s.

[125] An excellent example of a practical guide for consumers, enabling them to choose socially and ecologically responsible producers, is the brochure *Shopping for a Better World*, which has a large circulation in the Anglo-Saxon world. Published by the Council on Economic Priorities and regularly updated, it presents a detailed survey and

comparison of the quality of products in tests of goods and services), counselling of consumers (general and individual advice for customers on ways of defending themselves against poor products and inadequate services) and, last but not least, public action in favour of progressive legislation in the field of consumer protection (consumer rights and the liability of the producers for their products). In the final analysis, it is necessary to promote the *sovereignty of the consumer*, which economic theory simply takes as a given fact, by establishing a suitable institutional framework and specific forms of support so that selective consumption can become a real prospect for the reflective individual.

(3) The economic citizen as a critical investor

Both well-situated 'property-owning citizens' with good incomes and small investors choose to put aside a larger or smaller part of their income, which is then available to the economy for the financing of investments. In a capitalist market economy built on private property the capital markets play a central role in the allocation of economic resources. Nowadays they exert an enormous global pressure not only on the entire financial world but also on the real economy. They discipline the big institutional investors (insurance companies and organizations providing financial services) and, through the stock exchange, also force the public limited companies active in the real economy to constantly increase the shareholder value, i.e. the internal value of the company as assessed by the market quotation.[126] Even small investors are nowadays performance-oriented in their activities on the stock exchange. Capitalism has never functioned better by its own terms and the corresponding 'value-orientation' and speculative mentality was never so widespread as at the present moment. But, on the other hand, the interest of many citizens in ethical investment has never been so great, particularly in the capitalist country par excellence, the USA. This interest represents a countermovement to the speculative mentality and to the desire for 'quick money'.

All forms of economic action must be defined as *speculation* which do not aim at a productive creation of value (production of goods or the provision of services) but solely at the exploitation of expected price differences between the times of buying and selling on the stock exchanges and the markets for commodities and foreign exchange. By

evaluation of the most important producers of consumer goods according to certain criteria (information policy, social commitment, observance of women's rights, animal experiments, protection of the environment, armaments production etc.).

[126] On globalization see Section 9.3; on the problem of the strict orientation of corporate management on share-holder value see Section 10.1 (4).

making use of secondary financial instruments (such as options and futures) speculative business activities can largely be carried out independently of the real economic earnings expectations on which they are ultimately based. But they are never entirely independent and for this reason 'unfounded' exaggerated expectations of returns will occasionally be corrected by rapid drops in prices. The 'game' therefore depends on the 'players' buying in phases of speculative appreciation in value and selling again before the prices begin to fall.

The speculative mentality is compatible with republican-ethical convictions only to a very restricted degree, as it encourages a far-reaching autonomy of the motives for increasing private capital at the expense of all other practical considerations, so that the investor is *solely* interested in the increase of capital value achieved in whatever way. It is not least for this reason that the speculative markets are comparatively often the scene of shady dealings on or beyond the borders of legality, although this fact should not be used to condemn speculation as such.[127]

The republican-ethical sense of responsibility is therefore equivalent to the readiness to limit the private pursuit of profit in favour of (at least an additional) consideration of the practical effects and ethical aspects of capital allocation. In view of the enormous significance of the capital markets in the modern global economy it is evident that the behaviour of private investors provides an excellent opportunity not only to let savings 'work' where they have the most meaningful effects from an ethical point of view but also to 'signalize' to the market the direction a human, social and ecological allocation of capital and value creation should take.

The problem is that the information normally provided by banks and stock exchanges provides the investor with little orientation. As a private citizen he is here again dependent on institutional support. Three approaches suggest themselves: the ethically aware investor can (a) delegate the problem to the professional financial administrators of *ethical investment funds* of the kind that has long existed in the Anglo-Saxon world and is gradually gaining ground in continental Europe as well; (b) base his personal investment decisions on the qualitative information of specialized independent *rating agencies*; or (c) join one of the increasingly numerous *associations of critical shareholders* of large companies in order to participate with other like-minded investors in the partially public meetings of the shareholders (general meetings) and to advocate

[127] See H. B. Peter, 'Spekulation', in Enderle *et al.* (eds.), *Lexikon der Wirtschaftsethik*, col. 1014–20.

ethically responsible business practices on the part of the company in which he has invested his capital.

How far economic civic commitment should in practice go in professional and private life is a decision for which, in a free society, a politically mature citizen is in principle himself personally responsible. As far as the observation of the legitimacy of personal actions involving moral obligations towards other affected persons plays no direct part, it is a matter of the demands individuals make on their own idealism in order to 'signalize' their sense of responsibility. Then we can probably speak with Kant less of 'unremitting' than of 'meritorious' obligations to show solidarity.[128] Although it is scarcely possible to prescribe the obligations of the individual citizen in this regard, it is at least appropriate to set up certain institutional 'halt signs' which will reduce the opportunities for ethically less acceptable tendencies to develop, and, vice versa, to create incentives which will strengthen the motivation to pursue ethically more acceptable tendencies. This leads us definitively away from questions of economic civic ethics to the issues of regulatory ethics.

[128] See Kant, 'Metaphysics of Morals', p. 75.

9 Regulatory ethics

> How can the modern industrialized economy be given an order which both functions *and* respects the dignity of man?[1]

Market economy, understood as the institutionalized form of complex economic activity based on the division of labour and competition, is always more than just the market mechanism. There is no such thing as *the* market economy, as a market order can by no means be specified in terms of market coordination alone. The justification of a certain order of the market economy consists in embedding the market in an overall conception, taking into account both the market and the non-market elements of well-coordinated socio-economic interactions in a society. The determination of such a conception, and in particular of the precise role which can be ascribed to the market as a partial coordination mechanism within it, is the task of institutional politics. The problem is obviously of a normative kind: as with every legitimate form of politics, *regulatory politics* must be oriented on justified normative principles. The clarification of the corresponding orientational problems is the task of regulatory *ethics*.[2] This provides the critical-normative reflection on foundations in regard to the ethical-rational justification of institutional politics. Institutional ethics would be pointless or at least hopeless, if the modern economy had the character of a totally autonomous, self-directed system emancipated from all control in the real lifeworld.[3] No direct

[1] W. Eucken, *Grundsätze der Wirtschaftspolitik*, 6th rev. edn, ed. E. Eucken and K. P. Hensel (Tübingen: Mohr Siebeck, 1990; 1st edn 1952), p. 14 (my italics).

[2] In the context of political economy the concept of order ethics (Ordnungsethik: translated here as regulatory ethics) is virtually unknown outside the German-speaking world and uncommon even among the founders of the ordoliberal conception, and where it has occurred to date there is scarcely any precise development of its ethical dimensions. But see R. Clapham, 'Zur Rolle der Ordnungsethik für das Konzept der sozialen Markwirtschaft', *Jahrbuch für Neue Politische Ökonomie* 8 (1989), pp. 30–41; Ph. Herder-Dorneich, 'Ordnungstheorie – Ordnungspolitik – Ordnungsethik', ibid., pp. 3–12.

[3] On the distinction between the (economic) system and the lifeworld see the earlier treatment in Section 4.2.

empirical statement is involved here; what is constitutive of the regulatory-ethical questions at issue is rather the following twofold premise:

- On the one hand, a modern, complexly organized economy essentially requires systemic elements of market coordination if it is to maintain its coordinative capacity and efficiency (functional premise).[4]
- On the other hand, if it is to serve life, an economic system must, in principle, be subordinated to the ethical and political integration of a well-ordered society; it can therefore only have the character of a societal subsystem (normative premise).

Without the functional premise there would be no particular ethical problem in regard to the economic order over and beyond the general regulatory problems of a well-ordered society. However, without the normative premise, the systemic 'self-containment' of an economic system evolving with a dynamics of its own would be immune to all political influence and deprived of all human meaning and value orientations; it would literally be beyond good and evil. The roles would then be reversed and the self-referential systems logic of the market and its unregulated dynamics would inevitably become the dominant regulatory principle for the whole of society. The 'market conformity'[5] of all actions, including those in the entire domain of institutional politics, would then in fact become the supreme norm (or the inherent necessity) governing society and would convert it into a total market society in which regulatory ethics would be impossible.[6]

There may actually be a real tendency towards a subordination of politics to the logic of the market. However, it is one matter to recognize this as a fundamental institutional-ethical *problem* and challenge and a completely different matter to elevate it to normative status and to see in its uncontrolled expansion the appropriate regulatory *solution*, as is happening at the moment under the neoliberal flag. For a societal shaping of the economy to be at all possible the fundamental normative orientation of regulatory ethics can only be towards asserting the indispensable *primacy of politics over the logic of the market*. This includes rather than excludes the attribution of a limited control and incentive function to the market mechanism in so far as it is purposeful and responsible in regard to the priority of the regulatory ethical point of view. But the specific extent to which the functional systems logic of the market can be 'unleashed'

4 For this reason institutional models which attempt to do without market coordination and instead transfer the pattern of a household economy (oikos) deriving from small life communities to the entire (national) economy, in the form of variants of a central administrative economy, are not taken into consideration in what follows.

5 We will take a closer look at the problems involved in the criterion of 'market conformity' towards the end of Section 9.1.

6 On the concept of the market society see Section 4.3 (3).

institutionally and the determination of the framework within which the market should 'rule' is, in a modern society, ultimately a matter of deliberative public debate among politically mature economic citizens, as we have seen in the previous chapter. Without the primacy of ethical politics over the logic of the market it would be impossible from the start to make the institutional embedding of the market economy in the principles of a well-ordered society of free and equal citizens a topic of the 'public use of reason'. How else could a market 'order which both functions and respects the dignity of man' (Eucken) be established and adapted to the changing social requirements and challenges with good reasons? In a free and democratic society it is the supreme and most noble task of regulatory politics to subject the latently 'self-centred' market processes to the fair and life-serving rules of a well-ordered civil society and in this way to 'civilize' them.[7] The ideal site of regulatory politics justified by institutional ethical principles of this kind is the unlimited public sphere in which all politically responsible state and economic citizens of republican conviction participate.[8]

In spite of the immense body of literature on institutional theory and politics, very few authors perceive the fundamental significance of such a politico-philosophical approach to the problem of order from the perspective of the lifeworld or grasp the central role played in this approach by the need for an ethically justifiable integration of the economic system in rational forms of the formation of the political and economic will.[9] Instead, the systematic orientation of the literature on the politico-economic order, particularly in the standard textbooks,[10] is still largely dominated by the old 'systems debate' involving the dualistic polarity between the systemic principles of a market economy vs. those of a

[7] For a characterization of the civil society see Section 7.3.

[8] Precisely speaking, therefore, the institutional framework as such is not the 'systematic site of morality' as Homann puts it (Homann/Blome-Drees, *Wirtschafts- und Unternehmensethik*, p. 35), but only the site of moral *implementation*. The ideal site of moral *justification* is the unrestricted public sphere of all mature citizens.

[9] Such an approach was already proposed in Ulrich, *Transformation*, p. 371ff., 'against the fiction of the reducibility of institutional politics to *mere* systems control' (p. 372). The focus of attention in this work was directed towards the relationship between the politico-economic communication order (democratic communication rights of all economic citizens) and the disposal order (rights of property and disposal).

[10] It is symptomatic of the contemporary trend that in a widely used German handbook of economics institutional politics is dealt with under the headword 'order economics' *(Ordnungsökonomik)*, a term (probably inspired by the new institutional economics) just as unusual in the earlier literature as the term 'order ethics'. See M. E. Streit, 'Ordnungsökonomik', in *Gabler Volkswirtschafts-Lexikon* (Wiesbaden: Gabler, 1990), pp. 814–43. In spite of the extensive treatment and the numerous individual references to normative questions, Streit's article scarcely takes into account the fundamental ethical problem behind his references and in this regard thus reproduces the weaknesses of the earlier handbooks.

centrally planned economy.[11] 'Mixed economic orders' were also regarded as possible, although the judgement on them generally was more or less prejudiced and lacking in reflection, depending on the ideological standpoint of the author concerned. As a result of the breakdown of the centrally planned economies in the (now defunct) real existing socialism and the increasing 'competition between regulatory frameworks', such 'third ways'[12] have often been regarded as completely impossible. Typological distinctions between alternative economic orders have seemed more or less pointless since only the one ('pure' or 'free') market economy has survived.[13] Resolute advocates of such a point of view even expressly discredit the aims and objectives of a social market economy (in the sense of the German model) as a dubious 'compromise formula'[14] or even as a 'magic formula' or an 'empty phrase'.[15] Under these circumstances the only valid economy is a 'market economy without adjectives' (Vaclav Klaus). Regulatory ethics is confronted here with an ideology-critical task of the greatest topicality, a matter on which the institutional economics of the old neoclassical type seems almost blind on account of its one-sided paradigmatic 'predecision' in favour of market solutions.

[11] For an exemplary, clear and systematic textbook presentation, which remains unsurpassed to this day, see H. G. Schachtschabel, *Wirtschaftspolitische Konzeptionen* (Stuttgart: Kohlhammer, 1967), p. 26ff. The regulatory-ethical systematics of Rich, *Business and Economic Ethics*, p. 435ff., also focuses on the systems debate, but it does so with an impressively comprehensive ethical-critical thoroughness and includes the consideration of 'third ways', founded on a clear terminological demarcation between 'basic system' and the (political) 'order' of an economy.

[12] The founders of ordoliberalism and the social market economy understood their conceptions to be a 'third way' between Manchester liberalism (laissez-faire, laissez-passer) and socialism. The concept was coined as early as the 1930s by Wilhelm Röpke, *Die Lehre von der Wirtschaft*, 13th edn (Berne *et al.*: Haupt, 1994; 1st edn 1937), p. 330. Later, however, Röpke found the concept misleading.

[13] One of the few economists writing on institutional theory who, after 1989, continued to regard various fundamentally different forms of the market economy order as feasible and sees the talk of *the one* market economy as problematic is K. G. Zinn, *Soziale Marktwirtschaft: Idee, Entwicklung und Politik der bundesdeutschen Wirtschaftsordnung* (Mannheim: Bibliographisches Institut, 1992), p. 16f. We now see more and more critics of the ideology of market economy as the surviving and 'only possible' economic order. See among others John Gray, *False Dawn: The Delusions of Global Capitalism* (London: Granta Books, 1998).

[14] See G. Schwarz, 'Die ordnungspolitische Verwahrlosung der Schweiz', *Neue Zürcher Zeitung*, N° 58, 10/11 March 1990, p. 25. A longer version with the same title has been published in G. Radnitzky/H. Bouillon (eds.), *Ordnungstheorie und Ordnungspolitik* (Berlin: Springer, 1991), pp. 221–38.

[15] So, for example, G. Radnitzky, 'Soziale oder freie Marktwirtschaft', *Neue Zürcher Zeitung*, N° 120, 26/27 May 1990, p. 93; Radnitzky, 'Marktwirtschaft: frei oder sozial?', in Radnitzky/Bouillon (eds.), *Ordnungstheorie und Ordnungspolitik*, pp. 47–75. The ideological charge of such academic (!) contributions is revealed in the simple *magic anti-formula* Radnitzky sweepingly opposes to the 'magic formula of the social market economy' he rejects: 'The free, private [sic!] market economy is in itself social.'

In what follows the basic regulatory problem sketched above will first be elaborated more precisely and the treatment of the paradigmatic positions of the contemporary political debate will then be critically examined (Section 9.1). As it will be shown that none of the existing positions meets the systematic requirements of an integrative regulatory ethics, the central ideas and the constitutive starting points for a comprehensive regulatory-ethical shaping of the institutional framework of a life-serving market economy which is 'vital' in every sense of the word will be systematized. The proposed basic conception is necessarily formal, i.e. it is restricted to an ideal ordering of the fundamental aspects. The specific determination of the contents of a 'correct' economic order will be understood and treated as a public concern of deliberative politics (Section 9.2). Finally, after having focused on the national level so far, the orientational ideas on regulatory ethics developed here will be confronted with what is probably the central challenge of our time, the increasing globalization of the economy with all its consequences for the lifeworld (Section 9.3).

9.1 The basic problem of regulatory ethics: market logic and 'vital policy'

As has been said, the initial systematic problem of regulatory ethics lies in the characteristic fundamental tension between the lifeworld aspects and the systemic aspects of every market economy order.

On the one hand it is necessary to clarify by political deliberation the preconditions for the acceptability of market coordination. What is at issue is the integration of the market forces in the ethical principles and rules of a well-ordered society. The guiding aspects are the legitimacy (deontological-ethical aspect) and meaningfulness of the market economy for human ends (teleological-ethical aspect). In both orientational dimensions of a life-serving development the market forces need 'instruction'. The 'visible hand' of the competitive incentives offered to or effected upon the economic agents by the market's framework (rather than the market's 'invisible hand' alone) should guide their actions and the overall economic development towards the desired regulatory political results. In this regard regulatory policy is '*vital policy*', as Alexander Rüstow, one of the pioneers of ordoliberalism, put it.[16] Consequently, a

[16] See A. Rüstow, 'Wirtschaftsethische Probleme der sozialen Marktwirtschaft', in P. M. Boarman (ed.), *Der Christ und die soziale Marktwirtschaft* (Stuttgart/Cologne: Kohlhammer, 1955), pp. 53–74, at p. 74: 'Vital policy' takes into consideration 'all the factors ... on which the happiness, well-being and contentment of man truly depend'.

market economy which is 'vital'[17] in this sense must always be understood instrumentally: what counts is the regulation of the market in order to ensure its human, social and ecological compatibility. Where market solutions as such do not 'promote a life worthy of a human being'[18] but obstruct it, a political limitation of the market is required, even if it goes hand in hand with a loss of efficiency and prosperity (for whom?) from a 'purely' economic point of view.

On the other hand, where the market should 'rule' in accordance with vital policy guidelines – and this should always be the case only within limits – it is necessary to create the institutional preconditions for workable competition. Its effectiveness must then be enforced against those economic agents who would prefer to seek protection against the strong winds blowing on the market by using their political or economic power to evade competition and to acquire free 'rents'[19] without any corresponding performance. They would then lead a more comfortable economic life at the expense of others – a tendency not alien to many entrepreneurs, as Adam Smith has already sharply observed:

> To widen the market and to narrow the competition is always the interest of the dealers. To widen the market may frequently be agreeable enough to the interest of the publick; but to narrow the competition must always be against it, and can serve only to enable the dealers, by raising their profits above what they naturally would be, to levy, for their own benefit, an absurd tax upon the rest of their fellow-citizens.[20]

We do not, of course, agree with Smith's sweeping thesis that a restriction of competition is always damaging to the public interest, as it ignores possible aspects of market limitation which are justifiable in terms of vital policy. His argument must to this extent, therefore, be regarded as economistic. Apart from this Smith recognizes in principle that maintaining an 'open' market, in as far as it is in 'the interest of the public', has to be understood as a political task. A superordinate set of rules is needed to guarantee the constitutive preconditions for a well-functioning market system and to protect competitive performance against attempts 'to narrow the competition'. In this regard regulatory policy is *competition*

[17] Röpke, *Lehre von der Wirtschaft*, p. 331, speaks of the 'morally vital question'.

[18] 'Vital is whatever promotes the "vita humana" and a life which is worthy of a human being.' See A. Rüstow, 'Paläoliberalismus, Kommunismus und Neoliberalismus', in F. Greiss/F. W. Meyer (eds.), *Wirtschaft, Gesellschaft und Kultur. Festgabe für Alfred Müller-Armack* (Berlin: Duncker & Humblot, 1961), pp. 61–70, at p. 68.

[19] A whole special domain of institutional economics has developed which deals with this problem; see J. M. Buchanan/R. D. Tollison/G. Tullock (eds.), *Toward a Theory of the Rent-Seeking Society* (College Station: Texas University Press, 1980).

[20] Smith, *Wealth of Nations*, p. 267.

policy. Its guiding principle in this case is not the restriction of the market in accordance with lifeworld criteria, but, on the contrary, the assertion of the market forces (open markets and workable competition) in order to ensure the efficacy of competition in accordance with the requirements of vital policy. In this impersonal manner the willingness of all economic agents to participate in performance-based competition can be encouraged.

This 'Janus face' of regulatory policy is constitutive for an understanding of the tensions arising between 'vital policy' and competition policy. Regulatory politics stands at the intersection between the (in principle prior) claim to embed the market in the lifeworld of a well-ordered society on the one hand (vital policy) and the claim to develop the (in principle subordinate) systemic logic of the market on the other (competition policy). The regulatory framework of the market must mediate between both claims. The answer to the question how precisely the relationship between these two basic regulatory tasks should be interpreted and the corresponding practical solution of the problem of mediation be found determines the characteristic paradigms of political economy as represented by various schools and their specific conceptions of a 'good' framework of the market.

In view of the often flowing transitions and the wide variety of possible standpoints it is not easy to order the various institutional conceptions systematically. The standard literature offers an unsatisfactory picture, as it largely reproduces the systematic presentations of the 1950s and 1960s. It is particularly symptomatic that in this tradition the thought patterns of neoliberalism and ordoliberalism are often given as one approach, or the latter is merely presented as a sub-variant of the former and is only seldom clearly distinguished from it.[21] This is legitimate in regard to the theoretical developments in the years immediately following the Second World War, as the ordoliberals initially described themselves as neoliberals. The reason why they increasingly characterized themselves from the 1960s on as ordoliberals can be found precisely in the mutation of their opponents, whom they formerly called old or paleoliberals, into 'neoliberals' of a very different kind, as Rüstow once expressly complained:

As the present day representatives of that paleoliberalism now unfortunately call themselves neoliberals, although our neoliberalism arose quite specifically in

[21] Earlier than most other theorists of institutional politics Reinhard Blum recognized the widening gap between an ordoliberalism which was in itself ambivalent and a neoliberalism which was 'relapsing' into pure economism. His careful treatment of the historical and intellectual development can be found in R. Blum, *Soziale Marktwirtschaft: Wirtschaftspolitik zwischen Neoliberalismus und Ordoliberalismus* (Tübingen: Mohr Siebeck, 1969), particularly pp. 100 and 116ff.

opposition and contradistinction to old liberalism, this all greatly serves, of course, to promote confusion.[22]

Since then a genuine paradigmatic dividing line has developed between ordoliberalism on the one hand and neoliberalism (in the recent sense of the word) on the other. With the rise of Reagonomics and Thatcherism in the 1980s in the Anglo-Saxon world and the beginning of the 1990s in continental Europe, the more recent variant of neoliberalism has established itself in real politics as the dominant paradigm. In spite of certain superficial similarities on essential points this turns out to be the precise opposite of the ordoliberal philosophy of order. It is therefore necessary to clearly distinguish the neoliberal conception in this contemporary sense from both the ordoliberal and the old or paleoliberal conception of the market economy order.

In what follows we will concentrate on the systematic task of working out the corresponding paradigmatic dividing lines as precisely as possible. The typology proposed rests upon two 'divisive' points of view which complement one another. The first is the instance of harmonization that guarantees the maintenance of 'good order' in the economic cosmos of the market; it is fundamental for the distinction between paleoliberalism and neoliberalism. The second is the central criterion for the shaping of the regulatory framework; it determines the dividing line between neoliberalism and ordoliberalism (Figure 9.1).

(1) Paleoliberalism

In old or paleoliberalism the good order of the market is guaranteed by a belief in harmony founded on metaphysics and natural law. To this extent it stands in the tradition of classical liberalism – but no longer in its time. The concept 'paleoliberalism' will be used here systematically only for pre- and post-classical *laissez-faire* thinking, above all in the 19th century and the early part of the 20th century up to the disillusioning experience of the Great Depression and the Keynesian turn in economic thinking. That it can, admittedly, still be found today in certain economic contexts is a fact we shall discuss shortly.[23]

Paleoliberals radically attribute to the market an inbuilt capacity for self-organization and the harmonization of interests, whereas every claim

[22] A. Rüstow, 'Wirtschaft als Dienerin der Menschlichkeit', in Aktionsgemeinschaft soziale Marktwirtschaft (ed.), *Was wichtiger ist als Wirtschaft* (Ludwigsburg: Hoch, 1960), pp. 7–16, at p. 7.

[23] On the accompanying revolutionary political developments see the account at the end of Section 5.1.

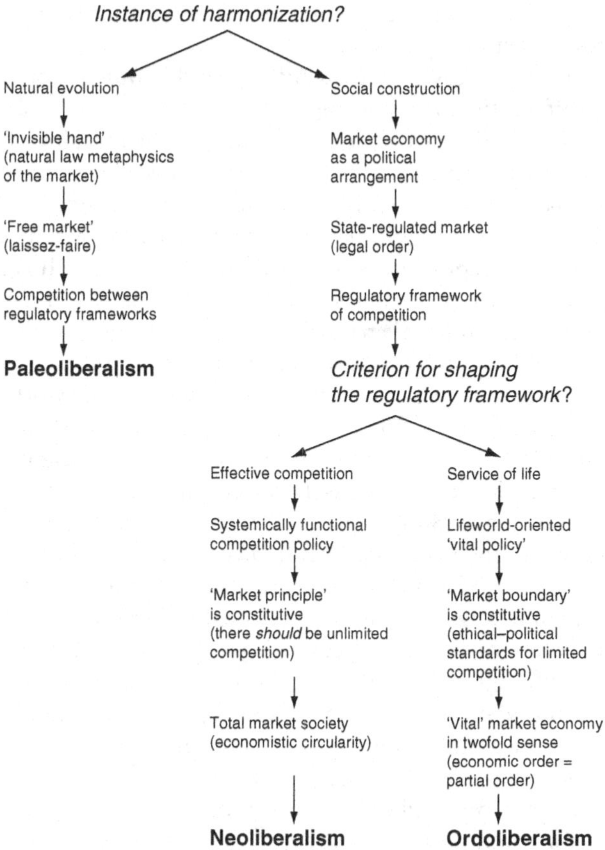

Figure 9.1. The systematic dividing lines between paleo-, neo- and ordoliberalism (ideal-typical conception)

to shape the economic and social order by political means is met with profound scepticism. They have a naturalistic understanding of the market economy, in which they have converted the metaphysical trust of classical theorists in a well-ordered economic cosmos of the market guided by 'the invisible hand' of God into a dogmatic form of 'pseudo-theological'[24] *market fundamentalism*. What is more, they have done so

[24] See O. von Nell-Breuning, 'Neoliberalismus und katholische Soziallehre', in Boarmann (ed.), *Der Christ und die soziale Marktwirtschaft*, pp. 107–22, at p. 114. The most thorough criticism of paleoliberalism comes from the ordoliberal Alexander Rüstow; see Rüstow, *Versagen des Wirtschaftsliberalismus*.

without being aware of or even having reflected at all upon the religious deep structures of such a position.

It is evidently necessary to defend Adam Smith's much more comprehensive and differentiated position against this kind of market fundamentalism. As a classical theorist Smith fully reflected the thinking of his time and also pointed beyond it into the future. Those who still advocate paleoliberal positions today are, in contrast, the representatives of anachronistic and outmoded thought patterns which deny the wholly different experiences and conceptual possibilities of modern society. It is true that in Smith's thinking the metaphysics of the market rooted in natural law played a fundamental role; it is true that he shared the optimistic deism of Scottish moral philosophy; it is true that he interpreted the driving force of liberal market dynamics as an expression of a teleological world process desired and designed by God.[25] But, as we have seen, Smith saw the market as an only partial substitute for the socio-moral integrative forces of a liberal society (which by themselves were too weak). Consequently, as a moral philosopher, Smith clearly distanced himself in almost every respect from a strictly economic-liberal *laissez-faire* position; this is particularly evident from his advocacy of the priority of justice, as we have already seen. On taking a closer look, we must rather recognize Smith as the founding father of ordoliberalism.[26] A good case can also be made for the view that although Smith does not elaborate on the integration of his deontological moral philosophy and his liberal political economy his work implies a political-philosophical conception which comes close to the central idea of republican liberalism developed in Chapter 8.[27]

Paleoliberals are more likely to be found among the pre-Smithian economists, for example the Physiocrats[28] with their emphasis on *ordre*

[25] For details see H.-D. Kittsteiner, 'Ethik und Teleologie: Das Problem der "unsichtbaren Hand" bei Adam Smith', in: F.-X. Kaufmann/H.-G. Krüsselberg (eds.), *Markt, Staat und Solidarität bei Adam Smith* (Frankfurt/New York: Campus, 1984), pp. 41–73; see also Patzen, 'Zur Diskussion des Adam-Smith-Problems', p. 47ff.

[26] Apart from the account in Section 2.2 and 5.1 see on this thesis Ulrich, 'Der kritische Adam Smith'.

[27] In the following sentence, for example, Adam Smith formulates the core of republican civic virtue: 'and he is certainly not a good citizen who does not wish to promote, by every means in his power, the welfare of the whole society of his fellow citizens.' See Smith, *Moral Sentiments*, p. 231. For the academic discussion on the republican aspect of Smith's thought see D. Brühlmeier, 'Adam Smith als politischer Denker im Kontext vom Liberalismus, Institutionalismus und Republikanismus', in Meyer-Faje/Ulrich (eds.), *Der andere Adam Smith*, pp. 277–302, especially p. 287ff. and *Adam Smith: Denker der Freiheit* (Sankt Augustin: Academia, 1992), p. 36ff. On republican liberalism see Section 8.1.

[28] See the illuminating account of the doctrinal history in A. Bürgin, *Zur Soziogenese der politischen Ökonomie: Wirtschaftsgeschichtliche und dogmenhistorische Betrachtungen* (Marburg: Metropolis, 1993), p. 327ff.

naturel in the economic cycle, or among the epigones of Smith who were less well versed in philosophy and the human sciences. On account of the antiquated nature of this school of thought there are virtually no strict paleoliberals left today, at least among economic experts. Distinctive paleoliberal elements can, however, still be discerned in the work of Friedrich A. von Hayek and his followers, particularly in their profound belief in the evolutionary self-organizing powers of the market and their corresponding scepticism in regard to any kind of 'rationalistic' claims of organization through society. They are the authors of the denunciation of all such approaches as 'constructivism'.[29]

Alienated from its religious deep structures and yet at the same time still imprisoned within it, paleoliberalism leads to symptomatic fallacies, of which only the most important will be pointed out here. Whereas for the classical protagonists of liberal political economy, above all Adam Smith, the 'prestabilized harmony' (Leibniz) created in the world by God was the self-evident *precondition* for the ethically good results of a functioning market, the paleoliberals exaggerated the status of the market mechanism. They saw it alone as the guarantee of (almost) all good in the world and misunderstood societal harmony quite simply as an automatic *consequence* of a deregulated 'free' market. The market itself thus became the highest instance in the (secularized) world, taking the place of the Creator.[30]

Even professional economists whose thinking otherwise tends to be more neoliberal are not always immune to paleoliberal 'relapses'. This is being demonstrated at present in a highly topical fashion in connection with the discussion on the globalization of the markets. A surprising number of economists welcome the menacing approach or, in some cases, the reality of a literally unrestricted global competition for the location of industry, even in its most radical form, as a desirable global competition between the regulatory frameworks. These economists of a new paleoliberal type, who have themselves evidently become addicted to the market's logic, encounter the growing call to embed uncontrolled global competition in equally global human, social and ecological standards at a supranational level with striking normative scepticism. What they in fact welcome is, in the final analysis, the end of the primacy of politics over the logic of the market – and hence the (temporary) victory of

[29] See Hayek, 'The Errors of Constructivism', p. 3ff.; on Hayek see also Section 5.1. We will refrain from a more detailed criticism of Hayek's economic philosophy here in view of its limited relevance for an enlightened (*political*-liberal) institutional ethics. We refer the reader instead to R. Kley, *Hayek's Social and Political Thought* (Oxford: Clarendon, 1994).

[30] See Büscher, 'Gott und Markt', p. 135f.

the markets over politics. The resultant 'systems Darwinism'[31] is not then felt to be a threat but is rather seen as a guaranteed way of compelling the national economies – against their supposed tendency towards 'fossilization' – to undertake a healthy 'fitness' course. They will then be in a position both to pursue their own particularist national interests and, guided by the invisible hand, nonetheless contribute to an increase in the diffuse well-being of the world to the benefit of all. We will come back to this point later.[32]

(2) *Neoliberalism*

From Hayek's point of view neoliberalism in the modern sense of the term must also be classified as 'constructivist'. Neoliberalism clearly regards the market economy, and particularly its competitive aspect, as a political arrangement and as a purposive and rational form of social organization which cannot establish or stabilize itself but must be regulated and implemented by the state. The state has the task of establishing the frame conditions of a well-functioning market economy. For neoliberalism it is precisely to this end, and only to this end, that the state is necessary and acceptable as an authoritative instance with power to regulate competition, whereas paleoliberalism believes it can manage without such an external instance. But apart from requiring the state to guarantee these preconditions, neoliberalism consistently demands that the state should not intervene in the market in specific situations; economic policy must be restricted as far as possible to a policy regulating the institutional framework in a general fashion.

Although ordoliberals would certainly agree that the state must fulfil the task of regulating the institutional framework, they would see the specific content of this task in a very different light. Ordoliberalism, which we will examine in more detail in (3), must be distinguished from neoliberalism in regard to the second typological aspect, namely the criterion for the shaping of a good regulatory framework. For the neoliberals the sole or at least the decisive criterion is the efficiency of the market in the sense of *effective competition*[33] that stimulates economic performance. To this extent regulatory policy is competition policy. In regard to the

[31] Herder-Dorneich, 'Ordnungstheorie', p. 9.

[32] We will deal specifically with the problems of globalization in regard to regulatory politics in Section 9.3.

[33] Advocates of the new institutional economics of the neoclassical type, whose basic axiomatic assumptions largely concur with the neoliberal conception of order, would speak of the criterion of *transaction cost minimization*. For an account and a critique of this criterion see Ulrich, *Transformation*, p. 247ff.

domestic market this is directed towards stabilizing competition and keeping it open by preventing cartel agreements, and in regard to the external markets it is aimed at maintaining or improving the competitive capacity of the national institutional frameworks at the international level – and virtually nothing more. The essential elements of the frame conditions are the legal preconditions regulating trade (primarily the guarantee of property rights, freedom of trade, liability and contract rights),[34] the fiscal conditions (taxes and duties) and the infrastructural preconditions necessary for an economic performance which is competitive in regard to quality and costs (availability of human capital and services, transportation networks and telecommunications). Beyond these factors the state may at best take a minimum of regulatory measures to stabilize general cyclical developments and to promote economic growth, to protect the natural environment and to guarantee the social security of all citizens. Even such regulations are, however, almost always encountered with profound scepticism and trust tends to be placed instead in the self-healing powers of the market. An instructive example is the problem of mass unemployment and the continuing optimistic view of the neoliberals that the best employment policy lies in undertaking no special measures beyond labour market deregulation and vocational training.

Furthermore, in almost exactly the same way as the paleoliberals, the neoliberals suspect that state activities are inefficient and regard them strictly through economic glasses; the republican aspect of the res publica is lost from sight. Accordingly neoliberals favour denationalization and privatization wherever they see them as efficient. They have less fear of private power than of state power. Their understanding of fundamental rights is privatistically restricted, following the Hobbesian tradition in emphasizing negative rights to freedom, particularly the unrestricted and inviolable right to the possession of private property. On the other hand, in the domain of the polity and even more of the economy, they usually

[34] For an exemplary position see A. Schüller, 'Die institutionellen Voraussetzungen einer marktwirtschaftlichen Ordnung', in R. Vaubel/H. D. Barbier (eds.), *Handbuch Marktwirtschaft* (Pfullingen: Neske, 1986), pp. 34–44. The conception of the fundamental preconditions for the market economy which must be guaranteed by the state runs along completely Hobbesian lines: 'The prevention of violence and deceit, the protection of property, the guarantee of contractual freedom, the enforcement of contracts and the rule of law' (p. 35). As property-rights claims he lists 'decision, acquisition, liability and transfer rights' (p. 36). Without any political-ethical justification of the legitimacy of his position he further states: '*Private property* is obviously an indispensable condition for an efficient market economy . . . The strength of property rights is decisive for the development and performative capacity of the (sic!) market-economic order' (p. 39). Yet there is no mention of the possible reasons for a limitation of 'property-rights claims' or of the communication and social rights of those affected by such claims.

judge an extension of the citizens' communication and participation rights sceptically, particularly in regard to workers' participation in economic decision-making, as this is suspected of being inefficient (for the owners of capital!). Social rights are decisively rejected.[35] For the same reasons 'vital policy' as characterized above is rejected as incompatible with a liberal order or generally regarded as irrelevant.

It is virtually pointless to assign the neoliberal conception of order sketched here to particular representatives of institutional order theory in the economic sciences, as it largely reflects the general convictions of contemporary mainstream economics. At the deep structure level there is a far-reaching congruency between the neoliberal world-view and neoclassical axiomatics in the sense of pure economics, and particularly the new institutional economics based on Pareto and contract theory. For this reason it is enough to refer back to the earlier treatment for a precise analysis.[36] The Nobel prize winner James Buchanan, whose constitutional economics is the basis for the work of most representatives of normative institutional economics, can therefore be regarded as the first pioneer of neoliberal institutional order theory.

The regulatory essence of neoliberal theory has been most clearly elaborated to date in writings which lie at the intersection between academic institutional order theory and real politics. A textbook example is provided by the 'regulatory political programme' published jointly by a group of Swiss top managers and professors of economics, which indeed provides a pointed and precise programmatic statement of neoliberal order theory:

> A consistent economic order policy requires the state to restrict itself to the shaping of an institutional framework and to avoid selective interventions in economic processes. This framework must guarantee a functioning price system and effective competition. The state must define private property rights and their limits in regard to other economic agents, guarantee freedom of contract, implement liability rules, create the preconditions for a stable currency and keep the markets open. A stable institutional framework leaves the individual the greatest possible, lastingly guaranteed freedom and this promotes personal initiative and self-responsibility.[37]

Let us briefly take a closer look at this programmatic neoliberal statement. The first sentence contains the fundamental credo against all kinds of

[35] On the systematics of fundamental rights see Section 7.1. [36] See Section 5.3.

[37] F. Leutwiler/S. Schmidheiny *et al.*, *Schweizerische Wirtschaftspolitik im internationalen Wettbewerb: Ein ordnungspolitisches Programm* (Zürich: Orell Füssli, 1991), p. 11. This programme is also the foundation on which the supplementary manifesto *Mut zum Aufbruch (Courage for a New Departure)*, ed. by Pury/Hauser/Schmid, is based.

state intervention in the 'free' market. The second sentence states that regulatory policy must be primarily or even exclusively competition policy and be guided solely by the logic of the market. The third sentence presents with almost unsurpassable clarity the Hobbesian understanding of the obligations of the state, on which the manifest possessive individualism is based,[38] supplemented by the corresponding interest in the maintenance of the value of money and open markets. Finally, the fourth and last sentence illuminates the correspondingly restricted economic-liberal understanding of freedom, which is usually expressed in the uninhibited talk of 'a free market economy' and is understood neither as socially constituted nor as a problem of justice.[39]

The decisive objection from the point of view of economic ethics concerns the circularity of the justification: the institutional framework which is supposed to legitimize the market is itself ultimately justified from the purely economic standpoint of the efficiency of that market. As early as 1955 *Oswald* v. *Nell-Breuning* raised the accurate objection against the neoliberal position:

> ... the standards economic politics ought to follow cannot be derived *from the economy itself.*[40]

But precisely this is typical of the neoliberal approach. It is characterized less by the criterion of the social and vital-political control of the dynamics of the market than by the control of all economic agents *through* the market. The state alone stands outside competition in as far as this is necessary so that it can pursue a vigorous competition policy designed to ensure that the market 'rules'. Basically, the central idea behind this conception of order is not the ordering (and limitation!) of competition in the service of life but the ordering of the entire society in accordance with the 'market principle' and thus the implementation of a total market society.

As has been said, this is expressed particularly by the fact that nowadays, in view of the globalization of the market, the neoliberals accord the highest economic and socio-political priority to the international competitiveness of the national economies. Some neoliberals, who at the

[38] See Section 5.3 (1) and (3).

[39] Hoppmann provides a good example of such a (purely negative) understanding of freedom; he describes 'a person as "free" if he is not subjected to the will of another, if nobody can force him to do or not to do something in a particular way'. E. Hoppmann, 'Freiheit, Ordnung und Moral', *Orientierungen zur Wirtschafts- und Gesellschaftspolitik* 51 (1992), pp. 53–9, at p. 55. Cf., meanwhile, the understanding of freedom in the political liberalism of Rawls in Section 7.2.

[40] Nell-Breuning, 'Neoliberalismus', p. 119.

national level are clear advocates of regulatory policies to enforce competition and to ensure the openness of the market, evidently find it difficult to recognize precisely the consequences of their own conception of institutional politics at the supranational level; instead they surprisingly often and uncritically share the paleoliberal hope that a global 'competition between the regulatory frameworks' will have beneficial effects. Here, in view of the epochal challenge to regulatory politics resulting from globalization, an underlying closeness of neoliberalism to paleoliberalism manifests itself, which has its roots partly in shared ideological deep structures. The superficial primacy of politics over the inherent logic of the market, be it in regard to the general understanding of democratic politics[41] or to the specific conception of regulatory policy, is ultimately sacrificed to the primacy of the market. In view of this economistic understanding of institutional politics it is self-evident that the regulation of the market is only compatible with 'proper economic order policy' (as is sometimes said in neoliberal circles) in as far as it 'facilitates or improves the capacity [of the market] to function effectively'.[42] What is desirable above all else from this perspective is, a priori, the deregulation of all restrictions on the market competition, without the need for any particular justification, as the question of legitimation gets lost in the fog of diffuse efficiency categories such as 'the public interest'.[43] In their zeal for deregulation the neoliberals are then ultimately led to pin their hopes more or less on the metaphysical promise of salvation of the *ordre naturel*. For the vital-political task of shaping and guiding the market there is then neither room nor need.

(3) Ordoliberalism and the social market economy

The ordoliberal approach is, at least in principle, very different. Although the ordoliberals – and particularly Walter Eucken and Franz Böhm – approved of strict competition policy long before the neoliberals of modern stamp, in contrast to the latter they believed that the criterion for the shaping of the regulatory framework must be found in the usefulness of the market for non-economic ends. As Wilhelm Röpke, together with

[41] The primacy of the contractarian logic of market exchange in the economic theory of democracy was demonstrated in Section 5.3 (3), using Buchanan's constitutional economics as a central example.

[42] See, for example, H.-J. Ewers/T. Wein, 'Grundsätze für eine Deregulierungspolitik', *Wirtschaftsdienst* 70 (1990), pp. 320–8, at p. 321.

[43] For a criticism of this category mistake see Section 5.2.

Rüstow the main advocate of an ordoliberalism oriented on vital policy, emphasizes:

In other words, the market economy is not everything. It must find its place within a higher order of things which is not ruled by supply and demand, free prices and competition.[44]

The economy has to be placed in the service of 'values beyond the economy', in 'the service of human dignity'; this is 'the true purpose of the economy'.[45] The implicit or explicit core idea is, therefore, a market economy in the service of life. As probably the most consistent advocate of the primacy of the service of life 'beyond economics' Rüstow even formulates the following acid test:

We must be ready and would be ready to speak out in favour of an economic system which is worthy of being preferred for reasons beyond economics even if it were less productive than other systems. We would and must then be ready to accept economic sacrifices as the price.[46]

In the same sense Röpke expressly rejects 'economism' as 'an incorrigible mania of making the means the end'.[47] All ordoliberals have a clearly instrumental understanding of the market economy as a partial order which must be embedded in a more comprehensive overall societal order. The latter must, furthermore, provide it with ethical-political guidelines. The ordoliberals agree with Eucken in assuming the 'interdependence of the orders'.[48] At the centre of these manifold social partial orders stands the 'vital order' as the orientational core:[49]

The economy is the means, the vital situation the end.[50]

Vital policy thus possesses constitutive[51] significance for the everyday practical alignment of the market dynamics in the sense that competition in the market economy should be permitted or implemented only as a means of social coordination or as an incentive for economic performance where it serves the purposes of vital policy. In other words, vital policy

44 Röpke, *Humane Economy*, p. 6.
45 Rüstow, 'Wirtschaft als Dienerin der Menschlichkeit', p. 8. 46 Ibid., p. 9.
47 Röpke, *Humane Economy*, p. 107.
48 See Eucken, *Grundsätze der Wirtschaftspolitik*, p. 180ff.
49 The concept of vital order is adapted from Rüstow's vital policy and used by H.-G. Krüsselberg, 'Soziale Marktwirtschaft: Idee und Wirklichkeit', *Orientierungen zur Wirtschafts- und Gesellschaftspolitik* 41 (1989), pp. 56–64, at p. 59.
50 H. G. Krüsselberg, 'Ordnungstheorie – Zur Konstituiersung und Begründung der Rahmenbedingungen', in Biervert/Held (eds.), *Ethische Grundlagen der ökonomischen Theorie*, pp. 100–33, at p. 112, following several other formulations by Rüstow.
51 This must be distinguished from Eucken's (*Grundsätze*, p. 254ff.) 'constituting principles' of the competitive order, which have only a *functional* significance for the superordinate vital-political ends.

determines the *normative* preconditions which, in contrast to competition policy, do not merely guarantee the *functional* conditions for effective competition, but correspond to 'the way in which certain professions, above all the medical, submit to strict rules of competition to the point of including them among the standards of professional behavior', i.e. in the example 'the medical profession's *deontology*'.[52] What is quite clearly at issue is 'that we do *not allow* competition to become the dominating principle'.[53] Röpke leaves no doubt as to the justification:

> It cannot be denied that the market places the constant competitive struggle for self-assertion and self-advancement in the center of the stage. Nor can it be denied that such all-pervasive competition has a disturbing tendency to lead to consequences to which we cannot remain indifferent, especially from the moral point of view.[54]

The practical consequence is 'to *delimit* and moderate ... competition and market economy'.[55] Rüstow took up exactly the same position as early as the beginning of the 1930's when he introduced the concept of the boundary of the market, untiringly emphasizing:

> that the boundary of the market, the market framework, is the true human domain and is a hundred times more important than the market itself. The market itself has only a serving function. ... The market is a means to an end and not an end in itself, whereas the boundary of the market comprises many things which are an end in themselves and possess a human value of their own.[56]

It is the non-delegable task of state policy to guarantee life-serving preconditions befitting human dignity – among other things 'just starting conditions' and 'a distribution of opportunities that is as fair as possible'[57] – and, where necessary, to set *limits* to market coordination. For this reason ordoliberals understand 'the market economy as a state activity'[58] which can and must be shaped by socio-political regulation. To this extent it is, together with competition, a 'constitutional institution',[59] and this means that it must be ordered legally and subjected to the same constitutional principles as all other institutions of the state. The market economy must

52 Röpke, *Humane Economy*, p. 127 (my italics). 53 Ibid., p. 129 (my italics).
54 Ibid., p. 127.
55 This is the literal translation from the German original of Röpke, *Jenseits von Angebot und Nachfrage*, p. 174. In the Engl. edn *Humane Economy*, p. 129, there can be found the postulate 'of stressing the need to circumscribe and moderate it [i.e. the market economy] and of showing once more its dependence upon moral reserves'.
56 Rüstow, 'Paläoliberalismus, Kommunismus und Neoliberalismus', p. 68.
57 Rüstow, 'Wirtschaftsethische Probleme der sozialen Marktwirtschaft', p. 68.
58 L. Miksch, *Wettbewerb als Aufgabe: Grundsätze einer Wettbewerbsordnung*, 2nd edn (Godesberg: Küpper, 1947), p. 12.
59 F. Böhm, *Freiheit und Ordnung in der Marktwirtschaft* (Baden-Baden: Nomos, 1980), p. 257.

be understood as a legal order down to the core of the competition order:[60]

The sole ambition of the competition order is to guarantee the best possible satisfaction of *permissible* needs.[61]

It is the task of the superordinate legal and social order to determine what is allowed in a free society or what legitimate needs are. The competition order must only guarantee constitutionality internally 'by ensuring that price formation is free of arbitrary influences or the interference of those in positions of power'.[62] To prevent concentration of private economic power is therefore a top priority of competition policy for the ordoliberals, too. As Böhm puts it, their aim must be to ensure 'that competing economic agents have *no power* over the market',[63] and this makes a strong and neutral state necessary.[64] Only such a state can achieve what is needed to ensure legitimate and fair competition:

A state that wants to protect its competition order from ruin therefore must already combat the rise, not just the misuse of economic power.[65]

For:

as soon as economic power arrives on the scene the legal order runs into great difficulties, no matter how excellent it is.[66]

For this reason Eucken formulates the first political principle of economic politics as follows:

The politics of the state should be directed towards dissolving economic power groups or limiting their functions. Every consolidation of power groups strengthens the neo-feudal diminution of the state's authority.[67]

It is true that the neoliberals also see the need to keep competition power-free as the central task of competition policy. But in the context of the power question the ordoliberals alone also clearly oppose the instrumentalization of the state for private economic purposes, thus clearly distancing themselves, on the one hand, from the economistic understanding of

[60] See ibid., p. 70, and Eucken, *Grundsätze*, pp. 52, 307. For this reason it is justified to include 'the principle of a state-constituted economy' among the principles of a modern constitutional state. See Ph. Mastronardi, *Strukturprinzipien der Bundesverfassung? Fragen zum Verhältnis von Recht und Macht anhand des Wirtschaftsstaatsprinzips* (Basel: Helbing & Lichtenhahn, 1988).

[61] Böhm, *Freiheit und Ordnung*, p. 70 (my italics). [62] See ibid., p. 69.

[63] Ibid., p. 71 (my italics).

[64] See Rüstow, 'Wirtschaftsethische Probleme der sozialen Marktwirtschaft', p. 63.

[65] Böhm, *Freiheit und Ordnung*, p. 74. [66] Ibid., p. 72.

[67] Eucken, *Grundsätze*, p. 234.

politics as the continuation of business with other means and, on the other hand, revealing remarkable parallels to the understanding of the state and politics in the political liberalism of Rawls. Röpke makes it quite clear:

Whoever still tries to understand liberalism as a primarily economic conception is captured in an 'economistic' narrow-mindedness evidently obsolete today. (...) *Political and cultural liberalism* ... is primary, economic liberalism secondary.[68]

Up to now we have emphasized the basic vital-political orientation of the ordoliberals in their best contributions to the topic. So far, so good. The crux of ordoliberalism, however, lies in the fact that its advocates fail to sustain the primacy of vital policy over competition policy. Eucken, Böhm and others who are primarily interested in the competition order simply place the two regulatory domains *alongside* one another or do not touch upon the relationship between them at all. Eucken characterizes the competition order as 'the one side' and 'a desire for social and ethical order' as 'the other side' and speaks only vaguely of the connection between the two.[69] From the point of view of regulatory ethics such indeterminacy leads to ambivalence at the decisive point. Although, as we have shown, a consistent ordoliberal standpoint focuses on a fair and life-serving ordering *of* competition, Böhm, for example, is so enthusiastically in favour of competition that he at times regresses to the neoliberal conception of order *through* competition, as when he sweepingly celebrates competition as 'the greatest and most ingenious instrument of disempowerment in history'[70] – a formulation which is particularly popular among neoliberals. Yet competition can only – if at all – play this historical part if it is effectively permeated by the principles of the well-ordered society, but not when it rules the whole of society, thus converting it into a total market society. For this very reason, according to the ordoliberal conception, properly understood, the market must be subordinated to vital-political principles. Its rule can, therefore, only be conditional and restricted.

Böhm's much quoted formulation cannot be easily harmonized with his fundamental postulates on the role of power in society and the market.

[68] W. Röpke, *Civitas Humana: A Humane Order of Society* (London: William Hodge, 1948); cit. German edition *Civitas Humana: Grundfragen der Gesellschafts- und Wirtschaftsreform* (Erlenbach-Zurich: Rentsch, 1944), p. 51 (italics orig.). On the neoliberal understanding of politics see Section 5.3 (3); on political liberalism Section 7.2. and 8.1.

[69] See Eucken, *Grundsätze*, p. 370.

[70] F. Böhm, 'Demokratie und ökonomische Macht', in Institut für ausländisches und internationales Wirtschaftsrecht (ed.), *Kartelle und Monopole im modernen Recht* (Karlsruhe, 1961), vol. I, pp. 3–24, at p. 22.

That we are not, however, simply dealing with a careless use of language is unfortunately confirmed by what can be called the *vital-political sin* of the ordoliberals, their failure to clearly rank secondary the criterion of *market conformity* after vital-political criteria, which we can succinctly describe as 'vital conformity'. The criterion of market conformity, which stems from Röpke, declares that the interventions of the state in the market should happen in such a way:

> that they do not do away with the price mechanism and the resultant self-organization of the market, but take their place as new 'data' within the mechanism and are assimilated by it.[71]

The criterion of market conformity was not in fact regarded by the ordoliberals as a primary norm but only as a secondary condition in competition policy alongside the more comprehensive criterion of conformity with the institutional order. They have, however, failed to clarify the ambiguity of the criterion of market conformity precisely, and this has opened the door to a tendency to regress to a neoclassical, neoliberal view of the market. Market conformity can, namely, mean two different things:

- *Market conformity from a consistently vital political point of view.* The good intention of the ordoliberals consisted at first in the desire – which is essential for 'thinking in terms of orders' (Eucken) – to avoid unsystematic or even erratic state interventions. These only tackle economic political problems ad hoc and mostly with individual measures designed to correct symptoms after the fact, thus weakening the 'vital' (in a twofold sense) controlling effect of the price signals of the market. Instead the signalling and controlling function of market prices should be used for vital-political ends wherever possible and be reinforced within this framework by general incentives and monitoring procedures which operate indirectly. In this sense, for example, the taxes designed to influence the use of energy and to reduce pollution utilize the controlling function of the market in an ecologically beneficial way ('market-based environmental policy'). Understood in this way, an economic policy which is in conformity with the market can stand in the service of vital policy and quite simply embodies the functional premises formulated at the beginning of this chapter, but it does not possess an inherent normative value.
- *Market conformity from a neoclassical, neoliberal point of view.* If we read the criterion of market conformity through the glasses of

[71] Röpke, *Gesellschaftskrisis der Gegenwart*, p. 259. Along the same lines Eucken, *Grundsätze*, p. 254, calls the 'establishment of a well-functioning price system based on total competition' the fundamental principle of the competition order.

neoclassical theory, it takes on a much more restricted meaning. According to the economic maximum theorem the 'natural' (i.e. power related) equilibrium price is after all the guarantee of 'the most efficient' allocation of scarce resources.[72] This means that general political control measures which are market-conform in the sense discussed above but nevertheless change the 'natural' results of distribution, in particular the social distribution of work, income and property, by definition reduce the efficiency of the market. From the point of view of equilibrium theory regulatory measures with (re)distributional effects therefore 'distort' the 'optimal' allocation of goods and resources by the market and hence its supposedly impartial efficiency. If, in accordance with the economistic tradition, market efficiency is now regarded as the decisive embodiment of the way to serve the public interest, the efficiency function of the market is then no longer compatible with its vital-political control function (which is of course irrelevant from a neoliberal point of view).[73] All that is apparently permissible now is the implementation of economic-political measures which help to stabilize the 'equilibrium' of the market in a distributionally 'neutral' manner (the so-called neoclassical synthesis of market liberalism and Keynesian stability politics). On the other hand the criterion of market conformity excludes all regulatory measures with distributional effects and hence any regulated form of structural change.

This second, radical interpretation of the criterion of market conformity – or system conformity[74] – destroys the foundations of the ordoliberal conception: the primacy of vital policy and the corresponding instrumental view of the market as a mechanism which can and must be regulated in

[72] See the account in Section 5.2. On the following neoclassical version of the criterion of market conformity see also Katterle, *Alternativen zur neoliberalen Wende*, pp. 32ff., 68ff.

[73] For this reason the radical neoclassical theorists of the market, first Ludwig von Mises, then F. A. von Hayek and Milton Friedman, have asserted the strict incompatibility of all control measures with the 'optimal' allocation of goods through the free market and have preached for a return to the laissez-faire principle. See L. von Mises, *Liberalism: In the Classical Tradition* (New York: Irvington, 1985; 1st German edn Jena, 1927; reprinted St Augustin 1993); von Mises, *A Critique of Interventionism* (New York: Crown, 1977; 1st German edn Jena 1929).

[74] The extension of the criterion of market conformity to *system conformity*, which was already proposed in 1955 by Thalheim, does as little to change the situation as the (more sensible) concept of *conformity to the institutional order*, as long as ordering *through* competition is conceived, in neoclassical fashion, as the constitutive principle of the market, the system or the order. Thalheim did at least propose a relativizing distinction between various *degrees* of conformity and regards a limited acceptance of regulatory measures which 'are inadequate for the system but do not destroy it' as possible. See K. C. Thalheim, 'Zum Problem der Einheitlichkeit der Wirtschaftspolitik', in K. Muhs (ed.), *Festgabe für Georg Jahn* (Berlin: Duncker & Humblot, 1955), pp. 557–87, particularly p. 586f.

the service of vital politics. The primacy of vital policy is now made 'impossible', as the principle of market conformity re-establishes the economistic idea of inherent necessity. It is presumably not by chance, for example, that Eucken states, in a form which could be regarded as a definition of the neoliberal position, that:

> the competition order should not only recognize but actively promote the *inherent laws* which are expressed in the economic process.[75]

A detailed study of the writings of the ordoliberals reveals numerous proofs that they have all too often failed to avoid a 'regress'[76] to the old neoclassical thinking at this critical point. (This also helps us to understand why, in the German-speaking countries, radical neoliberalism of the contemporary type has developed out of an inconsistent ordoliberalism and not the other way round!) An exemplary false conclusion by Eucken will serve to explain the seemingly slight difference and its far-reaching consequences. At the beginning of a chapter on 'The Politics of Ordering the Economy as Social Politics' he writes:

> The creation of a well-functioning system for the regulation of an economy based on the division of labour is . . . the most important precondition for the solution of all (sic!) social problems.[77]

A few pages further on he reinforces the point:

> We should attempt to establish *social justice* by creating a well-functioning overall order and particularly by subjecting the acquisition of income to the strict rules of competition, risk and liability.[78]

This is a relapse to the old market-liberal tradition: social justice is considered to be an almost automatic *consequence of* control through the market (which must at first be established politically but is nonetheless strictly oriented on the achievement of efficiency) instead of being appreciated as a necessary vital-political *prerequisite for* truly life-serving market competition. In a functioning market no ethical problems seem to arise, not even in the market for 'the acquisition of income' (i.e. the employment market) – ordoliberals and neoliberals apparently agree on this point, although they at the same time fail to see all the internal (power-based) effects of the market.[79] The logical consequence is that

[75] Eucken, *Grundsätze*, p. 369 (my italics). For the background and a critique of the idea of inherent necessity see Chapter 4.
[76] See Blum, *Soziale Marktwirtschaft*, p. 100, who also provides a historical treatment.
[77] Eucken, *Grundsätze*, p. 314. [78] Ibid., p. 317 (my italics).
[79] On the market-internal effects, which are highly relevant from an economic-ethical standpoint (as a consequence of the status quo problem), see Sections 5.3 (2) and (3).

not even compromises between 'optimal' market efficiency and ethical-practical viewpoints are required for socio-political ends. As a result the priorities set by the ordoliberals in the relationship between vital policy and the inherent necessities of the market are overthrown and the neoliberal primacy of the market is asserted. And as this reversal of positions remains unchallenged, the noble professions of theorists such as Rüstow and Röpke only pay lip service to the priority of vital policy; they are more or less ornamental accessories which can be reserved for the soapbox. Oswald von Nell-Breuning reminds the ordoliberals in vain of their own starting point:

> In our opinion the statement that a good economic policy is the best social policy turns the facts upside down. We must put it the right way round: whether an economic policy is good or bad depends on the degree to which it contributes, by ethical and cultural standards, to a satisfactory and positive *shaping* of social life.[80]

Anyone who takes the ordoliberal priority of the vital-political point of view seriously (assuming that we can continue to use the term ordoliberal at all in view of the relapse to a neoliberal position) can only draw the conclusion that (in the neoclassical sense of the term) '*even interventions which are not in conformity with the market must be regarded as possible instruments of a responsible economic politics*', as the theologian and philosopher of economic and social ethics Egon E. Nawroth has pointed out to the neoliberals.[81] To determine the superordinate criteria for these interventions and to make use of the price signals of the market (market conformity in the non-classical sense) without violating the principle of 'vital conformity' is precisely the central task of a vital-political conception of order. What ultimately counts in a market economy in the service of life is the conformity of all the economic measures with the overall vital-political order.[82]

The vital-political sin of the ordoliberals at a point so important for politico-economic practice receives further impetus from Alfred Müller-Armack's conception of the *Soziale Marktwirtschaft*, which he himself

[80] Nell-Breuning, 'Neoliberalismus', p. 118 (italics in the original text).

[81] See E. Nawroth, *Die wirtschaftspolitischen Ordnungsvorstellungen des Neoliberalismus* (Cologne: Heymanns, 1962), p. 23 (italics in the original text); see also Nawroth, *Die Sozial- und Wirtschaftsphilosophie des Neoliberalismus* (Heidelberg: Kerle, 1961). Similarly, and with specific reference to Nawroth, Blum, *Soziale Marktwirtschaft*, p. 82f.

[82] This view is already adopted in G. Weisser, 'Für oder gegen Marktwirtschaft – eine falsche Frage', reprinted in Weisser, *Beiträge zur Gesellschaftspolitik* (Göttingen: Schwartz, 1978), pp. 654–72, at p. 659f. Similarly, and with special emphasis on the need to include the social order, H. Lampert, '"Denken in Ordnungen" als ungelöste Aufgabe', *Jahrbuch für Nationalökonomie und Statistik* 206 (1989), pp. 446–56.

characterizes as an 'irenic formula'[83] and an open 'economic style'.[84] Originally presented in 1946, it was at first strongly influenced by the ideas of the ordoliberals but remained vague, ambivalent and even contradictory at decisive points, thereby strengthening the tendency to regress to neoclassical economic liberalism.[85] In his response to Nawroth's criticism, Müller-Armack speaks out decidedly against 'a neoliberalism which sees the mechanism of competition as the exclusive principle for shaping the market'[86] and characterizes the social market economy as 'a constructively [!] conceived third way'.[87] He occasionally refers expressly to Röpke's and Rüstow's primacy of vital policy,[88] particularly in regard to what he, in 1959, termed the 'second phase' of the social market economy with its primarily socio-political tasks. On the other hand, he also expressly emphasizes the importance of the 'principle of market conformity' (understood in the narrow sense) for social politics:

> In its economic policy the state undertakes social restructuring and social interventions. The fundamental idea is to adapt these interventions to the market system in such a way that they are subjected to the principle of *market conformity*. This means that in spite of the interventions of state economic policy the functioning of the market... is not disturbed (sic!) and, if possible, is even improved.[89]

With all due respect for Müller-Armack's contributions to German economic policy in regard to the social market economy, it must nevertheless be said that from a systematic point of view his position ultimately differs from that of the neoliberals only on account of its more 'pragmatic' and less dogmatic basic stance:

> Experience has shown that the market economy can tolerate a fair degree of measures which are not in conformity with the market without damaging its essential nature.[90]

[83] See A. Müller-Armack, *Genealogie der Sozialen Marktwirtschaft: Frühschriften und weiterführende Konzepte* (Berne *et al.*: Haupt, 1974), pp. 150 and 225.
[84] Ibid., p. 120.
[85] Both Blum, *Soziale Marktwirtschaft*, p. 90ff., and Katterle, *Alternativen zur neoliberalen Wende*, p. 32ff., come to this conclusion. Blum places the conception of the social market economy *between* ordoliberalism and neoliberalism and finally sees it more in the latter category: 'Seen from the perspective of ordoliberalism ... the social market economy is a form of "revisionism" which suggests that it should be characterized as neoliberal but not as ordoliberal.' Blum, ibid., p. 121f.
[86] Müller-Armack, *Genealogie*, p. 148. Along the same lines he emphasizes elsewhere that the social market economy 'has absolutely nothing to do with the previous forms of pure liberalism' (ibid., p. 203f.).
[87] Ibid., p. 161, obviously in critical allusion to Hayek. Some pages later (p. 168), however, he acclaims Hayek's very different 'constitution of liberty'.
[88] See ibid., pp. 128, 138. [89] Ibid., p. 120f. (italics in the original text).
[90] Ibid., p. 123.

These 'measures which are not in conformity with the market', in particular the (post factum) *corrections* in the distribution of income and other social policies which go even further, are ultimately only 'supplements'[91] to the competition order resulting from compromise – instead of being preconditions which constitute the vital-political order. It is of course a fact that in Germany and other countries this corrective task has been shouldered politically by the Social Democrats, whereas Müller-Armack unhesitatingly asserts 'that economico-political decisions . . . are primarily questions of economic rationality'.[92] This comes very close to an advocacy of the circular economistic arguments legitimating the market system which are characteristic of the neoliberal conception.

We can also surmise that both the fiction of the public good deriving from the utilitarian principle and the social-democratic programme for the correction of the outcomes of the market economy lie behind Ludwig Erhard's programmatic formula 'prosperity for all'.[93] But basically Erhard followed the tradition of Adam Smith in understanding social justice and, in particular, full employment as *preconditions* for legitimate economic freedom. Accordingly, Horst Friedrich Wünsche, the last expert member of the Ludwig Erhard Stiftung (Bonn) to be appointed personally by Erhard, refutes the dominant political opinion of the day that economic efficiency and social justice can only be kept in balance by compromise, and he calls this 'a fundamental weakness of contemporary institutional policy'.[94]

It is a short step from such a 'weak' regulatory idea of mediation between vital policy and competition to the discrediting of the social market economy as a *dubious* compromise.[95] Some economists of repute who regard themselves as standing in the tradition of ordoliberalism or the social market economy, such as Egon Tuchfeldt, bluntly fought against the growing call in the 1970s for an active state policy in favour of the distribution of employment. They took up F. A. von Hayek's

[91] See, for example, ibid., p. 132; for a criticism see also Katterle, *Alternativen*, p. 40.

[92] Müller-Armack, ibid., p. 204.

[93] It is not difficult to find in Erhard's work *Wohlstand für alle* (p. 226ff., for example) statements in which a belief in the harmonious effects of economic growth is clearly recognizable.

[94] See H. F. Wünsche, 'Die immanente Sozialorientierung in Adam Smiths Ordnungsdenken – ein Paradigma für die Soziale Marktwirtschaft', in Meyer-Faje/Ulrich (eds.), *Der andere Adam Smith*, pp. 249–74, at p. 257f. See also Meyer-Faje/Ulrich, 'Verlorene Massstäbe in der Ordnungspolitik', *Hamburger Jahrbuch für Wirtschafts- und Gesellschaftspolitik* 35 (1990), pp. 53–74. In recent years the Ludwig Erhard Stiftung has failed, however, to come out clearly against the neoliberal undermining of the social market economy, although this would be an important step.

[95] See the position of G. Schwarz and G. Radnitzky mentioned at the beginning of Chapter 9.

argument that such a policy lacks market conformity and therefore amounts to 'rationalist constructivism'.[96] Of the original *integrative* core idea of a vital-political constitution of the market, as conceived by Rüstow and Röpke, only a pale reflection remains, which at best corresponds to the basic position of a *corrective* economic ethics.[97]

There is, moreover, a further, perhaps more serious deficit which the ordoliberals and the founders of the social market economy share with the old and the neoliberals, on which they have never really reflected: the systematically inadequate and antiquated political-philosophical foundation of their conception of institutional politics. We devote our attention to this deeper-lying issue in what follows.

9.2 Deliberative order politics: the market framework as a site of morality – whose morality?

Some people seem to think that the principal function of economics is to prepare the domination of society by 'specialists' in economics, statistics, and planning, that is, a situation which I propose to describe as *economocracy* – a horrible word for a horrible thing.[98]

Judgement on the market conformity or inconformity of proposed reforms of the institutional framework is a matter for the experts on the inherent logic of the market: the economists. Regulatory policies, or at least its core, then seem to be an issue of purely economic institutional theory or 'institutional economics'. Taking the usual scientistic self-understanding of mainstream economics as a 'value-free' science, the experts suppose that the practical significance of an economic theory of institutional politics lies in making an analytical contribution to the task of putting economic politics on a scientific footing. This is to be done on the basis of a 'purely' economic logic without any consideration of modern political philosophy. Paradoxically, the implicit normative ideal of such a superficially value-free 'rationalization' of politics is precisely the *end of politics*: fundamental ethical-political questions of a well-ordered

96 See E. Tuchfeldt, 'Soziale Marktsteuerung und Globalsteuerung', in Tuchfeldt (ed.), *Soziale Marktwirtschaft im Wandel* (Freiburg i.B.: Rombach, 1973), pp. 159–88, at p. 182ff.; Tuchfeldt objects expressly to the 'false image of man' according to which participants in the economy would act as 'politically mature citizens' out of a 'positive attitude towards the public good'!

97 See Section 3.1. The fact that the ordoliberal conception of Eucken must be seen as a corrective rather than an integrative approach to economic ethics is noted by H. G. Nutzinger, 'Unternehmensethik zwischen ökonomischem Imperialismus und diskursiver Überforderung', in Forum für Philosophie Bad Homburg (ed.), *Markt und Moral*, pp. 181–214, at p. 194f.

98 Röpke, *Humane Economy*, p. 149.

society and market economy are reduced to the quest of the experts for *systemic control* of the economic system in terms of purely functional rationality. Those who are not experts have little to contribute and should kindly leave the matter to the professionals in the field, as the amateurs could disturb the functional rationality of the system only by making 'unobjective' political claims upon it. In this technocratic model of rational economic politics even the politicians are left only with the task of implementing what the system experts regard as objective. All power to the economic expertise! is the 'economocratic' motto (Röpke).[99]

Such a reduced understanding of scientifically rationalized politics willingly or unwillingly leads to the depoliticization of politico-economic regulatory questions instead of seeing them as a matter of deliberative politics in accordance with the ideal of the public use of reason by mature economic citizens and subjecting them unconditionally to debate. This depoliticization corresponds to an academic disregard for the normative deep structure of the 'objectively' valid economic logic inherent in the market and for the societal power relations which it uncritically reflects.[100] Those who make regulatory proposals which do not correspond entirely to this inherent logic are usually accused immediately by the 'professionals' of misunderstanding how 'the' market economy functions. For the technocrats *market conformity* thus serves as a filter for serious arguments that reduces all talk of the institutional framework as the site of (the implementation of) morality in the market economy to a farce: the idea of the market's inherent necessity dominates and silences the free public use of reason by the economic 'amateur' – not always but frequently enough.

This economistic pre-understanding of economic politics and the corresponding scepticism towards democracy – presented in a deliberately exaggerated form here – are still shared to a more or less pronounced degree, precisely in regard to questions of regulatory politics, by a large majority of economists. Among them we find advocates of all three conceptions of order presented in the previous section. It is therefore necessary to consider (1) the problematic relationship of the founders of ordoliberalism to democracy, and (2) the underlying economism even of the most recent conceptions of a 'democratic economic politics' of the neoliberal type. It is, however, only on the basis of a political-philosophical conception of deliberative democracy that (3) we can arrive at a workable

[99] For the background in the history of science and for a criticism of the scientistic-technocratic understanding of the question of putting politics on a scientific footing see Ulrich, *Transformation*, p. 145ff., especially 153ff.

[100] See Section 4.2.

understanding of *deliberative order politics*, which can then provide the foundation for the justification of an institutional framework for the market with ethical substance. Its formal task is to put the constitutive norms of such a framework in concrete terms. We will distinguish three constitutive normative tasks.

(1) The democracy deficits of ordoliberal regulatory ethics

The above mentioned tendency of the ordoliberals to relapse into economistic thought patterns can presumably be traced back to their problematically ambivalent relationship to the democratic social order and their predilection for various 'economic styles' of elitist (institutional) politics. To take an example, Alfred Müller-Armack, who is by no means a 'pure' economist, expressly demands that politics be placed 'on a scientific footing' in the sense described above and sees the main goal of such a scientifically based politics in the 'calm objectification (!) and concrete improvement of our life conditions'. He does not ask the decisive question in this context, namely *who* decides what can be judged an 'improvement'.[101] Instead he immediately enquires instead about the 'ultimate criterion of such an order'. His answer that this criterion cannot be 'might or right, majority or freedom, democracy or dictatorship, but only one thing: humaneness'[102] reveals, from the perspective of modern political philosophy and ethics, an obscure separation of the human social order from right, freedom and democracy. It is all too reminiscent of a problematic elitist understanding of state leadership, now transferred to economic politics. This is not a rash judgement. With the same elitist touch (and a questionable personalistic understanding of history) Müller-Armack finds it necessary to remind us that 'the function of the whole' of our 'modern economic system' is 'the work of minorities'.[103] He warns of the danger of too much democracy in the 'mass society':

> The demand for democratization, which has nowadays become an almost general creed, must be guided by the insight that this democratization should know its limits and not turn into a dictatorship of the majority.[104]

It is not surprising, therefore, that the founder of the social market economy in post-war Germany has, as a 'professional political economist',

[101] All quotations are from Müller-Armack, *Genealogie*, p. 211f.
[102] Ibid., p. 212. [103] Ibid., p. 168.
[104] Ibid. In the following sentence he refers, moreover, to F. A. von Hayek, whose radical scepticism towards democratic politics and all ideas of social justice is well known. See Hayek, *Law, Legislation and Liberty, vol. II: The Mirage of Social Justice* (Chicago: The University of Chicago Press, 1976), p. 78.

spoken out decisively against workplace democracy at the management level in exactly the same manner as the majority of his colleagues who subscribe to a 'value free' science.[105] The ordoliberals are no better than Müller-Armack in this regard. Röpke, who refers to the similar views of Böhm[106] as a confirmation of his position, considers it:

> necessary to reject firmly any attempt to do away with subordination in decisions involving the success of the enterprise or to put part of the responsibility upon people who are not qualified for it by virtue of any expert knowledge, training, or talent and who assume no corresponding risks.[107]

In a similar style Röpke also inveighs against 'a mass democracy cut loose from the moorings of natural law and tradition' and 'its extraordinary dangers to liberty'.[108] As a protective dyke he recommends the 'esteem of the natural law'.[109] This at least permits us to recognize the normative convictions which underlie the position of the 'professional political economist'. It also helps to explain why he elsewhere characterizes the goal of the ordoliberal 'third way', as a matter of course and without further justification, as that of '*natural order*'[110] in a manner reminiscent of the old liberals.[111] This ultimate criterion for the (de-)regulation of the market economy in fact corresponds much better with trust in the 'invisible hand' and hence in market conformity as a regulatory political principle than with the cultural construct of democratic institutional politics.

(2) *The economism of democratic institutional politics of the neoliberal type*

Only one line of the natural law tradition in economic-philosophical thinking is apparently completely unbiased in regard to democracy: the Hobbesian contractarian tradition and its contemporary refinement in

[105] See Müller-Armack, *Genealogie*, pp. 227ff. and 168f.

[106] F. Böhm, 'Das wirtschaftliche Mitbestimmungsrecht der Arbeiter im Betrieb', *Ordo* 4 (1951), pp. 21–250. See also the confirmation of his negative attitude twenty-four years later in Böhm, 'An die Leser des Jahrbuchs Ordo', *Ordo* 26 (1975), pp. 3–11.

[107] Röpke, *Humane Economy*, p. 299f.

[108] Ibid., pp. 70 and 66. It must be taken into account that during the Cold War in the late 1950s it corresponded to the spirit of the times to inveigh against de-individualization and supposedly collectivist tendencies in the West. On this point see the volume *Masse und Demokratie*, ed. A. Hunold (Erlenbach-Zürich/Stuttgart: Rentsch, 1957), which contains contributions by Röpke and Rüstow and also by Hayek.

[109] Röpke, Humane Economy, p. 8.

[110] Röpke, *Lehre von der Wirtschaft*, p. 330 (my italics).

[111] On the long shadow of natural law thinking in economics see Ulrich, *Transformation*, p. 184ff.

J. M. Buchanan's *Constitutional Economics.*[112] In contrast to most of the other approaches to institutional politics it is characterized, at least at first sight, by an unrestricted approval of the primacy of democratic politics (at the constitutional level) over the logic of the market (post-constitutional level). Karl Homann builds upon it in his 'institutional ethics' and accordingly postulates:

> *Systematically the political order precedes the market.* Nowadays this political order can only be a *democracy.*[113]

Economists who stand on the paradigmatic ground of constitutional economics agree completely, therefore, with the critique of an elitist understanding of institutional politics that is sceptical towards democracy, as described above.[114] Bruno S. Frey and Gebhard Kirchgässner, in particular, have taken up Buchanan's constitutional economics and developed a textbook model of a two-stage conception of democratic economic politics along these lines. Moving beyond the anti-democratic reflexes of the traditional economic theory of 'rational' economic politics, which seems tailor-made for a benevolent dictatorship, they have arrived at an understanding of the economic order as the subject matter of a 'basic societal consensus' which must be achieved by democratic means.[115]

One of the merits of this approach is that it does accord democracy a systematic role in institutional politics. Frey and Kirchgässner also go beyond the prevalent model-platonistic predecision, in mainstream economics that all forms of participation by employees in companies are to be regarded as necessarily inefficient because they increase transaction costs. Instead they follow the research results of critical economists and admit the empirical possibility that democratic decision-taking processes in the economy can be efficient and, consequently, that they are also worthy of discussion by 'professional economists' from the point of view of institutional policy.[116]

112 See the presentation and critique in Section 5.3, especially subsection (3).

113 Homann/Blome-Drees, *Wirtschafts- und Unternehmensethik*, p. 54 (italics in the original text).

114 For a largely concurring criticism of the traditional economic, and especially the ordo-liberal, understanding of institutional politics see G. Kirchgässner, 'Wirtschaftspolitik und Politiksystem: Zur Kritik der traditionellen Ordnungstheorie aus der Sicht der Neuen Politischen Ökonomie', in D. Cassel/B. T. Ramb/H. J. Thieme (eds.), *Ordnungspolitik* (Munich: Vahlen, 1988), pp. 53–75.

115 See B. S. Frey, *Theorie demokratischer Wirtschaftspolitik* (Munich: Vahlen, 1981); 2nd rev. edn by B. S. Frey/G. Kirchgässner, *Demokratische Wirtschaftspolitik: Theorie und Anwendung* (Munich: Vahlen, 1994).

116 See ibid. (1994), p. 77ff.

Nevertheless this 'constitutional' conception of democratic economic politics based on Buchanan by no means overcomes economism. On the contrary, it ultimately derestricts it and extends it to the sphere of politics, as we have seen earlier.[117] Characteristically Kirchgässner's[118] critique of ordoliberal institutional politics then starts from the point that the ordoliberals wish to restrict economic logic to the market sphere and do *not* subordinate their understanding of politics to the economic paradigm. Kirchgässner's objection makes sense only as long as the ordoliberal texts are scientistically reinterpreted as features of *empirical-analytical* theory (of real politics), but he fails to realize that the ordoliberals rightly postulated the necessary 'boundary of the market' (Rüstow) with *critical-normative* intent. The primacy of politics, adequately conceived as democratic however, over the inherent logic of the market cannot otherwise be maintained.

The problematic point of understanding democracy in the economic theory of democratic economic politics is then that it postulates the primacy of politics over the logic of the market only superficially. As in the entire economic theory of politics democratic legitimacy continues to be reduced categorially to Pareto-efficiency; the democratic social contract is conceived as a generalized exchange of advantages.[119] As a result every participant is granted an absolute veto right[120] in defence of his property and interests. There is no other conceivable solution on the basis of methodological and normative individualism. Such an economic conception of politics has nothing in common with a well-grounded understanding of republican deliberative democracy.[121] At best it provides an ideal-typical model of the actual tendency towards an unbounded market society and the consequent reduction of politics to the continuation of business with other means.[122] Insofar it cannot be denied that this conception has a certain empirical content.

Applied uncritically for normative purposes, however, such a conception of democracy denies the existence of the decisive problem of just

[117] See Section 5.3 (3).

[118] See Kirchgässner, 'Wirtschaftspolitik und Politiksystem', p. 55ff.

[119] This is the position of Frey/Kirchgässner, *Demokratische Wirtschaftspolitik*, 28f.; see also Homann/Blome-Drees, *Wirtschafts- und Unternehmensethik*, p. 54f.

[120] This is expressly stated in Homann/Blome-Drees, ibid., p. 56. By equating this Pareto-efficient exchange of advantages in the same sentence with the 'legitimation requirements of consensus' they make a clear category mistake which they cannot in fact avoid within their paradigm.

[121] We need only recall here the decisive normative premises of a political liberalism of philosophical origin (Rawls): moral persons, genuinely equal basic liberties of all citizens, primacy of basic rights over benefit calculation and over the exchange of mutual political advantages, public use of reason, etc. See Section 7.2.

[122] For details see Sections 5.3 (2) and (3).

starting conditions in a well-ordered society. It simply starts from the status quo of the given distribution of power and resources and assumes, in a circular argument, that this is a sufficient foundation for legitimation. In this way the constitutive role of democratic politics for the legitimation of the market economy, which constitutional economics expressly claims to advocate, is silently revoked – in its place the *h-o-test* constitutes what is the 'right' politics.[123] Thus the experts on the inherent logic of pure economics unexpectedly return to the political stage through the back door, this time with the offer of value-free 'information' in their pockets:

> To this end [the determination of a basic societal consensus] agreements and institutions are needed which are productive for all. *The economic-political advisors can offer information on such regulations which are advantageous for all.*[124]

It is clear what kind of proposals these h-o-advisors have to offer democratic economic politics. Regulatory reforms are generally regarded as efficient as far as they are 'in conformity with the market' (in the narrow neoclassical sense elucidated above) or amount to *more market* (deregulation). In contrast, those reforms involving vital-political regulatory measures with distributional effects on income, property, places of employment etc. which are not in conformity with the market or even require restrictions of the market are inevitably labelled 'inefficient' in accordance with the 'pure' Paretian economic logic. In practically all the current politico-economic debates – for example on the chronic problem of mass unemployment or on the shareholder-value doctrine[125] – the dominant views of the economic advisors accordingly favour a market harmony which is far removed from considerations of real-life practical and socio-political questions of distribution: the questions to what end and for whom specifically the market should produce its beneficial effects, and who is to pay the price, are hardly ever asked.[126]

But of course, the proposals of the Pareto-economic political advisors are no more value-free[127] than those of alternative advisors who take other regulatory criteria as their starting point. Against the self-(mis)understanding of the Pareto economists it must be said that regulatory

[123] See Section 5.3 (1). Elsewhere, however, Kirchgässner emphasizes that a h-o-tested democracy which assumes that individuals act strictly in their own interests would be 'incapable of functioning'; democracy 'is dependent on . . . the moral behaviour of its citizens'. See G. Kirchgässner, 'Einige Bemerkungen zur Rolle der Wirtschaftsethik', *Ethik und Sozialwissenschaften* 5 (1994), pp. 40–2, at p. 41.

[124] Frey/Kirchgässner, *Demokratische Wirtschaftspolitik*, p. 28 (my italics).

[125] See Section 10.1 (4).

[126] On 'inherent necessity' as the justification of this phenomenon see Section 4.3.

[127] This is the clearly expressed conviction of Kirchgässner, *Homo oeconomicus*, p. 3: 'Economics is a value-free science in the sense of Max Weber.'

reforms cannot be classified as competitively neutral, regardless of the criteria they use.[128] It is precisely the point of such reforms that they *should change* the rules and the incentive structures of the market – and with them the comparative market positions of competitors. The desired forms of behaviour are made more economical or profitable and the undesirable forms more expensive or less profitable, in order to persuade the economic agents to adapt their strategies accordingly. The effects of the market's regulatory framework rest upon exactly this process. Starting from a particular status quo the comparative cost advantages and disadvantages of competitors and their relative competitive positions are thus changed. We have already discussed in Chapter 8 a practically relevant example of environmental policy reform (ecologically motivated taxes and levies on energy), whose introduction has met with so much resistance in almost all countries from the energy-intensive branches of the economy.

Precisely this non-existent competitive neutrality of the institutional framework makes market-based regulatory policies possible – by means of changes in the price signals to the market players. Yet it is expressly (mis-) taken by Homann and Blome-Drees as the basis for their Paretian 'institutional ethics':

> Under competitive conditions the moral norms must apply *equally to all*; i.e. they must be *competitively neutral* so that no competitor can achieve advantages by taking up an outsider position [i.e. by moral free-riding].[129]

By mistakenly equating the (adequately assumed) *impartiality* of general institutional rules which are valid for everyone with their *competitive neutrality* Homann overlooks a central regulatory problem: all those reforms aiming to establish an impartial and hence ethically based framework for the market are not capable of achieving a consensus among homines oeconomici who wish only to maximize their own private advantages, precisely because they are not competitively neutral.[130] Inversely, a reform proposal which finds the approval of all would only be possible

[128] See the account in Section 8.2.

[129] Homann/Blome-Drees, *Wirtschafts- und Unternehmensethik*, p. 147 (my italics), in a similar vein ibid., p. 114. What is more, with this postulate the authors explode their own Paretian approach and implicitly adopt a deontological-universalistic moral point of view. The impartiality and the consensus potential of the *state* of an institutional framework cannot be meaningfully founded on the criterion of Pareto efficiency, as the latter can only meaningfully refer to *changes* in social conditions, i.e. can be applied only *in relation to* a given status quo. See Section 5.3 (3).

[130] In contrast, their paradigmatic founding father, J. M. Buchanan, is fully aware of this problem, although he cannot solve it within his paradigm, as we have already seen in Section 5.3 (3).

according to Paretian logic if the actually desired changes in the relative competitive position do not occur. The 'regulatory ethics' which results from a corresponding 'scientific' political counselling' consists in the defence of the status quo.[131]

Consequently, ethically meaningful institutional reforms designed to achieve a greater human, social and ecological compatibility of the market incentives can only be brought about *counter to the h-o-test* and to competitive neutrality. They demand from the affected economic agents, and especially from the most powerful among them, that they do not strictly defend their own particular interests but take on their share of responsibility for the improvable state of the regulatory framework even though they have to accept private disadvantages to a reasonable degree. In other words, the economic citizens' republican sense is indispensable if the institutional framework of the market is ever to become an essential site of (the implementation of) morality. Economic and state citizens of republican conviction are and will remain the ultimate site of morality.

The systematic consequences are considerable. The idea of localizing morality strictly in the regulatory framework and relieving the economic players entirely of moral demands, not only in the market but also in their political strategies,[132] breaks down – and with it the 'institutional-ethical' principle which supposedly runs 'efficiency in the moves of the game, morality in the rules'.[133] The attempt to found a regulatory ethics without morality and a democratic economic politics without an ethical-normative conception of deliberative politics has failed. The economistic circularity of 'pure' institutional economics which the economic theory of democratic politics was meant to overcome has reasserted itself.

[131] Exactly this point is made by Kirchgässner elsewhere ('Einige Bemerkungen', p. 40) in a criticism of Homann. The objection is, however, equally valid for the conception of Frey/Kirchgässner in their *Demokratische Wirtschaftspolitik* as it has the same paradigmatic foundation.

[132] Homann/Blome-Drees (*Wirtschafts- und Unternehmensethik*, p. 148) with reference to the strategies of economic agents in regard to institutional policy: 'We do not assume an originally moral interest here either, as we would then depart from the domain of economic argumentation.' How very true!

[133] Ibid., p. 35. The consistency of this principle with their premise on the basic individual attitude (in accordance with the footnote above) could be maintained only if we assume that the human *subjects* of political morality are not identical with the purely strategically interested economic gents; these would only be the literal *objects* of the ethical rules of the game. But this also means that they cannot be the sovereign of a democratic society either! For an elucidation of the same democratically intolerable separation of 'democracy' from the sovereign who establishes the constitution in Kant see Section 8.1, particularly n. 43.

(3) Deliberative order politics and its constitutive normative tasks

What the economic theory of democratic politics claims to present but is incapable of sustaining on the basis of its own paradigm is the perfectly correct starting point: the fundamental normative orientation of all regulatory politics guided by rational ethics will lead to the ensurement of the primacy of political ethics over the logic of the market. Institutional ethics begins beyond (or with a critique of) the elevation of the market mechanism to the highest regulatory principle.

In accordance with the republican-liberal conception developed in Chapter 8 the systematic site of regulatory-ethical discourse is deliberative politics organized around the regulative idea of the unlimited public use of reason by all politically mature economic citizens. We can describe this site of moral justification as the (ideal) politico-economic communicative community. The general motivational and institutional preconditions essentially include the reciprocal dovetailing of republican civic sense with a complex network of 'open spaces' and 'forums'. As crystallization points of the politico-economic debate, these networks lend argumentative force to the republican public sphere, which itself cannot be institutionalized. The network provides the communicative infrastructure in which lifeworld claims to exercise influence over the national, regional, local and individual economy (companies) are publicly debated and clarified. The quality of this infrastructure of deliberative regulatory politics can be measured by the central idea that all normative predecisions and requirements which determine the normative logic of the market must be unconditionally accessible to argument. They must be subjected to the only truly incontrovertible 'necessity' or, more properly, principle of a free democratic society, namely the legitimation claims of the public sphere. It is the primary critical-normative orientational task of regulatory ethics to stress the importance of such an infrastructure for deliberative order politics:

> Regulatory ethics develops ... conceptions of such networks in which communicative reason can unfold. In this way it ties up with lifeworld elements in the economy ... and contributes to their development.[134]

The orientational horizon of regulatory ethics understood in this way lies primarily in *opening up* the procedures of politico-economic decision-making on regulatory policies for critical civic debate. The *closure* of this process by means of binding decisions is a matter for deliberative

[134] A. Biesecker, 'Lebensweltliche Elemente der Ökonomie und Schlussfolgerungen für eine moderne Ordnungsethik', *Berichte des Instituts für Wirtschaftsethik* N° 61 (St Gallen: Institute for Economic and Business Ethics, 1994), p. 21.

regulatory politics at the practical level. Apart from the critical-reflective accompaniment of public debates, regulatory ethics can at best propose formal guiding ideas of a moderately abstract kind which might help to structure an ethically meaningful regulatory framework of the market in practice. Its competence in this point does not of course include the socio-technical methods of functional system control, in particular competition policies. Rather, its main task is to critically reflect on the *constitutive normativizing tasks* in regard to a vital-political framework which must be determined in deliberative praxis.

The constitutive role of regulatory politics does not refer to the market mechanism as such, as this is nothing other than the 'natural system' (Adam Smith) of the reciprocal exchange of advantages. What must be normatively constituted is rather the set of rules under which the system dynamics can be allowed to 'take its course' and at the same time limited in its operations and directed towards the service of life.[135] The political constitution of the market economy thus also includes the justified limitation of legitimate market control. Both can only be implemented in real-life politics, of course, in as far as the primacy of politics over the market is a given fact.[136]

The constitutive significance of normative points of view for a 'vital' market economy in the twofold meaning of the concept can only be grasped on the basis of a socio-economic view of the problem of the *rational* institutional ordering of the economy.[137] For as soon as an ethically disintegrated, autonomous economic rationality perspective is allowed, this will inevitably begin to take a course of its own and, in accordance with the apparently 'ethics-free' inherent logic of the economy, will necessarily free itself, at the intellectual level already, of nearly all vital-ethical claims. The crucial point of regulatory ethics in regard to a workable arrangement of an ethically and (socio-) economically rational market economy lies, therefore, in an integrative understanding of rational (and reasonable) economic activity. The mediation between ethical-political reason and economic rationality will no longer be conceived as a compromise in the form of the two-world conception of ethics

[135] Thus, the postulate of the political constitution of the market-economic order serving the vital interests of society in the sense intended here is not the same as the theory of the institutional-political constitution of the market as such (for a critical comment see Thielemann, *Prinzip Markt*, pp. 25, 298ff.). The former is based on the insight that the market is not a neutral instrument for all and any kinds of social coordination. For this reason competitive policy, which brings only the inherent logic of the market into play, must be overlaid by a vital policy determined in public deliberation.

[136] We take up this question again in Section 9.3.

[137] We refer back here to the socio-economic rationality conception of integrative economic ethics; see Section 3.3.

and economics; on the contrary, the ethical aspects of service to life will be seen as constitutive preconditions of every properly understood *idea* of socio-economically 'efficient' solutions to regulatory political problems.[138] It is the never-ending practical task of the public use of reason in deliberative order politics to determine the concrete meaning of economic reason in a society.

In this sense at least three kinds of constitutive normativizing tasks for vital policy can be distinguished: They concern (a) the subjective rights of all economic citizens in the market process, (b) the calculation norms involved in cost–benefit evaluations at the individual and company level, and (c) the boundary norms limiting the sphere of influence of the market. Only a brief sketch of these three constitutive factors can be offered here.

(a) Rights: Economic citizen's basic rights are undoubtedly of constitutive significance for the institutional framework of the market. We have already dealt with them in detail above.[139] Subjective or personality related rights often determine in a decisive way who as a participant in the market is 'inviolable' and who is not. These include property and tenants' rights, the rights of entrepreneurs, employees and consumers, and also the rights of citizens who do not participate in a business exchange but are affected by its external effects. They can often only defend themselves against the encroachments of ruthless economic actors by means of liability claims and rights of information, protection and complaint. Economic citizenship rights thus serve – over and beyond the legal protection of moral basic rights in economic life – to achieve a fair balance of power by strengthening the weaker market partner or the 'externally' disadvantaged individual. As we have seen in the discussion of the right to an unconditional basic income, well-ordered economic citizens' rights can replace a large number of special vital policy norms with generally 'civilized' relationships or at least ensure fair and clear preconditions for the solution of conflicts of interest in specific situations.

[138] Rich, *Business and Economic Ethics*, p. 594, has the same intention when he formulates the regulatory political maxim: 'Yet, what matters in assessing the life-serving aspect and *thus the economic rationality* of the economy is its *total efficiency*. An essential part of it results from human, social, and ecological accomplishments' (my italics). But as Rich does not understand this 'total efficiency' as an idea of socio-economic rationality which, in view of social value and interest conflicts, must involve discourse and deliberation (in regard to questions of justice!), his concept of overall and life-serving 'economic rationality' still carries overtones of the fiction of an objectively determinable 'general welfare' (ibid., next sentence) optimum (the utilitarian fiction of the public good). Who determines 'total efficiency' under such conditions?

[139] See Section 7.3.

The relationship between property rights and the opposing rights of economic citizens is particularly problematic.[140] The capitalist market economy[141] as it has developed and still exists today is essentially determined by codes regulating property and disposal rights. As Max Weber quite clearly saw, property closes down the communication with third parties and provides the property-owners with 'monopolized advantages' in social action.[142] Anyone who possesses the 'exclusive' private rights to dispose of a resource must render account to nobody for the way in which he uses or disposes of his right, provided he stays within the boundaries of legality. This applies as long as an exclusive property right or a partial dispositional right is not 'diluted' by information, participation, prosecution and compensation rights of third parties. Such 'whittling down' of property rights through the communication rights of others, which are of course also disposition rights, changes the starting position (the status quo) for negotiations on an exchange of advantages in the market and hence diminishes the 'efficiency' with which the property owners can assert their interests against the resistance of the others (and, incidentally, also diminishes the value of their property). On the other hand, if exclusive disposition rights permit a property-owner to close down communication with others, he can then escape the obligation to legitimize his actions and simply save himself the trouble of justifying his disposition or compensating those who suffer disadvantages as a result of his actions.[143]

What is necessary here from a regulatory point of view is a communicative rationalization of the economic order in the form of a precise specification of the general and special communication rights of the economic citizen and of the procedures for the formation of the political will in regard to the institutional framework of the market.[144] General communication rights apply to the rights of information and participation in the

[140] On the point that private property is only justifiable as a *limited* economic citizenship right see Section 7.3 (2b).

[141] We agree with Koslowski (*Ethik des Kapitalismus*, p. 8f.) when he considers the concept of the market economy (which sounds harmless enough) to be 'analytically not sharp enough' as a characterization of the existing economic and social order and regards the concept *capitalism* as a more precise description of its basic features: 'market economy, private property and economic individualism (individual profit and benefit maximization as the purpose of economic action).'

[142] See Weber, *Economy and Society*, vol. I, p. 44.

[143] This is also the normative premise behind possessive individualism, on which the entire (transaction cost theoretical) efficiency thesis of the *economics of property rights* is based. For a representative account see E. G. Furubotn/S. Pejovich, 'Property Rights and Economic Theory: A Survey of Recent Literature', *Journal of Economic Literature* 10 (1972), pp. 1137–62. See also the account and critique in Ulrich, *Transformation*, pp. 243–54.

[144] For a more detailed account see Ulrich, ibid., p. 371ff.

politico-economic process to which every economic citizen is entitled, whereas we can speak of special communication rights when particular persons are directly affected by a specific action of others whose decisions impinge upon their rights of communication, participation, protest or complaint in a concrete situation. Special communication rights should, of course, also enjoy general validity without respect of persons, but they can only be invoked by those who are directly affected by a decision.

Whereas special communication rights (in the sense mentioned) are on the same systematic level as the private dispositional rights colliding with them, the situation is different in the case of the general politico-economic communication rights. From a discourse-ethical point of view the order regulating politico-economic deliberation has in principle priority over the order regulating property and disposition rights. The debate among citizens on the regulatory framework should after all take place without restrictive conditions and may not be subjected to the partly closed communication conditions of an existing dispositional order. That would amount to a relapse into the Hobbesian pseudo-discourse determined by the relations of power.[145]

Taking the actual political status quo as a starting point, it will, above all, be necessary to neutralize as far as possible the influence of property relationships on public deliberation and so to eliminate the economic power to distort, close down, or prevent communication. The property

[145] The consequence (as regulative idea) is a three-stage institutional-ethical model which goes further than the two-stage model of constitutional economics (social contract versus market contract) by distinguishing at the level of the social contract between the primary level of the politico-economic order regulating communication and the subordinate dispositional order. The former fulfils vital-political tasks of orientation and legitimation, the latter functional tasks of system control. For details see Ulrich, *Transformation*, p. 131ff.; Ulrich, 'Towards an Ethically-based Conception', p. 36ff. Karl-Otto Apel, *Diskurs und Verantwortung*, p. 294ff., assumes that this three-level-model would equate the 'regulative principle' of the normative order of the levels, which he regards as thoroughly right, with a 'sociological finding' (p. 294). In spite of my detailed discussion of the regulatory problem (*Transformation*, p. 371ff.), Apel accuses me of neglecting what he calls 'the problem of establishing the conditions of application' (p. 295). His objection that 'Ulrich's three-level-conception ... implies absolutely monstrous idealizations' (p. 295) is groundless, as neither the supposed empirical reductionism nor the neglect of the specific systemic effects (which must indeed be taken into account empirically) can be found anywhere in my writings. What is more, his reproach reflects back on his own position, as his talk of 'establishing the conditions of application' implies the ('monstrously idealistic'!) assumption that the *regulative idea* of discourse could at some stage actually be *established* in real circumstances – but that can in principle never be the case! Yet the primacy of politico-economic discourse over the logic of the market is, as a regulative idea, constitutive of all institutional ethics and is consequently indispensable. To call this 'a monstrous idealization' would be a category mistake which Apel, in my opinion, encourages with his problematic conception of 'the application of discourse ethics'. See the critique in Section 3.1.

question thus remains the 'capital issue' of a well-ordered society and economy.[146]

(b) Calculation norms: What is at issue here is the need to change the incentive structures of the market at the central 'site' of cost calculation of all the market participants in accordance with vital-political points of view. It is essential that all the cost elements on which the market strategies of the economic players are based, as well as the price signals of the market on which they orientate their activities, are to be understood as normatively determined. It is not simply a question of overlaying the 'natural' prices of resources and goods, which, in the ideal-typical case, would be arrived at as equilibrium prices on the unregulated market, with 'constructivist' (Hayek) administrative price controls. Such a paleoliberal perspective falsely assumes that uncontrolled 'natural' market prices have the ethical dignity of impartiality and lead to the objectively most efficient allocation of scarce resources. Behind this view the old metaphysics of the market of natural law comes to light. It overlooks, however, two constitutive normative requirements.

Firstly, the fact is ignored that the dividing line between the costs and benefits of an economic activity that are taken into account and those which, as *external effects* (social or ecological costs or possibly even benefits), are not a part of the actor's calculation has always been normatively determined. The agents themselves are interested in the internalization of external benefits as long as the costs of internalisation do not exceed the return.[147] But the situation is different with the internalization of external costs. As soon as these costs become unreasonable for those directly affected or, for vital-political reasons, price signals of the market are needed to provide other incentives, regulatory *apportionment norms* (or standards) are necessary for the internalisation of the external costs in the (business) calculations of the economic agents.[148]

146 For an outline of a corresponding conception of partly neutralized private property and company law (corporate law) see Ulrich, *Transformation*, p. 387ff. On the thesis of the 'selectivity' of the political and administrative system to the benefit of powerful particularist interests, which has long been corroborated by political science, see the overview in P. Ulrich, *Die Grossunternehmung als quasi-öffentliche Institution: Eine politische Theorie der Unternehmung* (Stuttgart: Poeschel, 1977), pp. 59–67.

147 A standard example is the case of free parking at a shop or shopping centre. The owner will dispense with charges if the cost of collecting the parking fees and the loss of turnover resulting from the loss of customers is higher than the expected return.

148 In the political discussion on the costs of transport and ecological measures the term *'cost truth'* ('Kostenwahrheit') is being increasingly used. Behind this concept we can recognize the natural law fiction of objectively 'true' prices. In view of the normative constitution of all definitions of costs one should, strictly speaking, rather talk of normative 'cost validity'.

Secondly, we should note that natural equilibrium prices are nothing other than the expression of a certain power equilibrium determined by the competitive potential and solvency of the participants in a deal. The ethical legitimacy or illegitimacy of the starting position of the participants has a powerful effect on pricing in the market and thus on the allocational and distributional outcomes. We are concerned here with the problem of *market-internal effects*, which has been discussed earlier.[149] Barter agreements reached on the 'free' market merely 'consolidate' the balance of power. In this regard calculation norms justified by vital policy provide a subsidiary correction of the power relationships or at least a reduction of the effects of power on the mechanism of price formation, in as far as the economic rights of the participants are not fairly distributed. Such a change in the calculation norms can be achieved in two ways, depending on the nature of the concentration and exploitation of power which is involved.

- *Pricing norms*: they limit internal (power) effects by making it impossible for the stronger party to a contract to use his power to force through prices against the weaker party which are unjustifiable from a vital-political standpoint. A typical example is the institutional regulation of price ranges on the market for rented housing in order to protect tenants who, on account of their lack of mobility, are usually in a weaker negotiating position when faced with rent increases even on a 'functioning' market. This kind of state guarantee of as-if-market prices corresponds, for example, to the establishment by the Swiss government of a 'price controller', who is entitled to control the prices of powerful suppliers, including the monopolistically fixed prices of state enterprises, and to bind them to given pricing standards.
- *Apportionment norms*: just like external effects need to be internalized, undesirable market-internal effects need to be neutralized. Instead of first accepting the price formation in the market and only subsequently correcting or compensating for the problematic social distributional effects by means of redistributional public welfare arrangements, it usually makes better vital-political sense to change the primary distribution at the start, as far as this is possible, by means of price regulation (e.g. subsidies for socially or ecologically desirable activities and levies on undesirable activities) or the fixing of tax scales (e.g. progressive income tax scales).[150] This is, among other things, conceivable in regard to politically motivated interventions in the employment

[149] See Section 5.3 (2).

[150] As they do not directly change pricing on the market or the incentive structures and relations of power on which pricing is based, re-distribution norms cannot be assigned to

market, which have already been tested, although only rather timidly. We are concerned here, for example, with financial incentives to entrepreneurs for measures designed to preserve jobs (company models for the redistribution of working hours instead of dismissals) and against 'downsizing' policies with mass dismissals, which are all too often rewarded by the market. The aim is to achieve social redistribution and structural allocation effects, while at the same time taking into account and weighing up the reciprocal dynamic effects, in particular the undesirable weakening of other incentives. Leaving aside natural law premises (of 'market conformity'), there is no rational case for giving the vital-political aspect of just redistribution any less importance than the aspect of efficient allocation (for whom?) in regard to constitutive regulatory tasks.[151]

(c) Boundary norms: We speak of boundary norms in adaptation of Rüstow's concept of the 'boundary of the market'. Their purpose is to limit the social spheres in which the market should be the dominant force, in order to prevent market competition from becoming a 'tyrannic' organizing principle in life spheres where it is not appropriate and reasonable.[152] In principle, the state-enforced limitation of the market is called for whenever, for vital-political reasons, the good life and just social coexistence are judged to require not only fairness *in* the market but also the freedom of individuals *from* the compulsion to self-assertion under market conditions.[153] Various kinds of boundary setting norms must be distinguished, depending on the form and grade of intervention:

- *Threshold or limiting values*: here minimum or maximum values are determined and prescribed by the state for certain indicators of the vital-political tolerability of market outcomes. Examples are ecologically motivated emission limits (air pollution control) or the permissible degree of contamination of foodstuffs. But this also includes regulations with regard to market internal effects, for example standardized minimum wages or maximum working hours (for socio-political

the domain of economic institutional politics in the narrow sense, but are part of a complementary social politics which is situated beyond the boundaries of the market. It will be one of the vital-political goals to keep the need for subsequent corrections (of the 'primary' distribution) through social politics as low as possible by minimizing the socially intolerable market-internal effects.

151 Norms of distributional justice and of social security cannot simply be understood as 'regulative principles', as in Eucken's terminology, which is too narrowly restricted to competitive politics; see also S. Katterle, 'Marktwirtschaft und Ethik', *Discussion Papers of the Faculty of Economics* N° 302 (Bielefeld: University of Bielefeld, 1995), p. 4.

152 See Walzer, *Spheres of Justice*, p. 17ff.; cf. Section 7.3 (2b).

153 See the considerations in Section 6.2 on the meaning orientation of economic activity in an advanced economy.

reasons). Finally, minor norms like the determination of speed and weight limits for vehicles (in regard to transportation policy) can be regarded as regulations in terms of limiting values.

- *Norms for the spatial and temporal delimitation of the market*: markets have always been more or less limited geographically and temporally, for example by means of customs duties, limited opening hours and working time or regional planning. Regulations of this kind are, at least in European countries, currently controversial (e.g. in regard to work on Sundays); nevertheless they should be regarded as constitutive vital-policy decisions. In a globalizing economy, new spatial and temporal restrictions on the market may be even more desirable in the future (e.g. protection of local or regional markets in developing countries from world-wide competition).[154]
- *Admission norms*: these make the right to participate in a specific market, above all as suppliers, dependent on the fulfilment of certain controlled preconditions, for example general personal data (e.g. age, for child and youth protection), professional qualification standards (for the protection of clients), safety, hygiene and health standards, employment or environmental conditions. Conditions or prohibitions can refer directly to certain problematic products whose uncontrolled purchase is socially undesirable (alcohol, tobacco, drugs, weapons).
- *Exclusion of the market*: for certain goods the market can be totally excluded and replaced by a different, usually administrative source of supply. This is essential in the case of *public goods* for whose production and utilization the market is in principle unsuited, but for which there is nonetheless a public need (e.g. infrastructure services which must be available extensively regardless of commercial considerations). These must be distinguished from (quasi-private) *merit goods*, which can in principle be supplied and demanded on the market, although for vital-political reasons it is desirable that their use should not depend on the purchasing power or willingness of the citizens (in particular health care, education services and cultural goods). The distinction between private goods to be supplied by the market on the one hand, and public or merit goods on the other, cannot be made by purely analytical means; it must rather be understood as a normative decision with constitutive significance for a market economy in the service of life.[155]

[154] See below, Section 9.3 (2).

[155] The concept of merit goods goes back to R. Musgrave, *The Theory of Public Finance* (New York: McGraw-Hill, 1959). For a defence in economic-ethical perspective see W. Ver Eecke, 'The Concept of a "Merit Good": The Ethical Dimension in Economic Theory and the History of Economic Thought or the Transformation of Economics into Socio-Economics', *Journal of Socio-Economics* 27/1 (1998), pp. 133–53.

The more the progressive economization of all areas of life leads to the almost ubiquitous domination of the market, the more important fundamental vital-political decisions become, in order to determine when and where exactly a competitive regime is desirable and how strictly it should work. *The only compelling force in fair competition should be that of the better offer – but competition need not dominate all aspects of our lives.*

9.3 The global question: competition of national market frameworks or supranational sites of regulatory morality?

We have not yet considered whether or to what extent the indispensable ethical primacy of politics over the market in regard to the regulatory framework exists at all in reality. The rapidly advancing globalization of the markets and hence of competition we are witnessing gives rise to doubts about the sovereignty of state politics to a hitherto unknown degree. The national state seems, so to speak, to be abdicating as the 'site' and instance of regulatory politics in the contemporary world. During the fifty years after the Second World War a more or less well developed social welfare state existed, above all in the advanced industrial societies of Western Europe, founded upon a broad-based 'social democratic' consensus.[156] This state saw it as its task to achieve a socio-political and, increasingly, an ecological integration of the market dynamics. In spite of the continuing radically unequal distribution of income and property, the old social question seemed, in principle, to have been solved in these welfare societies, permitting a great majority of the population to enjoy an at least modest share in the economic prosperity of the nation and, in view of the prospects of steady economic growth and an analogous solution of the ecological question, ensuring the approval of the vast majority of the population for the 'real existing' market economy.

But in the past two decades everything has changed. There is no longer any steady growth of real incomes but only of unemployment. And there is clear evidence that the redistribution of wealth is taking place in the opposite direction, from the poorer to the richer strata of the population.[157] Almost forgotten existential concerns and the threat of social decline have now become a 'normal' risk even well into the middle class,

[156] See Dahrendorf, *Life Chances*, p. 106.

[157] For an abundance of international empirical evidence on disturbing socio-economic developments see L. Thurow, *The Future of Capitalism: How Today's Economic Forces Will Shape Tomorrow's World* (London: Brealey Publishing, 1996). For the central European countries in particular see H. Afheldt, *Wirtschaft, die arm macht: Vom Sozialstaat zur gespaltenen Gesellschaft* (Munich: Kunstmann, 2003).

which is also losing ground. On the one hand, a narrow apex of the rich and super rich climbs higher up the ladder of prosperity and, on the other hand, an ever growing part of the population plunges down the social ladder into precarious employment and new poverty. The two-thirds society is in the process of becoming reality together with a multiplicity of concomitant symptoms, including growing homelessness, criminality and the manifold manifestations of social collapse which are already an observable fact in the countries that are 'most advanced' in this respect: the homes of Reagonomics and Thatcherism. The fundamental differences in the social structure of advanced and 'under-developed' countries are becoming blurred.[158] Whereas the welfare states of the Western European countries continue (for the moment) to foot the bill in spite of the prevailing financial crises, this task has been largely abandoned in the USA and Great Britain. And the political will to carry out an ecological reform of the market economy has also waned virtually to zero.

Instead the slogans setting the tone are now: deregulation, privatization and 'more market'; reduction of 'excessive' social welfare costs and the 'slim state'; 'revitalization' and 'high performance must be rewarded' – all of this with the aim of preserving or regaining 'international competitiveness', which will then supposedly lead ultimately, by means of increased company profits and economic growth, to the creation of new jobs. There is said to be a merciless global *locational competition* for capital investors, manufacturing and service industries bringing employment to the working population and urgently needed revenues from taxation to the state sector. The higher national unemployment becomes, the more the general economic interests of the nation and the particular interests of the capital owners whose enterprises 'provide labour' seem to coincide – a view embodied in the concept of shareholder value and usually measured by the market capitalization of companies on the stock exchange.[159] If returns on investment are unsatisfactory, 'downsizing', rationalization and the reduction of wage costs are called for. Should there be resistance from those affected or even public protests, the powerful and demanding shareholders or their representatives in top management then threaten to transfer production abroad and, without turning a hair, present the supposedly 'irrefutable' argument that global competition compels them to reduce the cost of labour at the local place of business. Thus,

[158] The bitter expression 'the third-worldization of the USA', coined by J. Galtung in the 1980s, has been confirmed by numerous empirical indicators presented by critical economists. 'America is uniquely a first world economy with a third world economy inside of it.' This is the judgement of Thurow, *Future*, p. 173.

[159] For more on this point see Section 10.1 (4).

the uncompromising 'market economy without adjectives' (i.e. without an embedding vital policy) postulated by the neoliberals is increasingly becoming reality and has in the meantime apparently not only ceased to be a 'social' but also a 'free' market economy. Wherever one looks, one finds inherent economic necessity or at least thinking in its terms.

Market globalization is the phenomenon that lies (apparently or really) behind all these implied realities. What is going on can be defined from a general perspective of social sciences as:

> the intensification of worldwide social relations which link distant localities in such a way that local happenings are shaped by events occurring many miles away and vice versa.[160]

In the ideal-typical final state, global markets require the production factors, particularly capital and technology but also labour and natural resources, to be mobile on a worldwide scale. And this results in a worldwide alignment of factor prices – because investment always takes place where the costs are lower (although only temporarily) and the prospects of profit higher than anywhere else.[161] As has been said, the global market inexorably demands this process of alignment, in so far as it is not prevented from completing a work that does not always bring blessings for all.

According to the neoclassical theory of external trade these 'blessings' lie quite simply in the maximization of the diffuse *public good of the world*, which can be expected thanks to the globally unlimited, 'optimal' (most economical) allocation of all production factors. And notably enough: the theoretical model of the perfect global market also functions, as always in 'pure' economics, as a normative orientational ideal. As we have long known, aspects of distribution and hence of justice are ignored in such a utilitarian fiction of the public good. Will social disintegration be the price of world-market integration even for advanced countries?[162]

In what follows let us consider more closely (1) the mechanisms of globalization and their problematic consequences, before we turn (2) to the urgent practical question as to where (if at all) the 'sites' for a reestablishment of the primacy of politics over the logic of global markets can be found.

[160] A. Giddens, *The Consequences of Modernity* (Cambridge: Polity, 1990), p. 64, quoted in D. Held, 'Editor's Introduction' in Held (ed.), *Political Theory Today* (Cambridge: Polity, 1991), pp. 1–21, at p. 9.

[161] See Thurow, *Future of Capitalism*, p. 166f.

[162] Evidence for this danger is given in D. Rodrik, *Has Globalization Gone Too Far?* (Washington DC: Institute for International Economics, 1997).

(1) Global competition between industrial locations and regulatory frameworks – the great neo-(paleo-) liberal experiment

Only one market exists to date in reality which comes fairly close to the theoretical ideal model now that the communicational and technological infrastructure allows us to observe what is happening in the stock exchanges virtually all over the world in real time: the global capital market. There is a simple reason for this, apart from the already mentioned technological preconditions. Capital is a highly mobile factor which reacts 'most sensitively' to changing business location conditions of all kinds in as far as they affect the calculation of the risks and returns of the investors. If these conditions deteriorate substantially in a country there is a massive 'flight of capital' and if they improve noticeably the international capital flows in billions to the attractive locations. The volatility of such capital flows exercises an enormous disciplinary effect on all concerned and – this is the decisive point – has an impact both on the real economies producing goods and providing services and on the national instances responsible for economic and currency policies:

- The *companies* are disciplined, above all, by the big investment funds (pension funds, banking institutes, private equity funds): the shares of companies whose performance is too low in an international comparison, i.e. which have only a small return on equity, are eliminated from the portfolios of the funds. Their quotation on the stock exchange then comes under pressure, and this, in turn, does not only endanger the professional position of the managers responsible but also conjures up the danger of an unfriendly takeover of the company, thus threatening its very existence. Consequently, the maintenance of the shareholder value at almost any cost is the order of the day.
- The *national authorities* responsible for economic and currency policies are disciplined, above all, by the possibility of massive speculation on the part of international foreign exchange dealers against the national currency. With the possible exception of the USA, they are forced to stabilize the currency as a means of fighting inflation, maintaining favourable interest levels and keeping the country attractive as an important 'location' for industrial investment which will help to create employment. If their success and their expectations for the future in this regard decline only a little or if other countries noticeably improve their locational conditions in comparison, the global financial markets 'punish' the country that is supposed to be falling behind virtually overnight. As a result, an international competition between the institutional frameworks at the state level, including the political frame

conditions, is set in motion which cuts the ground from under the feet of an autonomous vital policy.

What is more, the export-oriented branches of the economy with their often influential associations hand on the enormous pressure of international competition to which they are subjected to the domestic political instances. In this way globalization has a double effect, from the outside and the inside, which promotes the end of 'national' economic politics. The domestic side of this pressure is often taken insufficiently into account, and will therefore be briefly elucidated here.

The big companies are operating more and more on a worldwide level, transforming themselves into transnational corporations and developing an identity of 'unencumbered *corporate* selves'[163] or 'homeless wanderers', whose economic interests are no longer tied up with the national economic interests of the citizens of a particular state. Moreover, a substantial part (probably more than a third but less than half)[164] of the international flow of goods and capital nowadays takes place within these companies (intra-firm trade) and further undermines their already loose national connections. As a variation on the well-known slogan of an earlier president of General Motors ('What is good for GM is good for America') we can say that what is good for GM need not necessarily be good for America any longer. Now the far-reaching dissolution of the ties between the interests of the companies and those of the country of origin has a fatal effect. Formerly the big manufacturers were not only interested in low (wage) costs in their home country but also shared the collective interest in high domestic demand as long as they realized a substantial part of their turnover on the domestic market. This motivated them to take a certain degree of interest in the national economic cycle. And that was precisely the basis for the employers' acceptance of the 'social democratic consensus'[165] they have nowadays gradually abandoned. The reason is simple: the domestic market for goods is far less important for globally oriented companies than the share of costs arising in the country of origin (headquarters) and hence interest in low wages in the 'home' country predominates over the interest in domestic demand for their

163 This takes up the notion of Sandel, 'The Procedural Republic and the Unencumbered Self': unencumbered *corporate* selves are the antipodes to 'corporate citizens' in a true sense of the term, as we will see in Section 10.2 (4). The difference is similar to that between the two concepts of the person underpinning economic vs. republican liberalism; cf. Section 8.1.

164 See W. Milberg, 'Foreign Direct Investment and Development: Balancing Costs and Benefits', *International Monetary and Financial Issues for the 1990s*, Vol. XI (New York: UNCTAD, 1999), pp. 99–116; figures of transnational intra-firm trade at p. 104.

165 See Dahrendorf, *Life Chances*, p. 106ff.

products. This tends to lead to the collapse of the already rather weak motivational impulse to show consideration for the domestic economy in the country of origin. Consequently transnational firms more and more reject obligations of national solidarity, which, from their perspective, seem in any case rather old-fashioned.[166] Nonetheless, by threatening to transfer production to a cost-favourable location abroad, they at the same time put strong pressure on the national and regional economic policies of their home country in order to 'improve' the domestic conditions of production.

For obvious reasons the actual loss of sovereignty of the economic-political (and socio-political) authorities at home is thoroughly welcomed by the export branches of the economy not only because it strengthens their position and facilitates the assertion of company interest, but also because it fits in with their economistic free trade convictions, according to which the 'invisible hand' of the growing global market is good for the economy and its positive overall effects will ultimately be to the benefit of all countries and peoples – the only open question is when and in what form this will be realized in practice.

Those who share this conviction and welcome the global competition between the institutional frameworks and the corresponding loss of significance of the national economic- and socio-political authorities seem to overlook the fact that they are actually abandoning their usual neoliberal basic position and relapsing into a paleoliberal understanding of the market at the international level, and that they are thus reverting to the old free-trade doctrine that led to the Great Depression and the collapse of the world economy in 1929. Trust in the competition between the institutional frameworks is after all the equivalent of the natural-law conviction that more reasonable outcomes can be expected from a policy of the *survival of the fittest* involving unregulated and politically uncontrolled struggles between companies, states and entire economic blocks (EU, NAFTA, ASEAN, etc.) than from the ordoliberal and neoliberal conceptions of (global) competition as a (supra) state concern.[167] Market-radical supporters of world-wide locational competition do not therefore see such a development towards a global Darwinistic competition between regulatory frameworks as a danger but regard it as essentially 'efficient' (for whom?). Consequently they are consistent in their scepticism not only in regard to the practical feasibility but also to the

[166] See C. Koch, *Die Gier des Marktes: Die Ohnmacht des Staates im Kampf der Weltwirtschaft* (Munich/Vienna: Hanser, 1995), p. 90.

[167] For an understanding of competition as a 'state concern' (Miksch) see Section 9.1 (3).

truly neoliberal (!) goal of an international competition order as such, not to mention ordoliberal ideas of vital policy:

> The harmonization of competition rules leads to a weakening of the international regulatory competition. In this way the solution of the still open question as to the optimal [sic!] competition policy is made considerably more difficult.[168]

Another position is making increasing political headway that fits in better; not with the ordoliberal but at least with the *neoliberal* philosophy. It postulates that the competition between the institutional frameworks should prevail only in regard to those aspects which, according to the neoliberal conception, are not constitutive for the functional efficiency of competition, in particular in regard to all regulations represented by the social and vital-political 'adjectives' of the market economy. On the other hand a uniform global competition order is regarded as a necessary precondition for a functioning (and fair) competition between locations.[169] The practical consequence is the growing understanding of the World Trade Organization (WTO) set up in 1995 not only as an extended agreement on free trade (like the earlier GATT) but as a supranational authority on competition. Apart from the task of eliminating customs duties and technical obstacles to trade, it should concentrate, analogously to traditional national competition policy, on guaranteeing effective competition and a functioning price system (including a global currency system) in accordance with generally valid rules, on protecting property rights and freedom of contract throughout the world and on keeping the markets open. To put it briefly, it should lead global competition from a 'natural state' to a 'legal state'.[170]

In spite of the advantages of this neoliberal conception of regulated globalization in comparison with the paleoliberal doctrine of total competition of locations and institutional frameworks, the same objection remains at the global level of the WTO as at a national level: the circular argument of the economistic justification is not overcome.[171] Yet again

[168] H. Hauser/K.-U. Schanz, *Das neue GATT. Die Welthandelsordnung nach Abschluss der Uruguay-Runde*, 2nd edn (Munich/Vienna: Oldenbourg, 1995), p. 277f.

[169] See E.-U. Petersmann, 'Why Do Governments Need the Uruguay Round Agreements, NAFTA and the EEA?', *Aussenwirtschaft* 49 (1994), pp. 31–55, at p. 55: '"Competition between rules" also requires "competition between government policies".'

[170] See E.-U. Petersmann, 'Proposals for Negotiating International Competition Rules in the GATT-WTO World Trade and Legal System', *Aussenwirtschaft* 49 (1994), pp. 231–77, at p. 264: 'As a framework agreement and code of conduct, the WTO Agreement sets out the basic rights and duties of its member countries and lays down a new legal basis for international movements of goods, services, persons, trade-related investments and intellectual property rights.'

[171] For the real-life consequences of IMF, World Bank and WTO policies in developing countries see J. Stiglitz, *Globalization and its Discontents* (New York: Norton, 2002).

the world economy order is judged one-sidedly by the criteria of market efficiency and the protection of property rights – and hence by the contractarian ideal of mutual advantage under the given global starting conditions. From a neoliberal point of view, this is not only 'just'[172] but also serves the maximization of the 'global public good'. Too little account is taken of vital-political points of view such as:

- global justice and the maintenance of humane living conditions in countries or regions of the world which, on account of a poor starting point in regard to educational standards, infrastructure or simply because of an unfavourable geographical situation, have little chance of becoming competitive in the worldwide competition of 'locational qualities' (rule of law and observation of human rights, particularly of workers' rights, priority for meeting basic needs or the development of the basic capabilities of the layers of the population with little purchasing power);[173]
- the intrinsic value of cultural traditions and life forms which differ from an entrepreneurial life form (lack of cultural neutrality of competition);[174]
- the planetary ecological problems in view of the indisputable fact that the Western lifestyle cannot be generalized to the global level without overstraining or destroying the natural resources of the earth, which itself gives rise to a serious problem of justice (socio-ecological sustainability).

In regard to the last mentioned problem complex there are at least recognizable endeavours to include the establishment of 'ecological legitimacy criteria' for internationally exchanged goods and their production conditions in the WTO agreements with the aim of restricting *eco-dumping* beyond national borders.[175] In the short or long term there will be an urgent need to undertake analogous efforts in order to create barriers and to determine minimal standards for the prevention of *social dumping* in the form of so-called 'social clauses', particularly with reference to core labour standards as defined by the International Labour Organization (ILO). It is namely questionable from a vital-political point

[172] From the neoliberal point of view every restriction on the freedom of contract or exchange at the international level is regarded from the start as 'discrimination' and thus as 'unjust'. As has been shown in Section 5.3 however, nothing can be said about the justice and injustice of exchange relationships without a deontological-ethical judgement on the *starting conditions* of the exchange.

[173] For details on the unequal structural starting points see Sachs, *The End of Poverty*, p. 57ff., and the *Human Development Reports* issued by the United Nations Development Programme (New York: Oxford University Press, different years). On basic needs and basic capabilities see Section 7.3.

[174] See Section 6.3. [175] See e.g. Hauser/Schanz, *Das neue GATT*, p. 267ff.

of view when the WTO on the one hand imposes trade sanctions on countries which attempt to gain competitive advantages for the export trade of their national industries by means of subsidies but on the other hand does not permit sanctions against countries which, for example, tolerate violations of fundamental workers' rights by their companies and in this way achieve an unfair advantage in international competition.[176]

From a neoclassical and neoliberal point of view, however, the need for ecological and social legitimacy criteria is restricted to the prevention of negative external effects from one country to another, as such spillovers would reduce the efficiency of the market. But as long as the 'imperfections of the market' take effect only at the national level, the supranational ecological and, in particular, social standards continue to be rejected as 'inefficient' and as a concealed form of protectionism (by countries with well-developed welfare systems), as they serve to prevent the 'optimal' international division of labour in accordance with the comparative competitive advantages of the competing countries:

> We renew our commitment to the observance of internationally recognized [!] core labour standards. (...) We believe that economic growth and development fostered by increased trade and further trade liberalization [!] contribute to the promotion of these standards. We reject the use of labour standards for protectionist purposes, and agree that the comparative advantage of countries, particularly low-wage developing countries, must in no way be put into question.[177]

In such an economistic perspective every country can and should 'optimize' its ecological and social standards as follows:

> The government determines the ecological standard in such a way that, for example, the resulting environmental quality (its utility in accordance with the preferences of the population) corresponds exactly to the direct costs of the standard plus the indirect costs in the form of companies which close down and move abroad. Then there is no further incentive to attract further companies by lowering the standard. The loss of environmental quality would be greater than

[176] The *ILO Declaration on Fundamental Principles and Rights at Work* (1998) covers four areas: (a) freedom of association and the right to collective bargaining; (b) the elimination of forced and compulsory labour; (c) the abolition of child labour; and (d) the elimination of discrimination in the workplace. For the political state of the discussion on social clauses see A. Chan/R. Ross, 'Racing to the Bottom: International Trade without a Social Clause', *Third World Quarterly* 24/6 (2003), pp. 1011–28; C. Granger/J.-M. Siroën, 'Core Labour Standards in Trade Agreements: From Multilateralism to Bilateralism', *Journal of World Trade* 40/5 (2006), pp. 813–36.

[177] World Trade Organization, *Singapore Ministerial Declaration* (Geneva: WTO, 1996). Obviously, the order of priority between the declared 'commitment' and the 'believed' economic logic either remains ambivalent or is hidden in a utilitarian and contractualistic idea of 'internationally recognized' standards.

the benefits arising from the establishment of companies and the diminution of the direct costs of the standard.[178]

With this form of environmental economics or analogous 'social economics' the economistic idea of maximizing the public good returns with a vengeance, quite apart from the questionable assessment of environmental quality or social conditions on the basis of (whose?) subjective preferences.

An *ordoliberal* further development of the WTO is now appearing on the horizon, going beyond this kind of regulatory economism and moving in the direction of a programme promoting a step by step vital-political orientation of global competition in accordance with criteria that are not purely economistic. This could lead to the acknowledgment of the insight that an adequate consideration of all the vital-political lifeworld issues must be seen as an ethically and politically justified precondition for a legitimate global economy and not merely as the hoped-for consequence of free competition following its own logic in harmony with the market.[179] The diagnosis and the danger of serious social and ecological follow-up costs of an unregulated globalization are so evident that they require no further elucidation after the detailed general critique of economism and the institutional-ethical considerations on the primacy of vital policy presented above.

We can see, furthermore, that a globalization of the market which is not subject to vital-political restrictions is also rather questionable for the individual national economies from a macro-economic point of view. Even in countries like Germany and Switzerland with an above-average export-based economic structure and (according to the usual world rankings) a comparatively very good position in regard to the international competitiveness of some of their industries, a one-sided export orientation ignores the obviously ambivalent internal effects on the domestic economy. The advantage of acquiring contracts for the export industries and their domestic (in as far as these are also internationally competitive!) or foreign suppliers must be weighed against the fact that

[178] N. Berthold/J. Wilpert, 'Umwelt- und Sozialklauseln: Gefahr für den Freihandel?', *Wirtschaftsdienst – Zeitschrift für Wirtschaftspolitik* 76 (1996), pp. 596–604, at p. 599. Berthold and Hilpert (p. 601) regard the universal validity of 'minimal social standards which are as a rule identical with human rights' as justified. But the decisive question of where the borderline lies between what the authors regard as justifiable minimal standards and supposedly 'unfair' international standards that destroy comparative competitive advantages is left unanswered. For a critique of this kind of 'optimizing' environmental economics see Ulrich, *Transformation*, p. 219ff.

[179] On this confusion of preconditions and consequences of the market as a belated intellectual expression of the deistic religious background to classical political economy see Section 9.1 (1).

local trade and industry provide by far the largest number of jobs and continue to depend on the purchasing power of the domestic clients.[180] But the enormous global pressure to reduce costs tends to cause a drop in real wages of the low and middle income groups, as was (and still is) the case in a striking fashion in the USA and Great Britain, the two torch bearers of the great neoliberal or even paleoliberal experiment. An at least partial conflict of interests between the import-oriented and the export-oriented branches of industry as well as between the companies and employees active in them then arises, which in fact contradicts the thesis of the common good so sweepingly advocated by the radical supporters of globalization.

In view of the complexity of the overall internal effects of globalization in the economic, social and ecological domains, it is permissible to doubt the usefulness of such a one-sided economic-political criterion as the *international competitiveness* of an entire economy, which cannot in any case be clearly operationalized.[181] Even from a purely macroeconomic perspective the assumed parallelism and clear causation of the various economically relevant bases (balance of payments, strength of currency, share of world markets, export-import quotas, gross national product, employment levels etc.) are not given. It is, for example, often the case that an increase in the export quota is accompanied by an increase in imports; but if an internal relationship between the two quantities exists and the growing exports (of stronger branches) are interpreted as a sign of increased international competitiveness, the accompanying growth of imports cannot at the same time be taken as an indication of the loss of competitiveness (of other branches). This would be the case, however, if the international flow of goods is to have any significance at all as an indicator. Furthermore, changes in the exchange rate regularly thwart efforts to achieve 'an increase in international competitiveness' especially in the case of highly competitive countries. Recent studies have in fact shown that entire economies (nations) do not provide a meaningful basis for the explanation of international competitiveness. Although the politico-economic institutional framework of a state is a relevant and influential factor, another element turns

[180] A radical version of that 'dilemma of globalization' is raised with Hans-Werner Sinn's thesis of a growing 'bazaar' character of export-based economies like Germany. See H.-W. Sinn, 'The Dilemma of Globalisation: A German Perspective', *Économie Internationale* 100 (2004), pp. 111–20; Sinn, 'The Pathological Export Boom and the Bazaar Effect: How to Solve the German Puzzle', *World Economy* 29/9 (2006), pp. 1157–75.

[181] On this point see U. van Suntum, 'Internationale Wettbewerbsfähigkeit einer Volkswirtschaft: Ein sinnvolles wirtschaftspolitisches Ziel?', *Zeitschrift für Wirtschafts- und Sozialwissenschaften* 106 (1986), pp. 495–507.

out to be far more significant, namely the presence or absence of regionally concentrated branches ('clusters'). Some of these are particularly competitive at the international level because of the complex coincidence of a variety of (partially historical) factors, not least of which is the local internal competition between the market leaders in the respective branches.[182]

Finally, from a vital-political perspective, it must be asked whether low wage levels at home, which are usually regarded as a means of increasing international competitiveness, can at the same time be a means of achieving a higher wage level at a later stage – or could it perhaps be the case that the welfare of the *nation as a whole* has ceased to be the aim of national competitiveness? Ultimately we are faced here with a symptomatic economistic reversal of ends and means. Behind the conclusion by analogy from the successful market position of an individual company to the national economy as a whole the old economistic fiction of the public good manifests itself. For this reason economists who have examined the concept more closely increasingly consider that it is:

> advisable ... to eliminate the concept of international competitiveness of a national economy from the vocabulary of economics or at least to use it much more carefully than hitherto.[183]

The significance of international competition between the national institutional frameworks for the location of industry is clear in only one regard: there is a grave danger of a disastrous vital-political downward spiral. Every affected state may then feel compelled to offer the companies in its economic sphere short-term comparative cost advantages by creating more favourable frame conditions (in particular lower taxes, social dues and environmental requirements), thus forcing other states to follow suit if they are to remain competitive and to maintain their share of the world market. Consequently, under the conditions of globalization, the incorporation of the market in a vital-political order is impossible in a single state.

(2) Searching for the sites of supranational regulatory politics

Adopting the perspective of integrative economic ethics and the corresponding socio-economic idea of rationality, we have described the vital-political regulatory tasks as constitutive for a market economy in the

182 On this point see M. E. Porter, *The Competitive Advantage of Nations* (New York: Free Press, 1990); P. Krugman, *Geography and Trade* (Cambridge MA/London: MIT Press, 1991); for a survey see Hao Ma, 'Toward Global Competitive Advantage: Creation, competition, cooperation, and co-option', *Management Decision* 42/7 (2004), pp. 907–24.

183 Suntum, 'Internationale Wettbewerbsfähigkeit', p. 503f.

service of life, thus rendering the primacy of politics over the logic of the global market indispensable. If this institutional-ethical claim is to be upheld the following vital-political principle must then be observed: *the spaces in which the institutional preconditions for observance of the primacy of politics are given must be identical with the spaces in which a market operates.*

The requirements of this principle can be met essentially in two different ways:

– Those who advocate a global market must (if they are not economistically narrow-minded) also support a global vital-political framework. But then the difficult question arises as to the institutional 'site' of global vital policy and as to whether such a framework can be created at all in view of the enormously divergent interests of all the states and regions of the world.
– Those who reject global vital policy or regard it as unrealizable for the moment cannot (if they are not economistically narrow-minded) approve of a sweeping and unlimited globalization of competition either. They will instead welcome the limitation of transnational markets to those areas in which a normative instance exists for the legitimation and implementation of a vital-political framework that is binding on all participants in the market.[184]

The second path might be more realistic and advisable as it permits an evolutionary step-by-step vital-political learning process on the transnational political stage. World-wide regulatory agencies able to ensure the compatibility of market dynamics with today's and the future's vital-political requirements in the human, social and environmental spheres – and all this compatible with democracy – are not yet in sight. The direct leap from the national to the global level is accordingly too great to remain politically controllable. Suitable world-wide political institutions and procedures of *global governance* which meet the requirements of a free democratic basic order and do not restrict the fundamental rights of modern citizens but, on the contrary, expand them transnationally, are in part not even at the planning stage; their development must consequently be seen as an epochal challenge.[185] We need only consider how weak the political will is even in the European Union to legitimate the developing political union by means of a European constitution that could guarantee its citizens uniform personality and political as well as

[184] For a similar position in regard to a 'Europe of social states' see H. Afheldt, *Wohlstand für niemand? Die Marktwirtschaft entlässt ihre Kinder*, 2nd edn (Munich: Kunstmann, 1999), p. 216.

[185] On this point see D. Held, 'Democracy, the Nation State and the Global System', in Held (ed.), *Political Theory Today*, pp. 197–235.

economic citizenship rights.[186] But this constitutional framework is necessary if the guiding ethical ideas of deliberative order politics are to be fulfilled.[187]

There is, hence, a need for the creation of an *intermediary level* in the form of large multinational regions which are controllable from a regulatory-political point of view.[188] The already existing or developing transnational economic blocs (EU, ASEAN, NAFTA, MERCOSUR, etc.) could take on this obvious but to date scarcely realized 'vital' political task and implement its ideas internally in the course of time. In many areas such multinational units could implement generalizable vital-political standards at a supra-regional level more easily than national governments, since these are all too often subject to the pressure of the particular interests of powerful industries at the national level. It would be a precondition that individual states are not granted a right of veto. Well-ordered global markets could then be achieved by networking and adapting the established supra-regional vital orders. They could be created step by step in those economic sectors in which a worldwide political agreement on and implementation of global institutional frameworks has been reached.

The vital-political learning path sketched above opens up the vision of a future multi-layered economy whose principle would not be the unconditional deregulation of global markets but the differentiation of various economic sectors, 'localized' at the regional, national or global level depending on the vital-political priorities they have from a cultural, social, ecological *and* national-economic point of view. In this way it would be possible to create, alongside one another, a network of various locally limited and protected markets, national domestic markets or supranational markets within multinational economic units such as the EU and, finally, some open global markets with a corresponding transnational order.

Now we must ask which vital-political aspects are decisive in the context of such a multi-stage ordering of the economic sphere. In accordance with the formal normativization tasks treated in the previous section three areas can be distinguished: boundary norms, subjective rights and calculation norms.

[186] The fact that this fundamental democratic deficit is so seldom questioned in the EU can probably be explained only by the weak republican, grass-roots democratic tradition in most of the EU countries and particularly in those which dominate the Union. See Section 8.1, especially n. 13.

[187] See below Section 9.2 (3a).

[188] For a similar position see Afheldt, *Wohlstand für niemand?*, p. 211f.

- *Boundary norms*: these are naturally of fundamental significance for the purpose of delimiting markets geographically. The idea may sound provocative against the background of the (still) dominant ideologies of free trade and globalization, but what is needed, *horribile dictu*, is a new protectionism (now justified in vital-political terms).[189] In contrast to the traditional form of protectionism, this by no means serves to protect powerful national branches from (international) market competition but aims solely at implementing fair vital policy and competition policy requirements for all players in regionally restricted markets. If for some reason such a geographical market boundary setting cannot be realized on a specific regulatory level, in particular on account of the threat of uncontrollable business transfers to locations outside this regulatory sphere, it is then, and only then, necessary to ensure regulation at the next higher level, in accordance with the principle of ethical displacement[190] (subsidiarity principle). Certain normative minimal standards, especially for the prevention of social dumping ('social clauses') and ecological dumping ('environmental clauses'), must in any case be implemented as speedily as possible at a worldwide economic level, be it in the context of the WTO or some other, maybe UN institution.
- *Rights*: the already mentioned institutionalization of comparable personality and citizenship rights is of decisive vital-political importance in every legitimate transnational market.[191] The customary and all too frequent but dubious practice nowadays of subordinating questions of human rights to inter-state commercial interests and thus building up international business relationships from the start on the basis of moral free riding can be brought to an end only in this way. Transnational 'guest companies' must be prevented from achieving unfair competitive advantages by exploiting workers under inhumane conditions or by taking advantage of the lack of environmental regulations in developing countries with weak or corrupt governments and thus enabling them to exercise pressure for the reduction of employment, social or environmental standards in their countries of origin too (threat of moving abroad). It will, therefore, be necessary to subject them contractually to the maintenance of defined basic rights as a general condition for admission to a sphere of the market regulated in accordance

189 For clear support of this position see T. Lang/C. Hines, *The New Protectionism: Protecting the Future Against Free Trade* (London: Earthscan Publications, 1993), particularly pp. 125ff. and 154. In a similar vein Afheldt, *Wohlstand für niemand?*, p. 219.

190 See R. T. De George, *Competing with Integrity in International Business* (New York/ Oxford: Oxford University Press, 1993), p. 97f.

191 On the categories of moral rights see Section 7.1.

with vital-political principles. It would be best if the economically powerful blocs operating globally would themselves require 'their' globally active companies to apply the standards for the maintenance of human and citizens' rights valid in domestic business (particularly in the EU and NAFTA) to their operations beyond the national borders. Particular attention should be paid to the observation of children's rights (restricted employment of children and youths) and general workers' rights in the guest countries and regions.[192]

- *Calculation norms*: in an economic association of world regions these norms fulfil internally the same manifold tasks stated in Section 9.2 in a national perspective. They serve the purpose both of internalizing external effects and of achieving the best possible neutralization of the market-internal (power) effects. Particular importance as a criterion for the delimitation of local or regional market areas must be accorded to the implementation of political measures controlling and restricting transport for ecological reasons, as this can create decisive incentives for the increased local production of goods involving intensive transportation.[193] Externally, at the level of the relationships between large regional or global units, central importance must rather be attributed to agreements on inter-regional principles regulating exchange in regard to fair trade and the implementation of socially and ecologically acceptable production standards for export articles. As a transitional step towards the improvement of transparency on the vital-political production conditions of imports, particularly for buyers in other regions of the world, a system of voluntary labels could be introduced which would be awarded whenever higher production standards than those required in the land of origin were met.

192 See the proposal for ten corresponding international basic rights in T.J. Donaldson, 'Rights in the Global Market', in Freeman (ed.), *State of the Art*, pp. 139–62, and Freeman, *The Ethics of International Business* (New York/Oxford: Oxford University Press, 1990). Donaldson's proposal is not, however, in accordance with the citizenship rights systematics advocated here and is, from this point of view, incomplete. For endeavours on the world-political level the 'UN Draft Norms on the Responsibilities of Trans-National Corporations' is as important as it is controversial. See *Draft Norms on the Responsibilities of Transnational Corporations and other Business Enterprises with Regard to Human Rights*, adopted by the United Nations Sub-Commission for the Promotion and Protection of Human Rights (SCHR) in August 2003 (UN-Doc. N° E/CN.4/Sub.2/2003/12). For a discussion see F. Wettstein/S. Waddock, 'Voluntary or Mandatory: That is (Not) the Question. Linking Corporate Citizenship to Human Rights Obligations for Business', *Zeitschrift für Wirtschafts- und Unternehmensethik* 6/3 (2005), pp. 304–20.

193 For these ideas on the regulated regionalization of transport see also Afheldt, *Wohlstand für niemand?*, p. 215.

Without doubt the regulatory political project outlined here, involving the creation of a multi-staged network of local, national, supranational and global economies, will take decades to achieve. But from a vital-political point of view it is surely a more convincing alternative than the rather different line adopted at present of approving unconditionally the global competition between existing institutional frameworks. Republican-ethical support for the vital-political project can come, above all, from two directions:

- firstly, from a critical global public sphere, whose enormous political potential has already been demonstrated in a number of situations, such as, for example, the case of the Brent Spar oil platform;[194]
- secondly, through the increased republican-ethical self-commitment and the acceptance of political responsibility for the institutional framework by the major actors in the potentially unlimited global market: the big transnational corporations. These companies, whose importance as the 'site' of the morality of economic activity inevitably grows with the declining power of the nation states, is the next focus of our attention: corporate ethics is now called for.

[194] For the rise of a transnational civil society see M. Kaldor, *Global Civil Society: An Answer to War* (Cambridge: Polity, 2003).

10 Corporate ethics

'The business of business is business' is a well-known rhetorical formula. Business people should concern themselves with their business and nothing else, as this is also the best way of serving the public interest. The formula suggests that good business management is characterized purely and simply by a strict observance of the commercial criteria of success on the market. Richard De George calls this 'the myth of amoral business'.[1] According to this myth business people do not need to preoccupy themselves explicitly with ethical questions in regard to their activities, since these are amoral (i.e. free of morals and not immoral) matters which cannot be adequately judged from a moral point of view.

However, the formula does contain implicitly an idea of corporate ethics in regard to the socially correct function and the legitimacy of business activities. It states that the 'business of business' consists in selling goods and services of all kinds at a profit. Ultimately business is neither an aesthetic, charitable nor political affair, but simply business. The standard by which good business is measured is the achieved or achievable net profit, no more no less. Thus the maximization of profit seems to be the natural goal and the constitutive principle of 'free entrepreneurship'. According to the myth of amoral business it is precisely the strict observance of the so-called *profit principle* by the entrepreneur which ensures that the private economy serves the general interests of society in the best possible way. The profit principle is, therefore, in itself a good thing, at least under the conditions of a functioning competitive market.

The manner of talking about the 'business of business' obviously serves the purpose of normatively justifying the 'profit principle'. It characterizes profit orientation as a form of action which is not only permissible but even imperative. Even the most radical advocates of a private economy 'free' of ethics implicitly or explicitly seek to legitimize their standpoint by

[1] See De George, *Business Ethics*, p. 3ff.

claiming that this focus best serves the public interest. How else could they assert that in spite of, or even precisely on account of, their pursuit of 'pure' private profit they have no moral qualms whatsoever? No matter what position we adopt towards the 'business of business' formula, we are automatically involved in an economic-ethical discourse about the correct social role of entrepreneurial activity. And, whether we reflect upon it or not, we inevitably have a certain normative 'social theory' at the back of our minds, i.e. a comprehensive economic and socio-philosophical understanding of a corporation's position in society and of the corresponding economic order.

These institutional-ethical premises of all corporate ethics have a profound impact on the normative ideas as to how responsible managers should act in concrete situations. It is therefore important in corporate ethics to take these premises into consideration. The institutional basic conception of a corporation and the way it is embedded in a legitimate overall regulatory conception need to be adequately determined. Only then is it possible to decide which forms of corporate activity are responsible and which 'non-economic' moral demands on the management can be regarded as reasonable in spite of the corporation's need to assert itself under competitive conditions.[2]

It is striking how rarely this insoluble bond between the institutional ethics of business enterprise and the responsible ethics of managers is really taken into account. The fundamental normative question as to how the social function of a corporation should be determined and legitimated is usually settled from the outset by reference to its historical, factually given constitution. And quite often this answer is simply tacitly and unquestioningly assumed. In this way critical reflection is abandoned in the face of the normative force of the factual.[3] In academic discussions on corporate ethics this abandonment of reflection often remains unquestioned because it corresponds to the customary institutional separation of the disciplines of business administration and political economy. The separation is simply reproduced by restricting corporate ethics to management ethics, i.e. to an ethics of corporate management under the

[2] On the understanding of the supposed problem of the (im)possibility of moral action under competitive conditions as a problem of reasonable expectation see Section 4.3 (3).

[3] Steinmann/Löhr, *Grundlagen der Unternehmensethik*, p. 100f., start explicitly from the thesis that, 'in a given historical situation', the democratically established institutions 'permit' 'the "abandonment of justification" by persons endowed [by these institutions] with freedom of action' (i.e. the management). 'The entrepreneur or manager to whom the question of legitimation is addressed can answer it in principle by reference to the existing laws.' However, Steinmann and Löhr (ibid., p. 103) do at least postulate the need for reflection on the question of legitimacy *outside* corporate ethics, namely in 'economic ethics' (which is assigned to the level of political economy).

'given' but nonetheless normative ideas of corporate action. Horst Steinmann and Albert Löhr, for example, state:

> that the profit principle is a historico-structural given in the competitive economy which a single company cannot afford to question.[4]

They thus assume that in the context of the historically 'given' economic order and constitution of the company the profit principle already has a general ethical 'presumption of correctness'[5] in its favour and thereby quietly convert a factual into a *normative* 'given'. Although they state that this presumption of correctness must be tested again in every 'individual case', corporate ethics can, in their opinion, only be concerned with a 'situationally correct application of the profit principle'.[6] We will examine what that means precisely in detail later.

In contrast, the knowledge-constitutive interest of *integrative corporate ethics* consists precisely in critical reflection on the ethical preconditions for the legitimate pursuit of profit without abandoning reflection in the face of pre-established normative 'presumptions of correctness' or empirically given inherent necessities. Integrative corporate ethics does not, therefore, start from a 'situationally correct application' but from a foundational critique of the profit principle. This means a critical discussion of all the normative requirements for ethically rational economic activity in and by corporations, including both the basic preconditions for legitimacy and life-serving orientations of corporate value creation.[7] Corporate ethics is thus conceived as a rational ethics of corporate economic activity as a whole. It involves critical work on the normative premises of the self-definition of business administration as a (not entirely) autonomous discipline and on its efforts to seal itself off from such reflection. Corporate ethics will achieve its greatest practical

[4] Ibid., p. 130; similarly Homann/Blome-Drees, *Wirtschafts- und Unternehmensethik*, p. 182f.

[5] See Steinmann/Oppenrieder, 'Unternehmensethik', p. 174, Steinmann/Löhr, 'Einleitung', p. 8, and *Grundlagen der Unternehmensethik*, p. 107; similarly Homann/Blome-Drees, *Wirtschafts- und Unternehmensethik*, p. 39, with reference to the first mentioned source.

[6] Steinmann/Löhr, *Grundlagen der Unternehmensethik*, p. 107; see also A. Löhr, *Unternehmensethik und Betriebswirtschaftslehre* (Stuttgart: Metzler, 1991), p. 234.

[7] For a fundamental critical examination see Ulrich, 'Unternehmensethik – diesseits oder jenseits der betriebswirtschaftlichen Vernunft?' and 'Unternehmensethik – Führungsinstrument oder Grundlagenreflexion?', in Steinmann/Löhr (eds.), *Unternehmensethik*, pp. 189–210, at p. 194f. More recently Freeman, *The Politics of Stakeholder Theory*, p. 418f., has arrived at a similar standpoint. He also postulates the need for critical reflection on the institutional-ethical premises of business ethics and proposes seeing 'the role of the business ethicist as reinventing the corporation'. This involves a 'moral discourse' on 'the ideas of the value-creating activity of business'. This means 'giving up the role of finding some moral bedrock for business'.

significance when it effectively serves as an integrative mode of critical (self-) reflection within 'normal' business economic thinking.

Such a fundamentally critical approach develops the specific corporate ethical consequences from the outcome of the general ethical critique of economism which we have already elaborated in Part II. It in no way confuses the levels of institutional politics and corporate policy respectively as 'sites' of morality. It rather represents a systematic consideration of the insoluble reciprocal relationships between socially responsible corporate management and the institutional ethics of market economy.

In the treatment of the topic it will, therefore, be necessary to include this inner relationship between the institutional-ethical premises and the corporate-ethical discussion, both in regard to the positions to be criticized and to the context of the proposed conception of integrative corporate ethics. First of all the various attempts to interpret and justify the entrepreneurial 'profit principle' and the underlying corporate understanding must be closely studied in the context of a critique of economism (Section 10.1). It will then be possible to systematically order and to reflect upon the basic corporate-ethical positions advocated at present in terms of their more or less critical treatment of the supposed 'profit principle'. The foundational critique of these positions then leads us to the approach of integrative corporate ethics (Section 10.2). This in turn opens up again the question of dealing fairly with the partially conflicting 'claims' of various stakeholders (groups of claimants) in the corporations. At the same time it opens up the way to an understanding of the social institution 'enterprise' as a pluralistic arrangement for the creation of value which is not economistically restricted but firmly embedded in republican-ethical principles. Corporate policy can then be understood as a genuinely political undertaking to be oriented by the regulative idea of ethical discourse on business legitimacy as well as on the reasonableness of moral demands on the company (Section 10.3). Finally the structural and mental preconditions for a corresponding corporate culture of integrity and responsibility and the consequences for a robust integrative 'ethical programme' in corporations will be briefly developed (Section 10.4).

10.1 The basic problem of corporate ethics: 'profit principle' and legitimate business activity

Under what preconditions can the pursuit of 'private' profit by a corporation be justified? How far are the (side) effects of the pursuit of profit on all those affected justifiable and, vice versa, how far are the claims of those involved tolerable for the corporation in view of its need to assert itself in a competitive economy? In consideration of the complexity of ethical legitimacy questions in general, as developed in the earlier chapters, and of the institutional-ethical questions in particular, an easy sweeping solution cannot be expected from the outset. Nonetheless such a sweeping answer still plays a central role not only in the pre-understanding of many business practitioners but also in academic discussions on the topic. Since the neoliberal turn the tendency to offer simple solutions has probably even increased, namely in the form of the validity claim of the so-called profit principle as the highest norm (or indeed principle) of legitimate entrepreneurial activity.

The talk of the 'profit principle' derives from a specific tradition of Business Administration in the German-speaking countries, which cannot be found so directly either in the Anglo-Saxon or any other theoretical tradition. The prominent role of the 'profit principle' can be traced back to the Nestor of (neo-)classical German business economics, Erich Gutenberg. In the first volume of his 'Grundlagen der Betriebswirtschaftslehre' (Fundamentals of Business Administration) he attributes central importance to the 'erwerbswirtschaftliche Prinzip' ('principle of economic acquisition') – a concept which he uses as an equivalent of the profit principle:

> If we ask how companies in the market economy system are in a position to produce exactly the kinds and quantities of goods which are needed without central instructions and directives the answer will be: the effect is achieved by the operation of a principle which has nothing to do directly with meeting the overall economic need, namely the *economic acquisition principle*. It is not completely identical with the *principle of profit maximization*, although this is its culmination. The acquisitive principle provides the *maxim* according to which the heads of autonomous companies make their business decisions and decide whether these decisions were *right* or *wrong*.
>
> The system is based on a very important *assumption*, namely that in a national economy the provision with goods and services is best ensured when each individual company attempts *in the long term to realize the greatest possible profit* on the invested capital (. . .). Furthermore, the view is advocated that this system at the same time has the *tendency* to employ the production factors labour, land and capital fully.
>
> *Experience* has shown that these *ideas* do not always correspond to reality and, in particular, that what happens in the market economy empirically does not accord with the *hypothetical* borderline case of total competition. But this does not rule out the possibility that the system of free companies in a free market economy was projected in accordance with the *idea* of total competition.[8]

The key words italicised in the text indicate the inadequately qualified methodological status of the 'profit principle' as sketched here.[9]

[8] Gutenberg, *Grundlagen der Betriebswirtschaftslehre*, p. 464 (my italics). [9] Ibid., p. 467.

Level \ Methodological status	*Empirical thesis*	*Normative postulate*
Personal action orientation	(1) Motive: subjective pursuit of profit	(2) Moral duty: capitalist entrepreneurial ethos
Systemic functional mechanism	(3) 'Inherent necessity': objective profit requirements	(4) Institutional rules of the game: 'profit principle'

Figure 10.1. Possible interpretations of entrepreneurial profit orientation

Gutenberg describes it imprecisely and ambiguously as a (normative) 'idea', a 'principle' and 'maxim' constitutive of corporate actions within the system and at the same time as a methodical ('hypothetical') 'assumption' or an empirical 'tendency'. We will return to the nonetheless clearly determinable methodological status of the profit principle in Gutenberg later; for the moment we will analyse and systematize the different interpretative variants of the corporate profit principle. A two-dimensional differentiation of four possible definitions of what can be understood by the profit principle – or, more neutrally formulated, the profit orientation of the corporations – suggests itself. On the one hand we are dealing either with an empirical thesis or with a normative postulate; and on the other hand either with a personal action orientation or with an (impersonally operative) systemic functional mechanism of the market economy order. These two distinctions allow us to combine the four systematic interpretative possibilities for the profit orientation of corporations in a single matrix (Figure 10.1).[10]

In what follows these four possible interpretations of the 'profit principle' will be subjected to a critical examination of their foundations (Subsections 1–4). Furthermore, the methodological status of the 'profit principle' in the theory of business administration will be elucidated and its uselessness as the starting point for corporate ethics demonstrated (5).

[10] First presented in P. Ulrich, 'Unternehmensethik und 'Gewinnprinzip'. Versuch der Klärung eines unerledigten wirtschaftsethischen Grundproblems', in H. G. Nutzinger (ed.), *Wirtschaftsethische Perspektiven III* (Berlin: Duncker & Humblot, 1996), pp. 137–71.

(1) *Profit orientation as a motive for entrepreneurship: the personal pursuit of profit*

This interpretation presents an empirical-analytical hypothesis in regard to the actual motives of entrepreneurial action, which does not give rise to any particular problems from the point of view of economic ethics. It is of no consequence whether it can be proved empirically that the pursuit of profit is the dominant motive of entrepreneurs (or managers employed by companies) or whether the motivational situation is complex, including a moral dimension, so that the pursuit of profit is only one motive among others. The latter viewpoint corresponds after all to the opinion of such famous social economists as, for example, Adam Smith,[11] Amartya Sen,[12] Amitai Etzioni,[13] Jon Elster[14] and indeed of most social scientists.

Regardless of the empirical situation: the validity of ethical demands does not depend on the objective case (social validity) but on whether the validity claim can be inter-subjectively or trans-subjectively justified in a binding fashion (normative validity). The attempt to reinterpret the question of the actual intentions of entrepreneurs as a normative requirement of corporate ethics would be a category mistake from a philosophical-ethical point of view. What matters in (economic and corporate) ethics is precisely the critical questioning of factually given motives for action in regard to legitimacy and accountability.

In this sense a generally exaggerated or situatively illegitimate pursuit of profit by individuals is at most a matter requiring corporate ethical clarification or criticism. This however, already presumes the existence of a critical normative idea of corporate ethics beyond the 'profit principle'. If, moreover, such individual-ethical attempts at clarification do little or nothing to change the behaviour of business leaders in practice, we may well characterize such endeavours as 'unrealistic' from an empirical perspective. Yet this does not give rise, in principle, to any problems of justification but merely to a pragmatic problem of motivation.[15]

(2) *Profit orientation as the moral duty of the entrepreneur: the capitalistic entrepreneurial ethos*

This interpretation of the corporate profit orientation must be seen in the context of the religious and intellectual historical developments. These

[11] See Smith, *Theory of Moral Sentiments*. [12] See Sen, *On Ethics and Economics*, p. 16ff.
[13] See A. Etzioni, *The Moral Dimension: Toward a New Economics* (New York: Free Press, 1988).
[14] See Elster, *Cement of Society*, p. 202ff.; Elster, 'Possibility of Rational Politics', p. 120.
[15] On the relationship between moral questions of justification and of motivation see the fundamental treatment in Section 1.2.

led in the early modern period to the crystallization of a specifically capitalistic entrepreneurial ethos which raised the profit orientation to the level of an identity-shaping virtue. What happened basically is that the internalized practical and mental constraints of an acquisitively oriented life style were elevated in exaggerated fashion to the normative level, as we have seen above.[16] In its strictest form striving for the maximization of profit is interpreted not only as the moral right but even as the moral duty of the entrepreneur. The most famous formulation of this ethos can be found in the much quoted sentence of Milton Friedman:

The social responsibility of business is to increase its profits.[17]

The historical development of this metaphysical-economistic conviction is absolutely constitutive for the concept of the entrepreneur. In this concept a powerful historical combination of the corresponding capitalistic ethos with the specific life and social form of the early modern bourgeoisie takes effect.[18] Even today this thought pattern is amazingly widespread among the leaders of the economy.[19] As proof of its topicality we can take the remarks made by Gerd Habermann in the name of the influential Arbeitsgemeinschaft Selbständiger Unternehmer (Working Group of Independent Entrepreneurs) in Germany, who expressly professes his commitment to the traditional entrepreneurial ethos in the following words:

Thus the commercial *entrepreneur* also has a specific *ethos* on which he must model his actions, if he wishes to act in accordance with his social function and duty. His *greatest social responsibility* is to offer goods and services in the most economic manner possible. His *imperative as an entrepreneur* is, therefore: Produce! Be useful for your customers! *Be successful*! Be enterprising! In this respect there is no contradiction between *what is required economically* and *what is morally right*: *both coincide*. It does not contradict morality, therefore, but is in fact the moral duty of the entrepreneur to do everything that is in accordance with his company's rationale in order to keep the company 'fit', even if this means carrying out measures

16 On this point see Sections 4.1. and 5.1; on the reasons for the historical 'victory' of this life form see also Section 6.3.

17 This is the title of Friedman's essay in *The New York Times Magazine*, 13 September 1970, pp. 32–3, 122, 124 and 126; reprinted, e.g., in Gibson (ed.), *Business Ethics*, pp. 206–11, and in other readers. One should note that Friedman does not use the adjective 'social' loosely (in the sense of 'economic') but really means comprehensive social responsibility. Thus the credo expressed in the title cannot be fully derived from Friedman's argument saying that corporate executives are the agents of the business owners and therefore are obliged to maximize profits for their principals.

18 See P. Ulrich, 'Unternehmerethos', in Enderle *et al.* (eds.), *Lexikon der Wirtschaftsethik*, col. 1165–76.

19 See Ulrich/Thielemann, *Ethik und Erfolg*, p. 34ff., and 'How do Managers Think?', p. 883ff.

which are painful for individual employees. The precondition is, however, that, as a producer, the entrepreneur observes the more general moral and legal rules, as is required of everyman. Conflicts will only arise if he fails in this respect. Within these rules, however, *the entrepreneurial activity itself is the first moral duty.*[20]

The fact that an employer here elucidates his understanding of himself and his role as a businessman – his entrepreneurial ethos – certainly deserves personal respect, but what he says must, nonetheless, be subjected to critical reflection. Such reflection points out the difference between corporate *ethics* and the mere statement of a pre-existent entrepreneurial *ethos* characterized by conventional moral awareness. And this difference is constitutive of corporate ethics; modern business and economic ethics must be conceived generally at the post-conventional level and cannot be satisfied with the uncritical reproduction of a conventional professional ethos.[21] A corporate ethical 'profit principle' cannot be rationally grounded at the conventional level.

The fact that Habermann argues at the level of a conventional moral awareness can be recognized precisely by the manner in which he refers to 'general moral and legal rules, as ... required of everyman'; they are assumed to be pre-existent, generally known and unproblematic. Friedman's postulate cited above reveals exactly the same conventionalist restriction: it is the duty of business leaders:

to make as much money as possible while conforming to the basic rules of the society, both those embodied in the law and those embodied in ethical custom.[22]

Beyond the existing ethical 'customs' and legal rules an autonomous ethical-critical reflection on the principles of responsible action seems neither necessary nor conceivable under the conditions of economic self-assertion. Even if the measures which must be carried out in a corporation are possibly 'painful', 'what is required economically' cannot conflict with the observation of moral duties, as it is embedded in 'more general rules' and is itself the 'first moral duty' (Habermann) of the entrepreneur. The existing rules of the game of competition in the market economy must simply be accepted and observed but not questioned in regard to their ethical justifiability or any kind of accountability in concrete social situations. Friedman, again, has clearly pointed this out in a variant formulation of his postulate:

There is one and only one social responsibility of business – to use its resources and engage in activities designed to increase its profits *so long as it stays within the*

[20] Habermann, 'Teilen oder produzieren?' (my italics). See also the reply of Ulrich, 'Zwei Ebenen unternehmerischer Verantwortung'.
[21] On this point see Sections 1.2, 1.3 and 1.5.
[22] Friedman, 'Social Responsibility of Business', p. 32.

rules of the game, which is to say, engages in open and free competition without deception or fraud.[23]

But what actually justifies the strictly binding character of the rules of the game? The answer to this question leads us from the action-theoretical and individual-ethical to the system-theoretical and institutional-ethical interpretation of the entrepreneurial pursuit of profit. Again we must distinguish between an empirical and a normative version.

(3) Profit orientation as a systemically determined inherent necessity: the requirement of profit as 'not open to debate'

Here the necessity of a – strict or limited – entrepreneurial pursuit of profit is justified by reference to the actual conditions of self-assertion on the market to which the corporations are subject, as an inherent necessity which is given in the existing system of competitive economy. This is then assumed as a factual premise and thus as a condition for the possibility of all corporate ethics in the framework of a 'modern' economic system. Albert Löhr, for example, argues that insight into the necessity of corporate ethics:

leaves the question fully open as to whether it is at all *possible* for the company to engage in independent ethical reflection under the rules of the competitive economy. (...) How far this [the demand to make a profit or to renounce the maximization of profit] is possible or ought to be possible in an individual case is of course an *empirical* question, which will always depend on the capacity of the individual company for economic survival.[24]

Here the normative question of the justifiability of the profit principle is empiristically reinterpreted as a problem of 'room for manoeuvre' which, on account of the general compulsion to achieve a profit, makes corporate ethics only partially 'possible'.[25] The range of a corresponding *corporate ethics under market constraints* is reduced to delimiting normatively the 'situationally just application of the profit principle'.[26] The profit principle itself is seen as a historico-structural given of the competitive

[23] M. Friedman, *Capitalism and Freedom*, p. 133. (my italics).
[24] Löhr, *Unternehmensethik und Betriebswirtschaftslehre*, p. 277f. (italics in the original text). Professor Albert Löhr is president of the *Deutsche Netzwerk Wirtschaftsethik*, the German branch of the European Business Ethics Network (EBEN).
[25] See ibid., p. 278. On this 'possibility theorem' see above Section 4.3 (2).
[26] This is again the standpoint of Löhr, ibid., p. 234ff., and Steinmann/Löhr *Grundlagen der Unternehmensethik*, p. 107ff.

economy, which is 'not open to debate' in regard to the claims of corporate ethics.[27]

We have already dealt in detail with the argument of inherent necessity in a general form and have in the process elaborated the logical primacy of the (subjective) choice of ends over the resulting (!) market constraints.[28] It is not competition in the market economy as such which forces economic agents to follow a certain line in their business activities; it is rather the case that they subject themselves or the heads of their companies to concrete practical constraints by setting their own goals. The more strictly interest in profit is pursued, the more pressing these constraints logically become. In the borderline case premising the maximization of profit the constraints seem almost total or deterministic. The (lack of) 'room for manoeuvre' is thus not primarily an empirical question of given external factors; it increases or decreases in the minds of the entrepreneurs, depending on the degree to which profit orientation is regarded as the normative basis guiding economic activities and on the assumed order of importance between this profit orientation and 'outside' interests.[29] The problem of the more or less clearly perceived (im)possibility of taking interests 'external to the company' into account must therefore be seen as a conflict affecting two aspects of the normative validity claims: on the one hand the *accountability* of the corporations to those affected by their activities and on the other hand the *reasonableness* of certain moral demands on the entrepreneur.

This means that the supposedly empirical compulsion for corporations to pursue profit unconditionally cannot be normatively justified and that it must also be open to critical ethical examination at the level of the individual company. The fundamental corporate ethical problem is not the empirical (im)possibility of moral action but precisely the opposite, namely the normative 'possibility' (admissibility) of the pursuit of profit; the latter must be subjected to the categorical *legitimacy proviso*, as we shall see more precisely later. Only in as far as the entrepreneurial pursuit of profit stands the test of legitimacy, which must always be established in

[27] See Steinmann/Löhr, *Grundlagen der Unternehmensethik*, p. 130. With this exclusion of critical reflection on the *fundamental* justifiability of the profit principle from corporate ethics, however, they contradict their own – better – thesis that ethical considerations are systematically prior to the profit principle not only at the institutional level but also at the company level (p. 107).

[28] See Section 4.3 (3).

[29] Weber, *Economy and Society*, vol. I, p. 139. It is perhaps of interest in this context that Erich Gutenberg, *Unternehmung als Gegenstand*, p. 11, was aware of this voluntarist aspect. After all, he defined a company as 'the result of a purposeful *will* which combines goods for a *uniform end*' (my italics). See the similar statement by Schumpeter in Section 4.3 (3).

concrete situations, can it be ethically approved and permitted, i.e. regarded as legitimate or 'possible' in the ethical sense. In contrast, no reference to the functional demands of the system or to any practical constraints which exist in regard to the pursuit of assumed entrepreneurial goals can directly justify the 'acceptance' of the violation of the moral rights of other persons – this is the humanistic essence of all genuinely liberal ethics. Corporate ethics must also categorically support and sustain this insight instead of sacrificing it from the start to the 'system conditions' of the market economy.

(4) Profit orientation as a regulatory-political rule of the game: the normatively constituted profit principle

It is a known fact that inherent necessities are not pleasant; they are easier to bear in life if a meaning and a normative dignity of their own can be attributed to them. For this reason virtually all the advocates of economic determinism tend to attribute normative force to it and to the accompanying profit principle. The assumption that the questioning of the 'profit principle' at the company level is impossible leads to the thesis that it is also unnecessary; profit-oriented business controlled by regulatory means seems to be sufficient and ethically superior. Thus Steinmann and Löhr, for example, alternate between empirical reference to the 'situative historical boundary conditions of the market economy' which must be observed 'for the conceptional foundation of a corporate ethics'[30] and the normative claim that it is necessary:

> to realize that the system imperatives as the fundamental framework conditions for the actions of companies must in principle already be justified; otherwise it would not be ethically acceptable to call upon the individual economic agents to implement them.[31]

Indeed! But what precisely are the 'already justified system imperatives'? At all events Löhr's vague reference to 'welfare-theoretical considerations' and an 'economically *optimal overall situation* in a society (Pareto optimum)'[32] can clearly be criticized as economism. The

[30] See Steinmann/Löhr, *Grundlagen der Unternehmensethik*, p. 130.
[31] Löhr, *Unternehmensethik und Betriebswirtschaftslehre*, p. 237.
[32] See ibid., p. 237f. (my italics). Like Karl Homann (see below) Löhr, ibid., p. 275, approves 'the call to make profits' (with certain subsidiary conditions) and argues polemically – and not particularly convincingly in view of the economism behind his arguments – against critical reflection on the foundations of the profit principle: 'Those who wish . . . to 'transform' the profit principle not only express (often thoroughly justifiable) criticism of the market economy but at the same time implicitly demand inefficiency' (p. 238). What kind of efficiency in the realization of which and whose values is being defended here? Anonymous efficiency can be intended only as *general* efficiency and thus falls under the economistic fiction of the common good.

utilitarian welfare theory has no dimension of justice ethics whatsoever and is thus clearly unworkable as an institutional-ethical justification of the profit principle. Hidden behind it is the economistic fiction of harmony and the common good in its many variants, which we have already subjected to detailed criticism from an economic-ethical point of view both at the fundamental level of economic theory (Chapter 5) and in the context of regulatory ethics (Chapter 9). Here we can restrict ourselves to pointing out how economism in institutional policies affects attempts to provide a corporate-ethical justification of the profit principle. At least three manifestations can be distinguished: (a) economic determinism of the institutional framework, (b) the business administrative doctrine of formal goals and (c) the shareholder-value doctrine.

(a) The first, particularly distinctive variant can be characterized as *economic framework determinism*. It is advocated especially by Karl Homann. This argumentative strategy is based on the assumption that the institutional framework of the market – as a well-constructed normative practical and legal context determined by the politico-economic order – should have an effect upon the entrepreneur directly through the market mechanism in deterministic fashion, thus disciplining him morally from the outside. Accordingly, for Homann, the institutional framework is *the* 'systematic site of morality'[33] in the market economy, whereby 'in the normal case'[34] the need for ethical self-discipline on the part of the entrepreneur is totally superfluous. It is not surprising, therefore, that Homann also adopts Steinmann and Löhr's general 'presumption of correctness'[35] for the profit principle. Yet, in contrast to them,[36] he advocates the most stringent form:

> Profit maximization thus falls under an ethical 'presumption of correctness' [provided there is a suitable institutional framework].[37]

For Homann the consequence is:

> the insight [sic!] . . . that the companies in a market economy ought to maximize their profits for ethical reasons.[38]

[33] Homann, 'Wettbewerb und Moral', p. 55, Homann/Blome-Drees, *Wirtschafts- und Unternehmensethik*, p. 35.

[34] Homann/Blome-Drees, ibid., p. 117.

[35] See Steinmann/Löhr, *Grundlagen der Unternehmensethik*, p. 107.

[36] As opposed to Homann, Steinmann and Löhr do not normally apply their 'presumption of correctness' to the strict *maximization* of profit; on the contrary they wish to subject it to corporate ethical restrictions. On the resultant *corrective* corporate ethics see below Section 10.3 (3).

[37] Homann/Blome-Drees, *Wirtschafts- und Unternehmensethik*, p. 39, with reference to Steinmann/Löhr, 'Einleitung', p. 8.

[38] Homann/Drees, ibid., p. 183, in an explicit rejection of the critical foundational approach developed here.

> Long-term maximization of profit is, therefore, *not a privilege* of the entrepreneurs for which they must continually apologize; it is rather their *moral duty* because – presuming the existence of a suitable institutional framework – it is precisely this behaviour which best serves the interests of the consumers, the general public.[39]

However, quite apart from the economistic reductionism involved in the terms 'general public' and 'consumers' and the total indeterminacy as to the normative characteristics of 'a suitable institutional framework', we are faced here with a purely 'model-theoretical'[40] or 'paradigmatic'[41] assumption, as Homann admits. Considered 'pragmatically',[42] the institutional framework can scarcely ever be perfect. It then follows logically from the deterministic premises on the framework that 'regulatory deficits have an impact at the level of practical action'; here corporate ethics comes 'into play'. And it is only in the event of such deficits that a subsidiary 'need for moral responsibility of the entrepreneur can be identified'[43] – 'as a temporary helping hand precisely ... where the market and competition fail to function'.[44]

But where does the market economy 'function' and where does it fail to do so? Homann glosses over the fact that the determination of 'deficits in institutional policies' is always based on a normative statement. The entrepreneur is obviously not free to ignore this when he has to decide whether, in a concrete situation, he should 'temporarily' practise a corporate ethical self-limitation of the strict profit maximization he strives for 'in the normal case'. Homann's *stopgap conception of corporate ethics* is therefore self-contradictory. It assumes the need for general corporate-ethical reflection and with it, if it is to make any sense at all, a renunciation of profit maximization on principle. This means, however, that the normative assumption of a 'profit principle' based on institutional ethics must already be abandoned at the level of corporate ethics.

(b) The second manifestation of institutional or corporate political economism is the well-known theoretical notion in business administration that the maximization of profit does not represent the special

39 Ibid., p. 38f. (emphasis in the original text). There is an almost identical formulation at p. 51.

40 Homann, 'Wettbewerb und Moral', p. 35.

41 Ibid., p. 39: 'Paradigmatically, the competitive process from the initial production facilities to the market outcomes is situated in a quasi *determined* context' (my italics). We should recall that such a 'paradigmatic' *as-if* construction has no claim to normative validity. See Section 4.3.

42 Ibid., pp. 38, 48.

43 Last three citations from Homann/Blome-Drees, *Wirtschafts- und Unternehmensethik*, p. 116f.

44 Homann, 'Wettbewerb und Moral', p. 48.

interests of particular parties or the 'practical goal' of the owners of capital. It must instead be understood as an objective *'formal goal' of a corporation* in regard to the general public interest. This is the traditional academic standard justification of the 'profit principle' in business administration studies.[45] The purpose of this separation of 'practical' and 'formal' goals is to attribute to the latter the character of a value-neutral objective and hence purely formal criterion of 'rational' management,[46] which supposedly leaves everything open from an ethical point of view. As it is formulated in traditional business administration studies the term 'formal goal' simply states *that* a company should orientate its actions on the (supposedly formal and incontestable) 'profit principle'; it is the 'practical goal' alone which then determines *how* this should happen. Steinmann and Löhr also adopt this position when they assert:

> that the ethical questionability of entrepreneurial action does not lie in the pursuit of the profit principle as such, but in the question of the *means by which* profits are made.[47]

Only these means (entrepreneurial strategies and operative combinations of production factors) are seemingly 'accessible to ethical reflection'[48] at the company level. Now the point of the talk about 'the formal goal of profit' becomes clear. As long as ethically unproblematic means are available, the pursuit of profit accordingly can – as an ethically deproblematized goal – be permitted without restriction. The conception of a formal goal then logically ends with the call for the *maximization* of profit.[49]

[45] See E. Kosiol, *Die Unternehmung als wirtschaftliches Aktionszentrum: Einführung in die Betriebswirtschaftslehre* (Reinbek: Rowohlt, 1972), p. 226f. Kosiol speaks explicitly of 'the maximization of profit as a formal goal' and attempts to justify this by arguing that here 'financial profit should not be seen as an ultimate goal but only as a means to a higher end' (p. 226).

[46] Again Kosiol, ibid., p. 54, explicitly states: 'The formal goal ... is the expression of the rationality of an action.'

[47] Steinmann/Löhr, *Grundlagen der Unternehmensethik*, p. 112, and the introductory passages to this statement, ibid., p. 101ff. They are forced into this position for systematic reasons, as there would otherwise be no foundation for the 'presumption of correctness' on which their corporate ethics is based. For a concurring standpoint see the business administrator Schneider, *Unternehmensethik und Gewinnprinzip*, p. 81: 'The fact *that* profits are made cannot give rise to ethical misgivings but only the question *how* (with what activities and means) they are achieved and used.'

[48] Steinmann/Löhr, 'Realistische Idee', p. 315; this argument in turn derives from the 'impossibility theorem', according to which the entrepreneurial striving for profit is sweepingly classified as an inherent necessity; 'only the decision as to the specific means by which a company should make a profit ... is open to choice' (Löhr, *Unternehmensethik und Betriebswirtschaftslehre*, p. 276).

[49] Steinmann/Löhr, *Grundlagen der Unternehmensethik*, p. 125, also speak of the 'formal goal of the *maximization* of profit' (my italics), but this is in no way consistent with their corrective approach to corporate ethics, which we will examine more closely in Section 10.2 (3).

It is easy to recognize the old economistic fiction of the common good behind this traditional theoretical attempt of business economists (and ethicists!) to arrive at an ethical-political neutralization of the pursuit of profit as such. Within the framework of economistic premises of harmony the demand for the maximization of profit is unquestionably not neutral in regard to values and interest, as the *quantity* of the achievable profit cannot be isolated from the ethical *quality* of the means and strategies used. What always matters from an ethical point of view, therefore, is primarily the ranking of the 'formal' pursuit of profit in relation to conflicting considerations of the values involved. It is not only the manner in which profit is made (means) but the normative premise *that* profit ought to be made at all in a particular situation which requires justification from a corporate ethical standpoint. This is, incidentally, admitted by Steinmann and Löhr in extreme cases:

> From this precedence [of ethical considerations over the profit principle] the final consequence might even be that a company must be closed down for ethical reasons.[50]

Here the status of the profit principle, which is otherwise taken as formal, is correctly regarded as a *material* value orientation which can conflict with other value standpoints of higher rank and can as such be ethically questionable. But this does not apply only to the borderline cases of a generally valid context. Every ethically (and not merely strategically) motivated self-limitation of a company in favour of the protection of prior legitimate interests (moral rights) of those affected inevitably involves a loss of profit in the sense of a renunciation of a 'possible' maximization of profit. Those who decide for profit maximization also decide against the acceptance of such opportunity costs and thus implicitly against conflicting value standpoints of all kinds. The supposedly formal goal cannot therefore be pursued in isolation from material value preferences – and the latter cannot be chosen without having a decisive impact on the former.

But it is also generally the case that the renunciation of profit maximization out of consideration for market-external value standpoints can in some situations be compensated for by increasing entrepreneurial performance in other situations. A static, mono-causal and mechanistic conception of entrepreneurial self-assertion under competitive conditions, as is particularly typical of the economic determinism criticized above, fails to grasp the true complexity and elasticity both of the entrepreneurial performative process and of the dynamics of competition. It is

[50] Ibid., p. 107.

scarcely ever the case that an ethically motivated decision to restrict the profit target in a specific situation leads to existential problems due to the failure of self-assertion in the market. It is, therefore, all the more reasonable to expect companies to renounce the strict and inconsiderate maximization of profit when this is ethically necessary.

(c) As the last of the three manifestations of the profit principle and of regulatory-political economism that has come into the foreground in recent years we must name the doctrine of the maximization of *shareholder value*.[51] Over and beyond the euphemistic effects of a technical term it involves a more precise rendering of the profit principle in two respects.

On the one hand the concept of shareholder value even leads to a radicalization of the profit principle as it 'makes the expectations of the investors the sole standard by which successful entrepreneurial activity is measured'.[52] It speaks out clearly in favour of the preferential treatment of the interests of one group of claimants over all the other stakeholders – including the management itself[53] – as the guideline for entrepreneurial action. The talk of a 'formal goal' of business activity is then abandoned on the surface, but the corresponding underlying harmonistic assumptions are in fact radicalized. The overall harmonization of societal interests is conceived in terms of a total market society, in accordance with the neoliberal model, entirely by means of efficient capital allocation. The only responsibility the management has is the best possible exploitation of the capital at its disposal, as all decisions on the use of capital for social (i.e. 'non-economic') ends is exclusively a private concern of the owners, more or less in accordance with the following motto:

> What are you doing with my money? I didn't invest in your company for philanthropic, humanitarian, or social objectives. I invested for profits. I'll make my own decisions about other uses of my money.[54]

51 The concept appeared on the scene after the publication of A. Rappaport, *Creating Shareholder Value* (New York: Free Press, 1998; 1st edn 1986).

52 A. Bühner, 'Shareholder Value', *Die Betriebswirtschaft* 53 (1993), pp. 749–69, at p. 749.

53 In view of the separation of ownership and (management) control in most companies, the best possible identification of the personal interests of the managers with those of the owners, i.e. the creation of an 'owner-oriented attitude', is achieved in the shareholder value approach by postulating (1) a substantial share of capital for the executives and (2) strict dependence of their compensation on the shareholder return performance. It also (3) welcomes strong pressure of the capital market on management including the danger of an (unfriendly) takeover and (4) lively competition on the employment market for corporate executives. See Rappaport, *Creating Shareholder Value*, p. 3. On the stakeholder approach see below Section 10.3 (2).

54 The viewpoint of an anonymous shareholder, quoted in M. Anshen, 'The Socially Responsible Corporation: From Concept to Implementation', in Anshen (ed.), *Managing the Socially Responsible Corporation* (New York: Macmillan, 1974), pp. 1–22, at p. 7. Anshen himself is critical of this line of argument, which was taken earlier by Friedman in *Capitalism and Freedom* and 'Social Responsibility of Business'.

This expresses the *strictly privatistic model of entrepreneurship* as an undertaking of owners for the optimal investment of capital, which is the underlying foundation both of the shareholder value approach as an institutional-ethical premise and of the ideal of a capitalist life form. Those who propagate the uncompromising management of companies in accordance with the conception of shareholder value also postulate, whether they are aware of it or not, the corresponding regulatory model of a market economy without adjectives of the Anglo-Saxon type.[55]

On the other hand, the shareholder value conception excludes the possibility of seeing the maximization of short-term profits in the bookkeeping of a corporation as the target. This supposedly implies a mitigation of the profit principle. Now, the central aim is rather a long-term 'sustainable' increase in the value of a corporation, which accords with the basic position of the traditional entrepreneurial ethos in regard to investment. In the case of corporations quoted on the stock exchange, the market capitalization of a company is usually seen as the indicator of its value, as this more or less fittingly reflects the evaluation of its overall future profit potential by the capital market. The adoption of the long-term economic[56] perspective aimed at establishing the preconditions for sustainable success is at the same time seen as evidence for the ethical quality of management policy and its orientation on the common good:

> Shareholder value as the *long-term financial goal* of an enterprise must – from an emphatically strategic point of view – be in *harmony* with the interests of the other stakeholders and particularly of the employees. The *conflicts* are to be found *in the short and middle term.*[57]

The interests of the other stakeholders, however, are not seen to be valid in terms of their legitimacy and the corresponding claims, but are only taken into account instrumentally as a means of increasing the shareholder value. This is the specifically economistic aspect of this doctrine. The confusion of categories in the thinking of some supporters of this

[55] In contrast to other business administrators Klaus Spremann reflects upon the institutional-ethical dimension of the approach. See K. Spremann, 'Wertsteigerung als Managementprinzip in Europa?', in K. Höfner/A. Pohl (eds.), *Wertsteigerungsmanagement. Das Shareholder-Value-Konzept: Methoden und erfolgreiche Beispiele* (Frankfurt/New York: Campus, 1994), pp. 303–19: 'The reception of the shareholder value in the practice of European management marks the beginnings of a transition to a different economic model of which the European social community has hitherto had little experience' (p. 307).

[56] For an interpretation of the long-term economic thought pattern and its widespread acceptance by top managers see Ulrich/Thielemann, 'How Do Managers Think?', p. 891ff.; more thoroughly ibid., *Ethik und Erfolg*, p. 37ff.

[57] R. Volkart, 'Langfristige Shareholder-Orientierung', *Neue Zürcher Zeitung*, N° 154 of 5 July 1996, p. 23 (italics in the original).

conception and the extent to which that thinking is characterized by the old utilitarian fiction of the common good is expressed in the following not untypical statement of an economist, who even explicitly postulates the instrumentalist simplification of the treatment of the conflict of interests in regard to the creation of value in a company:

Whether and how the corporation can take into account and satisfy the ever-present and unlimited claims of all possible stakeholders depends exclusively [sic!] on whether or not these stakeholders make a productive contribution to the actual purpose of the corporation. If they do, they must be rewarded in accordance with the marginal productivity. (. . .) If they do not, the corporation digs its own grave in competitive situations if it accepts (or is forced to accept) the demands of unproductive stakeholders.[58]

Note how clearly the business-ethical impossibility theorem shines through behind the descriptive form of this statement. The cynical dismissal of 'unproductive stakeholders' also indicates that the author lacks all awareness of the possible legitimacy of stakeholder claims from a business-ethical point of view.[59] True to the shareholder value doctrine he asserts without modification:

The interests of the shareholders and of the general public in efficient capital allocation run parallel to one another.[60]

Even if the category mistake and the ideological premises lying behind this kind of economistic *nirvana economics* are ignored, an unprejudiced evaluation of the circumstances must lead to the realization that the conception does not even guarantee an orientation of management on the long-term interests of a corporation. The demands of the stock exchange for an increase in the shareholder value must always be met in the short-term, particularly in the home of the doctrine, the USA, where managements are measured by proofs of success presented on a quarterly basis. This is perfectly possible with financial and accounting methods (such as, e.g. reducing owned capital or – more dubiously – undermining the substance of the corporation or its scarcely measurable 'human capital' in favour of higher returns). Hence the potential for pursuing intelligent long-term perspectives for the creation of value in the interest of the shareholders is restricted. This applies all the more to the potential for considering the interests of the 'unproductive stakeholders'

[58] H. Kleinewefers, 'Wie der volkswirtschaftliche Nutzen maximiert wird', *Neue Zürcher Zeitung*, N° 154 of July 5 1996, p. 23.
[59] For a further critique of instrumentalism as a form of economism see Section 10.2 (1). On the relations between stakeholders as source of legitimation see Section 10.3 (1).
[60] Kleinewefers, 'Wie der volkswirtschaftliche Nutzen', p. 23.

(Kleinewefers). Ultimately the difference between the shareholder value doctrine and the classical principle of profit maximization remains vague in practice.

(5) The profit principle as a methodical as-if construction

In conclusion let us return to Erich Gutenberg. On closer analysis, none of the four possible interpretations of the profit principle discussed above can be attributed to him. What is decisive and methodically adequate for him is rather the view that the profit principle is *assumed* to be the starting point of rational entrepreneurial activity, an assumption which does not necessarily describe reality but ultimately has to do with a 'hypothetical borderline case' and a certain viewpoint.[61] Gutenberg's position on the practical significance of the principle of profit maximization is rather cautious and can well be seen from today's perspective as a clear criticism of the shareholder value doctrine or – to use his terminology – the acquisitive principle:

> Surely nobody today would assume that leaving the overall economic development to the implementation of this principle would be sufficient to achieve the degree of economic and social perfection in which Adam Smith and Bastiat still believed. Nobody today, in times of great economic and social tension, would be naïve enough to see profit as the sole means of overcoming this tension. (. . .) The history of the capitalist system is not lacking in excesses resulting from action in accordance with the principle of economic acquisition.[62]

As the reference to 'excesses' in 'the history of the capitalist system' clearly proves, Gutenberg definitely distanced himself from attempts to attribute a normative quality to the profit principle. He later refers (without closer justification) to the *system-constitutive function* of this principle as the decisive reason for its 'essential' claim to validity. By means of the 'assumption' referred to above, however, he attributes above all a *theory-constitutive* importance to the principle for the discipline of business administration. Along these lines the discipline could conceive itself as an (internally value-free) 'pure' functional analysis of the productivity relationships between the different production factors (factor-theoretical approach of business administration). And this amounts to the elimination of all ethical problems in business practice from 'modern' business administration studies.

It is thus clear why Gutenberg did not provide a fundamental and critical normative reflection on the problem even though he unmistakably

[61] See the lengthy quotation from Gutenberg at the beginning of Section 10.1.
[62] Gutenberg, *Grundlagen der Betriebswirtschaftslehre*, p. 468f.

recognized the limits to the validity of the profit principle. He was solely interested in the 'constitution of the object of knowledge of *theoretical* business administration'. Its purpose is not to determine what is right when all the aspects of real life are taken into account, but what is right in an acquisitive economy from an ideal-typical point of view, for example, 'theoretically right buying and selling'.[63] But what is theoretically right? That depends, as Gutenberg very clearly sees, on the theory-constitutive 'standpoint' of the economist. He expressly distinguishes the business administrative standpoint from other 'possible standpoints' such as 'political economy, sociology and ethics' (p. 24f.) and defines it in terms of the economic 'rationality principle' (p. 28ff.). In business administration theory, as Gutenberg emphasizes, this has nothing to do with the *subjective* interest of managers in making profits, but constitutes the *objective* logic of capital investment: 'a process consisting of transforming money into concrete commodities and back to money again' (p. 33), which Gutenberg expresses with the brief Marxian formula M-C-M (p. 43).[64] Gutenberg thus understands the standpoint of business administration theory as the impersonal standpoint which constitutes the 'liberalist-capitalist system' and demonstrates that actions which are right from the point of view of business administration theory are 'right measures in themselves' (p. 39). They are right 'in themselves' because 'the psycho-physical subject can contravene them. (...) But this must not lead to disturbances and limitations in the theory' (p. 41). Gutenberg was one of the first economists to state quite clearly that pure economic or business administration theory has the methodological character of an 'as-if construction' – 'as if a psycho-physical subject is not present at all. In this way the latter is eliminated from the enterprise as an object of business administration theory' (p. 42).[65]

In principle we are dealing here quite simply with the usual economic determinism of neoclassical theory elucidated above. It has neither empirical nor normative content justifiable from a rational-ethical point

63 See Gutenberg, *Unternehmung als Gegenstand*, p. 40 (my italics). All the following page numbers in brackets refer to this book.

64 Gutenberg does not, however, refer explicitly to Karl Marx and does without the apostrophe after the second M (M') which for Marx symbolizes the value added.

65 Here the practical purpose of the '*as-if*' methodology manifests itself, namely the elimination of 'outside' interest (Max Weber) from the (theoretical) considerations. For more detail on this point see P. Ulrich, 'Der spezielle Blick der allgemeinen BWL für die ökonomischen Dinge der Unternehmensführung', in W. Kirsch/A. Picot (eds.), *Die Betriebswirtschaftslehre im Spannungsfeld zwischen Generalisierung und Spezialisierung. Edmund Heinen zum 70. Geburtstag* (Wiesbaden: Gabler, 1989), pp. 137–54.

of view, but is axiomatically given in the form of 'as-if' assumptions.[66] It is, therefore, hardly possible to accuse Gutenberg of justifying the normative-practical validity claims of a 'profit principle' by devious ideological means. This happens only when his theory is reinterpreted to provide a supposedly normative basis for corporate ethics. The latter should not, however, continue the methodologically mistaken normative application of the as-if constructs of 'pure' business administration theory or economics. It is rather the task of business ethics to show up the lack of ethical justification in these (background) theories and to take the legitimacy question of entrepreneurial activity seriously from the outset – as an independent problem which cannot be reduced in economistic fashion.

The demonstrated failure of the various attempts to justify a 'profit principle' that could itself be regarded as the embodiment of the correct ethical orientation leads to the following interim conclusion: *The strict maximization of profit cannot, in principle, provide a legitimate orientation for entrepreneurial activity*, as it directly involves the subordination of all value standpoints or claims that conflict with the pursuit of profit. Every approach of corporate ethics which does not categorically make entrepreneurial orientation on success or profit dependent upon reservations as to their legitimacy must be regarded as an economistic simplification. *The legitimate pursuit of profit is always a morally bounded pursuit of profit.*

Primarily this has nothing to do with the specific character of the achievement of profit as such; it applies to all (particularistic) value orientations. From an ethical point of view they can never be elevated one-sidedly to the level of a principle. Ultimately there is only one principle: the moral principle (understood in the rational-ethical sense), as it first permits the rational treatment of specific conflicting value standpoints – including those advocating the logic of the market and success. This is perhaps the most important message of a corporate ethics free of all ideology: the pursuit of profit is always only the *object* of corporate-ethical reflection. It represents one value and one dimension of entrepreneurial value creation (in the full sense of the word) among others, but it cannot at the same time itself be the overall *criterion* for justifying business activity. The whole point of corporate ethics is precisely the unreserved critical examination of ethical aspects that might deserve priority over the pursuit of profit. With this principled subordination of the possibly but not necessarily legitimate and certainly not impartial interest in profit to ethical principles corporate ethics is linked to the republican ethos of economic citizenship.[67] This accords fully with

[66] See Section 4.3 (1). [67] See Section 8.1.

the position of the Erlangen philosopher Paul Lorenzen, who was probably the first to point out that 'the principle of maximum profit' is incompatible with a republican corporate ethics:

The maximum principle makes it impossible to understand a corporation as being primarily a part of the republic.[68]

In summary of the discussion so far we can conclude that republican corporate ethics takes a position beyond the profit principle as its starting point.

10.2 Instrumentalist, charitable, corrective or integrative corporate ethics?

Attitudes towards the 'profit principle' play such a fundamental part in the discussions on the foundations of corporate ethics that the most important approaches can be ordered systematically in accordance with the degree to which they relate to this principle and its underlying economistic premises. Basically four approaches can be distinguished (Figure 10.2).

The first three approaches – which can be characterized as instrumentalist, charitable and corrective corporate ethics – remain devoted to the 'profit principle', each in its own specific way and to its own degree. The fourth variant – integrative corporate ethics – is the only one to take a position beyond the unjustifiable 'profit principle' as its starting point. Instead it subjects the pursuit of profit by companies consistently to the demand for corporate ethical legitimation. The degree to which the inherent value of ethical points of view and the need to overcome the profit principle are recognized increases from one approach to the next in the order given below.

(1) Instrumentalist corporate ethics: a contribution to entrepreneurial success

Whereas a strictly economistic conception of the 'profit principle' elevates it to the normative level and sees it as the embodiment of ethically responsible entrepreneurship, the instrumentalist thought pattern apparently accepts and even calls for the consideration of ethical standpoints as a relevant aspect of intelligent management.[69] Its advocates see no

[68] Lorenzen, 'Philosophische Fundierungsprobleme', p. 62.

[69] This characterization of the instrumentalist position follows the results of the qualitative empirical study of Ulrich/Thielemann, *Ethik und Erfolg*, p. 46ff., and 'How Do Managers Think?'. This study demonstrates that the instrumentalistic thought pattern can often be found both among top managers and academic business administrators.

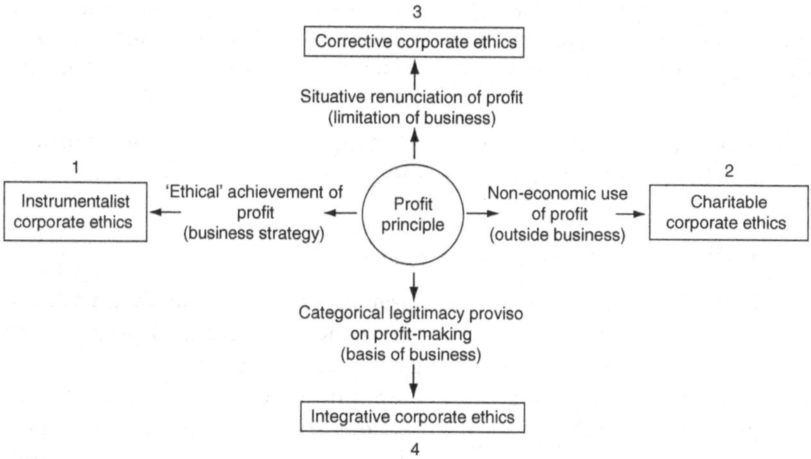

Figure 10.2. Corporate ethical approaches and their relationship to the profit principle

necessary conflict between the acceptance of ethical considerations and the pursuit of profit and success. The two are rendered compatible with the help of the by no means novel insight that 'ethics' can be a 'profitability factor'[70] or even a 'critical success factor'.[71] 'Investment' in 'ethics' in the sense of the toleration of opportunity costs for the moment is justified by the strategic aim of safeguarding the profit potential in the long-term. The term 'ethics' must be put in inverted commas here because the interest is not in the inherent value of ethical points of view but in their *function* as a means of guaranteeing entrepreneurial success. In certain circumstances it can make sense 'to take ethical claims into account'. In this way ethics is converted into an instrument of management or a good investment from a long-term economic perspective:

> The renunciation of profits which are possible today but ethically questionable thus becomes a long-term *investment* designed to improve the share of the market, turnover and profit. It becomes an *instrument* which guarantees the future of the company.[72]

[70] This is already noted with critical intent (and with 'ethics' predominantly in inverted commas) in A. Lisowsky, 'Ethik und Betriebswirtschaftslehre', *Zeitschrift für Betriebswirtschaft* 4 (1927), pp. 253–58, 363–72, 429–42, at p. 432.

[71] This is the rather uncritical, instrumentalist view of F. Hofmann/W. Rebstock, 'Unternehmensethik. Eine Herausforderung an die Unternehmung', *Zeitschrift für Betriebswirtschaft* 59 (1989), pp. 667–87, at p. 667.

[72] K.M. Leisinger, 'Nicht alles Legale ist auch legitim', *Übersee Rundschau* 41 (1989), vol. 162, pp. 42–5, at p. 45 (my italics). The thesis of *the long-term economic* harmony between ethical and entrepreneurial points of view is also implicit in the shareholder-value doctrine criticized above.

The active management of values and moral controlling is an element of modern company management in modern societies... Companies must *invest in morality* if they wish to guarantee their survival in society and hence in the market.[73]

This is in accordance with the concurring results of several empirical studies which show that a large majority of top managers agree with the thesis:

Sound ethics is good business in the long run.[74]

Here we are obviously not, or at least not primarily, dealing with an ethical maxim, but with a kind of strategic intelligence. For such *soft strategies* two practical directions suggest themselves:

- In the external relations of a corporation 'ethical behaviour' can improve the unstable or even precarious societal *acceptance* of corporate strategies confronted by an increasingly critical public sphere. Acceptance is, however, exclusively measured by the non-occurrence of manifest public resistance and thus refers solely to the category of (factual) social 'standing', 'good reputation', 'goodwill' and 'image' of the company. Categorially, acceptance has nothing to do with legitimacy in the sense of ethically grounded normative validity. The strategies of the customary public relations departments designed to ensure acceptance of the corporation lack the unreserved communicative orientation.[75]
- In the internal relations between the managers of companies and their employees 'ethical' concessions to the personal inherent value of the employees can improve their *motivation*. The cultivation of human relations or human resources[76] in this sense is strategically all the more relevant for success the more decisive the 'human capital' is as a factor determining innovation and productivity. Again, what counts in this

[73] J. Wieland, 'Warum Unternehmensethik?', in Forum für Philosophie Bad Homburg (ed.), *Markt und Moral*, pp. 215–39, at p. 228 (my italics).

[74] See R. C. Baumhart, 'How Ethical Are Businessmen?', *Harvard Business Review* 39 (1961), N° 4, pp. 6–19 and 156–76, at p. 10; S. N. Brenner/E. A. Molander, 'Is the Ethics of Business Changing?', *Harvard Business Review* 55 (1977), N° 1, pp. 57–71, at p. 62; H. Becker/D.J. Fritzsche, 'Business Ethics: A Cross-Cultural Comparison of Managers' Attitudes', *Journal of Business Ethics* 6 (1987), pp. 289–95, at p. 293. Ulrich/Thielemann, 'How Do Managers Think?', p. 891f.

[75] On the categorial difference between orientation on communication and on success see Section 2.5 (1); on the difference between legitimacy and acceptance see Section 5.3 (2) and on its specifically corporate ethical aspects, particularly in the context of the public relations of companies, see below Section 10.3 (1).

[76] On the difference between the approaches of 'human relations' and 'human resources' see R. E. Miles, 'Human Relations or Human Resources?', *Harvard Business Review* July/August (1965), pp. 148–63.

approach is not, or not primarily, the inherent human value of the employees from the viewpoint of the normative logic of interpersonal relations, but their instrumental value within a business rationale.

Let it be clearly understood: neither the realistic content of such soft strategies is in dispute here, nor is the possibility that company managers can develop principles of behaviour from such considerations which can also in part be welcome – so to speak as accidental side effects – from an ethical standpoint. What makes good sense strategically, however, is the object of and not the standard for ethical-critical examination, as we established at the end of the previous section. As long as this categorial difference and order of priorities is maintained, there is nothing to be said against the search for additional arguments based on intelligent self-interest. These can demonstrate to entrepreneurs that the observation of moral principles may not always but certainly can often serve a functional purpose in ensuring the long-term potential for success and profit of their companies. Yet we cannot overlook the fact that in instrumentalist corporate ethics the pursuit of success enjoys lexical priority, so that 'ethics' is subordinated to the economic precondition that it 'pays off' in the long run. Conditional ethics is not ethics at all, as it violates the inherent value of knowable moral duties, which provide the very foundations for the primacy of ethics.[77] And what about all those conflictual situations in which ethics does not pay off in the long run?

As the qualitative empirical study mentioned above has shown, most of the instrumentalists have deeper-lying convictions[78] which prevent them from seeing cases of conflict as a particular problem, although the threat of conflict is real and its solution the whole point of corporate ethics. Instead they trust ultimately that the 'invisible hand' of the market itself will guarantee the ethical quality of entrepreneurial activity. The very fact that ethically motivated entrepreneurial behaviour or success-oriented behaviour with morally beneficial side effects can often 'pay off' in the long run is interpreted as a sign that the market economy itself in principle guarantees the harmony of ethics and the entrepreneurial pursuit of success. This concealed background economism is a clear indication of the early modern entrepreneurial ethos and its Calvinist roots.[79] The

[77] In this respect we agree fully with Löhr, *Unternehmensethik und Betriebswirtschaftslehre*, p. 255: 'Giving up the "old" primacy of ethics is not a necessary consequence of the insight that economic action is also necessary, but is simply the abandonment of a rational and comprehensive orientation of human action in general.'

[78] For the phenomenon of *background economism* touched upon here see Ulrich/Thielemann, 'How Do Managers Think?', p. 889f., and *Ethik und Erfolg*, pp. 71ff. and 95ff.

[79] See above Sections 4.1. and 5.1.

entrepreneur or manager who places his trust in instrumentalist corporate ethics thus ultimately defends his conventional entrepreneurial ethics. He consequently tends to see in all possible places 'signs' which confirm and deproblematize his harmonistic world-view and his understanding of himself and his role in society. The instrumentalist conception is thus a corporate-ethical position which is seriously advocated with personal conviction and by no means empty rhetoric designed to conceal indifference or even cynicism in regard to the inherent value of ethical claims.[80]

Of course a scientific corporate ethics cannot simply reflect or reproduce such a position but must arrive at a critical interpretation. This is the only way of understanding instrumentalism. There is no objection to building the 'business case' for corporate ethics, but this cannot be the sum total of an unconditional and critical corporate ethics.

(2) Charitable corporate ethics: ethics 'post festum'

This second concept also involves economistic simplifications, although in a different manner than instrumentalism. In contrast, however, it does at least achieve a partial break with the profit principle. According to this thought pattern entrepreneurial activity should at first also be guided strictly by the 'principle' of profit maximization. The justification (or attempted legitimation) of this still economistic understanding of entrepreneurial activity is now, however, that non-economic value claims made on a company can and should be met, *after* (and only after) a profit has been made. The allocation of a share of profits made for cultural, social, scientific or other 'good' purposes is, therefore, not justified, as in the case of instrumentalism, by its strategic usefulness (e.g. for the promotion of the image of a company in the public sphere), but is now expressly motivated by the cultural, social or human value of generous charitability – and, what is more, not in spite of but precisely on account of the strict priority of profit maximization. Corporate ethics then takes the form of *donation ethics* or a charitable (alms) ethics 'post festum', i.e. after the competitive battle on the market has been brought to a successful conclusion.[81]

Consequently, in this conception, the achievement of the greatest possible financial surplus is interpreted as the precondition for 'doing good'.

[80] The above-mentioned American studies on the moral consciousness of top managers clearly tend towards this misinterpretation; for a critical reinterpretation see Ulrich/Thielemann, 'How Do Managers Think?', p. 890ff.

[81] The terms 'post festum' and 'alms' can be found literally in Habermann, 'Teilen oder produzieren?'. Partial economism and donation ethics can very well be advocated by one and the same person.

Only those who achieve surpluses can use them for good ends.[82]

The question of how the share of profits donated for good ends has been achieved, that is to say of the ethical quality of business strategies, is totally ignored, as the 'invisible hand' of the market alone is responsible for this side of the deal in this corporate ethical thought pattern. The problem of corporate ethics is thus characteristically split into two parts. For the process of profit-making the principle of profit maximization continues to be binding; the possibility and the necessity of taking ethical standpoints into account is only recognized in the subsequent profit-spending. The separation of the two aspects is, however, less clear than it might seem at first sight. The profits which will be available *later* for charitable purposes will be all the higher the more consistently a company reinvests its *present* surpluses instead of distributing them. Therefore, in the long-term economic perspective, the 'possibility' of immediate charitability disappears in this conception; 'first of all' the profits must always be maximized.

This kind of corporate ethics 'post festum' fails above all to recognize, however, that essential natural and socio-cultural preconditions or qualities of the good life and just social coexistence which are affected or harmed by the strict pursuit of profit maximization (e.g. irreversible ecological damage or the psychosomatic consequences of inhuman working conditions for the working population) do not have the character of purchasable goods. Consequently, the disregard for their inherent value cannot be made good or compensated for subsequently with money. The same economistic simplification of the problems of corporate ethics can be found in the well-known *cake metaphor*, according to which the 'profit cake' (or, at the national level, the 'social product cake') must first be baked before it can be distributed; the greater the cake the more can be distributed for non-economic purposes such as environmental protection and social welfare. But, to stay with the metaphor, if a cake is to be edible, what counts is not only its size but also and primarily the 'recipe' used in making it. What lies behind the cake metaphor is, once again, the utilitarian fiction of an ethically neutral formal goal of maximum profit (or social product), from which all ethically justified claims can subsequently be met.[83]

[82] See Schneider, 'Unternehmensethik und Gewinnprinzip', p. 870. See also the reply by Ulrich, 'Schwierigkeiten mit der unternehmensethischen Herausforderung'.

[83] For a critique of the fiction of the formal goal specifically encountered in business administration see Section 10.1 (4b); for a critique of the utilitarian fiction of the common good on which it is based see Section 5.2.

Splitting off (ethical) 'profit-spending' in this way from the normative conditions of profit-making was originally also characteristic to a large extent of the postulate of *corporate social responsibility* (CSR). CSR achieved wide acceptance in the academic community of business administration as well as in business practice in the 1960s and 1970s, above all in the USA, as a counterpoint to the principle of profit maximization. But this postulate too was frequently relativized (more or less ironically) as follows:

Corporate responsibility is fine, if you can afford it.[84]

In spite of the heatedness of the discussions on corporate social responsibility at that time we are by no means dealing here with a radical antithesis but merely with a partial revision of the old economistic position. Apart from the charity principle characterized above this conception soon came to include as its second central idea the more comprehensive *stewardship principle*, according to which a company should exercise the freedom and powers of decision, the competence and the resources entrusted to it by society for the general good of all those directly concerned and, ultimately, of the general public.[85] Whereas, in the exclusively charitable conception the claims of social responsibility were restricted to humanitarian 'corporate giving', the stewardship principle increasingly exceeded this purely charitable understanding of corporate ethics. For the first time the fundamental idea that company executives were responsible for a variety of social matters ('corporate community involvement') and for the effects of entrepreneurial activities on all the groups of claimants (stakeholders) became popular.

(3) Corrective corporate ethics: situative self-limitation of the entrepreneurial pursuit of profit

Once the relevance of ethical standpoints for entrepreneurial policies has been partially recognized it is only a small step to a stronger variant of the postulate of socially responsible management, which leads to a limitation of the profit principle in regard to the process of *achieving* success. Thus actual business morals, i.e. behaviour patterns in the market, become the focus of business ethics. Ethics – and this is precisely the point at which

84 For a critical approach to this standard argument, in which the above-mentioned splitting off of profit-spending from profit-making is also manifest, see R. E. Freeman, *Strategic Management: A Stakeholder Approach* (Boston: Pitman, 1984), p. 40.

85 On this point see W. C. Frederick/J. E. Post/K. Davies, *Business and Society: Corporate Strategy, Public Policy, Ethics*, 7th edn (New York *et al.*: McGraw Hill, 1992), p. 34ff.

economism is surpassed – can now 'cost something', without these costs having the character of an investment.[86] This is a complete reversal of instrumentalist corporate ethics, and it is now seen as the true 'sign' of what is ethically right. Consequently, the precondition that there is a conflict between the ethical orientation of business activities and the entrepreneurial pursuit of success is already included in the definition of corporate ethics: corporate ethics then only just *begins* with the voluntary self-limitation of the pursuit of profit, whereby the aim of profit maximization is implicitly or explicitly abandoned. This approach is characteristically recorded in an ethics codex which, as a form of a moral self-commitment of company executives (or entire branches of industry), defines the moral guidelines and 'limits' to be imposed upon the pursuit of success.

This conception of corrective corporate ethics forms the basis – usually implicitly rather than explicitly – of the predominant part of Anglo-Saxon business ethics. In an explicitly elaborated form its leading advocates in the German-speaking discussion on corporate ethics are Horst Steinmann and his collaborators, to whose position we restrict our discussion here for analytical purposes.[87] As we have seen above they posit 'in general' – or in their earlier formulation 'in the normal case' – the 'ethical presumption of the correctness'[88] of the profit principle; if this presumption of correctness is seriously questioned in 'individual', 'exceptional' or 'conflictual cases'[89] as a result of ethical doubts of those affected or by manifest conflicts, corporate ethics must then be activated as a situational corrective of the profit principle:[90]

> Seen in this way, the relationship of the profit principle and corporate ethics is one of rule and exception.[91]

[86] In similar fashion Löhr, *Unternehmensethik und Betriebswirtschaftslehre*, p. 284: 'Ethics costs money'.

[87] First Steinmann/Oppenrieder, 'Brauchen wir eine Unternehmensethik?', and Steinmann/Löhr, 'Realistische Idee'. For a critique of their original position see Ulrich 'Unternehmensethik – Führungsinstrument oder Grundlagenreflexion?'. On the general conception of corrective business ethics and its predominant self-understanding as 'applied' ethics see Section 3.1.

[88] Steinmann/Löhr, *Grundlagen der Unternehmensethik*, p. 107. And earlier 'Einleitung' in Steinmann/Löhr (eds.), *Unternehmensethik*, p. 8; similarly Steinmann/Oppenrieder, 'Brauchen wir eine Unternehmensethik?', p. 174.

[89] Steinmann/Löhr, 'Realistische Idee', p. 308.

[90] This is at least the original position of Steinmann/Oppenrieder, 'Brauchen wir eine Unternehmensethik?', p. 173, and Steinmann/Löhr, 'Realistische Idee', p. 308.

[91] Steinmann/Oppenrieder, 'Brauchen wir eine Unternehmensethik?', p. 174. For a critique of this ethics in exceptional cases see Ulrich, 'Unternehmensethik – Führungsinstrument oder Grundlagenreflexion?', p. 194ff.

The omnipresence of ethically problematic internal and external effects (of the market), however, speaks in favour of considering the supposed exceptional case as the normal case in everyday practice.[92] More recently Steinmann and Löhr have consequently restricted the normative validity claims of their presumption of correctness to the more neutral formulation that this presumption is only valid 'in general' and that in 'individual cases' the corporate ethical question 'must again be posed'. This leads them to the following fitting conclusion, which is scarcely compatible with the profit principle:

> To this extent ethical considerations have systematic priority over the profit principle not only at the institutional but also at the corporate level.[93]

The 'general presumption of correctness' attached to the profit principle thus turns out by and large to be empty rhetoric without any clear orientational force for business activities. It would be just as easy to speak of a 'general presumption of *in*correctness' in regard to the profit principle. Regardless of whether the corporate ethical glass is characterized – so to speak – as half empty or half full, neither the one nor the other 'general presumption' can change the fact that the categorical proviso on the legitimacy of entrepreneurial activities applies in every individual case.

But why do Steinmann and Löhr continue to use this rhetoric at all, disregarding the fact that the talk of the 'profit principle' is thus deprived of any clear meaning and can certainly no longer be equated with the maximization of profit?[94] And how can they advocate at one and the same time the 'profit principle' and the thesis that a corporate ethics which 'costs money' is 'possible'? This second question seems all the more urgent as they also continue to claim 'that the profit principle ... is not open to debate for an individual company',[95] as we have seen in Section 10.1.

The solution of this riddle can be found in the *fiction of the formal goal* criticized earlier, under which the 'profit principle' is subsumed in the

[92] On the ethical relevance of market 'internal effects' see Section 9.2.(3), lit.b).

[93] Steinmann/Löhr, *Grundlagen der Unternehmensethik*, p. 107.

[94] Their position also lacks clarity on this point; see n. 49 in this chapter. Löhr alone, *Unternehmensethik und Betriebswirtschaftslehre*, p. 278, explicitly points out that the 'demands of the profit principle ... can never be fulfilled in practice in the sense of a maximization of profit'. Löhr's justification, however, is not ethical; he argues instead that profit maximization is an 'ideal norm' (sic!) which 'logically' can never be completely fulfilled under real conditions, but only to the 'best possible' extent. Here, once again, the category mistake of the empiricist (im)possibility thesis manifests itself, when Löhr refers to profit maximization instead of ethics. See above Section 10.1 (3).

[95] Steinmann/Löhr, *Grundlagen der Unternehmensethik*, p. 130.

tradition of business administrative theory. This fiction continues to be applied in the conception of (corrective) corporate ethics. Whereas, as we have shown, the formal goal is based on the thesis of economic determinism and the determinism of the institutional framework, the entrepreneurs are more or less free in their choice of practical goals.[96] Precisely this fact, that the supposed economic determinism is ineffective at this level, is used as an argument against an exclusive reliance on an institutional framework. An institutional framework, it is argued, cannot 'canalize or regulate' the 'choice of practical goals' by corporations 'in advance' in a manner which makes personal ethical responsibility at the level of individual entrepreneurial actions irrelevant. For this reason corporate ethics is necessary as a 'constructive supplement to the law', i.e to the institutional framework provided by the state.[97]

The talk of a formal goal in business administration theory suggests not only that this goal leaves 'everything open' in regard to the choice of practical goals by the entrepreneurs but also that the corporate ethical decisions to be taken can be *restricted* to the determination of the practical goals. Thus corporate ethics is once again reduced by half, although in a different manner than is the case with the charitable variant, and the profit principle as such need not be subjected to ethical reflection at the level of entrepreneurial decision-taking. The profit principle is consequently deproblematized, as if it were an interest-neutral, indeed purely 'formal', marginal factor in corporate policy without consequences in real-life practice. But, as we have already seen, we are in fact dealing here with a remnant of regulatory and corporate political economism in this conception of corrective corporate ethics.[98] This amounts to an abandonment of reflection in regard to the normative core of the historically given market economy 'conditions'. This abandonment of reflection is also characteristic of the two-world conception on which *applied ethics* is based, with its separation of the ethics (which is to be applied) and the economic logic of the market (which is conceived in non-ethical terms).[99]

The only possible systematic consequence is that not only the 'practical goals' of business activity, i.e. the strategies and means with which 'money is made', but also the 'formal goal' (which is not value and interest neutral), and consequently the pursuit of profit as such, must

[96] Ibid., p. 101ff.; literally at p. 104. [97] See ibid., p. 101f. [98] See Section 10.1 (4).

[99] Steinmann/Löhr, *Grundlagen der Unternehmensethik*, p. 94ff., expressly understand this approach (fittingly and not by chance) as 'applied corporate ethics'. We refer back here to the detailed critique of the conception of applied business ethics in Section 3.1, especially subsection (2).

always be subject to a complete (and not purely situational) and unconditional self-critical reflection on the part of the business leaders. The profit principle – regardless of whether it is advocated strictly or with reservations, and whether it is presented as an empirical inherent necessity or a rule of the game that can be ethically justified – must therefore be abandoned once and for all as a basic norm of corporate ethics. Instead, every kind of entrepreneurial pursuit of success and profit must be subordinated *in principle* (and not merely ad hoc) to the priority of the *condition* that economic actions must be legitimate and that economic actors must behave responsibly towards all who are potentially affected. This, however, passes beyond the approach of corrective corporate ethics, which remains fixated on the dubious 'general presumption of correctness' in regard to the profit principle.

(4) Integrative corporate ethics: fundamental critical reflection on the entrepreneurial pursuit of profit

The pursuit of a freely chosen corporate goal is always and only legitimate to the extent that it is 'possible' from an ethical perspective, i.e. legitimate in the light of the moral rights of all who are affected by it. Every serious form of corporate ethics which has not been reduced from the start to apologetics begins by asserting the principle that entrepreneurs may only pursue those entrepreneurial aims which are ethically legitimate and involve the acceptance of accountability. What is at issue is, no more and no less, the requirement that the pursuit of success and profit must be categorically subordinated to the normative precondition of legitimacy, or in brief, to the *legitimacy proviso*. This – and not the 'profit principle' – must be recognized as the supreme principle of corporate ethics.

The integrative approach to corporate ethics aims at placing the entrepreneurial pursuit of success from the start and from the bottom up on a sound normative 'business foundation' (legitimacy basis) instead of conceiving ethics, as in the corrective approach, merely as the external limitation of a profit principle which can 'normally' be taken as justified. Whereas in corrective corporate ethics the relationship between ethics and the pursuit of success is conceived of horizontally, as being on one level, so that the problems which arise can only be solved by compromise, it is shifted by ninety degrees to the vertical position in the integrative approach. The moral content of the business model itself is now conceived as the ethical core of good business. This is the solid 'value ground' on which corporate policies and business strategies that are already in themselves ethical and 'replete with values' can be built. Or to put it less metaphorically: the integrative approach understands corporate ethics as the constitutive normative precondition of every legitimate entrepreneurial activity and not merely as a corrective (subsidiary to the law) justifying the occasional self-limitation of economic activities for which the profit principle is seen to be constitutive. The 'possibility problem' of corporate ethics is thus to be understood basically as a problem of legitimating freely chosen entrepreneurial business ends and goals.[100]

Integrative corporate ethics sees itself as a *permanent process of unconditional critical reflection and the shaping of sound normative foundations for entrepreneurial activity in the service of life*. The corporation should willingly commit itself to securing its existence and achieving its commercial success exclusively with competitive strategies of value creation which are socially legitimate and meaningful. This general basic norm of integrative corporate ethics can be termed *business integrity*. Business integrity is always put to the hardest test when business strategies which are both financially promising and at the same time ethically sound cannot be found or developed. In such cases the logical consequence is to renounce the opportunity for profit and to endeavour to secure the existence of the company by other means with a better normative 'substructure'.

The first systematic site for the realization of morally sound business policies (oriented on meaningfulness and accepting the premises of legitimacy) is the freely chosen entrepreneurial *task of value creation*.[101] We will return to this point in a moment. But first of all we must widen the normative conditions for the possibility of an orientation of entrepreneurial activity towards the service of life involved in the integrative understanding of corporate ethics. These normative conditions can no longer be restricted to the room for manoeuvre of individual companies which is empirically given in the existing institutional framework of the market. In order to avoid an uncritical abandonment of reflection in the face of the 'inherent necessities', it is necessary to supplement the ethos of business integrity at a second level of fundamental reflection within corporate ethics. At this level the normative validity claims of the existing 'rules of

[100] See Section 4.3 (3). We will take a closer look at the necessary corporate-ethical legitimation discourse in Section 10.3.

[101] In management jargon the concept of 'mission' has become fashionable for the supreme goal of enterprise, for which the term 'freely chosen task of value creation' is taken here. It is perhaps not by chance that the word *mission* calls to mind the religious origins of the early modern business ethos, which also contains the site of morality within its inner justification of the entrepreneurial pursuit of success (see Section 4.1). Integrative business ethics maintains this constitutive role of the traditional entrepreneurial ethos but overcomes the old economistic simplification of the problems involved. This is achieved by means of an explicit rational-ethical reflection on the normative 'business foundations'. As the concept of 'mission' is normally understood nowadays in a purely strategic sense, it is avoided here.

the game' of competition are critically examined and the *republican share of responsibility of the 'private economy'* for the framework conditions of the various branches of industry is evaluated. In particular, this refers to the overall institutional conditions under which companies can be reasonably expected to face the demands of competitive self-assertion. The systematic consequence is that integrative corporate ethics must itself be conceived from the start as involving two stages – in addition to and not in place of the (undisputed) two-stage character of institutional ethics and corporate ethics. The integration of ethics and the logic of business success are seen as the entrepreneurial challenge of business integrity (first stage), which must however be supported at the regulatory political level. To this end the company managers must see beyond the mere observance of business integrity and acknowledge their republican-political share of responsibility (second stage) at the level of the company and the industrial federation (Figure 10.3).[102]

1st Stage: The entrepreneurial task of value creation (business integrity)

The basic function of every company, which distinguishes it from other types of social organization, is and remains of course the provision of goods and services for customers in return for payment. But from the point of view of serving life this is not a sufficient determination of the purpose of economic enterprise. Beyond that, integrative corporate ethics begins by orienting business activity meaningfully on a 'vision' of real-life practical values which ought to be created, be it on the level of fulfilling fundamental human needs or on the level of enlargening the abundance of human life (as outlined in Chapter 6). This can take the form of a contribution to the quality of the private life of the consumers of goods or services or – more sophisticatedly – of a better fulfilment of a fundamental social task (e.g. nutrition, the provision of living space, of traffic facilities, health and education services, etc.).[103] Commitment to an idea of value creation which aims to make a genuine contribution to the quality of life

[102] On the conception and the dissemination of republican ethical consciousness as the second stage of integrative corporate ethics see Ulrich/Thielemann, *Ethik und Erfolg*, pp. 86ff., 161f., and 'How Do Managers Think?', p. 677f. Steinmann/Löhr, 'Unternehmensethik als Ordnungselement', p. 143f., also argue to an increasing degree for 'a republican understanding of the role of companies'. A consistent republican corporate ethics is not, however, compatible with their 'presumption of correctness for the profit principle'. On the political and philosophical foundations of republicanism see Chapter 8.

[103] For the second focus see C. K. Prahalad/A. C. Hammond, 'Serving the World's Poor, Profitably', *Harvard Business Review* 80/9 (2002), pp. 48–57.

2nd stage of responsibility: **republican corporate citizenship**

Critical questioning of given conditions of competition which lead to corporate ethical dilemmas

1st stage of responsibility: **business integrity**

Search for profitable forms of socio-economically meaningful and legitimate economic activity under the conditions set by the regulatory framework

▶ **Entrepreneurial task of value creation**
Corporate aim to serve life on a sound normative 'business basis'
(legitimacy premise and the imparting of meaning)

▶ **Share of responsibility at the branch and regulatory political level**
for ethically responsible standards and frame conditions of competition
(*ordo*liberal commitment to a market economy serving vital political purposes)

Figure 10.3. Internal two-stage conception of corporate ethics

in society is itself already an expression of the basic republican ethical stance of entrepreneurs.

A corresponding example of *focus on societal function* by a company could be a 'global player' in food production that extends business activities to under-developed or poorly developed countries where a substantial part of the population suffers from under-nourishment. Obviously it makes sense for this company to see the real-life meaning of its activities in making a substantial contribution to the improvement of the general food supply (rather than in selling luxury goods to the moneyed class). The company thereby takes into account the internal effects of its activities on the existing, mostly small-scale structures established by local producers and tradesmen by carefully integrating them into the new supply system (instead of simply using its superior power and efficiency on the market to bring about their ruin). Another example would be a car producer who sees his new societal function in developing innovative and integrative transport systems which make the transport network in general more efficient and take ecological factors into account (instead of simply bringing more and more private cars onto the jammed streets).[104]

[104] On the idea of a functionally oriented entrepreneurial policy see E. Jantsch, 'Unternehmung und Umweltsysteme', in B. Hentsch/F. Malik (eds.), *Systemorientiertes Management* (Berne *et al.*: Haupt, 1973), pp. 27–46, at p. 33, more or less in accordance with the motto: 'We transport people' instead of 'We produce cars'.

Value creation understood in this way and guided by the need for meaningful business activity gives companies their *raison d'être*. This *raison d'être* can be recognized and its realization pursued only by people who have not lost touch with real life and who develop a vision founded on personal experience as to how important needs or concerns can be better satisfied with innovative methods. The secret of success of great entrepreneurs thus often lies in their profound conviction as to the human or social significance of their actions and in the persistence or even obsession with which they pursue the vision or their life project. A good example is the Migros cooperative built up by Gottlieb Duttweiler, for decades (and still) the leading retail chain in Switzerland.[105] It is not surprising that more recent examples can be found in the field of nature-and-health-conscious products, for which only a marginal market among the advocates of an alternative life form was originally prophesied, but which have won acceptance from a broad spectrum of customers thanks to the initiative of committed and visionary entrepreneurs like The Body Shop[106] or Tom's of Maine.[107]

From the perspective of integrative corporate ethics the essential systematic point here is that in the creation of value by companies the service of life is understood to be the constitutive ethical *and* functional foundation of business success. The categorical primacy of the service of life over the achievement of profit must be maintained as it is the ultimate justification of business activity. The starting point is not strategic calculation but the real life practical question: 'What do we stand for?'[108] The sounder the ethical foundation of a business model, the easier it will usually be to find a synthesis between ethics and the market strategies determined by the logic of success. And the more convincingly this synthesis is achieved, the easier it will be for the management of companies to provide good reasons for the justification of their actions and hence of business success in conflict situations. And if this is no longer possible on account of the challenge of changed socio-economic conditions, the management will be in a favourable position to find a new ethical and strategic synthesis which preserves the sound principles behind its idea of value creation. The definition of the goal of value creation at the same

105 See G. Duttweiler, *Überzeugungen und Einfälle* (Zurich: Ex Libris, 1978); H. Munz/ Gottlieb Duttweiler Institut (eds.), *Das Phänomen Migros: Die Geschichte der Migros-Gemeinschaft* (Zürich: Ex Libris, 1973).

106 See A. Roddick, *Body and Soul* (London: Crown, 1991).

107 See T. Chappell, *The Soul of a Business: Managing for Profit and the Common Good* (New York: Bantam, 1993).

108 See R. E. Freeman/D. R. Gilbert, *Corporate Strategy and the Search for Ethics* (Englewood Cliffs: Prentice Hall, 1988), p. 70f.

time provides the management from a systematic point of view with the possibility to make a strategic and ethically reflected choice between the specific 'practical constraints' of the market to which it submits itself.[109] The determination of an entrepreneurial idea which is based on the creation of practical values for everyday life and avoids at the outset ethically questionable areas of business is, therefore, the best precaution against the risk of an ethical dilemma involving a choice between the 'constraints' arising from the need for self-assertion on the market and unforeseen moral 'demands'. The most intelligent policy for companies is, therefore, to build up new business strategies from the start at a point of intersection of possible syntheses of business policy which also have a future from an ethical point of view:

> We cannot connect ethics and strategy unless there is some point of intersection between the values and ethics that we hold and the business practices that exemplify these values and ethics. In order to build strategy on ethics and avoid a process that looks a lot like post hoc rationalization of what we actually did, we need to ask: "What do we stand for?" in conjunction with our strategic decisions. We can't wait until later.[110]

Whenever a corporation plans a new (comprehensive or partial) business strategy, it is important that it should choose its strategies not only in accordance with its evaluation of the potential for success on the market but also with a critical reflection on the ethical 'value' of strategic business alternatives and the corresponding specific practical constraints of the market. In other words: decisions on business strategies must always be embedded in the ethical value orientations of the corporation and meaningfully justified by them.

A comprehensive entrepreneurial conception of value creation will not be restricted to the consideration of the direct use of the products or services for customers offered on the market. It will also integrate the conditions of production, the market internal effects on suppliers and competitors and the entire market external (social and ecological) consequences of the use of its products and services after sale. In other words, in its assessment of value creation an ethically well-grounded business strategy will take into account the whole 'value chain' of production and the entire life cycle of the products offered, from the raw materials to the ways of transportation, production methods and the conditions of use, including the recycling of reusable parts or materials and waste disposal. It will only offer those products on the market for which it can take on the

[109] On this point see the fundamental treatment in Section 4.3 (3a).
[110] Freeman/Gilbert, *Corporate Strategy*, p. 98f.

responsibility in regard to the entire life cycle and to all the foreseeable side effects. This principle of *product stewardship* can be understood as a concrete fulfilment of the stewardship principle in the context of the entrepreneurial conception of value creation mentioned above.[111]

2nd Stage: the co-responsibility of the private economy at the branch and regulatory political level (republican corporate citizenship)

The reasonableness of the demand that an individual company should operate in accordance with a life-serving conception of value creation depends essentially on the institutional framework under which it must assert itself in competition. It is the in part already existing 'organized irresponsibility'[112] of the politically constituted economic order which first imprisons the companies structurally within the confines of an 'inherently necessary', ethically dilemmatic situation. Leading figures in the business world with republican convictions, who take the creation of value in the service of life seriously, will not in such cases simply shrug their shoulders and point to the practical constraints of self-assertion under the given competitive conditions. Instead they will welcome and initiate ethically justified reforms of the institutional framework.

Experience shows that the quality of the institutional framework of the market economy cannot be much better than what the wielders of real political economic power desire – and these are not least the leading figures in the economy and, in particular, the politically influential trade organizations (branch associations). Entrepreneurs and top managers who are really interested in company policies with a high social and economic potential for the consideration of values consequently recognize their share of responsibility as men and women of republican commitment for the ethical quality of the 'rules of the game' and the regulatory framework under which they wish to play 'the game of competition'. The regulatory-political responsibility of the heads of corporations and associations is justified and motivated, in as far as it is born of republican and ethical convictions (and only then), by their *enlightened self-interest* in an institutional framework for competition which encourages and rewards entrepreneurial behaviour of higher ethical value with cost advantages and, vice versa, imposes 'disincentives' or cost

[111] See above Section 10.2 (2). The principle of product stewardship is reflected, for example, in the *Responsible Care* Programme of the International Association of Chemical Industries. On this point see De George, *Competing with Integrity*, p. 93f.

[112] See Beck, *Gegengifte*, p. 96ff.

disadvantages on business behaviour which is less valuable from a vital-political point of view.

Under the real existing framework conditions of the market economy the opposite is all too often the case. Behind such symptomatic 'failures of the market' a *failure of the regulatory-political framework* can always be identified. Entrepreneurs and top managers can and should consequently see it as an aspect of professional, i.e. ethically guided, intelligence, when they do not simply put up with problems in the tension field of ethics and the entrepreneurial need for self-assertion caused by organizational weaknesses of the system. They should contribute instead, out of shared republican convictions, to an institutional reversal of incentives.[113] The adoption of such an ethical standpoint, be it at the national or supranational level, can ultimately be seen as the real test of truthfulness to corporate ethical principles.

Below the level of state institutional policies the possibility of self-regulation and self-commitment by entire branches of the economy in the form of ethically oriented *branch agreements* can also be considered in as far as they do not violate the higher regulations of vital policy or the competitive order. Ethically justified branch agreements can be easily distinguished from the usually impermissible cartel agreements, as the latter create gratuitous income for the participating companies at the expense of third parties, whereas the former observe the legitimate interests of third parties by binding competition to the prior conditions of vital policy.[114] In accordance with the familiar subsidiarity principle and a corresponding step by step 'ethical displacement'[115] branch standards are an expression of the autonomous collective self-commitment of a branch of the economy, either as a (provisional) compensation for the lack of legal regulations or for the implementation of competitive conditions which are of higher ethical value in comparison to the existing laws. The first case is particularly relevant in international competition between 'global players' wherever supranational social and ecological standards are largely lacking. For instance, in the footwear and apparel manufacturing industry, most competitors' problems with child labour led to the Fair

[113] At this point Homann/Blome-Drees, *Wirtschafts- und Unternehmensethik*, p. 162, also abandon their otherwise economistic conception of politics as the continuation of business with other means and postulate 'the moral commitment of a company above all in the acceptance of political responsibility and less in one-sided prior concessions in competition'.

[114] See the analogous distinction between old and new protectionism in Section 9.3 (2). See also M. Osterloh, *Interorganisationales Lernen in ethischen Branchenvereinbarungen*, Diskussionsbeitrag N° 18 (Zurich: Institut für betriebswirtschaftliche Forschung an der Universität Zürich, 1995), p. 7.

[115] See De George, *Competing with Integrity*, p. 97f., and, following him, Steinmann/Löhr, 'Unternehmensethik als Ordnungselement', p. 157.

Labour Association.[116] Another example is the already mentioned self-commitment programme Responsible Care of the International Association of Chemical Industries. The second case is of significance, among other things, in branches whose technological or structural development is so rapid that the existing laws limp behind the problems that arise with a certain time lag (e.g. in medical technology, bio- and genetic technology, food technology, information and communication technology).

The practical sense of an ethical branch agreement can be seen in making the more advanced corporate ethical commitment of one or more competitors the standard of the entire branch. In this way a common solution to the dilemma of choice between morally desirable and strategically advantageous behaviour can be found and ethically valuable innovations can be protected against exploitation by competitors with lower standards of self-commitment. By means of agreement on ethical branch standards business practices which undermine these standards can be declared to be avoidable forms of moral free riding and hence of unfair competition. Such branch agreements must, of course, take into account the reasonableness of the demands made on all the members and, for example, provide for transitional arrangements.

Ethical branch agreements cannot and do not want to be competitively neutral in any case.[117] They rather serve the purpose of raising the standards of fair competition so that they take into account the higher value of the ecological, social or human aspects of the overall situation. Yet the effective reach of such branch agreements is limited: possible moral free riders (companies or individuals) may lack the good will to orient their economic behaviour on these higher values and the maximum sanction available to a branch association is the exclusion of non-cooperative firms. They are probably most effective in 'low-cost situations', in which the direct cost disadvantages of members over non-members of the association as a result of the ethical self-commitment can be compensated for at least

[116] See S. Zadek, 'The Path to Corporate Responsibility', *Harvard Business Review* 82 (2004), N° 12, pp. 125–32.

[117] On the misunderstanding as to the competitive neutrality of generally valid framework conditions see the treatment in Sections 8.2 and 9.2 (2). Steinmann/Löhr, *Grundlagen der Unternehmensethik*, pp. 108, 122, and 'Unternehmensethik als Ordnungselement', p. 158, make an analogous mistake in regard to branch agreements. Their leading question 'Is a competitively neutral revision of a branch codex possible?' can be answered positively only if a planned revision leaves the relative competitive positions of the branch members unchanged and hence implies *no* incentive for a change of behaviour in the desired republican-ethical direction. But then this (pseudo) reform is meaningless from a vital-political point of view.

partially by indirect advantages, for example in the provision of information or the improvement of a company's reputation.[118]

In 'high-cost situations', however, branch agreements cannot satisfactorily regulate the losses that can be reasonably expected of their members. The same is true for the case when fundamental socio-political issues are involved, which are a matter for public deliberation and cannot be left to the responsibility of the private economy. In such cases an 'ethical displacement' to the level of institutional policies regulated by the state is necessary.

The assumption of responsibility at both the branch and regulatory-political level is often hindered by economistic thought patterns which attribute a normative quality to the competitive constraints of a deregulated 'free market' and claim that these ensure the ethicality of corporate behaviour. In this manner the ability to distinguish between a life-serving institutional framework for the market which takes vital-political aspects into account and state interventionism which falsifies the conditions of competition is fogged over.[119] This confusion can be overcome only with the help of a consistent ordoliberal conception of institutional politics in which vital policy is regarded as a constitutive precondition for a life-serving market economy. Otherwise the market would lack a meaningful orientation for the improvement of its efficiency. But precisely this corporate ethical subordination of profit interests to the 'vital' (Rüstow) concerns of the res publica is of decisive importance if the institutional framework of the market is not to degenerate politically to a mere site for the continuation of the pursuit of profit with political means.[120] Without economic citizens of republican conviction in the executive suites of companies, whose public spirit makes them fundamentally willing to grant the ethical principles of the res publica systematic priority over their private economic interests, neither institutional nor corporate ethics can be put into practice. This indivisible relationship between business integrity and republican co-responsibility is the essence of well-conceived *corporate citizenship*.[121]

[118] Such 'low-cost situations' limit the extent of the loss of turnover and profit required of the members and thus also reduce the danger of an erosion of ethical branch agreements. On the concept of the 'low-cost situation' see Section 4.3 (3b).

[119] On the relatively undifferentiated level of awareness of institutional politics among some top managers see Ulrich/Thielemann, *Ethik und Erfolg*, p. 137ff.

[120] On ordoliberal 'vital policy' see Section 9.1 (3), on political economism Section 5.3 (3).

[121] This interpretation of corporate citizenship is more thoroughly developed in P. Ulrich, 'Republikanischer Liberalismus und Corporate Citizenship: Von der ökonomistischen Gemeinwohlfiktion zur republikanisch-ethischen Selbstbindung wirtschaftlicher Akteure', in H. Münkler/H. Bluhm (eds.), *Gemeinwohl und Gemeinsinn, Bd. IV: Zwischen Normativität und Faktizität* (Berlin: Akademie Verlag, 2002), pp. 273–91. For an English approach that comes comparatively near to such an integrative view (but still lacks an explicit politico-philosophical perspective) see S. Zadek, *The Civil Corporation: The New Economy of Corporate Citizenship* (London: Earthscan, 2001).

Thus the integrative circle between corporate and institutional ethics is closed again.

Although an enlightened understanding of the ethical problems of this kind has not yet made much impact on the private economy – which is not so private in some vital-political respects – there are growing signs that the truly 'leading' figures in the economy are in part beginning to develop a new awareness of the preconditions for life-serving corporate value creation and a new understanding of their role. They are tired of being the 'whipping boys of the nation' and wish instead for a life in which they can stand up for their business practices without a bad conscience or the burden of moral tension, both publicly and in their private lives. These 'new entrepreneurs'[122] wish to be in a position to give honest and convincing answers to the critical ethical questions of their fellow citizens on their professional activities. This applies particularly in regard to those who possibly have legitimate demands to make on the companies they manage: the claimant groups or the stakeholders.

10.3 Deliberative corporate policy-making: the 'stakeholder dialogue' as a site of business morality

With the insight that an ethically justifiable profit principle does not exist, the normative question as to how managers should properly deal with the partially similar, partially conflicting value conceptions, 'claims' and interests of the various claimant groups or stakeholders becomes an open one again. Experience shows that business activity is often at the heart of value and interest conflicts in society. On account of the impact of their activities in a wide variety of social contexts big corporations, above all, are being subjected to a growing 'public exposure'.[123] On the one hand they are under more or less strong pressure as a result of people's expectations that, apart from their basic function of producing goods or services for the market in return for payment, they should fulfil a variety of other socio-economic functions for the providers of their capital (shareholder value and interest on loan capital), employees (workplaces, good wages and social benefits, good immaterial working conditions) and suppliers (fair and stable supply opportunities), as well as for the communities in which they are located, the state and the general public

[122] On this new corporate-ethical thought pattern, which can be found among about 10% of the top managers in the study mentioned above, see Ulrich/Thielemann, Ethik und Erfolg, p. 81ff., and 'How Do Managers Think?', p. 888f.

[123] See Th. Dyllick, *Management der Umweltbeziehungen: Öffentliche Auseinandersetzungen als Herausforderung* (Wiesbaden: Gabler, 1989), p. 15ff.; similarly J. Post, *Corporate Behavior and Social Change* (Reston VA: Reston Publishing Co., 1978).

(taxation, contributions to the infrastructure, cultural and charitable activities). On the other hand there are often equally intense conflicts over the distribution of negative external effects of all kinds, in particular ecological costs (e.g. emission of pollutants, high noise levels and spoiling of the countryside by the production plants), but also social costs (e.g. as a result of the reduction of workplaces). Under these circumstances the private autonomy of privately constituted corporations under company law turns out to be a legal fiction. Big corporations, above all, have long become quasi-public institutions. Although their property basis is private, the effects of their operations are predominantly of public relevance.[124]

In the context of integrative corporate ethics companies must, therefore, be regarded in principle as enterprises for pluralistic value creation, regardless of their legal form, as they have a considerable impact on the lives and existential conditions of a variety of reference groups and must accordingly submit their activities to pluralistic legitimation by all the affected parties. This means that the question of the quality of the value creation to be achieved by the companies – which values should the companies create? – is no longer sufficient. Inevitably, the question of the just *distribution* of the value creation (benefits) as well as the value consumption (costs) for all stakeholders must also be asked. For whom are the values to be created? And who should bear which (internal and external) costs of the value creation process?

No simple criterion is conceivable which would permit a decision on the ethically correct solution of the multiplicity of value and interest conflicts resulting from entrepreneurial activity, after we have rejected the harmonistic fiction of the 'profit principle'. Instead, recourse must be had to processes of argumentative justification of normative validity claims. It is essential that the practical character of the resulting *corporate politics*, in every sense of the word, be taken seriously. Corporate policy-making must ultimately be understood as the real (sub-)politics of the corporation, which in turn must be conceived in the discourse-ethical categories of ethically rational politics, and that means as deliberative politics.[125] The model of *deliberative corporate policy-making* suggests itself here. Of course it is and remains the task of company executives to propose a meaningful conception of value creation for their company. But in order to guarantee a legitimate distribution of value creation and value consumption and hence the integrity of the business, the proposals must be put up for discussion unconditionally and justified in a deliberative process involving all the 'stakeholders' and other affected parties.

[124] See Ulrich, *Grossunternehmung als quasi-öffentliche Institution*, p. 159ff.
[125] On the model of deliberative politics see Section 8.2.

It is doubtless the case that the corporate-ethical postulate of the *stakeholder dialogue* can in certain circumstances lead to serious problems for company executives in regard to the reasonableness of stakeholder claims. To avoid any misunderstanding, this does not amount to a rigorous demand that the company managers should abandon the pursuit of success and profit in a heroic act of self-denial and become benevolent altruists instead. It is a matter of course that the interest of corporations in income and profit are also good prospective 'candidates'[126] for *possibly* legitimate claims, particularly when the satisfaction of numerous other claims depends upon them. From an ethical point of view the corporation itself and all the persons dependent directly or indirectly upon its self-assertion on the market cannot reasonably be expected to forego their claims unconditionally. The corporate ethical *legitimation discourse* can, therefore, also be seen from the perspective of the corporation as a *discourse on reasonableness*, i.e. on the justice and adequacy of the demands made upon the corporation.[127] It can, moreover, be assumed that good entrepreneurial models of value creation, which are guided by the high quality fulfilment of authentic needs of potential customers, will usually be found thoroughly worthy of recognition in the legitimacy test.

Thus the corporate-ethical fundamental condition of the legitimacy of business activity in regard to all those affected by no means makes it impossible for companies to pursue strategically clever, success-oriented actions within the framework of decisions on aims and behavioural principles which are found to be legitimate. It is rather the whole point of legitimacy premises to ensure that corporate policy on the purposes and goals of business activities reveal a sense of responsibility towards all the stakeholders and that the managers can be reasonably expected to fulfil them. For this reason it is essential that the 'inviolable' rights of all participants and other affected persons should be clarified first. They are the criterion for an impartial and responsible treatment of the conflicting claims of all parties. Which of these claims can be regarded as justifiable (i.e. as moral rights) and to what extent, these are questions that can be cleared up only in a process of deliberation about the concrete situation.

In what follows we examine and define more clearly the so-called stakeholder approach in regard to its soundness as the 'site' of the corporate ethical legitimation discourse (1). We then go into the possibilities for ensuring the observance of binding stakeholder rights in the context of an autonomous corporate ethical self-commitment (2).

[126] Thielemann, *Das Prinzip Markt*, p. 130.
[127] On the concept of the discourse on reasonableness see Section 4.3 (3).

(1) *Stakeholder relationships as the site of the corporate-ethical discourse on legitimacy and reasonableness*

The concept of a stakeholder was probably first used in 1963 at the Stanford Research Institute (SRI) as a play on words extending the concept of a 'stockholder' (who today is more frequently called a shareholder). Its use was apparently proposed by the Swedish social scientist Eric Rhenman, who was resident at the SRI at the time. He first used the concept in a publication in 1968.[128] Its career really took off, however, only after it was taken up by R. E. Freeman as 'a new way of thinking about strategic management'.[129]

The stakeholder approach is quite simply the well-known concept of the claimants group which a company must take into account.[130] It became most prominent in the form of the behavioural theory of the firm by Cyert and March,[131] which is in turn based upon the inducement-contribution theory of March and Simon.[132] The approach models 'the business firm as a political coalition'[133] (coalition theory of the firm) between the corporation (or more generally: any organization) and its coalition partners (stakeholders) as a contractual balance of services and services in return. Each coalition partner offers the corporation certain services or resources it needs (contribution), as long as the service in return (inducement) is rewarding from the perspective of the partner concerned. Corporate policy is accordingly interpreted as maintaining a (negotiational) balance between the company executives and all the groups whose 'contributions' are needed by the company for the production of its services.

Stakeholder theories can thus be understood as generalized or extended forms of the coalition theory. There are, however, several variants which must be distinguished from one another by their criteria for the delimitation of the claimant groups involved. The key question is:

128 See E. Rhenman, *Industrial Democracy and Industrial Management* (London: Tavistock, 1968), p. 24ff. Rhenman defines stakeholders as 'individuals or groups who depend on the company for the realisation of their personal goals' (p. 25).

129 See Freeman, *Strategic Management*, pp. vi, 31, 41 and 49, who incidentally also points out the rather unclear origin of the concept and the impulses which came from Rhenman's *Industrial Democracy*.

130 This is already the basis of the understanding of corporate politics (as discussed in the partially conflicting interests of the various claimant groups) in the first edition of Ulrich/ Fluri, *Management*, in 1975.

131 R. M. Cyert/J. G. March, *A Behavioral Theory of the Firm* (Englewood Cliffs NJ: Prentice Hall, 1963). They do not use the term stakeholder, but speak usually of 'coalition members' or, with March and Simon (see the next footnote) of 'organizational participants'.

132 J. G. March/H. A. Simon, *Organizations* (New York: John Wiley & Sons, 1958); the concept can be found even earlier in H. A. Simon/D. W. Smithburg/ V. A. Thompson, *Public Administration* (New York: Alfred A. Knopf, 1950).

133 J. G. March, 'The Business Firm as a Political Coalition', *Journal of Politics* 24 (1962), pp. 662–78.

Who is to be considered as a stakeholder and who is not? Basically there are two possible answers, each with two subvariants:[134]

(a) *The power-based strategic conception*: those groups are characterized as stakeholders which have a *potential for influence* on the corporation either on account of their powers of disposition over limited resources or on account of their power to impose sanctions (potential for threat) if the corporation does not give in to their claims. In a narrower variant only those claimants are taken into account who have *effective* power over the corporation *at the moment*; in a more comprehensive variant all groups are included which are directly or indirectly *affected* by the activities of the corporation, even though they may not be in a position at this moment in time to assert their interests effectively; it could well be that they have a latent though not manifest power potential, which they can one day develop and assert.

(b) *The critical normative conception*: those groups are characterized as stakeholders who have *legitimate claims* on the corporation. These claims may be special rights founded on contractual agreements (employment, cooperation, manufacturing or purchase contracts) or general moral rights of those affected by the actions or lack of action of the corporation. The moral obligations of the corporation in its relationship with its contractual partners go beyond the legal obligations arising from the contract. In certain circumstances – and quite apart from the agreed services and services in return – the *solidarity* of a corporation towards its partners may be called for, should they run into difficulties and become existentially dependent on the goodwill of the stronger partner.[135] In the narrower variant of

[134] Instead of the following two basic conceptions Donaldson and Preston propose a threefold division between a *descriptive*, an *instrumental* and a *normative* application of the stakeholder theory. This systematics is not followed here, as the 'instrumental' or strategic view always rests upon the description of potential (empirical) operational relationships. See T. Donaldson/L. E. Preston, 'The Stakeholder Theory of the Corporation: Concepts, Evidence and Implications', *Academy of Management Review* 20/1 (1995), pp. 65–91.

[135] On the concept of solidarity see Section 1.2. Typical examples of such emergency situations, in which a possible duty of solidarity of the stronger partner towards the weaker must be considered, are: (1) The moral duty of a company which dismisses employees to take their existential concerns seriously and to support them in the search for a new job or in the solution of financial problems, particularly when they are not in a position to help themselves; (2) the moral duty of a bank which has given a company a large credit not to withdraw the credit without considering the existential need of the company to survive economically. It is also necessary to consider the fact that in the broader sense of the normative critical stakeholder conception (see above) the duty of solidarity cannot be restricted to the circle of those directly affected by the direct operations of the company, but must in principle be extended to every person in need of care and support, in accordance with Kant's conception of the 'meritorious' duty to exercise solidarity (Kant, 'Metaphysics of Morals', p. 75). See also the comments at the end of Section 8.3.

the critical normative conception only the contractual partners and others directly affected by the actions of the corporation are regarded as stakeholders. In the broader variant every (politically) mature person has in principle the right to 'address' the issue of the moral justification of the actions of a corporation, to raise objections and to demand a public justification of questionable company activities which are of public interest. From this perspective a definite list of the stakeholders is no longer possible; the stakeholders are then quite simply all those participants in the *deliberative public realm* of a free democratic society who wish to make argumentative 'claims' on a company and to enter into a dialogue with its executives in their role as citizens.

In its descriptive nature the strategic conception follows fully the tradition of the behaviourist coalition theory and is distinguished from it only by its 'practical', i.e. instrumentalist perspective.[136] In contrast, the critical normative conception has a completely different methodical status. Here we are dealing with a regulative idea in the light of which we must examine critically who should be entitled to make justified claims on a company (and not merely who can assert his claims effectively). It is not enough 'to have a stake' (i.e. an interest) in company affairs and the power to push it through; the only acceptable criterion is now the ethically justified legitimacy of claims. Thus, it would be more appropriate to speak of a 'claimholder approach' than a stakeholder approach.[137] The recognition of the unconditional republican political duty of corporations to legitimate their activities logically leads to the comprehensive perspective of the stakeholder (or claimholder) approach as that conception which sees the corporation against the horizon of an in principle unlimited public legitimation discourse in a modern civil society. And it sees this discourse as the systematic site of corporate political morality. The business integrity of company executives must prove its worth in the public process of deliberation among politically mature economic citizens, and only here can it find the justification for its actions.

Against this (discourse-ethically illuminated) horizon it is now possible to examine more closely exemplary interpretations and applications of the stakeholder approach in *management theory* in regard to their ethical content. It will scarcely come as a surprise that here the strategic perspective is predominant. As long as this is accurately perceived and reflected upon, the theorists and practitioners of management know what they are doing. Confusion arises, however, when the strategic stakeholder conception is equated with, or at least not sufficiently distinguished from, a

[136] For a general critique of instrumentalist corporate ethics see Section 10.2 (1).

[137] See the concurring view in B. Waxenberger/L. Spence, 'Reinterpretation of a Metaphor: from Stakes to Claims', *Strategic Change* 12 (2003), pp. 239–49.

business-ethical conception. No less a scholar than R. E. Freeman, who is an acknowledged source of reference both as a theorist of management and as a representative of American business ethics, originally confused these two perspectives in his often quoted and adopted standard definition. The difference between the narrower and the broader variant of the power-oriented strategic conception also remains blurred:

A stakeholder in an organization is (by definition) any group or individual who can affect or is affected by the achievement of the organization's objectives.[138]

The inclusion of everyone 'who is affected' points only at first sight to a corporate ethical aspect of the stakeholder conception. It is symptomatic of his strategic perspective that Freeman does (or at least did) not take the fact that people are affected seriously from a systematic point of view, neither as an independent reason for the legitimacy of claims nor as the source of the moral obligation of the corporation towards those who do not have the power to influence its decisions. Instead he sees the relevance of those who are affected solely as part of a long-term calculation of the risks which might possibly follow from continual strategic disregard for their concerns and thus reduces the two groups to one, i.e. those 'who can affect':

I make the definition symmetric because of the changes which the firm has undergone in the past few years. Groups which 20 years ago had no effect on the actions of the firm can affect it today largely because of the actions of the firm which ignored the effects on these groups. Thus, by calling those affected groups 'stakeholders', the ensuing strategic management model will be sensitive to future change, and able to turn 'external changes' into internal changes.[139]

This reductionist line of thought unmasks the approach, which is suggestively presented as ethical in content, as a power-based, strictly strategic and hence instrumentalist way of thinking. In the final analysis, therefore, the additional clause in Freeman's definition ('or is affected') only apparently serves to solve the ethical problems of this 'hard' strategic perspective.[140]

[138] Freeman, *Strategic Management*, p. 46 and in similar vein, ibid., p. 25. In the third sentence after the definition quoted above the strategic perspective is clarified. Freeman now only writes: 'Groups which can affect that [strategic] direction and its implementation must be considered in the strategic management process' (ibid., p. 46).

[139] Ibid., p. 46.

[140] As Goodpaster aptly remarks, Freeman could have chosen the simpler formulation that the stakeholder approach takes into account all 'who can actually or *potentially* affect the company'. See K. E. Goodpaster, 'Business Ethics and Stakeholder Analysis', *Business Ethics Quarterly* 1/1 (1991), pp. 55–71, at p. 59 (my italics). Yet Goodpaster's viewpoint ultimately remains within the confines of a conventional understanding of corporate ethics, including acceptance of the 'profit principle' (and thus of a corrective corporate ethics), which Freeman, 'Politics of Stakeholder Theory', p. 410ff., equally aptly criticizes from his more recent and fundamental perspective (see below).

Those who are negatively affected by certain consequences of the actions or lack of action of a company, but have no means of influencing the course of events in order to escape the burden of negative effects or at least to secure compensation, remain excluded from the strategic considerations of the company – unless its executives attribute to them a latent power potential with possibly acute long-term consequences. On the other hand, according to Freeman, even a terrorist group can in certain circumstances be counted as a stakeholder, if it can acquire strategic influence over the management of a corporation.[141] As if he wanted to increase the confusion or to play down rhetorically the reduction of ethical to strategic categories Freeman then attempts to place the strategic conception in the conceptual vicinity of the critical-normative interpretation:

> 'Stakeholder' connotes *'legitimacy'*, and while managers may not think that certain groups are 'legitimate' in the sense that their demands on the firm are inappropriate, they had better give 'legitimacy' to these groups *in terms of their ability to affect the direction of the firm.*[142]

Here the ethical category *legitimacy* is explicitly reduced to the strategic category of *acceptance.* By blurring instead of clarifying the categorial difference between strategic and ethical rationality Freeman's stakeholder theory in its original form (which was accepted almost unanimously by management theorists) has contributed much to the continuing confusion in the treatment of the problem, as it encourages supposedly normative interpretations which, however, lack a corporate-ethical foundation.[143] By way of illustration we can give a brief sketch of two exemplary variations of such a categorially ambiguous or even mistaken normative turn.

- Some management theorists have proposed an extension of the shareholder-value approach to a *stakeholder-value approach,*[144] which on the one hand takes into account the changed strategic conditions

141 See Freeman, *Strategic Management*, p. 53.

142 Ibid., p. 45. Although Freeman points out the normative nature of the concept of legitimacy in the sense of justified claims, he then dismisses the concept from further consideration with a dubious line of argument: 'For the present time I shall put these questions aside, not because they do not bear fruitful research, but rather, I believe, that first we must understand the weaker sense of "stakeholder legitimacy": if you want to be an effective manager, then you must take stakeholders into account' (p. 45).

143 Recently, Freeman has himself pointed to the weaknesses of his early book; see R. E. Freeman, 'The Stakeholder Approach Revisited', *Zeitschrift für Wirtschafts- und Unternehmensethik* 5/3 (2004), pp. 228–41.

144 See P. Gomez, *Wertmanagement: Vernetzte Strategien für Unternehmen im Wandel* (Düsseldorf: Econ, 1993), p. 23ff. See also M. Janisch, *Das strategische Anspruchsmanagement: Vom Shareholder Value zum Stakeholder Value* (Berne *et al.*: Haupt, 1993).

determining success but, on the other hand, is meant at the same time to be in keeping with a well-meant normative intention:

In the further development [of the shareholder-value approach] the stakeholder value [stands] in the foreground. The strategy is designed to create value for all the stakeholder groups of the corporation.[145]

No matter how good the intention might be from a corporate-ethical point of view – the problems which consequently arise in regard to the normative clarification of the conflicting claims of owners and employees, customers and suppliers, local communities and other affected persons cannot be mastered by an approach which leaves no systematic space for the categories of ethical rationality but simply puts a 'strategic method of value management'[146] in their place. The corresponding socio-technical 'strategies' have acquired their supposedly normative orientational force deviously along the path of economistic reductionism. This is achieved partly with the help of the utilitarian fiction of the common good ('creating value for all'), which ignores the question of legitimate claims and the just solution of conflicts at the decisive point, as the creation of 'stakeholder values' is after all made dependent on the prior generation of shareholder value. Or it is subordinated to the contractualist exchange of advantages, as in the inducement-contribution theory of March and Simon, which ignores the status-quo problem of given power relationships and reduces the problem of reaching just solutions to power-based bargaining.[147] The listing of supposedly objective and determinable 'ideas on the benefits for the strategic claimant groups'[148] and the methodical approach via empirical-analytical 'benefit analysis',[149] understood as the starting point for the generation

[145] Gomez, *Wertmanagement*, p. 30.

[146] See ibid., p. 107ff.; similarly Janisch, *Anspruchsmanagement*, p. 260ff.

[147] On this see Section 5.2 (utiliarianism) and Section 5.3 (contractualism). Contractualist ideas are indicated, among other things, by Gomez (*Wertmanagement*, p. 103) with his reference to a 'process of bargaining on goals'; utilitarian ideas can be seen in Janisch's definition of the 'strategic management of claimant groups' as the 'optimal shaping of the relationships with the individual claimant groups' (*Anspruchsmanagement*, p. 263). Optimal for whom? The practical part of Gomez's *Wertmanagement* (p. 107ff.), or in English *value management*, scarcely ever refers to the conflicting value claims of the claimant groups, which can be reconciled with the declared programme of the 'stakeholder-value approach' only against the background of economistic premises. The *generation* of value should and must obviously be achieved by the strictly strategic pursuit of success, so that afterwards the *distribution* of the value creation can take into account as many claims as possible. On this implicitly *charitable* corporate ethics see Section 10.2 (2).

[148] Janisch, *Anspruchsmanagement*, p. 142ff. Here 'benefit' is expressly defined as the 'measure of the satisfaction of needs'.

[149] Ibid., p. 144.

of benefits 'for all', calls to mind the assumptions of a benevolent dictator as the arbitrator of conflicts on social values and interests, here evidently embodied by the company management.[150]

– Under the headings 'two-way public relations',[151] 'dialogue-oriented corporate communications'[152] or simply 'corporate dialogue'[153] *public relations theory* has increasingly taken over the ideas of the stakeholder dialogue, and specifically the broader variant relating to the public sphere. Here too, however, the decisive categorial difference between legitimation discourse and strategies designed to secure acceptance are often blurred over rather than clarified and made fruitful for practical purposes. It is surprising that even acknowledged experts on corporate ethics speak uninhibitedly and uncritically of 'the *instrument* of corporate dialogue ... as a *means* of proactive public relations work'.[154] There can of course be no objection to the consideration of the legitimate strategic interests of corporations. But this approach fails to work out clearly the discourse-ethical primacy of an unconditional communicative orientation resulting from a legitimation discourse over the criterion of strategic success. And nonetheless it is asserted without qualification that this ultimately instrumentalized form of corporate dialogue is 'a manifestation of the ideal of the public use of reason'.[155] It is hardly surprising that in these texts the regulative idea

[150] On this unpolitical and undemocratic conception of elitist economic politics see Section 9.2.

[151] The leading promotor of a dialogue-based conception of corporate communications and public relations is J. E. Grunig (ed.), *Excellence in Public Relations and Communication Management* (Hillsdale NJ: Erlbaum, 1992). For a critical discussion see S. Zajitschek, *Corporate Ethics Relations: Orientierungsmuster für die legitime Gestaltung unternehmensexterner Beziehungen* (Berne *et al.*: Haupt, 1997), p. 213ff.

[152] See G. Bentele/H. Steinmann/A. Zerfass (eds.), *Dialogorientierte Unternehmenskommunikation. Grundlagen – Praxiserfahrung – Perspektiven* (Berlin: Vistas, 1996).

[153] See H. Steinmann/A. Zerfass, 'Privates Unternehmertum und öffentliches Interesse', in G. R. Wagner (ed.), *Betriebswirtschaft und Umweltschutz* (Stuttgart: Schäffer-Poeschel, 1993), pp. 3–26, at p. 4. Similarly A. Zerfass/A. G. Scherer, 'Unternehmensführung und Öffentlichkeitsarbeit: Überlegungen zur wissenschaftstheoretischen Grundlegung der Public-Relations-Forschung', *Die Betriebswirtschaft* 55 (1995), pp. 493–512, at p. 502.

[154] Steinmann/Zerfass, 'Privates Unternehmertum', p. 7 (emphasis changed). Bentele/Steinmann/Zerfass, *Dialogorientierte Unternehmenskommunikation*, p. 457, state even more clearly: 'The *strategic anchoring of communication through dialogue* results from the consideration that communicative processes in a business context are always to be understood as the means by which the strategic and operative management ought to be supported' (emphasis in the original).

[155] Steinmann/Zerfass, 'Privates Unternehmertum', p. 13. On the regulative idea of the public use of reason see Section 8.2; on the discourse-ethical primacy of the communicative orientation over the success orientation see Section 2.5.

of an unlimited critical public sphere as the (necessary rational ethical) site of legitimation plays no systematic part in the intended use of 'public reason'. It is rather the case that they at least harbour the always latent danger of the instrumentalization of dialogue for the strategic purposes of 'public relations work', as Markus Kaiser has aptly pointed out: This kind of ... corporate communication [is] less determined by an honest interest in mutual understanding than by the will to self-assertion through the most skilful refutation of critical objections.

The persuasive effect seems to be the *only* criterion for this kind of public relations work.[156]

However, as Apel has accurately pointed out, 'it is in principle impossible to discover *strategically* – for example by means of *negotiations* or *suggestive persuasion* – who is right'.[157] If it is not to be instrumentalized itself corporate ethics must unconditionally advocate a critical-normative stakeholder approach, rigorously uphold the essential categorial distinctions and provide fundamental reflections on a management theory in which categorial confusion and reductionism are avoided. More than twenty years ago the author of the present text proposed a discourse-ethically based conception of 'dialogue-oriented corporate politics', which understands corporate policy-making as genuine politics of corporations. The primary corporate-ethical orientation of actions must be seen in the development of the corporate communicative potential for achieving mutual consent in dealings with all the groups inside and outside the corporation who are affected by corporate activities. This includes the unconditional abandonment of restrictions on corporate political communication (in the sense of the creation of symmetrical communicative situations).[158]

Apart from the necessary clarification of the fundamental categorial difference between bargaining and argumentative communication and agreement (which requires no further treatment here), a discourse-ethical reinterpretation of the stakeholder approach is, above all, in a position to clear up two problems: on the one hand the

[156] M. Kaiser, 'Kulturelle Kommunikationspraxen als Leitbild einer wirtschaftsethisch reflektierten Unternehmenskommunikation', in: Bentele/Steinmann/Zerfass (eds.), *Dialogorientierte Unternehmenskommunikation*, pp. 109–45, at p. 118.

[157] Apel, *Diskurs und Verantwortung*, p. 283.

[158] This discourse-ethical approach to the understanding of corporate politics and the concept of a communicative potential for agreement as opposed to the concept of strategic potential for success were first developed in P. Ulrich, 'Konsensus-Management: Die zweite Dimension rationaler Unternehmensführung', *Betriebswirtschaftliche Forschung und Praxis* 35 (1983), pp. 70–84, above all at p. 78ff.

normative points of view which are at the heart of the 'stakeholder dialogue' (a) and, on the other hand, the special status of the general public sphere (b).[159]

(a) The normative aspects involved in a discursive examination of stakeholder claims are, on the one hand, *accountability* for the consequences arising from the recognition or rejection of the various claims of all concerned and, on the other hand, the question whether the corporation itself can be *reasonably expected* to recognize the claims made on it.[160] In contrast to the usual interpretation of the stakeholder approach the strategic potential to wield influence and power or utter threats has no normative power at all here. This potential cannot even be regarded as a source of (implicit or explicit) arguments but must, on the contrary, be eliminated from all attempts to arrive at a just solution of conflicts by means of communication and agreement. The acknowledgment of the 'uncompelled compulsion of the better argument'[161] is the indispensable normative minimum of ethical reason which can be reasonably expected of all (including the management itself) who wish to be recognized as participants in the deliberative processes on corporate policy.

(b) The contractualist approaches merely regard the *critical public sphere* as one stakeholder among others and thus classify the 'general public' as nothing more than a 'special interest group'. However, the unrestricted general public sphere involving all politically mature (economic) citizens must be understood, from a discourse-ethical point of view, as the notional 'meta-institution' (Apel) or the (highest) systematic site of corporate ethical legitimation. As a consequence of the reduced view of the public sphere as a mere 'stakeholder' the fact is regularly overlooked that, inversely, stakeholders are always at the same time part of the deliberative public sphere. Therefore, it is necessary to recognize them, on the one hand, as members of the public (politico-economic) communication community and, on the other hand, to remind them of their civic and ethical duties and responsibilities as mature citizens. The moral right of all stakeholders (in the widest sense of the concept) to 'intervene' in corporate politics has its roots in the fact that as (economic) citizens they are always the holders of possibly legitimate 'claims'

[159] On discourse ethics see Section 2.5. Even the most progressive variants of the Anglo-Saxon stakeholder approach are far removed from a discourse-ethical reinterpretation. Instead Freeman, 'Politics of Stakeholder Theory', in particular, has attempted to find a normative foundation for the approach behind Rawls' 'veil of uncertainty'.

[160] See Section 4.3 (3). [161] Habermas, 'Vorbereitende Bemerkungen', p. 137.

whose justifiability must be tested in the public deliberative processes of an open society. By publicly upholding their claims on the company as stakeholders they at the same time submit them to the critical public sphere for a general recognition of their worthiness. The management must similarly submit arguments on the unreasonableness of these claims to the same 'capacity for publicity' (Kant).[162] *Corporate ethics cannot, therefore, be enclosed within a 'private morality' of those directly involved in the dialogue on corporate politics.*

The fatal misjudgements of public protest against certain corporate actions to which a privatistic misunderstanding of corporate ethics and politics can lead were demonstrated in 1995 in the case of the disused oil platform Brent Spar. Shell as the owner wished to dispose of it cheaply by sinking it in the North Sea. Instead of taking the critical arguments of Greenpeace seriously the company evidently saw Greenpeace merely as a 'rival' and attempted to discredit it as a 'special interest group' which was pursuing its own (unfair) political interests, in spite of its reputation among ecologically conscious world citizens as an organization devoted to the protection of the environment. Shell could well have seen the Greenpeace arguments as possibly legitimate objections and recognized that its own arguments on the unreasonable cost must be unconditionally examined in the critical public sphere. But the possibility that the activists were expressing an idealistic concern, showing republican responsibility and defending the impartial public interests of the res publica, was dismissed at the outset by the company. This dismissive attitude was accompanied by the management's evident failure to understand the public expectation that the company should perceive and acknowledge a possibly justifiable moral obligation to avoid the deliberate pollution of the sea, quite apart from the question of the advantages and disadvantages of various methods of disposing of the Brent Spar.[163]

Theorists of management are only now beginning to take cautious first steps towards including this second dimension of rational management, which can only be grasped adequately with the discourse-ethical categories of rational communication, in their more comprehensive conceptions of management. In the meantime Knut Bleicher, for example, also

[162] See the account at the beginning of Section 8.2.

[163] See Ulrich, 'Brent Spar und der moral point of view: Reinterpretation eines unternehmensethischen Realfalls', *Die Unternehmung* 50/1 (1996), pp. 27–46. See also S. M. Livesey, 'Eco-Identity as Discursive Struggle: Royal Dutch/Shell, Brent Spar, and Nigeria', *The Journal of Business Communication* 38/1 (2001), pp. 58–91.

postulates the 'development of communicative potential' as the 'precondition for a dialogic corporate policy'.[164] However, he presents this task visually in a systematically unclear and unmediated form *alongside* the task of creating 'benefit potentials'[165] for all claimant groups in the utilitarian tradition and even speaks in an instrumentalist fashion of the 'activation of communicative potentials for purpose of the development of benefit potentials'.[166] In the conception of 'normative management' socio-technical thought patterns generally continue to be dominant, for example in the contractualist reduction of 'consensus management' to a 'power-balanced treatment of conflict'.[167] The admittedly extremely demanding step towards a totally new basis for normative management – in as far as this concept can still be regarded as suitable at all – on the solid foundations of integrative corporate ethics has scarcely been taken into consideration to date by management theorists. The effects of the 'myth of amoral business'[168] still seem to be too strong at the moment, as the customary strategically narrow interpretation of the stakeholder dialogue all too clearly reveals.

It is a positive sign, however, that R. E. Freeman, who sees himself as a mediator between strategic management theory and business ethics, has recognized the categorial weaknesses of his concept as presented above and has frankly admitted the need:

to revise this concept along essentially Kantian lines. That is, each of these stakeholder groups has a right not to be treated as a means to some end, and therefore

164 K. Bleicher, *Normatives Management: Politik, Verfassung und Philosophie des Unternehmens* (Frankfurt/New York: Campus, 1994), p. 228ff. The concept of 'normative management' was first proposed by Hans Ulrich, 'Die Bedeutung der Management-Philosophie für die Unternehmensführung', in H. Ulrich (ed.), *Management-Philosophie für die Zukunft* (Berne: Haupt, 1981), pp. 11–24.

165 The concept of 'benefit potential' was first introduced by Cuno Pümpin as an extension of the concept of market potential in his approach to strategic management that was implicitly based on the stakeholder-value conception. See C. Pümpin, *Das Dynamikprinzip: Zukunftsorientierungen für Unternehmer und Manager* (Düsseldorf: Econ, 1989), p. 46f.: 'We can define ... a benefit potential as a constellation latently or effectively present in the environment, the market or the company which can be developed through the activities of the company itself *to the advantage of all the reference groups of the company*' (my emphasis).

166 Bleicher, *Normatives Management*, p. 276. The visualization referred to in the text can be found in Figure IV.19 in ibid., p. 277.

167 See ibid., p. 237. I no longer use the concept of 'consensus management' first formulated in Ulrich, 'Konsensus-Management', in spite of its strategic success as a concept, as it is predominantly used in an instrumental fashion, although it was originally intended as a critique of theoretical foundations. Incidentally, Knut Bleicher also refers quite correctly in this context to the communicative-ethical categories of rationality which are essential to an understanding of the development and form of communicative potentials and 'consensus management'.

168 De George, *Business Ethics*, p. 3.

must participate in determining the future direction of the firm in which they have a stake.[169]

Freeman now corrects his original neglect of those affected by company activities who lacked the power to influence strategies and unreservedly emphasizes the central significance of the deontological-ethical aspect:

If our theory does not require an understanding of the rights of those parties affected by the corporation, then it will run afoul of our judgements about rights. (...) Property rights are not a license to ignore Kant's principle of respect for persons.[170]

The consequence for Freeman is also the categorical corporate-ethical *legitimacy proviso*, which we characterized in the preceding section as the deontological aspect of business integrity: management may not violate the moral rights of others in the measures it undertakes to secure the existence and the success of a corporation.[171] In recent years Freeman and other scholars have increasingly moved in the direction of a fundamental reflection on the legitimate rights of all stakeholders within the framework of institutional ethics and have recognized that the normative conception of the corporation as a whole has thus become an unavoidable theme of business ethics.[172]

(2) *Stakeholder rights as an institutional consequence of stakeholder relations from a corporate ethical perspective*

As in every ethical discourse, what counts essentially in a properly understood stakeholder dialogue is the public justifiability of claims, in this case

[169] W. M. Evan/R. E. Freeman, 'A Stakeholder Theory of the Modern Corporation: Kantian Capitalism', in T. C. Beauchamp/N. E. Bowie (eds.), *Ethical Theory and Business*, 3rd edn (Englewood Cliffs NJ: Prentice Hall, 1988), pp. 97–106, at p. 97. Along the same lines, a deontological turn to the stakeholder approach is also advocated in American business ethics by J. J. Brummer, *Corporate Responsibility and Legitimacy: An Interdisciplinary Approach* (New York: Greenwood, 1991), p. 144ff. Donaldson/Preston, 'Stakeholder Theory', also emphasize the fundamental significance of the normative basis of the stakeholder approach and the indispensable need to consider questions of justice, as well as more recent N. E. Bowie, *Business Ethics: A Kantian Perspective* (Malden MA: Blackwell, 1999), p. 82ff., and K. Gibson, 'The Moral Basis of Stakeholder Theory', *Journal of Business Ethics* 26/3 (2000), pp. 245–57.

[170] Evan/Freeman, 'Stakeholder Theory', p. 100.

[171] In the same sense Evan/Freeman. In the same manner as K. O. Apel introduced his supplementary principle into responsibility ethics, Evan/Freeman find it necessary to supplement their 'principle of corporate rights' (legitimacy principle) by a 'principle of corporate effects' (responsibility principle), without seeing that the two are identical, as a properly understood responsibility ethics always judges the acceptability of the consequences of actions in the light of the moral rights of all concerned. (See Section 2.5.)

[172] See Freeman, *The Politics of Stakeholder Theory*; cf. n. 7 in this chapter.

the reasonableness of claims made on the corporation and the accountability of the corporation for its plans of action to anybody involved or concerned. This in turn gives rise to the institutional ethical question as to how far institutionalized stakeholder rights must be ensured as a precondition and support of an unrestricted corporate dialogue. As a consequence of their 'Kantian turn' Evan and Freeman rightly go as far as to postulate a fundamentally different understanding both of the corporation as a social institution and of its legal constitution. They also draw institutional ethical consequences, which is still rather the exception in the Anglo-American discussion. This is expressed in two complementary proposals with differing long-term effects.

On the one hand they postulate a stakeholder board of directors made up of representatives of owners, employees, customers, suppliers and the local community, each elected by its own 'stakeholder assembly', and a representative of the 'metaphysical' overall interests of the corporation.[173] This proposal goes in the direction of a *pluralistic corporate constitution* and is largely identical with long-existing European models, although Evan and Freeman make no reference to them. As a quasi-public institution the corporation requires in principle a pluralist basis for legitimation, even though the legal and political will to introduce the necessary reforms is as yet scarcely visible. With the refutation of the profit principle, however, the conception of a corporate constitution representing strictly monistic interests is unmasked as a rather anachronistic, privatistic and economistic fiction. Until the situation changes it would at least be possible to establish an informal stakeholder advisory board as a regular forum for discussion, as Evan and Freeman propose.[174]

On the other hand they make an interesting proposal for the establishment of a Stakeholder Bill of Rights, which defines the inviolable basic rights of all stakeholders including their rights of participation in the election of the board; as a complement or counterbalance a Management Bill of Rights is suggested.[175] According to the rather cursory remarks of Evan and Freeman the stakeholders would be granted the right to free speech, the right to grievance procedures inside the corporation and if necessary in the courts, the right to civil disobedience, and other basic corporate political rights. The management would have the right to act upon its fiduciary duty as interpreted by the board. They also emphasize that these rights are unconditional and must also be guaranteed even at the cost of economic efficiency. Although Evan and Freeman do not refer specifically to republican ethical thinking, their

[173] See Evan/Freeman, 'Stakeholder Theory', p. 104. [174] Ibid., p. 105. [175] See ibid.

approach can be understood as an expression of the idea of general institutional or organizational citizen's rights developed earlier, which guarantee politically mature citizens working in complex organizations 'the normative faultline that appears with (the) ability to say no'.[176] If we carry this idea on corporate rights to its logical conclusion we arrive at the central notion of an *open corporate constitution oriented on basic rights*, which goes beyond the establishment of employee rights (Bill of Employee Rights)[177] and guarantees every stakeholder, indeed every individual who feels he/she is affected by corporate actions, rights of hearing, appeal and grievance and, in the case of the infringement of legitimate claims, rights of compensation.[178]

For their part managements of republican conviction are in a perfectly good position to observe certain institutional civic basic rights of their employees and of all the other stakeholders as an act of autonomous corporate ethical self-commitment in anticipation or supplementation of legally guaranteed economic citizenship rights. They can also work for the realization of a corresponding collective self-regulation for their entire branch of industry. They would then be acting in accordance with the irrefutable insight that the moral rights of all who are affected by corporate actions must be respected regardless of the given legal situation.[179] At the same time already existing, legally guaranteed, general basic rights could be given concrete form in regard to their special significance for 'the world of organizations' and their general validity confirmed.

In what follows we restrict ourselves to the dimension of organizational and management ethics oriented on the *basic rights of employees*.[180] The special entitlement of employees to respect for their personal dignity and

[176] Habermas, *Between Facts and Norms*, p. 324. On the concept of the 'organizational' or 'institutional citizen' see Section 8.3 (1).

[177] On the postulate of institutionalized employee rights in the Anglo-Saxon world see especially D. Ewing, *Freedom Inside the Organisation* (New York: McGraw-Hill, 1977); Th. Donaldson, *Corporations and Morality* (Englewood Cliffs NJ: Prentice Hall, 1982), p. 129ff.; M. G. Velasquez, *Business Ethics* (Englewood Cliffs NJ: Prentice Hall, 1982), p. 319ff.; P. Werhane, *Persons, Rights and Corporations* (Englewood Cliffs NJ: Prentice Hall, 1985).

[178] For more details on this conception, which we first presented in 1986, see Ulrich, *Transformation*, p. 427ff.

[179] On the relationship between moral and legal rights see Section 7.1.

[180] For details on management ethics oriented on basic rights see Ulrich, 'Führungsethik'; on the more wide-reaching perspectives of an organizational ethics which is consistently built up on the principle of equal organizational rights for all and of an 'undivided ethics of cooperation', and thus leads ultimately to conceptions of self-administration, see P. Ulrich, 'Zur Ethik der Kooperation in Organisationen', in R. Wunderer (ed.), *Kooperation: Gestaltungsprinzipien und Steuerung der Zusammenarbeit zwischen Organisationseinheiten* (Stuttgart: Schäffer-Poeschel, 1991), pp. 69–89.

the protection of their inviolable basic rights is justified by their dependent situation within the organizational hierarchy. In this context we must think, above all, of two categories of organizational citizens' rights or employees rights which are worthy of protection.[181]

(a) *Elementary personality rights*:[182] these rights, which are generally guaranteed by every state under the rule of law, deserve to be expressly confirmed and more precisely elaborated in regard to their significance as fundamental rights of employees in corporations. They include:
   - firstly the protection of the mental and physical *inviolability of the person* from every form of disrespect for the personality, above all from sexual molestation or inhuman and health-damaging harassment of 'scapegoats' by superiors, colleagues or employees (mobbing);
   - secondly, protection from discrimination and arbitrary treatment, i.e. the right to equal treatment (without regard for sex, nationality, religious and political opinions, ethnic and social origins, etc.), to *equality of opportunity* in regard to objective criteria for the assessment of performance and payment (fair pay), to chances of promotion and general working conditions. In addition, all employees should be entitled to fair consideration of other non-material aspects of personal dignity and integrity and of interpersonal solidarity;
   - thirdly, everyone has the right to the protection of his *private sphere* and this applies equally to the organizational world. The private sphere must remain untouched outside the functional duties regulated by employment and performance contracts. No employee is accountable to his superior for his personal situation or convictions in as far as they are irrelevant to his contractually regulated tasks and activities. And the same applies, of course, inversely for the superior. Data protection within the company is of particular importance. Companies must refrain from registering and collecting personal data as far as they are not strictly necessary for operational procedures and from handing on the personal data which are internally necessary to third parties, unless the person concerned gives express permission. Furthermore, every individual on whom data are collected must be accorded the right of access to the information kept in his personal file.

181 The organizational citizens' rights which are now mentioned in the text should be understood as proposals for concrete norms and thus as the object of practical stakeholder discourse.

182 See also the more general treatment in Section 7.1.

(b) *Communication rights*: the citizens of a free and democratic society must also enjoy the right within a company to open and unfiltered information and to participation in all matters concerning themselves; they must also have the right to free and critical expression of their concerns or opinions without fear of sanctions. This applies particularly to situations in which they, as dependent employees, are expected by their superiors to show loyalty in ethically dubious matters. The top management should explicitly welcome the civil courage of its employees. The middle management, in particular, must be encouraged not to behave opportunistically but instead to express the moral doubts they may have about certain procedures in the company. In such cases they must also be protected against sanctions by their direct superiors. Although every employee is in principle required to show loyalty towards his employer within the framework of the duties regulated by his work contract, this loyalty reaches its ethical limit wherever company activities violate the basic rights of those affected or when moral goods of higher value are damaged. For this reason a management of republican conviction will not expect 'blind' obedience from its employees but will always promote critical loyalty.[183]

In order that the right to critical loyalty can be lived out in practice under conditions of hierarchical dependence, special protected channels of communication must be institutionalised. They enable the individual who is caught on the horns of a dilemma between his moral convictions and role expectations to raise his voice without having to fear personal disadvantage. Employees should be able to discuss their problems personally with an especially appointed person of trust, for example a company ombudsman, or with a confidential ethics committee. Or the company should have an ethics hot-line that can be used confidentially or even anonymously. After he has exhausted all the internal channels available to him in vain, the employee finally has the right to address himself to the critical public sphere and to make the dubious procedures in the organisation known publicly, particularly by informing the media (whistle-blowing), as we have stated earlier. The guarantee of unrestricted organizational citizenship rights and the institutionalization of suitable internal channels of communication ought, moreover, to prevent the development of most legitimate reasons for recourse to public 'whistle-blowing' against the company. They thus turn out to be thoroughly intelligent measures to protect the good reputation of the company.

[183] On this and what follows see Section 8.3 (1).

10.4 Elements of an integrative ethical programme for corporations

Beyond the guarantee of organizational citizens' rights for all employees and analogously for stakeholders outside corporations and beyond the creation of special communication channels for cases of need it should be the aim of organizational policies to develop comprehensive structural and corporate cultural preconditions in such a way that reflection and argumentation on ethical standpoints in every area and at all hierarchical levels can become a matter of course, a 'normal' element of thinking, speaking and acting for all concerned.

From a structural point of view the fundamental question is how the principle of 'organized responsibility'[184] can be put into practice. Just like general civic virtue, organizational citizens' virtue also requires institutional 'backing' if we are to avoid making excessive heroic demands on the virtue of individuals in organizational contexts.[185] Wherever possible and predictable, the specific *problems of opportunism* which employees and middle management can run into in the case of organized irresponsibility must be eliminated or at least minimized structurally. The problems of opportunism present in all hierarchically structured organizations arise in the field of tension between the individual advantages that can be achieved (particularly in regard to income and career opportunities) by means of uncritical, 'blind' loyalty on the one hand and the personal disadvantages which may possibly be suffered as a consequence of incorruptible moral integrity on the other. In severe cases the problems of opportunism place too heavy a demand on the moral strength of the organization members exposed to them. In practice this is an all too frequent cause of ethically wrong behaviour precisely on the part of ambitious managers.[186] There are essentially two kinds of organizational measures which lead to the structural elimination of opportunism problems:

- Firstly, ethical points of view must be consistently internalised in all *management systems* (e.g. behavioural principles and management guidelines, systems which provide incentives, judge performance and regulate remuneration and promotion). The incentive structures must be thoroughly shaped in such a way that ethically responsible action is

[184] See Tuleja, *Ethik und Unternehmensführung*, p. 263.
[185] See the consideration of this point at the end of Section 8.2.
[186] See S.W. Gellermann, 'Why "good" managers make bad ethical choices', *Harvard Business Review* 4 (1986), July/August, pp. 85–90; see also J.A. Waters, 'Catch 20.5: Corporate Morality as an Organizational Phenomenon', *Organizational Dynamics* (1978), pp. 3–19.

rewarded and inconsiderate behaviour serving solely personal enrichment and career goals demotivated. Ultimately, the consistent orientation of the entire controlling and auditing system on pluralistic aims of value creation (in accordance with the defined tasks of the corporation in regard to value creation) is required. It is conceivable to replace or at least supplement the customary profit accounts, which are oriented on the one-sided aspect of capital investment (maximization of shareholder value), by a value creation account which is at least formally neutral in regard to the distribution of the achieved value creation among all stakeholders. Ideally this will be embedded in a comprehensive conception of the social and ecological balancing of accounts.[187]

– Secondly, ambiguity or lack of clarity as to the ethical ranking of the *standards for action* must be avoided. Managers and employees at all levels of the hierarchy may never be presented solely and one-sidedly with high goals for performance and success by their immediate superiors within the framework of a modern success-oriented management system. At the same time the ethical premises and the framework conditions within which these goals are to be striven for must be defined. This can best be achieved by a combination of a general ethics code of the company and guidelines specifically designed for various areas, through which the particular opportunism problems of a field of activity can be combated in a concrete manner.

Structural 'ethical measures' of the kind mentioned are necessary but not sufficient.[188] In addition, less obvious endeavours must be undertaken for the development of a *culture of integrity and responsibility* which is deeply anchored in the self-understanding of the members of an organization and directly experienced in daily life. To put it more precisely, it is necessary to promote the personal and corporate cultural preconditions for morally responsible action among all the members of an organization by developing an ethical awareness which will *capacitate* and *sensitize* them for recognizing the moral aspects of their actions. And they

[187] On the social balancing of accounts see M. Dierkes, 'Gesellschaftsbezogene Berichterstattung: Was lehren uns die Experimente der letzten zehn Jahre?', *Zeitschrift für Betriebswirtschaft* 54 (1984), pp. 1210–35; on ecological balancing of accounts and controlling see H. Hallay/R. Pfriem, *Öko-Controlling. Umweltschutz in mittelständischen Unternehmen* (Frankfurt/New York: Campus, 1992).

[188] For conceptual details and the situation in German and Swiss corporations see P. Ulrich/Y. Lunau, '"Ethikmassnahmen" in schweizerischen und deutschen Unternehmen: Konzeptionelle Überlegungen und empirische Befunde', *Die Unternehmung* 51 (1997), pp. 49–65; full account in P. Ulrich/Y. Lunau/Th. Weber, 'Ethikmassnahmen in der Unternehmenspraxis', in P. Ulrich/J. Wieland (eds.), Unternehmensethik in der Praxis: Impulse aus den USA, Deutschland und der Schweiz (Berne *et al.*: Haupt, 1998), pp. 121–94.

must be *encouraged* to express ethical doubts, even when this requires the individual, in concrete cases of conflict, to adopt a critical role distance towards his organizational task. In such situations organizational citizens feel still called upon to act in accordance with their indivisible civic responsibility.

It is a logical consequence that managers must present and answer for their endeavours to create an organizational culture of integrity and responsibility to all organizational citizens. A 'culture' understood and legitimated in this way can of course grow slowly only until it provides a solid basis for responsible commitment in and by the corporation. But it is the indispensable fertile soil in which the *argumentative integrity*[189] of mature citizens can become the natural disposition of all role bearers even in a more or less clearly hierarchically structured organization. The experience in everyday practice of a frank and honest interpersonal communication between critical yet loyal organizational citizens as an effective element of corporate culture will in turn improve *business integrity* in activities at all organizational levels and in dealings with stakeholders. This inseparability of a sound culture of integrity from an (institutionally enabled or supported) open ethical culture of argument is seldom fully realized.[190]

There are important systematic consequences for a corporate integrity programme (ethics programme) that takes this context into account. On the one hand structures and decision processes must be *opened up* for ethical reflection and argumentation. The 'sites' must be institutionalised where the questions of accountability of the actors and reasonableness of the demands made upon them (in the complex relationships between management and employees, and ultimately all stakeholders) are discursively clarified on a hierarchically unrestricted and power-free base. All concerned must be empowered (i.e. entitled and enabled) and encouraged to participate in the corporate ethical dialogue. On the other hand, it is also necessary to *close* the complex organization to some degree against ethically irresponsible or undesired forms of behaviour by binding all corporate activity to declared, testable normative standards and replacing false incentive structures which encourage opportunism by a system of

[189] See Blickle, *Kommunikationsethik*, p. 10ff., and Section 2.5 (1).

[190] A remarkable *real life example* of a corporate ethical codex which does not simply depend on 'fixed values' but aims primarily at the structural and cultural realization of the preconditions for a dialogic handling of ethical questions in corporations is provided by SØR Rusche Ltd. See Th. Rusche, 'Das Diskursmodell der kommunikativen Unternehmensethik', in H. H. Hinterhuber/A. Al-Ani/G. Handbauer (eds.), *Das neue Strategische Management: Elemente und Perspektiven einer zukunftsorientierten Unternehmensführung* (Wiesbaden: Gabler, 1996), pp. 301–20.

'organized responsibility'. Of course, these standards must in turn be legitimated by corporate ethical dialogue and also kept open for ethical criticism. For this reason the 'opening up' of opportunities for ethical-critical argumentation must always enjoy priority over the 'closing down' of opportunities for action.

Establishing this priority between the opening and closing types of 'ethical measures' and their indispensable reciprocal relations is of decisive importance for the implementation of an ethically oriented management. This must be emphasized in view of the one-sided tendency which still exists both in practice and in scientific research to interpret ethical measures as a means of implementing authoritatively determined 'fixed values' from the top to the bottom of the hierarchy. Such a one-sided 'closing down' of behavioural room for manoeuvre in the organization not only negates the structural preconditions of its own legitimation. It also undermines precisely that moral capacity for the acceptance of responsibility by employees at all levels which it intends to achieve, as the management in this way indicates to them that it does not seriously believe that they are capable of autonomous responsibility. The corresponding, more or less 'irresponsible' behaviour as a result of this *authoritarian error* may not then be long in coming.

In the literature this weakness of one-sided, exclusive, heteronomously determined *compliance* programmes has in the meantime been recognized. The suggested alternative of an *integrity* approach[191] indeed places increasing trust in the moral autonomy of the employees at all levels. But it nonetheless attempts merely to replace the legalistic 'compliance standards' by internalised 'company values', as long as it fails to create at the same time the preconditions for an open dialogue on authentic values and legitimate standards. Ultimately, therefore, it simply chooses a more subtle method of establishing 'fixed values' in the organization from the top downwards, which strongly calls to mind the questionable (and rather unrealistic) conception of an authoritarian 'management of corporate culture'.[192]

A one-sided 'opening up' of room for communication, however, would be scarcely less problematic than a one-sided authoritarian 'closing down'

[191] See L. S. Paine, 'Managing for Organizational Integrity', *Harvard Business Review* March–April (1994), pp. 106–17.; see also H. Steinmann/T. Olbrich, 'Business Ethics in US Corporations', in Ulrich/Wieland (eds.), Unternehmensethik in der Praxis, pp. 63–89. For a critique of Paine's approach see also U. Thielemann, 'Compliance und Integrity – Zwei Seiten ethisch integrierter Unternehmenssteuerung', *Zeitschrift für Wirtschafts- und Unternehmensethik* 6/1 (2005), pp. 31–45.

[192] See Ulrich, 'Symbolisches Management'.

of undesired options for action, if the open culture of reflection and argumentation within a company had no binding consequences in the shape of an ethically oriented arrangement of structural incentives and management systems. Moral free riders – or in plain English: unscrupulous opportunists – could continue to use the openness of the situation for inconsiderately maximizing personal advantage instead of accepting their share of responsibility and allowing their actions to be guided by the legitimate behavioural principles and value dispositions arrived at in the corporate dialogues. The result of such a *laissez-faire error* would probably be the swift and disastrous disillusionment of precisely the more morally sensitive and responsible members of the company. In their eyes such organized irresponsibility would make it meaningless to take 'offers' of open ethical-critical communication in the everyday life of the corporation seriously as long as these did not lead to the acceptance of binding norms and 'rules of the game' by all the players. The top management itself would have to set a personal example here and ensure the observation of the rules throughout the company. It is, therefore, of decisive importance that a balance is found between 'ethical measures' which open up discourse and those which close down options.

In practice no conceptional standard has as yet been established for an adequately elaborated ethics programme to serve the purposes sketched out above. In summary, however, in can be said that an integrative ethics programme in the sense of a (fundamentally critical) integrative corporate ethics would ideally comprise the following systematically essential elements (Figure 10.4):

A) An enlightened and well-grounded corporate value creation task ensures a meaningful orientation of business strategy by defining genuine human or social needs the corporation strives to fulfil on the market ('mission statement').
B) Binding business principles declare in a verifiable form the self-commitment of the corporation to adopt only legitimate strategies and methods in the pursuit of success ('code of ethics'). These include the principles of the republican sharing of responsibility, particularly at the branch and institutional level, for the observation of fair rules of competition and of general public interests ('corporate citizenship').
C) Clearly defined and guaranteed moral rights of all stakeholders, and especially of the employees as organizational citizens, confirm the inviolable personality rights of all concerned and open up practicable opportunities for participation in a corporate ethical discourse which is, as far as possible, open and free of power and sanctions (corporate constitution, especially 'bill of employee rights').

A. Meaningful corporate value creation task
('mission statement')
B. Binding business principles
('code of ethics')
C. Guaranteed stakeholder rights
('bill of stakeholder rights', corporate constitution)
D. Discursive infrastructure
('sites' of open corporate ethical discourse)
E. Development of ethical competence
('ethics training' and a lived culture of responsibility)
F. Ethically consistent management systems
(incentive, performance assessment and auditing systems)

Figure 10.4. Elements of an integrative ethics programme for corporations

D) A discursive infrastructure institutionalizes within the organization the 'sites' for the argumentative clarification of questions of accountability and the reasonableness of demands made on participants in the course of corporate action in a context which is free of sanctions and open as to the outcomes ('forums' of corporate ethical dialogue, ethics committees etc.).
E) Measures for the development of ethical competence improve the ethical awareness of the employees at all levels and encourage them to engage in independent ethical reflection and argumentation ('ethics training'). These are embedded in a continuously cultivated and lived culture of integrity and responsibility.
F) An extensive examination and, if necessary, supplementation of the existing management systems within the corporation in regard to their consistency with the ethics programme supports the desired culture of integrity by ensuring that all the goal-setting, incentive and performance assessment procedures are free of contradictions. A suitable compliance programme and an ethical auditing carried out at regular intervals guarantee the observation of the defined principles and standards and the implementation of special ethical measures.

The path to such a comprehensive ethics programme must be understood as a learning process to be shaped according to the specific requirements of corporations in regard to the principles of organizational development. Is it worthwhile to follow this demanding path? The answer depends ultimately on the kind of corporation the participants wish to work in. The path we have sketched is the right one if a company consistently sees itself and wishes to establish a reputation as a good 'corporate citizen' who, in the final analysis, has *earned* his business success and his public standing by means of honest activities that create genuine values.

Bibliography

Ackerman, B./Alstott, A., *The Stakeholder Society* (New Haven: Yale University Press, 1999).

Adorno, T., 'Kritik', in Adorno, *Kleine Schriften zur Gesellschaft* (Frankfurt: Suhrkamp, 1971), pp. 10–19.

Afheldt, H., *Wirtschaft, die arm macht: Vom Sozialstaat zur gespaltenen Gesellschaft* (Munich: Kunstmann, 2003).

Wohlstand für niemand? Die Marktwirtschaft entlässt ihre Kinder, 2nd edn (München: Kunstmann, 1999).

Albert, H., 'Die Problematik der ökonomischen Perspektive', *Zeitschrift für die gesamte Staatswissenschaft* 117 (1961), pp. 438–67.

'Politische Ökonomie und rationale Politik' (first publ. 1967), in Albert, *Aufklärung und Steuerung* (Hamburg: Hoffmann & Campe, 1976), pp. 91–122.

Ökonomische Ideologie und Politische Theorie, 2nd edn (Göttingen: Otto Schwartz, 1972; 1st edn 1954).

Anshen, M., 'The Socially Responsible Corporation: From Concept to Implementation', in Anshen (ed.), *Managing the Socially Responsible Corporation* (New York: Macmillan, 1974), pp. 1–22.

Anzenbacher, A., *Einführung in die Ethik* (Dusseldorf: Patmos, 1992).

Apel, K.-O., 'Arnold Gehlens "Philosophie der Institutionen" und die Metainstitution der Sprache', in Apel, *Transformation der Philosophie*, vol. I (Frankfurt: Suhrkamp, 1976), pp. 197–221.

'Der transzendentalhermeneutische Begriff der Sprache', in Apel, *Transformation der Philosophie*, vol. II (Frankfurt: Suhrkamp, 1976), pp. 330–57.

'Die Konflikte unserer Zeit und das Erfordernis einer ethisch-politischen Grundorientierung', in Apel *et al.* (eds.), *Reader zum Funkkolleg: Praktische Philosophie/Ethik*, vol. I (Frankfurt: Fischer, 1980), pp. 267–92.

'Diskursethik vor der Problematik von Recht und Politik', in K.-O. Apel/ M. Kettner (eds.), *Zur Anwendung der Diskursethik in Politik, Recht und Wissenschaft* (Frankfurt: Suhrkamp, 1992), pp. 29–61.

'Lässt sich ethische Vernunft von strategischer Zweckrationalität unterscheiden?', in W. van Reijen/K.-O. Apel (eds.), *Rationales Handeln und Gesellschaftstheorie* (Bochum: Germinal, 1984), pp. 23–79.

'Limits of Discourse Ethics? An Attempt at a Provisional Assessment', in Apel, *Selected Essays, vol. II: Ethics and the Theory of Rationality* (New Jersey: Humanities Press, 1996), pp. 192–219.

'The Apriori of the Communicative Community and the Foundations of Ethics', in Apel, *Towards a Transformation of Philosophy*, pp. 225–300.

'Zur geschichtlichen Entfaltung der ethischen Vernunft in der Philosophie (I)', in K.-O. Apel/D. Böhler/K. Rebel (eds.), *Funkkolleg*, vol. I (Weinheim/Basle: Beltz), pp. 66–99.

Diskurs und Verantwortung (Frankfurt: Suhrkamp, 1988).

Towards a Transformation of Philosophy, transl. G. Adey/D. Frisby (London: Routledge, 1980).

Apel, K.-O./Kettner, M. (eds.), *Zur Anwendung der Diskursethik in Politik, Recht und Wissenschaft* (Frankfurt: Suhrkamp, 1992).

Arendt, H., *Eichmann in Jerusalem: A Report on the Banality of Evil* (New York: Penguin, 1994; 1st edn 1963).

The Human Condition (Chicago: University of Chicago Press, 1958).

Aristotle, *Nichomachean Ethics* (Cambridge: Cambridge University Press, 2000).

The Politics of Aristotle, ed. by P. L. P. Simpson (Chapel Hill: University of North Carolina Press, 1997).

Arrow, K., 'Methodological Individualism and Social Knowledge', *American Economic Review* 84/2 (1994), pp. 1–9.

Aufderheide, D., *Unternehmer, Ethos und Ökonomik. Moral und unternehmerischer Gewinn aus der Sicht der Neuen Institutionenökonomik* (Berlin: Duncker & Humblot, 1995).

Avineri, S./De-Shalit, A. (eds.), *Communitarianism and Individualism* (Oxford/ New York: Oxford University Press, 1992).

Bahro, R., *The Alternative in Eastern Europe* (London: NLB & Verso, 1978).

Baier, K., *Moral Point of View: Rational Basis of Ethics* (Ithaca/London: Cornell University Press, 1958).

Barber, B., 'An American Civic Forum: Civil Society between Market Individuals and the Political Community', *Social Philosophy and Policy* 13 (1996), pp. 269–83.

Strong Democracy: Participatory Politics for a New Age (Berkeley: University of California Press, 1984).

Baron, H., *The Crisis of the Early Italian Renaissance: Civic Humanism and Republican Liberty in an Age of Classicism and Tyranny* (Princeton: Princeton University Press, 1955).

Bastiat, F., *Economic Harmonies*, transl. from the French by W. H. Boyers; ed. by G. B. de Huszar (Princeton NJ: Van Nostrand, 1964).

Baumhart, R. C., 'How Ethical Are Businessmen?', *Harvard Business Review* 39 (1961), 4, pp. 6–19 and 156–76.

Baumstark, E., *Kameralistische Encyclopädie* (Ruggell, Liechtenstein: Topos, 1975; 1st edn 1835).

Bausch, Th., 'Wirtschaft und Ethik: Notizen zu einem dialogischen Brückenschlag', in Forum für Philosophie Bad Homburg (ed.), *Markt und Moral*, pp. 19–36.

Beck, U., *Gegengifte: Die organisierte Unverantwortlichkeit* (Frankfurt: Suhrkamp, 1988).

Politik in der Risikogesellschaft (Frankfurt: Suhrkamp, 1991).

Becker, G. S., *The Economic Approach to Human Behavior* (Chicago: University of Chicago Press, 1976).

Becker, H./Fritzsche, D. J., 'Business Ethics: A Cross-Cultural Comparison of Managers' Attitudes', *Journal of Business Ethics* 6 (1987), pp. 289–95.

Benhabib, S., 'Toward a Deliberative Model of Democratic Legitimacy', in Benhabib (ed.), *Democracy and Difference: Contesting the Boundaries of the Political* (Princeton: Princeton University Press, 1996), pp. 67–94.

Situating the Self (Cambridge: Polity, 1992).

Bentele, G./Steinmann, H./Zerfass, A. (eds.), *Dialogorientierte Unternehmenskommunikation. Grundlagen – Praxiserfahrung – Perspektiven* (Berlin: Vistas, 1996).

Bentham, J., *A Commentary on the Commentaries and a Fragment on Government*, ed. J. H. Burns and H. L. A. Hart (London: Athlone, 1977).

An Introduction to the Principles of Morals and Legislation, ed. J. H. Burns and H. L. A. Hart (London: University of London, Athlone, 1970; 1st edn 1789).

Berlin, I., *Two Concepts of Liberty* (Oxford: Clarendon, 1958), reprinted in Berlin, *Liberty* (Oxford: Oxford University Press, 2002), pp. 166–217.

Berthold, N./Wilpert, J., 'Umwelt- und Sozialklauseln: Gefahr für den Freihandel?', *Wirtschaftsdienst – Zeitschrift für Wirtschaftspolitik* 76 (1996), pp. 596–604.

Biervert, B./Held, M. (eds.), *Das Menschenbild der ökonomischen Theorie* (Frankfurt/New York: Campus, 1991).

Biervert, B./Wieland, J., 'Der ethische Gehalt ökonomischer Kategorien –Beispiel: Der Nutzen', in Biervert/Wieland (eds.), *Ökonomische Theorie und Ethik*, pp. 23–50.

Biesecker, A., 'Lebensweltliche Elemente der Ökonomie und Schlussfolgerungen für eine moderne Ordnungsethik', *Berichte des Instituts für Wirtschaftsethik* 61 (St Gallen: Institute for Economic and Business Ethics, 1994).

Binswanger, H. C., *Geld und Natur: Das wirtschaftliche Wachstum zwischen Ökonomie und Ökologie* (Stuttgart/Vienna: Weitbrecht, 1991).

Bleicher, K., *Normatives Management: Politik, Verfassung und Philosophie des Unternehmens* (Frankfurt/New York: Campus, 1994).

Blickle, G., *Kommunikationsethik im Management: Argumentationsintegrität als personal- und organisationspsychologisches Leitkonzept* (Stuttgart: Metzler-Poeschel, 1994).

Blum, R., 'Die Zukunft des Homo oeconomicus', in Biervert/Held, *Menschenbild*, pp. 111–31.

Soziale Marktwirtschaft: Wirtschaftspolitik zwischen Neoliberalismus und Ordoliberalismus (Tübingen: Mohr Siebeck, 1969).

Böhler, D., 'Diskursethik und Menschenwürdegrundsatz zwischen Idealisierung und Erfolgsverantwortung', in Apel/Kettner (eds.), *Zur Anwendung der Diskursethik in Politik, Recht und Wissenschaft*, pp. 201–31.

'Philosophischer Diskurs im Spannungsfeld von Theorie und Praxis', in K.-O. Apel/D. Böhler/K. Rebel (eds.), *Funkkolleg Praktische Philosophie/Ethik: Studientexte*, 3 vols (Weinheim/Basle: Beltz, 1984), vol. II, pp. 313–55.

'Über Diskursethik und (Markt-) Wirtschaftstheorie', in: J. P. Brune/D. Böhler/W. Steden (eds.), *Moral und Sachzwang in der Marktwirtschaft* (Munster: LIT, 1995), pp. 125–43.

Böhm, F., 'An die Leser des Jahrbuchs Ordo', *Ordo* 26 (1975), pp. 3–11.

'Das wirtschaftliche Mitbestimmungsrecht der Arbeiter im Betrieb', *Ordo* 4 (1951), pp. 21–250.

'Demokratie und ökonomische Macht', in Institut für ausländisches und internationales Wirtschaftsrecht (ed.), *Kartelle und Monopole im modernen Recht* (Karlsruhe, 1961), vol. I, pp. 3–24.

'Die Idee des Ordo im Denken Walter Euckens', *Ordo* 3 (1950), pp. xv–lxix, reprinted in Böhm, *Freiheit und Ordnung in der Marktwirtschaft* (Baden-Baden: Nomos, 1980).

Freiheit und Ordnung in der Marktwirtschaft (Baden-Baden: Nomos, 1980).

Böhm-Bawerk, E. von, 'Macht oder ökonomisches Gesetz?', *Zeitschrift für Volkswirtschaft, Socialpolitik und Verwaltung* 23 (1914), pp. 205–71.

Bohnen, A., *Die utilitaristische Ethik als Grundlage der modernen Wohlfahrtsökonomik* (Göttingen: Schwartz, 1964).

Boltanski, L./Chiapello, E., *The New Spirit of Capitalism*, transl. G. Elliott (London: Verso, 2005).

Boulding, K. E., *The Skills of the Economist* (Cleveland: Howard Allen, 1958).

Bowie, N. E., 'Business Ethics as a Discipline: The Search for Legitimacy', in Freeman (ed.), *State of the Art*, pp. 17–41.

Business Ethics: A Kantian Perspective (Malden MA/Oxford: Blackwell, 1999).

Brennan, G./Buchanan, J. M., 'The Normative Purpose of Economic "Science": Rediscovery of an Eighteenth Century Method', *International Journal of Law and Economics* 1 (1981), pp. 155–66, reprinted in Buchanan, *Economics Between Predictive Science and Moral Philosophy*, pp. 51–65.

The Reason of Rules: Constitutional Political Economy (Cambridge: Cambridge University Press, 1985).

Brennan, G./Lomasky, L., *Democracy and Decision: The Pure Theory of Electoral Preference* (Cambridge MA: Cambridge University Press, 1993).

Brenner, S. N./Molander, E. A., 'Is the Ethics of Business Changing?', *Harvard Business Review* 55 (1977), 1, pp. 57–71.

Brewing, J., *Kritik der Unternehmensethik* (Berne *et al.*: Haupt, 1995).

Brownlie, I./Goodwin-Gill, G. S. (eds.), *Basic Documents on Human Rights*, 5th edn (Oxford: Oxford University Press, 2006).

Brühlmeier, D., 'Adam Smith als politischer Denker im Kontext vom Liberalismus, Institutionalismus und Republikanismus', in Meyer-Faje/Ulrich (eds.), *Der andere Adam Smith*, pp. 277–302.

Adam Smith: Denker der Freiheit (Sankt Augustin: Academia, 1992).

Brummer, J. J., *Corporate Responsibility and Legitimacy: An Interdisciplinary Approach* (New York: Greenwood, 1991).

Brunner, E., *The Divine Imperative: A Study in Christian Ethics*, transl. O. Wyon (Philadelphia: Westminster Press, 1947); orig. *Das Gebot und die Ordnungen. Entwurf einer protestantisch-theologischen Ethik*, 4th edn (Zurich: Theologischer Verlag, 1978; 1st edn 1932).

Buchanan, J. M., *Economics Between Predictive Science and Moral Philosophy* (College Station: Texas University Press, 1987).

Freedom in Constitutional Contract: Perspectives of a Political Economist (College Station: Texas University Press, 1977).

The Limits of Liberty: Between Anarchy and Leviathan (Chicago/London: University of Chicago Press, 1975).

Buchanan, J. M./Tollison, R. D./Tullock, G. (eds.), *Toward a Theory of the Rent-Seeking Society* (College Station: Texas University Press, 1980).

Buchanan, J. M./Tullock, G., *The Calculus of Consent: Logical Foundations of Constitutional Democracy* (Ann Arbor: University of Michigan Press, 1962).

Bühner, A., 'Shareholder Value', *Die Betriebswirtschaft* 53 (1993), pp. 749–69.

Bürgin, A., *Zur Soziogenese der politischen Ökonomie: Wirtschaftsgeschichtliche und dogmenhistorische Betrachtungen* (Marburg: Metropolis, 1993).

Büscher, M., 'Gott und Markt – religionsgeschichtliche Wurzeln Adam Smiths und die "Invisible Hand" in der säkularisierten Industriegesellschaft', in Meyer-Faje/Ulrich (eds.), *Der andere Adam Smith*, pp. 123–44.

Campbell, C., *The Romantic Ethic and the Spirit of Modern Consumerism* (Oxford/ Malden MA: Blackwell, 1987).

Campbell, T. D., *Adam Smith's Science of Morals* (London: Allan & Unwin, 1971).

Chan, A./Ross, R., 'Racing to the Bottom: International Trade without a Social Clause', *Third World Quarterly* 24/6 (2003), pp. 1011–28.

Chappell, T., *The Soul of a Business: Managing for Profit and the Common Good* (New York: Bantam, 1993).

Clapham, R., 'Zur Rolle der Ordnungsethik für das Konzept der sozialen Markwirtschaft', *Jahrbuch für Neue Politische Ökonomie* 8 (1989), pp. 30–41.

Coase, R., 'The Problem of Social Cost', *The Journal of Law and Economics* 3 (1960), pp. 1–44.

Cohen, J., 'Deliberation and Democratic Legitimacy', in A. Hamlin/P. Pettit (eds.), *The Good Polity: Normative Analysis of the State* (Oxford: Basil Blackwell, 1989), pp. 17–34.

Cole, G. D. H., *Principles of Economic Planning* (London: Macmillan, 1935).

Cortina, A., 'Diskursethik und Menschenrechte', *Archiv für Rechts- und Sozialphilosophie* 76 (1990), pp. 37–49.

'Ethik ohne Moral: Grenzen einer postkantischen Prinzipienethik?', in Apel/ Kettner, *Zur Anwendung der Diskursethik*, pp. 278–95.

'The General Public as the Locus of Ethics in Modern Society', in Ulrich/ Sarasin (eds.), *Facing Public Interest*, pp. 43–58.

Craig, G. A., *Triumph of Liberalism: Zurich in the Golden Age, 1830–1869* (London: Collier Macmillan, 1988).

Cunliffe, J./Erreygers, G., 'Basic Income? Basic Capital! Origins and Issues of a Debate', *Journal of Political Philosophy* 11 (2003), pp. 89–110.

Cyert, R. M./March, J. G., *A Behavioral Theory of the Firm* (Englewood Cliffs NJ: Prentice Hall, 1963).

Dagger, R., *Civic Virtues: Rights, Citizenship, and Republican Liberalism* (New York/Oxford: Oxford University Press, 1997).

Dahrendorf, R., 'Citizenship and Social Class', in M. Bulmer/A. M. Rees (eds.), *Citizenship Today: The Contemporary Relevance of T. H. Marshall* (London: Routledge, 1996), pp. 25–48.

'Moralität, Institutionen und die Bürgergesellschaft', *Merkur* 7 (1992), pp. 557–68.

'The Changing Quality of Citizenship', in: B. Van Steenbergen (ed.), *The Condition of Citizenship* (London: Sage, 1994), pp. 10–19.

Die Chancen der Krise: Über die Zukunft des Liberalismus (Stuttgart: DVA, 1983).

Life Chances: Approaches to Social and Political Theory (Chicago: Chicago University Press, 1979).

The Modern Social Conflict: An Essay on the Politics of Liberty (New York/London: Weidenfeld & Nicolson, 1988).

De George, R. T., 'Will Success Spoil Business Ethics?', in Freeman (ed.), *State of the Art*, pp. 42–56.

Business Ethics, 3rd edn (New York: Macmillan, 1990).

Competing with Integrity in International Business (New York/Oxford: Oxford University Press, 1993).

Deci, E. L./Ryan, M. R., *Intrinsic Motivation and Self-determination in Human Behaviour* (New York: Plenum, 1985).

Demsetz, H., 'The Exchange and Enforcement of Property Rights', *Journal of Law and Economics* 7 (1964), pp. 11–64.

Dierkes, M., 'Gesellschaftsbezogene Berichterstattung: Was lehren uns die Experimente der letzten zehn Jahre?', *Zeitschrift für Betriebswirtschaft* 54 (1984), pp. 1210–35.

Donaldson, T./Preston, L. E., 'The Stakeholder Theory of the Corporation: Concepts, Evidence and Implications', *Academy of Management Review* 20/1 (1995), pp. 65–91.

Donaldson, T. J., 'Rights in the Global Market', in Freeman (ed.), *State of the Art*, pp. 139–62.

The Ethics of International Business (New York/Oxford: Oxford University Press, 1990).

Donaldson, T., *Corporations and Morality* (Englewood Cliffs NJ: Prentice Hall, 1982).

Donnelly, J., *Universal Human Rights in Theory and Practice* (Ithaca NY: Cornell University Press, 1989).

Downs, A., *An Economic Theory of Democracy* (New York: Harper, 1957).

Duttweiler, G., *Überzeugungen und Einfälle* (Zurich: Ex Libris, 1978).

Dworkin, R., *Taking Rights Seriously* (Cambridge MA: Harvard University Press, 1978).

Dyllick, Th., *Management der Umweltbeziehungen: Öffentliche Auseinandersetzungen als Herausforderung* (Wiesbaden: Gabler, 1989).

Elster, J., 'The Possibility of Rational Politics', in D. Held (ed.), *Political Theory Today* (Oxford: Polity, 1991), pp. 115–42.

The Cement of Society: A Study of Social Order (New York: Cambridge University Press, 1989).

Ulysses and the Sirens: Studies in Rationality and Irrationality (Cambridge: Cambridge University Press, 1979).

Enderle, G., 'Die Goldene Regel für Manager?', in Ch. Lattmann (ed.), *Ethik und Unternehmensführung* (Heidelberg: Physica, 1988), pp. 130–48.

'Wirtschaftsethik als "angewandte" Ethik', *Wirtschaft und Recht* 39 (1987), pp. 114–24.

Handlungsorientierte Wirtschaftsethik (Berne *et al.*: Haupt, 1993).

Sicherung des Existenzminimums im nationalen und internationalen Kontext (Berne *et al.*: Haupt, 1987).

Wirtschaftsethik im Werden: Ansätze und Problembereiche der Wirtschaftsethik (Stuttgart: Akademie der Diözese Rottenburg-Stuttgart, 1988).

Enderle, G. *et al.* (eds.), *Lexikon der Wirtschaftsethik* (Freiburg i.B.: Herder, 1993).

Engels, W. *et al.* (eds.), *Bürgersteuer – Entwurf einer Neuordnung von direkten Steuern und Sozialleistungen* (Bad Homburg: Schriftenreihe des Kronberger Kreises, 1986).

Engels, W./Mitschke, J./Starkoff, B., *Staatsbürgersteuer* (Wiesbaden: Karl Bräuer Institut, 1974).

Epikur, *Philosophie der Freude*, ed. J. Mewaldt (Stuttgart: Kröner, 1973).

Erhard, L., *Wohlstand für alle* (Düsseldorf: Econ, 1957).

Erreygers, G./Vandevelde, T. (eds.), *Is Inheritance Legitimate? Ethical and Economic Aspects of Wealth Transfers* (Berlin: Springer, 1997).

Etzioni, A., *The Moral Dimension: Toward a New Economics* (New York: Free Press, 1988).

The Spirit of Community: Rights, Responsibilities and the Communitarian Agenda (New York: Crown, 1993).

Eucken, W., *Grundsätze der Wirtschaftspolitik*, 6th rev. edn, ed. E. Eucken and K. P. Hensel (Tübingen: Mohr Siebeck, 1990; 1st edn 1952).

Evan, W. M./Freeman, R. E., 'A Stakeholder Theory of the Modern Corporation: Kantian Capitalism', in T. C. Beauchamp/N. E. Bowie (eds.), *Ethical Theory and Business*, 3rd edn (Englewood Cliffs NJ: Prentice Hall, 1988), pp. 97–106.

Ewers, H.-J./Wein, T., 'Grundsätze für eine Deregulierungspolitik', *Wirtschaftsdienst* 70 (1990), pp. 320–8.

Ewing, D., *Freedom Inside the Organisation* (New York: McGraw-Hill, 1977).

Ferguson, A., *An Essay on the History of Civil Society* (Edinburgh: Edinburgh University Press, 1966; 1st edn 1767).

Fetscher, I., 'Einleitung', in Th. Hobbes, *Leviathan* (Frankfurt: Suhrkamp, 1984), pp. IX-LXVI.

Fitzmaurice, M., 'Environmental Protection and the International Court of Justice', in V. Lowe/M. Fitzmaurice (eds.), *Fifty Years of the International Court of Justice* (Cambridge: Cambridge University Press, 1996), pp. 293–315.

Forst, R., *Kontexte der Gerechtigkeit, Politische Philosophie jenseits von Liberalismus und Kommunitarismus* (Frankfurt: Suhrkamp, 1994).

Forum für Philosophie Bad Homburg (ed.), *Markt und Moral: Die Diskussion um die Unternehmensethik* (Berne *et al.*: Haupt, 1994).

Frank, R. H./Cook, Ph. J., *The Winner-Take-All Society* (New York: Penguin, 1996).

Frankena, W., *Ethics* (Englewood Cliffs NJ: Prentice Hall, 1963).

Frankfurt, H., 'Freedom of the Will and the Concept of a Person', *Journal of Philosophy* 68 (1971), pp. 5–20.

Frankl, V. E., *Man's Search of Meaning* (New York: Washington Square Press, 1963).

The Will to Meaning: Foundations and Applications of Logotherapy (New York: Meridian, 1988).

Fraser, N., 'Struggles over Needs', in Fraser, *Unruly Practices: Power, Discourse and Gender in Contemporary Social Theory* (Minnesota: Minnesota University Press, 1989), pp. 161–87.

Frederick, W. C./ Post, J. E./ Davies, K., *Business and Society: Corporate Strategy, Public Policy, Ethics*, 7th edn (New York *et al.*: McGraw Hill, 1992).
Freeman, R. E., 'The Politics of Stakeholder Theory: Some Future Directions', *Business Ethics Quarterly* 4 (1994), pp. 401–21.
'The Stakeholder Approach Revisited', *Zeitschrift für Wirtschafts- und Unternehmensethik* 5/3 (2004), pp. 228–41.
Strategic Management: A Stakeholder Approach (Boston: Pitman, 1984).
Freeman, R. E. (ed.), *Business Ethics: The State of the Art* (New York/Oxford: Oxford University Press, 1991).
Freeman, R. E./Gilbert, D. R., *Corporate Strategy and the Search for Ethics* (Englewood Cliffs NJ: Prentice Hall, 1988).
Freire, P., *Pedagogy of the Oppressed* (New York: Seabury, 1971).
Frey, B. S., 'From Economic Imperialism to Social Science Inspiration', *Public Choice* 77 (1993), pp. 95–105.
Theorie demokratischer Wirtschaftspolitik (Munich: Vahlen, 1981); 2nd rev. edn: B. S. Frey/G. Kirchgässner, *Demokratische Wirtschaftspolitik: Theorie und Anwendung* (Munich: Vahlen, 1994).
Frey, B. S./Kirchgässner, G., 'Diskursethik, Politische Ökonomie und Volksabstimmung', *Analyse und Kritik* 15, pp. 129–49.
Friedman, M., 'The Methodology of Positive Economics', in Friedman, *Essays in Positive Economics* (Chicago: University of Chicago Press, 1953), pp. 3–43.
'The social responsibility of business is to increase its profits', *The New York Times Magazine*, 13 September 1970, pp. 32–3, 122, 124 and 126; reprinted, e.g., in Gibson (ed.), *Business Ethics*, pp. 206–11, and in other readers.
Capitalism and Freedom (Chicago/London: University of Chicago Press, 1962).
Fromm, E., *To Have or To Be?* (New York *et al.*: Harper & Row, 1976).
Furubotn, E. G./Pejovich, S., 'Property Rights and Economic Theory: A Survey of Recent Literature', *Journal of Economic Literature* 10 (1972), pp. 1137–62.
Gai, Dh. (ed.), *Decent Work: Objectives and Strategies* (Geneva: ILO, 2006).
Galbraith, J. K., *The Affluent Society* (Boston: Houghton Mifflin, 1958).
Galtung, J., *Human Rights in Another Key* (Cambridge: Polity, 1994).
Gauthier, D., *Morals by Agreement* (Oxford: Clarendon, 1986).
Gehlen, A., *Man, his Nature and Place in the World* (New York: Columbia University Press, 1988; 1st edn German, Bonn 1940).
Gellermann, S. W., 'Why "good" managers make bad ethical choices', *Harvard Business Review* 4 (1986), July/August, pp. 85–90.
Gentz, M., 'Wirtschaftsethik in der Unternehmensführung', in Wieland (ed.), *Wirtschaftsethik und Theorie der Gesellschaft*, pp. 92–108.
Gibson, K., 'The Moral Basis of Stakeholder Theory', *Journal of Business Ethics* 26/3 (2000), pp. 245–57.
Gibson, K. (ed.), *Business Ethics: People, Profit, and the Planet* (New York: McGraw-Hill, 2006).
Giddens, A., *The Consequences of Modernity* (Cambridge: Polity, 1990).
Giersch, H., 'Die Moral der offenen Märkte', *Frankfurter Allgemeine Zeitung*, 64, 16 March 1991.
Gilligan, C., *In a Different Voice: Psychological Theory and Women's Development* (Cambridge MA: Harvard University Press, 1983).

Gomez, P., *Wertmanagement: Vernetzte Strategien für Unternehmen im Wandel* (Düsseldorf: Econ, 1993).
Goodpaster, K. E., 'Business Ethics and Stakeholder Analysis', *Business Ethics Quarterly* 1/1 (1991), pp. 55–71.
Gorz, A., *Critique of Economic Reason* (London and New York: Verso, 1989).
Farewell to the Working Class (London: Pluto, 1982).
Reclaiming Work: Beyond the Wage-based Society (Cambridge: Polity, 2000).
Gouldner, A. W., 'The Norm of Reciprocity: A Preliminary Statement', *American Sociological Review* 25 (1960), pp. 161–78.
Granger, C./Siroën, J.-M., 'Core Labour Standards in Trade Agreements: From Multilateralism to Bilateralism', *Journal of World Trade* 40/5 (2006), pp. 813–36.
Gray, J., *False Dawn: The Delusions of Global Capitalism* (London: Granta Books, 1998).
Groeben, N./Schreier, M./Christmann, U., *Argumentationsintegrität (I): Herleitung, Explikation und Binnenstrukturierung des Konstrukts*, Bericht N° 28 aus dem Sonderforschungsbereich 'Sprache und Situation' (Heidelberg/Mannheim: University of Heidelberg, 1990).
Gross, P., *Die Multioptionsgesellschaft* (Frankfurt: Suhrkamp, 1994).
Grunig, J. E. (ed.), *Excellence in Public Relations and Communication Management* (Hillsdale NJ: Erlbaum, 1992).
Günther, K., *Der Sinn für Angemessenheit: Anwendungsdiskurse in Moral und Recht* (Frankfurt: Suhrkamp, 1988).
Gutenberg, E., *Die Unternehmung als Gegenstand betriebswirtschaftlicher Theorie* (Berlin/Vienna: Gabler, 1929).
Grundlagen der Betriebswirtschaftslehre, vol. I: *Die Produktion*, 22nd edn (Berlin/New York: Springer, 1976).
Gygi, F., 'Die schweizerische Wirtschaftsverfassung', *Zeitschrift für schweizerisches Recht*, N. F. 89 (1970), II, pp. 259–389.
Habermann, G., 'Teilen oder produzieren? Bemerkungen zum Ethos des Unternehmers', *Neue Zürcher Zeitung*, N° 211, 11/12 September 1993, p. 31f.
Habermas, J., 'A Reply to my Critics', in: J. P. Thompson/D. Held (eds.), *Habermas: Critical Debates* (Cambridge MA: MIT Press, 1982), pp. 219–83.
'A Reply', in A. Honneth/H. Joas (eds.), *Communicative Action: Essays on Jürgen Habermas' 'The Theory of Communicative Action'*, transl. J. Gaines and D. L. Jones (Oxford: Polity, 1991), pp. 214–64.
'Aspects of the Rationality of Action', in Th.F. Geraets (ed.), *Rationality Today* (Ottawa: Ottawa University Press, 1979), pp. 184–204.
'Civil Disobedience: Litmus Test for the Democratic Constitutional State', *Berkeley Journal of Sociology* 30 (1985), pp. 95–116.
'Discourse Ethics: Notes on a Program of Philosophical Justification' in Habermas, *Moral Consciousness and Communicative Action* (Cambridge: Polity, 1990), pp. 43–115.
'Konventionelle oder kommunikative Sittlichkeit?' in K.-O. Apel *et al.* (eds.), *Praktische Philosophie/Ethik I* (Frankfurt: Suhrkamp, 1980).
'Morality and Ethical Life: Does Hegel's Critique of Kant Apply to Discourse Ethics?', in Habermas, *Moral Consciousness and Communicative Action* (Cambridge: Polity, 1990), pp. 195–215.

'Reconciliation through the Public Use of Reason: Remarks on John Rawls' Political Liberalism', *Journal of Philosophy* 92 (1995), pp. 109–31.

'Technology and Science as "Ideology"', in Habermas, *Toward a Rational Society*, transl. J. Shapiro (Boston: Beacon Press, 1970), pp. 81–122.

'Three Normative Models of Democracy', in S. Benhabib (ed.), *Democracy and Difference: Contesting the Boundaries of the Political* (Princeton: Princeton University Press, 1996), pp. 21–30.

'Toward a Reconstruction of Historical Materialism', in: Habermas, *Communication and the Evolution of Society* (Oxford/Malden MA: Blackwell, 1991), pp. 119–20.

'Vorbereitende Bemerkungen zu einer Theorie der kommunikativen Kompetenz', in J. Habermas/N. Luhmann, *Theorie der Gesellschaft oder Sozialtechnologie – Was leistet die Systemforschung?* (Frankfurt: Luchterhand, 1971), pp. 101–41.

'What is Universal Pragmatics?', in Habermas, *Communication and the Evolution of Society* (Oxford/Malden MA: Blackwell, 1991), pp. 1–68.

Between Facts and Norms: Contributions to a Discourse Theory of Law and Democracy, transl. W. Rehg (Cambridge MA: MIT Press, 1996).

Justification and Application: Remarks on Discourse Ethics transl. C. P. Cronin (Cambridge MA: MIT Press, 1993).

The Inclusion of the Other, ed. C. Cronin and P. De Greiff (Cambridge MA: MIT Press, 1998).

The Structural Transformation of the Public Sphere, transl. Th. Burger (Cambridge MA: MIT Press, 1989).

Theorie des kommunikativen Handelns, 2 vols, (Frankfurt: Suhrkamp, 1981).

Theory of Communicative Action, 2 vols, transl. Th. McCarthy (Boston: Beacon Press, 1984).

Hallay, H./Pfriem, R., *Öko-Controlling. Umweltschutz in mittelständischen Unternehmen* (Frankfurt/New York: Campus, 1992).

Harsanyi, J. C., 'Morality and the Theory of Rational Behaviour', *Social Research* 44 (1977), pp. 626–56.

Hauser, H./Schanz, K.-U., *Das neue GATT. Die Welthandelsordnung nach Abschluss der Uruguay-Runde,* 2nd edn (Munich/Vienna: Oldenbourg, 1995).

Hausman, D. M./McPherson, M. S., *Economic Analysis and Moral Philosophy* (Cambridge/New York: Cambridge University Press, 1996).

Hayek, F. A. von, 'Competition as a Discovery Procedure', in von Hayek, *New Studies in Philosophy, Politics, Economics and the History of Ideas* (Chicago: University of Chicago Press, 1978), pp. 179–90.

'The Errors of Constructivism', in von Hayek, *New Studies,* pp. 3–22.

'The Pretence of Knowledge', in von Hayek, *New Studies,* pp. 23–34.

'The Results of Human Action but not of Human Design', in von Hayek, *Studies in Philosophy, Politics, and Economics* (Chicago: University of Chicago Press, 1967), pp. 96–105.

Law, Legislation and Liberty, vol. II: The Mirage of Social Justice (Chicago: The University of Chicago Press, 1976).

Held, D., 'Democracy, the Nation State and the Global System', in Held (ed.), *Political Theory Today,* pp. 197–235.

'Editor's Introduction' in Held (ed.), *Political Theory Today*, pp. 1–21.
Held, D. (ed.), *Political Theory Today* (Cambridge: Polity, 1991).
Held, M., 'Die Ökonomik hat kein Menschenbild' – Institutionen, Normen, Menschenbild', in Biervert/Held (eds.), *Menschenbild*, pp. 10–41.
Herder-Dorneich, Ph., 'Ordnungstheorie – Ordnungspolitik – Ordnungsethik', *Jahrbuch für Neue Politische Ökonomie* 8 (1989), pp. 3–12.
Herms, E., *Gesellschaft gestalten. Beiträge zur evangelischen Sozialethik* (Tübingen: Mohr Siebeck, 1991).
Hinkelammert, F., *The Ideological Weapons of Death: A Theological Critique of Capitalism* (Maryknoll NY: Orbis Books, 1986).
Hinsch, W., 'Einleitung' to the German edn of Rawls, *Die Idee des politischen Liberalismus*, ed. W. Hinsch (Frankfurt: Suhrkamp, 1992), pp. 9–44.
Hirsch, F., *Social Limits to Growth* (London: Routledge & Kegan Paul, 1977).
Hirschman, A. O., *Shifting Involvements: Private Interest and Public Action* (Princeton NJ.: Princeton University Press, 1982).
The Passions and the Interests: Political Arguments for Capitalism before its Triumph (Princeton NJ: Princeton University Press, 1977).
Hobbes, Th., *Leviathan*, ed. Edwin Curley (Indianapolis: Hackett, 1994).
Hobsbawm, E. J., *The Age of Capital, 1848–1875* (London: Encore, 1975).
Höffe, O., 'Ethik', in Höffe (ed.), *Lexikon der Ethik*, 4th edn (Munich: Beck, 1992), p. 61f.
'Humanität', in Höffe (ed.), *Lexikon der Ethik*, 4th edn, p. 124.
Ethik und Politik: Grundmodelle und Probleme der praktischen Philosophie (Frankfurt: Suhrkamp, 1979).
Kategorische Rechtsprinzipien: Ein Kontrapunkt der Moderne (Frankfurt: Suhrkamp, 1990).
Hofmann, F./Rebstock, W., 'Unternehmensethik. Eine Herausforderung an die Unternehmung', *Zeitschrift für Betriebswirtschaft* 59 (1989), pp. 667–87.
Hofmann, W., 'Zum Gesellschaftsbild der Nationalökonomie von heute', in Hofmann, *Universität, Ideologie, Gesellschaft, Beiträge zur Wissenschaftssoziologie* (Frankfurt: Suhrkamp, 1969), pp. 92–116.
Holleis, W., *Das Ungleichgewicht der Gleichgewichtstheorie: Zur Diskussion um die neoklassische Wirtschaftstheorie*, (Frankfurt/New York: Campus, 1985).
Hollstein, W., *Die Gegengesellschaft: Alternative Lebensformen*, 4th expanded edn (Bonn: Verlag Neue Gesellschaft, 1981).
Holzhey, H., 'Locke's Begründung des Privateigentums in der Arbeit', in H. Holzhey/G. Kohler (eds.), *Eigentum und seine Gründe*, Studia philosophica, Supplementum 12 (Berne: *et al.*: Haupt, 1983), pp. 19–34.
Homann, K., /Hesse, H., *et al.*, 'Wirtschaftswissenschaft und Ethik', in H. Hesse (ed.), *Wirtschaftswissenschaft und Ethik* (Berlin: Duncker & Humblot, 1988), pp. 9–33.
Homann, K., 'Entstehung, Befolgung und Wandel moralischer Normen: Neuere Erklärungsansätze', in F. U. Pappi (ed.), *Wirtschaftsethik – Gesellschaftswissenschaftliche Perspektiven* (Kiel: Universität Kiel, 1989), pp. 47–64.
'Ethik und Ökonomik: Zur Theoriestrategie der Wirtschaftsethik', in Homann (ed.), *Wirtschaftsethische Perspektiven I* (Berlin: Duncker & Humblot, 1994), pp. 9–30.

'Konsensethik', in *Gabler Volkswirtschafts-Lexikon* (Wiesbaden: Gabler, 1996), pp. 614–7.

'Philosophie und Ökonomik: Bemerkungen zur Interdisziplinarität', *Jahrbuch für neue politische Ökonomie*, vol. 7 (Tübingen: Mohr Siebeck, 1988), pp. 99–127.

'Wettbewerb und Moral', *Jahrbuch für christliche Sozialwissenschaften* 31 (1990), pp. 34–56.

'Wirtschaftsethik: Angewandte Ethik oder Ethik mit ökonomischer Methode', *Zeitschrift für Politik* 43 (1996), pp. 178–82.

'Wirtschaftsethik: Die Funktion der Moral in der modernen Wirtschaft' in Wieland (ed.), *Wirtschaftsethik und Theorie der Gesellschaft*, pp. 52–3.

Homann, K./Blome-Drees, F., *Wirtschafts- und Unternehmensethik* (Göttingen: Vandenhoeck & Ruprecht, 1992).

Homann, K./Pies, I., 'Wirtschaftsethik in der Moderne: Zur ökonomischen Theorie der Moral', *Ethik und Sozialwissenschaften* 5 (1994), pp. 3–12.

Hoppmann, E., 'Freiheit, Ordnung und Moral', *Orientierungen zur Wirtschafts- und Gesellschaftspolitik* 51 (1992), pp. 53–9.

'Moral und Marktsystem', *Ordo* 41 (1990), pp. 3–26.

Hosmer, L. T., 'Managerial Ethics and Microeconomic Theory', *Journal of Business Ethics* 3 (1984), pp. 315–25.

Huber, J., *Wer soll das alles ändern? Die Alternativen der Alternativbewegung* (Berlin: Rotbuch, 1980).

Hunold, A. (ed.), *Masse und Demokratie*, (Erlenbach-Zürich/Stuttgart: Rentsch, 1957).

Illich, I., *The Right to Useful Employment and its Professional Enemies* (London: Boyars, 1978).

International Labor Organization (ed.), *Economic Security for a Better World* (Geneva: ILO, 2004).

Employment, Growth and Basic Needs: A One-World problem (New York: Praeger, 1977).

Janisch, M., *Das strategische Anspruchsmanagement: Vom Shareholder Value zum Stakeholder Value* (Berne *et al.*: Haupt, 1993).

Jantsch, E., 'Unternehmung und Umweltsysteme', in B. Hentsch/F. Malik (eds.), *Systemorientiertes Management* (Berne *et al.*: Haupt, 1973), pp. 27–46.

Jaspers, K., *Einführung in die Philosophie*, 4th edn (Zurich: Artemis, 1963); Engl. *Way to Wisdom: An Introduction to Philosophy* (New Haven: Yale University Press, 1951).

Jonas, H., *The Imperative of Responsibility: In Search of an Ethics for the Technological Age* (Chicago/London: University of Chicago Press, 1984).

Kaiser, M., 'Kulturelle Kommunikationspraxen als Leitbild einer wirtschaftsethisch reflektierten Unternehmenskommunikation', in Bentele/Steinmann/Zerfass (eds.), *Dialogorientierte Unternehmenskommunikation*, pp. 109–45.

Kaldor, M., *Global Civil Society: An Answer to War* (Cambridge: Polity, 2003).

Kambartel, F., 'Arbeit und Praxis. Zu den begrifflichen und methodischen Grundlagen einer aktuellen politischen Debatte', *Deutsche Zeitschrift für Philosophie* 41 (1993), pp. 239–49.

'Bemerkungen zum normativen Fundament der Ökonomie', in J. Mittelstrass (ed.), *Methodologische Probleme einer normativ-kritischen Gesellschaftstheorie* (Frankfurt: Suhrkamp, 1975), pp. 107–25.

'Ist rationale Ökonomie als empirisch-quantitative Wissenschaft möglich? ', in J. Mittelstrass (ed.), *Methodenprobleme der Wissenschaften vom gesellschaftlichen Handeln* (Frankfurt: Suhrkamp, 1979), pp. 299–319.

'Rekonstruktion und Rationalität. Zur normativen Grundlage einer Theorie der Wissenschaft', in Schwemmer (ed.), *Vernunft, Handlung und Erfahrung*, pp. 11–21.

Kant, I., 'An Answer to the Question: What is Enlightenment?', in Kant, *Practical Writings*, pp. 11–22; 54–60.

'Critique of Practical Reason', in Kant, *Practical Philosophy*, pp. 139–271.

'Groundwork of the Metaphysics of Morals', in Kant, *Practical Philosophy*, pp. 37–108.

'Idea for a Universal History with a Cosmopolitan Purpose', in Kant, *Political Writings*, pp. 41–53.

'On the Common Saying: That may be correct in theory but it is of no use in practice', in Kant, *Practical Philosophy*, pp. 273–309.

'Toward perpetual peace', in Kant, *Practical Philosophy*, pp. 311–51.

'What is Orientation in Thinking?', in Kant, *Political Writings*, pp. 237–49.

Critique of Pure Reason, ed. and transl. P. Guyer and A. W. Wood (Cambridge: Cambridge University Press, 1998).

Political Writings, ed. H. Reiss, transl. H. B. Nisbet (Cambridge Edition of the Works of Immanuel Kant: Cambridge University Press, 1991).

Practical Philosophy, ed. and transl. Mary J. Gregor (Cambridge Edition of the Works of Immanuel Kant: Cambridge University Press, 1996).

Religion within the Limits of Reason Alone (New York: Harper, 1960).

Katterle, S., 'Marktwirtschaft und Ethik', *Discussion Papers of the Faculty of Economics*, N° 302 (Bielefeld: University of Bielefeld, 1995).

'Methodologischer Individualismus and Beyond', in Biervert/Held (eds.), *Menschenbild*, pp. 132–52.

Alternativen zur neoliberalen Wende. Wirtschaftspolitik in der sozialstaatlichen Demokratie (Bochum: SWI, 1989).

Keil, G., *Kritik des Naturalismus* (Berlin: de Gruyter, 1993).

Kerber, W., 'Homo oeconomicus: Zur Rechtfertigung eines umstrittenen Begriffs', in Biervert/Held (eds.), *Menschenbild*, pp. 56–75.

Kersting, W., 'Globale Rechtsordnung oder weltweite Verteilungsgerechtigkeit?', *Jahrbuch der deutschen Gesellschaft zur Erforschung des politischen Denkens* (Stuttgart: Metzler, 1996), pp. 197–246.

'Lexikalisch erfasst: Wirtschaftsethik und ethisches Wirtschaften', *Zeitschrift für Politik* 42 (1995), pp. 325–30.

'Moralphilosophie, angewandte Ethik und Ökonomismus. Bemerkungen zur wirtschaftsethischen Topologie', *Zeitschrift für Politik* 43 (1996), pp. 183–94.

'Spannungsvolle Rationalitätsbegriffe in der politischen Philosophie von John Rawls', in K.-O. Apel/M. Kettner (eds.), *Die eine Vernunft und die vielen Rationalitäten* (Frankfurt: Suhrkamp, 1996), pp. 227–65.

Die politische Philosophie des Gesellschaftsvertrags (Darmstadt: Wissenschaftliche Buchgesellschaft, 1994).

Kettner, M., 'Einleitung: Über einige Dilemmata angewandter Ethik', in Apel/Kettner (eds.), *Zur Anwendung der Diskursethik*, pp. 9–28.

'Rentabilität und Moralität. Offene Probleme in Karl Homann's Wirtschafts- und Unternehmensethik', in Forum für Philosophie Bad Homburg (ed.), *Markt und Moral*, pp. 241–67.

'Wie ist eine diskursethische Begründung ökologischer Rechts- und Moralnormen möglich?', in J. Nida-Rümelin/D. v. d. Pfordten (eds.), *Ökologische Ethik und Rechtstheorie* (Baden-Baden: Nomos, 1995), pp. 301–23.

Keynes, J. M., 'Economic Possibilities for Our Grandchildren', in Keynes, *Collected Writings, vol. IX, Essays in Persuasion* (London: Palgrave Macmillan, 1972; 1st edn 1930), pp. 321–32.

Kirchgässner, G., 'Bemerkungen zur Minimalmoral', *Zeitschrift für Wirtschafts- und Sozialwissenschaften* 116 (1996), pp. 223–51.

'Einige Bemerkungen zur Rolle der Wirtschaftsethik', *Ethik und Sozialwissenschaften* 5 (1994), pp. 40–2.

'Towards a Theory of Low-Cost Decisions', *European Journal of Political Economy* 8 (1992), pp. 305–20.

'Wirtschaftspolitik und Politiksystem: Zur Kritik der traditionellen Ordnungstheorie aus der Sicht der Neuen Politischen Ökonomie', in D. Cassel/B. T. Ramb/H. J. Thieme (eds.), *Ordnungspolitik* (Munich: Vahlen, 1988), pp. 53–75.

Homo oeconomicus: Das ökonomische Modell individuellen Verhaltens und seine Anwendung in den Wirtschafts- und Sozialwissenschaften (Tübingen: Mohr Siebeck, 1991).

Kittsteiner, H.-D., 'Ethik und Teleologie: Das Problem der "unsichtbaren Hand" bei Adam Smith', in F.-X. Kaufmann/H.-G. Krüsselberg (eds.), *Markt, Staat und Solidarität bei Adam Smith* (Frankfurt/New York: Campus, 1984), pp. 41–73.

Kleinewefers, H., 'Wie der volkswirtschaftliche Nutzen maximiert wird', *Neue Zürcher Zeitung*, 154, 5 July 1996, p. 23.

Kley, R., *Hayek's Social and Political Thought* (Oxford: Clarendon, 1994).

Vertragstheorien der Gerechtigkeit: Eine philosophischen Kritik der Theorien von John Rawls, Robert Nozick und James Buchanan (Berne *et al.*: Haupt, 1989).

Kliemt, H., 'Individualism, Libertarianism and Non-Cognitivism', *Analyse & Kritik* 8 (1986), pp. 211–28.

'The Veil of Insignificance', *European Journal of Political Economy* 2/3 (1986), pp. 333–44.

Knight, F. H., *Freedom and Reform: Essays in Economics and Social Philosophy* (New York/London: Harper & Brothers, 1947).

Knobloch, U., *Theorie und Ethik des Konsums* (Berne *et al.*: Haupt, 1994).

Koch, C., *Die Gier des Marktes: Die Ohnmacht des Staates im Kampf der Weltwirtschaft* (Munich/Vienna: Hanser, 1995).

Kohlberg, L., *Essays on Moral Development, vol. I: The Philosophy of Moral Development* (San Francisco: Harper & Row, 1981).

Koller, P., 'Menschen- und Bürgerrechte aus ethischer Perspektive', in B. S. Byrd/ J. Hruschka/J. C. Joerden (eds.), *Annual Review of Law and Ethics, vol. 3: Human Rights and the Rule of Law* (Berlin: Duncker & Humblot, 1995), pp. 49–68.

Kosiol, E., *Die Unternehmung als wirtschaftliches Aktionszentrum: Einführung in die Betriebswirtschaftslehre* (Reinbek: Rowohlt, 1972).

Koslowski, P., 'Grundlinien der Wirtschaftsethik', *Zeitschrift für Wirtschafts- und Sozialwissenschaften* 109 (1989), pp. 345–83.

'Über die Notwendigkeit von ethischen und zugleich ökonomischen Urteilen', *Orientierungen zur Wirtschafts- und Gesellschaftspolitik* 33 (1987), pp. 7–13.

Ethik des Kapitalismus, 3rd edn (Tübingen: Mohr Siebeck, 1986).

Principles of Ethical Economy, transl. D. W. Lutz (Dordrecht/Boston/London: Kluwer, 2001).

Krugman, P., *Geography and Trade* (Cambridge MA/London: MIT Press, 1991).

Krüsselberg, H. G., 'Ordnungstheorie – Zur Konstituierung und Begründung der Rahmenbedingungen', in B. Biervert/M. Held (eds.), *Ethische Grundlagen der ökonomischen Theorie* (Frankfurt/New York: Campus, 1989), pp. 100–33.

'Property-Rights-Theorie und Wohlfahrtsökonomik', in A. Schüller (ed.), *Property Rights und ökonomische Theorie* (Munich: Vahlen, 1983), pp. 45–77.

Krüsselberg, H.-G., 'Soziale Marktwirtschaft: Idee und Wirklichkeit', *Orientierungen zur Wirtschafts- und Gesellschaftspolitik* 41 (1989), pp. 56–64.

Küng, H., *A Global Ethic for Global Politics and Economics* (New York: Oxford University Press, 1998).

Global Responsibility: In Search of a New World Ethic (London: SCM/New York: Crossroad, 1991).

Künzli, A., *Mein und Dein: Zur Ideengeschichte des Eigentumsfeindschaft* (Cologne: Bund-Verlag, 1986).

Lampert, H., '"Denken in Ordnungen" als ungelöste Aufgabe', *Jahrbuch für Nationalökonomie und Statistik* 206 (1989), pp. 446–56.

Lang, T./Hines, C., *The New Protectionism: Protecting the Future Against Free Trade* (London: Earthscan Publications, 1993).

Leisinger, K. M., 'Nicht alles Legale ist auch legitim', *Übersee Rundschau* 41 (1989), vol. 162, pp. 42–5.

Whistleblowing und Corporate Reputation Management (München-Mering: Hampp, 2003).

Leutwiler, F./Schmidheiny, S. *et al.*, *Schweizerische Wirtschaftspolitik im internationalen Wettbewerb: Ein ordnungspolitisches Programm* (Zürich: Orell Füssli, 1991).

Lisowsky, A., 'Ethik und Betriebswirtschaftslehre', *Zeitschrift für Betriebswirtschaft* 4 (1927), pp. 253–58, 363–72, 429–42.

Livesey, S. M., 'Eco-Identity as Discursive Struggle: Royal Dutch/Shell, Brent Spar, and Nigeria', *The Journal of Business Communication* 38/1 (2001), pp. 58–91.

Locke, J., *Two Treatises of Government* (Cambridge: Cambridge University Press, 1967).

Löhr, A, *Unternehmensethik und Betriebswirtschaftslehre: Untersuchungen zur theoretischen Stützung der Unternehmenspraxis* (Stuttgart: M & P Verlag für Wissenschaft und Forschung, 1991).

Unternehmensethik und Betriebswirtschaftslehre (Stuttgart: Metzler, 1991).

Lorenzen, P., 'Philosophische Fundierungsprobleme einer Wirtschafts- und Unternehmensethik', in Steinmann/Löhr (eds.), *Unternehmensethik*, pp. 35–67.
Luhmann, N., *Die Wirtschaft der Gesellschaft* (Frankfurt: Suhrkamp, 1988).
Zweckbegriff und Systemrationalität, 2nd edn (Frankfurt: Suhrkamp, 1977; 1st edn 1968).
Ma, H., 'Toward Global Competitive Advantage: Creation, competition, cooperation, and co-option', *Management Decision* 42/7 (2004), pp. 907–24.
Maak, Th./Ulrich, P., 'Korruption – die Unterwanderung des Gemeinwohls durch Partikularinteressen: Eine republikanisch-ethische Perspektive', in M. Pieth/P. Eigen (eds.), *Korruption im internationalen Geschäftsverkehr: Bestandsaufnahme, Bekämpfung, Prävention* (Neuwied: Luchterhand, 1999), pp. 103–19.
Macpherson, C. B., *The Political Theory of Possessive Individualism* (Oxford: Clarendon, 1962).
Maihofer, W., 'Realität der Politik und Ethos der Republik', in: Apel/Kettner (eds.), *Zur Anwendung der Diskursethik*, pp. 84–126.
Manin, B., 'On Legitimacy and Political Deliberation', *Political Theory* 15 (1987), pp. 338–68.
March, J. G., 'The Business Firm as a Political Coalition', *Journal of Politics* 24 (1962), pp. 662–78.
March, J. G./Simon, H. A., *Organizations* (New York: John Wiley & Sons, 1958).
Margalit, A., *The Decent Society* (Cambridge MA: Harvard University Press, 1996).
Marshall, Th.M., 'Citizenship and Social Class', in Marshall (ed.), *Sociology at the Crossroads and Other Essays* (London: Heinemann, 1963), pp. 67–127.
Marx, K., *Capital*, transl. B. Fowkes, 3 vols (Harmondsworth: Penguin, 1976).
Mastronardi, Ph., *Strukturprinzipien der Bundesverfassung? Fragen zum Verhältnis von Recht und Macht anhand des Wirtschaftsstaatsprinzips* (Basel: Helbing & Lichtenhahn, 1988).
Mauss, M., *The Gift: Forms and Functions of Exchange in Archaic Societies*, transl. I. Cunnison (London: Cohen & West, 1966; French orig. 1924).
Maynor, J. W., *Republicanism in the Modern World* (Cambridge: Polity, 2003).
Mead, G. H., *Mind, Self and Society* (Chicago: University of Chicago Press, 1934).
Medick, H., *Naturzustand und Naturgeschichte der bürgerlichen Gesellschaft* (Göttingen: Vandenhoeck & Ruprecht, 1973).
Mendonça, W. P., 'Zwischen Rechten und Gütern. Zur liberalistischen Verkürzung der praktischen Vernunft bei John Rawls', in Demmerling/Gabriel/Rentsch (eds.), *Vernunft und Lebenspraxis*, pp. 329–51.
Meran, J., 'Ist es ökonomisch vernünftig, moralisch zu handeln?', in Ulrich (ed.), *Auf der Suche*, pp. 53–88.
Meyer, Th., *Fundamentalismus – Aufstand gegen die Moderne* (Reinbek: Rowohlt, 1989).
Meyer-Faje, A./Ulrich, P. (eds.), *Der andere Adam Smith: Beiträge zur Neubestimmung von Ökonomie als Politischer Ökonomie* (Berne *et al.*: Haupt, 1991).
Michelman, F. I., 'Law's Republic', *The Yale Law Journal* 97 (1988), pp. 1493–537.

'The Supreme Court 1985 Term. Foreword: Traces of Self-Government', *Harvard Law Review* 100 (1986), pp. 4–77.

Miksch, L., *Wettbewerb als Aufgabe: Grundsätze einer Wettbewerbsordnung*, 2nd edn (Godesberg: Küpper, 1947).

Milberg, W., 'Foreign Direct Investment and Development: Balancing Costs and Benefits', *International Monetary and Financial Issues for the 1990s*, Vol. XI (New York: UNCTAD, 1999), pp. 99–116.

Miles, R. E., 'Human Relations or Human Resources?', *Harvard Business Review* July/August (1965), pp. 148–63.

Mill, J. St., *Principles of Political Economy* (1848). Collected Works of John Stuart Mill, ed. J. M. Robson, vols. III-V (Toronto: University of Toronto Press, 1965ff.).

Mises, L. von, *A Critique of Interventionism* (New York: Crown, 1977; 1st German edn Jena 1929).

Human Action: A Treatise on Economics (London: William Hodge, 1949).

Liberalism: In the Classical Tradition (New York: Irvington, 1985; 1st German edn Jena 1927; reprinted St Augustin 1993).

Nationalökonomie: Theorie des Handelns und Wirtschaftens (Geneva: Union, 1940).

Planned Chaos (New York: Foundation for Economic Education, 1981).

Mitschke, J., 'Steuer- und Sozialpolitik für mehr reguläre Beschäftigung', *Wirtschaftsdienst* 75/2 (1995), pp. 75–84.

Steuer- und Transferordnung aus einem Guss (Baden-Baden: Nomos, 1985).

Mittelstrass, J., 'Was heisst: sich im Denken orientieren?', in Schwemmer (ed.), *Vernunft, Handlung und Erfahrung*, pp. 117–32

'Wirtschaftsethik als wissenschaftliche Disziplin?', in G. Enderle (ed.), *Ethik und Wirtschaftswissenschaft* (Berlin: Duncker & Humblot, 1985), pp. 17–32.

'Wirtschaftsethik oder der erklärte Abschied vom Ökonomismus auf philosophischen Wegen', in Ulrich (ed.), *Auf der Suche*, pp. 17–38.

Wissenschaft als Lebensform (Frankfurt: Suhrkamp, 1982).

Montesquieu, Ch. de, *The Spirit of Laws*, ed. by D. W. Carrithers, based on Th. Naugent's translation (London: Nourse, 1750) of the first French ed. (Berkeley CA: University of California Press, 1977; orig. Geneva: Barillot, 1748).

Müller-Armack, A., 'Die zweite Phase der sozialen Marktwirtschaft – Ihre Ergänzung durch das Leitbild einer neuen Gesellschaftspolitik' (1960), reprinted in Müller-Armack, *Genealogie der Sozialen Marktwirtschaft*, pp. 129–45.

Genealogie der Sozialen Marktwirtschaft: Frühschriften und weiterführende Konzepte (Berne *et al.*: Haupt, 1974).

Münkler, H., 'Politische Tugend. Bedarf die Demokratie einer sozio-moralischen Grundlegung?', in Münkler (ed.), *Die Chancen der Freiheit. Grundprobleme der Demokratie* (Munich/Zurich: Piper, 1992), pp. 25–46.

Munz, H./Gottlieb Duttweiler Institut (eds.), *Das Phänomen Migros: Die Geschichte der Migros-Gemeinschaft* (Zürich: Ex Libris, 1973).

Musgrave, R., *The Theory of Public Finance* (New York: McGraw-Hill, 1959).

Myrdal, G., *Das politische Element in der nationalökonomischen Doktrinbildung*, 2nd edn (Bonn-Bad Godesberg: Verlag Neue Gesellschaft, 1976), preface to the 1st German edn (Berlin 1932), not included in the English edn.

The Political Element in the Development of Economic Theory (London: Routledge & Kegan Paul, 1954).

Nadolny, S., *The Discovery of Slowness* (New York: Penguin, 1987).

Nawroth, E., *Die Sozial- und Wirtschaftsphilosophie des Neoliberalismus* (Heidelberg: Kerle, 1961).

Die wirtschaftspolitischen Ordnungsvorstellungen des Neoliberalismus (Cologne: Heymanns, 1962).

Nell-Breuning, O. von, 'Neoliberalismus und katholische Soziallehre', in Boarmann (ed.), *Der Christ und die soziale Marktwirtschaft*, pp. 107–22.

Nielsen, P. R., 'Arendt's Action Philosophy and the Manager as Eichmann, Richard III, Faust or Institution Citizen', *California Management Review* 26 (1984), pp. 191–201.

Nietzsche, F., *Werke*, vol. III, ed. K. Schlechta (Munich: Hanser, 1956).

Nozick, R., *Anarchy, State and Utopia* (New York: Basic Books, 1974).

Nussbaum, M., 'Aristotelian Social Democracy', in R. B. Douglass/G. M. Mara/ H. S. Richardson (eds.), *Liberalism and the Good* (New York *et al.*: Routledge, 1990), pp. 203–52.

Nutzinger, H. G., 'Unternehmensethik zwischen ökonomischem Imperialismus und diskursiver Überforderung', in Forum für Philosophie Bad Homburg (ed.), *Markt und Moral*, pp. 181–214.

Offe, C., 'Fessel und Bremse: moralische und institutionelle Aspekte "intelligenter" Selbstbeschränkung' in A. Honneth *et al.* (eds.), *Zwischenbetrachtungen im Prozess der Aufklärung* (Frankfurt: Suhrkamp, 1989), pp. 739–74.

Offe, C./Preuss, U. K., 'Democratic Institutions and Moral Resources', in Held (ed.), *Political Theory Today*, pp. 143–71.

Oser, F./Althof, W., *Moralische Selbstbestimmung: Modelle der Entwicklung und Erziehung im Wertebereich*, 2nd edn (Stuttgart: Klett-Cotta, 1994).

Osterloh, M., *Interorganisationales Lernen in ethischen Branchenvereinbarungen*, Diskussionsbeitrag 18 (Zurich: Institut für betriebswirtschaftliche Forschung an der Universität Zürich, 1995).

Paine, L. S., 'Managing for Organizational Integrity', *Harvard Business Review* March–April (1994), pp. 106–17.

Pateman, C., 'Democratizing Citizenship: Some advantages of a basic income', *Politics and Society* 32 (2004), pp. 89–106.

Patzig, G., 'Ein Plädoyer für utilitaristische Grundsätze in der Ethik', *Neue Sammlung* 13 (1973), pp. 488–500.

Ethik ohne Metaphysik, 2nd edn (Göttingen: Vandenhoeck & Ruprecht, 1983).

Patzig, M., 'Zur Diskussion des Adam-Smith-Problems – ein Überblick', in Meyer-Faje/Ulrich (eds.), *Der andere Adam Smith*, pp. 21–54.

Peter, H. B., 'Spekulation', in Enderle *et al.* (eds.), *Lexikon der Wirtschaftsethik*, col. 1014–20.

Peters, B., 'Der Sinn von Öffentlichkeit', in F. Neidhardt (ed.), *Öffentlichkeit, öffentliche Meinung, soziale Bewegung*, Special Issue of *Kölner Zeitschrift für*

Soziologie und Sozialpsychologie (Opladen: Westdeutscher Verlag, 1994), pp. 42–76.

Petersmann, E.-U., 'Proposals for Negotiating International Competition Rules in the GATT-WTO World Trade and Legal System', *Aussenwirtschaft* 49 (1994), pp. 231–77.

'Why Do Governments Need the Uruguay Round Agreements, NAFTA and the EEA?', *Aussenwirtschaft* 49 (1994), pp. 31–55.

Pettit, Ph., *Republicanism: A Theory of Freedom and Government* (Oxford: Clarendon, 1997).

Piaget, J., *Genetic Epistemology* (New York: Columbia University Press, 1970).

The Moral Judgement of the Child (New York: Free Press, 1932).

Pieper, A., *Einführung in die Ethik*, 2nd rev. edn (Tübingen: Francke, 1991).

Pies, I., *Normative Institutionenökonomik: Zur Rationalisierung des politischen Liberalismus* (Tübingen: Mohr Siebeck, 1993).

Pigou, A. C., *The Economics of Welfare* (London: Macmillan, 1920; new edn 1960).

Plessner, H., 'Conditio humana', in G. Mann/A. Heuss, (eds.), *Propyläen Weltgeschichte*, 10 vols (Berlin/Frankfurt: Propyläen, 1964), vol. I, pp. 33–86.

Pocock, J. G. A., 'Virtues, Rights and Manners. A Model for Historians of Political Thought', *Political Theory* 9 (1981), pp. 353–68.

The Machiavellian Moment: Florentine Political Thought and the Atlantic Republican Tradition (Princeton NJ: Princeton University Press, 2003; 1st edn 1975).

Polanyi, K., *The Great Transformation* (Boston: Beacon Press, 1957/2001, 1st edn 1944).

Porter, M. E., *The Competitive Advantage of Nations* (New York: Free Press, 1990).

Portmann, A., *Entlässt die Natur den Menschen?* (Munich: Piper, 1970).

Um das Menschenbild (Stuttgart: Reclam, 1964).

Post, J., *Corporate Behavior and Social Change* (Reston VA: Reston Publishing Co., 1978).

Prahalad, C. K./Hamel, G., 'The Core Competence of the Corporation', *Harvard Business Review* 68/3 (1990), pp. 79–91.

Prahalad, C. K./Hammond, A. C., 'Serving the World's Poor, Profitably', *Harvard Business Review* 80/9 (2002), pp. 48–57.

Pümpin, C., *Das Dynamikprinzip: Zukunftsorientierungen für Unternehmer und Manager* (Düsseldorf: Econ, 1989).

Pury, D. de, in 'David de Pury und wie er die Welt sieht' (Interview), *Tages-Anzeiger*, Zurich, 2 February 1996.

Pury, D. de/Hauser, H./Schmid, B., *Mut zum Aufbruch* (Zurich: Orell Füssli, 1995).

Radnitzky, G., 'Marktwirtschaft: frei oder sozial?', in G. Radnitzky/H. Bouillon (eds.), *Ordnungstheorie und Ordnungspolitik* (Berlin: Springer, 1991), pp. 47–75.

'Soziale oder freie Marktwirtschaft', *Neue Zürcher Zeitung*, 120, 26/27 May 1990, p. 93.

Rappaport, A., *Creating Shareholder Value* (New York: Free Press, 1998; 1st edn 1986).

Rawls, J., 'Justice as Fairness: Political not Metaphysical', *Philosophy and Public Affairs* 14 (1985), pp. 223–51.

'Kantian Constructivism in Moral Theory', *The Journal of Philosophy* 77/9 (1980), pp. 515–72.

'The Basic Liberties and Their Priority', in S. M. McMurrin (ed.), *The Tanner Lectures on Human Values 1982* (Salt Lake City/Cambridge: University of Utah Press/Cambridge University Press, 1983), pp. 3–87.

'The Basic Structure as a Subject', in A. I. Goldman/J. Kim (eds.), *Values and Morals* (Dordrecht: Reidel, 1978), pp. 47–71.

'The Domain of the Political and Overlapping Consensus', *New York University Law Review* 64 (1989), pp. 233–55.

'The Idea of an Overlapping Consensus', *Oxford Journal of Legal Studies* 7 (1987), pp. 1–25.

'The Idea of Public Reason' in Rawls, *Political Liberalism*, pp. 212–54.

'The Priority of Right and Ideas of the Good', *Philosophy and Public Affairs* 17 (1988), pp. 251–76, reprinted in Rawls, *Political Liberalism*, pp. 173–211.

A Theory of Justice, rev. edn (Cambridge, MA: Belknap Press of Harvard University Press, 1999).

Justice as Fairness: A Restatement (Cambridge MA/London: Harvard University Press, 2001).

Political Liberalism (New York: Columbia University Press, 1993).

Rentsch, Th., 'Wie ist eine menschliche Welt überhaupt möglich? Philosophische Anthropologie als Konstitutionsanalyse der humanen Welt', in Ch. Demmerling/G. Gabriel/Th. Rentsch (eds.), *Vernunft und Lebenspraxis, Philosophische Studien zu den Bedingungen einer rationalen Kultur* (Frankfurt: Suhrkamp, 1995), pp. 192–214.

Rhenman, E., *Industrial Democracy and Industrial Management* (London: Tavistock, 1968).

Rich, A., *Business and Economic Ethics: The Ethics of Economic Systems*, ed. G. Enderle (Leuven: Peeters, 2006).

Riklin, A., *Verantwortung des Akademikers* (St Gallen: VGS, 1978).

Rinderspacher, J. P., 'Warum nicht auch mal sonntags arbeiten?', in K. W. Dahm *et al.* (eds.), *Sonntags nie? Die Zukunft des Wochenendes* (Frankfurt: Campus, 1989), pp. 13–42.

Robbins, L., *An Essay on the Nature and Significance of Economic Science*, 2nd edn (London: Macmillan, 1949).

Rock, R./Rosenthal, K., *Marketing = Philosophie* (Frankfurt *et al.*: Peter Lang, 1986).

Roddick, A., *Body and Soul* (London: Crown, 1991).

Rodrik, D., *Has Globalization Gone Too Far?* (Washington DC: Institute for International Economics, 1997).

Röpke, W., *A Humane Economy: The Social Framework of the Free Market*, transl. E. Henderson (Chicago: Henry Regnery Co., 1960).

Civitas Humana: A Humane Order of Society (London: William Hodge, 1948); cit. German edn: *Civitas Humana: Grundfragen der Gesellschafts- und Wirtschaftsreform* (Erlenbach-Zurich: Rentsch, 1944).

Die Gesellschaftskrisis der Gegenwart (Erlenbach-Zurich: Rentsch, 1942; 5th edn 1948).

Die Lehre von der Wirtschaft, 13th edn (Berne *et al.*: Haupt, 1994; 1st edn 1937).
Rothschild, K., 'Macht: Die Lücke in der Preistheorie', in H. K. Schneider/ Ch. Watrin (eds.), *Macht und ökonomisches Gesetz*, vol. II (Berlin: Duncker & Humblot, 1973), pp. 1097–111.
Ruh, H., 'Modelle einer neuen Zeiteinteilung für das Tätigsein der Menschen. Strategien zur Überwindung der Arbeitslosigkeit', in H. Würgler (ed.), *Arbeitszeit und Arbeitslosigkeit: Zur Diskussion der Beschäftigungspolitik in der Schweiz* (Zurich: Verlag der Fachvereine, 1994), pp. 135–52.
Rusche, Th., 'Das Diskursmodell der kommunikativen Unternehmensethik', in H. H. Hinterhuber/A. Al-Ani/G. Handbauer (eds.), *Das neue Strategische Management: Elemente und Perspektiven einer zukunftsorientierten Unternehmensführung* (Wiesbaden: Gabler, 1996), pp. 301–20.
Rüstow, A., 'Paläoliberalismus, Kommunismus und Neoliberalismus', in F. Greiss/F. W. Meyer (eds.), *Wirtschaft, Gesellschaft und Kultur. Festgabe für Alfred Müller-Armack* (Berlin: Duncker & Humblot, 1961), pp. 61–70.
'Wirtschaft als Dienerin der Menschlichkeit', in Aktionsgemeinschaft soziale Marktwirtschaft (ed.), *Was wichtiger ist als Wirtschaft* (Ludwigsburg: Hoch, 1960), pp. 7–16.
'Wirtschaftsethische Probleme der sozialen Marktwirtschaft', in P. M. Boarman (ed.), *Der Christ und die soziale Marktwirtschaft* (Stuttgart/Cologne: Kohlhammer, 1955), pp. 53–74.
Das Versagen des Wirtschaftsliberalismus, 2nd edn (Düsseldorf: Küpper, 1950; 1st edn 1945); 3rd edn ed. F. P. and M. Maier-Rigaud (Marburg: Metropolis, 2001).
Sachs, J. D., *The End of Poverty: Economic Possibilities for Our Time* (London: Penguin, 2005).
Sandel, M. J., 'The Procedural Republic and the Unencumbered Self', *Political Theory* 1 (1984), pp. 81–96.
Democracy's Discontent: America in Search of a Political Philosophy (Cambridge MA: Harvard University Press, 1996).
Liberalism and the Limits of Justice (Cambridge/New York: Cambridge University Press, 1982).
Schachtschabel, H. G., *Wirtschaftspolitische Konzeptionen* (Stuttgart: Kohlhammer, 1967).
Scharpf, F. W., 'Für eine Subventionierung niedriger Erwerbseinkommen', *Wirtschaftsdienst* 74/3 (1994), pp. 111–8.
'Soziale Gerechtigkeit im globalen Kapitalismus', *Die neue Gesellschaft/ Frankfurter Hefte* 40 (1993), pp. 544–7.
Schelling, T. C., *Micromotives and Macrobehaviour* (New York: W. W. Norton, 1978).
Scherhorn, G., 'Autonomie and Empathie. Die Bedeutung der Freiheit für das verantwortliche Handeln: Zur Entwicklung eines neuen Menschenbildes', in Biervert/Held (eds.), *Menschenbild*, pp. 153–72.
'Konsumverhalten', in G. Enderle *et al.* (eds.), *Lexikon der Wirtschaftsethik* (Freiburg i. Br.: Herder, 1993), col. 545–51.
Schneider, D., 'Unternehmensethik und Gewinnprinzip in der Betriebswirtschaftslehre', *Zeitschrift für betriebswirtschaftliche Forschung* 42 (1990), pp. 869–91.

Schüller, A., 'Die institutionellen Voraussetzungen einer marktwirtschaftlichen Ordnung', in R. Vaubel/H. D. Barbier (eds.), *Handbuch Marktwirtschaft* (Pfullingen: Neske, 1986), pp. 34–44.

Schumpeter, J., *Capitalism, Socialism and Democracy* (London: Allen & Unwin, 1976).

Das Wesen und der Hauptinhalt der theoretischen Nationalökonomie (Leipzig: Duncker & Humblot, 1908).

History of Economic Analysis (London: Allen & Unwin, 1954).

Schwarz, G., 'Die ordnungspolitische Verwahrlosung der Schweiz', *Neue Zürcher Zeitung*, 58, 10/11 March 1990, p. 25. Extended version in G. Radnitzky / H. Bouillon (eds.), *Ordnungstheorie und Ordnungspolitik* (Berlin: Springer, 1991), pp. 221–38.

Schwemmer, O. (ed.), *Vernunft, Handlung und Erfahrung. Über die Grundlagen und Ziele der Wissenschaft* (Munich: Beck, 1981).

Seel, M., *Versuch über die Form des Glücks* (Frankfurt: Suhrkamp, 1995).

Sen, A., 'Rational Fools: A Critique of the Behavioral Foundations of Economic Theory', *Philosophy and Public Affairs* 6 (1977), pp. 317–44.

Commodities and Capabilities (Amsterdam: North-Holland Publishing, 1985).

Development as Freedom (Oxford: Oxford University Press, 1999).

On Ethics and Economics (Oxford/New York: Basil Blackwell, 1987).

Senghaas, D. (ed.), *Peripherer Kapitalismus: Analysen über Abhängigkeit und Unterentwicklung* (Frankfurt: Suhrkamp, 1974).

Sennett, R., *The Corrosion of Character: The Personal Consequences of Work in the New Capitalism* (New York: Norton, 1998).

Sewing, W., 'John G. A. Pocock und die Wiederentdeckung der republikanischen Tradition', Preface in J. G. A. Pocock, *Die andere Bürgergesellschaft. Zur Dialektik von Tugend und Korruption* (Frankfurt/New York: Campus, 1993), pp. 7–32.

Shapiro, I., *The Evolution of Rights in Liberal Theory* (Cambridge: Cambridge University Press, 1986).

Shue, H., *Basic Rights: Subsistence, Affluence and U. S. Foreign Policy* (Princeton: Princeton University Press, 1980).

Simon, H. A./Smithburg, D. W/Thompson, V. A., *Public Administration* (New York: Alfred A. Knopf, 1950).

Singer, M. G., *Generalization in Ethics* (London: Eyre and Spottiswoode, 1963).

Sinn, H.-W., 'The Dilemma of Globalisation: A German Perspective', *Économie Internationale* 100 (2004), pp. 111–20.

'The Pathological Export Boom and the Bazaar Effect: How to Solve the German Puzzle', *World Economy* 29/9 (2006), pp. 1157–75.

Sloterdijk, P., *Critique of Cynical Reason* (London/New York: Verso, 1987).

Smith, A., *An Enquiry into the Nature and Causes of the Wealth of Nations*, Glasgow Edition of the Works and Correspondence of Adam Smith, 2 vols. (Oxford: Oxford University Press, 1976).

The Theory of Moral Sentiments, Glasgow Edition of the Works and Correspondence of Adam Smith (Oxford: Oxford University Press, 1976; 1st edn 1759).

Spremann, K., 'Wertsteigerung als Managementprinzip in Europa?', in K. Höfner/A. Pohl (eds.), *Wertsteigerungsmanagement. Das Shareholder-*

Value-Konzept: Methoden und erfolgreiche Beispiele (Frankfurt/New York: Campus, 1994), pp. 303–19.

Steinmann, H./Löhr, A., 'Einleitung: Grundfragen und Problembestände einer Unternehmensethik', in Steinmann/Löhr (eds.), *Unternehmensethik*, 2nd rev. and exp. edn (Stuttgart: Schäffer-Poeschel, 1991), pp. 3–32.

'Unternehmensethik – eine "realistische Idee"', *Schmalenbachs Zeitschrift für betriebswirtschaftliche Forschung* 40 (1988), pp. 299–317.

'Unternehmensethik als Ordnungselement in der Marktwirtschaft?', *Schmalenbachs Zeitschrift für betriebswirtschaftliche Forschung* 47 (1995), pp. 143–79.

Grundlagen der Unternehmensethik, 2nd rev. and exp. edn (Stuttgart: Schäffer-Poeschel, 1994).

Steinmann, H./Olbrich, T., 'Business Ethics in US Corporations', in Ulrich/Wieland (eds.), *Unternehmensethik in der Praxis*, pp. 63–89.

Steinmann, H./Oppenrieder, B., 'Brauchen wir eine Unternehmensethik?', *Die Betriebswirtschaft* 45 (1985), pp. 170–83.

Steinmann, H./Zerfass, A., 'Privates Unternehmertum und öffentliches Interesse', in G. R. Wagner (ed.), *Betriebswirtschaftslehre und Umweltschutz* (Stuttgart: Schäffer-Poeschel, 1993), pp. 3–26.

'Privates Unternehmertum und öffentliches Interesse', in G. R. Wagner (ed.), *Betriebswirtschaft und Umweltschutz* (Stuttgart: Schäffer-Poeschel, 1993).

Stiglitz, J., *Globalization and its Discontents* (New York: Norton, 2002).

Streit, M. E., 'Ordnungsökonomik', in *Gabler Volkswirtschafts-Lexikon* (Wiesbaden: Gabler, 1990), pp. 814–43.

Streminger, G., *Der natürliche Lauf der Dinge: Essay zu Adam Smith und David Hume* (Marburg: Metropolis, 1995).

Sunstein, C. R., 'Beyond the Republican Revival', *The Yale Law Journal* 97 (1988), pp. 1539–90.

Suntum, U. van, 'Internationale Wettbewerbsfähigkeit einer Volkswirtschaft: Ein sinnvolles wirtschaftspolitisches Ziel?', *Zeitschrift für Wirtschafts- und Sozialwissenschaften* 106 (1986), pp. 495–507.

Taylor, Ch., 'Cross Purposes: The Liberal-Communitarian Debate', in N. L. Rosenblum (ed.), *Liberalism and the Moral Life* (Cambridge MA: Harvard University Press, 1989), pp. 159–82.

'What's Wrong with Negative Liberty?' in A. Ryan (ed.), *The Idea of Freedom: Essays in Honour of Isaiah Berlin* (Oxford: Oxford University Press, 1979), pp. 175–93; reprinted in Taylor, Ch., *Philosophy and the Human Sciences* (Cambridge: Cambridge University Press, 1985), pp. 211–29.

Teriet, B., 'Zeitsouveränität für eine flexible Lebensplanung', in J. Huber (ed.), *Anders arbeiten – anders wirtschaften* (Frankfurt: Fischer, 1979), pp. 150–7.

Thalheim, K. C., 'Zum Problem der Einheitlichkeit der Wirtschaftspolitik', in K. Muhs (ed.), *Festgabe für Georg Jahn* (Berlin: Duncker & Humblot, 1955), pp. 557–87.

Thielemann, U., 'A Brief Theory of the Market – Ethically Focused', *International Journal of Social Economics* 27/1 (2000), pp. 6–31.

'Die Differenz von Vertrags- und Diskursethik und die kategorialen Voraussetzungen ideologiekritischer Wirtschaftsethik', in J.-P. Harpes/

W. Kuhlmann (eds.), *Zur Relevanz der Diskursethik: Anwendungsprobleme der Diskursethik in Wirtschaft und Politik* (Münster: Lit, 1997), pp. 271–312.

'Compliance und Integrity – Zwei Seiten ethisch integrierter Unternehmenssteuerung', *Zeitschrift für Wirtschafts- und Unternehmensethik* 6/1 (2005), pp. 31–45.

'Integrative Wirtschafts- und Unternehmensethik als Reflexion des spannungsreichen Verhältnisses von Einkommensstreben und Moral', *Berichte des Instituts für Wirtschaftsethik* 67 (St Gallen: Institute for Economic and Business Ethics, 1994).

Das Prinzip Markt: Kritik der ökonomischen Tauschlogik (Berne *et al.*: Haupt, 1996).

Thurow, L., *The Future of Capitalism: How Today's Economic Forces Will Shape Tomorrow's World* (London: Brealey Publishing, 1996).

Tietzel, M., 'Moral und Wirtschaftstheorie', *Zeitschrift für Wirtschafts- und Sozialwissenschaften* 106 (1986), pp. 113–37.

Tuchfeldt, E., 'Soziale Marktsteuerung und Globalsteuerung', in Tuchfeldt (ed.), *Soziale Marktwirtschaft im Wandel* (Freiburg i.B.: Rombach, 1973), pp. 159–88.

Tugendhat, E., 'Gibt es eine moderne Moral?', *Zeitschrift für Philosophische Forschung* 50 (1996), pp. 323–38.

Vorlesungen über Ethik (Frankfurt: Suhrkamp, 1993).

Tuleja, T., *Beyond the Bottom Line* (New York: Facts on File, 1985).

Ulrich, H., 'Die Bedeutung der Management-Philosophie für die Unternehmensführung', in H. Ulrich (ed.), *Management-Philosophie für die Zukunft* (Berne *et al.*: Haupt, 1981), pp. 11–24.

Ulrich, P., 'Arbeitspolitik jenseits des neoliberalen Ökonomismus – das Kernstück einer lebensdienlichen Sozialpolitik', *Jahrbuch für christliche Sozialwissenschaften* 38 (1997), pp. 136–52.

'Brent Spar und der moral point of view: Reinterpretation eines unternehmensethischen Realfalls', *Die Unternehmung* 50/1 (1996), pp. 27–46.

'Business in the Nineties: Facing Public Interest', in Ulrich/Sarasin (eds.), *Facing Public Interest*, pp. 1–8.

'Der kritische Adam Smith – im Spannungsfeld zwischen sittlichem Gefühl und ethischer Vernunft', in Meyer-Faje/Ulrich (eds.), *Der andere Adam Smith*, pp. 145–90.

'Der spezielle Blick der allgemeinen BWL für die ökonomischen Dinge der Unternehmensführung', in W. Kirsch/A. Picot (eds.), *Die Betriebswirtschaftslehre im Spannungsfeld zwischen Generalisierung und Spezialisierung. Edmund Heinen zum 70. Geburtstag* (Wiesbaden: Gabler, 1989), pp. 137–54.

'Ethics and Economics', in L. Zsolnai (ed.), *Ethics in the Economy: Handbook of Business Ethics*, (Berne/Oxford: Peter Lang, 2002, 2nd edn 2003), pp. 9–37.

'Integrative Economic Ethics – Towards a Conception of Socio-Economic Rationality', in P. Koslowski (ed.), *Contemporary Economic Ethics and Business Ethics* (Berlin/Heidelberg/New York: Springer, 2000), pp. 37–54.

'Integrative Wirtschafts- und Unternehmensethik – ein Rahmenkonzept', in Forum für Philosophie Bad Homburg (ed.), *Markt und Moral*, pp. 75–107.

'John Stuart Mills emanzipatorischer Liberalismus', in P. Ulrich/M. Assländer (eds.), *John Stuart Mill: Der vergessene politische Ökonom und Philosoph* (Berne *et al.*: Haupt, 2006), pp. 253–82.

'Konsensus-Management: Die zweite Dimension rationaler Unternehmensführung', *Betriebswirtschaftliche Forschung und Praxis* 35 (1983), pp. 70–84.

'Republikanischer Liberalismus und Corporate Citizenship: Von der ökonomistischen Gemeinwohlfiktion zur republikanisch-ethischen Selbstbindung wirtschaftlicher Akteure', in H. Münkler/H. Bluhm (eds.), *Gemeinwohl und Gemeinsinn, Bd. IV: Zwischen Normativität und Faktizität* (Berlin: Akademie Verlag, 2002), pp. 273–91.

'Schwierigkeiten mit der unternehmensethischen Herausforderung', *Zeitschrift für betriebswirtschaftliche Forschung* 43 (1991), pp. 529–36.

'"Symbolisches Management": Ethisch-kritische Anmerkungen zur gegenwärtigen Diskussion über Unternehmenskultur', in Ch. Lattmann (ed.), *Die Unternehmenskultur* (Heidelberg: Physica, 1990), pp. 277–302.

'Towards an Ethically-Based Conception of Socio-Economic Rationality', *Praxiology: The International Annual of Practical Philosophy and Methodology, vol. V: Human Action in Business*, ed. W. Gasparski/L. V. Ryan (New Brunswick, N.J./London: Transaction, 1996), pp. 21–49.

'Unternehmensethik – diesseits oder jenseits der betriebswirtschaftlichen Vernunft?', in Ch. Lattmann (ed.), *Ethik und Unternehmensführung* (Heidelberg: Physica, 1988), pp. 96–116.

'Unternehmensethik – Führungsinstrument oder Grundlagenreflexion?', in Steinmann/Löhr (eds.), *Unternehmensethik*, pp. 189–210.

'Unternehmensethik und "Gewinnprinzip". Versuch der Klärung eines unerledigten wirtschaftsethischen Grundproblems', in H. G. Nutzinger (ed.), *Wirtschaftsethische Perspektiven III* (Berlin: Duncker & Humblot, 1996), pp. 137–71.

'Unternehmerethos', in Enderle *et al.* (eds.), *Lexikon der Wirtschaftsethik*, col. 1165–76.

'Wirtschaftsethik als Wirtschaftswissenschaft: Standortbestimmungen im Verhältnis von Ethik und Ökonomie', *Berichte des Instituts für Wirtschaftsethik* 23 (St Gallen: Institute for Economic and Business Ethics, 1988).

'Wirtschaftsethik auf der Suche nach der verlorenen ökonomischen Vernunft', in Ulrich (ed.), *Auf der Suche*, pp. 179–226.

'Zur Ethik der Kooperation in Organisationen', in R. Wunderer (ed.), *Kooperation: Gestaltungsprinzipien und Steuerung der Zusammenarbeit zwischen Organisationseinheiten* (Stuttgart: Schäffer-Poeschel, 1991), pp. 69–89.

'Zwei Ebenen unternehmerischer Verantwortung', *Neue Zürcher Zeitung*, 232, 6 October 1993, p. 39.

Die Grossunternehmung als quasi-öffentliche Institution: Eine politische Theorie der Unternehmung (Stuttgart: Poeschel, 1977).

Transformation der ökonomischen Vernunft: Fortschrittsperspektiven der modernen Industriegesellschaft, 3rd rev. edn (Berne *et al.*: Haupt, 1993; 1st edn 1986).

Ulrich, P. (ed.), *Auf der Suche nach einer modernen Wirtschaftsethik* (Berne *et al.*: Haupt, 1990).

Ulrich, P./Lunau, Y., '"Ethikmassnahmen" in schweizerischen und deutschen Unternehmen: Konzeptionelle Überlegungen und empirische Befunde', *Die Unternehmung* 51 (1997), pp. 49–65.

Ulrich, P./Lunau, Y./Weber, Th., 'Ethikmassnahmen in der Unternehmenspraxis', in Ulrich/Wieland (eds.), *Unternehmensethik in der Praxis*, pp. 121–94.

Ulrich, P./Sarasin, Ch. (eds.), *Facing Public Interest: The Ethical Challenge to Business Policy and Corporate Communications* (Dordrecht/Boston/London: Kluwer, 1995).

Ulrich, P./Thielemann, U., 'How Do Managers Think about Market Economies and Morality? Empirical Enquiries into Business-ethical Thinking Patterns,' *Journal of Business Ethics* 12 (1993), pp. 879–98; reprinted in an abridged version in Gibson (ed.), *Business Ethics*, pp. 52–60.

Ethik und Erfolg: Unternehmensethische Denkmuster von Führungskräften – eine empirische Studie (Berne *et al.*: Haupt, 1992).

Ulrich, P./Wieland, J. (eds.), *Unternehmensethik in der Praxis: Impulse aus den USA, Deutschland und der Schweiz* (Berne *et al.*: Haupt, 1998, 2nd edn 1999).

United Nations Development Programme (ed.), *Human Development Report* (New York/Oxford: Oxford University Press, different years).

Vaihinger, H., *Die* Philosophie *des 'als ob'*, 8th edn (Leipzig: Meiner, 1922), Engl. *The Philosophy of As If* (London: Routledge, 2000).

van der Veen, R. J., 'Real Freedom versus Reciprocity: Competing Views on the Justice of Unconditional Basic Income', *Political Studies* (1998), pp. 140–63.

Van Parijs, Ph., 'Reciprocity and the Justification of an Unconditional Basic Income. Reply to Stuart White', *Political Studies* (1997), pp. 327–30.

Real Freedom for All: What (if anything) can justify capitalism? (Oxford: Clarendon, 1995).

Vanberg, V., *Liberaler Evolutionismus oder vertragstheoretischer Konstitutionalismus?* (Tübingen: Mohr Siebeck, 1981).

Velasquez, M. G., *Business Ethics* (Englewood Cliffs NJ: Prentice Hall, 1982).

Ver Eecke, W., 'The Concept of a "Merit Good": The Ethical Dimension in Economic Theory and the History of Economic Thought or the Transformation of Economics into Socio-Economics', *Journal of Socio-Economics* 27/1 (1998), pp. 133–53.

Vogt, W., 'Zur Kritik der herrschenden Wirtschaftstheorie', in Vogt (ed.), *Seminar: Politische Ökonomie* (Frankfurt: Suhrkamp, 1973), pp. 108–205.

Volkart, R., 'Langfristige Shareholder-Orientierung', *Neue Zürcher Zeitung*, 154, 5 July 1996, p. 23.

Wagner, A., 'Zweiter Arbeitsmarkt mit neuem Anspruch?', in H. Seifert (ed.), *Reform der Arbeitsmarktpolitik – Herausforderung für Politik und Wirtschaft* (Cologne: Bund-Verlag, 1995), pp. 206–40.

Wagner, A./Weinkopf, C., 'Zweiter Arbeitsmarkt', *Die Neue Gesellschaft/ Frankfurter Hefte* 41 (1994), pp. 606–11.

Walras, L., *Éléments d'économie politique pure, ou théorie de la richesse sociale* (1874); Engl. transl.: *Elements of Pure Economics, or The Theory of Social Wealth* (Cambridge MA: Harvard University Press, 1954).

Walzer, M., 'The Civil Society Argument: A Path to Social Reconstruction', *Dissent* 38 (1991), pp. 293–304.

Spheres of Justice: A Defense of Pluralism and Equality (New York: Basic Books, 1983).

Waters, J. A., 'Catch 20.5: Corporate Morality as an Organizational Phenomenon', *Organizational Dynamics* (1978), pp. 3–19.

Waxenberger, B./Spence, L., 'Reinterpretation of a Metaphor: from Stakes to Claims', *Strategic Change* 12 (2003), pp. 239–49.

Weber, M., 'Die Wirtschaft der Weltreligionen', in Weber, *Gesammelte Aufsätze zur Religionssoziologie*, vol. I, 9th edn (Tübingen: Mohr Siebeck, 1988).

'"Objectivity" in Social Science and Social Policy', in *The Methodology of the Social Sciences: Max Weber*, transl. and ed. E. A. Shils and H. A. Finch (New York: Free Press, 1949), pp. 49–122.

'Politics as a Vocation', in *From Max Weber, Essays in Sociology*, pp. 77–128.

'Science as a Vocation', in *From Max Weber, Essays in Sociology*, pp. 129–56.

'The Evolution of the Capitalistic Spirit', in *General Economic History: Max Weber*, ed. I. J. Cohen, transl. F. H. Knight (New Brunswick/London: Transaction, 1981), pp. 352–69.

Economy and Society: An Outline of Interpretative Sociology, 2 vols., ed. G. Roth/C. Wittich (Berkeley: University of California Press, 1978).

From Max Weber: Essays in Sociology, ed. by H. H. Gerth/C. Wright Mills (London: Routledge, 1991; 1st edn 1948).

The Protestant Ethic and the Spirit of Capitalism, transl. T. Parsons (London: Unwin Hyman, 1930).

Weeks, J. F./Dore, E. W., 'Basic Needs: Journey of a Concept', in M. E: Crahan (ed.), *Human Rights and Basic Needs in the Americas* (Washington D.C.: Georgetown University Press, 1982), pp. 13–149.

Weisser, G., 'Die Überwindung des Ökonomismus in der Wirtschaftswissenschaft', in Weisser, *Beiträge zur Gesellschaftspolitik* (Göttingen: Schwartz, 1978; 1st edn 1954), pp. 573–601.

'Für oder gegen Marktwirtschaft – eine falsche Frage', reprinted in Weisser, *Beiträge zur Gesellschaftspolitik* (Göttingen: Schwartz, 1978), pp. 654–72.

'Wirtschaft', in W. Ziegenfuss (ed.), *Handbuch der Soziologie* (Stuttgart: Enke, 1956), pp. 970–1098, reprinted as a separate publication (Göttingen: Schwartz, 1989).

Wirtschaftspolitik als Wissenschaft: Erkenntniskritische Grundfragen der praktischen Nationalökonomie (Stuttgart: Kohlhammer, 1934).

Weizsäcker, C. C. von, 'Notes on Endogenous Change of Tastes', *Journal of Economic Theory* 3 (1971), pp. 345–72.

Werhane, P., *Persons, Rights and Corporations* (Englewood Cliffs NJ: Prentice Hall, 1985).

Wettstein, F./Waddock, S., 'Voluntary or Mandatory: That is (Not) the Question. Linking Corporate Citizenship to Human Rights Obligations for Business', *Zeitschrift für Wirtschafts- und Unternehmensethik* 6/3 (2005), pp. 304–20.

White, S., 'Liberal Equality, Exploitation, and the Case for an Unconditional Basic Income', *Political Studies* (1997), pp. 312–26.

'The Citizen's Stake and Paternalism', *Politics and Society* 32 (2004), pp. 61–78.

The Civic Minimum: On the Rights and Obligations of Economic Citizenship (New York/Oxford: Oxford University Press, 2003).

Wieland, J., 'Die Ethik der Wirtschaft als Problem lokaler und konstitutioneller Gerechtigkeit', in Wieland (ed.), *Wirtschaftsethik und Theorie der Gesellschaft*, pp. 7–31.

'Warum Unternehmensethik?', in Forum für Philosophie Bad Homburg (ed.), *Markt und Moral*, pp. 215–39.

Ökonomische Organisation, Allokation und Status (Tübingen: Mohr Siebeck, 1996).

Wieland, J. (ed.), *Wirtschaftsethik und Theorie der Gesellschaft* (Frankfurt: Suhrkamp, 1993).

Wimmer, R., *Universalisierung in der Ethik* (Frankfurt: Suhrkamp, 1980).

Wingert, L., *Gemeinsinn und Moral. Grundzüge einer intersubjektivistischen Moralkonzeption* (Frankfurt: Suhrkamp, 1993).

World Trade Organization, *Singapore Ministerial Declaration* (Geneva: WTO, 1996).

Wünsch, G., 'Wirtschaftsethik', in H. Gunkel, (ed.), *Religion in Geschichte und Gegenwart*, 2nd edn, vol. VI (Tübingen: Mohr Siebeck, 1932), col. 1964–1971; reprinted in G. Brakelmann/T. Jähnichen (eds), *Die protestantischen Wurzel der sozialen Markwirtschaft: Ein Quellenband* (Gütersloh: Gütersloher Verlagshaus, 1994), pp. 275–83.

Wünsche, H. F., 'Die immanente Sozialorientierung in Adam Smiths Ordnungsdenken – ein Paradigma für die Soziale Marktwirtschaft', in Meyer-Faje/Ulrich (eds.), *Der andere Adam Smith*, pp. 249–74.

'Verlorene Massstäbe in der Ordnungspolitik', *Hamburger Jahrbuch für Wirtschafts- und Gesellschaftspolitik* 35 (1990), pp. 53–74.

Yunus, M., *Banker to the Poor: Micro-Lending and the Battle against World Poverty* (New York: Public Affairs, 1999).

Zadek, S., 'The Path to Corporate Responsibility', *Harvard Business Review* 82 (2004), 12, pp. 125–32.

The Civil Corporation: The New Economy of Corporate Citizenship (London: Earthscan, 2001).

Zajitschek, S., *Corporate Ethics Relations: Orientierungsmuster für die legitime Gestaltung unternehmensexterner Beziehungen* (Berne *et al.*: Haupt, 1997).

Zerfass, A./Scherer, A. G., 'Unternehmensführung und Öffentlichkeitsarbeit: Überlegungen zur wissenschaftstheoretischen Grundlegung der Public-Relations-Forschung', *Die Betriebswirtschaft* 55 (1995), pp. 493–512.

Zinn, K. G., *Soziale Marktwirtschaft: Idee, Entwicklung und Politik der bundesdeutschen Wirtschaftsordnung* (Mannheim: Bibliographisches Institut, 1992).

Index of subjects

abundance of goods/of life 196–207, 212, 410
acceptance 50–1, 70, 173, 175, 179, 180, 184, 198, 289, 387, 400, 425, 427
accountability 140–1, 291, 299, 303, 386, 408, 429, 433, 439, 442
acquisition 119, 136, 201, 205, 213, 241
action 13–25, 39, 53–5, 57–60, 71–2, 115–16, 169–70, 216–21, 381–5, 420, 422–3, 437–42
  communicative 69, 105–7, 288–90, 303, 428
  economic 105–7, 135–44, 303–4, 312
  freedom of 14, 156, 189
  strategic 45–7, 67–8
altruism 70, 294–5, 420
arenas or forums for civic debate 77, 298, 302, 350
argumentation 4, 16, 41, 58–9, 76–8, 104, 108, 131, 136, 230, 296–7, 350, 428–30, 437, 440, 442
  factual 65
  process of 63–5, 76, 290, 293–4
  rational 64, 67
  unconstrained 65, 69, 77
as-if 135, 166, 169–71, 180–1, 292, 396–7
asymmetry of life chances / opportunities 210–11, 231, 239, 245
autonomy 4, 14–15, 24, 39, 47, 51, 54–6, 198–9, 226, 229, 241, 243, 282, 440

balance of interests 68, 70, 296
basic income (see income, unconditional basic)
basic needs approach 246–7
bill of rights 221, 433–4, 441
branch agreements 415–17
business ethics (see economic ethics/ business ethics; corporate ethics)
business model 408, 412
business principles 441
business strategy 403, 408–9, 412–14, 441

capabilities (approach)/capability 247–52, 254, 267
capital 132, 133–4, 253, 258, 282, 306, 312–14, 328, 360–3, 380, 390, 392–6, 418
capital market 132, 312–14, 362–3, 393
capitalism 117–19, 123, 128, 157, 158, 163, 209, 214, 353
categorical imperative 52–7, 58
citizen 1–2, 76–8, 179–82, 225–32
  economic xii, 239–64, 302–6
  institution(al)/organizational 306–10, 436–9, 441
  property-owning (bourgeois) 119, 154, 172, 274, 282
citizenship / civic rights (see rights)
citizenship status 240–4
civic capital / stakeholding 258–9
civic duties 225, 257, 286–7
civic humanism 277–8, 281, 283
civil associations 242
civil society 242–5, 252, 275, 287, 291, 317, 423
claims 62–78
  legitimate 14, 71–2, 141, 220–8, 304, 420, 422
  moral 20, 25, 34–42, 65, 143, 269
  validity 4, 65–9, 84, 99, 140–2, 169, 386
common good / public good 96, 113, 148–9, 153, 155, 157, 173–5, 178, 183, 232, 287, 296, 305, 307, 309, 311, 340, 369, 391
  fiction of the 112, 149, 158–66, 211, 361, 370, 388, 394, 426
communication 64–5, 71–8, 353–5

communistic fiction (of market liberalism) 164, 173
communitarianism 239, 275–6, 278, 281, 283–4, 287
community 198–9, 223–6, 280–84
  ideal communicative 65, 75–7
  moral 17–24, 35–9
  social 16–17
competition 97, 123–6, 147–8, 174, 301–2, 320–1, 331–41, 359
  constraints of 122, 130, 137, 140, 142, 212, 386, 417
  effective 326, 328–31
  global / locational 130, 158, 195, 212, 241, 267, 325–6, 360–71
  limitation of 144–6, 320, 415
  partiality of 128, 209–12
  self-assertion in 121–2, 131, 143–4, 214, 414
competition of cultures 207–12
competition of institutional frameworks 125, 318, 325–7, 330, 362–6, 370, 375
competition policy 320–1, 326, 329–30, 333–5, 364–5, 373
competitiveness 122, 125, 131–2, 190, 208, 219, 327, 329, 348, 360, 368–70
compliance 306, 440, 442
conception(s) of the good 15, 22, 24, 57, 190, 207, 229–31, 238–9, 245, 283, 286–7
conditio humana 13, 16–17, 32, 55, 189, 246
conscience 16, 20–1, 26–7, 49, 71, 92, 157, 222, 308, 418
consensus 65, 67, 69, 71, 85, 174–5, 229–31, 297–9, 345, 347–8, 359, 363
constitution 41, 78, 230, 332
  corporate 433–4, 441
  republican 284–7, 291
constraints (see also competition, constraints of) 197, 241, 250, 385–7, 412–14
  mental 115–16, 133, 383
consumption 197–8, 201–2, 205, 310–12
  compensatory 204
  defensive 204
contract theory 41, 167–8, 176–83, 224, 231, 234, 344–6
corporate citizen(ship) 414–18, 441–2
corporate ethics 376–9, 398
  charitable 402–4
  corrective 404–8
  instrumentalist 398–402
  integrative 408–18
corporate policy 419–23, 428–31
  deliberative 418–36
corporate social responsibility (CSR) 404
corporation 271, 363, 375–442
corruption 275, 304–6

deliberation (see politics, deliberative; democracy, deliberative; public, deliberative)
democracy 182–3, 229–31, 242, 343–9
  deliberative 267, 295–304
  economic theory of 291–4
  property-owning 235, 258
development policy 248–9, 275, 358, 367, 411
dialogue 71, 288, 418–33
difference principle 232–5
discourse 62–3, 141–4
  application 82–4
  corporate ethical 420–3
  fictive 74–8
  ideal 65–6
  legitimation 74, 427
  practical 66, 73, 84, 223–4
  public 74–8, 290
discourse ethics 62–78, 82–8, 106–7, 288–90
discrimination 29, 218, 224, 226, 435
disinterest, mutual 170, 175, 177, 184
disposal 248–9, 353
dissent, consensus-based regulation of 298–9
distribution 106, 162–6, 175, 181, 193–4, 219, 232–3, 238, 267, 336, 347, 419, 438

ecology 158, 164, 203, 226, 300, 310, 335, 348, 357, 359–60, 366–9, 373–4, 411, 415, 419, 430, 438
economic citizenship (see citizen, economic; rights, economic citizenship; ethics, economic citizen's)
economic determinism 126–39, 170, 387–9, 407
economic ethics / business ethics ix, xii, 1–3, 79–80, 107, 110
  corrective 80–2, 86–9
  functionalist 95–100
  integrative 3–5, 100–10
  topology of 269–71

economic growth 162–4, 194, 201, 203, 248–9, 359–60
economic optimum 162–6
economic progress 194–5, 206
economic reductionism 148–50, 174–84
economics
autonomous 81, 104
constitutional 179–83, 328, 344–7
institutional 328, 341–2
moral 91–5
neoclassical 159–67
normative 89–100
paretian 173–6
pure 90–1, 101–5, 135–6, 166–84
economism 5–7, 111–14, 148–9, 169–79, 330–4, 344–9, 364, 398
circularity of 89, 104, 111, 190, 329, 340, 349, 365
critique of 101–10, 114, 379
methodological 98–9, 135–6
political 182–3, 241
economy
domestic 363–4, 368–70
life-serving 1–2, 319, 334, 338, 370, 409–14
multi-layered 372
economy of abundance 196–202, 205–8, 250
economy of poverty 206, 210, 212
economy of vital necessities 191–4
effects
external 178–9, 203, 355, 367, 406, 419
market internal 175–6, 356–8, 368–70
efficiency 89–90, 106–7, 345–9
legitimacy and 105–7, 174–8, 236, 320, 352, 433
market 326, 335–8
Pareto- 173–84, 232, 346
emancipation (from competition) 196, 207–15, 250–1, 263
empathy / sympathy 18, 34, 49–50, 153, 310
employment 195, 202–4, 213, 257, 261–6
empowerment 195, 243, 247–9, 267, 302, 439
enlightenment 4, 29–30, 127, 167, 288–91
entitlement 224–6, 243–4, 247–52, 423
entrepreneurship 120, 209, 376, 393, 398
equality 167–8, 228–45
moral 34–7, 224–6, 235
equality of opportunity 167, 226–45, 435
equilibrium theory 164–6, 176–80, 335–6, 355–6
ethics 16–17, 25–31, 51–2, 66–7
applied 79–82, 86, 102, 407
deontological 57–63, 70–1, 96, 174, 187, 319, 432
duty 16, 54, 57–8, 281
economic citizen's xii, 8, 273–6, 299–300
individual 8, 269–71, 283, 285–6, 382
management 377, 434
political 78, 108, 182, 223, 245, 350
primacy of 47, 105–6, 317, 350, 401
rational 4–7, 30, 37–9, 43–4, 85, 101, 162, 190, 223, 245, 283, 378
regulatory / institutional xii, 7–9, 74, 269–70, 286, 302, 315–19, 349–52, 377–80, 410, 433
responsibility 58–9, 71–5
teleological 57–8, 60–3, 70, 186, 319
universally valid (minimal) 30–41, 304
virtue 22, 269–71, 283, 302
ethics codex or code of ethics 306, 308, 405, 441
ethics programme (in a corporation) 439–42
ethos 21–5, 120, 190
Calvinistic 116–20
communicative 63, 67
entrepreneurial 153, 382–5, 401–2
republican 283, 397
exchange of advantages 40, 234, 239, 287, 346, 351, 353, 426

fact of pluralism 229, 239, 277
free riding (moral) 17, 61, 217–18, 284, 301–2, 416–17, 441
freedom 13–14, 227–8, 282–3
arbitrary 180, 228, 241
economic 116, 229, 241, 244, 340
real (vs. formal) 194, 228–9, 237, 239, 243, 245, 247–8, 256, 258, 262, 266
greatest possible 228, 237, 243, 258, 260, 282, 328
individual / personal 14, 96–7, 123, 180–1, 225, 227
positive vs. negative 228, 245, 282–3
republican 282–3, 286–7, 290
fundamentalism 11, 27–30, 275, 287, 323

generalization principle (see also universalization) 35–7, 43, 53, 57–62
global governance 371–3
globalization 130, 250, 359–75
Golden Rule 44–8
good life 15, 22–6, 189–91, 214, 230, 277
goods 22, 106, 185
  consumer 197, 201, 202, 204
  material 197–200, 235
  merit 358
  primary 234–7
  public 358

happiness xiii, 22–3, 51, 57–8, 78, 151, 157, 161, 190, 200–1, 205, 311
hedonism 39, 201
  ethical vs. psychological 160–1, 169, 172
  paradox of 201–2
homo oeconomicus 88, 113, 135, 161, 170–2, 182, 274, 287, 292, 295, 300
human capital 265
human dignity xiii, 33, 35, 47, 55, 249, 331, 332

identity 33, 54, 56, 143, 170, 221, 252, 277, 363, 383
  cultural 23–4, 226
  needs of 246
  personal vs. social 16, 18, 23–4, 34, 35, 198–9, 201, 208, 275, 279–81
ideology
  critique of 4, 169, 318
  economistic 112, 183
  growth 163
image of man 55, 152, 169–73, 180, 277
impartial spectator 48–52, 65, 150, 198
incentive 94, 95, 97, 145, 171, 238, 256–7, 269, 301, 314, 316, 319, 331, 335, 348–9, 355–7, 374, 415, 437
  false 305, 309, 439
  structural 270, 441
income 123, 135, 140, 143, 202, 233–4, 240, 259–60, 295, 312, 336, 347, 356, 359, 369, 415, 420, 437, 442
  acquisition of 121, 195, 337
  distribution of 219, 238, 340, 359
  unconditional basic 253–9, 261–4, 352
individualism 173, 274–5, 280
  methodological 70, 168, 173, 175–7, 180, 183, 280, 292, 346
  normative 99–100, 169–5, 177, 180–1, 241, 346
  possessive 172, 180, 206, 208, 296, 310, 329
industrialization 158
inequality 157–8, 219–40
inherent necessities (see necessities, inherent)
inheritance 240, 254, 258
institutional 'backing' 302, 303, 308, 311
integrity 15, 33–4, 303, 437, 440
  argumentational 67, 74–5, 439
  business 8, 409–10, 417, 423, 432, 439
  culture of 379, 438–9, 442
  civic and political 283
International Labour Organization (ILO) 366
interpersonal relations 18, 20, 42
  normative logic of 2, 37–9, 43, 78, 113, 220, 401
investment 195, 204–5, 252, 258–9, 312–14, 360–2, 393, 396, 399, 405, 438
invisible hand 114, 126, 127, 148, 149, 150, 153–4, 157, 319, 323, 344, 364, 401, 403

justice 39, 41, 60, 107, 152, 154–5, 162–4, 167, 175, 178, 181–2, 184, 188, 193, 216–21, 229–40, 260, 266, 289, 294, 305, 324, 329, 361, 366, 388, 420
  corrective 219
  global 366
  political 217, 229
  primacy of 167, 231
  principles of 217, 232–4, 237, 258, 284, 287
  sense of 62, 152, 217, 231, 273, 286
  social 219, 232, 337, 340

labour 122, 124, 159, 193, 203–4, 216, 249, 251, 257, 262, 305–6, 315, 337, 360–1, 366–7, 380, 415
labour market 1, 56, 121, 124, 210, 219, 250, 255, 257, 259, 261–6, 327
law 20, 41, 53–5, 218
  international 217, 221
  natural 115, 222–3, 237, 253, 276, 277, 322–4, 344, 355, 357, 364
  positive 218, 222, 223
  rational 223
leadership 309, 343
legality 218, 313, 353
legitimacy 20, 21, 59, 70–1, 74, 84, 106, 216–20, 267–8, 289–90, 297–8, 301, 303–4, 408–9, 420–32

legitimate business activity 379–98
legitimation 78, 185–8, 229–30, 290–1, 299, 347, 419–20, 428
  contractualistic 178–80, 296, 429
  procedural 296, 297
  rational 296
liberalism 8, 154, 159, 168, 228–43, 273–88
  economic 8, 121–2, 154, 157, 228–40, 278–80
  neo- 278, 283, 326–30
  ordo- xiii, 132, 330–41
  paleo- 322–6
  political 8, 228–40, 278–80
  republican 8, 278–88
life form/plan/project/script 23, 26, 128, 190, 201, 208–15, 228, 230, 239, 247, 252, 267
  ascetic 201
  dual 251, 263
  emancipatory 207–12
  entrepreneurial (acquisitive) 146, 207–10, 257, 366
  hedonistic 201–2
  industrial 204–5
  undivided (of the economic citizen) 303
lifeworld 17, 18, 27, 35, 81, 85, 108, 110, 116, 120–1, 123, 128–30, 134, 186, 190–1, 196, 203, 212, 214, 251, 269, 315, 317, 319, 321, 350, 368

management
  consensus 431
  normative 431
management systems 437, 441–2
market (see also market economy; competition)
  boundary of the 332, 346, 357
  deregulation of the 163, 330, 347, 360, 372
  efficiency function of the 125, 336
  framework of the 254, 321, 349, 351, 353, 388, 409, 417
  logic of the 2–3, 102–5, 125, 133–9, 182–4, 316–17, 329, 345–6, 350
  legitimation of the 163, 179, 347
  metaphysics of the 149–50, 154
  partiality of the 133, 151, 159, 355
  primacy of the 330, 338
market conformity 316, 335–9, 341, 342, 344
market economy
  civilized ix, 7, 9, 243
  conditions of the 87, 98, 109, 113, 134
  free 124, 127, 151, 156, 318, 329, 361
  life-serving 319, 417
  social 330, 339–41, 343
  systemic character of the 126
market economy as a coercive context 120–32
market failure 86–9
market mechanism 128, 131, 149, 151, 325, 350
market regulations 117, 121, 357
market restrictions 146, 347, 358
maximization of personal benefit 99, 136, 143, 170, 172, 304
meaning of economic activity
  advanced 196–207
  elementary 191–5
means of life 192–3
moral consciousness 18–19, 37–42
moral disposition 13–19
moral psychology 37, 52
moral sentiments 49–50, 153
moral subject (see also person) 14, 41
morality 7–8, 13–25, 49–52, 75–8, 91–9, 101–3, 108–10, 280, 285, 287, 289, 294, 341–59, 383, 430
morality of the market 97–9, 147–84
motives 50–1, 91–4
  rational 15, 54, 292
  moral 91–4, 148, 294
  economic 92, 116, 120

natural state vs. cultural/legal state 276–7, 365
necessities of life 191–4, 196, 202, 203, 205, 212, 226, 255
necessities, inherent 4, 7, 73, 113, 115, 116, 125, 130–1, 135–6, 144, 145, 148, 149, 153, 187, 270, 337–8, 342, 378, 385–7, 408–9
  partiality of 132–4
  politics for the limitation of 145
  reasonable 139–42
  room for manoeuvre and 137–9
need satisfaction 160, 192, 200–3, 205, 234–5, 248, 310–11
needs 18, 39, 48, 90, 160–1, 173, 192–3, 196, 200–2, 204–5, 310, 333, 420, 441
  basic/elementary/existential 117, 192, 196, 199, 204, 246–7
  critique of 200–2, 207
negative income tax 240, 259–60
neutrality (of the political order) 230–1, 239, 277

norms 19, 20, 24, 40–2, 83, 85, 116, 129, 145, 217–18
admission 358
apportionment 355–7
boundary 357–8, 373
calculation 355–7, 374
pricing 356

order xii, 315
natural 127, 150, 344
political 78, 229–31, 338–40, 345, 370
original position 167, 168, 224, 231, 234, 273–4

Pareto criterion 169, 173–7, 180, 233–4
participation 199, 225–6, 242, 251–2, 261–3, 345, 436, 441
political 225–6, 282
rights of 76, 223, 225, 227, 328, 433
participation in the economic process 78, 251, 353
person 13–14, 18, 22–6, 34–6
autonomous 47, 54, 281
concept of the 279–82
mature 4, 423
moral (see also moral subject) 139, 152, 217, 231, 244
personal advantage (see utility)
point of view
developmental lines of the moral 43–4
discourse-ethical interpretation of the 66, 85, 354, 429
economic 6, 111, 161, 164, 166, 179
moral 14, 36–7, 39, 41–2, 47, 49, 51, 56, 62–6, 84–5, 142, 148, 175, 265
post-conventional 30–2, 46
rational-ethical 37, 41, 48, 51, 54, 66, 78, 107, 110, 147, 219
utilitarian 60
political economy 2, 48, 79, 90, 116, 126, 150–8, 166, 167, 169, 324–5, 377, 396
political philosophy ix, 167, 274, 275–7
politics
corporate 419, 428–30
deliberative 76–8, 288, 341–59
democratic 182–3, 345–9
institutional xiii, 145–6, 315–16, 329–30, 340–1, 344–6, 379, 417
primacy of 128, 130, 179, 316, 325–6, 330, 334, 336–9, 345–6, 350–1, 370–1
regulatory xiii, 315, 317, 319, 320–1, 329–30, 341–3, 350–2, 375
republican 288
positivism/scientism 81, 159
poverty (see also economy of poverty) 193–5, 202, 212, 241, 250, 252, 266, 360
power 21, 39, 75, 125, 131, 142, 175–6, 180, 302, 327, 333–4, 356, 422–5
preferences 234–5, 293–7, 310–11
price (signals of the market) 56, 121–2, 165, 312, 335–6, 338, 348, 355–6
principle 53
ethical/moral 21, 25, 30–2, 36–7, 39, 43, 48, 51–2, 54, 59, 174–5, 216, 222, 224, 397
market 88–9, 99, 148, 155, 159, 163, 166, 178, 287, 329
power 21, 216, 222
profit / economic acquisition 8, 119–20, 376–409, 418–19, 433
utilitarian 57–8, 161–4, 169, 340
principles of justice 217, 224, 232–40, 284, 286–7
private interest 70, 95, 147–8, 172, 173, 228, 283–4, 287, 298
privatization 299, 327, 360
profit maximization 140, 155, 391, 395, 402–5, 418–19
profit orientation (see also principle, profit/economic acquisition) 376–7, 381–95
profit-making 120, 404
profit-spending 403–4
property (rights) 180–1, 235, 243, 248, 252–4, 282, 328, 352–5, 365–6, 419, 432
protectionism 367, 373
public 229–31, 290, 296–8, 429
critical 93, 288–92, 308, 375, 400, 429–30, 436
deliberative 107–9, 302, 317, 354, 423, 429
republican 287–8, 350
unlimited 76–8, 108, 223, 317
public constitution of the private sphere 298–300
public opinion 289, 297
public relations 400, 427–8
publicity 77, 289, 300, 430
purchasing power 194, 199, 202, 205, 358, 369
pursuit of profit 313, 376–7, 379–80, 390–1, 417
entrepreneurial 119, 154, 382, 385–7, 404–9
legitimate 378, 397–8

quality of life 1, 196–7, 202–3, 410

rationality 89–90, 161, 169, 280
  communicative 64, 66–7, 69, 78, 184
  critique of (pure) economic 101–5, 114
  economic 3, 79–81, 88–91, 95–101, 111–14, 119–20, 182–4
  ethical-practical 79–80, 101, 156
  functional/instrumental (technical) 67–8, 130, 187, 342
  socio-economic 101–10
  strategic 29, 67–9, 285, 425
  systems 2, 114, 127–8, 132, 187
rationalization 26–7, 128–30
  communicative 76, 353
  economic 2, 120, 130, 159, 200
  ethical 31, 39, 49
  social 128–9
  technical 76
reason 30, 50, 54–5, 115, 280
  critique of (pure) economic 104–5, 110
  economic 1–2, 9, 101, 352
  ethical 2, 3, 51, 280, 285
  good 15–16, 21, 26–7, 41, 55, 63–4, 82–3, 94, 141–2, 296, 303, 412
  practical 19, 29–30, 54, 64
  public use of 230–1, 267, 283, 287–91, 297–304, 317, 342, 350–2, 428
reasonableness/reasonable expectation 84, 139–44, 414, 416, 420, 430, 433, 439, 442
reciprocity 34–40
  affective 50–1
  argumentative 63–5, 71, 78
  ethical/moral 35–7, 43, 45–8, 113, 168
  ethos of 34, 45
  incomplete 71–2
  strategic 43, 45–7
  universalization of 34–7, 43, 55–6
recognition 34, 37, 47, 51, 55–6, 64–5, 105, 168, 174, 178, 198, 220, 235, 262–3
reflection 11, 37, 63, 74, 76
  abandonment of 4, 62, 84, 87–9, 99–101, 104, 109, 112, 115, 131, 134, 136, 138, 149, 377–8, 407, 409
  critical 3–5, 27, 87, 95, 100–1, 114, 134, 138–9, 170, 193, 234, 281, 315, 378–9, 384, 409, 413
  ethical 31, 109, 385, 389–90, 397, 407, 437, 439, 442
  self- 9, 19, 33–4, 50, 202, 208, 310, 408
regulative idea 35, 57, 65, 71, 74–8, 101, 105–7, 110, 139, 169, 175, 220, 251, 268, 288–9, 295, 297, 350, 379, 423, 427
regulatory framework xii, 318, 321–2, 326, 330, 349, 351, 359, 364
relativism 11, 25, 28, 42
republicanism 182, 273–83, 288, 295, 302, 304
respect
  mutual 34, 263
  self- 16, 34, 48, 50–1, 198, 233, 240, 252
  worthiness of 198
responsibility 71–5, 218, 269–70, 303, 307, 310, 313
  civic 72, 288, 307, 439
  co-/shared 72–5, 142, 267, 283, 288, 300, 349, 409–10, 414–15, 417, 441
  organized 309, 414, 437, 439, 441
  role 72, 306–7
reversibility of perspectives/role reversibility 34–5, 45, 48, 50, 53, 63, 115, 141
rights 223, 352–5, 373–4
  basic 221, 225, 247, 249, 252, 266, 267, 373, 434–5
  civic 222–7, 276
  communication 78, 353–4, 436
  economic citizenship xii, 213, 226, 239, 245–6, 254–5, 260, 265, 267, 352–4, 371, 434
  equality of 61, 78, 286
  human 220–6, 246–7, 252, 373
  inviolable 78, 291, 420, 441
  legal 218, 220, 222
  moral 21, 35, 83, 216–18, 220–7, 234–5, 247, 304, 434, 441
  personality 225–6, 235, 435
  social 225–8, 250, 265, 328
rights vs. goods 234–7
role-taking 33–6, 63
rule of law 218, 220, 244
rule utilitarianism 60–2, 97

scarcity 106, 112, 160, 161, 196, 202–5
self 24
  autonomous 281
  encumbered vs. unencumbered 280–2, 363
self-assertion (see also competition, self-assertion in) 72, 73, 87–8, 99, 298
  legitimate 70, 72, 87–8
self-commitment 14–15, 50–1, 70, 293–4, 306, 309, 375, 405, 415–17, 434, 441
self-criticism 51, 293
self-determination 14–15, 39, 55, 189, 197, 245, 281, 282

self-interest 127, 135, 171, 174, 280
  enlightened / well-understood 45–6, 401, 414
self-limitation 93, 142–4, 145, 207–8, 209–10, 306, 389, 405
service of life 186–7, 191–2, 207, 338, 351, 358, 370, 409, 412, 414–15
shareholder value 8, 132, 312, 360, 362, 392–5, 425–6
sites of morality 7–8, 67, 77–8, 101, 108–10, 152, 223, 269–71, 288–91, 388
social contract 41, 167, 179–82, 346, 354
social policy (see also welfare state) 194–5, 213, 339
society (see also civil society) 26–7, 40–1, 76, 98–100, 117, 128
  free and democratic 78, 270, 276, 317, 436
  liberal/free 131, 273, 276–7, 298, 333
  market 2, 99, 125, 182, 211, 282, 316, 329
  open vs. closed 70, 77–8, 117, 430
  well-ordered 167, 217–19, 228–32, 236–7, 241, 243, 266–7, 273, 287, 317, 355
solidarity 21, 24, 33, 59, 71, 96, 194, 244, 265, 270, 275, 284, 308, 314, 364, 422
stakeholder 379, 392, 393–4, 418–34, 441
standards xii, 27, 355
  ecological 325, 415
  labour 367
  minimal 366, 373
  production 374
  social 367–8
status-quo problem 174, 178–9, 426
stewardship 404, 414
structural dependence 241, 249, 250
subject status 32–4, 234
subsidiarity 242, 373, 415
subsistence (level) 117, 191–3, 199, 249
sustainability 164, 233, 256–7, 366
sympathy (see empathy)
system 126, 139–40
  conformity to the 132–4, 336
  economic 92–3, 108, 129, 187–8, 251, 316–17

trade 117, 158, 175, 211, 327, 361, 364, 366–7, 373, 374

unemployment 1, 158, 193, 204, 257, 259–60, 264–5, 327, 359, 360
United Nations Development Programme (UNDP) 249
universalism 28, 287
universalization 29–32, 35–7, 39, 43, 60, 62, 65, 83, 148, 175, 224
utilitarianism 57–8, 160–9, 183, 232, 293, 361, 394, 403, 426
utility 41, 45, 47, 60, 68, 112, 160–5

value/value creation 26, 29–30, 56, 62, 89, 92, 112, 120–2, 159, 178, 185–7, 189–90, 207, 216–17, 312–13, 366, 378, 397, 402, 409, 410–14, 419–20, 438, 441
veil of ignorance 167–8, 224, 231, 273
virtue 22–3, 26, 50, 57, 152, 217–18, 270, 307
  (economic) citizen/civic xii, xii, 232, 244, 270, 273–4, 276, 278, 283, 284–6, 288, 292, 295, 300–3, 305–6, 437
  political 274, 277, 284
  republican 8, 283–4, 299, 303, 324
vital policy xiii, 319–21, 328, 330–41, 347, 351–9, 363, 366–7, 368, 370–5, 417–18

welfare state 195, 241, 250, 359–60
welfare theory 164, 166, 168, 173–6, 232, 388
whistle-blowing 310, 436
will 15–16, 18, 23, 24, 37, 41, 51–5, 65, 67, 138–9, 214, 217, 299–300, 416
work (see also labour) 117–19, 124–5, 195, 199–205, 212–13, 252, 261–5
World Trade Organization (WTO) 365–8, 373

Index of names

Ackerman, B. 258
Adorno, Th. 4
Afheldt, H. 359, 371–4
Al-Ani, A. 439
Albert, H. 81, 90, 104, 112, 162, 165–6, 169, 176
Alstott, A. 258
Althof, W. 4, 28, 38
Anshen, M. 392
Anzenbacher, A. 20, 201
Apel, K.-O. 19, 27, 42, 47, 55, 62–7, 72–6, 82, 84–8, 95, 138, 141, 184, 273, 285, 286, 354, 428, 429, 432
Arendt, H. 200, 203, 277, 308
Aristotle 22, 90, 116, 190, 192, 199, 203, 277, 284
Arrow, K. 170
Assländer, M. 258
Aufderheide, D. 96
Avineri, S. 276

Bahro, R. 205–6
Baier, K. 31, 37, 45, 47, 55
Barber, B. 282, 299, 302
Barbier, H. D. 327
Baron, H. 277
Bastiat, F. 155–6, 395
Baumhart, R. C. 400
Baumstark, E. 185
Bausch, Th. 140
Beauchamp, T. C. 432
Beck, U. 303, 309, 414
Becker, G. S. 171
Becker, H. 400
Benhabib, S. 35–7, 39, 70, 268, 281, 295–7, 299, 300
Bentele, G. 427, 428
Bentham, J. 58, 160–2, 164, 169
Berlin, I. 282
Berthold, N. 368
Biervert, B. 113, 160, 169, 182, 310, 331
Biesecker, A. 350
Binswanger, H. C. 130
Bleicher, K. 430, 431
Blickle, G. 67, 439
Blome-Drees, F. 96, 98–9, 133, 137, 148, 155, 171, 173–4, 300, 317, 345, 346, 348–9, 378, 388–9, 389, 415
Bluhm, H. 417
Blum, R. 113, 321, 337–9
Boarman, P. M. 319, 323
Böhler, D. 27, 42, 73, 84, 86, 140
Böhm, F. xii, 330, 333–5, 344
Böhm-Bawerk, E. von 176
Bohnen, A. 164
Boltanski, L. 209
Bouillon, H. 318
Boulding, K. E. 176
Bowie, N. E. 102, 432
Brakelmann, G. 118
Brennan, G. 135, 144, 171–2, 174, 293
Brenner, S. N. 400
Brewing, J. 140
Brownlie, I. 221
Brühlmeier, D. 324
Brummer, J. J. 432
Brune, J. P. 86
Brunner, E. 186
Buchanan, J. M. 135, 144, 168, 170–2, 174, 177, 181, 238, 276, 294, 320, 328, 330, 345–6, 348
Bühner, A. 392
Bulmer, M. 243
Bürgin, A. 324
Burns, J. H. 58, 160
Büscher, M. 151, 325
Byrd, B. S. 225

Campbell, C. 201
Campbell, T. D. 50, 198
Carrithers, D. W. 153
Cassel, D. 345

Chan, A. 367
Chappell, T. 412
Chiapello, E. 209
Christmann, U. 67
Clapham, R. 315
Coase, R. 165
Cohen, I. J. 118
Cohen, J. 295
Cole, G. D. H. 256
Cook, Ph. J. 209
Cortina, A. 95, 223, 230, 288
Crahan, M. E. 246
Craig, G. A. 121
Cunliffe, J. 258
Curley, E. 21
Cyert, R. M. 421

Dagger, R. 278
Dahm, K. W. 208
Dahrendorf, R. 200, 206, 228, 242–4, 251, 266–7, 359, 363
Davies, K. 404
De George, R. T. 310, 373, 376, 415, 431
Deci, E. L. 198
Demmerling, Ch. 186, 237
Demsetz, H. 248
De-Shalit, A. 276
Dierkes, M. 438
Donaldson, Th. 374, 422, 432, 434
Donnelly, J. 226, 247
Dore, E. W. 246
Downs, A. 291–2
Duttweiler, G. 412
Dworkin, R. 222, 224, 228
Dyllick, Th. 418

Eigen, P. 306
Elster, J. 143, 293–4, 382
Enderle, G. 45, 46, 82, 104, 137–8, 198, 226, 245, 313
Engels, W. 260
Epikur 196
Erhard, L. 163, 340
Erreygers, G. 258
Etzioni, A. 275, 284, 382
Eucken, E. 315
Eucken, W. xii, 121, 317, 330–7, 341, 357
Evan, W. M. 433–4
Ewers, H.-J. 330
Ewing, D. 434

Ferguson, A. 127
Fetscher, I. 170, 180
Finch, H. A. 159
Fitzmaurice, M. 227
Forst, R. 281–2, 287, 295
Frank, R. H. 209
Frankena, W. 19, 57, 59
Frankfurt, H. 310
Frankl, V. E. 189, 214
Fraser, N. 296
Frederick, W. C. 404
Freeman, R. E. 102, 374, 378, 404, 412–13, 421, 424–34
Freire, P. 249
Frey, B. S. 171, 294–5, 345–7, 349
Friedman, M. 135, 259, 336, 383–5, 392
Fritzsche, D. J. 400
Fromm, E. 197, 208
Furubotn, E. G. 353

Gabriel, G. 186, 237
Gai, Dh. 192
Galbraith, J. K. 204
Galtung, J. 225, 246–7
Gasparski, W. 100
Gauthier, D. 170
Gehlen, A. 13, 15, 75
Gellermann, S. W. 437
Gentz, M. 147, 148
Geraets, Th.F. 67
Gerth, H. H. 27
Gibson, K. 46, 383, 432
Giddens, A. 361
Giersch, H. 149
Gilbert, D. R. 412–13
Gilligan, C. 39
Goldman, A. I. 238
Gomez, P. 425, 426
Goodpaster, K. E. 424
Goodwin-Gill, G. S. 221
Gorz, A. 197, 200, 208, 213, 261–3
Gouldner, A. W. 34
Granger, C. 367
Gray, J. 318
Gregor, M. J. 4, 77, 274
Greiss, F. 320
Groeben, N. 67
Gross, P. 197
Grunig, J. E. 427
Gunkel, H. 118
Günther, K. 83, 134
Gutenberg, E. 120, 135, 380–1, 395–7
Guyer, P. 115
Gygi, F. 244

Habermann, G. 154, 383–4, 402
Habermas, J. 18, 21–2, 29, 33–7, 62–71, 75–8, 82–4, 85, 129, 139, 141, 198, 206, 214, 222–3, 227, 234–5, 273, 288, 291–5, 297, 298–9, 303, 308–9, 429, 434
Hallay, H. 438
Hamel, G. 124
Hamlin, A. 295
Handbauer, G. 439
Handke, P. 131, 143
Harpes, J.-P. 289
Harsanyi, J. C. 289, 293
Hart, H. L. A. 58, 160
Hauser, H. 124, 209–10, 328, 365, 366
Hausman, D. M. 103
Hayek, F. A. von 127, 156, 179, 325–6, 336, 339–40, 343–4, 355
Held, D. 139, 294, 361, 371
Held, M. 113, 169, 182, 310, 331
Hensel, K. P. 315
Hentsch, B. 411
Herder-Dorneich, Ph. 315, 326
Herms, E. 105, 211
Hesse, H. 82, 100
Heuss, A. 13
Hines, C. 373
Hinkelammert, F. 249
Hinsch, W. 229, 231
Hinterhuber, H. H. 439
Hirsch, F. 203, 204, 233
Hirschman, A. O. 153, 311
Hobbes, Th. 21, 126, 167, 168, 170, 172, 177–80, 182, 184, 224, 273, 275–6, 278, 296, 327, 329, 344, 354
Hobsbawm, E. J. 158
Höffe, O. 26, 53, 55, 58, 59, 178
Hofmann, F. 399
Hofmann, W. 211
Höfner, K. 393
Holleis, W. 165
Hollstein, W. 195, 211
Holzhey, H. 253
Homann, K. 15, 61, 82, 91–100, 133–7, 144, 148, 155, 171, 173–4, 182, 184, 300, 317, 345, 346, 348–9, 378, 387–9, 415
Honneth, A. 65, 143
Hoppmann, E. 149, 329
Hosmer, L. T. 102
Hruschka, J. 225
Huber, J. 211, 213
Hunold, A. 344
Huszar, G. B. de 155

Illich, I. 195, 208

Jähnichen, T. 118
Janisch, M. 425, 426
Jantsch, E. 411
Jaspers, K. 24
Joas, H. 65
Joerden, J. C. 225
Jonas, H. 71

Kaiser, M. 428
Kaldor, M. 375
Kambartel, F. 24, 200, 262
Kant, I. 3–4, 11, 16, 19, 30, 32–3, 36–7, 43, 47–8, 50–60, 62, 64–7, 71, 77, 115, 167–8, 178, 219, 230, 267, 274, 278, 283–90, 295, 314, 349, 422, 430, 432
Katterle, S. 133, 134, 182, 336, 339, 340, 357
Kaufmann, F.-X. 324
Keil, G. 126
Kerber, W. 169, 172
Kersting, W. 7, 97, 100–1, 167, 168, 183, 267, 273
Kettner, M. 72, 73, 82, 87, 95, 145, 273, 285, 300
Keynes, J. M. 196, 205–6, 211
Kim, J. 238
Kirchgässner, G. 93, 96, 145, 294–5, 345, 346–7, 349
Kirsch, W. 396
Kittsteiner, H.-D. 324
Klaus, V. 318
Kleinewefers, H. 394
Kley, R. 180–1, 325
Kliemt, H. 15, 145
Knight, F. H. 118, 280
Knobloch, U. 192
Koch, C. 364
Kohlberg, L. xiii, 28, 35, 38–42, 46, 281
Kohler, G. 253
Koller, P. 225
Kosiol, E. 390
Koslowski, P. 86, 88–9, 94, 100, 150, 151, 353
Krugman, P. 370
Krüsselberg, H.-G. 104, 160, 166, 324, 331
Kuhlmann, W. 289, 293
Küng, H. 30
Künzli, A. 253

Lampert, H. 338
Lang, T. 373

Lattmann, Ch. 45, 87, 93
Leisinger, K. M. 310, 399
Leutwiler, F. 328
Lisowsky, A. 399
Livesey, S. M. 430
Locke, J. 167, 253, 276
Löhr, A. 82, 87, 137, 163, 283, 377–8, 385–8, 390–1, 406
Lomasky, L. 293
Lorenzen, P. 283, 398
Lowe, V. 227
Luhmann, N. 65, 127, 139–40, 142, 164
Lunau, Y. 438
Luther 151, 196

Ma, H. 370
Maak, Th. 306
Macpherson, C. B. 172
Maier-Rigaud, F. P. & M. 150
Maihofer, W. 285
Malik, F. 411
Manin, B. 228, 295–7, 299
Mann, G. 13
March, J. G. 421, 426
Margalit, A. 33
Marshall, Th. M. 225, 243, 255
Marx, K. 113, 124, 128, 159, 200, 396
Mastronardi, Ph. 333
Matthew 45, 48
Mauss, M. 34
Maynor, J. W. 283
McMurrin, S. M. 230
McPherson, M. S. 103
Mead, G. H. 33, 35, 48, 63
Medick, H. 253
Mendonça, W. P. 237
Meran, J. 119
Mewaldt, J. 196
Meyer, F. W. 320
Meyer, Th. 29
Meyer-Faje, A. 48, 116, 151, 324, 340
Michelman, F. I. 278, 283, 292
Miksch, L. 332, 364
Milberg, W. 363
Miles, R. E. 400
Mill, J. St. 258
Mises, L. von 170, 182–3, 336
Mitschke, J. 260
Mittelstrass, J. 85, 104, 105, 112, 200
Molander, E. A. 400
Montesquieu, Ch. de 153, 278, 283
Moses 47
Muhs, K. 336
Müller-Armack, A. 1, 3, 320, 338–40, 343–4
Münkler, H. 278, 283, 417
Munz, H. 412
Musgrave, R. 358
Myrdal, G. 111–12, 162, 164, 166

Nadolny, S. 204
Nawroth, E. 338–9
Neidhardt, F. 295
Nell-Breuning, O. von 323, 329, 338
Nida-Rümelin, J. 145
Nielsen, P. R. 306
Nietzsche, F. 28
Nozick, R. 180, 228
Nussbaum, M. 251
Nutzinger, H. G. 341, 381

Offe, C. 143, 294
Olbrich, T. 440
Oppenrieder, B. 87, 378, 405
Oser, F. 4, 28, 38
Osterloh, M. 415

Paine, L. S. 440
Pappi, F. U. 91
Pareto, V. 173
Pateman, C. 258
Patzen, M. 49, 324
Patzig, G. 11, 15, 25–6, 58
Pejovich, S. 353
Peter, H. B. 313
Peters, B. 295
Petersmann, E.-U. 365
Pettit, Ph. 283, 295, 297
Pfordten, D.v.d. 145
Pfriem, R. 438
Piaget, J. 38, 42
Picot, A. 396
Pieper, A. 14
Pies, I. 61, 91, 94, 98, 171
Pieth, M. 306
Pigou, A. C. 162
Plessner, H. 13, 15
Pocock, J. G. A. 274, 277–8, 283, 292, 305
Pohl, A. 393
Polanyi, K. 113, 117, 121, 158, 182
Porter, M. E. 370
Portmann, A. 13, 15
Post, J. E. 404
Prahalad, C. K. 124
Preston, L. E. 422, 432
Preuss, U. K. 294

Pümpin, C. 431
Pury, D. de 124, 209, 210, 328

Radnitzky, G. 318, 340
Ramb, B. T. 345
Rappaport, A. 392
Rawls, J. 62, 77, 167–8, 170, 177, 217, 220, 222, 224, 227–41, 254, 258–9, 266, 273–4, 276–80, 283–4, 286, 299, 329, 334, 346, 429
Rebel, K. 27, 42
Rebstock, W. 399
Rees, A. M. 243
Reijen, W. van 47
Reiss, H. 4
Rentsch, Th. 186, 237
Rhenman, E. 421
Rich, A. 22, 113, 191, 193, 318, 352
Riklin, A. 9
Rinderspacher, J. P. 208
Robbins, L. 106, 112
Robson, J. M. 258
Rock, R. 185, 186
Roddick, A. 412
Rodrik, D. 361
Röpke, W. 111, 132, 318, 320, 330–6, 338, 339, 341–2, 344
Rosenblum, N. L. 275, 282
Rosenthal, K. 185, 186
Ross, R. 367
Rothschild, K. 176
Ruh, H. 213
Rusche, Th. 439
Rüstow, A. xiii, 150, 319–21, 323, 331–3, 338–9, 341, 344, 346, 357, 417
Ryan, A. 282
Ryan, L. V. 100
Ryan, M. R. 198

Sachs, J. D. 194, 366
Sandel, M. J. 275, 279–81, 363
Sarasin, Ch. 230, 288
Schachtschabel, H. G. 318
Schanz, K.-U. 365, 366
Scharpf, F. W. 259, 260
Schelling, T. C. 293
Scherer, A. G. 427
Scherhorn, G. 198, 310
Schmid, B. 124, 209–10, 328
Schmidheiny, S. 328
Schneider, D. 149, 390, 403
Schneider, H. K. 176
Schreier, M. 67
Schüller, A. 104, 327
Schumpeter, J. 90, 131, 140, 164–5, 183, 291–2, 386
Schwarz, G. 318, 340
Schwemmer, O. 4, 24
Seel, M. 23, 26, 199
Seifert, H. 264
Sen, A. 103, 249, 267, 292, 293
Senghaas, D. 249
Sennett, R. 209
Sewing, W. 274, 277, 305
Shapiro, I. 235
Shils, E. A. 159
Shue, H. 221, 227
Simon, H. A. 421, 426
Simpson, P. L. P. 277
Singer, M. G. 60, 62
Sinn, H.-W. 369
Siroën, J.-M. 367
Sloterdijk, P. 144
Smith, A. 18, 33–4, 43, 48–53, 65, 90, 116, 126–7, 147–8, 150–7, 198, 237, 324–5, 338–9, 340, 351, 382, 395
Smithburg, D. W. 421
Spence, L. 423
Spremann, K. 393
Starkoff, B. 260
Steden, W. 86
Steinmann, H. 82, 86–7, 137, 163, 283, 377–8, 385, 386, 387–8, 390–1, 405–7, 410, 415–16, 427–8, 440
Stiglitz, J. 365
Streit, M. E. 317
Streminger, G. 153
Sunstein, C. R. 278, 283, 292, 295, 296
Suntum, U. van 369, 370

Taylor, Ch. 275, 282, 286
Teriet, B. 213, 263
Thalheim, K. C. 336
Thielemann, U. 46, 74, 99, 122, 126, 130, 141, 146, 155, 165, 176, 178, 181, 183, 288–9, 302, 351, 383, 393, 398, 400–2, 410, 417–18, 420, 440
Thieme, H. J. 345
Thompson, J. P. 139
Thompson, V. A. 421
Thurow, L. 359–61
Tietzel, M. 293
Tollison, R. D. 320
Tuchfeldt, E. 340–1
Tugendhat, E. 15, 17–19, 22, 24, 28–9, 30, 36, 48, 56–7, 84, 128, 163, 208, 219–20, 222, 241, 245, 254, 265

Tuleja, T. 309, 437
Tullock, G. 168, 320

Ulrich, H. 431
Ulrich, P. 26, 30, 42, 46, 48, 50, 52, 58, 66, 74, 81, 87, 90, 93, 100, 103, 105, 111, 116–17, 119, 121, 128–9, 147, 149, 151–5, 161, 164–6, 192, 195–6, 201, 213, 224, 230, 233, 248, 254, 258, 286, 288, 297, 302, 306, 317, 324, 326, 340, 342, 344, 353–5, 368, 378, 381, 383–4, 393, 396, 398, 400–3, 405, 410, 417–19, 421, 428, 430–1, 434, 438, 440
Ulysses 304

Vaihinger, H. 135
van der Veen, R. J. 262
Van Parijs, Ph. 194, 228, 243, 245, 251, 255–8, 260, 262, 266–7
Van Steenbergen, B. 242
Vanberg, V. 179
Vandevelde, T. 254
Vaubel, R. 327
Velasquez, M. G. 434
Ver Eecke, W. 358
Vogt, W. 166
Volkart, R. 393

Waddock, S. 374
Wagner, A. 264, 266
Wagner, G. R. 137, 427
Walras, L. 90, 165, 166
Walzer, M. 226, 242, 255, 357
Waters, J. A. 437
Watrin, Ch. 176
Waxenberger, B. 423
Weber, M. 27, 29, 36, 45, 58, 76, 112, 117–20, 122–6, 129, 132, 133, 143, 149–51, 153, 154, 157, 159, 181, 191, 201, 209–10, 214, 254, 347, 353, 386, 396
Weber, Th. 438
Weeks, J. F. 246
Wein, T. 330
Weinkopf, C. 266
Weisser, G. xiii, 111–13
Weizsäcker, C. C. von 293
Werhane, P. 434
Wettstein, F. 374
White, S. 259, 262
Wieland, J. 92, 94, 147, 160, 400, 438, 440
Wilpert, J. 368
Wimmer, R. 45, 56, 60, 61
Wingert, L. 33–4, 234
Wood, A. W. 115
Wright Mills, C. 27
Wunderer, R. 434
Wünsch, G. 118, 154
Wünsche, H. F. 340
Würgler, H. 213

Yunus, M. 252

Zadek, S. 416, 417
Zajitschek, S. 427
Zerfass, A. 137, 427, 428
Ziegenfuss, W. 112
Zinn, K. G. 318
Zsolnai, L. 100